MODELS OF CITIES AND REGIONS

MODELS OF CITIES AND REGIONS

Theoretical and Empirical Developments

Edited by

A.G. Wilson, P.H. Rees and C.M. Leigh

School of Geography,
University of Leeds

JOHN WILEY & SONS
Chichester · New York · Brisbane · Toronto

Library of Congress Cataloging in Publication Data:

Main entry under title:

Models of cities and regions.

Includes index.
1. Cities and towns—Mathematical models—Addresses, essays, lectures. 2. Regional planning—Mathematical models—Addresses, essays, lectures. 3. Urban economics—Mathematical models—Addresses, essays, lectures. 4. Regional economics—Mathematical models—Addresses, essays, lectures. I. Wilson, Alan Geoffrey. II. Rees, P.H. III. Leigh, Christine Mary.
HT153.M62 301.36'01'51 77-5338

ISBN 0 471 99540 1

Printed and bound in Great Britain

Preface

A range of aspects of urban and regional modelling are dealt with in this book and it is useful to explain briefly how this particular set of topics came together. The original ambition of the editors was to implement and report upon a research project within which a set of urban and regional models were tested empirically for a single study area. Inevitably perhaps, it proved impossible to carry this out in a very neat way, but there were compensations: first, it was shown that most of the empirical work could be carried out, and secondly, that the research lead to a number of useful theoretical developments. Hence, in our subtitle, we record our concern with theoretical and empirical developments.

Within this broad framework, the points to be noted at the outset are as follows:

(1) Empirical work was carried out for a single study area for most of the types of model described in Urban and regional models in geography and planning (by A.G. Wilson, published by John Wiley in 1974). Thus, we report on the methods, trials and problems of empirical modelling. Such detailed accounts are rare in the literature, especially with largely secondary data bases and so we hope this is positively useful.

(2) The work was carried out for a single study area, West Yorkshire in the U.K. and there are two points to note in this respect. First, we hope that in the discussions of empirical methods, generality dominates the particularity of our study area. Secondly, by applying the latest modelling methods (from systematic fields of geography and related disciplines) to a single area, we offer the basis for a new kind of regional geography.

(3) Our empirical work generated many theoretical problems and some corresponding advances. We hope therefore that the book gives an account of how theoretical research can be carried out in an atmosphere informed by empirical work.

(4) The project involved academic staff, research staff sponsored by two research councils, and research students also sponsored by two research councils. The work reported on is a demonstration, therefore, of how such integrated work can be implemented. This is particularly important at a time when it seems increasingly difficult to organise large-scale research projects in universities.

Taken together, we hope that these points establish the nature of the book as a treatise on the details of research methodology and practice. As such, it is offered to a wide range of readers: teaching staff in higher education, research workers, professional planners and others in government, and to students.

A substantial number of acknowledgements are due. We are grateful to the Social Science Research Council for the grant which supported Graham Mountcastle and Paul Smith 1971-1974 and Terry Smith for the academic year 1972-1973. The Science Research Council supported a major project in transport planning in the University of Leeds and we have drawn on that for Chapter 9, though the bulk of the transport research will be reported elsewhere. At the outset of writing this book, the editors did not realise the rigours demanded in the production of camera ready copy for the publisher and are grateful to the authors for their collaboration in many aspects of this enterprise. For some of the co-authored chapters, it is useful to indicate the division of responsibility. In Chapter 3, John King was responsible for the sections on West Indian immigrants in Leeds under Philip Rees' supervision, and Philip Rees and Paul Smith jointly for the rest. In Chapter 5, Roger Mackett carried out the work on the Leeds-Lowry-type model and Graham Mountcastle on the West Yorkshire one. In Chapter 7, Paul Smith was responsible for the West Yorkshire shopping model, Roger Mackett for the Leeds shopping model, and Peter Whitehead for the public services research (the latter under Christine Leigh's supervision).

The production of the typescript for this book was masterminded by Rosanna Whitehead, and she also typed a large part of it. We are most grateful for the managerial and secretarial work on her part which has made this book possible. We also thank Pam Talbot for her share of the typing. Gordon Bryant, Geoff Hodgson and John Dixon have drawn most of the figures at various times and we are very grateful for their skills in many respects. We are also grateful to Wilf Robinson for much technical help.

AGW
PHR
CML

Leeds February 1977

List of Contributors

Peter W. Bonsall, Institute for Transport Studies, University of Leeds.

Arthur F. Champernowne, Institute for Transport Studies, University of Leeds.

Eric L. Cripps, Department of Planning, Bedford County Council.

Paul R. Goodman, Department of Transportation and Planning, West Yorkshire Metropolitan County Council.

Anthony Hankin, Runshaw Sixth Form College, Leyland, Lancashire.

John R. King, Department of Social Work, Lothian Regional Council.

Christine M. Leigh, School of Geography, University of Leeds.

Roger L. Mackett, Institute for Transport Studies, University of Leeds.

Graham D. Mountcastle, Social Development Division, City Housing Department, Birmingham.

Philip H. Rees, School of Geography, University of Leeds.

Ian Sanderson, Planning Department, Tyne and Wear County Council.

Martyn L. Senior, School of Geography, University of Leeds.

A. Paul Smith, Warrington New Town Development Corporation.

Terry B. Smith, Department of Town Planning, Leeds Polytechnic.

Frank Southworth, Institute for Transport Studies, University of Leeds.

Ronald Spence, Computing Department, Leeds City Council.

Peter J. Whitehead, Department of Transportation and Planning, West Yorkshire Metropolitan County Council.

Huw C.W.L. Williams, School of Geography, University of Leeds.

Alan G. Wilson, School of Geography, University of Leeds.

List of Figures

List of Tables

Contents

Chapter 1

Research methods for urban and regional modelling

A.G. Wilson

1.1 The model system

This book is concerned with quantitative methods of urban and regional analysis. The advance of such methods is now reasonably well known and documented (for example, Burton, 1963; Wilson, 1972-A; Davis, ed, 1972), and there is no need to give detailed history here. During the 1960's, most such work, especially in geography, mainly used statistical methods, though from 1964 onwards with the publication of Lowry's Model of metropolis and the development of models in transport engineering, another substantial stream of mathematical modelling work can be identified. This represents a shift from inductive to deductive methods which is commonly observed as a stage of development in many disciplines.

An urban and regional model system can be thought of as a number of interacting subsystems, each of which can be represented by a (sub) model. A comprehensive (or general) model related to the whole system. With the exception of the work of Lowry (1964) and models based on his, most urban and regional modelling research has been concerned with particular subsystems; and the models have been tested separately, usually on different areas. Further, simplification had to be made to achieve 'comprehensiveness' in the manner of Lowry, and restrictions to particular subsystems permitted more depth. Against this background, the research strategy generating this book can be summarised as follows: to develop the best available model for each subsystem, and to test each empirically for a common study area. In this way, we hoped to develop the building blocks of an improved general model. We also tested variants of the Lowry model, both for comparative purposes and because it provided an alternative research path. Finally, we have continually borne in mind the need to make the model system potentially useful for urban and regional planners. The theme of the book therefore is the development of research methods for building improved models of cities and regions and the empirical testing of such models. The subsystems considered are shown in Figures 1.1 and 1.2. The detailed rationale for this choice is given elsewhere (Wilson, 1974-A, Chapters 2 and 3). Choices also have to be made at the outset about scale: it can easily be seen that we have chosen to build models of population and the economy at a regional scale, and to concern ourselves with the spatial distribution of population and economic activities, and some related flows, mainly at an urban scale (though in some of our work we have also investigated intra-regional distribution and urban and intra-urban population models).

Figure 1.1 The main submodels, at different scales

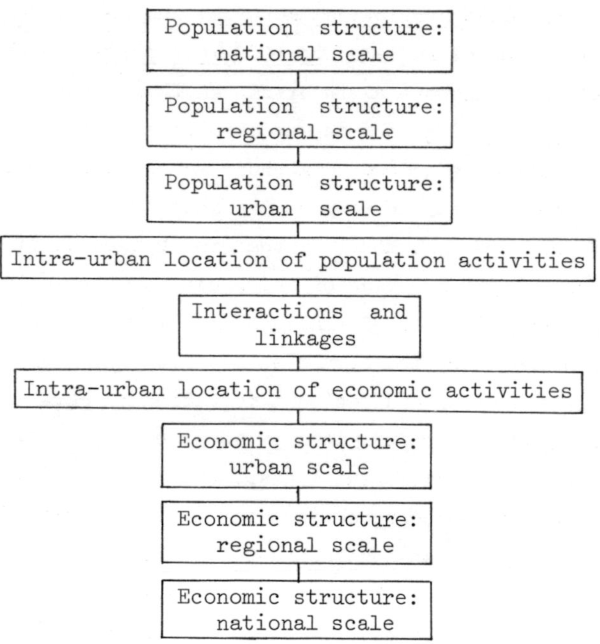

Figure 1.2 Intra-urban models

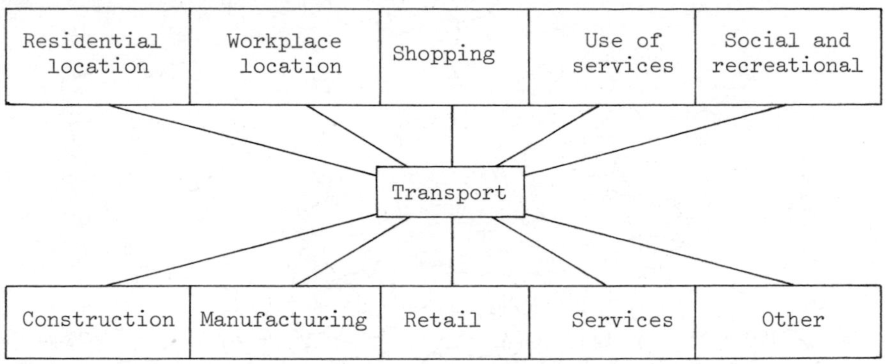

The structure of this scheme can be emphasised by noting the main headings under which are work is reported in detail, from Chapter 3 onwards: (i) population; (ii) the economy; (iii) 'Lowry model' development; (iv) residential location; (v) the utilisation of services; (vi) the distribution of economic activity; and (vii) transport. We have concentrated more on population and organisation activities, and less on physical stock such as housing and other buildings, though the models developed can be used to test the impact of marginal changes in such stock, which is one of the major tasks of urban and regional planning.

Another perspective on the nature of the model system we have developed and tested can be obtained from a description of the study area used for empirical testing. It is the West Yorkshire study region shown in Figure 1.3 with most of the urban work being concentrated on a further subdivision of Leeds shown in Figure 1.4.

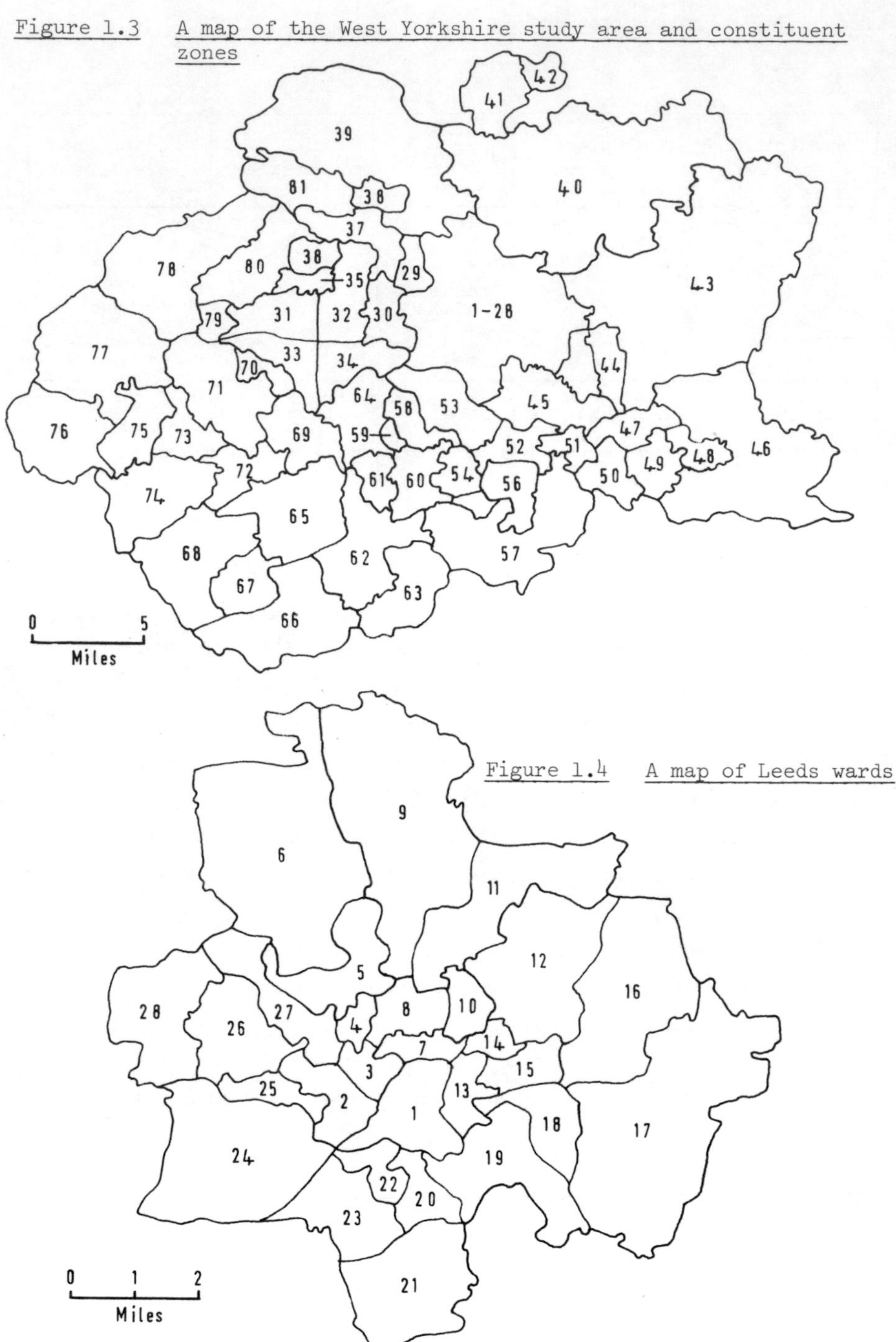

Figure 1.3 A map of the West Yorkshire study area and constituent zones

Figure 1.4 A map of Leeds wards

Key to Figures 1.3 and 1.4 Study area zones

1 to 28 Leeds Wards	29 to 81 Local Authorities		
1. City	22. Holbeck	40. Wetherby	61. Mirfield
2. Wellington	23. Beeston	41. Harrogate	62. Kirkburton
3. Westfield	24. Wortley	42. Knaresborough	63. Denby Dale
4. Hyde Park	25. Armley	43. Tadcaster	64. Spenborough
5. Meanwood	26. Bramley	44. Garforth	65. Huddersfield
6. Headingley	27. Kirkstall	45. Rothwell	66. Holmfirth
7. Blenheim	28. Stanningley	46. Osgoldcross	67. Meltham
8. Woodhouse		47. Castleford	68. Colne Valley
9. Moortown		48. Knottingley	69. Brighouse
10. Potternewton		49. Pontefract	70. Queensbury and Shelf
11. Allerton	29. Horsforth	50. Featherstone	71. Halifax
12. Roundhay	30. Pudsey	51. Normanton	72. Elland
13. Richmond Hill	31. Bradford 'A'	52. Stanley	73. Sowerby Bridge
14. Harehills	32. Bradford 'B'	53. Morley	74. Ripponden
15. Burmantofts	33. Bradford 'C'	54. Ossett	75. Hebden Royd
16. Crossgates	34. Bradford 'D'	55. Horbury	76. Todmorden
17. Halton	35. Shipley	56. Wakefield CB	77. Hepton
18. Osmondthorpe	36. Baildon	57. Wakefield RD	78. Keighley
19. East Hunslet	37. Aireborough	58. Batley	79. Denholme
20. Hunslet Carr	38. Otley	59. Heckmondwike	80. Bingley
21. Middleton	39. Wharfedale	60. Dewsbury	81. Ilkley

The West Yorkshire region is subdivided into the pre-April 1974 local authorities for the purposes of spatial analysis and Leeds City is subdivided into 28 wards as constituted in 1966. Our work also has relevance for the post-1974 local government boundaries, as our West Yorkshire region almost coincides with the new Metropolitan County, and the new County Districts are usually aggregates of the old local authorities. The relationship between the various boundaries are described in detail by Illingworth, Smith and Rees (1974). In practice, our work on particular submodels does not, unfortunately, have such a tidy empirical base. Ideally, we would work with the following spatial systems: (i) the whole of the West Yorkshire region (in its UK context)(System 1); (ii) local authorities within West Yorkshire (which includes the Leeds 'aggregate' case within its regional context)(System 2); and (iii) Leeds wards, probably with other local authorities in the region as 'external zones' (System 3). We should be equally systematic about time. Since our main source of data is the Census, we might consider using the cross-section points,

1951, 1961, 1966 and 1971, both for a series of comparative static model analyses and as an empirical basis for dynamic modelling. In fact, our spatial systems vary slightly from these ideal bases, largely because of the data problems. The population work relates largely to System 1 but the economic modelling partly to the whole Yorkshire and Humberside region, and partly to the West Riding conurbation area as defined for the Census. There are two Lowry model applications: to System 1 and to System 3. In the latter case, the size of the data and computing problems forced the omission of external zones. This restricted System 3 was also used for the residential location model and for most of the services work, though for some of the latter, the intra-Leeds zones were not wards, but were new aggregates of enumeration districts. A shopping model was tested for System 2. The transport model was based on System 3, with the addition that the old Bradford area was subdivided into four zones as in the West Yorkshire Transportation Study. Most of the empirical work used here for model testing relates to 1966 - the latest year for which Census data was available at the start of the study. Where possible, for dynamic modelling work we have also used earlier data and related our results to data from the 1971 Census as they have been published. We discuss the problems and possibilities of being more systematic, about spatial systems and trip periods, in our assessment of the empirical work at the end of Chapter 2.

In these first two chapters, we concentrate on describing the methods we have used and developed, the problems we have tried to solve, the advances we think we have made, and we give a general assessment of the developments reported. Although the empirical tests relate to a specific area, the problems we have attempted to tackle are of a more general nature, and some of our solutions are of general relevance. It is important, therefore, to emphasise these wider issues, especially in these opening chapters. The rest of this chapter is structured as follows. In Section 1.2, the '1970 state-of-the-art' which we took as our starting point is described. In Section 1.3.4, we outline the research problems which faced us and in Sections 1.4 and 1.5 we outline in general terms the research methods we have used, taking theory and empirical testing in turn. In Chapter 2, our main results are summarised

1.2 The starting point

With the exception of the work on Lowry-type models, the aim in relation to each submodel is to estimate the main variables implied by Figures 1.1 and 1.2 above. (Lowry-type models achieve this in a simplified way internally.) These main variables are functions of sets of other variables, some of which are potentially under the control of the planner, and it is such relationships which provide the basis of the use of these models in planning.

The starting points in our demographic model was the work of Rogers (1966, 1968). He in turn has built on the work of Leslie (1945) - showing how Leslie's ideas could be generalised and presented in a multi-regional framework. Population is categorised by age, sex, region and calendar time, and a typical variable would be $w_r^{iX}(t)$ - the population of sex X, in age group r, in region i at time t. These variables are arranged in a vector and the t+T population, for some increment, T, is obtained by multiplying that vector by a matrix of 'rates' - of birth, survival and migration. Submodels, or some other forms of estimating procedure, are needed for the rates themselves if the model is to be used for population forecasting. Nonetheless, our starting point in this case seemed clear.

Since our main focus has been the study of population activities, the main output of an economic model would be employment, and the typical variable would be $E_k^i(t)$, the employment in sector k in region i at time t. In both demographic and economic models, i is to be taken as the whole West Yorkshire study area in its regional context. The obvious starting point is a model which effectively represents the interdependence of different economic sectors, the Leontief input-output model, and the best known example of such a model was that of Artle (1959).

The Lowry (1964) model was more or less comprehensive, although a number of potentially predictable variables were taken as given exogenously, particularly the spatial distribution of basic employment. 'Basic' defines those parts of the economy which are not dependent in their locational behaviour on the local population - essentially, the industrial or 'exporting' sectors. The non-basic sectors are then broadly 'service' sectors. Lowry then ingeniously constructs a model on a few deceptively simple assumptions which represent a specification of submodel mechanisms and submodel interactions. Given total basic employment by sector, the equivalent population supported by these jobs could be calculated, making an assumption about an activity rate. Given a further assumption about population demand for services, a multiplier is calculated which leads to an estimate of total service employment and hence total population. In effect two very simple sets of assumptions, involving activity rates and an 'economic base' kind of mechanism, are being used to replace the more extended models of the sectors described earlier. The spatial distribution of activities in the Lowry model were produced using simple gravity models, but these were linked through an interesting iterative mechanism which also involve land use accounting. Initially, the spatial distribution of basic employment is assumed to be given and workers and their families are assigned to residences in a gravity like way around workplaces; the demand for services , measured in units of service employment, is then in turn distributed in a gravity-like way around these populations. This gives more people to be located, more services, and so on. The obvious iterative cycle usually soon converges in practice and has been shown by Garin (1966) to be equivalent to inverting a matrix. At each stage of the iteration, land use constraints, given maximum density and ' service' minimum size constraints must be satisfied. The model was applied in British contexts by Cripps and Foot (1970), Batty (1971) and by Echenique et.al. (1969), and the position achieved by 1970 was reviewed by Goldner (1971), and later by Batty (1972). A number of theoretical polishes had been added to the model (Wilson , 1969, 1971-A), and given the existing background of theoretical and empirical work, this seemed to be a line of research which we should pursue.

Most operational residential location models were based on gravity model principles, taking workplace locations as given. This often involved, as in the Lowry model, an extremely simple and unrealistic assumption about housing supply; that it always exactly met demand. Further, the models were very aggregative, taking no account of house type and price or household income. So our starting point was a disaggregated model in which houses and jobs were treated on the same basis, and as given, and the task of the model a residential workplace assignment model, was to assign workers and households to job and residential locations (Wilson, 1970-B). An alternative strategy was offered by the economic-theoretical modelling work of Harris (1962) and his co-workers, building on the concept of the Herbert and Stevens (1960) model, which in turn built on the work of Alonso (1960, 1964). Such models operated at a similar level of disaggregation to our own, could be tested, with a similar data base, and so we resolved to pursue that line of enquiry also.

The study of the location of services also typically involved gravity models, as described above in Lowry model context. The most common example was the shopping model, of which there has been many applications following the work of Huff (1964) and Lakshmanan and Hansen (1965). The alternative approaches are well described in a government report (Distributive Trades E.D.C., 1970). As with residential location, the models used tended to be too aggregative. In the field of public facility location (schools, libraries, health facilities and so on) there was much less work, though Scott (1971) and others were suggesting the possible uses of location-allocation methods.

Perhaps our weakest starting point related to the spatial distribution of economic activity. In the Lowry model, the location of the basic sector was taken as given exogenously, and this was not untypical, but a few workers such as Lakshmanan (1968) and Putman (1967) have tried to model such distributions, usually using econometric methods. Coversely, our strongest starting point related to the transport model. Development of such models started in North America in the 1950's and a wealth of experience has been gained. A typical starting point, in 1970, involving a reasonably disaggregated entropy maximising model, was provided by the SELNEC model (Wilson, Hawkins, Hill and Wagon, 1969).

It remains to indicate in principle how a model system of this kind could be used by planners. What are the controllable variables among the independent variables in each case? The demographic and economic variables are, as perhaps is well known from other perspectives, the most uncontrollable! A planner would not usually see himself as controlling birth and death rates, and he probably has relatively little influence over migration rates. Regional planners have more often been concerned to move jobs to people than vice versa. However, attitudes are perhaps changing to the control of birth rates. In the economic model, total product and hence employment, is influenced by the technical structure of the economy as represented by the input-output coefficients and final demand (including investment and net exports). The economic planner in principle, has a considerable degree of control over the various aspects of final demand, investment, export and imports, though this does not always seem to be exercised effectively in practice. But even though control may be weak, good models are essential so that the best possible population and economic forecasts can be made available for planning purposes.

The various location models can be treated together. They each present the usage of one or more facilities for a given supply pattern. The residential workplace assignment model will give T_{ij}^{kw}, the number of people living in a type k house in zone i and working in a type w job in zone j, given H_i^k, the distribution of housing by type and E_j^w, the distribution of jobs by type. A change in housing policy for example, would generate a new set of H_i^k's and the model would predict T_{ij}^{kw}'s - implicitly dealing with complicated matters such as 'filtering'. Various evaluation measures such as change in consumers' surplus achieved by this policy, can be calculated and used to help find the most effective policy. A similar analysis can be used to describe the way in which the shopping model would help in the design of shopping centre developments. The transport model predicts flows by person type by mode for a given pattern of the spatial distribution of people, jobs and services and a given supply of transport facilities. The planner can in principle change the spatial distribution and the pattern of transport facilities, and the model will predict the consequences of such changes and evaluation measures can be calculated.

The models themselves, of course, do not generate the solutions. The transport model was somehow thought by many people to 'favour' roads, because model-based analyses always produced highway solutions. But this is because only highway solutions were examined! The inventiveness of the designer and the policy maker is a crucial component of model-based planning. The 'best' plan can only be chosen if it is one of the alternatives which had been investigated. In all these cases, there is likely to be controversy about the evaluation measures to be adopted. Do all costs and benefits count equally? How are intangibles to be dealt with? The plan which maximises suppliers' profits may not be the one which maximises consumers' benefits (cf. Hotelling, 1929). But at the very least model outputs will supply much information which is relevant to planning decisions.

1.3 Research problems

With this background it is useful to summarise the research problems which faced us at the outset. Work on the demographic model started in the spring of 1971 (Costello, 1971; Donovan, 1971; Pearson, 1971). We assumed that we could, straightforwardly, build a Rogers' model for West Yorkshire. However, we found that Rogers had assumed that data would be available giving population in age groups of equal width, that width being equal to the projection period, say, of five years. The British Census data did not come in such a tidy form. There are two possible solutions - to develop a more general model which will take uneven data directly, or to 'smooth' the data using interpolation or some such method. Initially, we adopted the first of these methods, though in the end we used both. This forced us into a close examination of population data and how it related to the Rogers' model. Various new problems then began to present themselves. First, there were problems of rate measurement. A typical regional birth rate might be 'births in the region in a period' divided by 'initial population' or perhaps 'mid-year population'. But this set of births included those to mothers who had migrated into the region during the period; and the 'denominator' population included potential mothers who migrated elsewhere during the period. Thus, numerators and denominators in typical rate definitions did not match. Secondly, we began to realise that population flows existed which were not properly handled in existing models. Migration data, for example, relates to people who have 'migrated and survived to the end of the period' - so they can answer the migration question put to them on the Census form. But what about people who migrate during the period from i to j, but die in j before the end of the period? They appear in region j death statistics rather than i-j migration statistics. Thus, very quickly, we were faced with an extensive set of new theoretical problems.

The biggest problem associated with the task of building an economic model was lack of suitable data. Input-output models demand data on interindustry transactions and import and export flows across the regional boundaries. Such data only exist at the national scale. So the first job was to find regional data which could be used to adjust national input-output coefficients for use in a regional context. Then, by making a number of rather strong assumptions, it was possible actually to build the model.

There were a number of research problems associated with developments of the Lowry model. First, many of the submodels could be improved in an obvious way. We noted however, that relatively little rigorous testing, relative to the original model, had been carried out with Lowry model variants, and so with one of our case studies, we built an original Lowry model to provide a frame of reference. Further, many of the British applications had neglected one of Lowry's most interesting features - the land use accounting mechanism, and we were determined to build on this. One of the great attractions of the Lowry model is that it does contain a detailed mechanism for subsystem interaction. However, this seems rigid and unrealistic, especially when applied, as is common, in a comparative static way. So a further important aim was to build dynamic versions of the model.

For the residential-workplace assignment model the initial way ahead was clear: to build and to test empirically, the disaggregated spatial interaction model and the Herbert-Stevens model. The more fundamental theoretical question related to choosing the best of the two models, or possibly producing an eclectic synthesis from both. This raised general issues of the relationship between entropy maximising models and models based more firmly on economic theory which used mathematical programming methods. The initial way ahead was also clear for the service sector. We knew in principle how to disaggregate existing models such as the Huff-Lakshmanan-Hansen model, and how to investigate alternative models for the public sector. The difficulty was in finding suitable data for model calibration and testing. A similar consideration applied to the economic activity location sector, though as noted in the previous section, the starting point was a weaker one.

In the transport case, we could take a wealth of experience and, say, the SELNEC model as a starting point. Since no household-survey-based-transport study had been carried out in West Yorkshire, we could also make a virtue out of necessity by demonstrating how such a model could be constructed using mainly Census data and some parameters from other studies. This did leave use with a particular problem, however, for trip purposes other than work. There was also an important demonstration exercise to be carried on within geography: it is still common within that discipline for much more primitive forms of spatial interaction model to be used. Finally, there were some underlying theoretical problems here also, analogous to those associated with the residential workplace choice model: the entropy maximising basis had been criticised as being inadequate from the viewpoint of economic theory, and again there was the task of integrating this and the utility maximising approach.

It is clear from even this broad introduction that, while we always had a starting point using existing models which could be developed empirically, there were a host of theoretical problems whose solution could lead to a new generation of models. Fortunately, 1971 was a time when new and faster calibration techniques pioneered by authors such as Batty (1970) began to be available, and this facilitated much of our empirical development. We also were able to bear in mind two possible consequences of testing different submodels on a single study area. First, we should produce many of the components of an 'advanced general model' which might supercede that of Lowry. Secondly, we might begin to provide the basis for a new kind of regional geography, and one which would be particularly useful in a planning context. Traditionally, regional geography has been largely descriptive or offered only verbal explanations and theories. The 'new geography' was systematic. We are now perhaps near the points where the wheel turns full circle and the fruits of the revolution can be used to provide a regional geography whose basis is a set of quantitative models, but to which can be added the insights which were often gained from more traditional approaches.

1.4 Research methods 1: theory

The beginnings of our research strategy will now be clear. Given that we have identified some problems to be solved, it is useful to pause and to consider in broad terms the possible means of solution. It was argued in an earlier paper (Wilson, 1971-B) that there are six possible ways of making progress: (i) developments of existing lines of work; (ii) scale shifts; (iii) shifts in theory building style; (iv) the introduction of new concepts and integration of concepts; (v) shifts in model building technique; and (vi) developments arising from new fields and new problems.

These categories overlap somewhat of course. Most of the headings are self explanatory, and it will already be clear from the earlier discussion how we were set to proceed under some of them. The second usually implies a shift to a more micro scale in the search for deeper levels of explanation, and the third shifts from descriptive to inductive, or from inductive to hypothetico-deductive methods. Neither of these concern us much here: we mostly operate at a 'meso' scale (cf. Haggett, 1965) and would argue that important results stand in their own right at this scale; though for some purposes we have begun to explore alternative computer representations which allow micro level models to be built (Wilson and Pownall, 1974) and also recognise the need for meso-micro theoretical linkages (Wilson, 1972-B). The fifth heading concerns developments in model building technique. Given a reasonably advanced starting point, we did not feel that we were likely to make revolutionary strides forward here. But the continual improvement in computing capability is always important, as are the advances in calibration methods already referred to. And we are already mostly using hypothetico-deductive methods. The sixth heading, problems associated with new issues, concerns us marginally in our attempts to model public services. There are other such areas, concerned for example with energy and with resource depletion, for which our methods are relevant, but which take us beyond the scope of this book (cf. Cripps, Macgill and Wilson, 1974).

Our main thrust then relates to the remaining three headings. We have made it clear that we think it is always sensible to develop existing lines of work, and our prime method in this respect on a number of fronts, was disaggregation. This applied to our introduction of house types and price and job types and income in the residential workplace model, types of good and mode in the shopping model, and person type (in a highly disaggregated form) and mode in the transport model. Perhaps the most spectacular advances result from the introduction of new theoretical concepts, or the integration of old ones which were thought to be disparate or conflicting. Three major developments of this kind and a number of others are reported below. The demographic modelling problems described in Section 1.3 above, were solved by the introduction of accounting concepts and associated techniques for the estimation of missing elements. The two existing approaches to residential workplace modelling were reconciled by extending Suzanne Evans' (1973) results linking entropy maximising and linear programming models. And entropy maximising and utility maximising approaches to transport modelling have been reconciled by using some judgements about the level of resolution at which each should be applied. Other advances include the introduction of 'development' mechanism into Lowry-type models to make them fully dynamic and the initiation of some work in public service modelling.

The more general understanding of the nature of the theoretical problems we have faced has come from the application of the systems typology suggested by Weaver (1958) in a general scientific context to urban and regional analysis (Wilson, 1974-B, 1974-C). He argues that there are three kinds of system: simple, of disorganised complexity, and of organised complexity. The first is characterised by a small number of variables, say two, three or four and can be analysed by the methods of traditional mathematics. Science was dominated by the study of such systems up to the end of the Nineteenth Century. The second type of system on the other hand is described by a large number of variables perhaps millions, but the elements do not interact very strongly with each other, and so they are 'disorganised'. Particles in a gas form an example, and the methods for analysing such systems were invented by Boltzmann and Gibbs at the end of the Nineteenth Century and were entropy maximising methods. This is the analysis of structure by <u>statistical averaging</u>. There is an analogous Type II system in which changes in time can be analysed averaging system change as described by average rates. These have close connections to Markov methods introduced early this century. The third type of system is also complex and described by a large number of variables, but the elements now interact strongly so that statistical averaging methods are no longer satisfactory. New methods must now be invented, and no general ones are yet available. Weaver notes that many biological systems are Type III, and we can easily see that this is also likely to be true of many social and economic systems.

It should also be emphasised that the Weaver type of a system will depend on the level of resolution at which it is viewed. Thus, an individual and his behaviour pattern is a Type III system, and a collection of individuals also form such a system. But for a very large collection of individuals with respect to particular elements of their behaviour, say the journey-to-work, it may be possible to treat the system as Type II and hence to have standard methods of analysis available. This also connects to another ever present feature of complex systems: the theoretical aggregation problem. A theory may be available about a system element, such as a particle in a gas or an individual person's behaviour as a consumer say, but the development of an aggregate theory is usually not straightforward. Entropy maximisation provides a method of aggregation for some kinds of Type II system. Linear programming offers a method for certain kinds of economic system. The need for such a technique is something which we always have to bear in mind in connecting theoretical approaches at different levels of resolution.

It does not take much more thought to see where we stand with our own range of models in the Weaver scheme. Models of population and population activities can be treated as Type II systems. The demographic model is an account based <u>average rate</u> model, while most of the activity submodels can be constructed on an entropy maximising basis (with the new results linking programming with entropy maximising being used to improve the micro-theoretical basis without losing our ability to reaggregate). Economic systems, on the other hand, with strong interactions between firms, are much more likely to be Type III. The input-output model is thus seen as a Type II average rate approximation to such a system. And the difficulties in making theoretical advances in the analysis of the location of economic activity can be seen as part of a general problem in science relating to Type III systems.

1.5 Research methods 2: empirical tests

Some of our methods for empirical testing have already been mentioned in the previous section, and the details will be given in subsequent chapters, so that this section can be brief. The main point to emphasise about data is that with West Yorkshire as a study area, virtually no special surveys have been available to us in the course of the study. We have had to make the best of publicy available data - mainly from the Census. In particular, no household-interview-based transport study has been carried out in West Yorkshire (though one has at last started in 1975) and so we were deprived of much of the data available to most other model building exercises. This at least means that our project is a demonstration as to what can be achieved using public secondary sources but it undoubtedly left us in a position of considerable disadvantage. We would with hindsight, perhaps regard as doubtful the proposition that the advantages of working on our local area outweighed these disadvantages.

Methods of empirical testing are closely allied to methods of calibration: goodness-of-fit statistics for the first purpose are those used to obtain the best estimates of model parameters for the second. We are able to use standard least squares' regression techniques and associated goodness-of-fit statistics. More often, however, our parameters appear in non-linear models and maximum likelihood estimates have to be used. Since most of the models used can be represented as entropy maximising models, this turns out to be particularly convenient, since obtaining maximum likelihood estimates of the parameter is equivalent to solving the constraint equations used to set up the model.

1.6 Research strategy

We have identified three kinds of work in the development of an urban and regional model system: (a) the empirical development for our study area of existing models which had been tested elsewhere; (b) the empirical development of known but untested models; and (c) work on new theoretical problems leading to new models. These three categories obviously feed back on each other as shown in Figure 1.5.

Figure 1.5 Elements of research strategy

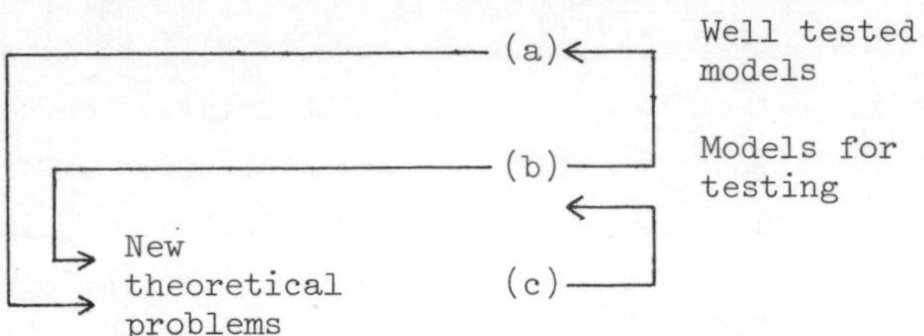

Empirical work in categories (a) and (b) inevitably suggests new category (c) problems. New models suggested in (c) - theoretical feedback to (b) and ultimately to (a). It is important to maintain a balance in an overall programme between these kinds of work. Thus for each submodel discussed above, we carried out our first empirical work under category (a) where possible, or failing that category (b). But we have tried to work on resulting problems in category (c), thus producing new models for testing. This strategy means that the predictions of any new models can always be compared to those of existing models, and it also minimises risk for the whole programme, because if an element of theoretical work fails, there is always the existing work to fall back on. There are no great diseconomies in this strategy either, because much of the effort goes into data collection and manipulation, and this is common to the different categories of research.

References

Alonso, W. (1960) A theory of the urban land market, Papers of the Science Association, 6, pp. 149-157.

Alonso, W. (1964) Location and land use, Harvard University Press, Cambridge, Mass.

Artle, R. (1959) Studies in the structure of the Stockholm economy, The Business Research Institute, Stockholm School of Economics, republished in 1965 by the Cornell University Press, Ithaca, New York.

Batty, M. (1970) Some problems of calibrating the Lowry model, Environment and Planning, 2, pp. 95-114.

Batty, M. (1971) Design and construction of a sub-regional land use model, Socio-Economic Planning Sciences, 5, pp. 97-124.

Batty, M. (1972) Recent developments in land use modelling: a review of British research, Urban Studies, 9, pp. 151-162.

Burton, I. (1963) The quantitative revolution and theoretical geography, The Canadian Geographer, 7, pp. 151-162.

Costello, S. (1971) The development of a generalised multi-regional model for demographic analysis and forecasting, M.Sc. thesis, Department of Computer Science, University of Leeds.

Cripps, E.L. and Foot, D.H.S. (1970) The urbanisation effects of a third London airport, Environment and Planning, 2, pp. 153-192.

Cripps, E.L., Macgill, S.M. and Wilson, A.G. (1974) Energy and materials flows in the urban space economy, Transportation Research, 8, pp. 293-305.

Davies, W.K.D. (ed.)(1972) The conceptual revolution in geography, University of London Press, London.

Distributive Trades E.D.C. (1970) Models for shopping studies, National Economic Development Office, London.

Donovan, S. (1971) The calibration of a regional migration flow model, M.Sc. thesis, Department of Computer Science, University of Leeds.

Echenique, M., Crowther, D. and Lindsay, W. (1969) A spatial model of urban stock and activity, Regional Studies, 3, pp. 281-312.

Evans, S.P. (1973) A relationship between the gravity model for trip distribution and the transportation problem in linear programming, Transportation Research, 7, pp. 39-61.

Garin, R.A. (1966) A matrix formulation of the Lowry model for intra-metropolitan activity location, Journal of the American Institute of Planners, 32, pp. 361-364.

Goldner, W. (1971) The Lowry model heritage, Journal of the American Institute of Planners, 37, pp. 100-110.

Haggett, P. (1965) Locational analysis in human geography, Edward Arnold, London.

Harris, B. (1962) Linear programming and the projection of land uses, Paper 20, Penn-Jersey Transportation Study, Philadelphia.

Herbert, J. and Stevens, B.H. (1960) A model for the distribution of residential activity in urban areas, Journal of Regional Science, 2, pp. 21-36.

Hotelling, H. (1929) Stability in competition, Economic Journal, 39, pp. 41-57.

Huff, D.L. (1964) Defining and estimating a trading area, Journal of Marketing, 28, pp. 37-48.

Illingworth, D.R., Smith, A.P. and Rees, P.H. (1974) Notes on the definition of the West Yorkshire study area and the new West Yorkshire metropolitan county, Working Paper 90, Department of Geography, University of Leeds.

Lakshmanan, T.R. (1968) A model for allocating urban activities in a state, Socio-Economic Planning Sciences, 1, pp. 283-295.

Lakshmanan, T.R. and Hansen, W.G. (1965) A retail market potential model, Journal of the American Institute of Planners, 31, pp. 134-143.

Leslie, P.H. (1945) On the use of matrices in certain population mathematics, Biometrika, 23, pp. 183-212.

Lowry, I.S. (1964) A model of metropolis, RM-4035-RC, Rand Corporation, Santa Monica.

Pearson, M.J. (1971) The computational estimation of migration flows, MSc thesis, Department of Computer Science, University of Leeds.

Putman, S.H. (1967) Intra-urban industrial location model design and implementation, Papers, Regional Science Association, 19, pp. 199-214.

Rogers, A. (1966) Matrix methods of population analysis, Journal of the American Institute of Planners, 32, pp. 40-44.

Rogers, A. (1968) Matrix analysis of inter-regional population growth and distribution, University of California Press, Berkeley and Los Angeles.

Scott, A.J. (1971) Combinatorial programming spatial analysis and planning, Methuen, London.

Weaver, W. (1958) A quarter century in the natural sciences, Annual Report, Rockefeller Foundation, New York.

Wilson, A.G. (1969) Developments of some elementary residential location models, Journal of Regional Science, 9, pp. 377-385.

Wilson, A.G. (1970-A) Entropy in urban and regional modelling, Pion, London.

Wilson, A.G. (1970-B) Disaggregating elementary residential location models, Papers, Regional Science Association, 24, pp. 103-125.

Wilson, A.G. (1971-A) Generalising the Lowry model, in Wilson, A.G. (ed.) Urban and regional planning, Pion, London, pp. 121-133.

Wilson, A.G. (1971-B) On some problems in urban and regional modelling, in Chisholm, M., Frey, A.E. and Haggett, P. (eds.) Regional forecasting, Butterworth, London.

Wilson, A.G. (1972-A) Theoretical geography - some speculations, Transactions, Institute of British Geographers, 57, pp. 31-44.

Wilson, A.G. (1972-B) Behavioural inputs to aggregative urban system models, in Papers in urban and regional analysis, pp. 71-90.

Wilson, A.G. (1974-A) Urban and regional models in geography and planning, John Wiley, London and New York.

Wilson, A.G. (1974-B) Towards a unified model of urban structure and development, to be published, Geography Papers, University of Michigan.

Wilson, A.G. (1974-C) Urban and regional models: some organising concepts to describe the state of the art, in Baxter, R., Echenique, M. and Owers, J. (eds.) Urban development models, MTP, Lancaster, pp.

Wilson, A.G., Hawkins, A.F., Hill, G. and Wagon, D.J. (1969) Calibrating and testing the SELNEC transport model, Regional Studies, 3, pp. 337-350.

Wilson, A.G. and Pownall, C.E. (1974) A new representation of the urban system for modelling and for the study of micro-level interdependence, Working Paper 64, Department of Geography, University of Leeds; to be published in Area.

Chapter 2

Some advances in urban and regional modelling

A.G. Wilson

2.1 The main developments

Perhaps the first point to be made is that we did manage to build and to test empirically a model of some kind or other for each of our main subsystems of interest. This involved a considerable amount of work in assembling relevant data from diverse secondary sources. This was perhaps particularly true of Chapter 4: it is very difficult to build an input-output model from secondary data. This kind of work also involves a considerable amount of computer programming, both in relation to the models themselves, and for calibration and testing. In many ways, this 'across-the-board' effect and its results represents the most important achievement reported here - a demonstration that the models can be built and tested using secondary data for a single region. But there have also been a number of theoretical advances and all in all, we feel we have made considerable progress towards the construction of a comprehensive urban model which would be useful to planners, and in the solution of a number of theoretical problems. Some of the theoretical work has implications beyond this particular study, and these advances are worth identifying in general terms. A more specific description of the main results is given in the remaining subsections of this chapter, and the results themselves are presented in detail in subsequent chapters.

In trying to solve the problems with the Rogers' model mentioned in Chapter 1, we have shown how <u>accounting</u> concepts can be introduced into spatial demographic analysis. The main results are given in three papers (Rees and Wilson, 1973, 1975-A; Wilson and Rees, 1974-A).

This work seemed to be so important that we devoted a greater share of effort to it than was originally intended. The results are important for demography, but also possibly more generally since although accounting techniques in model building are familiar, they are usually associated with Markovian assumptions and are not useful if much data is missing. We have shown how to avoid the assumptions and to solve, at least for this model, the missing data problems. In terms of the methods discussed in Section 1.4 of the previous chapter, this virtually represents the introduction of a new concept.

Secondly, we were successful in two ways in the <u>integration</u> of what were previously seen as very different concepts and approaches in the fields of residential location and transport modelling respectively. In the first case, we were able to build on the work of Evans (1973) to show how entropy maximising models and some linear programming models were members of the same family, and to deduce some results about dual variables which enabled us to reconcile the spatial interaction and Herbert-Stevens approaches. This also has wider implications: entropy maximising models can nearly always be seen as suboptimal or 'imperfect market' versions of (possibly economic) optimising or programming models, and vice versa. Thus, given the existence of one type of model, we have a procedure for developing the other, and intepretation involving concepts such as 'rent' which were previously thought to apply only to one type can, with suitable modification, be applied to the other. It becomes possible to relate 'phenomenological' and 'economic' approaches and to build models which have the advantages of each: the 'fitting' properties of the first with the 'interpretative' properties of the second. The main results are described by Senior and Wilson (1974-B) and Wilson and Senior (1974).

The second kind of integration also connects phenomenological and economic approaches but in the transport context and using a different method. It has been argued by Beckmann (1973), that spatial interaction models should be derived from the theory of consumers' behaviour and utility maximising theory. However, to attempt to do so directly involves characterising every possible trip for each individual as a 'good' in the economic sense. This leads either to an unreasonably high number of variables, or to simplifications which are unrealistic. We have attempted to integrate the two approaches by identifying carefully the scale to which each method applies. If we adopt a coarse scale, with main variables as trip frequency and trip expenditure for each individual, then it is possible to apply the theory of consumer behaviour at this scale and to estimate frequencies and expenditures as demand functions, while still applying entropy maximising methods to trip distribution and modal choice. This then has repercussions for the 'disaggregation' topic to be discussed next. The principles of this work are described in Wilson (1973-B) and Southworth (1974-A).

We noted in Section 1.4 that progress could often be made by disaggregating known models, and this has been a feature of much of our work. This has applied to our works on demographic models (Wilson and Rees, 1974-A), the Lowry model (Mackett, 1974-C), residential location (Senior and Wilson, 1974-A), services (Mackett, 1973-B; Smith, 1973; Whitehead, 1975-A) and transport (Southworth, 1974-B, 1975).

2.2 Accounting and demography

The introduction of accounting concepts solved the problems referred to in Section 1.4. All population flows are systematically identified in a set of accounts; and it is possible then to define rates within which numerators always match denominators. There are two ways of doing this: either by dividing each accounting element by the corresponding row sum (which is the usual basis in Markov-type modelling) or by taking some known counts of events in a period, such as births or deaths in a region, and dividing that by a corresponding at risk population. The first course was impossible because of inevitable data gaps in the accounts; in fact all the requisite data would only be available in countries which adopted an efficient population registration system. So we adopted the second, initially approximating the at risk population but also adding a procedure for calculating missing flows based on approximate rates. Estimates of rates and missing flows, and hence at risk populations are improved within an iterative procedure. In this way a full set of accounts can be built up for an historical period. The new theoretical concepts not only improve the model, but also enable the best use to be made of the available data.

As noted in Section 2.1 the main theoretical ideas are outlined in three papers (Rees and Wilson, 1973, 1975-A; Wilson and Rees, 1974-A), and they are presented in more detail in a recent book (Rees and Wilson, 1977). The origins of some of the work are described in Rees (1972) and Wilson (1972), with comments on possible notations in Rees (1973-A). As part of this work, we did successfully generalise the Rogers' model to free it from any restrictions on age group sizes and projection periods (Wilson, 1972) and such a model was successfully implemented (Smith and Mountcastle, 1973-A, 1973-B). The account-based model can easily be compared with alternative spatial demographic models - especially those of Rogers (1966) and Stone (1970) - and this is done in Rees (1974) and Rees and Wilson (1974-A). The account-based model in its most complete form is very detailed and can be cumbersome to handle. However, it is useful to develop simpler models as approximations of it rather than using alternative procedures. This has been done for dealing with small area populations and for ethnic groups (Rees and King, 1974). Also, it is necessary to build submodels to be used for projection purposes in demographic models. Stillwell (1975) has begun to explore the migration aspects of this.

Potentially, there is much data available for spatial demographic models - on population stocks and some flows from the Census, and on event-counts from Registrar-General's returns. In one particular case, concerned with Leeds immigrant births, King (1974-A, 1974-B) assembled the data himself from local sources. However, it is never available in ideal form, and many of our papers on empirical work devote much space to the problems of manipulating data for use in model development. The empirical work was carried out for four kinds of areas: the West Riding of Yorkshire (Smith and Rees, 1974), the West Yorkshire study area (Chapter 3 below), and Leeds City for immigrants only (Rees and King, 1974; King, 1974-A, 1974-B) and the small area of Hunslet within Leeds (Chapter 3 below). The fits to data seem remarkably good, although a full test of some of the assumptions cannot be carried out for lack of data. Nearly all the empirical work was carried out for the period 1961-1966, as only 1966 Census data was available to us for most of the project. Occasionally, it was possible to do some preliminary work using 1971 Census data.

The details of study areas and time periods are given in Chapter 3 below. The variety of study areas adopted partly reflects the need for analysis at different spatial scales, but also illustrates some of the difficulties in carrying out this kind of research. Most of our initial work was on the West Riding of Yorkshire instead of our own West Yorkshire study area, as the data was much more conveniently available. Also, as the theoretical development of the model proceeded in parallel with the early empirical work (each feeding on the other), this meant that the computer programmes were developed in rather *ad hoc* fashion. They were specific to the main regions involved, and development for a new spatial system, such as all the local authorities within our area, involved much programme rewriting. These faults are being rectified with the development of a suitably general programme within a new and ongoing SSRC sponsored research project (Rees, 1973).

2.3 Economic model building

As with the demographic model, an effective economic model can only be built if the underlying set of *accounts* can be constructed. The general shape of these accounts is shown in Figure 2.1.

Figure 2.1 Main elements in economic accounts

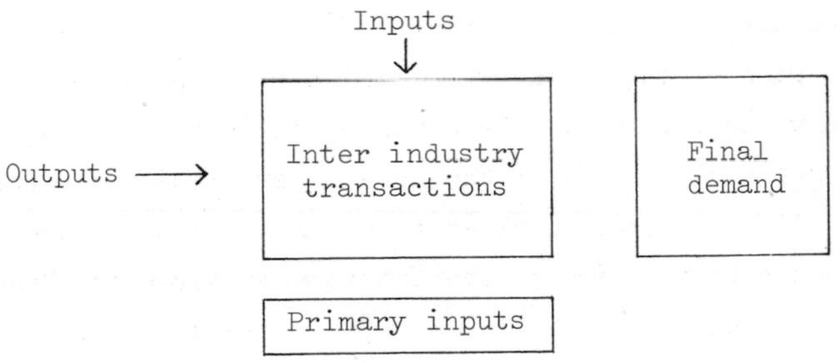

The elements of the accounts are usually shown in monetary units, though eventually we would hope to convert them to employment units so that the model can 'generate' jobs as part of a more comprehensive model. If $\underline{Z} = \{Z_{mn}\}$ represents the interindustry transactions (where m and n are sector labels), $\underline{Y} = \{Y_m\}$, final demand and $\underline{X} = \{X_m\}$, total product, then

$$\Sigma_n Z_{mn} + Y_m = X_m \tag{2.1}$$

If we define a set of coefficients a_{mn}, assumed to be constant, such that

$$a_{mn} = Z_{mn}/X_n$$

then Equation (2.1) can be written

$$\Sigma_n a_{mn} X_n + Y_m = X_m \tag{2.2}$$

or in matrix notation,

$$\underline{aX} + \underline{Y} = \underline{X} \tag{2.3}$$

so that, in the usual equation of the input-output model

$$\underline{X} = (\underline{I} - \underline{a})^{-1}\underline{Y} \tag{2.4}$$

where $\underline{I}$ is the unit matrix. The problem in building such a model for a region like West Yorkshire is that hardly any of the elements of $\underline{Z}$ and $\underline{Y}$ in equations such as (2.1) are known from data. The task of building the model is an exercise in making the best use of incomplete data from a wide variety of sources. It turns out to be necessary to complete the 'primary inputs' part of the accounts, shown in Figure 2.1, to achieve this purpose also.

The accounts presented in Chapter 4 were developed empirically for a two region example: the West Yorkshire conurbation and the rest of the world for 1963. The conurbation is the Census definition and was chosen because much of the data is available only for such a region. It is somewhat smaller than our usual study area. The year was chosen because it was the latest year for which Census of Production data existed in 1970, when the research started and also it was a year for which national input-output coefficients were known.

Final demand is usually taken as consisting of consumer expenditure investment, public authorities' expenditure and exports. The main sources of data (not always for 1963, and usually 'national' rather than regional, but adjustable to that year and to the conurbation), are the Family Expenditure Survey, the Department of Employment Earnings Survey, the Census of Production and Inland Revenue Reports. The task of assembling consistent estimates from these sources is complicated by the fact that the common expenditure breakdown is usually by commodity while we want it by industry. For investment, the main sources are the Census of Production and the 1963 input-output tables, together with the results of other research workers. Public authorities expenditure is obtained by taking regional proportions of input-output tables and the National Income Blue Book. Exports are estimated in two parts: using national propensities applied to the region of overseas flows, and applying proportions to the Road Goods Survey by commodity for the rest. Primary inputs are made up of labour, measured as income from employment, gross trading profits and imports. Analogous procedures are used to those sketched for final demand above. No data is available directly on inter-industry transactions. These have to be constructed indirectly by adjusting national input-output coefficients using provisional row and column totals established with the elements and estimates calculated to date. All estimates are then 'forced' together to give a consistent picture. Thus, the achievement with this model is not so much innovation in theory, but that a regional model can be assembled at all from the jigsaw puzzle of data available.

2.4 Building on the Lowry model

The original Lowry (1964) model consisted of two linked spatial interaction models to locate people and services and set of constraints relating to land use accounts and minimum size of service establishments. We noted in Section 1.4 that the submodels could be improved in obvious ways, and this was done in both case studies. We also noted that in most previous British studies, the constraints' procedures had been neglected. We retained them, again in both case studies, and used methods developed a few years ago (Wilson, 1969) to incorporate them systematically and consistently. Indeed, we should note that Lowry's original twelve equation model is deceptively simple because of the way adjustments are made if any constraints are infringed. A full explicit account of the equation system shows this (Wilson, 1974-A, Chapter 11). Beyond these basic improvements, different methods were used in each of our case studies and we describe each in turn.

The first was an inter-urban study whose zones were the 51 local authorities within our West Yorkshire region (Mountcastle, 1974). First, a run was carried out of the original Lowry model to provide a frame of reference. This was then modified slightly to include zonal areas as attractiveness factors within the spatial interaction models. This was necessary because Lowry's study area was based on equal sized grid squares and his version relied on this property. Perhaps the most important early results arose from the manipulation of the service minimum size constraints and experiments on the way in which service categories were defined. Three categories were used - following Lowry - referring to area scale: local, neighbourhood and metropolitan. The adjustment of the minimum size constraint for the third of these was particularly important and could be an essential model parameter measuring the effects of scale economies for large scale services. There was a basic weakness in using land area as an attractiveness factor. The zones varied in size from 700 acres to 75,000 and in the case of the largest zones, much of the land, while theoretically available for residential development, was not so in practice. A new variable was introduced to represent 'land not on the market for development'. This was then used both to improve the fits of the more primitive forms of the model, and also as a basis for dynamic modelling work. If it became possible to predict how such a set of variables changed through time, then the dynamic basis of the model would be that much stronger. In the dynamic version of the model, attractiveness terms were introduced which were functions of accessibilities. These developments together led to a very much extended form of Lowry model, and a series of results and interpretations are presented in Chapter 5. While the submodels usually remain inferior to those described as the basis of partial subsystem work in other chapters, this experience with these forms of the Lowry model did give us deeper insights into the nature of subsystem interactions and provided the beginning of dynamic modelling work. The empirical tests, especially for the more refined forms of the model, were satisfactory. There were the usual problems of assembly of data and, in particular for this case study, of obtaining detailed land use data, but these were overcome satisfactorily.

The second case study was concerned with wards within Leeds City, though for parts of the work, an external zone system was added also (Mackett, 1973-B,1974-A,1974-B,1974-C). The data problems were worse in this case as less data is available for wards within an authority than for whole authorities. Special precedures had to be used, for example, to estimate small area employment (Mackett, 1973-A). The additional improvements in this case study were concerned with disaggregated social groups, housing stock, dynamic mechanisms and closure by external zones. The disaggregation is one of those adopted in the residential location models of Chapter 6, and as well as being obviously useful in the interest of realism, it enables interesting dynamic mechanisms to be introduced. Housing stock was introduced explicitly into the constraint mechanisms in conjunction with occupancy rates as an alternative to densities and this also racilitates the introduction of dynamic mechanisms. In the dynamic version of the model, three different types of movers are used (house-job,house-only,job-only) and their impact on house and job vacancies is noted also. This supply is formed from net additions together with vacancies. A mechanism is introduced to allow higher social groups to have first choice of vacant dwellings over lower social groups. Finally, a full external zone system is introduced. The version of the model which is 'dynamic plus external zones' consist of a very large number of equations - almost a twenty-fold increase on Lowry's original twelve and is near the limits of computer capacity even for a relatively modest spatial system of 28 main zones. Again, and especially given the poor quality of much of the data, the empirical results are satisfactory. The details are given in Chapter 5.

2.5 Residential location: entropy maximising - linear programming integration

We noted in Section 1.4 that the obvious starting point was the empirical development and testing of a disaggregated residential location model (Wilson, 1970). This involved the production of an array of variables T_{ij}^{kw}, the number of people located in a type k house in zone i, working in a type w job in zone j. A number of minor theoretical improvements were added in the light of early empirical experience. The original model implicitly assumes one worker per household. In the model presented in Chapter 6 below, we have added a further superscript, n, taking values 1 or 0, to denote working heads of households and dependent workers respectively. In a later version of the model (Senior, 1977), non-working heads of households are also recognised explicitly. Secondly, we noticed that expenditure by people on housing (as a proportion of their income) in the model was not necessarily consistent with assumed house prices and stock because each total was derived separately from empirical information. We added a correction factor to allow for this.

Harris (1962) had shown in principle how to disaggregate the original model of Herbert and Stevens (1960), and this brought it to a level of resolution very similar to that of the disaggregated spatial interaction model. Thus, with the data assembled for testing our own model, we could also test this version of the Herbert-Stevens model, and this we proceeded to do. The methods used to integrate the two models are worth stating explicitly. The details are given in Chapter 6 below and in two papers (Senior and Wilson, 1974-B; Wilson and Senior, 1974). The principles only will be indicated here using the simplest version of the models (and the one-worker per household assumption). The spatial interaction version of the model is:

$$T_{ij}^{kw} = A_i^k B_j^w H_i^k E_j^w e^{-\beta^w c_{ij}} e^{-\mu^w \{p_i^k - q^w(w - c'_{ij})\}^2} \qquad (2.5)$$

where H_i^k is the number of type k houses in zone i, E_j^w the number of type w (taken as wage w) jobs in zone j, c_{ij} the travel costs from i to j, c'_{ij} the money component of these, p_i^k the price of a type k house in zone i and q^w the average proportion of income, after deduction of transport costs, spent by a w-income household on housing. A_i^k and B_j^w are balancing factors, and β^w and μ^w are sets of parameters to be estimated. The model can be written more simply as

$$T_{ij}^{kw} = A_i^k B_j^w H_i^k E_j^w e^{\mu^w b_{ij}^{kw}} \qquad (2.6)$$

if we define

$$b_{ij}^{kw} = \frac{-\beta^w c_{ij}}{\mu^w} - \{p_i^k - q^w(w - c'_{ij})\}^2 \quad (2.7)$$

The β^w parameters have now been absorbed within the b_{ij}^{kw}'s. The balancing factors are calculated to ensure that:

$$\Sigma_{jw} T_{ij}^{kw} = H_i^k \quad (2.8)$$

$$\Sigma_{ik} T_{ij}^{kw} = E_j^w \quad (2.9)$$

and μ^w is estimated to ensure that:

$$\Sigma_{ijk} T_{ij}^{kw} b_{ij}^{kw} = B^w \quad (2.10)$$

where B^w is an observed value. The B^w's in practice, will be estimated to ensure that:

$$\Sigma_{ijk} T_{ij}^{kw} c_{ij} = C^w \quad (2.11)$$

where the C^w's are observed values.

The disaggregated Herbert-Stevens model obtains the T_{ij}^{kw} which maximise a bid rent <u>net</u> of journey to work costs,

$$Z = \Sigma_{ijkw} T_{ij}^{kw}(b_{ij}^{kw} - c'_{ij}) \quad (2.12)$$

subject to constraints (2.4) and (2.5) - a version of the transportation problem of linear programming.

The integration of the two models is now obtained by using Evans' (1973) results that for the same b_{ij}^{kw} in the two models, the limit as each $\mu \to \infty$ of T_{ij}^{kw} in (2.5) is the T_{ij}^{kw} given by (2.12). To make the correspondence exact, the constraint (2.10) would have to be replaced by:

$$\Sigma_{ijkw} T_{ij}^{kw}(b_{ij}^{kw} - c'_{ij}) = Z \quad (2.13)$$

where Z will now take a suboptimal value relative to that in Equation (2.12). That is the entropy maximising (EM) model equivalent to a linear programming (LP) model can be obtained by using the objective function, such as (2.12) as a constraint, such as (2.13), with a suboptimal value, and maximising an appropriate entropy function. The integration in this particular case is achieved by assuming a bid rent function of the form (2.7), but it is now clear that other forms of bid rent functions could be tested within the EM model. Thus, to summarise, the LP models can be taken as members of the family of corresponding EM models with certain parameters taking infinite values.

This theoretical development was taken a stage further by investigating dual concepts. The constraints (2.8) and (2.9) have sets of dual variables, α_i^k and ν_j^w, associated with them in the LP problem which can be interpreted as rents and subsidies. They have Lagrangian multiples $\lambda_i^{k(1)}$ and $\lambda_j^{w(2)}$, associated with them in the EM model and indeed

$$A_i^k H_i^k = e^{-\lambda_i^{k(1)}} \tag{2.14}$$

and

$$B_j^w E_j^w = e^{-\lambda_j^{w(2)}} \tag{2.15}$$

It has been conjectured, and shown to be true in particular cases (Senior and Wilson, 1974-A, 1974-B) that:

$$\lambda_i^{k(1)}/\mu \to \alpha_i^k \text{ as } \mu \to \infty \tag{2.16}$$

and

$$\lambda_j^{w(2)}/\mu \to \nu_j^w \text{ as } \mu \to \infty \tag{2.17}$$

where μ is the parameter (Lagrangian multiplier) associated with Equation (2.13). A more detailed investigation shows that these quantities can be interpreted as rents and subsidies in the EM model, representing some kind of imperfect market. These interpretations are presented in more detail in Chapter 6.

The study area used for the range of empirical tests on these models was Leeds City (pre-1974) divided into its wards. The main source of data was the 1966 Census, but it will be clear from the list of variables following Equation (2.5) that considerable data demands are made. The <u>Family Expenditure Survey</u> had to be used, and data on house prices by zone had to be collected directly from local estate agents. This made it difficult to consider an extension of the study area. Six house types were used - three tenure groups and two 'condition' indices, and six w groups - though we had to use socio economic groups rather than income groups directly because of data reasons. The empirical results obtained were reasonably satisfactory. The β^w and μ^w parameters had the expected behaviour between groups and the goodness-of-fit statistics were adequate. Further progress now awaits the development of a dynamic framework so that these models can be applied to the people who are actually active within the housing market at particular times. The accounting basis of such a model has been explored (Wilson, 1974-A, Chapter 11), but further development awaits improved data and probably requires special surveys.

2.6 Services

We consider separately the supply of private and public goods, and in the introduction to Chapter 7 we discuss in detail the distinctions between them. In the former case, we concentrate on the supply and use of shopping facilities and in the latter, we discuss the provision of fire services within a comprehensive framework for the analysis of the spatial distribution of local authority services. We noted in Section 1.4 that our main task in building a shopping model was to disaggregate the commonly used model. The aggregate model can be written

$$S_{ij} = A_i e_i P_i W_j^{\alpha} e^{-\beta c_{ij}} \tag{2.18}$$

where S_{ij} is the flow of cash from residents of i to shops in j, e_i is the average per capita expenditure on shopping goods in zone i, P_i is the population of zone i, W_j measures the attractiveness of shops in j and c_{ij} is the cost of travel from i to j. A_i is a set of balancing factors calculated to ensure that

$$\Sigma_j S_{ij} = e_i P_i \tag{2.19}$$

and α and β are parameters to be estimated. This model fails to take account of the difference in shopping behaviour for different types of good (say to be labelled n) and by different modes of transport (to be labelled k). Accordingly, we have adapted a disaggregated version of Equation (2.13) which can be written, using an obvious notation as:

$$S_{ij}^{kn} = A_i^n e_i^n P_i (W_j^n)^{\alpha^n} e^{-\beta^{kn} c_{ij}^{kn}} \tag{2.20}$$

c_{ij}^{kn} will be usually taken as c_{ij}^{k} and independent of n.

Such a model has been calibrated for an area consisting of 51 (pre-1974) local authorities, within our West Yorkshire region, and separately for wards within Leeds city. In Chapter 7 we describe both applications. Six of the 51 authorities in the larger areas had a very small amount of sales and were neglected, and rings of external zones were added in this case to close the spatial system. The data, as ever, was not readily available, and it was particularly difficult to obtain interaction data so that an observed total expenditure could be calculated and the parameters β^{kn} estimated by solving

$$\Sigma_{ij} S_{ij}^{kn} c_{ij}^{k} = C^{kn} \tag{2.21}$$

for known C^{kn}. For the West Yorkshire case, we make use of a variety of partial data made available to us by particular local authorities, and in the Leeds case, we used survey data collected by our own students as part of another exercise. To estimate α^n, we were able to use the results of Batty and Mackie (1972) who showed that the equation to solve here was

$$\Sigma_j S_{*j} \log W_j^n = \Sigma_j \overline{S_{*j}^{obs}} \log W_j^n \tag{2.22}$$

for each n. We were thus able to generate an adequate set of results although as always we would have preferred to have had better data. The results and their interpretation are described in detail in Chapter 7 and in papers (Mackett, 1973-B; Smith, 1973). These models provide the basis for the planning of shopping centre location, though it is necessary for that purpose to be more explicit about the objective function to be optimised. As in Hotelling's (1929) linear example, different answers are obtained if consumers' welfare or retailers' profits, respectively are maximised and we have started some theoretical work to explore this issue in a 'spatial interaction model world' (Wilson, 1974; Coelho and Wilson, 1976).

In the case of public goods provided by a local authority, we have shown that different principles are involved and Whitehead

(1973, 1975-A, 1975-B) has presented a framework within which available resources can be related to need. An example is presented using fire services.

2.7 The spatial distribution of economic activity

It was noted in Section 1.3 of Chapter 1 that we had our weakest starting point for this submodel. Further, since this is evidently a Weaver Type III system, and the data available was poor even relative to much of our other data, we did not expect to make progress beyond the use of existing techniques. What we have tried to do is to apply all of these systematically. We have calculated indices of localisation and specialisation in the manner of Isard (1960), and built differential shift models on the lines, for example, of those of Lakshmanan (1968). Finally, we have grouped areas using a factor analysis procedure. The results are reported in detail in Chapter 8.

Basically our work hinged upon the collection and presentation of data sources, principally through the construction of disaggregated employment accounts since this was the most readily available form of stock data available for analysis at a variety of spatial scales, though most work related to the intra-regional scale. The building of these basic accounts permitted analysis of the spatial and sectoral patterns of activity in the economy as well as allowing some simple considerations of dynamics. We were able to derive a series of standard indices from the accounts (activity rates, localisation and specialisation indices, Tress scores and Lorenz curves, cf. Isard, 1960), as well as measures of geographical association and structural similarity. We also examined changes through time in the structure of the region by analysing shifts and shares for the period 1959-66 (cf. Lakshmanan, 1968). We attempted a regionalisation of the study area, based on the 'stock' data using principal components analysis. This allowed us to investigate 'latent' structures and frameworks in typology of subregions. Finally we attempted to link the accounting framework with some measures of interaction, basically following the work of Putman (1970) on accessibilities.

2.8 Transport: disaggregation and entropy maximising-utility maximising integration

The structure of a conventional transport model is shown in Figure 2.2 below.

Figure 2.2 The structure of a conventional transport model

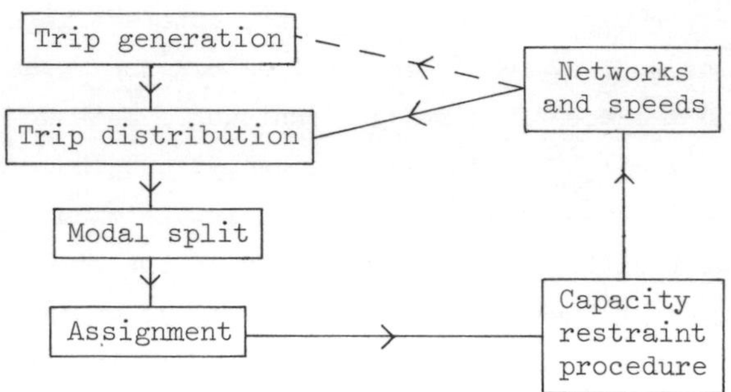

As part of our work, we have built such a conventional model (cf. for example, the SELNEC model described in Wilson, Hawkins, Hill and Wagon, 1969) and then extended it in a number of ways, partly by confronting a current theoretical controversy. The conventional model is described briefly first, and then our innovations.

For trip generation, we used the category analysis procedure (Wootton and Pick, 1967; Goodman, 1973, 1974). This estimates O_i^h and D_j, the number of trips originating in zone i from households of type h, and the total number of trips attracted to zone j. We adopted the 108 h-categories used by Wootton and Pick; six income groups, six family size-employment structure groups, and three car ownership groups. It is at this point that transport models connect to land use and activity submodels, since these trip productions and attractions depend on the spatial distribution of households by type and of economic activities.

The conventional trip distribution and modal split models are of the form

$$T^{*n}_{ij} = A^n_i B_j O^n_i D_j e^{-\beta^n C^n_{ij}} \qquad (2.23)$$

where T^{*n}_{ij} is the number of trips from i to j by person of type n, (usually taken as car-owner/non car-owner), O^n_i is an aggregate of O^h_i, D_j as before, and C^n_{ij} the average cost of travel from i to j as perceived by a person of type n. The β^n's are parameters to be estimated and A^n_i's and B_j's are balancing factors. Modal split is:

$$M^{kn}_{ij} = T^{kn}_{ij}/T^{*n}_{ij} = \frac{e^{-\lambda^n c^k_{ij}}}{\Sigma_{k\varepsilon\gamma(n)} e^{-\lambda^n c^k_{ij}}} \qquad (2.24)$$

where T^{kn}_{ij} is T^{*n}_{ij} split by mode k, c^k_{ij} is the cost of travel from i to j by mode k, and the λ^n's are parameters to be estimated. $\Sigma_{k\varepsilon\gamma(n)}$ denotes the sum over modes available to person of type n. A^n_i and B_j are calculated to ensure that:

$$\Sigma_j T^{*n}_{ij} = O^n_i \qquad (2.25)$$

and

$$\Sigma_{in} T^{*n}_{ij} = D_j \qquad (2.26)$$

and the β^n's such that

$$\Sigma_{ij} T^{*n}_{ij} C^n_{ij} = C^n \qquad (2.27)$$

where C^n is an observed total travel expenditure for people of type n. The λ's reflect sensitivity to the trade off between modal cost differences and are calibrated similarly. The C^n_{ij}'s are usually taken as some average of the modal costs available to people of type n, for example as in Wilson (1970):

$$e^{-\beta^n C^n_{ij}} = \Sigma_{k\varepsilon\gamma(n)} e^{-\beta^n c^k_{ij}} \qquad (2.28)$$

The c_{ij}^{k}'s themselves are 'generalised costs': weighted sums of money expenditure and different kinds of time. These trip matrices are then loaded onto modal networks. They have been calculated on the basis of assumed costs c_{ij}^{k}. If these costs now turn out to be incompatible with link flows, they are adjusted as part of the capacity restraint procedure, and new networks variables adopted, as indicated in Figure 2.2. These are then fed back to the distribution model as shown, and the whole scheme is iterated. The dotted line in the figure indicates that we would also like the trip generation submodel to be part of such a scheme: the number of trips produced would then be a function of supply as well as demand and would in that sense be 'elastic'. The models as described have been calibrated and tested for a spatial system which is more or less System 3 of Chapter 1 consisting of 51 local authorities within our West Yorkshire study area, with Bradford divided into four zones and Leeds into its 28 wards making 81 zones in all. The results are presented in Chapter 9.

A number of theoretical innovations were then introduced and tested empirically. The first arises from the observations that the generation and distribution models operate at different levels of resolution for no very good reason. In particular, the C^{n} term in Equation (2.7) might be a C_{i}^{h} term to match O_{i}^{h}. Then, Equation (2.3) becomes

$$T_{ij}^{*h} = A_{i}^{h} B_{j} O_{i}^{h} D_{j} e^{-\beta_{i}^{h} c_{ij}^{h}} \qquad (2.29)$$

O_{i}^{h} is used directly from the generation model. This of course, generates a large number of matrices and parameters β_{i}^{h} for calibration. Indeed, it could be argued that so many extra parameters have been added that the fit is bound to be good! This situation is dealt with in two ways. First, the h-classes are regrouped when there are no significant differences in trip making behaviour (Southworth, 1974-B). Secondly, we recognise that O_{i}^{h} and C_{i}^{h} between them describe the demand for trips by h-type residents of zone i, but at a level of resolution coarser than the T_{ij}^{*h} level. This means that utility maximising procedures can be used at this scale and O_i^h and C_i^h can be estimated as demand functions in terms of such variables as accessibility. We have done this by elementary methods so far using linear regression analysis (Wilson, 1973-B; Southworth, 1974-A, 1974-B, 1975). Since the β_i^h parameters are known when C_i^h is known, this means that it is the parameters in the C_i^h model - say the regression coefficients - which are the parameters of the model: the β_i^h's simply become intermediate variables. This means that important steps have been made towards the modelling and preduction of spatial interaction model parameters. No longer will they necessarily be constant over time.

2.9 An assessment

The main advances reported on in this book have been outlined in this chapter and the main achievements were highlighted in Section 2.1. At least two of our main theoretical advances, in spatial demography and the relationships between entropy maximising and linear programming models, have generated ideas and applications well beyond those originally conceived. The results associated with transport modelling and developments of the Lowry model may generate a similar response. In general, we have often been able to disaggregate and, by adding more detail in this way, make the various models more useful for application in urban and regional planning. And we have been able to carry out effective empirical work in relation to all models.

Our biggest disappointment has been the failure to ensure that all empirical work was carried out for mutually consistent spatial and temporal bases. The study areas should always have been the 'ideal' ones detailed in Section 1.1, and all analyses should have been carried out for 1951, 1961, 1966 and 1971 - the Census years. It will be clear by now that the difficulties in assembling a more restricted data base were considerable and that an ideal data base proved beyond our resources. Indeed, the construction of an ideal data base for 1951-71 from secondary sources alone is probably an impossibility. It is significant also that the West Yorkshire local planning authorities did not themselves have such a data base, although that situation should at least improve when the surveys for the new West Yorkshire Transportation Study have been carried out later in 1975.

This has meant that we have not been able to develop empirically a fully integrated comprehensive model since this would demand a superior data base, though some progress was made in the theoretical design of such a model (Wilson, 1974-A, Chapter 11). It also meant that the amount of effort we had left to attempt explicitly to use our models in a planning context was less than we would have liked, although the potential usefulness of the models is clear and is in any case detailed at the appropriate points in Chapters 3-9 below.

The argument presented in this book leads to the identification of three topics where more work would be fruitful, but implies that the volume of such work would have to be considerable. First, there is the need for better data systems. This is a field in which there is much work, but as often as not it seems to be on system design rather than assembly of a comprehensive set of data (the 'grid squares' work being a good example). Solutions to these problems may be prerequisites for the next two issues. The second concerns the development of an effective comprehensive model - properly integrated and internally consistent. This is not simply a matter of stringing together the submodels we already have within the context of a better data system. Sometimes there are 'conflicts' between submodels (for example between the residential location and transport models which often each separately and differently predict the 'journey to work') which can only be reduced if the whole model is made explicitly and fully dynamic. So 'dynamic modelling' is an important ongoing issue. The third topic concerns the use of models by planners. Experience since the 1968 Planning Act has emphasised that the analytical demands of the structure planning process are rightly very high. Local authorities have found it very difficult to meet these; and indeed one of the reasons for a 'sub-surface' backlash against structure planning may be feeling that old style intuition and 'muddling through' may be more comfortable. Good information and model systems go a long way towards meeting these demands. This is true of the models we report here. Further theoretical advances will be important, but the present generation of models could be used much more. The trends towards corporate planning and the development of management information systems and planning within housing and social services departments, will help because these will create demands for the same sorts of information from the planners as structure plans. But what is needed is a greater number of planners trained in these new techniques and more experience within local authorities of model based planning. It is difficult for a University research team to fulfil this role or even to exert much pressure. What is perhaps needed is more initiative from Central Government.

References

Batty, M. and Mackie, S. (1972) The calibration of gravity, entropy and related models of spatial interaction, Environment and Planning, 4, pp. 205-233.

Beckmann, M.J. (1973) The soft science of predicting traveller behaviour, Transportation Planning and Technology, 1, pp. 175-181.

Bonsall, P.W. (1974) Implementation of various cost functions in the tree building algorithms, Working Paper 95, Department of Geography, University of Leeds.

Bonsall, P.W., Cripps, E.L., Goodman, P.R., Hankin, A., Mackett, R.L., Sanderson, I., Senior, M.L., Southworth, F., Spence, R., Williams, H.C.W.L. and Wilson, A.G. (1974) A transport model for West Yorkshire, Working Paper 87, Department of Geography, University of Leeds.

Coelho, J.D. and Wilson, A.G. (1976) The optimum location and size of shopping centres, Working Paper 136, Department of Geography, University of Leeds; to be published in Regional Studies.

Evans, S.P. (1973) A relationship between the gravity model for trip distribution and the transportation problem of linear programming, Transportation Research, 7, pp. 39-61.

Goodman, P.R. (1973) Trip generation - a review of the category analysis and regression models, Working Paper 36, Department of Geography, University of Leeds.

Goodman, P.R. (1974) A category analysis trip generation model for West Yorkshire, Working Paper 61, Department of Geography, University of Leeds.

Harris, P. (1962) Linear programming and the projection of land uses, Paper 20, Penn-Jersey Transportation Study, Philadelphia.

Herbert, J. and Stevens, B.H. (1960) A model for the distribution of residential activity in urban areas, Journal of Regional Science, 2, pp. 21-36.

Hotelling, H. (1929) Stability in competition, Economic Journal, 39, pp. 41-57.

Illingworth, D.R. (1975) Demographic accounts and their relationship to the life histories of individuals, Working Paper 103, Department of Geography, University of Leeds.

Illingworth, D.R., Smith, A.P. and Rees, P.H. (1974) Notes on the definition of the West Yorkshire study area and the new West Yorkshire Metropolitan County, Working Paper 90, Department of Geography, University of Leeds.

Isard, W. (1960) Methods of regional analysis, MIT Press, Cambridge, Massachusetts.

King, J.R. (1974-A) The fertility of immigrants in Leeds, Working Paper 58, Department of Geography, University of Leeds.

King, J.R. (1974-B) Immigrant fertility trends and population growth in Leeds, Environment and Planning, 6, pp. 509-546.

Lakshmanan, T.R. (1968) A model for allocating urban activities in a state, Socio-Economic Planning Sciences, 1, pp. 283-295.

Lowry, I.S. (1964) A model of metropolis, RM-4035-RC, Rand Corporation, Santa Monica.

Mackett, R.L. (1973-A) The estimation of employment in small areas within the city, Working Paper 29, Department of Geography, University of Leeds.

Mackett, R.L. (1973-B) Shopping in the city - the application of an intra-urban shopping model to Leeds, Working Paper 30, Department of Geography, University of Leeds.

Mackett, R.L. (1974-A) A residential location model incorporating spatially varying levels of information, Regional Studies, 8, pp. 257-265.

Mackett, R.L. (1974-B) Some observations on the use and disaggregation of activity allocation models in structure planning, Working Paper 80, Department of Geography, University of Leeds.

Mackett, R.L. (1974-C) The development of an extended Lowry model for application at the city scale, Working Paper 81, Department of Geography, University of Leeds.

Mountcastle, G.D. (1974) The Lowry model and its application to West Yorkshire, Working Paper 83, Department of Geography, University of Leeds.

Mountcastle, G.D., Stillwell, J.C.H. and Rees, P.H. (1974) A user's guide to a programme for calibrating and testing spatial interaction models, Working Paper 79, Department of Geography, University of Leeds.

Neidercorn, J.A. and Bechdolt, B.V. (1969) An economic derivation of the 'gravity law' of spatial interaction, Journal of Regional Science, 9, pp. 273-282.

Putman, S. (1970) Developing and testing an intra-regional model, Regional Studies, 4, pp. 473-490.

Rees, P.H. (1972) The distribution of social groups within cities: models and accounts, in Wilson, A.G. (ed.) Patterns and processes in urban and regional systems, Pion, London, pp. 165-216.

Rees, P.H. (1973-A) A revised notation for spatial demographic accounts and models, Environment and Planning, 5, pp. 147-155.

Rees, P.H. (1973-B) The spatial analysis of demographic growth in British regions, Research proposal to SSRC.

Rees, P.H. (1974) A family of demographic accounts, Working Paper 68, Department of Geography, University of Leeds.

Rees, P.H. and King, J.R. (1974) A simple model for population projection applied to ethnic groups and small area population, Working Paper 76, Department of Geography, University of Leeds.

Rees, P.H. and Wilson, A.G. (1973) Accounts and models for spatial demographic analysis 1: aggregate population, Environment and Planning, 5, pp. 61-90.

Rees, P.H. and Wilson, A.G. (1974-A) A comparison of available models of population change processes, Regional Studies, 9, pp. 39-61.

Rees, P.H. and Wilson, A.G. (1974-B) A computer programme for constructing spatial demographic accounts for aggregate population: user's manual, Working Paper 60, Department of Geography, University of Leeds.

Rees, P.H. and Wilson, A.G. (1975) Accounts and models for spatial demographic analysis 3: rates and life tables, Environment and Planning, 7, pp. 199-231.

Rees, P.H. and Wilson, A.G. (1977) Spatial population analysis, Edward Arnold, London.

Rogers, A. (1966) Matrix methods of population analysis, Journal of the American Institute of Planners, 72, pp. 40-44.

Senior, M.L. (1973) Approaches to residential location modelling 1: ecological and spatial interaction approaches, Environment and Planning, 5, pp. 165-198.

Senior, M.L. (1974-A) Approaches to residential location modelling 2: urban economic models and some recent developments, Environment and Planning, 6, pp. 369-409.

Senior, M.L. (1974-B) Some reflections on Houghton's model and the Herbert-Stevens model, Working Paper 56, Department of Geography, University of Leeds.

Senior, M.L. (1977) Approaches to residential location modelling: empirical and theoretical developments of disaggregated models, intended Ph.D. thesis, Department of Geography, University of Leeds.

Senior, M.L. and Wilson, A.G. (1974-A) Disaggregated residential location models: some tests and further theoretical developments, in Cripps, E.L. (ed.) Space-time concepts in regional science, Pion, London, pp. 141-172.

Senior, M.L. and Wilson, A.G. (1974-B) Exploration and syntheses of linear programming and spatial interaction models of residential location, Geographical Analysis, 6, pp. 209-237.

Smith, A.P. (1973) Retail allocation models: an investigation into patterns of shopping in the Rotherham sub-region, Working Paper 50, Department of Geography, University of Leeds.

Smith, A.P. (1974) A computer version of a spatial demographic account building model: user's manual, Working Paper 51, Department of Geography, University of Leeds.

Smith, A.P. and Mountcastle, G.D. (1973-A) A computer version of a generalised Rogers' model 1: data preparation and model test for an English or Welsh county, Working Paper 31, Department of Geography, University of Leeds.

Smith, A.P. and Mountcastle, G.D. (1973-B) A computer version of a spatial demographic model 2: a user's manual, Working Paper 33, Department of Geography, University of Leeds.

Smith, A.P. and Rees, P.H. (1974) Methods for constructing spatial demographic accounts for a British region, Working Paper 59, Department of Geography, University of Leeds.

Southworth, F. (1973) Recent developments in trip distribution and modal split transportation models - a review, Working Paper 38, Department of Geography, University of Leeds.

Southworth, F. (1974-A) The calibration of a trip distribution - modal split model with origin-specific decay parameters, Working Paper 77, Department of Geography, University of Leeds.

Southworth, F. (1974-B) A disaggregated trip distribution model with elastic frequencies and expenditures, Working Paper 97, Department of Geography, University of Leeds.

Southworth, F. (1975) Highly disaggregated modal split models, Working Paper 108, Department of Geography, University of Leeds.

Spence, R. (1974) Computational aspects in the development of a large scale package of transport analysis programme, Working Paper 82, Department of Geography, University of Leeds.

Stillwell, J.C.H. (1975) Models for inter-regional migration: a review, Working Paper 100, Department of Geography, University of Leeds.

Stone, R. (1970) Mathematical models of the economy and other essays, Chapman and Hall, London.

Whitehead, P.J. (1973) Public facilities: some geographical and economic considerations, Working Paper 41, Department of Geography, University of Leeds.

Whitehead, P.J. (1975-A) A model framework to investigate spatial differences in local government service provision, Working Paper 96, Department of Geography, University of Leeds.

Whitehead, P.J. (1975-B) A spatial interaction model of library usage, Working Paper 105, Department of Geography, University of Leeds.

Wilson, A.G. (1969) Developments of some elementary residential location models, Journal of Regional Science, 9, pp. 377-385.

Wilson, A.G. (1970) Entropy in urban and regional modelling, Pion, London.

Wilson, A.G. (1972) Multi-regional models of population structure and some implications for a dynamic residential location model, in Wilson, A.G. (ed.) Patterns and processes in urban and regional systems, Pion, London, pp. 217-242.

Wilson, A.G. (1973-A) Travel demand forecasting: achievements and problems, in Brand, D. (ed.) Special Report 143, Highway Research Board, Washington DC, pp. 283-306.

Wilson, A.G. (1973-B) Further developments of entropy maximising transport models, Transportation Planning and Technology, 1, pp. 183-193.

Wilson, A.G. (1974-A) Urban and regional models in geography and planning, John Wiley, London and New York.

Wilson, A.G. (1974-B) Towards a unified model of urban development, to be published, Fiftieth Anniversary Symposium Proceedings, Department of Geography, University of Michigan.

Wilson, A.G. (1974-C) Urban and regional models: some organising concepts to describe the state of the art, in Baxter, R., Echenique, M. and Owers, J. (eds.) Urban development models, MTP, Lancaster, pp. 41-60.

Wilson, A.G. (1974-D) Retailers' profits and consumers' welfare in a spatial interaction shopping model, in Masser, I. (ed.) Theory and practice in regional science, Pion, London, pp. 42-59.

Wilson, A.G. (1974-E) Urban and regional analysis in Leeds - the structure of a research programme, Working Paper 84, Department of Geography, University of Leeds.

Wilson, A.G. (1975-A) Some methods for building dynamic models in urban and regional analysis, in Karlquist, A., Lundquist, F. and Snickars, F. (eds.) Dynamic allocation of urban space, Saxon House, Farnborough, pp. 15-40.

Wilson, A.G. (1975-B) Some new forms of spatial interaction models: a review, Transportation Research, 9, pp. 167-179.

Wilson, A.G., Hawkins, A.F., Hill, G. and Wagon, D.J. (1969) Calibrating and testing the SELNEC transport model, Regional Studies, 3, pp. 337-350.

Wilson, A.G. and Pownall, C.E. (1974) A new representation of the urban system for modelling and for the study of micro level interdependence, Working Paper 64, Department of Geography, University of Leeds; to be published in Area.

Wilson, A.G. and Rees, P.H. (1974-A) Accounts and models for spatial demographic analysis 2: age-sex disaggregated populations, Environment and Planning, 6, pp. 101-116.

Wilson, A.G. and Rees, P.H. (1974-B) Population statistics and spatial demographic accounts, The Statistician, 23, pp. 229-257.

Wilson, A.G. and Senior, M.L. (1974) Some relationships between entropy maximising models, mathematical programming models, and their duals, Journal of Regional Science, 14, pp. 207-215.

Wootton, H.J. and Pick, G.W. (1967) A model for trips generated by households, Journal of Transport Economics and Policy, 1, pp. 137-153.

Chapter 3

Population models

P.H. Rees, A.P. Smith and J.R. King

3.1 An introduction to population models

There is a continual need in both public and private planning activity for intelligence about the future numbers of people and of households with various characteristics. Pension schemes, housing plans and marketing strategies for example all require such information for the long, medium and short term future, respectively. Ideally, such forecasts of future population should be generated from a comprehensive model of urban or regional activity but as we noted in Chapter 1, we have to depend on more partial models at present. At the local scale population models are employed which are dependent on the size of and changes in the housing stock (Howell, 1974). At the urban or regional scale demographic models are employed that attempt to predict what happens in the processes of birth, death and migration. Such models produce detailed estimates of the populations of each sex and age group, and these estimates can be converted into household estimates given knowledge of the housing stock. Potentially, such models can be connected to employment and housing indicators by linking the migration estimates to those variables.

This chapter is devoted to a description of several applications of demographic models in particular geographical contexts. Some existing and some new concepts in population modelling are briefly reviewed below, and then in Sections 3.2, 3.3 and 3.4 a detailed description is given of how the new concepts can be used with only a restricted data base. The results of the operational accounting model are discussed in Section 3.5. A demographic projection model which uses the accounting framework in part is described in Section 3.6 and an application to a particular ethnic group is described in Section 3.7. The chapter concludes with an assessment of what can be learnt from this experience with population models firmly based on accounting principles.

Demographic models have a long history of application but only in the last two decades have they been applied in a regional or multi-regional context. An extensive review of demographic modelling is given in Illingworth (1976, Chapter 2) and a detailed discussion of the accounting bases of and the interrelationships among a series of demographic models is presented by Rees and Wilson (1975-A). A review of the way in which cohort survival models have been revised and extended is provided in Rees and Wilson (1977-A, Chapter 2), and the connections between the models of Rogers, Stone and Rees and Wilson are described in the same reference in Chapter 12. The reader is referred to those works for further details beyond the brief review which follows.

Two terms require definition before we survey the range of demographic models available for urban and regional analysis: accounts and models. Demographic accounts are descriptions of the numbers of transitions of persons or events between initial origin states and final destination states that take place in a period. The state definitions involve life state, regional location, age, sex, and numerous socioeconomic characteristics. Demographic models are representations of the process of change in these states by the multiplication of an initial population stock by a set of rates representing one or more of the demographic processes of death/survival, birth/maternity and migration. The rates used in demographic models may be derived explicitly from demographic accounts or from data files. Whichever approach is used all demographic models have an accounts basis which may be examined to test the consistency of the model (Rees and Wilson, 1975-A). On the other hand a large variety of models can be derived from any one set of accounts.

We can distinguish the following types of demographic models. (i) Simple closed system cohort-survival model The closed system type of model developed by Leslie (1945, 1948) and others, takes into account births and deaths as a source of population change but ignores migration and hence fares badly in situations where there exists a strong migration imbalance. (ii) Single and multi-regional cohort survival models These regional models developed largely by Rogers (1966, 1968, 1971) deal more effectively with migration, but often omit several possible demographic event sequences: birth and migration; migration and death; and survival within the last age group. (iii) Rogers' revised multi-region model based on life table rates Some of the above problems have been overcome by Rogers (1973). He has modified and extended his multi-regional cohort survival model using life table concepts. (iv) Stone's demographic accounting model In a major innovation in the demographic field, Stone (1971) produced a model in which all the various demographic flows are correctly specified. However, a major problem in applying Stone's accounting framework has been the matching of available data to the conceptual requirements of the model. (v) Accounts based model Rees and Wilson (1973, 1975-B; Wilson and Rees, 1974) have developed an accounts based model in which most of these problems of compatibility between data and accounts are resolved. (vi) A transition rate model Rees and Wilson (1977-A, Chapters 6, 12 and 13) have developed versions of the multi-regional cohort survival model in which the rates are explicitly generated from equivalent multi-regional, age and sex disaggregated population accounts.

The accounting basis of types (i), (ii) and (iii) is implicit, and this can lead to difficulties when the models are made operational. The type (iv) model has an accounting basis but is insufficiently disaggregated to deal with many regions within a country. So attention here is focused on types (v) and (vi) in which the accounting basis is explicit and disaggregated, and in which considerable attention is paid to the connections between data and accounts, and between accounts and models. We begin our discussion with an example of a type (v) model in the next section. The characteristics of population accounts and the accounts based model used to construct them should become clear as the West Yorkshire example is described.

3.2 The accounting framework and the associated accounts based model

Figure 3.1 shows the accounting framework adopted for the West Yorkshire Study Area (WYSA)[1]. The period of study adopted is the

(1) This is the common study area of 51 local authority areas employed in the studies reported in this book. It is roughly coterminous with the West Yorkshire Conurbation, the study area of the West Yorkshire Transportation Study, and the new Metropolitan County of West Yorkshire (see Illingworth, Smith and Rees, 1974 for details). A map and list of authorities is given in Figure 1.3 in Chapter 1.

Figure 3.1 A population accounts table for the West Yorkshire Study

Column heading: SURVIVAL BY AGE GROUP AT CENSUS DATE 1966

Column regions: WEST YORKSHIRE — REGION 1 | REST OF ENG.&WALES — REGION 2 | REST OF THE WORLD — REGION 3 (each with age groups 0–4, 5–9, 10–14, 15–19, . . ., 85–89, 90–94, 95+ numbered 1, 2, 3, 4, . . ., 18, 19, 20)

	REGION	AGE GROUP		WEST YORKSHIRE — REGION 1 (1 2 3 4 … 18 19 20)	REST OF ENG.&WALES — REGION 2 (1 2 3 4 … 18 19 20)	REST OF THE WORLD — REGION 3 (1 2 3 4 … 18 19 20)
EXISTENCE AT CENSUS DATE 1961	WEST YORKSHIRE – REGION 3	0 – 4	1	$K_{12}^{\epsilon(1)\delta(1)}$	$K_{12}^{\epsilon(1)\delta(2)}$	$K_{12}^{\epsilon(1)\delta(3)}$
		5 – 9	2	$K_{23}^{\epsilon(1)\delta(1)}$	$K_{23}^{\epsilon(1)\delta(2)}$	$K_{23}^{\epsilon(1)\delta(3)}$
		10 – 14	3	$K_{34}^{\epsilon(1)\delta(1)}$	$K_{34}^{\epsilon(1)\delta(2)}$	$K_{34}^{\epsilon(1)\delta(3)}$
		15 – 19	4			
		⋮		⋱	⋱	⋱
		85 – 89	18	$K_{18,19}^{\epsilon(1)\delta(1)}$	$K_{18,19}^{\epsilon(1)\delta(2)}$	$K_{18,19}^{\epsilon(1)\delta(3)}$
		90 – 94	19	$K_{19,20}^{\epsilon(1)\delta(1)}$	$K_{19,20}^{\epsilon(1)\delta(2)}$	$K_{19,20}^{\epsilon(1)\delta(3)}$
		95+	20	$K_{29,20}^{\epsilon(1)\delta(1)}$	$K_{29,20}^{\epsilon(1)\delta(2)}$	$K_{20,20}^{\epsilon(1)\delta(3)}$
	REST OF ENG.&WALES – REGION 2	0 – 4	1	$K_{12}^{\epsilon(2)\delta(1)}$	$K_{12}^{\epsilon(2)\delta(2)}$	$K_{12}^{\epsilon(2)\delta(3)}$
		5 – 9	2	$K_{23}^{\epsilon(2)\delta(1)}$	$K_{23}^{\epsilon(2)\delta(2)}$	$K_{23}^{\epsilon(2)\delta(3)}$
		10 – 14	3	$K_{34}^{\epsilon(2)\delta(1)}$	$K_{34}^{\epsilon(2)\delta(2)}$	$K_{34}^{\epsilon(2)\delta(3)}$
		15 – 19	4			
		⋮		⋱	⋱	⋱
		85 – 89	18	$K_{18,19}^{\epsilon(1)\delta(1)}$	$K_{18,19}^{\epsilon(2)\delta(2)}$	$K_{18,19}^{\epsilon(2)\delta(3)}$
		90 – 94	19	$K_{19,20}^{\epsilon(2)\delta(1)}$	$K_{19,20}^{\epsilon(2)\delta(2)}$	$K_{19,20}^{\epsilon(2)\delta(3)}$
		95 +	20	$K_{20,20}^{\epsilon(2)\delta(1)}$	$K_{20,20}^{\epsilon(2)\delta(2)}$	$K_{20,20}^{\epsilon(2)\delta(3)}$
	REST OF THE WORLD – REGION 3	0 – 4	1	$K_{12}^{\epsilon(3)\delta(1)}$	$K_{12}^{\epsilon(3)\delta(2)}$	
		5 – 9	2	$K_{23}^{\epsilon(3)\delta(1)}$	$K_{23}^{\epsilon(3)\delta(2)}$	
		10 – 14	3	$K_{34}^{\epsilon(3)\delta(1)}$	$K_{34}^{\epsilon(3)\delta(2)}$	
		15 – 19	4			
		⋮		⋱	⋱	
		85 – 89	18	$K_{18,19}^{\epsilon(3)\delta(1)}$	$K_{18,19}^{\epsilon(3)\delta(2)}$	
		90 – 94	19	$K_{19,20}^{\epsilon(3)\delta(1)}$	$K_{19,20}^{\epsilon(3)\delta(2)}$	
		95 +	20	$K_{29,20}^{\epsilon(3)\delta(1)}$	$K_{29,20}^{\epsilon(3)\delta(2)}$	
BIRTHS IN 1961-66 (BY AGE GROUP OF MOTHER AT C.D.1961)	WEST YORKSHIRE — REGION 1	⋮		⋮	⋮	⋮
		10 – 14	3	$K_{31}^{\beta(1)\delta(1)}$	$K_{31}^{\beta(1)\delta(2)}$	$K_{31}^{\beta(1)\delta(3)}$
		15 – 19	4	$K_{41}^{\beta(1)\delta(1)}$	$K_{41}^{\beta(1)\delta(2)}$	$K_{41}^{\beta(1)\delta(3)}$
		⋮		⋮	⋮	⋮
		40 – 44	9	$K_{91}^{\beta(1)\delta(1)}$	$K_{91}^{\beta(1)\delta(2)}$	$K_{91}^{\beta(1)\delta(3)}$
		45 – 49	10	$K_{101}^{\beta(1)\delta(1)}$	$K_{101}^{\beta(1)\delta(2)}$	$K_{101}^{\beta(1)\delta(3)}$
		⋮		⋮	⋮	⋮
	REST OF ENG.& WALES – REGION 2	⋮		⋮	⋮	⋮
		10 – 14	3	$K_{31}^{\beta(2)\delta(1)}$	$K_{31}^{\beta(2)\delta(2)}$	$K_{31}^{\beta(2)\delta(3)}$
		15 – 19	4	$K_{41}^{\beta(2)\delta(1)}$	$K_{41}^{\beta(2)\delta(2)}$	$K_{41}^{\beta(2)\delta(3)}$
		⋮		⋮	⋮	⋮
		40 – 44	9	$K_{91}^{\beta(2)\delta(1)}$	$K_{91}^{\beta(2)\delta(2)}$	$K_{91}^{\beta(2)\delta(3)}$
		45 – 49	10	$K_{101}^{\beta(2)}$	$K_{101}^{\beta(2)\delta(2)}$	$K_{101}^{\beta(2)\delta(3)}$
		⋮		⋮	⋮	⋮
	REST OF THE WORLD – REGION 3	⋮		⋮	⋮	
		10 – 14	3	$K_{31}^{\beta(3)\delta(1)}$	$K_{31}^{\beta(3)\delta(2)}$	
		15 – 19	4	$K_{41}^{\beta(3)\delta(1)}$	$K_{41}^{\beta(3)\delta(2)}$	
		⋮		⋮	⋮	
		40 – 44	9	$K_{91}^{\beta(3)\delta(1)}$	$K_{91}^{\beta(3)\delta(2)}$	
		45 – 49	10	$K_{101}^{\beta(3)\delta(1)}$	$K_{101}^{\beta(3)\delta(2)}$	
		⋮		⋮	⋮	
TOTALS				K_{*1}^{*1} K_{*2}^{*1} K_{*3}^{*1} K_{*2}^{*1} . . . K_{*18}^{*1} K_{*19}^{*1} K_{*20}^{*1}	K_{*1}^{*2} K_{*2}^{*2} K_{*3}^{*2} K_{*4}^{*2} . . . K_{*18}^{*2} K_{*19}^{*2} K_{*20}^{*2}	K_{*1}^{*3} K_{*2}^{*3} K_{*3}^{*3} K_{*4}^{*3} . . . K_{*18}^{*3} K_{*19}^{*3}
				POPULATION	POPULATION	SURVIVING OUT – MIGRAN

ea in K notation (sex superscript omitted)

<table>
<tr><td colspan="3">DEATH IN PERIOD 1961-66 (BY AGE GROUP AT DEATH)</td><td rowspan="3" colspan="2">TOTALS</td></tr>
<tr><td>EST YORKSHIRE — REGION 1</td><td>REST OF ENG. & WALES — REGION 2</td><td>REST OF THE WORLD — REGION 3</td></tr>
<tr><td>5 – 9, 10 – 14, 15 – 19, . . . 85 – 89, 90 – 94, 95+
2, 3, 4, 18, 19, 20</td><td>0 – 4, 5 – 9, 10 – 14, 15 – 19, . . . 85 – 89, 90 – 94, 95+
1, 2, 3, 4, 18, 19, 20</td><td>0 – 4, 5 – 9, 10 – 14, 15 – 19, . . . 85 – 89, 90 – 94, 95+
1, 2, 3, 4, 18, 19, 20</td></tr>
<tr><td>$^{)\delta(1)}$ $K_{12}^{\epsilon(1)\delta(1)}$
$K_{22}^{\epsilon(1)\delta(1)}$ $K_{23}^{\epsilon(1)\delta(1)}$
$K_{33}^{\epsilon(1)\delta(1)}$ $K_{34}^{\epsilon(1)\delta(1)}$
. . .
$K_{18,18}^{\epsilon(1)\delta(1)}$ $K_{18,19}^{\epsilon(1)\delta(1)}$
$K_{19,19}^{\epsilon(1)\delta(1)}$ $K_{19,20}^{\epsilon(1)\delta(1)}$
$K_{20,20}^{\epsilon(1)\delta(1)}$</td><td>$K_{11}^{\epsilon(1)\delta(2)}$ $K_{12}^{\epsilon(1)\delta(2)}$
$K_{22}^{\epsilon(1)\delta(2)}$ $K_{23}^{\epsilon(1)\delta(2)}$
$K_{33}^{\epsilon(1)\delta(2)}$ $K_{34}^{\epsilon(1)\delta(2)}$
. . .
$K_{18,18}^{\epsilon(1)\delta(2)}$ $K_{18,19}^{\epsilon(1)\delta(2)}$
$K_{19,19}^{\epsilon(1)\delta(2)}$ $K_{19,20}^{\epsilon(1)\delta(2)}$
$K_{20,20}^{\epsilon(1)\delta(2)}$</td><td>$K_{11}^{\epsilon(1)\delta(3)}$ $K_{12}^{\epsilon(1)\delta(3)}$
$K_{22}^{\epsilon(1)\delta(3)}$ $K_{23}^{\epsilon(1)\delta(3)}$
$K_{33}^{\epsilon(1)\delta(3)}$ $K_{34}^{\epsilon(1)\delta(3)}$
. . .
$K_{18,18}^{\epsilon(1)\delta(3)}$ $K_{18,19}^{\epsilon(1)\delta(3)}$
$K_{19,19}^{\epsilon(1)\delta(3)}$ $K_{19,20}^{\epsilon(1)\delta(3)}$
$K_{20,20}^{\epsilon(1)\delta(3)}$</td><td>$K_{1*}^{1*}$
K_{2*}^{1*}
K_{3*}^{1*}
.
.
.
K_{18*}^{1*}
K_{19*}^{1*}
K_{20*}^{1*}</td><td>POPULATION</td></tr>
<tr><td>$^{)\delta(1)}$ $K_{12}^{\epsilon(2)\delta(1)}$
$^{\epsilon(2)\delta(1)}_{22}$ $K_{23}^{\epsilon(2)\delta(1)}$
$K_{33}^{\epsilon(2)\delta(1)}$ $K_{34}^{\epsilon(2)\delta(1)}$
. . .
$K_{18,18}^{\epsilon(2)\delta(1)}$ $K_{18,19}^{\epsilon(2)\delta(1)}$
$K_{19,19}^{\epsilon(2)\delta(1)}$ $K_{19,20}^{\epsilon(2)\delta(1)}$
$K_{20,20}^{\epsilon(2)\delta(1)}$</td><td>$K_{11}^{\epsilon(2)\delta(2)}$ $K_{12}^{\epsilon(2)\delta(2)}$
$K_{22}^{\epsilon(2)\delta(2)}$ $K_{23}^{\epsilon(2)\delta(2)}$
$K_{33}^{\epsilon(2)\delta(2)}$ $K_{34}^{\epsilon(2)\delta(2)}$
. . .
$K_{18,18}^{(2)\delta(2)}$ $K_{18,19}^{\epsilon(2)\delta(2)}$
$K_{19,19}^{\epsilon(2)\delta(2)}$ $K_{19,20}^{\epsilon(2)\delta(2)}$
$K_{20,20}^{\epsilon(2)\delta(2)}$</td><td>$K_{11}^{\epsilon(2)\delta(3)}$ $K_{12}^{\epsilon(2)\delta(3)}$
$K_{22}^{\epsilon(2)\delta(3)}$ $K_{23}^{\epsilon(2)\delta(3)}$
$K_{33}^{\epsilon(2)\delta(3)}$ $K_{34}^{\epsilon(2)\delta(3)}$
. . .
$K_{18,18}^{\epsilon(2)\delta(3)}$ $K_{18,19}^{\epsilon(2)\delta(3)}$
$K_{19,19}^{\epsilon(2)\delta(3)}$ $K_{19,20}^{\epsilon(2)\delta(3)}$
$K_{20,20}^{\epsilon(2)\delta(3)}$</td><td>$K_{1*}^{2*}$
K_{2*}^{2*}
K_{3*}^{2*}
.
.
.
K_{18*}^{2*}
K_{19*}^{2*}
K_{20*}^{2*}</td><td>POPULATION</td></tr>
<tr><td>$^{3)\delta(1)}$ $K_{12}^{\epsilon(3)\delta(1)}$
$^{\epsilon(3)\delta(1)}_{22}$ $K_{23}^{\epsilon(3)\delta(1)}$
$K_{33}^{\epsilon(3)\delta(1)}$ $K_{34}^{\epsilon(3)\delta(1)}$
. . .
$K_{18,18}^{\epsilon(3)\delta(1)}$ $K_{18,19}^{\epsilon(3)\delta(1)}$
$K_{19,19}^{\epsilon(3)\delta(1)}$ $K_{19,20}^{\epsilon(3)\delta(1)}$
$K_{20,20}^{\epsilon(3)\delta(1)}$</td><td>$K_{11}^{\epsilon(3)\delta(2)}$ $K_{12}^{\epsilon(3)\delta(2)}$
$K_{22}^{\epsilon(3)\delta(2)}$ $K_{23}^{\epsilon(3)\delta(2)}$
$K_{33}^{\epsilon(3)\delta(2)}$ $K_{34}^{\epsilon(3)\delta(2)}$
. . .
$K_{18,18}^{\epsilon(3)\delta(2)}$ $K_{18,19}^{\epsilon(3)\delta(2)}$
$K_{19,19}^{(3)\delta(2)}$ $K_{19,20}^{\epsilon(3)\delta(2)}$
$K_{20,20}^{\epsilon(3)\delta(2)}$</td><td></td><td>$K_{1*}^{3*}$
K_{2*}^{3*}
K_{3*}^{3*}
.
.
K_{18*}^{3*}
K_{19*}^{3*}
K_{20*}^{3*}</td><td>IN-MIGRANTS</td></tr>
<tr><td>$^{)\delta(1)}$
$^{)\delta(1)}$

$^{)\delta(1)}$
$^{)\delta(1)}$</td><td>⋮
$K_{31}^{\beta(1)\delta(2)}$
$K_{41}^{\beta(1)\delta(2)}$
⋮
$K_{91}^{\beta(1)\delta(2)}$
$K_{101}^{\beta(1)\delta(2)}$
⋮</td><td>⋮
$K_{31}^{\beta(1)\delta(3)}$
$K_{41}^{\beta(1)\delta(3)}$
⋮
$K_{91}^{\beta(1)\delta(3)}$
$K_{101}^{\beta(1)\delta(3)}$
⋮</td><td>⋮
$K_{3*}^{\beta(1)*}$
$K_{4*}^{\beta(1)*}$
⋮
$K_{9*}^{\beta(1)*}$
$K_{10*}^{\beta(1)*}$
⋮</td><td>BIRTHS</td></tr>
<tr><td>$^{)\delta(1)}$
$^{)\delta(1)}$

$^{)\delta(1)}$
$^{)\delta(1)}$</td><td>⋮
$K_{31}^{\beta(2)\delta(2)}$
$K_{41}^{\beta(2)\delta(2)}$
⋮
$K_{91}^{\beta(2)\delta(2)}$
$K_{101}^{\beta(2)\delta(2)}$
⋮</td><td>⋮
$K_{31}^{\beta(2)\delta(3)}$
$K_{41}^{\beta(2)\delta(3)}$
⋮
$K_{91}^{\beta(2)\delta(3)}$
$K_{101}^{\beta(2)\delta(3)}$
⋮</td><td>⋮
$K_{3*}^{\beta(2)*}$
$K_{4*}^{\beta(2)*}$
⋮
$K_{9*}^{\beta(2)*}$
$K_{10*}^{\beta(2)*}$
⋮</td><td>BIRTHS</td></tr>
<tr><td>$^{\delta(1)}$
$^{)\delta(1)}$

$^{)\delta(1)}$
$^{)\delta(1)}$</td><td>⋮
$K_{31}^{\beta(3)\delta(2)}$
$K_{41}^{\beta(3)\delta(2)}$
⋮
$K_{91}^{\beta(3)\delta(2)}$
$K_{101}^{\beta(3)\delta(2)}$
⋮</td><td></td><td>⋮
$K_{3*}^{\beta(3)*}$
$K_{4*}^{\beta(3)*}$
⋮
$K_{9*}^{\beta(3)*}$
$K_{10*}^{\beta(3)*}$
⋮</td><td>INFANT IN-MIGRANTS</td></tr>
<tr><td>$K_{*2}^{*\partial(1)}$ $K_{*3}^{*\partial(1)}$ $K_{*4}^{*\partial(1)}$ . . . $K_{*18}^{*\partial(1)}$ $K_{*19}^{*\partial(1)}$ $K_{*20}^{*\partial(1)}$</td><td>$K_{*1}^{*\partial(2)}$ $K_{*2}^{*\partial(2)}$ $K_{*3}^{*\partial(2)}$ $K_{*4}^{*\partial(2)}$ . . . $K_{*18}^{*\partial(2)}$ $K_{*19}^{*\partial(2)}$ $K_{*20}^{*\partial(2)}$</td><td>$K_{*1}^{*\partial(3)}$ $K_{*2}^{*\partial(3)}$ $K_{*3}^{*\partial(3)}$ $K_{*4}^{*\partial(3)}$ . . . $K_{*18}^{*\partial(3)}$ $K_{*19}^{*\partial(3)}$ $K_{*20}^{*\partial(3)}$</td><td colspan="2">K_{**}^{**}</td></tr>
<tr><td>DEATHS</td><td>DEATHS</td><td>NON-SURVIVING OUT-MIGRANTS</td><td colspan="2">ALL PERSONS</td></tr>
</table>

five year period between the Census of 1961 (April 23/24) and the Sample Census of 1966 (April 24/25). Three regions are recognised in the accounts which partition the world completely: West Yorkshire (region 1), which is the focus of interest, the rest of England and Wales (region 2) and the rest of the world (region 3). The population is disaggregated into males (M) and females (F), although Figure 3.1 applies generally to either sex (x=M or F). Each sex is disaggregated into 20 age groups of five years interval, from 0-4 years (at last birthday) to 90-94 with the last open ended as 95 and over.

The notation adopted in Figure 3.1 is as follows. The general term employed is $K_{r\ s}^{\alpha(i)\omega(j)x}$ where K represents population; α is the superscript label which represents the initial life state in the period which can either be β for birth or ε for existence; ω is the superscript which represents the final life state in the period which can be δ for death or σ for survival. Attached to each of the life state superscripts are locational labels (i, j, k) representing the region where the life state is initially adopted. The superscript x represents sex and has two values M and F. The initial age group associated with $\alpha(i)$ is labelled r and the final age group associated with $\omega(j)$ is labelled s.

There are four particular forms of this general variable, each of which occupies one of the four quadrants into which Figure 3.1 is divided. (i) $K_{rs}^{\varepsilon(i)\sigma(j)x}$ are persons in existence at the start of the period in region i in age group r who end the period surviving in region j in age group s. The sex x is assumed not to change! (ii) $K_{rs}^{\varepsilon(i)\delta(j)x}$ are persons of sex x in existence at the start of the period in region i in age group r who die in the period in region j in age group s. (iii) $K_{rs}^{\beta(i)\sigma(j)x}$ are the persons of sex x born in region i in the time interval who survive in region j in age group s at the end of the period. The subscript r is used to refer to the age group of mother either at time of maternity/birth or at the beginning of the period. (iv) $K_{rs}^{\beta(i)\delta(j)x}$ are the persons of sex x born in region i to mothers in age group r who die before the end of the period in region j and in age group s.

In Figure 3.1 the arrangement of each of these types of population flow is shown for the three region, 20 age group set of accounts for West Yorkshire. The existence-survival submatrices in the top left hand quadrant of the table contain terms in a single diagonal, one above the principal diagonal, together with one term measuring the number of survivors within the last age group in the principal diagonal. The existence-death submatrices in the top right quadrant of the table contain terms both in the principal diagonal (people dying in the age group they were in at the start of the period) and in the diagonal one above (people dying in the age group one older than the one they started the period in). Only a single partial column of terms appears in the bottom half of the table in both the birth-survival quadrant and the birth-death quadrant in this simple age group/time period arrangement. Terms appear only in the third to tenth row of each of these submatrices - only women who were in the age group 10-14 to 45-49 at the beginning of the period are considered to be at risk of giving birth in the ensuing five year period. This arrangement, with the age group interval equal to the time period length, is known as the 'simple case' of population accounts. The submatrices labelled with two region 3 superscripts involving persons beginning and ending their existence in the period in region 3, the rest of the world, have been left blank. The numbers are difficult to estimate and are not of real interest.

Appended to each row of the accounts matrix are row totals which are regional population totals in a time t age group for the first two sets of rows, and which are total in-migrants from the rest of the world in the case of the third sets of rows. The fourth and fifth sets of rows give the birth totals for the regions by age group of mother at the start of the period, and the sixth set of rows shows the total of infants (persons born in the period) in-migrating from the rest of the world, having been born there.

The sets of column totals refer to: in the first and second block of columns, end of period regional populations in age groups; in the third block of columns, the numbers of surviving out-migrants to the rest of the world; in the fourth and fifth block of columns, the number of regional deaths in the period by age group at time of death; and in the final block of columns, the numbers of out-migrants to the rest of the world who died there, by age group at death.

In order to convert the symbolic terms of Figure 3.1 into numbers we need to make use of an accounts based model, a set of procedures that constructs from available demographic data a population accounts matrix. The general structure of the accounts based model used for the age disaggregated, simple case will be described for both historical and projection modes. For greater detail the reader should refer to Wilson and Rees (1974); Smith and Rees (1974); and Rees and Wilson (1977-A, 1977-B).

It should be helpful to begin by extending the content of Figure 3.1 to indicate those items of the accounts table which can be supplied exogenously to the model and those which have to be generated endogenously. Figure 3.2 reveals that there are in fact three groups of procedures involved: those involving external data estimation which yield the numbers in A type submatrices; those involving the estimation of 'minor flows' contained in B type submatrices; and those concerned with the estimation of the remaining 'major flows' in C type submatrices. It is convenient to add to these another stage, that involving calculation of the populations at risk and death rates, making four major stages overall, as presented in Figure 3.3.

Stage (1) Estimation of known flows

In Section 3.3 we will see how the various items are measured. For the moment, we may assume that at the end of this step, as indicated in Figure 3.3, figures will have been estimated for migration and survival flows, infant migration, births by age group of mother, deaths, and opening population stocks.

Stage (2) Calculation of populations at risk of death and death rates

The minor flow equations involve regional death rates and in order to calculate these, we must work out the populations at risk of death. The population at risk as we have seen is a weighted sum of the elements in the accounts table. The population at risk of dying can be defined in general terms as

$$\hat{K}_{rs}^{D*i} = \Sigma_{\alpha j\omega ku}\; {}^{i}_{s}\theta_{rs}^{D\alpha(j)\omega(k)}\; K_{ru}^{\alpha(j)\omega(k)} \qquad (3.1)$$

where the $\hat{K}^{D}$ is the population at risk of dying and the θ's are the weights or the proportions of the period a particular (jk,ru) flow was exposed to dying in age group s in region i. The summation is over all relevant states j, k and u. The populations at risk of dying for the simple case used in our operational model are

Figure 3.2 The West Yorkshire population accounts table with stocks and flows classified according to estimation procedure

Starting State \ Ending State		Survivors at census date 1966			Death in period 1961-1966			Totals
		West Yorkshire	The rest of England and Wales	The rest of the world	West Yorkshire	The rest of England and Wales	The rest of the world	
Existence at census date 1961	West Yorkshire	C	A	A	C	B	B	A
	The rest of England and Wales	A	C	A	B	C	B	A
	The rest of the world	A	A	D	B	B	D	D
Birth in period 1961-1966	West Yorkshire	C	A	A	C	B	B	A
	The rest of England and Wales	A	C	A	B	C	B	A
	The rest of the world	A	A	D	B	B	D	D
Totals		C	C	D	A	A	D	D

A Known stocks or flows (estimated from data).
B Minor flows estimated from model equation.
C Major flows or stocks estimated from an accounting equation.
D Flows or stocks not considered.

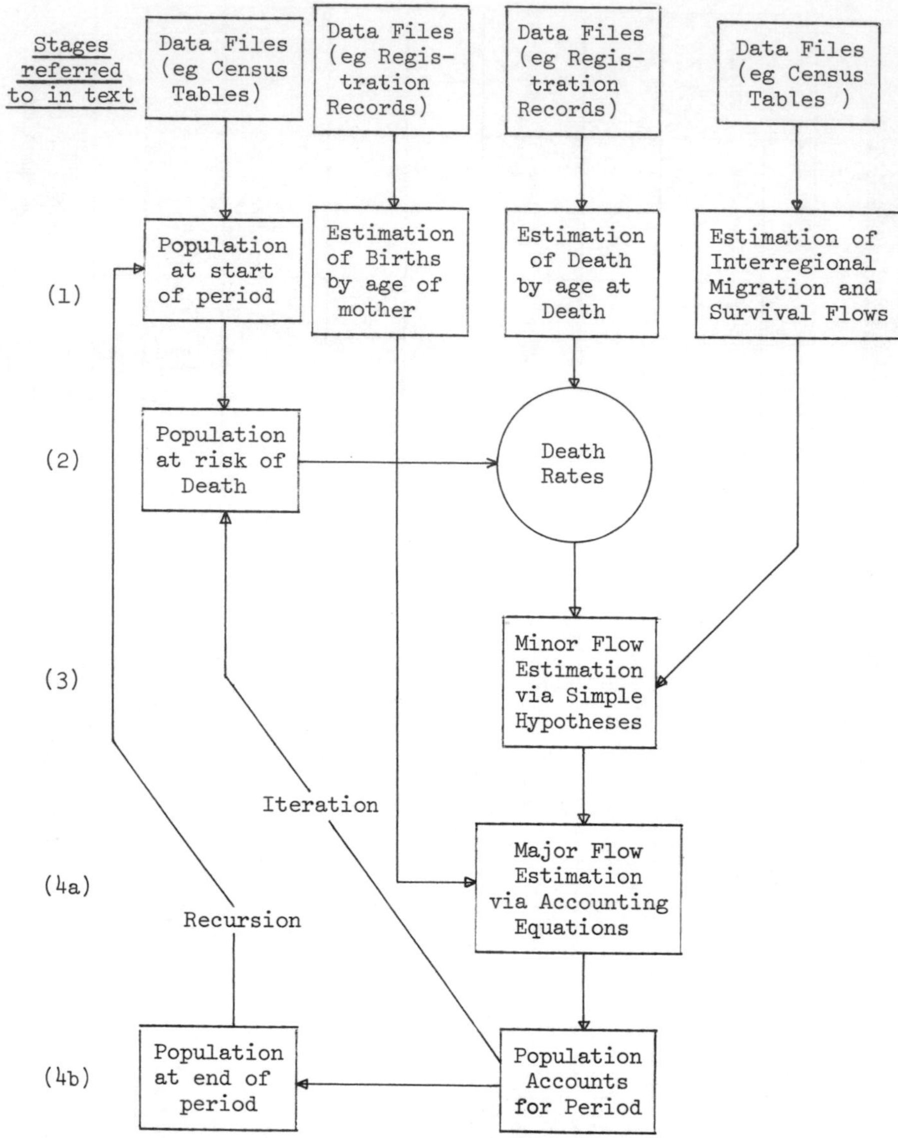

Figure 3.3 The general structure of the accounts based model in 'historical' mode

specified in Section 3.4. Four kinds of population at risk of dying must be defined. $\hat{K}^{D*i}_{s-1s}$ and $\hat{K}^{D*i}_{ss}$ are the populations at risk corresponding to each element in an existence-death submatrix in Figure 3.1. Slightly different definitions are needed for the first age group transition (r=0 to s=1) and for the last (r=R and s=R), R being the general label we use for the last age group. Death rates corresponding to these populations at risk are then calculated:

$$d^{*i}_{s-1s} = K^{\varepsilon(*)\delta(i)}_{s-1s} \Big/ \hat{K}^{D*i}_{s-1s} \tag{3.2}$$

$$d^{*i}_{ss} = K^{\varepsilon(*)\delta(i)}_{ss} \Big/ \hat{K}^{D*i}_{ss} \tag{3.3}$$

$$d^{*i}_{01} = K^{\beta(*)\delta(i)}_{*1} \Big/ \hat{K}^{D*i}_{01} \tag{3.4}$$

and

$$d^{*i}_{RR} = K^{\varepsilon(*)\delta(i)}_{RR} \Big/ \hat{K}^{D*i}_{RR} \tag{3.5}$$

These equations require deaths figures broken down by age group transition. However, in stage (1) we assumed estimation of $K^{*(*)\delta(i)}_{RR}$ figures only. Deaths by age group at death must be transformed into deaths by age transition using c_{rs} coefficients. The methods used are detailed in Section 3.4.

The flows in the table which are unknown can be divided into two categories - minor flows involving migration and then death, $K^{\varepsilon(i)\delta(j)}_{rs}$, $i\neq j$, or birth migration and death, $K^{\beta(i)\delta(j)}_{rl}$, $i\neq j$, which are usually fairly small in size, and major flows in which people remain in one region through out the period, $K^{\varepsilon(i)\delta(i)}_{rs}$, $K^{\beta(i)\delta(i)}_{rl}$, $K^{\varepsilon(i)\sigma(i)}_{rs}$ and $K^{\beta(i)\sigma(i)}_{rl}$. The minor flows are calculated using a set of minor flow equations incorporating a hypothesis about the rate at which people die, while the major flows are calculated using the general accounting equations, in Stage (4) below. These accounting equations are identities that show how the elements of any row or column are related to a constraining row or column total.

Stage (3) Estimation of minor flows

In general, we multiply the population at risk of dying in a particular interregional age transition by the death rate for the region of destination and corresponding age transition:

$$K^{\acute{\varepsilon}(i)\delta(j)}_{rs} = d^{*j}_{rs} \hat{K}^{D\varepsilon(i)\delta(j)}_{rs} \tag{3.6}$$

The simple case equations are given in Section 3.4.

Stage 4 Estimation of major flows via accounting equations

We now make use of the accounting equations in order to estimate the major flows. There are four groups of relationships:

(i) Initial populations

$$K_{r*}^{\varepsilon(i)*(*)} = K_{rr+1}^{\varepsilon(i)\sigma(i)} + \Sigma_{j\neq i} K_{rr+1}^{\varepsilon(i)\sigma(j)} + K_{rr}^{\varepsilon(i)\delta(i)} + K_{rr+1}^{\varepsilon(i)\delta(i)}$$

$$+ \Sigma_{j\neq i} K_{rr}^{\varepsilon(i)\delta(j)} + \Sigma_{j\neq i} K_{rr+1}^{\varepsilon(i)\delta(j)}, \quad r < R \tag{3.7}$$

and where R is the last age group

$$K_{R*}^{\varepsilon(i)*(*)} = K_{RR}^{\varepsilon(i)\sigma(i)} + \Sigma_{j\neq i} K_{RR}^{\varepsilon(i)\sigma(j)} + K_{RR}^{\varepsilon(i)\delta(i)} + \Sigma_{j\neq i} K_{RR}^{\varepsilon(i)\delta(j)} \tag{3.8}$$

(ii) Births

$$K_{r*}^{\beta(i)*(*)} = K_{r1}^{\beta(i)\sigma(i)} + \Sigma_{j\neq i} K_{r1}^{\beta(i)\sigma(j)} + K_{r1}^{\beta(i)\delta(i)} + \Sigma_{j\neq i} K_{r1}^{\beta(i)\delta(j)}$$

$$\lambda < r < \mu \tag{3.9}$$

where λ is the first and μ is the last age group from which mothers can start the period and give birth in it.

(iii) Deaths

$$K_{*s}^{*(*)\delta(i)} = K_{s-1s}^{\varepsilon(i)\delta(i)} + K_{ss}^{\varepsilon(i)\delta(i)} + \Sigma_{j\neq i} K_{s-1s}^{\varepsilon(i)\delta(j)} + \Sigma_{j\neq i} K_{ss}^{\varepsilon(i)\delta(j)}$$

$$1 < s \tag{3.10}$$

and

$$K_{*1}^{*(*)\delta(i)} = K_{11}^{\sigma(i)\delta(i)} + \Sigma_{j\neq i} K_{11}^{\varepsilon(j)\delta(i)} + \Sigma_{r=\lambda}^{\mu} K_{r1}^{\beta(i)\delta(i)}$$

$$+ \Sigma_{j\neq 1} \Sigma_{r=\lambda}^{\mu} K_{r1}^{\beta(j)\delta(i)} \tag{3.11}$$

(iv) Final Populations

$$K_{*s}^{*(*)\sigma(i)} = K_{s-1s}^{\varepsilon(i)\sigma(i)} + \Sigma_{j\neq i} K_{s-1s}^{\varepsilon(i)\sigma(i)} \quad 1 < s < R \tag{3.12}$$

$$K_{*R}^{*(*)\sigma(i)} = K_{R-1R}^{\varepsilon(i)\sigma(i)} K_{RR}^{\varepsilon(i)\sigma(i)} + \Sigma_{j\neq i} K_{R-1R}^{\varepsilon(j)\sigma(i)} + \Sigma_{j\neq i} K_{RR}^{\varepsilon(j)\sigma(i)} \tag{3.13}$$

$$K_{*1}^{*(*)\sigma(i)} = \Sigma_{r=\lambda}^{\mu} K_{r1}^{\beta(i)\sigma(i)} + \Sigma_{j\neq i} \Sigma_{r=\lambda}^{\mu} K_{r1}^{\beta(j)\sigma(i)} \tag{3.14}$$

Now we can begin by working out the terms involving death: for $1 < s < R$

$$K_{s-1s}^{\varepsilon(i)\delta(i)} = K_{s-1s}^{\varepsilon(*)\delta(i)} - \Sigma_{j\neq i} K_{s-1s}^{\varepsilon(j)\delta(i)} \tag{3.15}$$

and

$$K_{ss}^{\varepsilon(i)\delta(i)} = K_{ss}^{\varepsilon(*)\delta(i)} - \Sigma_{j\neq i} K_{ss}^{\varepsilon(j)\delta(i)} \tag{3.16}$$

and for s = 1 the (s-1, s) transition equation becomes

$$K_{*1}^{\beta(i)\delta(i)} = K_{*1}^{\beta(*)\delta(i)} - \Sigma_{j\neq i} K_{*1}^{\beta(j)\delta(i)} \qquad (3.17)$$

In order to breakdown Equation (3.17) by age group we must use e_{r1}^{i} coefficients that distribute infant deaths among the various age categories of mother. The coefficients can be applied to either the left or right hand side of Equation (3.17) to yield $K_{r1}^{\beta(i)\delta(i)}$ where r refers to age group of mother.

We are now in a position to work out the birth and survival terms:

$$K_{r1}^{\beta(i)\sigma(i)} = K_{r*}^{\beta(i)*(*)} - \Sigma_{j\neq i} K_{r1}^{\beta(i)\sigma(j)} - K_{r1}^{\beta(i)\delta(i)} - \Sigma_{j\neq i} K_{r1}^{\beta(i)\delta(j)}$$

$$\lambda < r < \mu \qquad (3.18)$$

$$K_{rr+1}^{\varepsilon(i)\sigma(i)} = K_{r*}^{\varepsilon(i)*(*)} - \Sigma_{j\neq i} K_{rr+1}^{\varepsilon(i)\sigma(j)} - K_{rr}^{\varepsilon(i)\delta(i)} - K_{rr+1}^{\varepsilon(i)\delta(i)}$$

$$- \Sigma_{j\neq i} K_{rr}^{\varepsilon(i)\delta(j)} - \Sigma_{j\neq i} K_{rr+1}^{\varepsilon(i)\delta(j)}, \quad 1 < r < R \qquad (3.19)$$

$$K_{RR}^{\varepsilon(i)\sigma(i)} = K_{R*}^{\varepsilon(i)*(*)} - \Sigma_{j\neq i} K_{RR}^{\varepsilon(i)\sigma(j)} - K_{RR}^{\varepsilon(i)\delta(i)} - \Sigma_{j\neq i} K_{RR}^{\varepsilon(i)\delta(j)} \qquad (3.20)$$

Finally, we complete the first iteration though the accounts by calculating the end of period population.

$$K_{*1}^{*\sigma(i)} = \sum_{r=\lambda}^{\mu} K_{r1}^{\beta(i)\sigma(i)} + \Sigma_{j\neq i} \sum_{r=\lambda}^{\mu} K_{r1}^{\beta(j)\sigma(i)} \qquad (3.21)$$

$$K_{*s}^{*\sigma(i)} = K_{s-1s}^{\varepsilon(i)\sigma(i)} + \Sigma_{j\neq i} K_{s+s}^{\sigma(j)\sigma(i)} \qquad (3.22)$$

and

$$K_{*R}^{*\sigma(i)} = K_{R-1R}^{\varepsilon(i)\sigma(i)} + \Sigma_{j\neq i} K_{R-1R}^{\varepsilon(j)\sigma(i)} + K_{RR}^{\varepsilon(i)\sigma(i)} + \Sigma_{j\neq i} K_{RR}^{\varepsilon(j)\sigma(i)} \qquad (3.23)$$

It is necessary to recycle from Stage (2) through to Stage (4) until convergence in the final population estimates or accounts matrix terms is achieved.

This account-based model can be converted without much difficulty from the historical mode described above into a projection mode, the structure of which is illustrated in Figure 3.4. The first step becomes the preparation of forecast rates of death, birth, migration and birth and migration events, rather than the input of these in the form of historical totals. The second step changes from one involving calculation of death rates to one involving the calculation of projected total deaths and total births. The remainder of the model is then as before. A further discussion of the structure of the model in

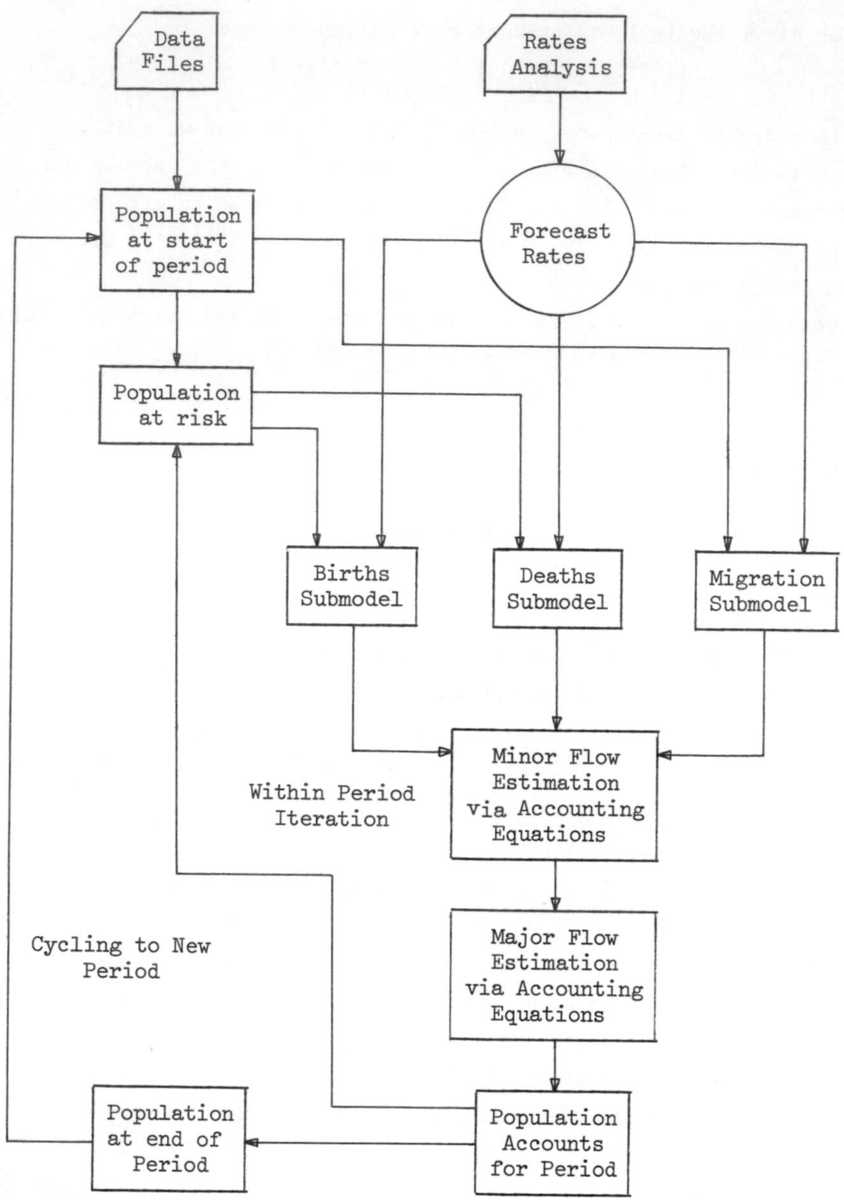

Figure 3.4 The accounts based model in a projection framework

projection mode is given in Wilson and Rees (1974) and Rees and Wilson (1976-A). In both historical and projection models, as the corresponding figures show, it is a straightforward matter to apply the model to a series of periods by using the closing stocks of one period as the opening stocks of a subsequent period.

3.3 Data requirements and estimation procedures for demographic accounts and models

One of the most important steps in building an operational model is to match data requirements with the data available from official or private sources. Estimates have to be made from published demographic data of model variables. In the ensuing discussion attention is focused on the data available in published form at county level in the Sample Census of 1966. Equivalent data is obtainable at local authority level, and better data is available in the Census of 1971. So, in most cases, less 'data gap filling' will be required than described here. However, some will always be required and the techniques employed here may prove useful to the reader in other contexts. At the end of the section the further procedures needed in constructing data for a study area (West Yorkshire) from local authority data will be described.

In preparing population accounts tables the initial requirement is the count of relevant population stocks at the initial point in time. One of the advantages of choosing a five year intercensal period as the accounting period is that the required population stocks are easily derivable from the Census of Population. However, several adjustments are necessary before census data can be introduced into the model. First, population data must be adjusted to the correct basis - from enumerated to usually resident. Secondly, it must be corrected for any underenumeration at the census. Thirdly, further correction is required, for any regional boundary changes over the accounting period. Fourthly, it may be necessary to disaggregate or aggregate census data so that it corresponds to the accounts required. We discuss each adjustment in turn.

Census authorities use two population concepts: <u>enumerated</u> (de facto) population consists of all the people actually present in a location on census night: and <u>usually resident</u> (de jure) population is the number of people counted by place of normal residence irrespective of their location on census night. The latter is the more relevant concept for accounts since death, birth and migration statistics are all recorded on this basis. Note also that care must be taken in the treatment of groups whose place of usual residence is difficult to define - students, members of the armed forces and vagrants. For the West Yorkshire Study, we have simply estimated a concept adjustment factor by dividing the total usually resident population by the total enumerated population.

$$\text{Concept adjustment factor} = \frac{\text{Total usually resident population}}{\text{Total enumerated population}} \qquad (3.24)$$

Adjustment for underenumeration is not normally required if using census figures. However, post-enumeration checks revealed that the 1966 Sample Census contained an underenumeration of around 67,000 in the 10% sample owing to the deficiencies in the sampling frame. No regional breakdown figure was available and so we applied a national inflation factor to the regional age and sex disaggregated populations. This factor can be calculated as follows:

$$\text{Inflation factor} = \frac{\text{Revised estimate of enumerated population}}{\text{1966 Sample Census enumerated population}}$$

$$= \frac{47,805,510}{47,135,510} = 1.0142143 \qquad (3.25)$$

Boundary changes at the regional level have been quite common in the past, although none affect West Yorkshire in the 1961 to 1966 intercensal period. Furthermore, as far as population stocks are concerned when boundary changes do occur, the populations of the new regions at previous census dates are normally also given.

Population stock information provided by official sources varies according to the scale of the region. There are three principal scales as shown in Figure 3.5: national, comprising England and Wales, Scotland and Northern Ireland; regional, comprising Standard Regions, conurbations and Standard Region remainders; and local, including Counties, County Boroughs and two categories of small local authorities prior to reorganisation. The local level now consists of metropolitan counties and districts, non-metropolitan counties and districts; Greater London Council and the London boroughs.

In estimating the missing figures, several techniques are available. For example, if we wish to disaggregate age group information further, we can employ deconsolidation factors derived from higher regional scales. In general

Figure 3.5 Age group information available in published form for population stocks at various scales at a full census England and Wales

National	Regional	Local	Accounts	National	Regional	Local	Accounts	National	Regional	Local	Accounts
(1)	(2)	(3)	(4)	(1)	(2)	(3)	(4)	(1)	(2)	(3)	(4)
0	0	0	0- 4	40	40-44	40-44	40-44	80	80-84	80-84	80-84
1	1	1		41				81			
2	2	2		42				82			
3	3	3		43				83			
4	4	4		44				84			
5	5	5	5- 9	45	45-49	45-49	45-49	85	85-89	85-89	85-89
6	6	6		46				86			
7	7	7		47				87			
8	8	8		48				88			
9	9	9		49				89			
10	10	10	10-14	50	50-54	50-54	50-54	90	90-94	90-94	90-94
11	11	11		51				91			
12	12	12		52				92			
13	13	13		53				93			
14	14	14		54				94			
15	15	15	15-19	55	55-59	55-59	55-59	95	95 and over	95 and over	95 and over
16	16	16		56				96			
17	17	17		57				97			
18	18	18		58				98			
19	19	19		59				99			
20	20	20	20-24	60	60-64	60-64	60-64	100			
21	21	21		61				101			
22	22-24	22-24		62				102			
23				63				103			
24				64				104			
25	25-29	25-29	25-29	65	65-69	65-69	65-69	105			
26				66				106			
27				67				107			
28				68				108			
29				69				109 and over			
30	30-34	30-34	30-34	70	70-74	70-74	70-74				
31				71							
33				72							
33				73							
34				74							
35	35-39	35-39	35-39	75	75-79	75-79	75-79				
36				76							
37				77							
38				78							
39				79							

Note: Less information is available for the Sample Census of 1966

$$\omega_r^i = \omega_p^i \left[\frac{\omega_r^I}{\Sigma_{r\varepsilon p}\omega_r^I} \right] \tag{3.26}$$

where ω_r^i represents the smaller region population of r, the finer age group interval, ω_p^i is the same variable for age group p of a coarser interval, and $[\omega_r^I/\Sigma_{r\varepsilon p}\omega_r^I]$ is a deconsolidation proportion for the rth age group for the larger region[(1)]. Such deconsolidation proportions can be arranged in a deconsolidation matrix, which is then applied to a population vector. In our West Yorkshire application for instance, the 1966 Sample Census does not give a breakdown of local authority populations over the age of 75. This can be achieved by employing the finer age breakdown available for the Yorkshire and Humberside region.

We can represent these four sets of adjustments to the enumerated population vectors as a series of operators by which the population vector is multiplied. Let $\underline{B}$ be the matrix of enumerated to usually resident adjustment factors, $\underline{U}$ be the matrix of underenumeration correction factors, $\underline{R}$ be the matrix of regional aggregation coefficients and $\underline{D}$ be the matrix of age group deconsolidation proportions. The population stock adjustment process can then be formally stated as

$$\underset{R_2 x N_2}{\underline{\hat{\omega}}(t)} \equiv \underset{R_2 x R_1}{\underline{D}} \; \underset{R_1 x R_1}{\underline{U}} \; \underset{R_1 x R_1}{\underline{B}} \; \underset{R_1 x N_1}{\underline{\omega}(t)} \; \underset{N_1 x N_2}{\underline{R}} \tag{3.27}$$

where $\underline{\omega}(t)$ is the input population matrix of age groups and regions derived from the census and $\underline{\hat{\omega}}(t)$ is adjusted population vector. There are R_1 age groups and N_1 zones for which enumerated population data is available. These are adjusted for residence basis and underenumeration by matrices with relevant factors in the principal diagonal and zeros elsewhere. The $\underline{D}$ matrix transforms the R_1 age groups into R_2 age groups and the $\underline{R}$ matrix transforms the N_1 regions into N_2 regions.

Birth and death totals are counts of events that take place within a specified period, in specified regions. Children born are classified by sex, and their mothers are classified by age group at the time of birth. Persons who die are classified by sex and age at time of death. Such classifications, however, are not those required by the model. For the accounts based model we ideally require that

---

(1) We use ω to represent population here, rather than K (employed earlier in defining the accounts matrix) in order to keep the description simple.

Figure 3.6 Information available on age group at death at various scales England and Wales

National	Regional	Local	Accounts	National	Regional	Local	Accounts	National	Regional	Local	Accounts
(1)	(2)	(3)	(4)	(1)	(2)	(3)	(4)	(1)	(2)	(3)	(4)
0	0			40	35-44			80	75		
1				41				81	and		
2	1- 4		0- 4	42			40-44	82	over		80-84
3				43				83			
4				44				84			
5				45				85			
6				46				86			
7			5- 9	47			45-49	87			85-89
8				48				88			
9				49				89			
10	5-14			50	45-54			90			
11				51				91			
12			10-14	52			50-54	92			90-94
13				53				93			
14				54				94			
15				55				95			95
16				56				96			and
17			15-19	57			55-59	97			over
18				58				98			
19				59				99			
20	15-24			60	55-64			100			
21				61				101			
22			20-24	62			60-64	102			
23				63				103			
24				64				104			
25				65				105			
26				66				106			
27			25-29	67			65-69	107			
28				68				108			
29				69				109			
30	25-34			70	65-74			110			
31				71				and			
32			30-34	72			70-74	over			
33				73							
34				74							
35				75							
36				76							
37			35-39	77			75-79				
38				78							
39				79							

The solid lines show what breakdown is available in published sources while the broken lines indicate that which is available as unpublished information.

deaths, recorded by sex and age group at death, be cross classified by age group at the beginning of the accounting period. Births should be classified by age group of mother at the start of the period.

Figure 3.6 shows the age (at death) classifications provided in the published mortality statistics for various spatial scales. At the national scale, statistics are available for each single year of age up to 110. At the regional scale, a ten year age group breakdown is published, but a further breakdown into five year age groups is available. Finally, at the local scale, deaths are only disaggregated by sex normally, but again a five year breakdown is available on request.

In order to make estimates of the deaths in the proper cohorts for the study area accounts {column (4)} we have employed data from each of the three scales {columns (1) to (3)}. It is necessary to adjust death statistics from a single calendar year base to one of an intercensal five year period. This is achieved by converting calendar year data to single 'census year' data and then summing over the whole census period. The relationship between calendar and 'census' years is expressed diagramatically in Figure 3.7.

Figure 3.7 The relationship between calendar years and 'census' years

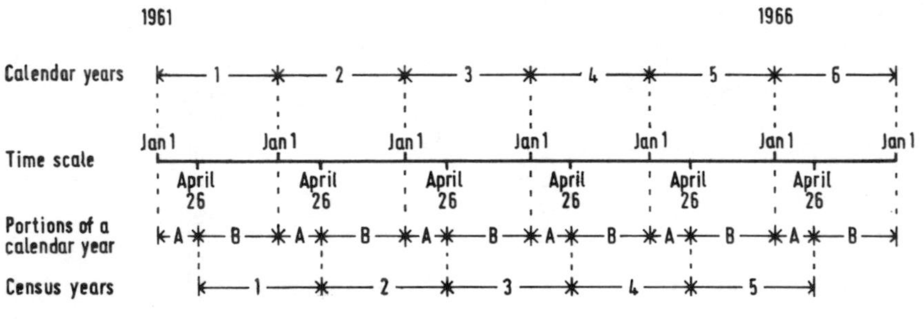

Calendar years are divided into two parts: A (1 January to census date) and B (census date to 31 December). Deaths in each census year are then estimated as

$$K^{*(*)\delta(i)}(\lambda) = F_B(\theta_\lambda)K^{*(*)\delta(i)}(\theta_\lambda)+F_A(\theta_{\lambda+1})K^{*(*)\delta(i)}(\theta_{\lambda+1}) \quad (3.28)$$

where λ is an index that labels 'census' year, θ is an index that labels a calendar year, and θ_λ is the label for the calendar year, the majority of which falls in 'census' year λ. $F_B(\theta_\lambda)$ and $F_A(\theta_{\lambda+1})$ indicate the proportion of calendar year deaths in question falling in portions A and B of the year. These factors can be simply estimated from a count of days in each portion, or as here, we can use national scale information available for each quarter from the Registrar General's Statistical Review in order to allow for the seasonal variation in deaths. Monthly data can also be used.

We can now go on to show how this adjusted information can be transformed into that required by the accounts base model. The procedure developed for our particular West Yorkshire case study is applicable to any similar region within England and Wales.

For the intercensal period the following items of information are available, or can be easily estimated: $K^{*(*)\delta(c)x}_{s-1s}$, $K^{*(*)\delta(c)x}_{ss}$ = national scale (or region c for country) deaths of sex x for each five year age group transition s-1 and ss[(1)]; $K^{*(*)\delta(I)x}_{*\upsilon}$ = deaths in standard region I (in this case Yorkshire and Humberside) of sex x in υ (ten year) age groups; $K^{*(*)\delta(i)x}_{**}$ = deaths in local area i (in this case West Yorkshire) by sex x; we wish to estimate: $K^{*(*)\delta(i)x}_{s-1s}$ and $K^{*(*)\delta(i)x}_{ss}$ = local scale deaths of sex x for each age group transition s-1, s and s, s for the intercensal period 1961-1966. We first work out the national age transition death rates

$$d^{*cx}_{s-1s} = K^{*(*)\delta(c)x}_{s-1s} \Big/ \hat{K}^{D*cx}_{s-1s} \tag{3.29}$$

and

$$d^{*cx}_{ss} = K^{*(*)\delta(c)x}_{ss} / \hat{K}^{D*cx}_{ss} \tag{3.30}$$

We can then use these national rates to estimate deaths in age transitions at the regional scale, constraining the estimates to add up to the correct known regional, age at death totals. The required equations are

$$K^{*(*)\delta(I)x}_{s-1s} = A^{Ix}_{\upsilon} d^{*cx}_{s-1s} \hat{K}^{D*Ix}_{s-1s}, \qquad s \in \upsilon \tag{3.31}$$

and

$$K^{*(*)\delta(I)x}_{ss} = A^{Ix}_{\upsilon} d^{*cx}_{ss} \hat{K}^{D*Ix}_{ss}, \qquad s \in \upsilon \tag{3.32}$$

---

(1) These are not directly available but can be estimated using information for age groups that are a single year in length and k coefficients (see Smith and Rees, 1974, pp 31-32).

subject to

$$\Sigma_{s\varepsilon\upsilon}\left[A_{\upsilon}^{Ix}d_{s-1s}^{*cx}\hat{K}_{s-1s}^{D*Ix}+A_{\upsilon}^{Ix}d_{ss}^{*cx}K_{ss}^{D*Ix}\right] = K_{*\upsilon}^{*(*)\delta(I)x} \quad (3.33)$$

so that

$$A_{\upsilon}^{Ix} = K_{*\upsilon}^{*(*)\delta(I)x}/\Sigma_{s\varepsilon\upsilon}\left[d_{s-1s}^{*cx}\hat{K}_{s-1s}^{D*Ix}+d_{ss}^{*cx}\hat{K}_{ss}^{D*Ix}\right] \quad (3.34).$$

A_{υ}^{Ix} is therefore a balancing factor which ensures that estimated deaths in the five year are groups and transitions add up to observed totals in ten year age groups.

Regional death rates can now be calculated as in Equations (3.29) and (3.30) and subsequently used to estimate local scale deaths

$$K_{s-1s}^{*(*)\delta(i)x} = A^{ix}d_{s-1s}^{*Ix}\hat{K}_{s-1s}^{D*ix} \quad (3.35)$$

and

$$K_{ss}^{*(*)\delta(i)x} = A^{ix}d_{ss}^{*Ix}\hat{K}_{ss}^{D*ix} \quad (3.36)$$

where A^{ix} is the balancing factor which satisfies the constraint

$$\Sigma_{s}(K_{s-1s}^{*(*)\delta(i)x}+K_{ss}^{*(*)\delta(i)x}) = K_{**}^{*(*)\delta(i)x} \quad (3.37)$$

and is derived as

$$A^{ix} = K_{**}^{*(*)\delta(i)x}/\Sigma_{s}(d_{s-1s}^{*Ix}\hat{K}_{s-1s}^{D*ix}+d_{ss}^{*Ix}\hat{K}_{ss}^{D*ix}) \quad (3.38)$$

It should be noted that these estimation equations employ population at risk of dying terms and as a result must be involved in the main iterative structure of the accounts based model. Figure 3.8 shows the structure of the table of death statistics that result for the West Yorkshire Study Area. The column totals in the table are the total number of deaths recorded in a five year age group over the five year intercensal period 1961-1966. This number has been distributed, by the methods described above, between the two initial age groups (equivalent to birth cohorts) from which the deceased could have come. The row totals add together all the deaths that occur to persons classified by five year initial age groups. The additional task of allocating these deaths to initial regional locations is performed by the accounts based model.

Procedures similar to those outlined above can be used to estimate the number of births to each age group transition of mothers. Figure 3.9 shows what information is available at various scales on births.

Figure 3.8 Deaths in West Yorkshire classified by age group at death and by age group at the beginning of the period

Age group at start of period	Age group at death										Totals
	0- 4	5- 9	10-14	15-19	20-24	25-29	30-34	35-39	40-44	45-49	
	1	2	3	4	5	6	7	8	9	10	
Born 0	1,844										1,844
0- 4 1	323	73									396
5- 9 2		53	48								101
10-14 3			53	81							134
15-19 4				73	80						153
20-24 5					78	104					182
25-29 6						106	137				243
30-34 7							168	215			383
35-39 8								266	396		662
40-44 9									439	560	999
45-49 10										739	1,748
Totals	2,167	126	101	154	158	210	305	481	835	1,299	

Age group at start of period	Age group at death										Totals
	50-54	55-59	60-64	65-69	70-74	75-79	80-84	85-89	90-94	95+	
	11	12	13	14	15	16	17	18	19	20	
45-49 10	1,009										1,748
50-54 11	1,159	1,545									2,704
55-59 12		1,747	2,334								4,801
60-64 13			2,680	3,578							6,258
65-69 14				3,817	4,865						8,682
70-74 15					5,210	5,692					10,902
75-79 16						5,744	5,866				11,610
80-84 17							5,456	4,297			9,753
85-89 18								2,946	1,582		4,528
90-94 19									844	288	1,132
95+ 20										174	174
Totals	2,168	3,292	5,014	7,395	10,075	11,436	11,322	7,243	2,426	462	66,669

Figure 3.9 Information available on age group of mother at birth of child at various scales, England and Wales

National	Regional	Local	National	Regional	Local
10	Under 20	Under 20	35	35-39	35-39
11			36		
12			37		
13			38		
14			39		
15			40	40-44	40-44
16			41		
17			42		
18			43		
19			44		
20	20-24	20-24	45	45 and over	45 and over
21			46		
22			47		
23			48		
24			49		
25	25-29	25-29	50		
26			51		
27			52		
28			53		
29			54		
30	30-34	30-34	55 and over		
31					
32					
33					
34					

The solid lines show what breakdown of births by age group of mother at time of birth is available in published sources. The broken lines indicate the age groups for which unpublished information is available.

By using the national single year of age information some idea of the number of births occurring to mothers in five year age group transitions can be made (see Smith and Rees, 1974, pp. 31-32). Then if local information on births by five year age group of mother is available, the following equations can be used to estimate births in a mother's age group transition,

$$K^{\beta(i)*(*)x}_{s-1*}(K^{\varepsilon(*)m(i)}_{s-1s}) = A^{ix}_{s} b^{*cx}_{s-1s} \hat{K}^{B*iF}_{s-1s} \qquad (3.39)$$

and

$$K^{\beta(i)*(*)x}_{s*}(K^{\varepsilon(*)m(i)}_{ss}) = A^{ix}_{s} b^{*cx}_{ss} \hat{K}^{B*iF}_{ss} \qquad (3.40)$$

where

$$A^{ix}_{s} = K^{\beta(i)*(*)x}_{**}(K^{\varepsilon(*)m(i)}_{*s})/(b^{*cx}_{s-1s}\hat{K}^{B*iF}_{s-1s}+b^{*cx}_{ss}K^{B*iF}_{ss}) \qquad (3.41)$$

The K notation term for births has been extended by appending a term that defines the mothers involved: $K_{s-1s}^{\varepsilon(*)m(i)}$ refers to females in age group s-1 who give birth in region i in age group s; and $K_{ss}^{\varepsilon(*)m(i)}$ refers to women in age group s who give birth in region i in age group s. The balancing factor A_s^{ix} ensures that the two birth terms sum to the observed local live births by age groups at time of birth. Once births in an age transition have been calculated they can be summed by the initial or time t age group

$$K_{s-1*}^{\beta(i)*(*)x} = K_{s-1*}^{\beta(i)*(*)x}(K_{s-1s-1}^{\varepsilon(*)m(i)}) + K_{s-1*}^{\beta(i)*(*)x}(K_{s-1s}^{\varepsilon(*)m(i)}) \quad (3.42)$$

These are the terms that appear as row totals in the birth rows of the accounts table (see the tables in Section 3.5). From them, we derive the e_{r1}^{i} coefficients which are used to disaggregate the $K^{\beta(i)ix}$, $K^{\beta(i)jx}$, $i \neq j$, $K^{\beta(i)\delta(i)x}$ and $K^{\beta(i)\delta(j)x}$, $i \neq j$ terms by age group of mother at the beginning of the accounting period:

$$e_{r1}^{i} = \frac{K_{r1}^{\beta(i)*(*)x}}{K_{*1}^{\beta(i)*(*)x}} \quad (3.43)$$

and these are applied thus

$$K_{r1}^{\beta(i)\varepsilon(i)x} = e_{r1}^{i} K^{\beta(i)\varepsilon(i)x} \quad (3.44)$$

to all the terms in the births half of the accounts table.

From the description of the accounts based model given in Section 3.2 it will be appreciated that it is essential to have some estimate of the migration of persons between regions in order to fill in either the historical or the projected accounts matrix. It is fortunate that such information is often available for selected periods. Regional input-output tables are very difficult to construct because of the lack of equivalent interregional inter-industry transfer statistics.

Figure 3.10 shows the submatrices for which we require migration estimates and their relation to available data. All the terms involving migration and death in the right half of the accounts matrix are generated in the model. The submatrices on the left hand side of the accounts matrix are of two kinds: those the terms of which can be estimated from figures given in the census tables on migration; and those involving out-migration to the rest of the world.

Figure 3.10 Migration flows: the sources of the estimates

Initial state \ Final state		Survival at census date 1966			Death in period 1961-66			Totals
		West Yorkshire	Rest of England and Wales	Rest of the world	West Yorkshire	Rest of England and Wales	Rest of the world	
Existence at census date 1961	West Yorkshire		Recorded in MST and MRR census tables	Part recorded in MST tables rest must be estimated from RGSR tables		Estimated in ab model	Estimated in ab model	population
	Rest of England and Wales	Recorded in MST and MRR census tables		Part recorded in MST tables rest must be estimated from RGSR tables	Estimated in ab model			population
	Rest of the world	Recorded in MST and MRR census tables	Recorded in MST and MRR census tables		Estimated in ab model	Estimated in ab model		RGSR tables CI act Statistics in-migrants
Births in period 1961-66	West Yorkshire		Estimated from MT census tables	Part estimated from MT census tables and part from RGSR tables		Estimated in ab model	Estimated in ab model	Births
	Rest of England and Wales	Estimated from MT census tables		Part estimated from MT census tables and part from RGSR tables	Estimated in ab model		Estimated in ab model	Births
	Rest of the world	Estimated from MT census tables	Estimated from MT census tables		Estimated in ab model	Estimated in ab model		RGSR tables CI act Statistics infant-migrants
Totals		population	population	surviving out-migrants	deaths	deaths	non-surviving out-migrants	

Note MST - Migration Summary Tables MR - Migration Tables, Part II MRR - Migration Regional Report
RGSR - Registrar General's Statistical Review CI - Commonwealth Immigrant ab - accounts based model

In order to estimate the terms in submatrices involving the rest of the world we must use information for zones in the rest of the world covered by the UK census (Scotland, Northern Ireland, Isle of Man, Channel Islands) and we must use information on the migration movements recorded annually in the Registrar General's Statistical Review for zones not included in the UK census (The Republic of Ireland, the Commonwealth countries bar the UK, the other countries of the world). More detailed information is available in the Commonwealth Immigrant Act Statistics for persons migrating into the UK from the Commonwealth. The migration information available in the census tables is of the existence, migration and survival type ($K^{\varepsilon(i)\sigma(j)}$ type data) needed in the accounts. The number of infant migrants is not given directly in the census migration tables but information on the number of children under five years of age in migrant households is given. A guess is made that half of these were born before the migration of the household and half afterwards. The migration movement statistics relate to the accounts table in a less direct fashion. They are the sums of the terms in several submatrices of the accounts. For example, the Registrar General's Statistical Review, Tables S1, S2 and S3, provide accounts of the number of movements made out of the UK to the rest of the world. Assuming we were interested in the UK accounts and called the UK region i, this movement, total could be labelled M^{iR}. The terms in the accounts would $K^{\varepsilon(i)\sigma(R)}$, $K^{\varepsilon(i)\delta(R)}$, $K^{\beta(i)\sigma(R)}$ and $K^{\beta(i)\delta(R)}$, neglecting age and sex for the moment. The relation between the M and K terms is as follows:

$$M^{iR} = K^{\varepsilon(i)\sigma(R)} + K^{\varepsilon(i)\delta(R)} + K^{\beta(i)\sigma(R)} + K^{\beta(i)\delta(R)} + RM^{iR} \qquad (3.45)$$

where RM^{iR} refers to all repeat migrations made by the persons already listed in the accounts terms. The M^{iR} information can be used to constrain $(K^{\varepsilon(i)\sigma(R)} + K^{\varepsilon(i)\delta(R)} + K^{\beta(i)\sigma(R)} + K^{\beta(i)\delta(R)})$ estimates - these cannot exceed M^{iR}. The relations between the migrants represented in the accounts matrix and the migrations counted crossing international borders are more fully explored in Rees (1974).

There are a great many more points of detail involved in estimating migrant flows, and these are dealt with in part in Rees (1971), Smith and Rees (1974) and Rees and Wilson (1977-B). To get from the items recorded in the published census tables and annual reviews to the data needed in the accounts based model involves a great many operations.

These can be structured in a similar manner to Equation (3.27):

$$\underset{R_2 x N_2}{\underline{\hat{m}}(t+T)} = \underset{R_2 x R_1}{\underline{D}} \; \underset{R_1 x R_1}{\underline{U}} \; \underset{R_1 x N_1}{\underline{m}(t+T)} \; \underset{N_1 x N_2}{\underline{R}} \qquad (3.46)$$

where $\underline{m}(t+T)$ is the initial vector of migrants disaggregated by age group at time t+T and $\underline{\hat{m}}(t+T)$ is the adjusted vector. The regional aggregation/disaggregation operator $\underline{R}$ involves operations like breaking down the UK to rest of the world flow into West Yorkshire to the rest of the world, the rest of England and Wales to the rest of the world, and the rest of the UK to the rest of the world flows. The $\underline{B}$ operator is not relevant as migration is necessarily measured on a usual residence basis. The age group deconsolidation operator $\underline{D}$ involves a complex set of operations (spelled out in Smith and Rees, 1974) which can be summed up in the $\underline{D}$ operator for females involved in the West Yorkshire to the rest of England and Wales flow given in Equation (3.47).

$$\underline{D} = \begin{bmatrix} 0.5236 & 0 & 0 & 0 \\ 0.4764 & 0 & 0 & 0 \\ 0 & 0.1196 & 0 & 0 \\ 0 & 0.2365 & 0 & 0 \\ 0 & 0.1992 & 0 & 0 \\ 0 & 0.1933 & 0 & 0 \\ 0 & 0.1199 & 0 & 0 \\ 0 & 0.1315 & 0 & 0 \\ 0 & 0 & 0.3194 & 0 \\ 0 & 0 & 0.3403 & 0 \\ 0 & 0 & 0.3403 & 0 \\ 0 & 0 & 0 & 0.2732 \\ 0 & 0 & 0 & 0.2701 \\ 0 & 0 & 0 & 0.1768 \\ 0 & 0 & 0 & 0.1441 \\ 0 & 0 & 0 & 0.1042 \\ 0 & 0 & 0 & 0.0616 \\ 0 & 0 & 0 & 0.0254 \\ 0 & 0 & 0 & 0.0065 \\ 0 & 0 & 0 & 0.0011 \end{bmatrix} \qquad (3.47)$$

The matrix has four columns representing the four initial age groups by which the migration flows were disaggregated: 5-14, 15-44, 45-49, 60 and over, and twenty rows representing the age groups needed in the accounts.

In the above discussion we have concentrated on the application of the accounts based model to one unit at the local authority or county scale. In fact, it is possible to apply the same techniques to non-standard regions in the form of local authority aggregates. The additional data manipulation in the majority of cases merely involves aggregation of local authority figures to totals for the desired region. Figure 3.11 illustrates for our West Yorkshire application the relationship between the study area, the West Riding county and the remainder of the accounts system showing the position of the various regions employed in the relevant census tables.

Figure 3.11 The relationship between regions used in the West Yorkshire accounts and those used in the principal data sources

Regions used in West Yorkshire accounts	Regions used in census and allied tables
West Yorkshire	51 local authorities in the West Riding of Yorkshire
Rest of England and Wales	England and Wales minus West Yorkshire or Rest of the West Riding of Yorkshire plus England and Wales minus the West Riding of Yorkshire
Rest of the world	Scotland Elsewhere in the British Isles ie Northern Ireland Irish Republic Isle of Man Channel Islands Abroad

The population stocks are obtained by aggregating the relevant local authority figures and subtracting from England and Wales population figures the West Yorkshire totals.

For 1966

$$K_{r*}^{\varepsilon(EW-WY)*(*)x} = K_{r*}^{\varepsilon(EW)*(*)x} - K_{r*}^{\varepsilon(WY)*(*)x} \qquad (3.48)$$

where EW refers to England and Wales and EW-WY refers to England and Wales minus West Yorkshire. Total birth and death figures for each sex are available for each calendar year for single local authorities and merely require the appropriate aggregation.

Suitable migration figures present greater problems. We need in our West Yorkshire example to estimate six sets of flows and each requires its own procedures. Migration from West Yorkshire to the

Rest of England and Wales is calculated as the sum for all the 51 local authorities making up West Yorkshire of 'Emigration to all areas' less 'Emigration to Scotland' less the sum of migrations to other local authorities within the West Yorkshire Study Area. Migration from the Rest of England and Wales to West Yorkshire is computed as the sum for all the 51 local authorities of 'Immigrations from all areas' less the sum of immigrations from other local authorities within the study area, less immigrations from elsewhere in England and Wales, less 'Immigrations from Scotland', less 'Immigrations from Elsewhere in the British Isles', less 'Immigrations from Abroad'. In the case of these flows 'all areas' refers to all areas of the world whereas in the previous set of flows 'all areas' refers only to all areas in Great Britain. Migration from the rest of the world to West Yorkshire is the sum for all the 51 local authority areas of 'Immigrations from Scotland' plus 'Immigrations from Elsewhere in the British Isles' plus 'Immigrations from Abroad'. Out-migration to the rest of the world is not recorded in the census tables directly and must be found as a sum for all local authorities of 'Emigrations to Scotland' plus estimates of emigrations to Northern Ireland, to the Irish Republic, to the Isle of Man and Channel Islands, and to areas 'Abroad' (see Smith and Rees, 1974; Rees and Wilson, 1977-A, Appendix 1 for details). Estimates are made of the numbers of emigrants to the rest of the world from England and Wales, and from these estimates are subtracted the estimates of the West Yorkshire to rest of the world flows to yield the number of migrants from the rest of England and Wales to the rest of the world. Immigration from the rest of the world to the rest of England and Wales is worked out by subtracting the estimate of the flow to West Yorkshire from that for England and Wales as a whole. All these migrant flows can be estimated by sex group fairly easily but a variety of different deconsolidations have to be used to generate five year age group numbers (see Smith and Rees, 1974, for details).

3.4 An operational model for West Yorkshire

So far we have presented a description of the procedures and methods of estimation involved in a demographic accounts based model. The task of this section is to piece these segments together by summarising the progression of events in an operational model in historical mode. This structure is described with reference to two flow charts, Figures 3.12 and 3.13, which are based directly on a computer program, described in Smith (1974), developed from the concepts presented in this chapter. The concepts and techniques involved have been described or alluded to in previous sections of the chapter. They are repeated here in a single sequence to give the reader an idea of what the operational model now looks like. It will be useful to any reader intending to develop his or her own accounting model and computer program. Others may find it more worthwhile to omit the section and to look at its results in Section 3.5.

Here we give a step by step account of the operational model. The flow charts reveal that an iterative method of solution is required. A single procedure is followed through each iteration with the exception of the first, and the steps involved in the first and subsequent iterations are given below with reference to flow charts.

<u>Path for first iteration</u>

(1), (2), (3a), (4a), (4b) ...... (4m), (5), (6), (7), (8), (9), (11)

<u>Path for subsequent iterations</u>

(3b), (4f), (4j), (4k), (4l), (4m), (5), (6), (7), (8), (9), (10), (11)

<u>Step One: assembly of known data</u>

The first step is to assemble those data items which are available directly from sources or which can be easily estimated from such data. Preliminary estimation is necessary because the classification of stocks and flows used by official bodies does not comply with the required breakdown as presented in the accounts table. These preliminary estimation techniques have been discussed in Section 3.3. The data items required for the operational accounts based model are shown in Figure 3.14.

<u>Step Two: adjustment of known data for underenumeration and concept differences</u>

Population stocks must be adjusted in order to take account of the concept change from census enumerated to usually resident population, and to correct for census underenumeration

$$K_{s-1*}^{\varepsilon(i)*(*)x}(\text{corrected}) = K_{s-1*}^{\varepsilon(i)*(*)x}.u \qquad (3.49)$$

where u is an appropriate factor. Migration flows should also be similarly corrected in order to allow for underenumeration in the

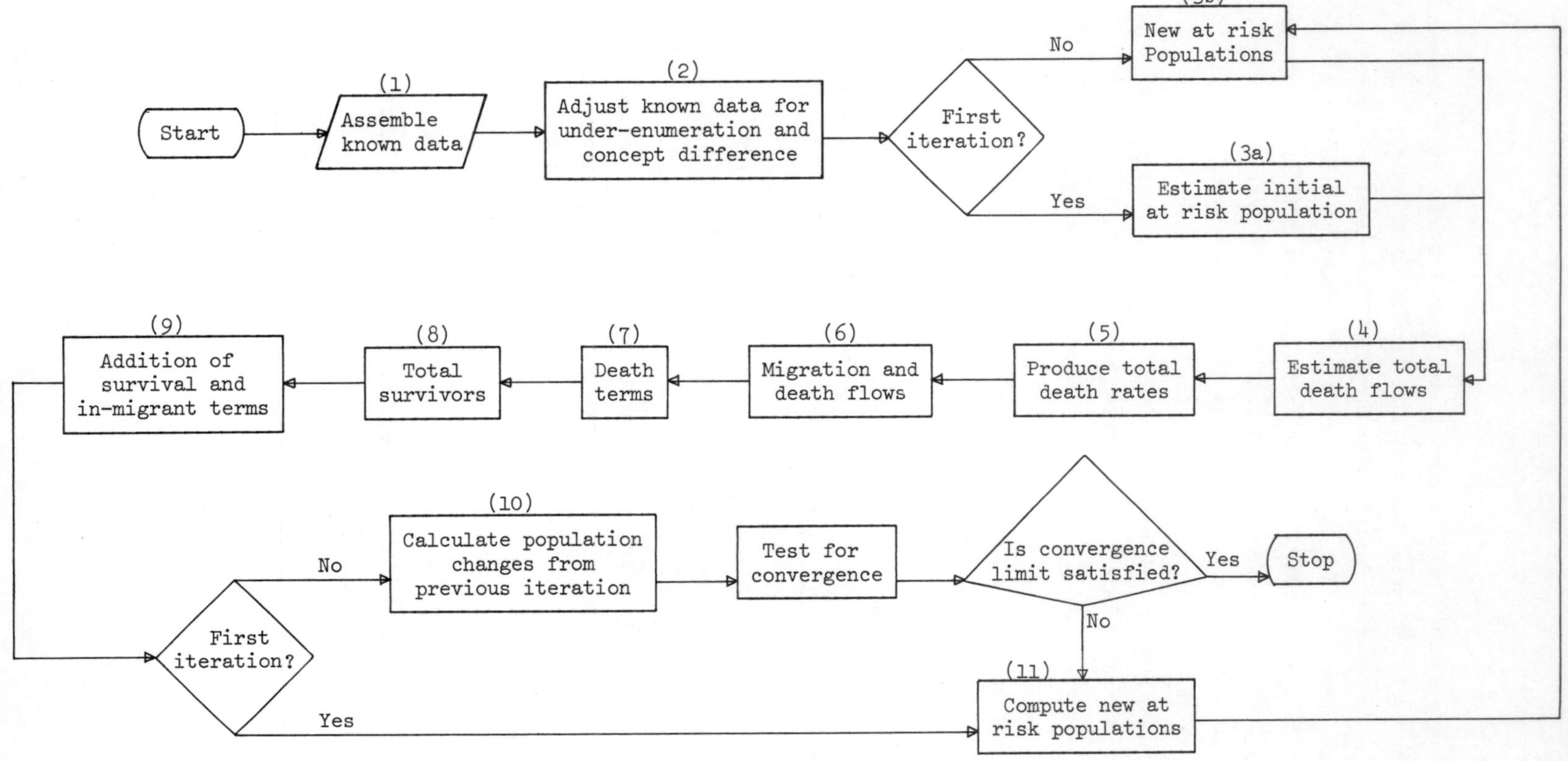

Figure 3.12 A flow chart illustrating sequential model procedure

Figure 3.13 The detailed procedures for total death flow estimation - Step 4

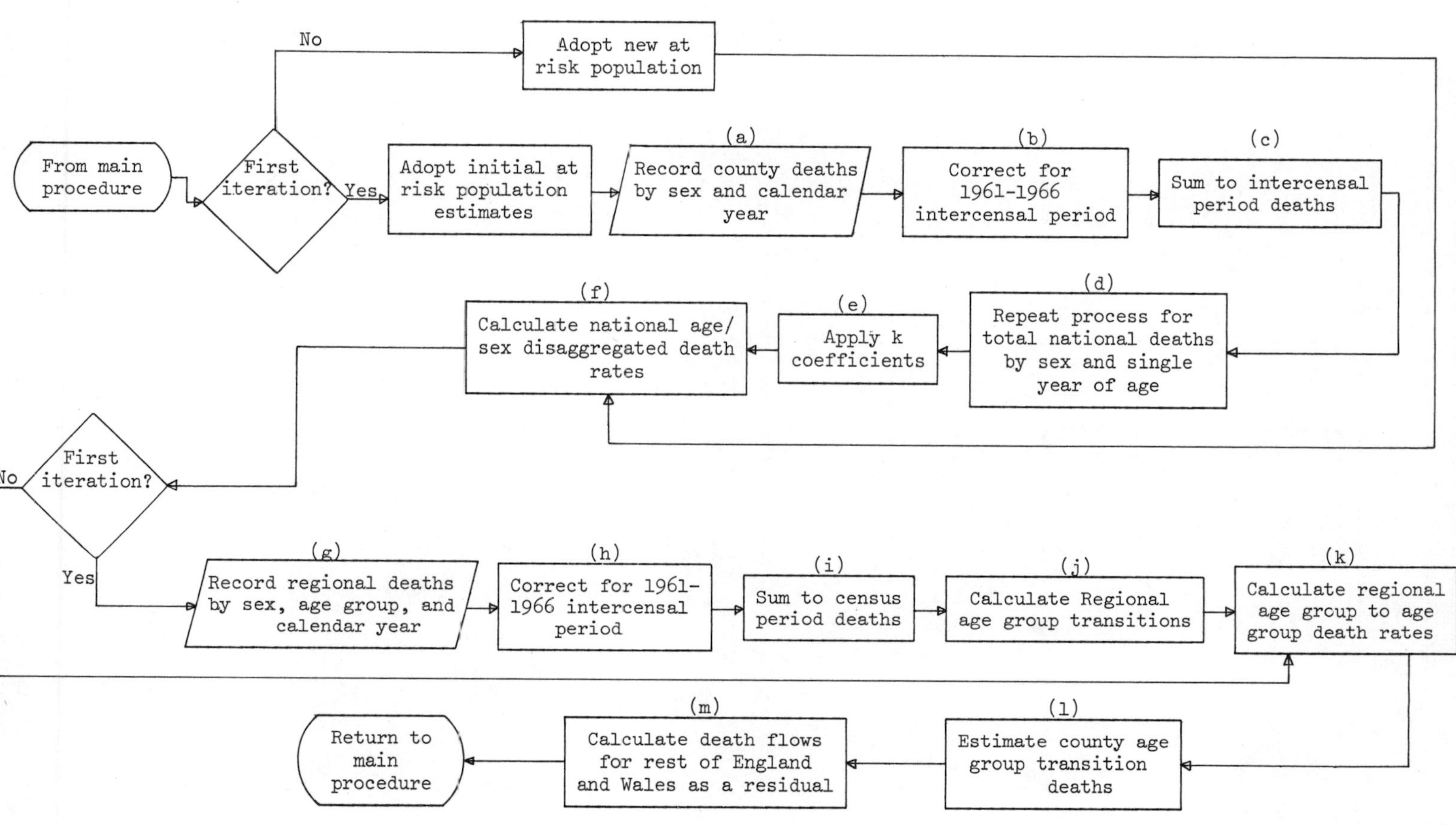

Figure 3.14 The data items required for the operational accounts based model

Sequence number	Nature of item	Variables	Ranges of subscripts and superscripts
(1)	Study area population, census date 1961	$K^{\varepsilon(i)*(*)x}_{s-1*}$	s-1 = 1, 20 x = M, F
(2)	Rest of England and Wales population, census date 1961	$K^{\varepsilon(c-i)*(*)x}_{s-1*}$	s-1 = 1, 20; x = M, F c-i means the country less zone i
(3)	Total study area births by sex, 1961-1966	$K^{\beta(i)*(*)x}_{**}$	x = M, F
(4)	Total rest of England and Wales births by sex, 1961-1966	$K^{\beta(c-i)*(*)x}_{**}$	x = M, F c-i means the country less zone i
(5)	Total study area deaths by sex, age group and calendar years (1961, 1962, ..., 1966)	$K^{*(*)\delta(i)x}_{*s}(*, \theta)$	s = 1, 20; x = M, F θ = 1961, ..., 1966
(6)	Total England and Wales deaths by sex by calendar year, by five year age group and single year of age	$K^{*(*)\delta(c)x}_{*s}(y, \theta)$	s = 1, 20; x = M, F θ = 1961, ..., 1966 y = 1, ..., 5
(7)	Total England and Wales deaths by sex by calendar year, for the last age group (s=21)	$K^{*(*)\delta(c)x}_{*21}(*, \theta)$	x = M, F θ = 1961, ..., 1966

(8)	Coefficients for converting s age group deaths into s-1, s and s1s deaths, based on census period calendar year and single year of age geometry	$k_{s-1s}(y, \theta)$	s = 1, ..., 20;
			y = 1, ..., 5;
			θ = 1961, ..., 1966

(9)	Correct factors to adjust enumerated population to usually resident and to allow for underenumeration	b u	concept adjustment factor underenumeration correction factor
(10)	Population at risk weights for deaths	${}^{i}_{s}{}^{\theta}D^{jk}_{ru}$	These represent the proportions of a time period a particular (jk, ru) population flow is exposed to dying in age group s in region i
(11)	Total regional deaths by sex, calendar year, and age group	$K^{*(*)\delta(I)x}_{*\upsilon}(\theta)$	I = standard region υ = 1, ..., 9 (ie 0-4 5-9, 10-14, 15-24, 25-34, 35-44, 45-54 55-64, 65 and over) x = M, F θ = 1961, ..., 1966
(12)	Regional population census date 1961	$K^{\varepsilon(I)*(*)x}_{s-1*}$	I = standard region s-1 = 1, ..., 20 x = M, F
(13)	Regional population census date 1966	$K^{*(*)\sigma(I)x}_{*s}$	I = standard region s-1 = 1, ..., 21 x = M, F
(14)	Total births by sex for region, 1961-1966	$K^{\beta(I)*(*)x}_{**}$	I = standard region x = M, F
(15)	Migrants by sex and by 21 age groups for a three by three region matrix	$K^{\varepsilon(i)\sigma(j)x}_{*s}$ where s=1, the variable is $K^{\beta(i)\sigma(j)x}_{*1}$	i ≠ j s = 1, ..., 21 x = M, F; i = i, c-i, w-c; j = i, c-i, w-c

1966 Sample Census.

$$K_{*s}^{\varepsilon(i)\sigma(j)x}(\text{corrected}) = K_{*s}^{\varepsilon(i)\sigma(j)x}.u \qquad (3.50)$$

Step Three: calculation of at risk population

Populations at risk of dying, for age group transitions s-ls-l and s-ls, are required before going on to death rate estimation. The method of estimation varies according to the iteration in which it occurs.

In the first iteration, initial estimates of the at risk population are derived simply using the following equations:

$$\hat{K}_{s-1s-1}^{D*ix}(\text{initial}) = 0.5\ K_{s-1*}^{\varepsilon(i)*(*)x} \qquad \text{for } s-1=1,\ 19 \qquad (3.51)$$

$$\hat{K}_{s-1s}^{D*ix}(\text{initial}) = 0.5\ K_{s-1*}^{\varepsilon(i)*(*)x} \qquad \text{for } s-1=1,\ 19 \qquad (3.52)$$

and, for special cases, using rather different expressions:

$$\hat{K}_{01}^{D*ix}(\text{initial}) = K_{**}^{\beta(i)*(*)x} \qquad (3.53)$$

$$\hat{K}_{2020}^{D*ix}(\text{initial}) = K_{20*}^{\varepsilon(i)*(*)x} \qquad (3.54)$$

In subsequent iterations at risk populations must be estimated from the output of the previous iteration, and this takes place in Step 11, the last of each iteration.

Step Four: estimation of total death flows

Total death flows are estimated in three stages, proceeding from national through regional to county level. By using the k coefficients defined in Step One and in Section 3.3, we can estimate national deaths in each age group to age group transitions (s-ls and s,s) and from these obtain national death rates by age group transition. Applying these with recorded regional death totals enables us to estimate regional death flows by transition plus the corresponding rates. Finally, these are used with study area death totals to arrive at estimates of the desired study area death flows for both transitions; s-ls-l and s-ls.

Certain of the following steps are required only in the first iteration and this is indicated where appropriate. Further, rate estimations in the first iteration require the use of the initial at risk population estimates produced in Step Three, but, in subsequent iterations the estimates computed in Step (11) of the previous iteration are substituted.

(a) Recording of study area deaths by sex and calendar year (First iteration only)

These have already been recorded as $K_{**}^{*(*)\delta(i)x}(*,\theta)$.

(b) Correction for 1961-1966 census period (first iteration only)

The calendar year deaths for 1961 to 1966 must be converted into an estimate of deaths within intercensal period (that is 23/24 April 1961 to 24/25 April 1966). Calendar year (θ) deaths are first converted into 'census' year deaths:

$$K_{**}^{*(*)\delta(i)x}(*,\lambda) = K_{**}^{*(*)\delta(i)x}(*,\theta).F_B^x(\theta) + K_{**}^{*(*)\delta(i)x}(*,\theta+1).F_A^x(\theta+1) \quad (3.55)$$

where, $F_B^x(\theta)$ and $F_B^x(\theta)$ indicate proportions of calendar year deaths, falling in portions A and B of the calendar year θ. λ is an index that labels each 'census' year. Factor values are estimated from national quarterly death figures and from a count of days.

(c) Summing over 'census' years to yield intercensal period deaths (First iteration only)

$$K_{**}^{*(*)\delta(i)x}(*,*) = \Sigma_{\lambda=1}^{5} K_{**}^{*(*)\delta(i)x}(*,\lambda) \quad (3.56)$$

(d) Repetition for total national deaths by sex and single year of age (First iteration only)

That is $K_{*s}^{*(*)\delta(c)x}(Y,\theta)$ is converted into $K_{*s}^{*(*)\delta(c)x}(Y,\lambda)$. In the case of last age group (age greater than or equal to 100) $K_{*21}^{*(*)\delta(c)x}(*,\theta$ is converted to $K_{*21}^{*(*)\delta(c)x}(*,\lambda)$ and summed over λ to $K_{*21}^{*(*)\delta(c)x}(*,*)$.

(e) Production of estimates of national deaths by transition by application of k coefficients (First iteration only)

$$K_{s-1s}^{*(*)\delta(c)x}(*,*) = \Sigma_Y\Sigma_\lambda k_{s-1s}(Y,\lambda)K_{*s}^{*(*)\delta(c)x}(Y,\lambda) \quad (3.57)$$

$$K_{ss}^{*(*)\delta(c)x}(*,*) = \Sigma_Y\Sigma_\lambda k_{ss}(Y,\lambda)K_{*s}^{*(*)\delta(c)x}(Y,\lambda) \quad (3.58)$$

where $k_{s-1s}(Y,\lambda) = (1.0-k_{ss}(Y,\lambda))$.

The twentieth age transition is open ended and so all deaths occurring to persons age 100 or over at death, $K_{*21}^{*(*)\delta(c)x}(*,*)$, are added for each sex to those occurring to persons age 95 or over at death.

(f) Calculation of national age/sex disaggregated death rates (all iterations)

For the ss transition the death rate is

$$d_{ss}^{*cx} = K_{ss}^{*(*)\delta(c)x}/\hat{K}_{ss}^{D*cx} \qquad (3.59)$$

For the s-1s transition the death rate is given by

$$d_{s-1s}^{*cx} = K_{s-1s}^{*(*)\delta(c)x}/\hat{K}_{s-1s}^{D*cx} \qquad (3.60)$$

For the special case (0,1) the equation that yields the death rate is

$$d_{01}^{*cx} = K_{*1}^{\beta(*)\delta(c)x}/\hat{K}_{01}^{D*cx} \qquad (3.61)$$

We set the values of $\hat{K}_{ss}^{D*cx}$ and $\hat{K}_{s-1s-1}^{D*cx}$ to the initial estimates in the first iteration and subsequently to the 'average' population at risk estimates.

(g) Recording of regional deaths by sex, age group, and calendar year (First iteration only)

These have already been recorded as $K_{*\upsilon}^{*(*)\delta(I)x}(*,\theta)$.

(h) Correction for 1961-1966 census period (First iteration only)

$K_{*\upsilon}^{*\delta(I)x}(*,\theta)$ is converted to $K_{*\nu}^{*\delta(I)x}(*,\lambda)$ as before.

(i) Summing to intercensal period deaths (First iteration only)

Summation is accomplished thus:

$$K_{*\upsilon}^{*\delta(I)x}(*,*) = \Sigma_{\lambda=1}^{5} K_{*\upsilon}^{*\delta(I)x}(*,\lambda) \qquad (3.62)$$

(j) Calculation of regional age group to age group transitions (all iterations)

The following equations are used:

$$K_{s-1s}^{*\delta(I)x} = \frac{d_{s-1s}^{*cx}\hat{K}_{s-1s}^{D*Ix}K_{*\upsilon}^{*(*)\delta(I)x}}{\left[\Sigma_{s\varepsilon\upsilon}d_{s-1s}^{*cx}\hat{K}_{s-1s}^{D*Ix}+\Sigma_{s\varepsilon\upsilon}d_{ss}^{*cx}\hat{K}_{ss}^{D*Ix}\right]} \qquad (3.63)$$

and

$$K_{ss}^{*\delta(I)x} = \frac{d_{ss}^{*cx}\hat{K}_{ss}^{D*Ix}K_{*\upsilon}^{*(*)\delta(I)x}}{\left[\Sigma_{s\varepsilon\upsilon}d_{s-1s}^{*cx}\hat{K}_{s-1s}^{D*Ix}+\Sigma_{s\varepsilon\upsilon}d_{ss}^{*cx}\hat{K}_{ss}^{D*Ix}\right]} \qquad (3.64)$$

where, initially $\hat{K}_{s-1s}^{D*Ix}$ and $\hat{K}_{ss}^{D*Ix}$ are estimated by half the initial age group populations (see Step Eleven) and where, for all subsequent iterations $\hat{K}_{s-1s}^{D*Ix}$ and $\hat{K}_{ss}^{D*Ix}$ are set to mid-point estimates (see Step Eleven).

(k) Calculation of regional age group to age group death rates (all iterations)

For ss transitions the death rate is calculated thus:

$$d_{ss}^{*Ix} = K_{ss}^{*(*)\delta(I)x} / \hat{K}_{ss}^{D*Ix} \tag{3.65}$$

and for s-ls transitions thus

$$d_{s-ls}^{*Ix} = K_{s-ls}^{*(*)\delta(I)x} / \hat{K}_{s-ls}^{D*Ix} \tag{3.66}$$

The special case of the 0, 1 transition is dealt with thus:

$$d_{01}^{*Ix} = K_{01}^{\beta(*)\delta(I)x} / \hat{K}_{01}^{D*Ix} \tag{3.67}$$

setting $\hat{K}_{s-ls}^{D*Ix}$ and $\hat{K}_{ss}^{D*Ix}$ to the initial estimates in the first iteration, and subsequently to the estimates produced in Step Eleven of the previous iteration.

(l) Calculation of study area age group to age group transition deaths (all iterations)

The following equations are used:

$$K_{s-ls}^{*(*)\delta(i)x} = \frac{d_{s-ls}^{*Ix}\hat{K}_{s-ls}^{D*ix}K_{**}^{*(*)\delta(i)x}}{\left[\Sigma_{s=1}^{20} d_{ss}^{*Ix}\hat{K}_{ss}^{D*ix} + \Sigma_{s=1}^{20} d_{s-ls}^{*Ix}\hat{K}_{ss}^{D*ix}\right]} \tag{3.68}$$

and

$$K_{ss}^{*(*)\delta(i)x} = \frac{d_{ss}^{*Ix}\hat{K}_{ss}^{D*ix}K_{**}^{*(*)\delta(i)x}}{\left[\Sigma_{s=1}^{20} d_{ss}^{*Ix}\hat{K}_{ss}^{D*ix} + \Sigma_{s=1}^{20} d_{s-ls}^{*Ix}\hat{K}_{s-ls}^{D*ix}\right]} \tag{3.69}$$

where, initially $\hat{K}_{ss}^{D*ix}$ and $\hat{K}_{s-ls}^{D*ix}$ are as set in Step Three, and subsequently, are derived from Step Eleven of the previous iteration.

(m) Calculation of transitional death flows for rest of England and Wales as a residual (all iterations)

This is accomplished very simply by:

$$K_{s-ls}^{*(*)\delta(c-i)x} = K_{s-ls}^{*\delta(c)x} - K_{s-ls}^{*\delta(i)x} \tag{3.70}$$

$$K_{ss}^{*(*)\delta(c-i)x} = K_{ss}^{*\delta(c)x} - K_{ss}^{*\delta(i)x} \tag{3.71}$$

Step Five: total death rates

Study area rates are determined thus:

$$d_{s-ls}^{*ix} = K_{s-ls}^{*(*)\delta(i)x} / \hat{K}_{s-ls}^{D*ix} \tag{3.72}$$

$$d_{ss}^{*ix} = K_{ss}^{*(*)\delta(i)x} / \hat{K}_{ss}^{D*ix} \tag{3.73}$$

and rates for the rest of England and Wales thus:

$$d^{*(c-i)x}_{s-1s} = K^{*(*)\delta(c-i)x}_{s-1s}/\hat{K}^{D*(c-i)x}_{s-1s} \qquad (3.74)$$

$$d^{*(c-i)x}_{ss} = K^{*(*)\delta(c-i)x}_{ss}/\hat{K}^{D*(c-i)x}_{ss} \qquad (3.75)$$

Again, in the first iteration the initial at risk population estimates (Step Three) are used, while in subsequent iterations the estimates provided in Step Eleven of the previous iteration are substituted.

Step Six: estimation of migration and death flows

The previously established death rates are applied to recorded interzonal migration flows.

$$K^{\varepsilon(i)\delta(j)x}_{s-1s} = 0.25(d^{*ix}_{s-1s}K^{\varepsilon(i)\sigma(j)x}_{s-1s}/(1.0 - 0.17675d^{*ix}_{s-1s}) \qquad (3.76)$$

$$K^{\varepsilon(i)\delta(j)x}_{ss} = \left[d^{*ix}_{ss}(0.25K^{\varepsilon(i)\sigma(j)x}_{s-1s}+0.17675K^{\varepsilon(i)\delta(j)x}_{s-1s})\right]/ (1.0-0.1465d^{*ix}_{ss}) \qquad (3.77)$$

These equations are applied to the four sets of interzonal migrants not involving emigration to the rest of the world. In the equations applied to emigrants to the rest of the world origin zone death rates rather than destination zone death rates are applied.

There are two special cases:

$$K^{\varepsilon(i)\delta(j)x}_{01} = 0.25d^{*ix}_{01}K^{\beta(i)\sigma(j)x}_{01}/(1.0-0.106d^{*ix}_{01}) \qquad (3.78)$$

$$K^{\varepsilon(i)\delta(j)x}_{2020} = 0.5d^{*ix}_{2020}K^{\delta(i)\sigma(j)x}_{2020}/(1.0-0.25d^{*ix}_{2020}) \qquad (3.79)$$

Step Seven: calculation of death terms

Within region deaths are estimated as a residual: in-migration and death flows are subtracted from total deaths of the zone.

$$K^{\varepsilon(i)\delta(i)x}_{ss} = K^{\varepsilon(*)\delta(i)x}_{ss} - \Sigma_{j\neq i}K^{\varepsilon(j)\delta(i)x}_{ss} \qquad (3.80)$$

$$K^{\varepsilon(i)\delta(i)x}_{s-1s} = K^{\varepsilon(*)\delta(i)x}_{s-1s} - \Sigma_{j\neq i}K^{\varepsilon(j)\delta(i)x}_{s-1s} \qquad (3.81)$$

Similar equations are used for the rest of England and Wales.

Step Eight: estimation of total survivors

For the first age group, we use:

$$K^{\beta(i)\sigma(i)x}_{*1} = K^{\beta(i)*(*)x}_{*1} - K^{\beta(i)\delta(i)x}_{*1} - \Sigma_{j\neq i}K^{\beta(i)\sigma(j)x}_{*1} - \Sigma_{j\neq i}K^{\beta(i)\delta(j)x}_{*1} \qquad (3.82)$$

For age groups two to twenty we employ:

$$K_{s-1s}^{\varepsilon(i)\sigma(i)x} = K_{s-1*}^{\varepsilon(i)*(*)x} - K_{s-1s-1}^{\varepsilon(i)\delta(i)x} - K_{s-1s}^{\varepsilon(i)\delta(i)x} - \Sigma_{j\neq i} K_{s-1s}^{\varepsilon(i)\sigma(j)x}$$

$$- \Sigma_{j\neq i} K_{s-1s-1}^{\varepsilon(i)\delta(j)x} - \Sigma_{j\neq i} K_{s-1s}^{\varepsilon(i)\delta(j)x} \qquad (3.83)$$

For the last age group the following version of Equation (3.83) is used:

$$K_{20*}^{\varepsilon(i)\sigma(i)x} = K_{20*}^{\varepsilon(i)*(*)x} - K_{20*}^{\varepsilon(i)\delta(i)x} - \Sigma_{j\neq i} K_{20*}^{\varepsilon(i)\sigma(j)x} - \Sigma_{j\neq i} K_{20*}^{\varepsilon(i)\delta(j)x} \qquad (3.84)$$

Similar equations are used for the rest of England and Wales.

Step Nine: addition of survival and in-migration terms

We use:

$$K_{*s}^{*(*)\sigma(i)x} = K_{s-1s}^{\varepsilon(i)\sigma(i)x} + \Sigma_{j\neq i} K_{s-1s}^{\varepsilon(j)\sigma(i)x} \qquad (3.85)$$

A similar equation is used for the rest of England and Wales. This yields time t+T survivors for each zone by 21 age groups for the 20 time t age group populations have all aged and have been augmented by the (t, t+T births) new 0-4 age group. In order to be consistent, the last two age groups are added together:

$$K_{*20}^{*(*)\sigma(i)x}(\text{new}) = K_{*20}^{*(*)\sigma(i)x}(\text{old}) + K_{*21}^{*(*)\sigma(i)x}(\text{old}) \qquad (3.86)$$

Step Ten: iteration control

In iterations other than the first, a test is required for convergence of the final population stocks of the present and previous iterations. In the first iteration this is not necessary and we go straight on to the estimation of new at risk populations. The convergence test takes the form:

$$\left| (K_{*s}^{*(*)\sigma(i)x}(n-1) - K_{*s}^{*(*)\sigma(i)x}(n)) / K_{*s}^{*(*)\sigma(i)x}(n-1) \right| < 0.01, \text{ for all age groups} \qquad (3.87)$$

where i = County and i = rest of England and Wales; n = iteration number.

If the convergence limit (in this case 0.01 or 1%) is reached for all age groups and for both zones then the iteration finishes. If not we carry on to produce a new set of at risk population estimates for a further iteration.

Step Eleven: production of new at risk population estimates

Coefficients introduced earlier in the paper are identified in Step Eleven and applied to the relevant time period flows in order to produce an estimate for each zone and each age group transition of the population at risk of dying during the time period.

(a) Study area and rest of England and Wales at risk population

The population at risk for the s-1, s-1 age group transition is given as follows:

$$\hat{K}^{D*ix}_{s-1s-1} = 0.5K^{\varepsilon(i)\sigma(i)x}_{s-1s} + 0.293K^{\varepsilon(i)\delta(i)x}_{s-1s-1} + 0.3535K^{\varepsilon(i)\delta(i)x}_{s-1s} + 0.25(\Sigma_{i\neq j}K^{\varepsilon(i)\sigma(j)x}_{s-1s} + \Sigma_{j\neq i}K^{\varepsilon(j)\sigma(i)x}_{s-1s} + 0.1465(\Sigma_{i\neq j}K^{\varepsilon(i)\delta(j)x}_{s-1s-1} + \Sigma_{j\neq i}K^{\varepsilon(j)\delta(i)x}_{s-1s}) + 0.17675(\Sigma_{i\neq j}K^{\varepsilon(i)\delta(j)x}_{s-1s} + \Sigma_{j\neq i}K^{\varepsilon(j)\delta(i)x}_{s-1s}) \quad (3.88)$$

The numbers 0.5, 0.293, ..., 0.17675 are the factors that measure the exposure to risk of the population flows they precede. The risk is in respect of dying in region i in age group transition s-1, s-1.

The population at risk for the s-1, s transition is provided by the following equation:

$$\hat{K}^{D*ix}_{s-1s} = 0.5K^{\varepsilon(i)\sigma(i)x}_{s-1s} + 0.3535K^{\varepsilon(i)\delta(i)x}_{s-1s} + 0.25(\Sigma_{i\neq j}K^{\varepsilon(i)\sigma(j)x}_{s-1s} + \Sigma_{i\neq j}K^{\varepsilon(j)\sigma(i)x}_{s-1s}) + 0.17675(\Sigma_{i\neq j}K^{\varepsilon(i)\delta(j)x}_{s-1s} + \Sigma_{j\neq i}K^{\varepsilon(j)\delta(i)x}_{s-1s}) \quad (3.89)$$

In the special case of the 20, 20 age group transition we employ:

$$\hat{K}^{D*ix}_{2020} = K^{\varepsilon(i)\sigma(i)x}_{2020} + 0.5K^{\varepsilon(i)\delta(i)x}_{2020} + 0.50(\Sigma_{i\neq j}K^{\varepsilon(i)\sigma(j)x}_{2020} + \Sigma_{j\neq i}K^{\varepsilon(j)\sigma(i)x}_{2020}) + 0.25(\Sigma_{i\neq j}K^{\varepsilon(i)\delta(j)x}_{2020} + \Sigma_{j\neq i}K^{\varepsilon(j)\delta(i)x}_{2020}) \quad (3.90)$$

For the special case of the 0, 1 transition (birth to the first age group) we use:

$$\hat{K}^{D*ix}_{01} = 0.5K^{\beta(i)\sigma(i)x}_{01} + 0.212K^{\beta(i)\delta(i)x}_{01} + 0.25(\Sigma_{i\neq j}K^{\beta(i)\sigma(j)x}_{01} + \Sigma_{j\neq i}K^{\beta(j)\sigma(i)x}_{01}) + 0.106(\Sigma_{i\neq j}K^{\beta(i)\delta(j)x}_{01} + \Sigma_{j\neq i}K^{\beta(j)\delta(i)x}_{01}) \quad (3.91)$$

(b) Estimates of regional at risk populations

Since the region is not a zone for which accounts are being explicitly prepared (it was introduced in order to tighten up certain estimation techniques) it is not possible to estimate its set of at risk populations in the manner spelled out above. Instead an approximation must be used: the mid period estimate.

In general we use:

$$\hat{K}^{D*Ix}_{s-1s-1} = 0.5K^{\varepsilon(I)*(*)x}_{s-1*} + 0.5(K^{*(*)\sigma(I)x}_{*s} - K^{\varepsilon(I)*(*)x}_{s-1*}) \quad (3.92)$$

$$\hat{K}^{D*Ix}_{s-1s} = \hat{K}^{D*Ix}_{s-1s-1} \qquad (3.93)$$

In this special case of the 0, 1 transition we employ:

$$\hat{K}^{D*Ix}_{01} = 0.5(K^{*(*)\sigma(I)x}_{*1}) \qquad (3.94)$$

This new set of population at risk estimates then replaces that of the previous iteration in Step Three of the model procedure and the next iteration is begun.

The procedure and equations of the operational model just described have been incorporated in a computer program written on 1900 Series Fortran IV for the Leeds University 1906A ICL computer. A detailed manual presenting the various features and structure of the program along with operating instructions for users has been presented by Smith (1974). The manual is designed both for those users wishing to adopt a black-box approach and for those requiring a more detailed explanation of the internal workings of the program.

3.5 Discussion of the results of the accounting model

The full accounts table produced using the operational model described in Section 3.4 for our three region case study comprising West Yorkshire, the Rest of England and Wales and the Rest of the World, and involving disaggregation by sex and by 20 five year age groups is now presented. The female accounts are first presented in a full accounts matrix format in Figure 3.15. As reproduced here Figure 3.15 may be a little difficult to read, but we present the accounts matrix and table in this format so that the reader may appreciate in full the structure of a multi-regional, age-sex disaggregated set of accounts. The numbers for both females and males are also given in Figure 3.17 and 3.18 in more readable format. It can be seen in Figure 3.15 that the accounting relationships hold in that rows and columns sum to their respective totals (although one or two discrepancies are introduced by rounding procedures). The rows sum to the totals given in the right hand column - time t (census date 1961) population stocks, or in the case of the rows in the bottom half of the table to 1961-1966 intercensal births. Similarly columns sum either to the end of period (census date 1966) population stocks or to the total deaths which occurred in each region over the accounting period.

Figure 3.15 constitutes the end product of a great deal of effort, both theoretical and empirical. What sort of picture of population change do the accounts present for the metropolitan region that is West Yorkshire in the first half of the 1960's? The first and most obvious product that the accounts provide is a better estimate of the census date 1966 population than that of the Sample Census of 1966 itself, which was severely underenumerated. The accounts do use Sample Census 1966 information, on migration flows, for example so that they cannot be entirely divorced from that mid-decade census but the births and deaths statistics are independent of it. However, if Britain had a population register, it would have been possible to estimate the migration flows independently of the end of period census, and thus population accounts could potentially constitute an independent check on the census and vice versa.

Secondly, the accounts make possible a direct check on the components of population change for each age-sex group. Let us, for example, analyse the change occurring in the numbers of women in the 20-24 year old age group in West Yorkshire. The census date 1966 population is estimated as 65,005. If we look up the 20-24 age group column in the accounts table we see that 57,084 both survived the five year period and stayed within West Yorkshire, that 5,715 migrated into the metropolitan region from the rest of England and Wales and that some 2,206 came from further afield. We can thus say that West Yorkshire itself contributed 87.8% of the 1966 population, the rest of England and Wales 8.8% and the rest of the world 3.4%. We have been able to break down the population of survivors into the stayer and in-migrant components.

The 57,084 stayers and survivors were at census date 1961 members of the 15-19 year old age group population of 66,659 girls in West Yorkshire. What happened to those 9,575 girls (66,659-57,084) who didn't survive and stay in West Yorkshire? Some 5,852 migrated to the rest of England and Wales and survived there; some 3,569 migrated to the rest of the world and survived there. Deaths to this cohort of women numbered 68 before age 20 in West Yorkshire, 75 between ages 20 and 25 in West Yorkshire, 3 before age 20 and 3 after age 20 in the rest of England and Wales, and 2 before age 20 and 2 after age 20 in the rest of the world, making a total of 153 deaths, 73 before age 20

Figure 3.15 The population accounts table for West Yorkshire 1961-196

SURVIVAL BY AGE GROUP AT CENSUS DATE 1966 — FEMALES

			West Yorkshire	Rest of England & Wales	Rest of the World
Existence at census date 1961	West Yorkshire	0-4	72604	3250	1297
		5-9	80805	2965	1071
		10-14	74356	2005	3021
		15-19	57804	5062	3588
		20-24	56892	4464	2162
		25-29	53730	4339	2091
		30-34	60600	2760	1000
		35-39	66764	1831	1091
		40-44	64067	1568	327
		45-49	70543	1737	360
		50-54	71256	1782	378
		55-59	66640	1089	320
		60-64	58499	1273	182
		65-69	46103	1061	146
		70-74	32610	839	114
		75-79	18797	509	80
		80-84	7763	348	4
		85-89	1749	122	
		90-94	170	25	
		95+	12	2	
	Rest of England & Wales	0-4	3040	1634736	27696
		5-9	3000	1492294	25861
		10-14	2000	1646679	16063
		15-19	5776	1709844	13165
		20-24	4095	1325944	48473
		25-29	4000	1284239	46484
		30-34	2080	1305326	22073
		35-39	3990	1513020	24096
		40-44	1516	1445988	8070
		45-49	1695	1520865	8605
		50-54	1673	1509003	8581
		55-59	1223	1366584	7005
		60-64	930	1183210	3963
		65-69	793	958322	3394
		70-74	645	693311	2682
		75-79	466	410507	1920
		80-84	275	183684	11
		85-89	113	50567	
		90-94	20	6963	
		95+	5	880	
	Rest of the World	0-4	2010	40647	
		5-9	1733	42383	
		10-14	1605	49348	
		15-19	2206	90494	
		20-24	2636	71623	
		25-29	2374	64480	
		30-34	1276	34443	
		35-39	1201	32230	
		40-44	424	16400	
		45-49	393	15100	
		50-54	351	13349	
		55-59	204	7514	
		60-64	141	4951	
		65-69	100	3701	
		70-74	82	2774	
		75-79	53	1806	
		80-84	30	974	
		85-89	10	293	
		90-94	2	65	
		95+	0	12	
Birth in period 1961-1966	West Yorkshire	0-4			
		5-9			
		10-14	2090	95	45
		15-19	9460	370	300
		20-24	20900	535	434
		25-29	18305	388	299
		30-34	10024	200	162
		35-39	4293	82	66
		40-44	769	75	12
		45-49	26	0	0
		50-54 … 95			
	Rest of England & Wales	0-4			
		5-9			
		10-14	67	64944	914
		15-19	452	436317	6140
		20-24	853	629952	8865
		25-29	480	433885	6107
		30-34	244	235872	3319
		35-39	100	96224	1754
		40-44	30	17239	243
		45-49	1	574	0
		50-54 … 95+			
	Rest of the World	0-4			
		5-9			
		10-14	29	754	
		15-19	997	5063	
		20-24	265	7310	
		25-29	196	5036	
		30-34	107	2737	
		35-39	43	1117	
		40-44	8	290	
		45-49	0	7	
		50-54 … 95+			

TOTALS

Age group 1966	West Yorkshire: Total population (final)	Rest of England & Wales: Total population (final)	Rest of the World: Total surviving in-migrants
0-4	80885	1838667	26764
5-9	78843	1687943	28883
10-14	70590	1538682	26232
15-19	74990	1638912	8706
20-24	69805	1518689	8679
25-29	67360	1481738	5665
30-34	60884	1752985	4575
35-39	64393	1627538	2307
40-44	70610	1563192	2138
45-49	66000	1464488	6397
50-54	77343	1543882	8365
55-59	73219	1526324	8961
60-64	66867	1374797	7325
65-69	59520	1080638	4445
70-74	47986	895164	3544
75-79	33465	686823	2796
80-84	19395	430803	3880
85-89	8068	163388	
90-94	1877	50988	
95+	217	7876	

ocks and flows, females

DEATH IN PERIOD 1961 – 66 (BY AGE AT DEATH)

Column groups: WEST YORKSHIRE (15–19, 20–24, 25–29, 30–34, 35–39, 40–44, 45–49, 50–54, 55–59, 60–64, 65–69, 70–74, 75–79, 80–84, 85–89, 90–94, 95+) | REST OF ENGLAND & WALES (0–4, 5–9, 10–14, 15–19, 20–24, 25–29, 30–34, 35–39, 40–44, 45–49, 50–54, 55–59, 60–64, 65–69, 70–74, 75–79, 80–84, 85–89, 90–94, 95+) | REST OF THE WORLD (0–4, 5–9, 10–14, 15–19, 20–24, 25–29, 30–34, 35–39, 40–44, 45–49, 50–54, 55–59, 60–64, 65–69, 70–74, 75–79, 80–84, 85–89, 90–94, 95+) | TOTALS

TOTAL POPULATION (INITIAL) — West Yorkshire

West Yorkshire	Rest of England & Wales	Rest of the World	Totals
	6 1	1 1	77752
	1 1	0 0	68081
78	1 1	1 2	81280
80 75	3 3	2 2	66050
73 98	3 3	1 2	61710
100 129	3 4	2 2	60082
162 208	3 4	1 2	64750
258 384	5 8	2 3	70857
432 552	5 6	1 1	66950
728 995	8 11	2 2	74186
1144 1524	13 17	3 4	76112
1730 2310	19 25	4 5	72743
2675 3547	24 31	4 5	67227
3782 4821	35 45	6 7	56005
5158 5633	51 62	8 9	44292
5679 5795	67 74	10 11	31102
5300 4228	76 80	11 10	17924
2080 1542	51 36	8 5	6416
610 273	19 11	3 1	1324
166	4	0	105

TOTAL POPULATION (INITIAL) — Rest of England & Wales

West Yorkshire	Rest of England & Wales	Rest of the World	Totals
	5848 1430	49 12	1671580
	1031 940	9 8	1527634
1	1020 1601	25 40	1736517
3 3	1514 1670	43 47	1519805
3 4	1984 1962	29 35	1362090
4 5	1997 2579	35 46	1340098
4 5	3125 4307	25 34	1417796
6 9	5347 7954	42 63	1564622
5 6	8931 11107	25 31	1479879
8 11	14066 19256	39 54	1578638
13 17	21546 28533	60 80	1569457
15 21	31236 41790	79 106	1447860
20 27	46435 59700	75 98	1294457
30 39	65244 83689	111 145	1183767
46 52	91784 108850	162 195	897730
58 64	111770 115400	219 241	640644
60 61	109072 87771	255 232	367954
53 37	67671 37906	193 136	157136
25 14	23753 6683	93 53	39054
7	6089	25	6073

TOTAL OUT-MIGRANTS

West Yorkshire	Rest of England & Wales	Rest of the World	Totals
	88 21		54708
	15 13		44148
1	15 23		58954
1 1	47 52		52001
2 2	42 52		74305
2 3	49 53		66880
2 2	38 53		38044
2 3	56 84		37504
1 2	50 63		17020
2 3	69 94		15661
3 4	94 125		13026
3 3	84 113		7921
3 4	94 122		5395
4 5	123 161		4103
6 7	168 206		3243
7 7	206 226		2385
8 7	218 198		1435
5 3	123 86		520
2 1	50 28		148
0	16		28

TOTAL BIRTHS

West Yorkshire	Rest of England & Wales	Rest of the World	Totals
	0	0	3060
	3	3	20556
	5	5	29604
	3	3	20448
	2	2	9994
	1	1	4534
	0	0	812
	0	0	27

TOTAL BIRTHS

West Yorkshire	Rest of England & Wales	Rest of the World	Totals
	1160	8	67806
	7791	54	490790
	11249	76	850004
	7750	54	640361
	4212	29	243074
	1718	12	58480
	308	2	17048
	10	0	503

TOTAL INFANT OUT-MIGRANTS

West Yorkshire	Rest of England & Wales	Rest of the World	Totals
	7		790
	45		5307
	64		7802
	44		5270
	24		3000
	10		1170
	2		210
	0		7

TOTAL DEATHS | TOTAL DEATHS | TOTAL NON-SURVIVING IN-MIGRANTS and 80 after. The proportion of the 20-24 population that died in the five years was therefore 0.0023 or 0.23%. Note that although some 99.77% of the 15-19 year olds survived the five year period only 85.64% stayed within the region. The 99.74% figure would be the one that would interest the actuary employed by an insurance company; the 85.64% figure is the rate of interest to the metropolitan planner. The former figure we refer to as the 'survival-anywhere rate' and the latter figure the 'within-region survival rate'. The 'survival-anywhere rate' is related to the life table survival rate but it is not the same as it(1). The ratio of the within-region survival rate to the survival-anywhere rate is the probability of staying within the region given that a person survives five years. This conditional probability for 20-24 year old women in West Yorkshire is 85.64/99.74 or 0.8586.

The accounts table can also be used to examine with great precision the net balance of in-flows to and out-flows from the 20-24 female population. We can examine this balance, the change in the population, by looking at the gains and losses:

gains		losses			balance
surviving in-migrants from the rest of England and Wales	5,715	surviving out-migrants to the rest of England and Wales		5,852	-137
surviving in-migrants from the rest of the world	2,206	surviving out-migrants to the rest of the world		3,569	-1,363
		deaths:			-153
		in West Yorkshire	before 20	68	
			after 20	75	
		in the rest of England and Wales	before 20	3	
			after 20	3	
		in the rest of the world	before 20	2	
			after 20	2	
total gains	7,921	total losses		9,574	-1,653

The net loss to West Yorkshire through migration would appear to be -1,500 (-137+-1,363) but this is the loss due to the migration for survivors only. A further 10 persons are estimated to have been lost initially through migration; they subsequently died. This loss through

(1) The distinctions between transition rates based on age group accounts like those being discussed here and life tables rates are spelled out in Rees and Wilson (1975-B) and (1977-A).

migration followed by death is generally fairly small in size but is an important component of change in retirement regions (such as the Sussex coast, the Fylde coast).

Enough has been said to show the value of such accounts tables for describing historical population change. The rates of change involved can be ascertained through the calculation of transition rates, formed by dividing each element in the interior of the table by its corresponding row sum. The full table of these rates for the female population of West Yorkshire is shown in Figure 3.16. In the case of population flows from the rest of the world to West Yorkshire, and to the rest of England and Wales, admission rates, the population flow divided by the destination region sex/age group population, have been substituted. These transition rates can be used in a transition rate model such as that referred to in the Section 2.1 review. A variety of such models are available (see Rees and Wilson, 1977-A, Chapters 6, 12 and 13 for an extensive discussion) and they can be used to examine the implications of current patterns of population change. All involve using some of the rates in Figure 3.16 together with a set of fertility rates for each region within the system of interest.

We round off the presentation of the results of the West Yorkshire accounting model by displaying the full results (flows and transition rates) in vector format rather than the matrix format of Figure 3.15 and 3.16. If more than three regions were involved a matrix presentation would not really be legible. In the tables of population flows (Figures 3.17 and 3.18) the rows sum to the totals given on the right hand side. The column totals are presented as separate vectors at the base of each table. The transition rate tables, Figure 3.19 and 3.20 sum to unity along each row. The column totals have no relevance.

How accurate are the numbers presented in Figures 3.15 to 3.20 and how reliable is the accounts based model we have used to produce them? We can compare the final populations produced by the model with the populations counted in the Sample Census of 1966. However, the comparison cannot provide a definitive test of the model because the census figures for 1966 are themselves unreliable.

Figure 3.21 presents a comparison of population stocks as produced by the accounts based model with the corrected 1966 census equivalents for both West Yorkshire and the Rest of England and Wales. The

Figure 3.16 Transition rates for the West Yorkshire populati

SURVIVAL BY AGE GROUP AT CENSUS DATE 1966

FEMALES

EXISTENCE AT CENSUS DATE 1961

Origin region	Age group	WEST YORKSHIRE	REST OF ENGLAND & WALES	REST OF THE WORLD
WEST YORKSHIRE	0 - 4	93683	04213	01827
	5 - 9	93968	04213	01676
	10 - 14	91572	03554	04708
	15 - 19	95636	08779	05354
	20 - 24	88972	07232	03504
	25 - 29	88882	07231	03485
	30 - 34	93594	04274	01544
	35 - 39	93258	04274	01538
	40 - 44	95681	02342	00488
	45 - 49	94818	02342	00485
	50 - 54	93620	02341	00486
	55 - 59	91610	02321	00441
	60 - 64	88511	01893	00270
	65 - 69	82319	01894	00261
	70 - 74	73191	01894	00256
	75 - 79	60436	01895	00258
	80 - 84	43311	01896	[illegible]
	85 - 89	27255	01896	[illegible]
	90 - 94	12814	01915	[illegible]
	95 +	06629	01641	[illegible]
REST OF ENGLAND & WALES	0 - 4	00216	97690	01655
	5 - 9	00216	98006	01647
	10 - 14	00166	94838	04841
	15 - 19	00378	93904	05561
	20 - 24	00348	95882	03507
	25 - 29	00348	95834	03488
	30 - 34	00204	97718	01557
	35 - 39	00204	97382	01550
	40 - 44	00103	97988	00547
	45 - 49	00103	97215	00548
	50 - 54	00103	96148	00547
	55 - 59	00085	[illegible]	00484
	60 - 64	00072	91406	00308
	65 - 69	00072	86098	00307
	70 - 74	00072	77229	00299
	75 - 79	00072	64526	00296
	80 - 84	00072	48015	[illegible]
	85 - 89	00072	[illegible]	[illegible]
	90 - 94	00071	[illegible]	[illegible]
	95 +	00074	[illegible]	[illegible]
REST OF THE WORLD	0 - 4	02611	02967	
	5 - 9	02406	[illegible]	
	10 - 14	01927	[illegible]	
	15 - 19	03429	[illegible]	
	20 - 24	04268	[illegible]	
	25 - 29	03957	04866	
	30 - 34	01970	[illegible]	
	35 - 39	01093	02074	
	40 - 44	[illegible]	[illegible]	
	45 - 49	00525	00961	
	50 - 54	[illegible]	[illegible]	
	55 - 59	[illegible]	00519	
	60 - 64	[illegible]	00383	
	65 - 69	[illegible]	[illegible]	
	70 - 74	[illegible]	00335	
	75 - 79	[illegible]	[illegible]	
	80 - 84	[illegible]	00255	
	85 - 89	[illegible]	[illegible]	
	90 - 94	00153	[illegible]	
	95 +	[illegible]	[illegible]	

BIRTH IN PERIOD 1961–1966

Mother's region	Mother's age group	WEST YORKSHIRE	REST OF ENGLAND & WALES	REST OF THE WORLD
WEST YORKSHIRE	10 - 14	94706	01757	01471
	15 - 19	94690	01806	01459
	20 - 24	94691	01802	01462
	25 - 29	94690	01800	01462
	30 - 34	94691	01800	01458
	35 - 39	94605	01805	01459
	40 - 44	94704	01847	01478
	45 - 49	96296	00000	00000
REST OF ENGLAND & WALES	10 - 14	00100	96796	01362
	15 - 19	00100	96796	01362
	20 - 24	00100	96796	01362
	25 - 29	00100	96796	01362
	30 - 34	00100	96796	[illegible]
	35 - 39	00100	96796	01362
	40 - 44	00101	96794	01364
	45 - 49	00099	96796	01349
REST OF THE WORLD	10 - 14	03671	95443	
	15 - 19	03712	95402	
	20 - 24	03726	95406	
	25 - 29	03714	95415	
	30 - 34	03730	95195	
	35 - 39	03675	95470	
	40 - 44	03890	95218	
	45 - 49	00000	100000	

TOTALS

TOTAL POPULATION (FINAL)	TOTAL POPULATION (FINAL)	TOTAL SURVIVING IN-MIGRANTS

1-1966: females

DEATH IN PERIOD 1961 66 (BY AGE AT DEATH)

Age columns in each area: 0–4, 5–9, 10–14, 15–19, 20–24, 25–29, 30–34, 35–39, 40–44, 45–49, 50–54, 55–59, 60–64, 65–69, 70–74, 75–79, 80–84, 85–89, 90–94, 95+ (West Yorkshire columns visible from 15–19 only). Each row's two values fall on the diagonal of adjacent age columns.

TOTAL POPULATION (INITIAL)

Row	WEST YORKSHIRE	REST OF ENGLAND & WALES	REST OF THE WORLD	TOTALS
1		00007 00002	00003 0001	100000
2	66	00001 00001	00001 00001	100000
3	00097	00001 00002	00002 00002	100000
4	00102 00113	00005 00005	00003 00003	100000
5	00119 00159	00004 00005	00002 00003	100000
6	00167 00215	00006 00007	00003 00004	100000
7	00250 00321	00005 00007	00002 00003	100000
8	00364 00541	00007 00011	00003 00004	100000
9	00645 00824	00007 00009	00002 00002	100000
10	00982 01342	00011 00015	00002 00003	100000
11	01503 02007	00016 00022	00004 00005	100000
12	02378 03176	00026 00035	00006 00007	100000
13	03952 05276	00036 00047	00006 00008	100000
14	06753 08607	00062 00081	00010 00013	100000
15	11647 12718	00114 00141	00018 00021	100000
16	18259 18633	00216 00237	00032 00035	100000
17	30018 23591	00424 00386	00063 00057	100000
18	45008 24035	00794 00559	00119 00082	100000
19	61782 20654	01465 00829	00201 00110	100000
20	89613	02116	00080	100000

TOTAL POPULATION (INITIAL)

Row	WEST YORKSHIRE	REST OF ENGLAND & WALES	REST OF THE WORLD	TOTALS
1		00349 00095	00003 00001	100000
2	0	00064 00062	00001 00001	100000
3	00000	00058 00092	00001 00002	100000
4	0000 00000	00100 00110	00003 00003	100000
5	00000 00000	00115 00142	00002 00003	100000
6	00000 00000	00149 00192	00003 00003	100000
7	00000 00006	00220 00304	00002 00002	100000
8	00000 00001	00344 00512	00003 00004	100000
9	00000 0000[illegible]	00605 00753	00002 00002	100000
10	00001 00001	00897 01226	00003 00003	100000
11	00001 00001	01373 01818	00004 00005	100000
12	00001 00001	02159 02888	00005 00007	100000
13	00002 00002	03587 04612	00006 00008	100000
14	00003 00004	05911 07582	00010 00013	100000
15	00005 00006	10224 12125	00018 00022	100000
16	00009 00010	17231 17791	00034 00037	100000
17	00018 00016	20512 22943	00067 00061	100000
18	00034 00023	43605 24123	00123 00087	100000
19	00062 00034	58600 22009	00234 00132	100000
20	00108	87425	00362	100000

TOTAL OUT MIGRANTS

Row	WEST YORKSHIRE	REST OF ENGLAND & WALES	REST OF THE WORLD	TOTALS
1		00005 00001		100000
2		00001 00001		100000
3	0001	00001 00001		100000
4	002 0000[illegible]	00003 00003		100000
5	00003 00004	00003 00004		100000
6	00003 00005	00004 00005		100000
7	00003 00003	00003 00004		100000
8	00003 00005	00004 00005		100000
9	00002 00003	00003 00004		100000
10	00003 00004	00004 00006		100000
11	00004 00005	00006 00008		100000
12	00004 00005	00006 00008		100000
13	00004 00006	00007 00009		100000
14	00007 0001[illegible]	00011 00015		100000
15	00013 00015	00019 00023		100000
16	00021 000[illegible]	00032 00035		100000
17	00042 00038	00057 00052		100000
18	00074 00051	00078 00095		100000
19	00134 00073	00125 00070		100000
20	00000	00228		100000

TOTAL BIRTHS

Row	WEST YORKSHIRE	REST OF ENGLAND & WALES	REST OF THE WORLD	TOTALS
1		00000	00000	100000
2		00095	00095	100000
3		00017	00017	100000
4		00095	00095	100000
5		00018	00018	100000
6		00022	00022	100000
7		00000	00000	100000
8		00000	00000	100000

TOTAL BIRTHS

Row	WEST YORKSHIRE	REST OF ENGLAND & WALES	REST OF THE WORLD	TOTALS
1		01729	00012	100000
2		01729	00012	100000
3		01729	00012	100000
4		01729	00012	100000
5		01729	00012	100000
6		01729	00012	100000
7		01729	00011	100000
8		01686	00000	100000

TOTAL INFANT OUT MIGRANTS

Row	WEST YORKSHIRE	REST OF ENGLAND & WALES	REST OF THE WORLD	TOTALS
1		00886		100000
2		00868		100000
3		00839		100000
4		00834		100000
5		00837		100000
6		00854		100000
7		00952		100000
8		00000		100000

TOTAL DEATHS	TOTAL DEATHS	TOTAL NON SURVIVING IN-MIGRANTS	

Figure 3.17 Population accounts table for West Yorkshire 1961-1966: stocks and flows, males, vector format

	Age group time t (s-1)		K^{11M}_{s-1s}	K^{12M}_{s-1s}	K^{13M}_{s-1s}	$K^{1\delta(1)M}_{s-1s-1}$	$K^{1\delta(1)M}_{s-1s}$	$K^{1\delta(2)M}_{s-1s-1}$	$K^{1\delta(2)M}_{s-1s}$	$K^{1\delta(3)M}_{s-1s-1}$	$K^{1\delta(3)M}_{s-1s}$	K^{1*M}_{s-1*}
	0	Born	90,344	1,711	1,336	-	2,575	-	19	-	19	96,00
	1	0- 4	76,073	3,417	1,315	429	106	8	2	4	1	81,35
	2	5- 9	69,272	3,096	1,192	86	79	2	2	1	1	73,73
	3	10-14	78,836	2,654	2,856	90	201	1	3	2	4	84,64
	4	15-19	60,199	4,359	2,501	189	187	6	6	4	4	67,45
	5	20-24	51,064	4,566	2,504	157	161	6	6	4	4	58,47
	6	25-29	53,351	4,771	2,603	160	190	6	7	4	4	61,09
	7	30-34	59,599	2,883	1,173	218	306	4	6	2	3	64,19
REGION 1	8	35-39	67,177	3,268	1,328	377	584	8	12	4	6	72,76
	9	40-44	61,907	1,589	384	624	838	7	9	2	3	65,36
West	10	45-49	65,785	1,719	418	1,087	1,664	12	19	3	5	70,71
	11	50-54	63,720	1,717	413	1,941	2,787	22	32	6	9	70,64
Yorkshire	12	55-59	55,944	908	311	3,254	4,256	22	29	9	11	64,74
	13	60-64	41,096	1,023	121	4,442	4,965	44	51	6	7	51,75
	14	65-69	26,182	729	84	4,652	5,107	49	57	7	8	36,87
	15	70-74	15,881	514	59	4,960	4,475	58	62	8	7	26,02
	16	75-79	7,905	316	35	4,120	3,511	59	57	7	7	16,01
	17	80-84	2,676	156	17	2,965	1,990	52	42	6	5	7,91
	18	85-89	569	54	6	1,419	607	31	19	4	2	2,71
	19	90-94	44	9	1	297	78	9	4	1	1	41
	20	≥95	7	1	0	46	-	1	-	0	-	5

	Age group time t (s-1)		K^{21M}_{s-1s}	K^{22M}_{s-1s}	K^{23}_{s-1s}	$K^{2\delta(1)M}_{s-1s-1}$	$K^{2\delta(1)M}_{s-1s}$	$K^{2\delta(2)M}_{s-1s-1}$	$K^{2\delta(2)M}_{s-1s}$	$K^{2\delta(3)M}_{s-1s-1}$	$K^{2\delta(3)M}_{s-1s}$	K^{2*M}_{s-1*}
	0	Born	2,093	2,017,102	27,969	-	29	-	46,298	-	317	2,093,80
	1	0- 4	3,784	1,722,493	28,481	10	3	7,737	2,117	63	17	1,764,70
	2	5- 9	3,424	1,564,437	25,660	2	2	1,699	1,568	14	13	1,596,81
	3	10-14	2,789	1,752,282	61,584	2	3	1,766	4,048	30	70	1,822,57
	4	15-19	4,517	1,480,860	60,642	7	7	4,132	4,103	83	82	1,554,43
	5	20-24	5,047	1,305,783	57,850	7	7	3,544	3,462	77	75	1,375,85
	6	25-29	5,080	1,314,319	57,979	7	8	3,328	3,943	72	85	1,384,82
REGION 2	7	30-34	3,128	1,396,347	27,245	6	8	4,389	6,153	42	59	1,437,37
	8	35-39	3,359	1,492,452	29,071	9	14	7,176	11,103	69	107	1,543,36
Rest of	9	40-44	1,523	1,389,175	9,226	8	10	12,116	16,240	40	54	1,428,39
	10	45-49	1,614	1,449,246	9,714	13	20	20,627	31,614	68	105	1,513,02
England	11	50-54	1,604	1,403,344	9,735	23	34	36,697	52,944	124	180	1,504,68
	12	55-59	708	1,197,088	6,241	20	26	59,917	78,691	150	200	1,343,04
and Wales	13	60-64	594	870,811	2,869	30	34	80,066	89,837	124	143	1,044,50
	14	65-69	445	592,755	2,222	35	40	88,209	97,986	150	173	782,01
	15	70-74	327	374,571	1,562	42	41	97,844	98,782	175	188	573,53
	16	75-79	212	196,505	999	42	40	93,981	80,953	188	179	373,09
	17	80-84	112	73,431	529	39	32	72,546	49,691	176	144	196,70
	18	85-89	41	17,523	189	25	15	37,042	16,492	108	66	71,50
	19	90-94	8	1,836	43	8	14	9,248	2,654	41	20	13,86
	20	≥95	1	255	4	1	-	1,333	-	5	-	1,59

re 3.17 (cont)

Age group time t	(s-1)	K^{31M}_{s-1s}	K^{32M}_{s-1s}	$K^{3\delta(1)M}_{s-1s-1}$	$K^{3\delta(1)M}_{s-1s-1}$	$K^{3\delta(2)M}_{s-1s-1}$	$K^{3\delta(2)M}_{s-1s}$
0	Born	876	23,567	-	12	-	267
1	0- 4	2,315	52,856	6	2	117	32
2	5- 9	1,981	45,111	1	1	24	22
3	10-14	1,580	42,640	1	2	21	48
4	15-19	2,874	74,744	4	4	102	101
5	20-24	4,152	87,736	6	6	116	113
6	25-29	3,730	79,018	5	6	98	116
7	30-34	2,014	42,235	4	5	65	92
8	35-39	1,867	39,424	5	8	93	145
9	40-44	662	19,002	3	4	82	110
10	45-49	617	17,435	5	8	122	188
11	50-54	553	15,475	8	12	197	287
12	55-59	154	6,185	4	6	149	198
13	60-64	93	2,834	5	5	122	141
14	65-69	70	2,104	5	6	142	164
15	70-74	50	1,501	6	6	168	181
16	75-79	32	961	6	6	181	172
17	80-84	17	504	6	5	167	137
18	85-89	5	141	3	2	81	49
19	90-94	1	27	1	1	26	13
20	≥95	0	3	0	-	3	-

Age group time t+T	(s)	K^{*1M}_{*s}	K^{*2M}_{*s}	$K^{*\delta(1)M}_{ss}$	$K^{*\delta(1)M}_{s-1s}$	$K^{*\delta(2)M}_{ss}$	$K^{*\delta(2)M}_{s-1s}$	$K^{*\delta(1)M}_{*s}$	$K^{*\delta(2)M}_{*s}$
1	0- 4	93,314	2,042,380	446	2,617	7,862	46,584	3,063	54,446
2	5- 9	82,173	1,778,766	89	111	1,725	2,152	200	3,877
3	10-14	74,677	1,612,645	92	82	1,789	1,592	174	3,381
4	15-19	83,205	1,797,576	200	206	4,240	4,099	406	8,339
5	20-24	67,591	1,559,963	170	198	3,666	4,210	368	7,876
6	25-29	60,263	1,398,085	173	174	3,432	3,581	347	7,013
7	30-34	62,161	1,398,108	227	205	4,459	4,065	432	8,524
8	35-39	64,741	1,441,466	391	319	7,277	6,252	710	13,529
9	40-44	72,403	1,535,144	635	606	12,204	11,260	1,241	23,464
10	45-49	64,093	1,409,767	1,105	853	20,761	16,360	1,958	37,121
11	50-54	68,015	1,468,401	1,972	1,692	36,916	31,821	3,664	68,737
12	55-59	65,878	1,420,536	3,278	2,832	60,087	53,262	6,110	113,349
13	60-64	56,806	1,204,180	4,476	4,288	80,233	78,918	8,764	159,151
14	65-69	41,783	874,668	4,693	5,004	88,400	90,029	9,697	178,429
15	70-74	26,697	595,589	5,008	5,153	98,070	98,206	10,161	196,276
16	75-79	16,257	376,586	4,169	4,522	94,221	99,024	8,691	193,245
17	80-84	8,149	197,782	3,010	3,557	72,765	81,182	6,067	153,947
18	85-89	2,805	74,092	1,447	2,027	37,154	49,871	3,474	87,025
19	90-94	615	17,718	306	624	9,283	16,560	930	25,843
20	≥95	61	2,132	47	83	1,337	2,671	130	4,008

Figure 3.18 Population accounts table for West Yorkshire 1961-1966: Stocks and flows, females, vector format

	Age group time t (s-1)		K^{11F}_{s-1s}	K^{12F}_{s-1s}	K^{13F}_{s-1s}	$K^{1\delta(1)F}_{s-1s-1}$	$K^{1\delta(1)F}_{s-1s}$	$K^{1\delta(2)F}_{s-1s-1}$	$K^{1\delta(2)F}_{s-1s}$	$K^{1\delta(3)F}_{s-1s-1}$	$K^{1\delta(3)F}_{s-1s}$	K^{1*F}_{s-1*}
	0	Born	85,451	1,626	1,318	-	1,815	-	14	-	14	90,23
	1	0- 4	72,404	3,259	1,297	311	70	6	1	3	1	77,35
	2	5- 9	65,686	2,945	1,171	51	46	1	1	0	0	69,90
	3	10-14	74,356	2,885	3,823	51	78	1	1	1	2	81,20
	4	15-19	57,084	5,852	3,569	68	75	3	3	2	2	66,65
	5	20-24	54,912	4,464	2,162	73	98	3	3	1	2	61,71
	6	25-29	53,330	4,339	2,091	100	129	3	4	2	2	60,00
	7	30-34	60,609	2,768	1,000	162	208	3	4	1	2	64,75
	8	35-39	66,154	3,031	1,091	258	384	5	8	2	3	70,93
REGION 1	9	40-44	64,067	1,568	327	432	552	5	6	1	1	66,95
	10	45-49	70,341	1,737	360	728	995	8	11	2	2	74,1
West	11	50-54	71,256	1,782	370	1,144	1,524	13	17	3	4	76,11
	12	55-59	66,640	1,689	320	1,730	2,310	19	25	4	5	72,7
Yorkshire	13	60-64	59,499	1,273	182	2,657	3,547	24	31	4	5	67,2
	14	65-69	46,103	1,061	146	3,782	4,821	35	45	6	7	56,00
	15	70-74	32,418	839	114	5,159	5,633	51	62	8	9	44,2
	16	75-79	18,797	589	80	5,679	5,795	67	74	10	11	31,10
	17	80-84	7,763	340	46	5,380	4,228	76	69	11	10	17,9
	18	85-89	1,749	122	16	2,888	1,542	51	36	8	5	6,4
	19	90-94	170	25	3	818	273	19	11	3	1	1,3
	20	≥95	12	3	0	166	-	4	-	0	-	1

	Age group time t (s-1)		K^{21F}_{s-1s}	K^{22F}_{s-1s}	K^{23F}_{s-1s}	$K^{2\delta(1)F}_{s-1s-1}$	$K^{2\delta(1)F}_{s-1s}$	$K^{2\delta(2)F}_{s-1s-1}$	$K^{2\delta(2)F}_{s-1s}$	$K^{2\delta(3)F}_{s-1s-1}$	$K^{2\delta(3)F}_{s-1s}$	K^{2*F}_{s-1*}
	0	Born	1,985	1,915,117	26,950	-	21	-	34,197	-	238	1,978,5
	1	0- 4	3,618	1,634,736	27,696	8	2	5,848	1,418	49	12	1,673,3
	2	5- 9	3,289	1,491,294	25,061	1	1	1,031	940	9	8	1,521,6
	3	10-14	2,888	1,646,878	84,063	1	1	1,020	1,601	15	40	1,736,5
	4	15-19	5,715	1,419,744	83,165	3	3	1,514	1,670	43	47	1,511,9
	5	20-24	4,815	1,325,144	48,473	3	4	1,594	1,962	29	35	1,382,0
	6	25-29	4,669	1,284,239	46,484	4	5	1,997	2,579	35	46	1,340,0
	7	30-34	2,898	1,385,326	22,073	4	5	3,125	4,307	25	34	1,417,7
REGION 2	8	35-39	3,178	1,513,928	24,096	6	9	5,347	7,954	42	63	1,554,6
	9	40-44	1,516	1,445,988	8,070	5	6	8,931	11,107	25	31	1,475,6
Rest of	10	45-49	1,615	1,526,965	8,065	8	11	14,086	19,256	39	54	1,570,6
	11	50-54	1,613	1,509,003	8,591	13	17	21,546	28,533	60	80	1,569,
England	12	55-59	1,223	1,365,594	7,005	15	21	31,236	41,790	79	106	1,447,0
	13	60-64	930	1,183,210	3,963	20	27	46,435	59,700	75	98	1,294,
and Wales	14	65-69	793	950,322	3,394	30	39	65,244	83,689	111	145	1,103,
	15	70-74	645	693,311	2,682	46	52	91,784	108,850	162	199	897,
	16	75-59	466	418,507	1,920	58	64	111,770	115,400	219	241	648,
	17	80-84	275	183,684	1,137	68	61	109,072	87,771	255	232	382,
	18	85-89	113	50,567	461	53	37	67,671	37,906	193	136	157,
	19	90-94	28	6,963	122	25	14	23,753	8,803	93	53	39,
	20	≥95	5	808	19	7	-	6,009	-	25	-	6,

ure 3.18 (cont)

	Age group time	t (s-1)	K^{31F}_{s-1s}	K^{32F}_{s-1s}	$K^{3\delta(1)F}_{s-1s-1}$	$K^{3\delta(1)F}_{s-1s}$	$K^{3\delta(2)F}_{s-1s-1}$	$K^{3\delta(2)F}_{s-1s}$
	0	Born	865	22,224	-	9	-	196
	1	0- 4	2,019	49,647	4	1	88	21
	2	5- 9	1,733	42,383	1	1	15	13
	3	10-14	1,565	49,349	1	1	15	23
	4	15-19	2,286	90,494	1	1	47	52
	5	20-24	2,634	71,623	2	2	42	52
	6	25-29	2,374	64,408	2	3	49	63
	7	30-34	1,276	34,443	2	2	38	53
	8	35-39	1,201	32,238	2	3	56	84
GION 3	9	40-44	424	16,480	1	2	50	63
	10	45-49	393	15,100	2	3	69	94
est of	11	50-54	351	13,349	3	4	94	125
orld	12	55-59	204	7,514	3	3	84	113
	13	60-64	141	4,951	3	4	94	122
	14	65-69	109	3,781	4	5	123	161
	15	70-74	82	2,774	6	7	168	206
	16	75-79	53	1,806	7	7	206	226
	17	80-84	30	974	8	7	218	198
	18	85-59	10	293	5	3	123	86
	19	90-94	2	65	2	1	50	28
	20	≥95	0	12	0	-	16	-

	Age group time	t+T (s)	K^{*1F}_{*s}	K^{*2F}_{*s}	$K^{*\delta(1)F}_{ss}$	$K^{*\delta(1)F}_{s-1s}$	$K^{*\delta(2)F}_{ss}$	$K^{*\delta(2)F}_{s-1s}$	$K^{*\delta(1)F}_{*s}$	$K^{*\delta(2)F}_{*s}$
	1	0- 4	88,301	1,938,967	323	1,844	5,942	34,408	2,167	40,350
	2	5- 9	78,041	1,687,641	53	73	1,046	1,441	126	2,487
	3	10-14	70,708	1,536,622	53	48	1,035	955	101	1,990
	4	15-19	78,810	1,699,112	73	81	1,564	1,625	154	3,189
	5	20-24	65,085	1,516,091	78	80	1,638	1,725	158	3,363
	6	25-29	62,361	1,401,230	106	104	2,049	2,017	210	4,066
	7	30-34	60,374	1,352,985	168	137	3,167	2,647	305	5,814
	8	35-39	64,783	1,422,536	266	215	5,409	4,364	481	9,773
	9	40-44	70,533	1,549,197	439	396	8,986	8,046	835	17,032
LUMN	10	45-49	66,008	1,464,036	739	560	14,163	11,176	1,299	25,339
	11	50-54	72,349	1,543,802	1,159	1,009	21,652	19,361	2,168	41,013
TALS	12	55-59	73,219	1,524,134	1,747	1,545	31,339	28,675	3,292	60,014
	13	60-64	68,067	1,374,797	2,680	2,334	46,553	41,929	5,014	88,482
	14	65-69	60,570	1,189,436	3,817	3,578	65,401	59,853	7,395	125,254
	15	70-74	47,004	955,164	5,210	4,865	92,003	83,895	10,075	175,898
	16	75-79	33,145	696,923	5,744	5,692	112,042	109,118	11,436	221,160
	17	80-84	19,315	420,903	5,456	5,866	109,366	115,700	11,322	225,066
	18	85-89	8,068	184,998	2,946	4,297	67,845	88,038	7,243	155,883
	19	90-94	1,872	50,981	844	1,582	23,822	38,028	2,426	61,850
	20	≥95	217	7,876	174	288	6,028	8,842	462	14,870

Figure 3.19 Transition rates for the West Yorkshire population, 1961-1966: males, vector format

	Age group time t (s-1)		h^{11M}_{s-1s}	h^{12M}_{s-1s}	h^{13M}_{s-1s}	$h^{1\delta(1)M}_{s-1s-1}$	$h^{1\delta(1)M}_{s-1s}$	$h^{1\delta(2)M}_{s-1s-1}$	$h^{1\delta(2)M}_{s-1s}$	$h^{1\delta(3)M}_{s-1s-1}$	$h^{1\delta(3)M}_{s-1s}$	h^{1*M}_{s-1*}
	0	Born	0.94104	0.01782	0.01391	-	0.02682	-	0.00020	-	0.00019	1.0000
	1	0- 4	0.93508	0.04200	0.01617	0.00527	0.00131	0.00009	0.00003	0.00004	0.00001	1.0000
	2	5- 9	0.93955	0.04200	0.01616	0.00116	0.00107	0.00002	0.00004	0.00001	0.00001	1.0000
	3	10-14	0.93135	0.03136	0.03374	0.00106	0.00238	0.00002	0.00002	0.00002	0.00004	1.0000
	4	15-19	0.89244	0.06462	0.03708	0.00280	0.00278	0.00009	0.00009	0.00005	0.00005	1.0000
	5	20-24	0.87332	0.07809	0.04283	0.00269	0.00275	0.00010	0.00010	0.00006	0.00006	1.0000
	6	25-29	0.87323	0.07809	0.04261	0.00262	0.00311	0.00010	0.00011	0.00006	0.00007	1.0000
REGION 1	7	30-34	0.92839	0.04492	0.01828	0.00339	0.00477	0.00007	0.00010	0.00003	0.00005	1.0000
	8	35-39	0.92324	0.04491	0.01825	0.00519	0.00802	0.00011	0.00016	0.00005	0.00008	1.0000
West	9	40-44	0.94712	0.02431	0.00588	0.00955	0.01282	0.00010	0.00014	0.00003	0.00004	1.0000
	10	45-49	0.93030	0.02431	0.00591	0.01537	0.02354	0.00017	0.00026	0.00005	0.00007	1.0000
Yorkshire	11	50-54	0.90197	0.02431	0.00584	0.02747	0.03945	0.00031	0.00045	0.00009	0.00012	1.0000
	12	55-59	0.86408	0.01402	0.00481	0.05026	0.06574	0.00034	0.00045	0.00013	0.00018	1.0000
	13	60-64	0.79405	0.01977	0.00233	0.08583	0.09593	0.00085	0.00098	0.00012	0.00013	1.0000
	14	65-69	0.71002	0.01978	0.00228	0.12616	0.13850	0.00133	0.00154	0.00018	0.00021	1.0000
	15	70-74	0.61026	0.01976	0.00226	0.19059	0.17196	0.00221	0.00238	0.00029	0.00028	1.0000
	16	75-79	0.49349	0.01975	0.00222	0.25724	0.21919	0.00371	0.00354	0.00044	0.00042	1.0000
	17	80-84	0.33831	0.01975	0.00218	0.37483	0.25162	0.00656	0.00537	0.00077	0.00062	1.0000
	18	85-89	0.20994	0.01983	0.00225	0.52352	0.22390	0.01140	0.00696	0.00138	0.00083	1.0000
	19	90-94	0.09838	0.02058	0.00229	0.66930	0.17661	0.01962	0.00973	0.00235	0.00114	1.0000
	20	≥95	0.12460	0.01842	0.00000	0.83626	-	0.02073	-	0.00000	-	1.0000

	Age group time t (s-1)		h^{21M}_{s-1s}	h^{22M}_{s-1s}	h^{23M}_{s-1s}	$h^{2\delta(1)M}_{s-1s-1}$	$h^{2\delta(1)M}_{s-1s}$	$h^{2\delta(2)M}_{s-1s-1}$	$h^{2\delta(2)M}_{s-1s}$	$h^{2\delta(3)}_{s-1s-1}$	$h^{2\delta(3)}_{s-1s}$	h^{2*M}_{s-1}
	0	Born	0.00100	0.96337	0.01336	-	0.00001	-	0.02211	-	0.00015	1.000
	1	0- 4	0.00214	0.97608	0.01614	0.00001	0.00000	0.00438	0.00120	0.00004	0.00001	1.000
	2	5- 9	0.00214	0.97972	0.01607	0.00000	0.00000	0.00106	0.00098	0.00001	0.00001	1.000
	3	10-14	0.00153	0.96143	0.03379	0.00000	0.00000	0.00097	0.00222	0.00002	0.00004	1.000
	4	15-19	0.00291	0.95267	0.03901	0.00000	0.00000	0.00266	0.00264	0.00005	0.00005	1.000
	5	20-24	0.00367	0.94907	0.04205	0.00001	0.00001	0.00258	0.00252	0.00006	0.00005	1.000
REGION 2	6	25-29	0.00367	0.04909	0.04187	0.00001	0.00001	0.00240	0.00285	0.00005	0.00006	1.000
	7	30-34	0.00218	0.97146	0.01895	0.00000	0.00001	0.00305	0.00428	0.00003	0.00004	1.000
Rest of	8	35-39	0.00218	0.96701	0.01884	0.00001	0.00001	0.00465	0.00719	0.00004	0.00007	1.000
	9	40-44	0.00107	0.97255	0.00646	0.00001	0.00001	0.00848	0.01137	0.00003	0.00004	1.000
England	10	45-49	0.00107	0.95785	0.00642	0.00001	0.00001	0.01363	0.02089	0.00004	0.00007	1.000
	11	50-54	0.00107	0.93265	0.00647	0.00002	0.00002	0.02439	0.03519	0.00008	0.00012	1.000
and Wales	12	55-59	0.00053	0.89133	0.00465	0.00001	0.00002	0.04461	0.05859	0.00011	0.00015	1.000
	13	60-64	0.00057	0.83370	0.00275	0.00003	0.00003	0.07665	0.08601	0.00012	0.00014	1.000
	14	65-69	0.00057	0.75798	0.00284	0.00004	0.00005	0.11280	0.12530	0.00019	0.00022	1.000
	15	70-74	0.00057	0.65310	0.00272	0.00007	0.00007	0.17060	0.17223	0.00030	0.00033	1.000
	16	75-79	0.00057	0.52668	0.00268	0.00011	0.00011	0.25189	0.21698	0.00050	0.00048	1.000
	17	80-84	0.00057	0.37332	0.00269	0.00020	0.00016	0.36881	0.25262	0.00089	0.00073	1.00
	18	85-89	0.00057	0.24507	0.00264	0.00035	0.00021	0.51807	0.23066	0.00152	0.00093	1.00
	19	90-94	0.00059	0.13244	0.00307	0.00060	0.00029	0.66716	0.19146	0.00293	0.00145	1.00
	20	≥95	0.00063	0.15952	0.00254	0.00076	-	0.83369	-	0.00286	-	1.00

	Age group time t (s-1)		h^{31M}_{s-1s}	h^{32M}_{s-1s}	$h^{3\delta(1)M}_{s-1s-1}$	$h^{3\delta(1)M}_{s-1s-1}$	$h^{3\delta(2)M}_{s-1s-1}$	$h^{3\delta(2)M}_{s-1s}$
	0	Born	0.00913	0.01126	-	0.00013	-	0.00013
	1	0- 4	0.02846	0.02995	0.00008	0.00002	0.00007	0.00002
	2	5- 9	0.02687	0.02825	0.00002	0.00001	0.00002	0.00001
	3	10-14	0.01867	0.02340	0.00001	0.00002	0.00001	0.00003
	4	15-19	0.04261	0.04808	0.00006	0.00006	0.00007	0.00007
	5	20-24	0.07101	0.06377	0.00010	0.00010	0.00008	0.00008
	6	25-29	0.06106	0.05706	0.00009	0.00010	0.00007	0.00008
REGION 3	7	30-34	0.03138	0.02938	0.00006	0.00008	0.00005	0.00006
	8	35-39	0.02566	0.02554	0.00007	0.00011	0.00006	0.00009
Rest of	9	40-44	0.01013	0.01330	0.00005	0.00007	0.00006	0.00008
	10	45-49	0.00872	0.01152	0.00007	0.00011	0.00008	0.00012
World	11	50-54	0.00782	0.01028	0.00011	0.00017	0.00013	0.00019
	12	55-59	0.00238	0.00460	0.00007	0.00009	0.00011	0.00015
	13	60-64	0.00180	0.00271	0.00009	0.00010	0.00012	0.00013
	14	65-69	0.00190	0.00269	0.00015	0.00017	0.00018	0.00021
	15	70-74	0.00191	0.00262	0.00025	0.00024	0.00029	0.00031
	16	75-79	0.00203	0.00258	0.00040	0.00038	0.00048	0.00046
	17	80-84	0.00218	0.00256	0.00077	0.00062	0.00085	0.00070
	18	85-89	0.00187	0.00197	0.00115	0.00069	0.00113	0.00069
	19	90-94	0.00229	0.00198	0.00235	0.00114	0.00188	0.00093
	20	≥95	0.00000	0.00190	0.00000	-	0.00214	-

ure 3.20 **Transition rates for the West Yorkshire population, 1961-1966: for females, vector format**

	Age group time t (s-1)		h^{11F}_{s-1s}	h^{12F}_{s-1s}	h^{13F}_{s-1s}	$h^{1\delta(1)F}_{s-1s-1}$	$h^{1\delta(1)F}_{s-1s}$	$h^{1\delta(2)F}_{s-1s-1}$	$h^{1\delta(2)F}_{s-1s}$	$h^{1\delta(3)F}_{s-1s-1}$	$h^{1\delta(3)F}_{s-1s}$	h^{1*F}_{s-1*}
	0	Born	0.94695	0.01802	0.01461	-	0.02011	-	0.00016	-	0.00015	1.00000
	1	0- 4	0.93603	0.04213	0.01677	0.00403	0.00091	0.00007	0.00002	0.00003	0.00001	1.00000
	2	5- 9	0.93968	0.04213	0.01676	0.00073	0.00066	0.00001	0.00001	0.00001	0.00001	1.00000
	3	10-14	0.91572	0.03554	0.04708	0.00063	0.00097	0.00001	0.00002	0.00002	0.00002	1.00000
	4	15-19	0.85636	0.08779	0.05354	0.00102	0.00113	0.00005	0.00005	0.00003	0.00003	1.00000
	5	20-24	0.88972	0.07232	0.03504	0.00119	0.00159	0.00004	0.00005	0.00002	0.00003	1.00000
	6	25-29	0.88882	0.07231	0.03485	0.00167	0.00215	0.00006	0.00007	0.00003	0.00004	1.00000
ON 1	7	30-34	0.93594	0.04274	0.01544	0.00250	0.00321	0.00005	0.00007	0.00002	0.00003	1.00000
	8	35-39	0.93258	0.04274	0.01538	0.00364	0.00541	0.00007	0.00011	0.00003	0.00004	1.00000
est	9	40-44	0.95681	0.02342	0.00488	0.00646	0.00824	0.00007	0.00009	0.00002	0.00002	1.00000
	10	45-49	0.94818	0.02342	0.00485	0.00982	0.01342	0.00011	0.00015	0.00002	0.00003	1.00000
kshire	11	50-54	0.93620	0.02341	0.00486	0.01503	0.02002	0.00016	0.00022	0.00004	0.00005	1.00000
	12	55-59	0.91610	0.02321	0.00441	0.02378	0.03176	0.00026	0.00035	0.00006	0.00007	1.00000
	13	60-64	0.88511	0.01893	0.00270	0.03952	0.05276	0.00036	0.00047	0.00006	0.00008	1.00000
	14	65-69	0.83219	0.01894	0.00261	0.06753	0.08607	0.00062	0.00081	0.00010	0.00013	1.00000
	15	70-74	0.73191	0.01894	0.00256	0.11647	0.12718	0.00114	0.00141	0.00018	0.00021	1.00000
	16	75-79	0.60436	0.01895	0.00258	0.18259	0.18633	0.00216	0.00237	0.00032	0.00035	1.00000
	17	80-84	0.43311	0.01896	0.00255	0.30018	0.23591	0.00424	0.00386	0.00063	0.00057	1.00000
	18	85-89	0.27255	0.01896	0.00253	0.45008	0.24035	0.00794	0.00559	0.00119	0.00082	1.00000
	19	90-94	0.12814	0.01915	0.00230	0.61782	0.20654	0.01465	0.00829	0.00201	0.00110	1.00000
	20	>95	0.06629	0.01641	0.00000	0.89613	-	0.02116	-	0.00000	-	1.00000

	Age group time t (s-1)		h^{21F}_{s-1s}	h^{22F}_{s-1s}	h^{23F}_{s-1s}	$h^{2\delta(1)F}_{s-1s-1}$	$h^{2\delta(1)F}_{s-1s}$	$h^{2\delta(2)F}_{s-1s-1}$	$h^{2\delta(2)F}_{s-1s}$	$h^{2\delta(3)F}_{s-1s-1}$	$h^{2\delta(3)F}_{s-1s}$	h^{2*F}_{s-1*}
	0	Born	0.00100	0.96796	0.01362	-	0.00001	-	0.01728	-	0.00012	1.00000
	1	0- 4	0.00216	0.97690	0.01655	0.00000	0.00000	0.00349	0.00085	0.00003	0.00001	1.00000
	2	5- 9	0.00216	0.98006	0.01647	0.00000	0.00000	0.00068	0.00062	0.00001	0.00001	1.00000
	3	10-14	0.00166	0.94838	0.04841	0.00000	0.00000	0.00059	0.00092	0.00001	0.00002	1.00000
	4	15-19	0.00378	0.93904	0.05501	0.00000	0.00000	0.00100	0.00110	0.00003	0.00003	1.00000
	5	20-24	0.00348	0.95882	0.03507	0.00000	0.00000	0.00115	0.00142	0.00002	0.00003	1.00000
ON 2	6	25-29	0.00348	0.95834	0.03469	0.00000	0.00000	0.00149	0.00192	0.00003	0.00003	1.00000
	7	30-34	0.00204	0.97710	0.01557	0.00000	0.00000	0.00220	0.00304	0.00002	0.00002	1.00000
st of	8	35-39	0.00204	0.97382	0.01550	0.00000	0.00001	0.00344	0.00512	0.00003	0.00004	1.00000
	9	40-44	0.00103	0.97988	0.00547	0.00000	0.00000	0.00605	0.00753	0.00002	0.00002	1.00000
gland	10	45-49	0.00103	0.97219	0.00548	0.00001	0.00001	0.00897	0.01226	0.00003	0.00003	1.00000
	11	50-54	0.00103	0.96148	0.00547	0.00001	0.00001	0.01373	0.01818	0.00004	0.00005	1.00000
Wales	12	55-59	0.00085	0.94370	0.00484	0.00001	0.00001	0.02159	0.02888	0.00005	0.00007	1.00000
	13	60-64	0.00072	0.91406	0.00306	0.00002	0.00002	0.03587	0.04612	0.00006	0.00008	1.00000
	14	65-69	0.00072	0.86098	0.00307	0.00003	0.00004	0.05911	0.07582	0.00010	0.00013	1.00000
	15	70-74	0.00072	0.77229	0.00299	0.00005	0.00006	0.10224	0.12125	0.00018	0.00022	1.00000
	16	75-79	0.00072	0.64520	0.00296	0.00009	0.00010	0.17231	0.17791	0.00034	0.00037	1.00000
	17	80-84	0.00072	0.38015	0.00297	0.00018	0.00016	0.28512	0.22943	0.00067	0.00061	1.00000
	18	85-89	0.00072	0.32180	0.00294	0.00034	0.00023	0.43065	0.24123	0.00123	0.00087	1.00000
	19	90-94	0.00071	0.17472	0.00305	0.00062	0.00034	0.59600	0.22089	0.00234	0.00132	1.00000
	20	>95	0.00074	0.11750	0.00280	0.00108	-	0.87425	-	0.00362	-	1.00000

	Age group time t (s-1)		h^{31F}_{s-1s}	h^{32F}_{s-1s}	$h^{3\delta(1)F}_{s-1s-1}$	$h^{3\delta(1)F}_{s-1s}$	$h^{3\delta(2)F}_{s-1s-1}$	$h^{3\delta(2)F}_{s-1s}$
	0	Born	0.00959	0.01123	-	0.00010	-	0.00010
	1	0- 4	0.02611	0.02967	0.00005	0.00001	0.00005	0.00001
	2	5- 9	0.02480	0.02705	0.00001	0.00001	0.00001	0.00001
	3	10-14	0.01927	0.02842	0.00001	0.00001	0.00001	0.00001
	4	15-19	0.03429	0.05985	0.00002	0.00002	0.00003	0.00003
	5	20-24	0.04268	0.05182	0.00003	0.00004	0.00003	0.00004
	6	25-29	0.03957	0.04806	0.00003	0.00005	0.00004	0.00005
ON 3	7	30-34	0.01970	0.02429	0.00003	0.00003	0.00003	0.00004
	8	35-39	0.01693	0.02074	0.00003	0.00005	0.00004	0.00005
t of	9	40-44	0.00633	0.01117	0.00002	0.00003	0.00003	0.00004
	10	45-49	0.00529	0.00961	0.00003	0.00004	0.00004	0.00006
rld	11	50-54	0.00461	0.00851	0.00004	0.00005	0.00006	0.00008
	12	55-59	0.00280	0.00519	0.00004	0.00005	0.00006	0.00008
	13	60-64	0.00210	0.00383	0.00004	0.00006	0.00007	0.00009
	14	65-69	0.00194	0.00343	0.00007	0.00010	0.00011	0.00015
	15	70-74	0.00185	0.00309	0.00013	0.00015	0.00019	0.00023
	16	75-79	0.00170	0.00278	0.00021	0.00023	0.00032	0.00035
	17	80-84	0.00170	0.00255	0.00042	0.00038	0.00057	0.00052
	18	85-89	0.00158	0.00187	0.00074	0.00051	0.00078	0.00055
	19	90-94	0.00153	0.00163	0.00134	0.00073	0.00125	0.00070
	20	>95	0.00000	0.00177	0.00000	-	0.00228	-

Figure 3.21 A comparison of the population stocks at the end of the period generated by an accounts based model and those derived from the Sample Census 1966 for West Yorkshire

			West Yorkshire				Rest of England and Wales			
	Age Group	Age Group	1966 Census corrected population	1966 Accounts estimates	Difference Net	Difference %	1966 Census corrected population	1966 Accounts estimates	Difference Net	Difference %
	0- 4	1	91,830	93,314	+1,484	1.6	1,995,220	2,042,380	+47,160	2.4
	5- 9	2	83,570	82,173	-1,397	1.7	1,777,150	1,778,766	+1,616	0.1
	10-14	3	73,840	74,677	+837	1.1	1.611,880	1,612,645	+765	0.05
	15-19	4	83,880	83,205	-675	0.8	1,811,990	1,797,576	-14,414	0.8
	20-24	5	67,530	67,591	+61	0.1	1,528,180	1,559,963	+31,783	2.1
	25-29	6	62,520	60,263	-2,257	3.6	1,400,190	1,398,085	-2,105	0.2
	30-34	7	61,430	62,161	+731	1.2	1,368,060	1,398,108	+30,048	2.2
	35-39	8	64,650	64,741	+91	0.1	1,432,410	1,441,466	+9,056	0.6
	40-44	9	71,150	72,403	+1,253	1.8	1,524,760	1,535,144	+10,384	0.7
	45-49	10	65,660	64,093	-1,567	2.4	1,408,750	1,409,767	+1,017	0.1
MALE	50-54	11	68,410	68,015	-395	0.6	1,472,390	1,468,401	-3,989	0.3
	55-59	12	65,350	65,878	+528	0.8	1,423,150	1,420,536	-2,614	0.2
	60-64	13	57,070	56,806	-264	0.5	1,220,470	1,204,180	-16,290	1.3
	65-69	14	41,340	41,783	+443	1.1	883,000	874,668	-8,332	0.9
	70-74	15	27,230	26,697	-533	2.0	599,880	595,589	-4,291	0.7
	75-79	16	)	16,257)				376,586)		
	80-84	17	)	8,149)				197,782)		
	85-89	18	) 27,830	2,805)	+57	2.0	680,110	74,092)	-11,800	1.7
	90-94	19	)	615)				17,718)		
	>95	20	)	61)				2,132)		
Total			1,013,290	1,011,687	-1,603	0.16	22,137,590	22,205,584	+67,994	0.31
	0- 4	1	86,680	93,314	+1,621	1.9	1,894,490	1,938,967	+44,477	2.3
	5- 9	2	77,700	78,041	+341	0.4	1,682,880	1,687,641	+4,761	0.3
	10-14	3	71,290	70,708	-582	0.8	1,541,500	1,536,622	-4,878	0.3
	15-19	4	80,790	78,810	-1,980	2.5	1,755,180	1,699,112	-56,068	3.2
	20-24	5	65,280	65,085	-195	0.3	1,524,560	1,516,091	-8,469	0.6
	25-29	6	61,200	62,361	+1,161	1.9	1,358,760	1,401,230	+42,470	3.1
	30-34	7	60,710	60,374	-336	0.6	1,343,310	1,352,985	+9,675	0.7
	35-39	8	63,460	64,783	+1,323	2.1	1,427,060	1,422,536	-4,524	0.3
	40-44	9	72,020	70,533	-1,487	2.1	1,556,670	1,549,197	-7,473	0.5
	45-49	10	65,670	66,008	+338	0.5	1,473,490	1,464,036	-9,454	0.6
FEMALE	50-54	11	72,490	72,349	-141	0.2	1,546,210	1,543,802	-2,408	0.2
	55-59	12	72,030	73,219	+1,189	1.7	1,529,850	1,524,134	-5,716	0.4
	60-64	13	68,930	68,067	-863	1.3	1,396,820	1,373,797	-22,023	1.6
	65-69	14	59,960	60,570	+610	1.0	1,200,820	1,189,434	-11,386	0.9
	70-74	15	46,320	47,004	+684	1.5	948,980	955,164	+6,184	0.7
	75-79	16	)	33,145)				696,923)		
	80-84	17	)	19,315)				420,903)		
	85-89	18	) 61,700	8,068)	+917	1.5	1,358,030	184,998)	+3,651	0.3
	90-94	19	)	1,872)				50,981)		
	>95	20	)	217)				7,876)		
Total			1,086,230	1,088,830	+2,600	0.24	23,538,610	23,517,429	-21,181	0.09
Total both Sexes			2,099,520	2,100,517	-997	0.05	45,676,200	45,723,013	+46,813	0.102

comparison suggests that there is a close but varying correspondence between model and census figures. There is no marked general tendency for the model to either over or under estimate and the model estimates are often within the margin of error bounded by the census enumerated population and the figures corrected for underenumeration.

We have presented here the accounts based model estimates for the full 20 age groups although the 1966 Sample Census produces only a 16 age group breakdown, the last including persons of 75 years of age or more. If the census figures were broken down using, say a 1961 5 year breakdown for persons of 75 and over then the percentage difference would probably increase in the highest groups. As it is the percentage 'errors' are small although for each region and each sex they tend to be relatively high for the first age group. Both positive and negative differences occur but these tend to cancel one another out with the result that the total error for the England and Wales 1966 population is only of the order of 0.1 of a percent. Perhaps surprisingly the West Yorkshire figures appear to be as accurate in general as those of the Rest of England and Wales in spite of the much smaller numbers involved.

3.6 A population projection model(1)

We can build on the discussion so far to discuss the design of population forecasting models. We now therefore outline a model for projecting the population of a single region or for forecasting the future population of a social group in a region that takes cognisance of the principles of accounting and uses some of the transition rates for West Yorkshire presented in Section 3.5. The model has an accounting equivalent which shows the features of a proper accounts matrix, and employs survival anywhere rates generated from the West Yorkshire accounts.

The model has the basic feature of the Leslie closed system model (see Section 3.1): the multiplication of a vector of populations by a matrix of age-sex disaggregated survival rates. If differs from the 'closed system' cohort survival model in incorporating out-migration rates into the survival rate definition and in dealing with in-migration as a separate input. In this respect the new model resembles a single

(1) Full details of this model are given in Rees and King (1974).

region version of the multiregional cohort survival model. However, the survival rates differ from those in that model, being defined to be consistent with those derived from population accounts tables. Births are generated by multiplying a sequentially generated female population at risk by a set of age disaggregated fertility rates. The model incorporates infants born in the period who migrate into the equation that estimates the first age group.

The projection model consists of four equations expressed in matrix notation. The first calculates the numbers of persons who survive a period of interest within a region and adds to them the number who migrate into the region and survive there. The second works out the populations of women at risk of giving birth in the region in the period of interest. The third equation establishes how many children are born elsewhere who migrate into the region, most usually with their parents, and survive there. The fourth equation simply combines the numbers surviving the period with those born into the period in the final vector of population of the region at the end of the period.

The equations are

$$\underline{w}_S^x(t+T) = \underline{S}^x(t,t+T)\underline{w}^x(t)+\underline{I}_S^x(t,t+T) \qquad (3.95)$$

$$\underline{w}^F(t,t+T) = ((\underline{w}_S^F(t+T)+\underline{w}^F(t))0.5) \qquad (3.96)$$

$$\underline{w}_B^x(t+T) = \underline{F}(t,t+T)\underline{w}^F(t,t+T)\sigma^x(t,t+T)s_{01}^x(t,t+T)+\underline{I}_B^x(t,t+T) \qquad (3.97)$$

$$\underline{w}^x(t+T) = \underline{w}_S^x(t+T)+\underline{w}_B^x(t+T) \qquad (3.98)$$

The variables and their subscript labels in the equations have the following meaning. $\underline{w}_S^x(t+T)$: a column vector of population of sex x for a region who have survived the period. The survival of the population is denoted by the subscript S. The population refers to point in time t+T where t is the starting point of the period of interest and T is the length in time units of the period. The population is disaggregated by age group. $\underline{S}^x(t,t+T)$: a matrix of survival rates of persons of sex x over the period t to t+T. The rates refer to the survival from one age group into another. $\underline{w}^x(t)$: a column vector of population of sex x for a region at time t, the start of the period of interest. The population is broken down by age group. $\underline{I}_S^x(t,t+T)$: a column vector of persons of sex x, who migrate into the region and survive (S) there to the end of the period. The surviving in-migrants are disaggregated into age groups. $\underline{w}^F(t,t+T)$: a column vector of average female population of women at risk of giving birth in the period in the region. In this case the sex superscript x has been given the value of F indicating females. The letter M refers to males. $\underline{w}_B^x(t,t+T)$: a column vector of persons of sex x born (B) in the period t to t+T who end the period surviving in the region. $\underline{F}(t,t+T)$: a matrix of fertility rates (numbers born divided by numbers at risk) for both sexes for the region in the period t to t+T. The rates refer to particular age groups of women in the population at risk. It is possible to break down fertility rates by sex of the children born but this is not usually done. We disaggregate births by sex using a sex proportion σ^x. $\sigma^x(t,t+T)$: the proportion of births in the region in period t to t+T that are of sex x. $s_{01}^x(t,t+T)$: the probability that a person of sex x born in period t to t+T will survive in the region at the end of period. The person is considered as coming from age group 0 and surviving in age group 1. $\underline{I}_B^x(t,t+T)$: a column vector of persons of sex x who are born (B) elsewhere in the period t to t+T and who migrate into the region and survive there at the end of the period time t+T.

Laid out in matrix form Equation (3.95) is as follows:

$$\begin{bmatrix} 0 \\ w_2^x(t+T) \\ w_3^x(t+T) \\ \vdots \\ w_R^x(t+T) \end{bmatrix} = \begin{bmatrix} 0 & 0 & 0 & \dots & 0 \\ s_{12}^x & 0 & 0 & \dots & 0 \\ 0 & s_{23}^x & 0 & \dots & 0 \\ \vdots & \vdots & \ddots & & \vdots \\ & & & \dots\ s_{R-1R}^x & s_{RR}^x \end{bmatrix} \times \begin{bmatrix} w^x(t) \\ w_2^x(t) \\ w_3^x(t) \\ \vdots \\ w_R^x(t) \end{bmatrix} + \begin{bmatrix} 0 \\ I_{*2}^x \\ I_{*3}^x \\ \vdots \\ I_{*R}^x \end{bmatrix}$$

$$\underset{R\times 1}{\underline{w}_S^x(t+T)} = \underset{R\times R}{\underline{S}^x(t,t+T)} \times \underset{R\times 1}{\underline{w}^x(t)} + \underset{R\times 1}{\underline{I}_S^x(t,t+T)} \qquad (3.99)$$

The population vectors $\underline{w}_S^x(t+T)$ and $\underline{w}^x(t)$ have been disaggregated into R age groups. Note that no population is recorded in the first age group of the end of period population vector, nor in the first age group of the in-migrant vector in this particular representation of the matrix contents. The survival rates matrix is structured as in cohort survival models with the principal sub-diagonal occupied by survival rates. These survival rates have the general form s_{r-1r}^x and they measure the number of persons who survive from age group r-1 at the beginning of the period into age group r at the end of the period within the region. Note that survival rates are of this form only if the age group intervals involved are all equal and are equal to the period over which the projection is made.

Although equal age group intervals equal to the length of the period are the most convenient arrangement, sometimes lack of data or small populations in the age/sex groups so defined prevents the adoption of such a model structure. This is so when the age group length exceeds the period. One common case is five year age groups and a one year period. The matrix contents of Equation (3.95) now differ a little from those specified in Equation(3.99). It is now possible to survive within an age group as well as from one age group to the next. Figure 3.22, a Lexis diagram, in which age is plotted against time, shows what happens.

Figure 3.22 A Lexis diagram showing the five year age group and one year period arrangement

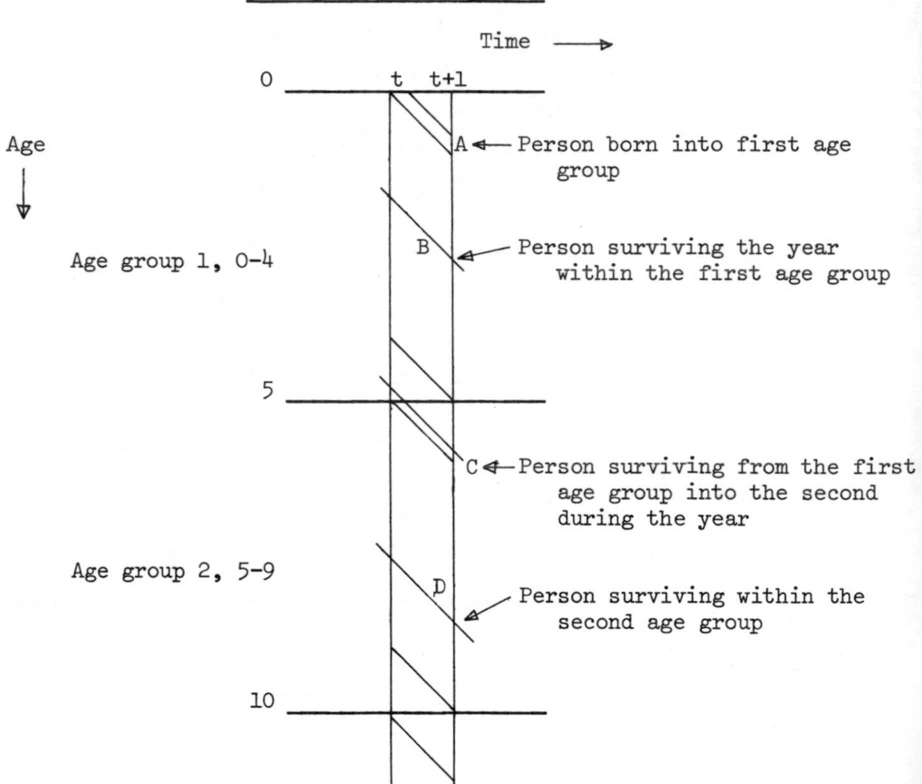

Person A is born during the year (t,t+1) and survives into the first five year age group (0-4 years) at the end of the year (t+1). The life-line labelled B is for a person who survives the year within the first age group. If the distribution of persons within the five year age group at the end of the year is rectangular (that is, even) some $4/5^{ths}$ of the persons in any age group (bar the last) will have survived within the age group and $1/5^{th}$ will have survived from the previous age group. In the case of the 5-9 age group at the end of the year the five year olds, represented by lifeline C, will have survived from the first age group. The six to nine year olds, represented by lifeline D, survive within the second age group. They were aged five to eight years at the start of the year.

The equivalent of Equation (3.95) is, under this five year age group, one year time period arrangement as follows:

$$\begin{bmatrix} w^x_{11}(t+1) \\ w^x_2(t+1) \\ w^x_3(t+1) \\ \vdots \\ \\ w^x_R(t+1) \end{bmatrix} = \begin{bmatrix} s^x_{11} & 0 & 0 & \dots & 0 \\ s^x_{12} & s^x_{22} & 0 & \dots & 0 \\ 0 & s^x_{23} & s^x_{33} & \dots & 0 \\ \vdots & \vdots & \vdots & & \vdots \\ 0 & 0 & 0 & \dots & s^x_{R-1R-1} \\ 0 & 0 & 0 & \dots & s^x_{R-1R}s^x_{RR} \end{bmatrix} \times \begin{bmatrix} w^x_1(t) \\ w^x_2(t) \\ w^x_3(t) \\ \vdots \\ \\ w^x_R(t) \end{bmatrix} + \begin{bmatrix} I^x_{11} \\ I^x_{*2} \\ I^x_{*3} \\ \vdots \\ \\ I^x_{*R} \end{bmatrix}$$

$$\underset{R\times 1}{\underline{w}}{}^x_S(t+1) = \underset{R\times R}{\underline{S}^x}(t,t+1) \times \underset{R\times 1}{\underline{w}^x}(t) + \underset{R\times 1}{\underline{I}}{}^x_S(t,t+1) \qquad (3.100)$$

where s^x_{rr} is the survival rate within age group r by persons of sex x. Survival involves both being alive at the end of the year and being resident in the same region at the start of the period. The subscript 1 has been added to $w^x_{11}(t+1)$ to indicate that these are only the survivors in the first age group and that the terms do not yet include persons born in the period.

The equation giving population at risk of giving birth, Equation (3.96) can be supplied with contents in the following form when five year age groups are employed with either a five year or a one year period.

$$\begin{bmatrix} w_1^F \\ w_2^F \\ w_3^F \\ \hline w_4^F \\ \cdot \\ \cdot \\ \cdot \\ w_{10}^F \\ \hline w_{11}^F \\ \cdot \\ \cdot \\ \cdot \\ w_R^F \end{bmatrix} = \left[\begin{bmatrix} w_{11}^F(t+T) \\ w_2^F(t+T) \\ w_3^F(t+T) \\ \hline w_4^F(t+T) \\ \cdot \\ \cdot \\ \cdot \\ w_{10}^F(t+T) \\ \hline w_{11}^F(t+T) \\ \cdot \\ \cdot \\ \cdot \\ w_R^F(t+T) \end{bmatrix} + \begin{bmatrix} w_1^F(t) \\ w_2^F(t) \\ w_3^F(t) \\ \hline w_4^F(t) \\ \cdot \\ \cdot \\ \cdot \\ w_{10}^F(t) \\ \hline w_{11}^F(t) \\ \cdot \\ \cdot \\ \cdot \\ w_R^F(t) \end{bmatrix} \right] \times [0.5]$$

$$\underset{R\times 1}{\hat{\underline{w}}^F} = ((\underset{R\times 1}{\underline{w}}{}_S^F(t+T) + \underset{R\times 1}{\underline{w}^F}(t)) \underset{1\times 1}{0.5}) \tag{3.101}$$

This expansion of Equation (3.96) computes the mid-point or average population of women in the period, and thus accounts for any addition to the population through immigration or subtraction from the population via emigration or death. It corresponds with the population denominator used in the calculation of age specific fertility rates, either exactly, if the mid-point population is used by the rate denominator, or approximately, if the mid-period population is used. An alternative population at risk should be used if cohort specific fertility rates are used. The population at risk equation then takes the form:

$$\begin{bmatrix} \hat{w}^F_{12} \\ \hat{w}^F_{23} \\ \hdashline \hat{w}^F_{34} \\ \vdots \\ \hat{w}^F_{10,11} \\ \hdashline \hat{w}^F_{11,12} \\ \vdots \\ \hat{w}^F_{RR} \end{bmatrix} = \left[\begin{bmatrix} w^F_2(t+T) \\ w^F_3(t+T) \\ \hdashline w^F_4(t+T) \\ \vdots \\ w^F_{11}(t+T) \\ \hdashline w^F_{12}(t+T) \\ \vdots \\ w^F_{R+1}(t+T) \end{bmatrix} + \begin{bmatrix} w^F_1(t) \\ w^F_2(t) \\ \hdashline w^F_3(t) \\ \vdots \\ w^F_{10}(t) \\ \hdashline w^F_{11}(t) \\ \vdots \\ w^F_R(r) \end{bmatrix} \right] \times [0.5]$$

$$\underset{R\times1}{\underline{\hat{w}}^F} = ((\underset{R\times1}{\underline{w}^F_S(t+T)} + \underset{R\times1}{\underline{w}^F(t)})\ \underset{1\times1}{0.5}) \qquad (3.102)$$

In Equation (3.102) the average population in a cohort that ages from one age group into another is considered to be the population at risk. The terms in the $\underline{w}^F_S(t+T)$ vector are listed one age group older than those in the $\underline{w}^F(t)$ vector. In both Equations (3.101) and (3.102) the vectors have two dashed lines between certain terms. The age groups between the two dashed lines are those in which women are at risk of giving birth. In the second, cohort case, the $\underline{w}^F(t)$ vector has to be marked off from age group three (10-14 years old) because these girls will enter the fertile age group four (15-19 years old) in part, if the period is less than five years in length and in total if the period is five years or longer. The two population at risk definitions can be clarified through display on a Lexis diagram as in Figure 3.23.

The population at risk of giving birth in age group 25-29, say, consists of the lifelines crossing line BD in Figure 3.23. Note that the women may be members of either the 20-24 year old cohort or the 25-29 year old cohort (the cohorts being defined at time t). The women of the 25-29 year old cohort (defined at time t) at risk in the five year period are represented by the lifelines crossing line CE. Line

Figure 3.23 A Lexis diagram showing the two kinds of population at risk

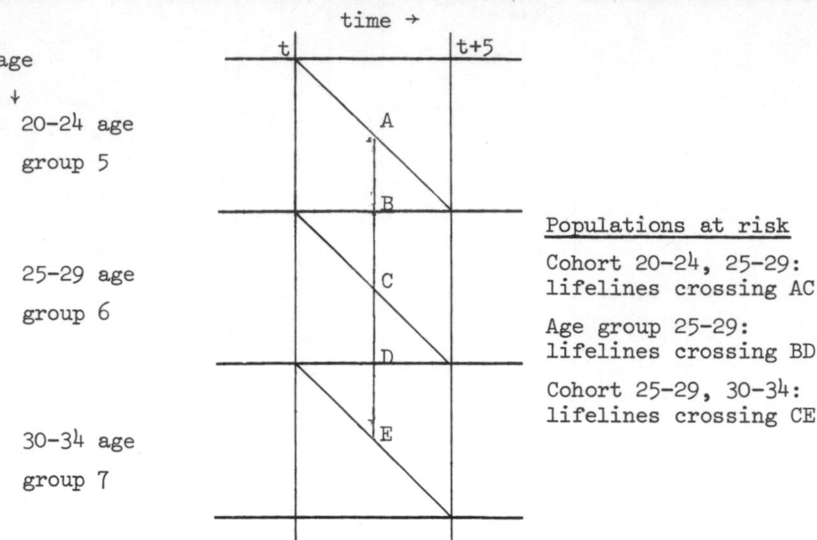

ABCDE is located at time $t+\frac{T}{2}$ or $t+\frac{5}{2}$ if the average population in the period is equal to the mid-point.

The vector of populations at risk of giving birth, calculated in Equations (3.101) or (3.102) is used together with the appropriate age-specific or cohort rates in Equation (3.97), which can be expanded as shown in Equation (3.103). The fertility rates occupy only the first row of the $\underline{F}$ matrix which is otherwise empty. Fertility rates are entered in the first row only where statistics are conventionally collected, namely, for age group 15-19 through to age group 45-49. Births do occur to women aged 10-14 and aged 50-54, but these are very few in number. They are conventionally counted in with the births to 15-19 year old women and the 45-49 year old women respectively. Because there are zeroes in the non-fertile age group positions in the first row of the $\underline{F}$ matrix, the populations at risk in age groups one to three and eleven to the last do not come into play and are, in effect, made redundant. Equation (3.103) is specified for age-specific fertility rates for five year age groups. Slightly different specifications are needed for cohort rates or for rates not specified by five year age groups.

$$\begin{bmatrix} w_{01}^{x}(t+T) \\ \hline 0 \\ \vdots \\ 0 \end{bmatrix} = \begin{bmatrix} 0 & 0 & 0 & f_4 & f_5 & \cdots & f_{10} & 0 & \cdots & 0 \\ \hline 0 & 0 & 0 & 0 & 0 & \cdots & 0 & 0 & \cdots & 0 \\ \vdots & \vdots & \vdots & \vdots & \vdots & & \vdots & \vdots & & \vdots \\ 0 & 0 & 0 & 0 & 0 & \cdots & 0 & 0 & & 0 \end{bmatrix} x \begin{bmatrix} \hat{w}_1^F \\ \hat{w}_2^F \\ \hat{w}_3^F \\ \hline \hat{w}_4^F \\ \hat{w}_5^F \\ \vdots \\ \hat{w}_{10}^F \\ \hline \hat{w}_{11}^F \\ \vdots \\ \hat{w}_R^F \end{bmatrix} x \begin{bmatrix} \sigma^x \end{bmatrix} \quad x \quad \begin{bmatrix} s_{01}^x \end{bmatrix} + \begin{bmatrix} \underline{I}_{01}^x \\ 0 \\ \vdots \\ 0 \end{bmatrix}$$

$$\underset{Rx1}{\underline{w}_B^x(t+T)} = \underset{RxR}{\underline{F}(t,t+T)} \; x \; \underset{Rx1}{\hat{\underline{w}}^F(t,t+T)} \; x \; \underset{1x1}{\sigma^x(t,t+T)} \; x \; \underset{1x1}{s_{01}^x(t,t+T)} + \underset{Rx1}{\underline{I}_B^x(t,t+T)} \qquad (3.103)$$

The births produced by multiplying $\underline{F}$ and $\underline{\hat{w}}^F$ together have to be sexed by multiplying by a sex proportion σ^x which is fairly constant over time and age and is represented by a scalar in Equation (3.103). The births of each sex have then to be survived over that fraction of the period remaining after birth by multiplication by an appropriate survival rate, s^x_{01}, which incorporates the risk of dying within the origin area, out-migrating and surviving, and out-migrating and dying just as did the $\underline{S}$ matrix of survival rates in Equation (3.95). To these survived, sexed births must be added the infants born outside the region in the period who migrate into the region and survive there, the I^x_{01} term.

The final model Equation (3.98) can be expanded thus in the five year equal age group/period case:

$$\begin{bmatrix} w^x_1(t+T) \\ w^x_2(t+T) \\ w^x_3(t+T) \\ \vdots \\ w^x_R(t+T) \end{bmatrix} = \begin{bmatrix} 0 \\ w^x_2(t+T) \\ w^x_3(t+T) \\ \vdots \\ w^x_R(t+T) \end{bmatrix} + \begin{bmatrix} w^x_{01}(t+T) \\ 0 \\ 0 \\ \vdots \\ 0 \end{bmatrix}$$

$$\underset{R\times 1}{\underline{w}^x(t+T)} = \underset{R\times 1}{\underline{w}^x_S(t+T)} + \underset{R\times 1}{\underline{w}^x_B(t+T)} \qquad (3.104)$$

or thus in the five year age group/one year period case

$$\begin{bmatrix} w^x_1(t+1) \\ w^x_2(t+1) \\ w^x_3(t+1) \\ \vdots \\ w^x_R(t+1) \end{bmatrix} = \begin{bmatrix} w^x_{11}(t+1) \\ w^x_2(t+1) \\ w^x_3(t+1) \\ \vdots \\ w^x_R(t+1) \end{bmatrix} + \begin{bmatrix} w^x_{01}(t+1) \\ 0 \\ 0 \\ \vdots \\ 0 \end{bmatrix}$$

$$\underset{R\times 1}{\underline{w}^x(t+1)} = \underset{R\times 1}{\underline{w}^x_S(t+1)} + \underset{R\times 1}{\underline{w}^x_B(t+1)} \qquad (3.105)$$

The demographic projection model has been presented here in matrix format. It is often useful, as well, as Wilson (1972) has pointed out, to express a matrix model in algebraic terms, particularly when a computer programme is being written for it. Readers interested in tracing through the algebraic equivalents of matrix Equations (3.95) to (3.98) are referred to Rees and King (1974). Also developed in that reference is the multi-regional version of the projection model presented here. The model can be converted from a single region basis to a multi-regional by adding locational superscripts to the main variables (our practice when describing the accounts based model) and by representing in-migration not as a flow but as a product of an out-migration rate multiplied by the population of the origin region.

It is fairly easy to show, using the multi-regional form of the model, the correspondence between model terms and accounts terms. The reader is again referred to Rees and King (1974) for details. There it is concluded that the only way that correspondence between model and accounts can be satisfied is to measure model rates from specifically constructed spatial population accounts. This, as we have demonstrated earlier in the chapter, is a fairly demanding procedure. So, often the rates input to projection models must be estimated in a cruder fashion but in a way that ensures that the right kind of rate (from an accounting point of view) is being measured.

This point can be illustrated by describing how the survival rates used in the projection example described in Section 3.7 involving the West Indian population in Leeds were obtained. No information on survival specific to the Leeds population or the West Indian population in Leeds was to hand. What was available was a population accounts table for a West Yorkshire Study Area and the associated transition rates (see Section 3.5). The probabilities of survival, and of migration and survival over the five year intercensal period 1961-1966 were calculated and added together to give the probability of survival anywhere. Three regions were involved: a West Yorkshire Study Area, the Rest of England and Wales and the Rest of the World, which we label WY, REW and RTW respectively. The procedure was

$$h_{s-1s}^{\varepsilon(WY)\sigma(*)x} = h_{s-1s}^{\varepsilon(WY)\sigma(WY)x} + h_{s-1s}^{\varepsilon(WY)\sigma(REW)x} + h_{s-1s}^{\varepsilon(WY)\sigma(RTW)x} \qquad (3.106)$$

For males in age group 20-24 at census date 1961, for example, the probabilities were

$$h_{56}^{\varepsilon(WY)\sigma(*)M} = 0.99437 = 0.86927 + 0.09117 + 0.03393 \quad (3.107)$$

An estimate was made of the probability of migrating out of Leeds CB and surviving the period 1961-1966 (the exact equations are in King, 1974-A), and this was subtracted from the West Yorkshire Study Area survival 'anywhere' probability to yield an estimated survival rate within Leeds for the 1961-1966 period:

$$s_{s-1s}^{LLx} = h_{s-1s}^{\varepsilon(WY)\sigma(*)x} - \Sigma_{j \neq L} h_{s-1s}^{\varepsilon(L)\sigma(j)x} \quad (3.108)$$

where L refers to Leeds. For the males in Leeds aged 20-24 at census date 1961 this works out as

$$s_{56}^{LLM} = 0.99437 - 0.26601 = 0.72836 \quad (3.109)$$

Note that s_{56}^{LLM} is a good deal lower than $h_{56}^{\varepsilon(WY)\sigma(WY)M}$ because a larger proportion of the population of a small area out-migrate from such an area than do from a larger area. The s_{s-1s}^{LLx} survival rates are used in the West Indian 'projection model'. By the time these are employed in the model we have been forced to assume that the probability of surviving anywhere for Leeds inhabitants in the intercensal period 1961-1966 is the same as the equivalent probability in the West Yorkshire Study Area; that the age disaggregation of migration out of Leeds is the same as out of the West Yorkshire Study Area; that the survival rates estimated for the whole of the Leeds population apply with no change to the West Indian population, and that the 1961-1966 survival rates so estimated are applicable for the next four intercensal periods (1966-197 1971-1976, 1976-1981 and 1981-1986) without change.

Only a formidable demographic information system and much accountin work could allow us to relax these assumptions and to calculate the survival rates for the West Indian population in Leeds more directly. In the absence of such a system and such work we can only state our belief that the true survival rates do not differ significantly from those used in the model.

In the next section we describe an example of the model in operation. This should give the reader unversed in abstract mathematics but familiar with numerical computation a better idea of how the model works.

3.7 The West Indian population of Leeds, 1961-1986

Leeds had, in 1971, a small community of 6,035 persons who were either born in the West Indies or whose parents were born there. They made up about 1.2% of the population of the city. The residential distribution within Leeds of persons born in the West Indies is shown in Figure 3.24. West Indians are concentrated in inner city districts north of the city centre, particularly in the Chapeltown area, but West Indian families are found in all wards of the city. So the projections of the West Indian population from 1971 to 1986 described in the next section have different implications for the various districts of the city.

Figure 3.24 The West Indian population of Leeds CB at census date 1971 (April 24/25)

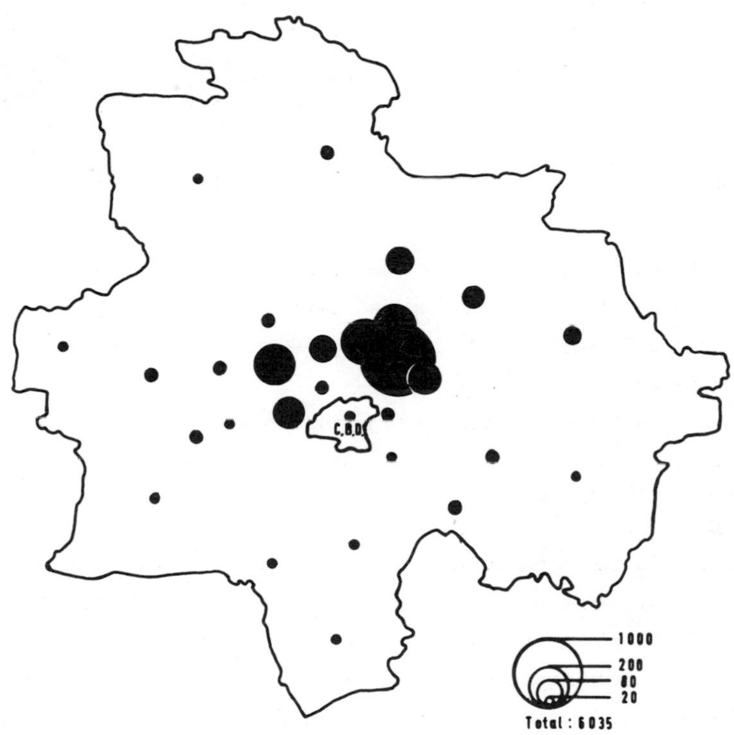

Recent measurement of the fertility rates of West Indian women (King, 1974-A, 1974-B) indicates that they have been experiencing levels of fertility about twice those of the British-born population although the levels are in the process of decline. We can examine what implications these fertility levels have for the size of the West Indian community by using the simple model for population projection outlined earlier. We show all the model equations for the first 'projection' period 1971-1976.

Equation (3.110) below contains the relevant figures for 1971-1976

$$\begin{bmatrix} 0 \\ 370 \\ 272 \\ 257 \\ 274 \\ 192 \\ 265 \\ 343 \\ 313 \\ 214 \\ 128 \\ 74 \\ 55 \\ 34 \end{bmatrix} = \begin{bmatrix} 0 & 0 & 0 & 0 & 0 & 0 & 0 & 0 & 0 & 0 & 0 & 0 & 0 & 0 \\ 0.861 & \cdot & \cdot & \cdot & \cdot & \cdot & \cdot & \cdot & \cdot & \cdot & \cdot & \cdot & \cdot & \cdot \\ 0 & 0.864 & \cdot & \cdot & \cdot & \cdot & \cdot & \cdot & \cdot & \cdot & \cdot & \cdot & \cdot & \cdot \\ 0 & \cdot & 0.830 & \cdot & \cdot & \cdot & \cdot & \cdot & \cdot & \cdot & \cdot & \cdot & \cdot & \cdot \\ 0 & \cdot & \cdot & 0.696 & \cdot & \cdot & \cdot & \cdot & \cdot & \cdot & \cdot & \cdot & \cdot & \cdot \\ 0 & \cdot & \cdot & \cdot & 0.758 & \cdot & \cdot & \cdot & \cdot & \cdot & \cdot & \cdot & \cdot & \cdot \\ 0 & \cdot & \cdot & \cdot & \cdot & 0.757 & \cdot & \cdot & \cdot & \cdot & \cdot & \cdot & \cdot & \cdot \\ 0 & \cdot & \cdot & \cdot & \cdot & \cdot & 0.859 & \cdot & \cdot & \cdot & \cdot & \cdot & \cdot & \cdot \\ 0 & \cdot & \cdot & \cdot & \cdot & \cdot & \cdot & 0.857 & \cdot & \cdot & \cdot & \cdot & \cdot & \cdot \\ 0 & \cdot & \cdot & \cdot & \cdot & \cdot & \cdot & \cdot & 0.917 & \cdot & \cdot & \cdot & \cdot & \cdot \\ 0 & \cdot & \cdot & \cdot & \cdot & \cdot & \cdot & \cdot & \cdot & 0.908 & \cdot & \cdot & \cdot & \cdot \\ 0 & \cdot & \cdot & \cdot & \cdot & \cdot & \cdot & \cdot & \cdot & \cdot & 0.896 & \cdot & \cdot & \cdot \\ 0 & \cdot & \cdot & \cdot & \cdot & \cdot & \cdot & \cdot & \cdot & \cdot & \cdot & 0.875 & \cdot & \cdot \\ 0 & \cdot & \cdot & \cdot & \cdot & \cdot & \cdot & \cdot & \cdot & \cdot & \cdot & \cdot & 0.851 & 0.688 \end{bmatrix} \begin{bmatrix} 412 \\ 314 \\ 247 \\ 257 \\ 173 \\ 267 \\ 351 \\ 334 \\ 220 \\ 131 \\ 75 \\ 63 \\ 20 \\ 24 \end{bmatrix} + \begin{bmatrix} 0 \\ 15 \\ 1 \\ 52 \\ 95 \\ 61 \\ 63 \\ 41 \\ 27 \\ 13 \\ 9 \\ 6 \\ 0 \\ 0 \end{bmatrix} \quad (3.11$$

for West Indian women. It is the 'numbers' version of Equation (3.99) where 'cd 1976' refers to 'census' date in April 1976, 'cd 1971' refers to census date April 24/25 1971 and '1971-1976' refers to the intercensa period between these dates.

We recall that multiplication of two matrices involving the followi operation

$$c_{ij} = \Sigma_k a_{ik} b_{kj} \qquad (3.11$$

where c_{ij} is the element in the ith row and j^{th} column of the product matrix $\underline{C}$, a_{ik} is the element in the ith row and k^{th} column of the first multiplicand matrix $\underline{A}$ and b_{kj} the element in the kth row and j^{th} column of the second multiplicand matrix $\underline{B}$. Each element of $\underline{w}_S^F$ (cd 1976) is similarly constructed. For example, the element in the fourth row of $\underline{w}_S^F$ (cd 1976) which refers to age group 15-19, is calculated as follows

$$w_4^F(\text{cd } 1976) = (0 \times 412) + (0 \times 314) + (0.830 \times 247) + (0 \times 257) + (0 \times 173) + (0 \times 367) + (0 \times 351) + (0 \times 334) + (0 \times 220) + (0 \times 131) + (0 \times 75) + (0 \times 63) + (0 \times 20) + (0 \times 24) + 52 \quad (3.112)$$

This reduces because of all the zero rates, to

$$w_4^F(\text{cd } 1976) = (0.830)\ 247 + 52 = 257 \quad (3.113)$$

The survival rates in the subdiagonal do not decline as a simple function of age as do life table survival rates or accounts based survival anywhere rates. They decline with age, then rise, then fall again. This is because the survival rates involve out-migration as well as death. The rate of out-migration is highest in the (3,4), (4,5) and (5,6) age group transitions (Smith and Rees, 1974, Figure 26). The first rows of the $\underline{w}_S^F$(cd 1976) vector, the $\underline{S}^F$ matrix and the $\underline{I}_S^F$ vector all contain zeros because we calculate these terms in later equations, but it is necessary to represent them there conceptually because we need to use all 14 age groups in the $\underline{w}_S^F$(cd 1971) vector.

Once the population of West Indian women at census date 1976 has been calculated we can work out the population at risk for use with the cohort fertility rates:

$$\begin{bmatrix} 391 \\ 293 \\ --- \\ 252 \\ 266 \\ 183 \\ 266 \\ 347 \\ 323 \\ 217 \\ 129 \\ --- \\ 75 \\ 59 \\ 27 \\ 12 \end{bmatrix} = \left[\begin{bmatrix} 370 \\ 272 \\ --- \\ 257 \\ 274 \\ 192 \\ 265 \\ 343 \\ 313 \\ 214 \\ 128 \\ --- \\ 74 \\ 55 \\ 34 \\ 0 \end{bmatrix} + \begin{bmatrix} 412 \\ 314 \\ --- \\ 247 \\ 257 \\ 173 \\ 267 \\ 351 \\ 334 \\ 220 \\ 131 \\ --- \\ 75 \\ 63 \\ 20 \\ 24 \end{bmatrix}\right] \times \begin{bmatrix} 0.5 \end{bmatrix}$$

$$\underline{\hat{w}}^F = (\underline{w}_S^F(\text{cd } 1976) + \underline{w}^F(\text{cd } 1971))\ 0.5 \quad (3.114)$$

The third equation for the West Indian population projections forecasts the number of births to women at risk using cohort fertility rates for five year cohorts derived from a study of the fertility of immigrants in Leeds (King, 1973, 1974-A, 1974-B). The numbers of females surviving in the first age group at the end of the intercensal period 1971-1976 is given in Equation (3.115) below.

$$\begin{bmatrix} 448 \\ \hline 0 \\ \cdot \\ \cdot \\ \cdot \\ 0 \end{bmatrix} = \begin{bmatrix} 0 & 0 & 0.349 & 0.698 & 0.818 & 0.809 & 0.526 & 0.397 & 0.172 & 0.078 & 0 & 0 & 0 & 0 & 0 \\ \hline 0 & 0 & 0 & 0 & 0 & 0 & 0 & 0 & 0 & 0 & 0 & 0 & 0 & 0 & 0 \\ \cdot & \cdot & \cdot & \cdot & \cdot & \cdot & \cdot & \cdot & \cdot & \cdot & \cdot & \cdot & \cdot & \cdot & \cdot \\ \cdot & \cdot & \cdot & \cdot & \cdot & \cdot & \cdot & \cdot & \cdot & \cdot & \cdot & \cdot & \cdot & \cdot & \cdot \\ \cdot & \cdot & \cdot & \cdot & \cdot & \cdot & \cdot & \cdot & \cdot & \cdot & \cdot & \cdot & \cdot & \cdot & \cdot \\ 0 & 0 & 0 & 0 & 0 & 0 & 0 & 0 & 0 & 0 & 0 & 0 & 0 & 0 & 0 \end{bmatrix} \times \begin{bmatrix} 391 \\ 293 \\ \hline 252 \\ 266 \\ 183 \\ 266 \\ 347 \\ 232 \\ 217 \\ 129 \\ \hline 75 \\ 59 \\ 27 \\ 12 \end{bmatrix} \times \begin{bmatrix} 0.490 \end{bmatrix} \times \begin{bmatrix} 0.907 \end{bmatrix} + \begin{bmatrix} 8 \\ \hline 0 \\ \cdot \\ \cdot \\ \cdot \\ 0 \end{bmatrix}$$

$$\underline{w}_B^F(\text{cd } 1976) = \underline{F}(1971\text{–}1976) \quad \times \quad \underline{w}^F \quad \times \quad \sigma^F \quad \times \quad s_{01}^F \quad + \quad \underline{I}_B^F \qquad (3.$$

Because cohort fertility rates are used there are non-zero entries in the first row of the $\underline{F}$ matrix from the third age group to the tenth (10-14 to 45-49). The total fertility rate assumed for West Indian women in the 1971-1976 period is calculated in this case by adding up all the individual cohort rates and is some 3.847. Note that we do not need to multiply each rate by five first as they refer to a five year period. This is well above the total fertility of all women either in Leeds or in England and Wales. A sex proportion of 0.490 for females is assumed, and a survival in Leeds rate of 0.907. A very small number of children in-migrating from elsewhere in the period is forecast.

The final step in this example is to combine the survivors vector with the infants vector by adding them together:

$$\begin{bmatrix} 448 \\ \\ 370 \\ 272 \\ 257 \\ 274 \\ 192 \\ 265 \\ 343 \\ 313 \\ 214 \\ 128 \\ 74 \\ 55 \\ 34 \end{bmatrix} = \begin{bmatrix} 0 \\ \hline 370 \\ 272 \\ 257 \\ 274 \\ 192 \\ 265 \\ 343 \\ 313 \\ 214 \\ 128 \\ 74 \\ 55 \\ 34 \end{bmatrix} + \begin{bmatrix} 448 \\ \hline \\ \\ \\ \\ \\ \\ \\ \\ \\ \\ \\ \\ \end{bmatrix}$$

$$\underline{w}^F(\text{cd } 1976) = \underline{w}_S^F(\text{cd } 1976) + \underline{w}_B^F(\text{cd } 1976) \qquad (3.116$$

In order to project the population of West Indian women in Leeds forward to 1986 forecasts have to be made of the contents of the survival rates matrix, the surviving in-migrant vector, the fertility rate schedule, the sex proportion, the survival rate for infants and the number of surviving in-migrant infants. The rates and numbers assumed are set out in Figures 3.25, 3.26, 3.27, 3.28, 3.29 and 3.30. The figures are discussed and justified at length in King (1974-A).

Figure 3.25 The survival rates assumed for West Indian women in Leeds

Age group at start of period		Age group at end of period		Survival rates		
No.	Age range	No.	Age range	1971-1976	1976-1981	1981-1986
1	0 - 4	2	5 - 9	0.86053	0.86053	0.86053
2	5 - 9	3	10 - 14	0.86415	0.86415	0.86415
3	10 - 14	4	15 - 19	0.83019	0.83019	0.83019
4	15 - 19	5	20 - 24	0.69573	0.69573	0.69573
5	20 - 24	6	25 - 29	0.75777	0.75777	0.75777
6	25 - 29	7	30 - 34	0.75697	0.75697	0.75697
7	30 - 34	8	35 - 39	0.85894	0.85894	0.85894
8	35 - 39	9	40 - 44	0.85562	0.85562	0.85562
9	40 - 44	10	45 - 49	0.91669	0.91669	0.91669
10	45 - 49	11	50 - 54	0.90820	0.90820	0.90820
11	50 - 54	12	55 - 59	0.89633	0.89633	0.89633
12	55 - 59	13	60 - 64	0.87484	0.87484	0.87484
13	60 - 64	14	65 & over	0.85106	0.85106	0.85106
14	65 & over	14	65 & over	0.68814	0.68814	0.68814

Figure 3.26 The surviving in-migrant vectors assumed for West Indian women in Leeds

Age group at start of period		Age group at end of period		In-migrants		
No.	Age range	No.	Age range	1971-1976	1976-1981	1981-1986
1	0 - 4	2	5 - 9	15	15	15
2	5 - 9	3	10 - 14	1	1	1
3	10 - 14	4	15 - 19	52	47	47
4	15 - 19	5	20 - 24	95	86	86
5	20 - 24	6	25 - 29	61	55	55
6	25 - 29	7	30 - 34	63	57	57
7	30 - 34	8	35 - 39	41	37	37
8	35 - 39	9	40 - 44	27	24	24
9	40 - 44	10	45 - 49	13	12	12
10	45 - 49	11	50 - 54	9	8	8
11	50 - 54	12	55 - 59	6	6	6
12	55 - 59	13	60 - 64	0	0	0
13	60 - 64	14	65 & over	0	0	0
14	65 & over	14	65 & over	0	0	0

Figure 3.27 The fertility rate schedules assumed

Assumption	Cohort age group at start of period		Age group at end of period		Cohort fertility rates for period		
	No.	Age group	No.	Age range	1971-1976	1976-1981	1981-1986
High Fertility Assumed	3	10 - 14	4	15 - 19	0.3488	0.3488	0.3488
	4	15 - 19	5	20 - 24	0.6975	0.6975	0.6975
	5	20 - 24	6	25 - 29	0.8180	0.8180	0.8180
	6	25 - 29	7	30 - 34	0.8090	0.8090	0.8090
	7	30 - 34	8	35 - 39	0.5260	0.5260	0.5260
	8	35 - 39	9	40 - 44	0.3970	0.3970	0.3970
	9	40 - 44	10	45 - 49	0.1720	0.1720	0.1720
	10	45 - 49	11	50 - 54	0.0780	0.0780	0.0780
Low Fertility Assumed	3	10 - 14	4	15 - 19	0.3488	0.1300	0.1300
	4	15 - 19	5	20 - 24	0.6975	0.2600	0.2600
	5	20 - 24	6	25 - 29	0.8180	0.7360	0.7360
	6	25 - 29	7	30 - 34	0.8090	0.7415	0.7415
	7	30 - 34	8	35 - 39	0.5260	0.4080	0.4080
	8	35 - 39	9	40 - 44	0.3970	0.1450	0.1450
	9	40 - 44	10	45 - 49	0.1720	0.0510	0.0510
	10	45 - 49	11	50 - 54	0.0780	0.0025	0.0025

Figure 3.28 The sex proportions

Sex	1971-1976	Period 1976-1981	1981-1986
Female	0.4895	0.4895	0.4895
Male	0.5105	0.5105	0.5105

Figure 3.29 The survival rate for infants

Age group at start of period		Age group end of period		Period		
No.	Age range	No.	Age range	1971-1976	1976-1981	1981-1986
0	Birth	1	0 - 4	0.90709	0.90709	0.90709

Figure 3.30 Numbers of surviving in-migrant infants

Age group at start of period		Age group end of period		Period		
No.	Age range	No.	Age range	1971-1976	1976-1981	1981-1986
0	Birth	1	0 - 4	8	8	8

We have assumed (Figure 3.25) constant survival 'in situ' rates over the three projection periods. The death rate component of these rates will undoubtedly decline slightly over time and the migration rate component will fluctuate. But as a first approximation these rates can be assumed constant without too much effect on the future population. The number of surviving in-migrants in Figure 3.26 is assumed to decline from 1971-1976, when dependents of earlier 1960's migrants will still be arriving, to a lower level in 1976-1981 and in 1981-1986 when only A and B voucher holders and their dependents will be arriving. We can in fact compare these in-migration vectors with those of out-migration and survival implied in our model. The rates of out-migration given in King (1974-A, Table 1) produce in 1971-1976 the following numbers of surviving out-migrants which can be compared with corresponding number of in-migrants.

Age transition (see Figure 3.24 for age ranges)	Surviving out-migrants	Surviving in-migrants	Net surviving in-migrants
1 - 2	55	15	-40
2 - 3	42	1	-41
3 - 4	42	52	10
4 - 5	78	95	17
5 - 6	41	61	20
6 - 7	64	63	-1
7 - 8	47	41	-6
8 - 9	45	27	-18
9 - 10	15	13	-2
10 - 11	9	9	0
11 - 12	5	6	1
12 - 13	4	0	-4
13 - 14	1	0	-1
14 - 14	3	0	-3
	451	383	-60

There is a net outflow likely under the assumptions we have adopted though the number of out-migrants may well be lower than those implied here if West Indians fail to move in the same numbers to growing suburban communities around Leeds with the same frequency as the whole population. To the net outflow as a result of migration must be added 29 deaths in the 1971-1976 period.

Most critical for this particular projection are the fertility rates assumed. Two sets of assumptions are made. In the first set (Figure 3.27) the high fertility rates of 1971 are assumed to continue in 1971-1976, 1976-1981 and 1981-1986. In the second set (Figure 3.27) the fertility rates are assumed to decline to a lower level in 1976-1981 and 1981-1986, to a level characteristics of the whole Leeds population in 1971. There is a strong evidence for such a decline occurring (King, 1974-A) and our guess would be that fertility among West Indian women is more likely to be nearer the second set of assumptions than the first. The sex proportion for births and survival rate for infants are assumed constant over the three projection periods.

Figure 3.31 A diagrammatic representation of the assumptions made in projecting the population of West Indian women

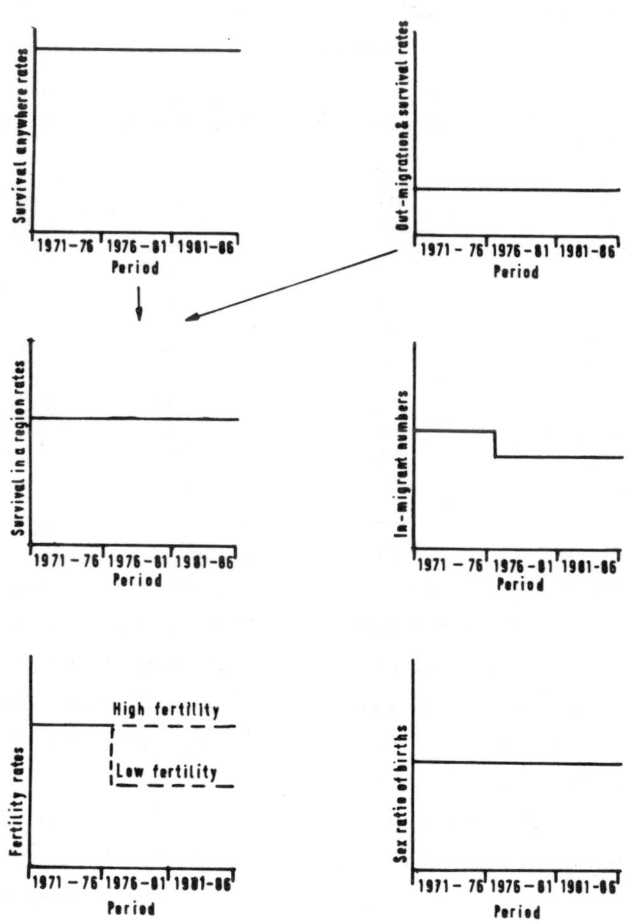

Figure 3.31 shows in simplified form the nature of the assumptions made in projecting the population of West Indian women. The projections are conditional on these assumptions proving correct. In the projections we do not foretell the future but rather say what it will be like if certain conditions hold.

If we run the model not only for the period 1971-1976 (as we have in Equations 3.110, 3.114, 3.115 and 3.116 but also for 1976-1981 and 1981-1986 for both the high and low fertility rate schedules we obtain the population stock figures given in Figure 3.32.

Figure 3.32 The population stocks of West Indian women in Leeds 1971, 1976, 1981 and 1986 under high and low fertility assumptions

Age group		High fertility assumption				Low fertility assumption			
No.	Age range	1971	1976	1981	1986	1971	1976	1981	1986
1	0 - 4	412	448	447	453	412	448	283	290
2	5 - 9	314	370	401	400	314	370	401	259
3	10 - 14	247	272	320	347	247	272	320	347
4	15 - 19	257	257	273	313	257	257	273	313
5	20 - 24	173	274	265	276	173	274	265	276
6	25 - 29	267	192	263	256	267	192	263	256
7	30 - 34	351	265	203	256	351	265	203	256
8	35 - 39	334	343	264	211	334	343	264	211
9	40 - 44	220	313	317	250	220	313	317	250
10	45 - 49	131	214	298	303	131	214	298	303
11	50 - 54	75	128	203	279	75	128	203	279
12	55 - 59	63	74	121	188	63	74	121	188
13	60 - 64	20	55	64	106	20	55	64	106
14	65 & over	24	34	70	103	24	34	70	103
Totals		2,888	3,239	3,509	3,741	2,888	3,239	3,345	3,437

These figures show that the West Indian female population is likely to increase by 853 under the high fertility assumption and by 549 under the low fertility assumption: note that all the difference in these increases is concentrated in the 0 - 4 and 5 - 9 age groups in 1986, the members of which will have been born in the 1976-1986 decade. There might be 853 West Indian girls aged under 10 in 1986 if fertility rates continue as they are and 549 if they fall in the way recent trends indicate.

A comprehensive view of the projected population in each age group for both women and men of West Indian origin is given in Figure 3.33 in the form of population pyramids for 1971, 1976, 1981

Figure 3.33 Age-sex pyramids for the projected population of West Indians in Leeds

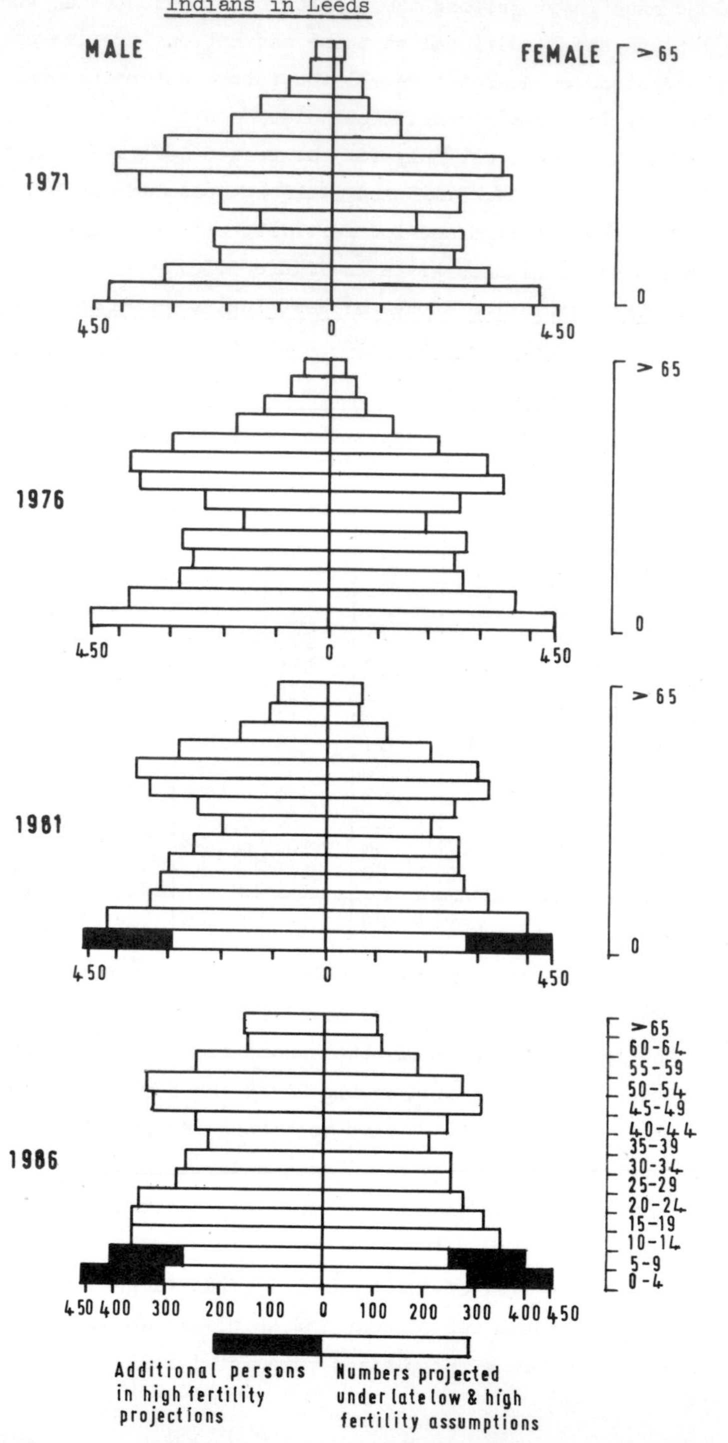

and 1986. They show that the population changes from one in 1971 whose age/sex structure is dominated by the differences between age groups in immigration propensity to a more normal form in 1986 either approaching a fairly even distribution of persons in the age groups prior to the outset of heavy mortality under the low fertility assumptions or a youthful one in the high fertility case. The high fertility histogram has the pyramidal form below age 40 in 1986 characteristic of a fairly rapidly growing population.

3.8 Concluding comments on the development of population models

Demographers have traditionally concentrated on the study of fertility and of mortality in a non-spatial, national context. We have attempted to demonstrate in this chapter that such concerns are not sufficient for the understanding of population change in cities and regions.

We have shown that a variety of single region or multi-region cohort survival models are available that give an explicit role to migration and show its effects on population change. We have demonstrated how consistent accounts of population change may be specified and how an associated accounts-based model may be designed. We have shown that despite heavy data demands accounting and cohort survival models can be made operational for real metropolitan regions (West Yorkshire) and for particular urban populations (the West Indian women of Leeds). Further developments of these models is, however, needed if they are to be useful planning tools. The population forecast needs to be converted to a household forecast. The demographic models need to be connected with housing, employment and residential location accounts and models. Perhaps the reader will take up this task. He will find the chapters that follow a useful grounding for this ambitious exercise.

References

General Register Office (1968-A) Sample Census 1966, England and Wales, Migration Summary Tables, Part I, HMSO, London.

General Register Office (1968-B) Sample Census 1966, England and Wales, Migration Regional Report, Yorkshire and Humberside, HMSO, London.

General Register Office (1969) Sample Census 1966, England and Wales, Migration Tables, Part II, HMSO, London.

Howell, J. (1974) The role of population forecasts and demographic analysis in new town planning, Paper presented at the Population Forecasting Seminar, Summer Annual Meeting, PTRC, University of Warwick

Illingworth, D.R. (1976) Testing some new concepts and estimation methods in population accounting, PhD thesis, Department of Geography, University of Leeds, in preparation.

Illingworth, D.R., Smith, A.P. and Rees, P.H. (1974) Notes on the definition of the West Yorkshire study area and the new West Yorkshire metropolitan county, Working Paper 90, Department of Geography, University of Leeds.

King, J.R. (1973) The social, economic and location characteristics of ethnic births in Leeds CB in 1971, Working Paper 47, Department of Geography, University of Leeds.

King, J.R. (1974-A) Immigrant fertility trends and population growth in Leeds, Environment and Planning, 6, pp. 509-546.

King, J.R. (1974-B) The fertility of immigrants in Leeds, Working Paper 58, Department of Geography, University of Leeds.

Leslie, P.H. (1945) On the use of matrices in certain population mathematics, Biometrika, 23, pp. 183-212.

Leslie, P.H. (1948) Some further notes on the use of matrices in population mathematics, Biometrika, 35, pp. 213-245.

Office of Population Censuses and Surveys (annual) The Registrar General's Statistical Review of England and Wales for the Year 19nn, Part II, Tables, Population, HMSO, London.

Office of Population Censuses and Surveys (1973) Population projections No 3 1972-2012, HMSO, London

Rees, P.H. (1971) How to make the Rogers' version of the demographic model operational for an English or Welsh county in about one hundred easy steps, Working Paper 8, Department of Geography, University of Leeds.

Rees, P.H. (1974) A family of demographic accounts, Working Paper 68, Department of Geography, University of Leeds.

Rees, P.H. and King, J.R. (1974) A simple model for population projections applied to ethnic group and small area population, Working Paper 76, Department of Geography, University of Leeds.

Rees, P.H. and Wilson, A.G. (1973) Accounts and models for spatial demographic analysis 1: aggregate population, Environment and Planning 5, pp. 61-90.

Rees, P.H. and Wilson, A.G. (1975-A) A comparison of available models of population change, Regional Studies, 9, pp. 39-61.

Rees, P.H. and Wilson, A.G. (1975-B) Accounts and models for spatial demographic analysis 3: rates and life tables, Environment and Planning, 7, pp. 199-231.

Rees, P.H. and Wilson, A.G. (1977-A) Spatial population analysis, Edward Arnold, London.

Rees, P.H. and Wilson, A.G. (1977-B) Spatial population analysis: methods and applications, in preparation.

Rogers, A. (1966) Matrix methods of population analysis, Journal of the American Institute of Planners, 32, pp. 40-44.

Rogers, A. (1968) Matrix analysis of inter-regional population growth and distribution, University of California Press, Berkeley and Los Angeles.

Rogers, A. (1971) Matrix methods in urban and regional analysis, Holden-Day, San Francisco.

Rogers, A. (1973) The mathematics of multi-regional demographic growth, Environment and Planning, 5, pp. 3-29.

Smith, A.P. (1974) A computer version of a spatial demographic account building model: user's manual, Working Paper 51, Department of Geography, University of Leeds.

Smith, A.P. and Rees, P.H. (1974) Methods of constructing spatial demographic accounts for a British region, Working Paper 59, Department of Geography, University of Leeds.

Stone, R. (1971) Demographic accounting and model building, OECD, Paris.

Wilson, A.G. (1972) Multi-regional models of population structure and some implications for a dynamic residential model, in Wilson, A.G. (ed), Patterns and processes in urban and regional systems, Pion, London.

Wilson, A.G. and Rees, P.H. (1974) Accounts and models for spatial demographic analysis 2: age/sex disaggregated populations, Environment and Planning, 6, pp. 101-116.

Chapter 4

Regional economic models

T.B. Smith and C.M. Leigh

4.1 Introduction

In this chapter the chief objective is to explain the process of constructing and developing a model of a regional economy, using West Yorkshire as an example. Initially at least, the amalgam of economic activities in the study area is treated as if it was located at a single point in space. Models that relate to the spatial allocation of activity are the concern of a later chapter (Chapter 8). The economic model building process is in effect an examination of a range or family of models that may be used to portray the working of a local economy. A crucial factor in the selection of a member of this family for a given situation is that of data availability. Much of this chapter will be concerned with describing attempts to overcome a serious lack of reliable and comprehensive information about the local economy. Such are the ramifications of this deficiency that substantial sections are devoted to the construction of a consistent set of social accounts for the West Yorkshire conurbation. Although this is a particular case, the problems discussed are fairly typical and general.

Accounts cannot be built in the abstract and, as usual, the choice of what can be regarded as data worthy of attention is conditioned by the theories and models currently available. Also of some importance is the recognition that information is only relevant in terms of the level of resolution that is being sought or is being imposed upon the observer.

Information relevant to different spatial resolution levels such as national, regional, sub-regional, local and neighbourhood levels is available for local economies. But this information will only be accessible to the observer at fixed scales, determined not only by the boundaries imposed on the map, but also by the sensitivity of tools that the observer has at his disposal. Unfortunately, in the West Yorkshire case the observer has little control over the data available to him from published sources, nor has he any choice in the sensitivity of the tools to be used. This suggests two possible lines of enquiry: firstly, to seek more disaggregated data; and secondly, to develop more sensitive tools. While it is probably best to pursue both areas of activity, in this chapter the principal emphasis is given to the first, although any implications that data constraints may have for new models will be noted.

4.2 Accounts and models

4.2.1 Conceptual aspects

In most empirical work using mathematical models, the construction of consistent tables of accounts for the area under study is an essential prerequisite which, if achieved, provides a substantial prop for the investigation of local social and economic problems as well as underpinning the work of the analyst in testing his suppositions and, hopefully, improving his models. The social and economic problems are, in their turn, often poorly defined or, more frequently, assumed to be well-known. In the case of West Yorkshire, however, it is fairly easy to present a list of questions large enough to justify the exercise of compiling some elementary social accounts. For example, until Woodward's recent work (Woodward, 1970) little was known in statistical terms about the relative sizes of the regional economies of the United Kingdom[(1)] and their states of health; considerable reliance had been placed upon the levels of local unemployment as a guide to public policy.

---

(1) The pioneers of regional social accounting in the United Kingdom were Deane, P. (1953) Regional variations in UK incomes from employment, Journal of the Royal Statistical Society, Series A, 116, pp. 123-135, and Stone, R. (1961) Social accounts at the regional level; a survey, in Regional Economic Planning, OEEC, Paris, pp. 263-296.

While Woodward's efforts to produce more comprehensive measures of regional economic fortune are of considerable value, there nevertheless remains a notable gap in statistical evidence at the metropolitan level. The content of this desired evidence should largely reflect the objectives of the various instruments of public policy such as the yield of taxes, the effects of government subsidies to agriculture and industry, the performance of the public corporations and the social services. In other words, the accounts should permit investigation of the following kinds of question. Firstly, how much product, or income, does the metropolitan economy generate, and how does this product vary over time? Secondly, how is this product distributed between private and public enterprise, ie. how much control does the planner really have? Thirdly, how is the income that is generated by the local economy distributed among various household categories (such as income groups)? Fourthly, how strong is the multiplier effect of public expenditure? Does increased consumer expenditure (due to government building projects for example) result in a higher regional product, or are there large leakages out of the economy as a consequence of inter-regional trading patterns? Finally and fifthly, what would be the impact of the introduction of a new activity into the economy, or the expansion of an existing activity?

A simple accounting framework that would in some ways encompass the features implied by the questions listed above might take the form set out in Figure 4.1. These accounts in effect represent a highly simplified model of the economy - a 'toy' model as Stone puts it (Stone, 1971) - which distinguishes three broad areas of activity: production, consumption and investment. When these sectors are laid out in matrix format as in the figure the result is, of course, a neat way of storing data about the transactions (normally in money units) that occur between the activities. Neatness is also rewarded with consistency, since the rows and columns of the accounts must balance.

Rudimentary as this set of accounts may seem, many different kinds of model can be constructed simply by giving emphasis to different parts of the matrix. The 'toy' model, for example, uses scalar quantities, one for each cell of the matrix shown in Figure 4.1, and this approach is to a large degree the model that is generated by the West Yorkshire social accounts described in this chapter, where broad aggregates like income from employment (or the transactions between consumption and production recorded in cell (2,1) of the accounts) are the chief concern. Alternatively, accounts presented at this level of aggregation can prove useful in tackling the first two questions raised above. The third question, however, would probably require that the consumption row and column be disaggregated to reveal the ways in which income accruing from labour is distributed among household groups; concomitantly, cell (1,2) of Figure 4.1 would reveal the patterns of consumer expenditure chosen by households.

Figure 4.1 The accounting system for Stone's 'toy' model

	Production	Consumption	Investment
Production	Cell (1,1)	Cell (1,2)	Cell (1,3)
Consumption	Cell (2,1)	Cell (2,2)	Cell (2,3)
Investment	Cell (3,1)	Cell (3,2)	Cell (3,3)

The fourth and fifth questions are less amenable to analysis, first because no foreign trade has been entered into the accounts; though the last question could be handled in a limited fashion, since the introduction of a new activity merely requires an additional row and column of the matrix.

Clearly, many other kinds of model could be built. For example, observers interested in ways in which the production sector of the economy functions - its technical relationships - would require further disaggregation of cell (1,1) with perhaps the addition of cells (1,3) and (3,1) if it was desired that the sector be observed through time. The interests and the objectives of the analyst can therefore be embodied in the accounting matrix by using different levels of aggregation in different permutations.

Even before this stage of the model-building process is reached, many assumptions have been made; to assess the extent of these assumptions consider the relationships portrayed in Figure 4.2.

Figure 4.2 Elementary relationships between theories, problems and account-building style

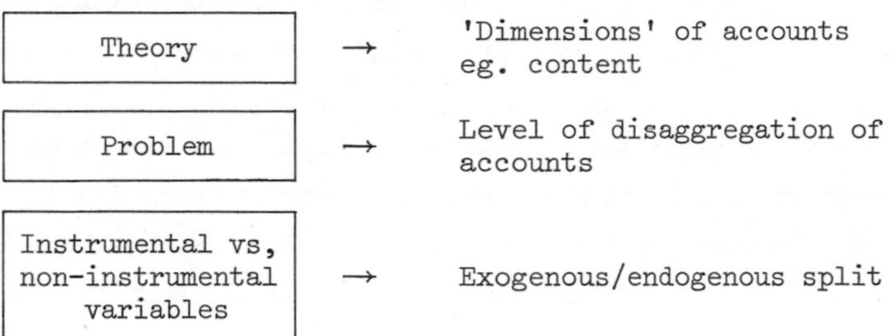

First, the dimensions of the accounts tend to be suggested by the nature of theories that underlie the particular problem area. In the case of a national economy, these theoretical underpinnings are provided by the notion of the circular flow of income (Lipsey, 1966). This notion tells the macro-economist that he should identify sectors of the economy such as consumption, production and saving and the flows that occur between them. While it may be difficult to implement an alternative strategy, given the inertia of existing stocks of data, it should be remembered that other options do exist. Some conspicuous examples which do not require that transactions be recorded in money terms are the information or communications approach to the study of urban growth, as presented by Meier (1962), and the representation of human activity by reference to energy production and consumption (as in Cripps, Macgill and Wilson, 1974).

Even if money units are retained, alternative conceptual schemes can be devised, for example as outlined in the concluding chapter of Isard and Langford's reflections and reminiscences on the Philadelphia input-output study (Isard and Langford, 1971).

It is perhaps worth noting the available theories that might be used to generate new accounting systems relevant to the study of urban and regional economies. Some have already been mentioned above - Meier's work, for example. Another contender is, of course, economic base theory - a device that implies a fairly crude set of accounts that distinguishes between activities that are orientated towards external markets and those that are purely locally-based. Despite all the limitations of base theory as an explanatory or forecasting tool, it does have the special advantage that it can generate accounts that record stocks - employees for example - as well as flows. This, to say the least, facilitates empirical implementation.

The second relationship depicted in Figure 4.2 has in some aspects been covered earlier within this section, when discussing possible developments of the 'toy' model. The question here takes the following form: are the problems, and the implicit disaggregations of the accounts, the same for a local economy as for a national economy? The answer is, to a large degree, determined by the openness of the economy in question; in this context openness applies not only to the volume of transactions that crosses the spatial boundaries of the economy (ie. trade) but also to those flows that pass into the final sectors, eg. consumption and investment. As an illustration, consider the attention paid in urban literature to the role of agglomeration economies and externalities. The latter are assumed to include the economies and diseconomies resulting from the co-location of professional, business and consumer services in central metropolitan areas; the former refer to interactions that occur between production plants of complementary industrial sectors. At a national level these complex relationships tend to be of fairly limited significance. Of greater concern to the macro-economic analyst would be the patterns of technology and productivity implied by the inter-sectoral flows. Agglomeration economies could however be dealt with in terms of the concentration, or vertical integration, of activities within a sector, and indeed this is a frequent area of study, especially with respect to the relationship between concentration, market power and efficiency - ie. the investigation of monopoly situations. But, in the analysis of local economies there is some evidence of concensus concerning the role of externalities, good and bad, in determining levels of income (the product) and future prospects (Thompson, 1968; Vernon, 1960; Goldberg, 1970; Moses and Williamson, 1967). Given this, the accounts required to promote further analytical investigation of the economy suggest that a detailed consideration of the intricacies of the production sector is not as valuable as might be expected. Rather, there is a case for more detailed information about the linkages between the production sector and the service infrastructure, which may be extended here to include the workforce and its demand patterns. As Thompson (1968) suggests, this is where one might expect to find the determinants of an area's middle and long-term prosperity, the manufacturing (production) sector, in effect, becomes the dependent variable of the analysis, while the service sector takes on the character of the independent variable.

The preceding remarks in some measure cover the third relationship shown in Figure 4.2. There, the implication is that the degree of control that the planner or analyst has over certain variables varies considerably with the spatial scale of the investigation, and that this variation can determine which variables can be regarded as endogenous and which can be regarded as exogenous. For example, when dealing with an urban economy, it is likely that over 50-60 percent of all transactions are made to the rest-of-the-world, and as noted above they are deemed to include consumption, saving and the government sector. Clearly, it would not represent a good investment in analyst-time if 50-60 percent of the information required to make forecasts had to be estimated independently. In urban models, Artle (1961) suggests that it is a considerable advantage to incorporate the household sector into the endogenous side of the account. More will be said of this transfer of sectors in later sections; for present purposes it serves to illustrate the more general point that a shift in the spatial scale of analysis can have important repercussions on the type of accounts required.

4.2.2 Options available

When faced with the task of effecting any empirical work on the metropolitan economy, the array of options available to the analyst is somewhat more restricted than the previous discussion might suggest. For instance, although there are theoretically three ways of arriving at a measure of gross domestic product at the national level, in practice only one - the income approach - turns out to be really feasible at an urban and regional level. Each approach is now described in more detail.

First, the production method measures the amount of activity that has taken place within the economy, during a year for example, by summing the value of goods and services produced. The components of the accounting identity are: C = goods and services sold to consumers; I = goods and services sold or retained as capital investment; G = goods and services absorbed by agencies of central government; X = goods and services exported; and M = goods and services imported. These components represent the final demand items of the accounts, because they are in effect withdrawals from the production sector of the economy, and do not constitute goods and services used to manufacture other goods and services. Not all firms, however, sell to these final demand sectors; indeed one of the features of urban economies is the existence of firms that produce and sell solely to other manufacturing or service industries (external economies). This last point would suggest that in modelling a large, or complex, urban economy the production method of accounting would require considerable disaggregation of the actual producing sectors rather than just the final demand categories. The product of an economy using this method is therefore the sum of the components, listed above, ie.

$$GDP = C + I + G + X - M \tag{4.1}$$

(Another, more difficult, approach would be to sum the value-added by each production process that any given good or service passes through; this is a daunting enough task at a national level, and so it will not be considered further here). The problems of trying to estimate the components of Equation (4.1) for a regional economy (let alone a metropolitan area) stem from the lack of suitable information concerning the regional distribution of trade. There are, of course, difficulties posed by the other components but these are common to the remaining two approaches and will be discussed below.

A second possible procedure involves summing the value of expenditures by the various broad categories laid down in the National Accounts 'Blue Book'[(1)]. Domestic expenditure comprises:

$$\text{Expenditure} = \begin{matrix}\text{Consumers'}\\ \text{expenditure}\end{matrix} + \begin{matrix}\text{Public authorities}\\ \text{current expenditure}\end{matrix} + \begin{matrix}\text{Capital}\\ \text{formation}\end{matrix}$$

$$+ \begin{matrix}\text{Value of physical}\\ \text{increase of stocks}\end{matrix} + \text{Net taxes} \qquad (4.2)$$

In this identity the item 'Net taxes' represents taxes paid minus any subsidies accruing. This, in effect, closes the system since it is obviously possible to finance deficits by borrowing. Note that unlike Equation (4.1) where the emphasis was on money received for the production of goods and services, Equation (4.2) does not require the explicit treatment of exports and imports - it represents the outgoing cash flows from a demand pool, a concept akin to that used by Leontief and Strout (1963) and Wilson (1970).

The third possible accounting relation of interest concerns the corollary of the demand pool; that is the supply pool, or income estimates. It is of the form

$$\text{Income} = \begin{matrix}\text{Wages and}\\ \text{salaries}\end{matrix} + \begin{matrix}\text{Income from}\\ \text{self-employment}\end{matrix} + \begin{matrix}\text{Gross trading}\\ \text{profits of companies}\end{matrix}$$

$$+ \begin{matrix}\text{Gross trading surpluses}\\ \text{of public corporations}\end{matrix} + \text{Rent} \qquad (4.3)$$

As in Equation (4.2), Equation (4.3) has components that account for any excess of outgoings over income; the trading profits and trading surplus items include any flows that may enter the economy from outside as inter-regional transfers. In theory, the three options listed above are in fact complementary and should sum to the same quantity. In practice, however, at a regional or sub-regional level this can rarely be achieved, since data are not available for every item. The best option seems at present to be one that uses the income equation as a constraint on the other two.

---

(1) Central Statistical Office, National Income and Expenditure, HMSO, (annual), hereafter referred to as the 'Blue Book'.

Having described the nature of the underlying social accounting equations, the range of models available to the analyst can be seen to follow as a result of the disaggregation mentioned in Section 4.2.1 above. Most of the succeeding discussion deals with flows between industries and flows between regions and the operational difficulties that have been encountered in these areas of local input-output analysis to date. It is also perhaps worth mentioning that the great bulk of work and writing in the field of urban and regional economic analysis has been concerned with the disaggregation of the production sectors of the economy. It is contended here, that the area of greatest need is in the disaggregation of the service and income-allocation sectors: no appreciable advances in the understanding of the macro-economic aspects of the local economy will be made until more detailed information on service linkages can be made available. However, having stated the need, the solution is by no means easy. To produce the required data, even at the national level, demands a significant advance in the accounting procedures used for measuring the product of the service sectors. The remaining paragraphs of this section are concerned with the treatment of trading relationships, modelling the exogenous sectors, and outlining the overall strategy developed for the West Yorkshire model.

The simplest kind of inter-industry model is the static, open, single-region variety developed by Leontief in the 1930's, referred to as the Leontief model below. The formal equation structure and the accounts system in which it is embodied were given in an earlier chapter (Chapter 2, Section 2.3); a similar set of equations is given here for reference. If $\underline{X} = \{X_{ij}\}$ represents inter-industry transactions (where i and j are sector labels); $\underline{Y} = \{Y_i\}$ final demand; and $\underline{G} = \{G_i\}$ total product or gross output, then

$$\Sigma_j X_{ij} + Y_i = G_i \tag{4.4}$$

If we define a set of coefficients a_{ij} assumed to be constant, such that $a_{ij} = X_{ij}/G_j$ then Equation (4.4) can be written

$$\Sigma_j a_{ij} G_j + Y_i = G_i \tag{4.5}$$

or in matrix notation

$$\underline{aG} + \underline{Y} = \underline{G} \tag{4.6}$$

so that, in the usual equation of the input-output model

$$\underline{G} = (\underline{I} - \underline{a})^{-1}\underline{Y} \qquad (4.7)$$

where $\underline{I}$ is the unit matrix.

Miernyk (1966) distinguished the static open model which he termed the square variety from the so-called dog-leg variant, the accounting system for which is shown below (Figure 4.3). The extensions to the original model represented by these accounts are concerned with separating the technical requirements of the local industries from the inter-regional trade patterns of the economy. The Leontief model, for instance, could argue with some conviction that the a_{ij} coefficients referred to the production technologies extant in the nation's production sectors; the dog-leg variant on the other hand explicitly recognises that the regional economy is not a self-contained production/consumption entity. In view of this, the coefficients underlying the regional transactions matrix in Figure 4.3 can now be redefined as regional requirements coefficients, and denote the internal or local requirements of industrial products from sector i per unit of output in sector j.

Figure 4.3 The dog-leg input-output model

Intermediate demands	Final demands		
Regional transactions matrix	Exports to sectors	Other final demands	Total gross output
Imports from sectors			
Other primary inputs			
Total gross outlay			

The two trade matrices (as opposed to the vectors of the Leontief model) also represent an increased interest in the sectoral distribution, rather than the regional distribution of trade. The main reason for such a disaggregation is that the volume of transactions that leaves the local economy is typically larger than the volume that is retained for internal use. Furthermore, a large proportion of this leakage is likely to be deliveries on intermediate account to other industries. Consequently, a knowledge of the distribution of this substantial proportion of external transactions will render the model more reliable for forecasting purposes, since the required exogenous estimates of final demand need not be complicated by the patterns of intermediate inter-regional trade.

Concomitantly, the structure of the imports matrix denotes that the analyst is concerned with the sectoral origin of the deliveries made to the local economy. Once again this emphasis reveals a concern for how the economy would behave under growth conditions; a typical problem might be to investigate the possible capacity constraints implied by a large increase in final demand. Such constraints might manifest themselves in two ways: on the one hand, the external supplying sector (in the rest-of-the-world region) might be unable to meet the increased demand for its products, which would raise the question of whether an additional local-industry expansion would be justified. Alternatively, the approach could be used to analyse the balance-of-trade characteristics of the local economy.

A second, more sophisticated approach involves the extension of the dog-leg model to encompass many regions. Two principle themes have dominated the form of the development: firstly, fixed coefficient models typified by the Moses-Chenery and Isard variants (Moses, 1955; Chenery, 1953; Isard, 1951); and secondly, the integrated gravity input-output multi-regional models formalised by Leontief and Strout (1963) and Wilson (1970).

Isard's version of the fixed coefficients model is underpinned by the accounting system shown in Figure 4.4.

Figure 4.4 The accounting system for the Isard fixed coefficient model

	Region 1	Region m	Region n	Final demand	Total
Region 1	$\underline{X}^{11}$	$\underline{X}^{1m}$	$\underline{X}^{1n}$	$\underline{Y}^{1}$	$\underline{G}^{1}$
Region k	$\underline{X}^{k1}$	$\underline{X}^{km}$	$\underline{X}^{kn}$	$\underline{Y}^{k}$	$\underline{G}^{k}$
Region n	$\underline{X}^{n1}$	$\underline{X}^{nm}$	$\underline{X}^{nn}$	$\underline{Y}^{n}$	$\underline{G}^{n}$
Primary inputs	$\underline{Z}^{1'}$	$\underline{Z}^{m'}$	$\underline{Z}^{n'}$		
Total	$\underline{G}^{1'}$	$\underline{G}^{m'}$	$\underline{G}^{n'}$		

where $\underline{G} = \{G^k\}$ is a column vector denoting gross outputs from industries in region k. This shows that the terms in the off-diagonal locations in the accounts table denote matrices of trade flows between regional economies and their constituent industries. A typical element of these accounts is given as X_{ij}^{km}, the flow from sector i in region k to sector j in region m. In order to turn the accounts into a matrix-operator model the usual input-output hypothesis is once again invoked, with the differences that the constant returns-to-scale assumption is now assumed to apply to trading flows as well as to technological flows. Thus, the extension of a_{ij} in Equation (4.5) is now

$$a_{ij}^{km} = \frac{X_{ij}^{km}}{\Sigma_k \Sigma_i X_{ij}^{km} + Z_j^m} \qquad (4.8)$$

Clearly, the usual Leontief technical coefficients will be identical to Isard's for all cases where k = m. To illustrate the form of the matrix of coefficients consider a two region, two industry model; the Isard $\underline{a}^{km}$ matrix will be as follows

$$\underline{a}^{km} = \left[\begin{array}{cc|cc} a_{11}^{11} & a_{12}^{11} & a_{11}^{12} & a_{12}^{12} \\ a_{21}^{11} & a_{22}^{11} & a_{21}^{12} & a_{22}^{12} \\ \hline a_{11}^{21} & a_{12}^{21} & a_{11}^{22} & a_{12}^{22} \\ a_{21}^{21} & a_{22}^{21} & a_{21}^{22} & a_{22}^{22} \end{array}\right] \qquad (4.9)$$

The important characteristic of this model is that there is a different coefficient for <u>every</u> element in the accounts table, which, as we shall see in discussing the Moses-Chenery model below, is its crucial weakness since it does not significantly reduce the data load required to implement the model empirically. As Hartwick (1971) demonstrates, Isard's model can be reformulated to incorporate a trade coefficient in addition to the usual technical coefficient. The partitioning of the total technical coefficient assumes the form

$$(s_{\dot{i}\dot{j}}^{km})(a_{\dot{i}\dot{j}}^{m}) = \left(\frac{X_{ij}^{km}}{\Sigma_k X_{ij}^{km}}\right) \text{x} \left(\frac{\Sigma_k X_{ij}^{km}}{\Sigma_k \Sigma_i X_{ij}^{km} + Z_j^m}\right) \tag{4.10}$$

where $s_{\dot{i}\dot{j}}^{km}$ is a trade coefficient representing the flow of output from industry i in region k to industry j in region m. This results in a technical coefficients matrix for each region m weighted by the trade factor $s_{\dot{i}\dot{j}}^{km}$. For clarity, our simple two region, two industry example is also reformulated as

$$(s_{\dot{i}\dot{j}}^{km})(a_{\dot{i}\dot{j}}^{k}) = \left[\begin{array}{cc|cc} s_{11}^{11}\,a_{11}^{1} & s_{12}^{11}\,a_{12}^{1} & s_{11}^{12}\,a_{11}^{2} & s_{12}^{12}\,a_{12}^{2} \\ s_{21}^{11}\,a_{21}^{1} & s_{22}^{11}\,a_{22}^{1} & s_{21}^{12}\,a_{21}^{2} & s_{22}^{12}\,a_{22}^{2} \\ \hline s_{11}^{21}\,a_{11}^{1} & s_{12}^{21}\,a_{12}^{1} & s_{11}^{22}\,a_{11}^{2} & s_{12}^{22}\,a_{12}^{2} \\ s_{21}^{21}\,a_{21}^{1} & s_{22}^{21}\,a_{22}^{1} & s_{21}^{22}\,a_{21}^{2} & s_{22}^{22}\,a_{22}^{2} \end{array}\right] \tag{4.11}$$

Although now conceptually neater, this reformulation still does not reduce the initial data requirements; its real advantage lies in its facility for separating the influences of trade and technology on the economy. This, of course, renders the reformulation more valuable in a forecasting context.

The Moses-Chenery variant differs from the Isard model in that now the sectoral destination of the trade flows between regions k and m is not known. The accounts table is similar to that shown in Figure 4.4 above, with the exception that the matrices of the Isard model ($\underline{X}^{km}$) are replaced by vectors representing the flow of goods from region k to region m without specifying the sectoral destination. In the two region, two industry case, the Moses-Chenery scheme of coefficients is as follows

$$(s_i^{km})(a_{ij}^m) = \left[\begin{array}{cc|cc} s_1^{11} a_{11}^1 & s_1^{11} a_{12}^1 & s_1^{12} a_{11}^2 & s_1^{12} a_{12}^2 \\ s_2^{11} a_{21}^1 & s_2^{11} a_{22}^1 & s_2^{12} a_{21}^2 & s_2^{12} a_{22}^2 \\ \hline s_1^{21} a_{11}^1 & s_1^{21} a_{12}^1 & s_1^{22} a_{11}^2 & s_1^{22} a_{12}^2 \\ s_2^{21} a_{21}^1 & s_2^{21} a_{22}^1 & s_2^{22} a_{21}^2 & s_2^{22} a_{22}^2 \end{array}\right] \quad (4.12)$$

Careful scrutiny of this matrix of coefficients reveals that it comprises relatively few unique terms, but that each combination of terms is unique. The unique terms are shown below

technical coefficients $\left[\begin{array}{cc|cc} a_{11}^1 & a_{12}^1 & a_{11}^2 & a_{12}^2 \\ a_{21}^1 & a_{22}^1 & a_{21}^2 & a_{22}^2 \end{array}\right]$

trade coefficients $\left[\begin{array}{c|c} s_1^{11} & s_1^{12} \\ s_2^{11} & s_2^{12} \\ \hline s_1^{21} & s_1^{22} \\ s_2^{21} & s_2^{22} \end{array}\right]$

From these matrices it now seems that some hope for constructing local input-output tables emerges; the technical coefficients could, in the first instance, be assumed to be identical as in national tables, and the trade coefficients, which merely give the proportion of each good that is consumed locally, could be the source of some experiments to generate different trade matrices. Hartwick concluded his own experiments with a test of the relative information content of the two models. His results show that the analyst has the choice between the accuracy (as measured by a high information level) of the Isard version and the practical feasibility of the Moses-Chenery model, due to its more realistic data demands.

The data demands implied by multi-regional input-output schemes have also generated another series of solutions by Leontief and Strout (1963) and Wilson (1970). Geographers had for some time used gravity models both to describe and to predict goods' flows (Starkie, 1967; Britton, 1967; Chisholm, 1973), as had econometricians (Linnemann, 1963), but the fusion of trade models with their inter-industry complements seems an outstanding advance. For all practical purposes, however, the model resulting from the integration of gravity, trade and input-output models is still as expensive in terms of data requirements as the Isard fixed-coefficients model. It cannot be denied, however, that the developments made by Leontief, Strout and Wilson have improved the forecasting capabilities of the models since change is now controlled by changes in the technology and distance-decay parameters.

As implied in an earlier section (4.2.1) most of the developments in input-output analysis at the regional and sub-regional level seem to have been geared to a greater understanding of the production sector of the 'toy' model, whereas it was felt that consumption and allocation mechanisms might prove more fruitful areas of development, particularly where the scale of the study was sub-regional or urban. It might also prove more viable politically. Recognising this, Artle proposed a model in 1961 that disaggregated those sectors of an inter-industry model that had usually been classed as exogenous, requiring extensive independent estimates of areas of concern to the planner, economist and geographer alike. Unfortunately, the availability of final demand data is usually even more limited than inter-industry or inter-regional information, given existing accounting systems. Artle's model is of some importance in the West Yorkshire context, since some of the data generation schemes employed in the work on this conurbation produced inputs of the kind specified by Artle. The model remains as a goal for urban input-output analysts, since to date very few implementations have been achieved with a UK data base, eg. for Anglesey, North Wales (Sadler and Archer, 1973) and Peterborough (Morrison, 1973). The structure of the Artle model is to be found in his 1961 paper on the structure of metropolitan economies (Artle, 1961, pp. 79-80).

To complete this catalogue of input-output models and their developments, there remain two types of model which regrettably are probably not feasible for urban and regional analysts unless information can be collected from surveys. Both fully dynamic models and the activity-analysis variant of the input-output model have been the subject of experiment at national and regional levels for over twenty years[1], but they remain essentially as directions to be worked towards, rather than areas of firm empirical achievement. The dynamic model is given greater emphasis here because of its improving prospects in this country since the work of Green (1971) was published. Green's contribution has been the assembly of investment flow matrices for UK industries for 1963 and 1968, using data from the Censuses of Production for those years.

The fully dynamic model hinges upon the following accounting relationships:

$$G_i - \Sigma_j X_{ij} - \Sigma_j D_{ij} - \Sigma_j K_{ij} = Y_i \qquad (4.13)$$

where G_i is gross output of industry i; $\Sigma_j X_{ij}$ is total intermediate demand $= \Sigma a_{ij} G_j$ where a_{ij} is the usual technical coefficient; D_{ij} is the flow of capital goods from industry i to industry j required to maintain stocks of capital equipment in j at existing levels, that is the flow of replacement capital goods. Moreover, $D_{ij} = d_{ij} G_j$ which implies that sales of replacement capital goods are proportional to output; K_{ij} is the flow of capital goods delivered by industry i to industry j that is required to expand the stock of capital goods held by industry j; and Y_i is final demand.

Miernyk (1970) used this accounting identity in a modified form for his work on the West Virginian economy. The modifications are concerned with the relationships embodied in the transactions represented by the K_{ij} terms in Equation (4.13) above. Unlike the D_{ij} transactions, the K_{ij} terms are usually considered to be related to changes in production levels rather than absolute production levels. Normally this would result in a set of first-order linear differential equations as depicted in matrix form:

$$\underline{G} - \underline{aG} - \underline{dG} - \underline{b\dot{G}} = \underline{Y} \qquad (4.14)$$

(1) Activity analysis is in effect the fusion of input-output analysis and mathematical programming, and has a lineage reaching back to Baumol's exposition in 1958 (Baumol, 1958). Recently, Broadbent has explored some rudimentary applications in the field of land-use accounting in Britain (Broadbent, 1973).

where $\underline{G}$ is, as before, gross output; $\dot{\underline{G}}$ is a vector containing the rates of change in $\underline{G}$; $\underline{a}$ is the technical coefficients matrix; $\underline{d}$ is the capital replacements coefficient matrix; $\underline{b}$ is the capital expansion coefficients matrix, where a typical element b_{ij} represents the demand by industry j for capital goods delivered by industry i per unit increase in output by industry j; and $\underline{Y}$ is final demand. In order to make the model of Equation (4.14) more tractable, Miernyk replaced the continuous rate-of-change variable $\dot{\underline{G}}$ by a first-order difference term:

$$\dot{\underline{G}} = \underline{G}_t - \underline{G}_{t-1} \tag{4.15}$$

where t is a time subscript. This allows Equation (4.14) to be written as:

$$\underline{G}_t - \underline{a}_t\underline{G}_t - \underline{dG}_t - \underline{b}(\underline{G}_t - \underline{G}_{t-1}) = \underline{Y}_t \tag{4.16}$$

or

$$\underline{G}_t = (\underline{I} - \underline{a}_t - \underline{d} - \underline{b})^{-1} (\underline{Y}_t - \underline{bG}_{t-1}) \tag{4.17}$$

where $\underline{I}$ is the identity matrix.

As Miernyk and other observers (such as Almon, 1967; Hewings, 1970) have pointed out, the viability of this model depends on the assumptions embodied in the capital coefficients matrices $\underline{d}$ and $\underline{b}$. Of crucial importance is their stability over time, and furthermore their stability as scale of output changes. With respect to this latter assumption, it is now well-documented that production technology (and thus capital requirements) contains several discrete steps, each step being encountered when the size of the production run increases beyond a certain threshold level (Woodward, 1957).

When tested in the field by Miernyk, the dynamic model produced forecasts that were only marginally different from a series of comparative-static forecasts with a fairly simple Leontief-type model. There remains, then, the question of the returns to scale offered by the dynamic version of the input-output model; the West Virginian example showed that the analyst must choose between costs of additional data collection, additional constant-returns assumptions, deeper understanding to be gained of the processes of growth and the strategic importance of capital investment in those processes. The urban analyst might also question the emphasis given to capital investment by the production sector, when many of the key problems of interest to him are concerned with the expenditure of public funds to increase or control the externalities (external economies of scale) that are the principal feature of urban development.

Finally, in Figure 4.5 an attempt is made to portray some of the interrelationships alluded to in the foregoing section. It should be noted that the axis labelled data costs represents the relative quantities of data required by the models shown; the axis labelled operational performance refers to the net benefits of each model improvement, and includes more reliable aggregate forecasts, more stable disaggregated forecasts and tractibility of solution method; and that the axis labelled level of disaggregation refers mainly to the spatial refinement of the models, ie. the size of the economy under study.

Figure 4.5 Input-output modelling: the relationships between data requirements, level of disaggregation and operational performance

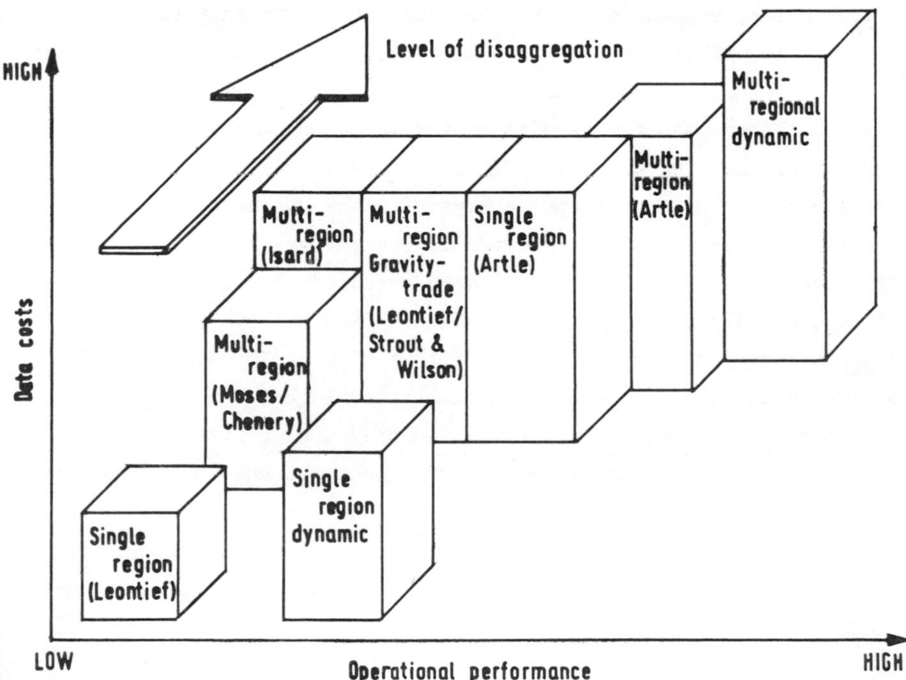

4.3 Data and objectives

In his foreword to a recent addition to the list of publications derived from the Cambridge 'Growth Model' (University of Cambridge, 1974), Professor Stone proffered some comments that are singularly apt in the context of the development of a model for West Yorkshire.

> "For most of us working in the social sciences, the assembly of data proves to be the most intractable problem. True, there are difficulties in formulating relationships and in estimating their parameters, but these, given abundant and reliable data, are not insurmountable. If the data are lacking, however, little can be achieved in practice by abstract speculation."

Local input-output modelling, and indeed most other attempts at studying the economy as a whole, vindicate this commentary. The reasons are not hard to find; in particular, the difficulties of collecting data on flow phenomena have already been mentioned. In more optimistic vein, however, we feel that some progress can be made, provided that objectives are continually kept under review. Put another way, it seems that a rigid adherence to the view that all the accounts must be complete, and that all the coefficients must be accurate to within fairly fine tolerances, will preserve the existing impasse in input-output analysis. Under such restrictions of attitude inter-industry studies of the local economy will remain expensive, daunting and rare exercises. Much recent discussion of the prospects for input-output analysis in the UK has focused on the relative merits of various methods of estimating the coefficients that embody the technical and trading relationships between industries. Broadly speaking, the debate has been between survey methods and non-survey methods. In the context of West Yorkshire and its slender data base, the debate is almost irrelevant - no matter how well the coefficients can be estimated they are of little consequence if no reliable information can be found on the transactions that occur between the industrial sectors and the final sectors (taken here as both the final demand and primary input sectors). The data collection task is as large for these flows as for the inter-industry portions of the model.

It was suggested earlier that a continual review of objectives might be useful. It could be that the simplicity or the elegance of input-output analysis is a mixed blessing which has promoted the use of input-output as a tool for forecasting, to the relative exclusion of other objectives. But clearly there are other valid objectives. For example, one that seems to have especial attraction for West Yorkshire involves the shift from a forecasting framework into a learning framework. From a strictly numerical point of view, this shift implies the use of the input-output framework to produce forecasts without numbers - in other words, the trend would be towards the kind of prediction that is found in technological forecasting, rather than in classical impact analysis.

Given the realisation that the end-product of an input-output model need not be restricted to tables of multipliers, what directions are possible for educational and planning activities? From an educational standpoint, it would seem practicable to build and run input-output models alongside other models of the same phenomena. This process, in effect represents learning by convergence, which on the one hand, may mean the rigorous application of the constraints embodied in each of the different but parallel models in order to produce maximally-consistent numerical forecasts. On the other hand learning by convergence might also mean that numerical forecasts are superceded by more abstract forms of prediction and learning. As an example, consider the way in which input-output forecasts are made: relationships between sectors are embodied in numerical form and the inverse matrix-multiplier provides an attractive summary of the end-product of a myriad of industrial linkages. Notice that all hypotheses must be converted into numbers before the operation can begin, and must be reconverted into tests or impacts at the end of the process. Herein, of course, lies the whole problem of input-output modelling. Given this, one obvious solution would then be to proceed directly from a set of perceived relationships (or hypotheses) about the local economy to a set of forecasts.

At present, only a few speculations can be offered about how such a learning model might be implemented. For instance, it should be possible to replace the a_{ij} coefficients of the traditional model with other, equally valid, mathematical relationships. An attractive possibility is provided by the work of Roberts (1971) on the use of signed digraphs which represent, in this context, elementary abstractions of the more usual numerical coefficients. Extension of this reasoning along the input-output forecasting chain implies that some kind of inverse-multiplier is required; the difference is, of course, that the inverse refers to a set of logical relationships.

While the tools of the logical inverse are scarcely known in urban and regional modelling, existing techniques could quite easily be used. To the authors' knowledge, it is mainly Karaska (1968, 1969) who seems to have attempted this kind of work that would break the reliance of input-output modelling upon extensive data sources. He was able to use the experience and the resources of the huge Philadelphia study, but his orientation was towards usable generalisations about the internal and external relations of the metropolitan economy.

4.4 Construction of the West Yorkshire social accounts matrix for 1963

4.4.1 Study area and sectoring schemes

The West Yorkshire input-output model described here is a two regional version which shows interactions between the West Yorkshire conurbation and the rest-of-the-world accounting systems for 1963, which was the only year for which consistent data was available at the start of the study. In its current form, therefore, imports to and exports from the West Yorkshire economy are collapsed into one row and one column of the accounts. The West Yorkshire conurbation area is shown in Figure 4.6 and will be seen to be slightly smaller than the more generally used West Yorkshire study area, since the data limitations, set by the Census, constrained us to work within this slightly smaller area.

The model uses 21 industrial sectors that correspond to the Standard Industrial Classification (SIC) orders I-XX, whilst orders XXI-XXIII are aggregated to form a miscellaneous services sector, order XXIV (public administration and defence) is excluded from the interindustry transactions table because it delivers all its output to the final demand sectors and hence all coefficients relating to this order are zero; similarly all its inputs come from the primary sector, that is, labour.

Key to local authorities

1 Bradford County Borough
2 Dewsbury County Borough
3 Halifax County Borough
4 Huddersfield County Borough
5 Leeds County Borough
6 Wakefield County Borough
7 Aireborough
8 Baildon
9 Batley
10 Bingley
11 Brighouse
12 Colne Valley
13 Denby Dale
14 Denholme
15 Elland
16 Heckmondwike
17 Holmfirth
18 Horbury
19 Horsforth
20 Keighley
21 Kirkburton
22 Meltham
23 Mirfield
24 Morley
25 Ossett
26 Pudsey
27 Queensbury and Shelf
28 Ripponden
29 Rothwell
30 Shipley
31 Sowerby Bridge
32 Spenborough
33 Stanley

Figure 4.6 West Yorkshire conurbation

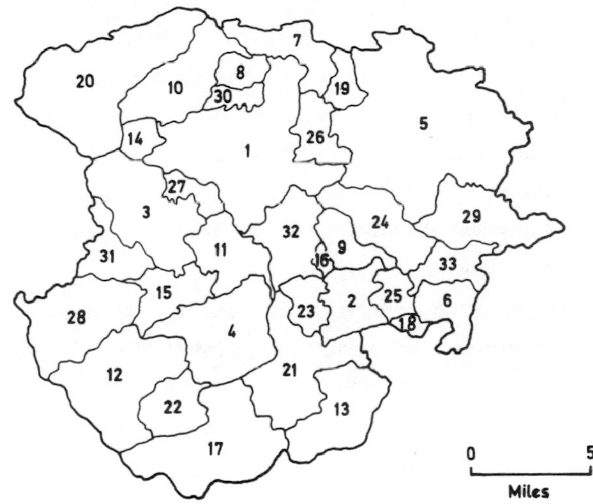

4.2.2 Gross output

Statistics on gross outputs for manufacturing industries in West Yorkshire (orders III-XVI) are obtainable from the Census of Production Summary Tables. Estimates of gross output figures for non-manufacturing industries could be obtained by applying the ratio: West Yorkshire employment (1963) in sector k/Great Britain employment (1963) in sector k; to the gross output figures for sector k obtainable from the 1963 Census of Production Summary Tables or, alternatively, the Input-Output Tables for the UK (Central Statistical Office, 1970). However, there were problems in deriving these estimates, since there was no readily available source of statistics on the sectoral distribution of employees in the West Yorkshire conurbation for the year 1963. It was necessary, therefore, to use 1966 employment data in the numerator of the above ratio as this was available from the Economic Activity Tables published in the Census.

Alternative methods of estimating the gross output of a sector in the West Yorkshire economy were explored, for example, by using the weights which were calculated by the Central Statistical Office and published in the Input-Output Tables for the UK 1963 (Central Statistical Office, 1970). These weights are estimates of the contribution of a given sector to Gross Domestic Product (GDP) in a given year, and as such they largely reflect changes in, and the distribution of, gross outputs of sectors. Consequently, the weights can be used to give estimates of gross output in years other than those recorded in the Census of Production (ie. 1954, 1958, 1963 and 1968). Such estimates, however, suffer from the same limitation as those involved in the ratio method described above, since they depend on the use of employment 'shares' (West Yorkshire versus the United Kingdom) to produce regional figures.

One further relevant source of information that should be mentioned is the calculation of Gross Regional Product per head for Yorkshire and Humberside, produced by Woodward (1970). Once again, this source is limited by the degree to which population or employment data must be used to derive data for the conurbation. However, Woodward's data is presented in the form of monetary values (£'s per head); this is a considerable advantage over other sources and was of great assistance in providing a check upon the calculations used to produce estimates of final demand.

4.4.3 Estimates of final demand

Final demand is taken to be the sum of consumption by households, investment flows, government expenditure and exports. The methods used for arriving at estimates of each of these for the West Yorkshire conurbation will now be discussed in turn.

(a) Consumption by households

Consumption by households is taken to be an exogenous variable. We describe below how the distribution of consumer expenditure was calculated using income-distribution weightings. A cross tabulation of commodity groups and expenditure categories is the principal table produced by this routine and represents a best estimate given national data and the regional distribution of income.

(i) Data sources

The major data sources available were as follows: National income 'Blue Book' - national expenditure control totals for each category of expenditure; Inland Revenue Report Command No. 3200 - distributions of incomes (after tax) by ranges for UK and West Yorkshire conurbation; Family Expenditure Survey - national cross-tabulation of expenditure category and household income; Input-Output Tables for UK 1963 - Table A (the make matrix[(1)]), and Table K (analysis of consumer expenditure by commodity group).

(ii) Data reconciliation

When using information from a diversity of sources there are inevitable differences in scope, date, definition and areal coverage

---

[(1)] Table A of the 1963 Input-Output Tables is known as the make matrix, a term coined by the Cambridge Growth Model Project team. Table A refers to the cross-tabulation of commodities by industrial sectors where a typical element represents the amount of a certain commodity, say vehicles, that is produced or made by each of the industrial sectors of the economy. Hence, the table has become known as the make matrix.

to be reckoned with. The income data presented more problems than the expenditure items, due mainly to the discrepancy between 'number of incomes' and 'number of tax cases' defined by the Inland Revenue. Incomes in this case refer to a person, or to persons, where a man and his wife are counted as one income. Tax cases, however, refer to the number of different types of assessable income, regardless of whether they are earned by one or more persons. For example, if a person earns a salary and has an additional income from investment and/or property, he will be recorded as a tax case for each class of income that he receives. One person may, therefore, be enumerated two or three times by the Inland Revenue although his <u>total disposable income</u> will not be entered in the appropriate range. To minimise the effects of this possible double or triple counting, only income from employment was used to construct weightings for national data; this procedure assumed that the number of persons not gaining an earned income was sufficiently small to allow its effect to be ignored. This introduced a number of biases, since the number of <u>earned</u> incomes in any range might underestimate the number of <u>disposable</u> incomes in that range. The effects of this bias can be minimised provided that the ranges chosen are fairly broad, so that the addition of a non-earned income to an earned income will be unlikely to alter a person's income-range. Secondly, large non-earned incomes will be rare (at least at the regional level) and mostly confined to the uppermost range, which will itself be open-ended and in consequence will ensure minimum underestimation.

A third, more serious, source of bias was introduced by using earned-income data only, for there might be a significant number of persons at the local level living on occupational pensions or property income. Further, it would not be reasonable to assume that these incomes were all in the upper ranges. Finally, tax returns would only be available for those persons earning sufficient to make them eligible to be assessed. This, of course, is probably the most serious bias in the data source, but can be overcome by using the 'Blue Book' personal income data; in this source PAYE records are used, and these permit an estimation of the numbers below the tax-limit. A reconciliation of raw Inland Revenue data with 'Blue Book' data to provide conversion factors for the raw regional tax data provided two compatible income distributions for the UK and the West Yorkshire conurbation.

The reconciliation problems presented by the remaining data sources were comparatively few; the categories of expenditure used by the 'Blue Book', the UK Input-Output Tables and the Family Expenditure Survey (FES) were all aggregated in a tidy manner, causing few problems. The FES, however, did present a break-down of expenditure for the provincial conurbations, but this information did not provide the same detailed disaggregation of purchases by income range that was available in national tables and was subsequently discarded.

(iii) Weighting and estimation procedures

Having, as far as possible, matched the data sources to each other, the calculation of the conurbation estimates was fairly straightforward. Let the state-variable be: C_{i}^{ym} the expenditure by persons (or households) in income group y, living in zone i, on consumer good m. To form the weights, the reconciled data sources were used to define: H_{i}^{y} the number of persons (or households) in income group y, resident in zone i; H_{*}^{y} the number of persons in income group y in the nation, where an asterisk denotes summation; and C_{*}^{*m} the expenditure by all income groups on good m.

The key premises of the weighting procedure are that a consumer's preferences are determined solely by the income group to which he belongs, and that this relationship can be consistently aggregated so that we may make use of the macro-premise that the distribution of consumer expenditure among categories of goods is determined by the distribution of consumers among income groups. Given these assumptions, the weighting procedure is simply

$$C_{i}^{*m} = \frac{H_{i}^{y}}{H_{*}^{y}} C_{*}^{*m} \qquad (4.18)$$

where C_{i}^{*m} is the amount spent on good m by consumers in zone i (West Yorkshire conurbation); C_{*}^{*m} is consumer expenditure on good m in the nation; H_{i}^{y} is the number of persons in income group y in zone i; and H_{*}^{y} is the number of persons in income group y in the nation. This now provides a vector of control totals for the remainder of the estimation routines. Recalling the state variable C_i^{ym}, it remains to estimate the regional cross-tabulation of expenditure by income groups, making use of the FES tables of expenditure by income. The elements of the FES tables p^{ym} are interpreted as conditional probabilities: either the probability of a unit of expenditure on good m being spent by persons in income group y, or the probability that a person in income group y will spend his money in expenditure category m. Clearly, the choice of probabilities will depend on the data available and, in this case, since the expenditure totals by goods are given by a prior estimate, then the more appropriate probability model would appear to be the former; ie. we would require that

$$\Sigma_y p^{ym} = 1 \tag{4.19}$$

rather than

$$\Sigma_m p^{ym} = 1 \tag{4.20}$$

Having chosen the more expedient though not necessarily the more correct model, the regional cross-tabulation of expenditure by income groups is readily obtained by multiplying by the control totals vector defined above. The matrix is presented in Table 4.1. Summing this matrix across the expenditure categories produces an estimate of total consumer spending attributable to each of the income groups in the West Yorkshire conurbation.

Given the decision to weight national data, the next objective in the estimation procedure was to calculate the inter-industry effects of the hypothesised basket of consumers' expenditure for West Yorkshire. This objective was effected by using Tables K and A of the UK Input-Output Tables for 1963. The former gives a breakdown of the national bill of consumers' expenditure into its implied commodity structure. Table 4.2 provides a regional version of Table K, whilst application of Table A, the make matrix, provided the final sequence in the estimation procedure; the outcome, Table 4.3, was a vector of flows from industries in the West Yorkshire conurbation to consumers in that region.

Table 4.1 Estimated consumer expenditure by incсme group: West Yorkshire, 1963 (£000's)

Income group (A) / Expenditure categories	<300	300 to 400	400 to 500	500 to 750	750 to 1,000	1,000 to 1,250	1,250 to 1,500	1,500 to 1,750	1,750 to 2,000	2,000 to 2,500	2,500 to 3,000	>3,000	Totals
Housing	2,483	2,584	3,273	4,057	2,659	5,028	5,784	4,285	4,729	4,606	4,861	6,517	50,866
Fuel	1,834	1,712	1,763	2,106	1,463	2,520	2,564	1,974	1,990	1,918	2,012	2,391	24,247
Food	4,771	3,798	5,657	7,246	5,708	11,819	13,286	10,144	10,688	10,170	11,816	14,472	109,576
Alcohol and drink	471	335	500	927	1,042	2,576	3,086	2,498	2,963	3,046	4,254	5,485	27,181
Tobacco	625	556	1,275	1,676	1,593	3,565	3,891	2,984	2,927	3,055	3,694	3,883	29,724
Clothing and footwear	747	846	1,422	1,897	1,778	4,005	4,901	4,102	4,825	4,642	5,390	7,761	42,318
Household durables	901	685	1,243	1,726	1,536	3,055	4,183	3,436	3,626	4,102	4,993	6,211	35,697
Other Goods	1,591	1,216	1,708	2,346	1,944	4,238	5,017	3,898	4,421	4,285	5,012	6,848	42,525
Transport and vehicles	237	216	394	648	811	1,974	2,629	2,564	3,021	7,902	3,646	4,963	29,013
Services	2,024	1,901	2,350	3,248	2,597	5,576	6,132	5,468	6,374	6,729	8,060	16,406	66,865
Totals	15,218	13,849	19,585	25,878	21,132	44,356	51,473	41,354	38,304	50,457	53,738	74,937	

Table 4.2 Sales to consumers by commodity group: West Yorkshire Conurbation, 1963 (£000's)

Sector & commodity classification		Housing	Fuel	Food	Alchohol and Drink	Tobacco	Clothing and Footwear	Household durables	Other goods	Transport and Vehicles	Services	Totals
I	1	–	–	43,522	–	–	–	–	1,793	–	–	45,315
	2	–	144	3,165	–	–	–	–	–	–	–	3,309
II	3	–	7,418	–	–	–	–	–	–	–	–	7,418
	4	804	–	–	–	–	–	–	–	–	–	804
III	5	–	–	2,603	–	–	–	–	–	–	–	2,603
	6	–	–	11,557	–	–	–	–	1,863	–	–	13,420
	7	–	–	2,895	–	–	–	–	–	–	–	2,895
	8	–	–	6,351	–	–	–	–	–	–	–	6,351
	9	–	–	36,671	–	–	–	–	–	–	–	36,671
	10	–	–	2,811	27,181	–	–	–	–	–	–	29,992
	11	–	–	–	–	29,724	–	–	–	–	–	
IV	12	–	1,512	–	–	–	–	–	–	7,055	–	8,567
	13	3,455	–	–	–	–	–	–	47	–	–	3,502
	14	–	720	–	–	–	–	–	–	–	–	720
	15	–	–	–	–	–	–	–	4,953	–	–	4,953
	16	–	–	–	–	–	–	–	2,736	–	–	2,736
	18	–	–	–	–	–	–	–	1,675	164	–	1,838
VI	29	–	–	–	–	–	–	1,289	–	–	–	1,289
	31	–	–	–	–	–	–	–	94	–	–	94
	32	–	–	–	–	–	–	–	2,406	–	–	2,406
	35	–	–	–	–	–	–	2,778	590	–	–	3,368
	36	–	–	–	–	–	–	4,223	991	117	–	5,331
IX	38	3,214	–	–	–	–	–	1,956	2,948	–	–	8,118
VIII	40	–	–	–	–	–	–	10,736	212	467	–	11,415
	42	–	–	–	–	–	–	1,067	118	117	–	1,301
X	44	–	–	–	–	–	1,972	–	1,227	–	–	3,199
	45	–	–	–	–	–	757	–	896	–	–	1,653
	46	–	–	–	–	–	8,991	–	–	–	–	8,991
	48	–	–	–	–	–	1,743	2,667	2,571	–	–	6,981
XI	49	–	–	–	–	–	688	–	1,392	–	–	2,079
XII	50	–	–	–	–	–	20,780	–	–	–	–	20,780
	51	–	–	–	–	–	6,950	–	–	–	–	6,950
XIII	52	241	–	–	–	–	–	–	–	–	–	241
	53	1,366	–	–	–	–	–	–	–	–	–	1,366
	54	–	–	–	–	–	–	–	1,061	–	–	1,061
XIV	55	–	–	–	–	–	–	6,668	–	–	–	6,668
	56	1,768	120	–	–	–	–	111	118	–	–	2,117
XV	58	2,813	–	–	–	–	–	–	1,156	–	–	3,968
	59	–	–	–	–	–	–	–	7,595	–	–	7,595
XVI	60	–	–	–	–	–	367	222	448	631	–	1,668
	61	804	–	–	–	–	–	1,223	4,505	–	–	6,531
XVII	62	31,580	–	–	–	–	–	–	–	–	268	31,847
XVIII	63	–	5,113	–	–	–	–	–	–	–	–	5,113
	64	–	9,218	–	–	–	–	–	–	–	–	9,218
	65	4,098	–	–	–	–	–	–	–	–	–	4,098
XIX	66	–	–	–	–	–	–	–	–	12,661	268	12,929
	67	–	–	–	–	–	–	–	–	3,013	100	3,113
	68	–	–	–	–	–	–	–	–	–	5,655	5,655
XX	69	–	–	–	–	–	69	–	–	–	5,889	5,958
XXI-XXIII	70	723	–	–	–	–	–	2,756	1,132	4,789	50,361	59,761
Totals		50,866	24,246	109,576	27,181	29,724	42,318	35,697	42,525	29,013	66,866	

I Agriculture, forestry and fishing
II Mining and quarrying
III Food, drink and tobacco
IV Chemicals and allied
V Metal manufacture
VI Engineering and electrical
VII Ships and marine engineering
VIII Vehicles
IX Other metal goods
X Textiles
XI Leather goods and furs
XII Clothing and footwear
XIII Bricks, pottery and glass
XIV Timber and furniture
XV Paper, printing, publishing
XVI Other manufacturing
XVII Construction
XVIII Gas, electricity, water
XIX Transport and communications
XX Distributions
XXI Insurance, banking, finance
XXII Professional business services
XXIII Miscellaneous services
XXIV Public administration and defence

Commodity/industry classification (1963)

1 Agriculture
2 Forestry and fishing
3 Coal mining
4 Other mining
5 Grain milling

6 Other cereal foodstuffs
7 Sugar
8 Cocoa, chocolate and sugar confectionary
9 Other food
10 Drink

11 Tobacco
12 Mineral oil refining
13 Paint and printing ink
14 Coke ovens
15 Pharmaceutical and toilet preparations

16 Soap, oils and fats
17 Synthetic resin and plstic materials
18 Other chemicals and allied industries
19 Iron and steel
20 Light metals

21 Other non-ferrous metals
22 Agricultural machinery
23 Machine tools
24 Engineer's small tools
25 Industrial engines

26 Textile machinery
27 Contractors' plant and machanical handling equipment
28 Office machinery
29 Other non-electrical machinery
30 Industrial plant and steel work

31 Other mechanical engineering
32 Scientific instruments
33 Electrical machinery
34 Insulated wires and cables
35 Radio and telecommunications

36 Other electrical goods
37 Cans and metal boxes
38 Other metal goods
39 Shipbuilding and marine engineering
40 Motor vehicles

41 Aircraft
42 Other vehicles
43 Production of man-made fibres
44 Cotton, etc, spinning and weaving
45 Wool

46 Hosiery and lace
47 Textile finishings
48 Other textiles
49 Leather, leather goods and fur
50 Clothing

51 Footwear
52 Cement
53 Other building materials, etc
54 Pottery and glass
55 Furniture, etc

56 Timber and miscellaneous wood manufactures
57 Paper and board
58 Paper products
59 Printing and publishing
60 Rubber

61 Other manufacturing
62 Construction
63 Gas
64 Electricity
65 Water supply

66 Road and rail transport
67 Other transport
68 Communications
69 Distributive trades
70 Miscellaneous services

71 Public administration, defence, health and education
72 Domestic services, etc, to households
73 Ownership of dwellings
74 Imports of goods
75 Imports of services

76 Sales by final buyer
77 Taxes on expenditure less subsidies
78 Income from employment
79 Gross profits and other trading income

Table 4.3 Industry requirements of estimated consumers' bill of goods at sellers' prices. West Yorkshire conurbation, 1963

Sectors	£000
I	21,380
II	5,690
III	45,020
IV	9,870
V	490
VI	3,680
VII	-
VIII	8,160
IX	3,830
X	12,010
XI	940
XII	6,560
XIII	1,290
XIV	4,920
XV	6,780
XVI	3,010
XVII	11,940†
XVIII	18,870
XIX	23,550
XX	115,622
XXI-XXIII	81,720
Imports	367,200†
Dwellings	50,800

For key to sectors see Table 4.2

† based on national data

(b) Estimates of investment flows

The estimates of gross fixed capital formation for West Yorkshire all involve the use of national data which are weighted to provide estimates for the sub-regional accounts. The principal data sources are: Census of Production, 1963 - aggregate investment figures; Input-Output Tables, 1963 - the commodity analysis and sector analysis of Gross Domestic Capital Formation which is also disaggregated by fixed and stock categories; and work by Michael Green on Capital Account Flows for 1963 and 1968 (Green, 1971).

(i) Estimating investment flows (demand pool)

The estimation of deliveries to and absorptions from the gross domestic fixed capital formation sector by West Yorkshire industries is perhaps the area of data development least suited to the weighting procedures that characterise the construction of the social accounts table. Investment expenditure is typically erratic, both in time and space, and in the absence of firm data at the sub-regional level, rigid and often unreal assumptions have to be made in order to progress with the social accounts. The approach adopted in this section may be seen as a microcosm of the approach adopted in the construction of the whole input-output model, since essentially it tackles a crucial data deficiency by setting up some numerical hypotheses and testing them with any corroborative material that may be available. In principle, this hypothesis testing loop should be reiterated until the underlying assumptions are either fully vindicated or discarded; needless to say, only enough data could be found to enable an initial, exploratory loop to be completed.

Having stated some reservations about the suitability of the tools and material available, what would constitute a viable set of objectives? In terms of the West Yorkshire model, the requirement is for a vector of deliveries from industrial sectors within the study area to a pool of investment goods in the rest-of-the-world sector - this may be called the demand side requirement. On the other hand, investment flows also enter the West Yorkshire economy from a supply pool of investment goods. Both approaches are depicted in Figure 4.7.

Figure 4.7 The demand and supply pools for investment goods

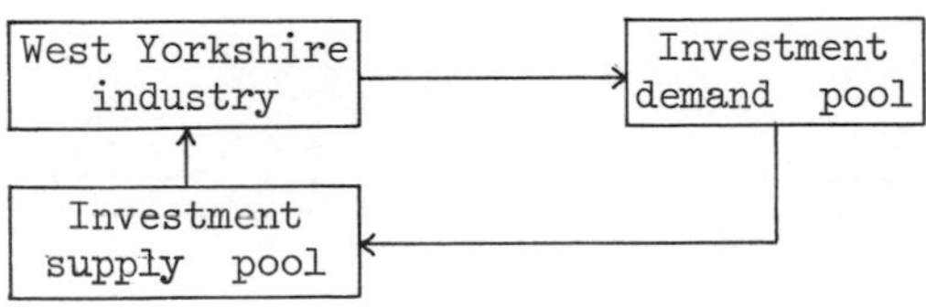

A fairly straightforward weighting of national data to provide regional estimates of deliveries to gross domestic capital formation is given in Table 4.4. These estimates require modification in two ways. Firstly, the figures include a large proportion of goods delivered to industries located outside West Yorkshire. Hence in order to estimate the internal use of these investment goods it would be appropriate to include some indication of the overall level of activity in the West Yorkshire economy which will measure, even if crudely, the region's propensity to import investment goods: eg. $G^{(r)}/G^{(n)}$, where $G^{(r)}$ is a measure of the region's gross output; and $G^{(n)}$ is a measure of the nation's gross output. Secondly, the above estimates of deliveries by sector must be converted into investment commodities (from Table A in the 1963 National Input-Output Tables) which can then be compared with investment demands made by local industries; that is, by subtracting demand from supply we can obtain an estimate of net investment for West Yorkshire.

Table 4.4 Estimated deliveries to gross domestic capital formation by industries in the West Yorkshire conurbation, 1963

Sector	Estimated Deliveries £m
I	0.0964
II	0.4212
III	-
IV	0.8804
V	0.2257
VI	54.0429
VII	-
VIII	6.5721
IX	2.2440
X	0.0568
XI	-
XII	-
XIII	0.1659
XIV	1.3105
XV	0.0320
XVI	0.2304
XVII	69.7878
XVIII	6.1370
XIX	1.3332
XX	6.7064
XXI-XXIII	4.8463
Total	£155.09m

For key to sectors see Table 4.2

(ii) Estimating investment absorptions (supply pool)

Once again the estimates for West Yorkshire must be derived from UK data in the 'Blue Book' which distinguishes three types of investment absorptions: vehicles, ships and aircraft (VSA); plant and machinery; and new buildings and works. Work carried out by Green (1971) and Woodward (1970) gives additional guides to weighting procedures for these categories. Green's work, in particular, allows a refinement of the weights used to estimate investment absorptions of plant and machinery in West Yorkshire, whilst Woodward suggests weighting schemes for the other two categories along the following lines:

(a) Vehicles, ships and aircraft

VSA investment can be distributed in proportion to railway and airline employees (investment in ships is not considered relevant in West Yorkshire), whilst investment in goods vehicles can be distributed in proportion to new registrations. As Woodward, himself, admits however, such weighting procedures are rather unsatisfactory when dealing with expenditure as erratic as investment. For this reason, we decided to retain the same assumptions that had been used to derive the vector of plant and machinery expenditure, ie. investment was considered to be proportional to output[1].

(b) Building and works

These data can be obtained from the Abstract of Regional Statistics (Yorkshire and Humberside)(Central Statistical Office, 1965) which provides control totals. The dwellings sector, while not an industrial sector in the usual sense, enters into the investment accounts here. The estimate was derived by using data on housing completions for the West Yorkshire conurbation (Ministry of Housing and Local Government, 1966) in the following weighting procedure for 1963

$$\text{Investment in dwellings in West Yorkshire} = \text{UK investment in dwellings: 'Blue Book'} \times \frac{\text{West Yorkshire completions}}{\text{UK completions}}$$

$$= £944\text{m} \times \left[\frac{9278}{307{,}714}\right] \qquad (4.21)$$

---

[1] In a previous section (4.2.2) it was noted that the West Virginian study assumed that constant-proportionality models could be used to replicate flows of replacement capital goods.

A detailed breakdown of the investment flow matrix to plant and machinery for West Yorkshire, following Green's method, is given in Table 4.5. Such an investment flow matrix has a typical element b_{ij} which gives the amount of commodity i required per unit output of industry j. We may, therefore, form a model for commodity i, as follows

$$L_i = \Sigma_j b_{ij} G_j \tag{4.22}$$

where L_i is total commodity i absorbed by industry j; and G_j is total output of industry j. In matrix form the model becomes

$$\underline{L} = \underline{bG} \tag{4.23}$$

There are several points to note about investment matrices. Firstly, the above model assumes constant proportionality between the amount of output delivered to gross domestic fixed capital formation in the nation vis-à-vis the region. In large sectors this may be a valid assumption, but in the case of small sectors the model outputs should be interpreted with care. Moreover, the model uses the simple input-output type of assumption that investment is related to the <u>level</u> of activity in the economy, rather than the rate of change of activity as in a true dynamic input-output model. Secondly, there is the related point that investment matrices assume constant coefficients, an assumption that is not always valid for, as Green points out, the stability of coefficients will be determined, to some extent, by the <u>size</u> of investment. However, stability (or a constant average relationship) may not be too unrealistic an assumption if the coefficient represents a medium to long term relationship, which is similar to offsetting investment costs over say five to ten years, and then taking the average annual rate, provided we know what irregularities, if any, occurred in the base matrix from which the initial coefficient were derived. Finally, it should be noted that technological changes effect the pattern of absorptions in the investment matrix as well as the pattern of inputs in the input-output table. Hence, in order to provide estimated data for the 1963 table we have been forced to invok some of the constant proportionality assumptions alluded to above. The first assumption that was made is that the amount of goods produce by industry i and delivered to gross domestic fixed capital formulatic

Commodity group / Industrial sector	18	22	23	25	26	27	28	29	30	31	32	33	34	35	36	38	40	55	56	61	Remainder	Totals
I	-	0.47	-	0.01	-	0.01	-	0.03	0.04	-	-	0.01	-	-	-	-	0.32	-	0.03	-	0.05	0.97
II	-	-	-	-	-	0.18	0.01	0.80	-	-	-	0.01	-	0.02	-	0.01	-	-	0.06	-	0.09	1.17
III	-	-	-	-	-	0.15	0.02	1.44	0.19	-	0.01	0.03	0.01	0.03	-	0.01	0.02	-	-	0.01	0.24	2.15
IV	-	-	-	-	-	0.06	0.03	0.61	1.72	0.02	0.06	0.08	0.02	0.07	-	0.02	0.01	0.01	-	0.01	0.30	3.03
V	-	-	0.08	0.01	-	0.43	0.02	0.52	0.89	0.29	0.02	0.06	0.02	0.03	-	0.01	0.01	-	-	0.01	0.60	2.99
VI	-	-	2.51	0.01	-	0.29	0.21	1.00	-	0.16	0.22	0.18	0.03	0.30	-	0.18	0.03	0.04	-	0.07	0.62	5.83
VIII	-	-	0.46	-	-	0.07	0.02	0.18	0.01	0.01	0.02	0.03	0.01	0.02	-	0.01	0.01	-	-	0.01	0.09	0.99
IX	-	-	0.11	-	-	0.07	-	0.08	-	-	-	-	-	-	-	-	-	-	-	-	-	0.26
X & XII	-	-	-	-	9.68	1.11	0.24	1.13	-	-	0.12	0.36	0.10	0.24	-	0.19	0.19	0.05	-	0.10	1.93	15.44
XV	-	-	-	-	-	0.36	0.05	0.65	-	-	0.01	0.02	0.01	-	-	0.05	0.01	0.01	-	0.02	0.20	1.39
XIII-XVI	-	-	-	-	-	0.38	0.04	0.68	0.10	-	0.02	0.04	0.02	0.01	-	0.03	0.02	0.01	0.01	0.01	0.20	1.64
XVII	-	-	-	0.01	-	1.24	0.06	0.22	-	-	0.01	0.01	-	0.01	-	0.05	0.01	0.01	0.16	0.02	-	1.81
XVIII	1.12	-	0.02	0.94	-	0.15	0.04	0.37	3.82	0.34	0.06	4.77	1.06	0.11	0.02	0.03	-	0.01	0.02	0.01	5.21	18.11
XIX	-	-	0.01	-	-	0.08	0.06	0.03	-	-	0.02	0.09	-	1.82	-	0.05	0.03	0.02	-	0.02	1.58	3.81
XX	-	-	-	-	-	0.43	0.21	1.45	-	-	-	-	-	1.31	0.19	0.65	0.04	0.05	0.04	0.07	0.84	5.27
XXI-XXIII	-	-	-	-	-	0.05	0.82	1.31	0.14	-	0.57	0.01	0.01	1.06	0.19	0.30	-	0.18	0.05	0.27	1.02	5.95
Totals	1.12	0.47	3.18	0.99	9.68	5.05	1.81	10.51	6.89	0.82	1.13	5.69	1.28	5.02	0.39	1.60	0.69	0.39	0.45	0.62	12.95	

For key to sectors and commodity groups see Table 4.2

is a constant proportion of output, irrespective of the size of industry i; this assumption is identical to the input-output hypothesis of constant returns to scale. As unreal as this may seem, it does permit an initial guess at the flows from industries in West Yorkshire. These have been given above in Table 4.4 (Deliveries to gross domestic capital formation). The next step is to check the validity of the assumption given any other corroborative evidence. The estimates for the supply side for West Yorkshire are given in Table 4.6.

Table 4.6 Summary of estimated absorptions of investment goods by West Yorkshire industries, 1963 (£m)

<table>
<tr><th>Investment absorptions \ Sector</th><th>Vehicles, ships and aircraft</th><th>Plant and machinery</th><th>Buildings and works</th><th>Total investment</th></tr>
<tr><td>I</td><td>0.27</td><td>0.97</td><td>0.73</td><td>1.97</td></tr>
<tr><td>II</td><td>0.08</td><td>1.17</td><td>0.45</td><td>1.70</td></tr>
<tr><td>III</td><td>0.54</td><td>2.15</td><td>1.48</td><td>4.17</td></tr>
<tr><td>IV</td><td>0.19</td><td>3.03</td><td>0.81</td><td>4.03</td></tr>
<tr><td>V</td><td>0.08</td><td>3.00</td><td>0.60</td><td>3.68</td></tr>
<tr><td>VI</td><td>0.60</td><td>5.82</td><td>1.99</td><td>8.41</td></tr>
<tr><td>VIII</td><td>0.04</td><td>0.99</td><td>0.51</td><td>1.54</td></tr>
<tr><td>IX</td><td>0.17</td><td>0.25</td><td>0.48</td><td>0.90</td></tr>
<tr><td>X</td><td>0.97</td><td rowspan="2">15.44</td><td>3.92</td><td rowspan="2">20.76</td></tr>
<tr><td>XI+XII</td><td>0.26</td><td>0.43</td></tr>
<tr><td>XIII</td><td>0.13</td><td>1.64</td><td>0.20</td><td>1.97</td></tr>
<tr><td>XIV</td><td>0.16</td><td>*</td><td>0.25</td><td>0.41</td></tr>
<tr><td>XV</td><td>0.13</td><td>1.38</td><td>0.58</td><td>2.09</td></tr>
<tr><td>XVI</td><td>0.03</td><td>*</td><td>0.14</td><td>0.17</td></tr>
<tr><td>XVII</td><td>1.05</td><td>1.81</td><td>0.34</td><td>3.20</td></tr>
<tr><td>XVIII</td><td>0.15</td><td>18.11</td><td>5.44</td><td>23.70</td></tr>
<tr><td>XIX</td><td>5.10</td><td>3.81</td><td>2.23</td><td>11.14</td></tr>
<tr><td>XX</td><td>3.02</td><td>5.27</td><td>3.89</td><td>12.18</td></tr>
<tr><td>XXI</td><td>3.29</td><td>5.95</td><td>24.66</td><td>33.90</td></tr>
<tr><td>Dwellings</td><td></td><td></td><td>28.46</td><td>28.46</td></tr>
<tr><td>Total absorptions</td><td>15.84</td><td>70.79</td><td>77.62</td><td>164.32</td></tr>
</table>

*For plant and machinery, data is only available for the composite sector XIII, XIV and XVI (bricks, timber and other manufactures).

For key to sectors see Table 4.2.

(c) Public authorities' current expenditure

Once again we are driven to make the assumption that the distribution of industrial demands generated by public authorities' current spending in West Yorkshire is directly proportional to the pattern of industrial demand displayed in the national Input-Output Tables (Table D). Again our strategy is to provide an initial guess, using national sources (that is, the 'Blue Book' and the Input-Output Tables) which can be adjusted by using more local knowledge or weightings.

The exact procedure adopted here consisted of the calculation of the proportion of output delivered to the public authorities by each of the industrial sectors of the UK economy. The application of these proportions, displayed in column 3 of Table 4.7, produced the required estimate of public authorities' expenditure. The second stage of this exercise - finding supporting evidence - could only take the form of checking the control total of the vector shown above. Two separate sources were available: the local authority financial statements for the base year and Woodward's estimates of expenditure per head for Yorkshire and Humberside, for 1961 and 1964 (Woodward, 1970). The latter proved a more tractable source than the former and was preferred in the final analysis. Neither, of course, could really provide what was wanted: a check on the commodity or industry implications of government expenditure.

Woodward found that in 1964 the total current expenditure by public authorities in Yorkshire and Humberside was £328.4m: a per capita expenditure of £71.4. By using the Registrar-General's mid-year-estimate for the base year (1963) a check could be made, although admittedly mismatched. The control total derived in this way was £122.9m. Comparison of this figure with the total at the foot of the fourth column in Table 4.7 shows a considerable discrepancy, which can be attributed to the size of the wage-bill paid by local and central government to its employees in West Yorkshire.

(d) Exports

Ideally, exports in the West Yorkshire model would be treated as the sum of two distinct items: firstly exports proper, ie. goods and services delivered to activities outside the United Kingdom and

Table 4.7 Estimating public authorities' expenditure, 1963

Sector	1 Sales to public authorities (£m)	2 Gross output (£m)	3 Proportion delivered to government a/c	4 Estimates for West Yorkshire conurbation (£m)
I	100.7	1666.7	0.060	1.12
II	32.1	1092.5	0.029	0.61
III	37.4	3163.8	0.012	1.00
IV	160.7	2604.6	0.062	3.93
V	8.5	1902.4	0.004	0.23
VI	383.1	4305.7	0.089	17.71
VII	133.0	379.1	0.351	-
VIII	345.3	2257.9	0.153	5.14
IX	15.9	1226.3	0.013	0.68
X	16.9	1741.8	0.010	5.51
XI	0.2	149.1	0.001	0.02
XII	21.4	808.2	0.026	1.80
XIII	2.3	733.1	0.003	0.04
XIV	22.6	620.5	0.036	0.92
XV	91.0	1531.1	0.059	2.38
XVI	26.0	758.9	0.034	0.41
XVII	291.0	3245.6	0.090	8.93
XVIII	82.3	1597.7	0.052	3.11
XIX	165.8	3647.7	0.045	4.26
XX	95.1	4761.5	0.020	3.62
XXI-XXIII	495.5	5297.0	0.094	15.52
XXIV	2736.0	2736.0	1.000	(55.62)
Total (all industries except XXIV)				76.93+

+The only product of sector XXIV is, in effect, its labour, and thus the only entry in the national accounts is made under the heading income from employment. Consequently, any deliveries of labour made by public employees in West Yorkshire will be recorded in the income from employment row of the primary inputs sector.

For key to sectors see Table 4.2.

secondly inter-regional flows, ie. goods delivered for intermediate use to activities within the United Kingdom but outside West Yorkshire. Both items present severe data problems but since we were essentially concerned with constructing a two region model (West Yorkshire versus the rest-of-the-world) the details of the inter-regional flows were not pursued further. Some estimates of exports are given in the trade matrices below (Section 4.4.6) and further reconciliation of our estimates of trade and corroborative evidence based on the National Institute of Economic and Social Research estimates (NIESR)(Brown, 1972, p.75) for inter-regional trade in the UK are dealt with in Section 4.4.6 below. It is worth pointing out that the estimation of exports represents a case where our objectives have had to be modified as a result of insurmountable data deficiences.

4.4.4 Estimates of primary inputs

The primary inputs sectors may be defined as (a) imports of goods and services; (b) taxes on expenditure minus subsidies and sales by final buyers; (c) income from employment; and (d) gross profits and other trading income, and our procedures for estimating them are discussed in turn.

(a) Imports

Imports are handled analogously to exports in the final demand estimates. National Input-Output Tables give a commodity breakdown of imports, but the imports absorbed by the West Yorkshire economy contain a substantial proportion of inter-regional flows as well as imports from overseas. Goods Traffic Surveys for 1962 and 1967 provide information on road imports. Alternatively we can assume that if the overseas import requirements of the imports to West Yorkshire is used to calculate estimates of overseas imports, these could be subtracted from estimates of total imports to provide a check on inter-regional flows. Again, further discussion of this procedure will be found in Section 4.4.6 below.

(b) Taxes and sales by final buyers

The distribution of taxes can be suitably derived by pro-rating the National Input-Output Tables. Similarly these tables are used to estimate sales by final buyers. Equally, however, these two categories can be included in a residuals sector, since by far the most important sectors of the primary inputs estimates are the estimates of income from employment and gross trading profits (which constitutes the pool from which taxes and other payments are funded).

(c) Income from employment

Inland Revenue data was used to estimate the control totals for the entry 'income from employment'. Information on the income paid by manufacturing industries in the West Yorkshire conurbation was obtained directly from the regional summaries published in the 1963 Census of Production. The remaining items (non-manufacturing and agricultural incomes) required special weighting procedures. The complete estimation procedure is described below.

The 1963 Census of Production Summary Tables provide the principal source of data for the entry 'income from employment', which is defined in the 'Blue Book' as the sum of wages and salaries and employers' national insurance contributions. The data from this source are limited, however, in that they only refer to manufacturing industries; totals for non-manufacturing sectors had to be estimated from what was available from other sources. These are discussed below.

The distribution of incomes from employment derived from firm data for 1963 is presented in Table 4.8.

Table 4.8 Income from employment derived from manufacturing industries in the West Yorkshire conurbation, 1963 (£m)

Sector	Wages and salaries paid	Sector	Wages and salaries paid
III	12.3	XI	2.5
IV	12.2	XII	19.6
V	11.9	XIII	4.1
VI	62.4	XIV	7.0
VIII	8.2	XV	13.9
IX	11.3	XVI	3.0
X	94.3	Total	262.7

For key to sectors see Table 4.2

The estimation of figures for the remaining, non-manufacturing sectors relied, of necessity, upon the use of employment data to provide weights for national data. The distribution of wage bills is directly related to the size of an industry's workforce. It seemed valid, therefore, to proceed with an employment-weighting scheme, which could be adjusted later to account for regional wage differentials.

The weighting procedure is summarised in Table 4.9. The first column represents the relevant 'Blue Book' data to which are applied a set of weights calculated as follows. Let $(n)Y^k$ be wages and salaries paid by industry k at the national level (n); let $(r)E^k/(n)E^k$ be the proportion of employment in industry k located in region (r); then our simple, unadjusted, weighted estimate of income from employment in non-manufacturing industry k is:

$$(r)Y^k = (n)Y^k\{(r)E^k/(n)E^k\} \qquad (4.24)$$

<u>Table 4.9</u> <u>The estimation of wages and salaries for non-manufacturing industries in the West Yorkshire conurbation, 1963</u>

Sectors	1 'Blue Book' wages and salaries (£m)	2 Employment ratio	3 Unadjusted wages and salaries (£m)	4 Adjusted (by wage differentials) (£m)
I	333	0.011	3.72	3.537
II	553	0.019	10.46	9.958
XVII	1280	0.031	39.29	37.404
XVIII	337	0.038	11.94	11.300
XIX	1518	0.026	39.08	37.204
XX	1904	0.038	72.65	69.163
XXI	686	0.029	19.92	18.964
XXIV	929	0.022	20.72	19.725
Public health (XXIII)	450			
Local authorities education (XXIII)	533	0.032	105.50	100.436
Other services (XXIII)	2367	-	-	
Total non-manufacturing	10890	-	323.28	308.000

For key to sectors see Table 4.2

The distribution of monetary values for West Yorkshire is shown in column 3 of Table 4.9. In this form, the estimates take no account of the money-wage differentials that exist within the UK. To remedy this, an adjustment was made using information from the Department of Employment's New Earnings Survey, 1968, which allowed the construction of an index of 95.20 for Yorkshire and Humberside's non-manufacturing industries (relative to a UK index of 100). Column 4 of Table 4.9 represents the application of this index.

The weighting procedure described above should, of course, be evaluated using an independent source of data. For this purpose the Inland Revenue's Survey of Personal Incomes for the 1964/65 tax year was consulted. The Inland Revenue's estimate of the total wages and salaries (before tax) subject to tax under Schedule D and E for the conurbation was £522.2m, a figure which implies that our estimated total wage-bill of £571m is plausible.

In general the Inland Revenue Surveys provided the most detailed information on incomes in West Yorkshire. Indeed, this source is the main constituent of the Central Statistical Office's 'Blue Book' tables on personal incomes. But, despite the considerable appeal of this level of disaggregation, there remained less-than-trivial problems of definition and accounting that eventually prompted us to make use of the 'Blue Book' figures first and then to use the conurbation data as a check. Some of the problems were overcome in the derivation of estimates of consumers' expenditure, and a further treatment of the intricacies involved in the reconciliation of Inland Revenue data with other sources is to be found in technical notes (Smith, 1974).

(d) Gross trading profits

Again this part of the primary inputs accounts has to be treated as three separate sections because of data restrictions: firstly, estimates for the manufacturing orders, secondly, agriculture and finally estimates for non-manufacturing orders excluding agriculture.

(i) Manufacturing orders

Net output figures can be derived from two sources and compared. Firstly the Census of Production provides data for the West Yorkshire conurbation for 1963. Alternatively it is feasible to apply rates calculated from national data (net output per head) to employment data for West Yorkshire and hence estimate gross trading profits for industries in the West Yorkshire conurbation. 'Blue Book' data on companies and public corporations required that a composite fuel and power sector (orders II and XVIII) be used. Table 4.10 gives the details of the estimates.

… profits for West Yorkshire industries, 1963

	1	2	3	4	5	6	7
Sector	Net output for West Yorkshire (£m)	Wages and salaries West Yorkshire (£m)	Net output per employee. West Yorkshire (£)	Net output per employee. National (£)	Estimated net output using employment weights (£m)	Gross trading profits (Col.1-2)	Special weightings for non-manufacturing sectors
Manufacturing industries							
III	31.4	12.3	1585	1679		19.1	
IV	26.4	12.2	1913	2388		14.2	
V	20.4	11.9	1324	1449		38.3	
VI	109.4	62.4	1288	1307		47.0	
VII	-	-	-	1060		-	
VIII	12.7	8.2	1209	1455	Firm data available from Census of Production	4.5	
IX	21.8	11.3	1354	1218		10.5	
X	169.8	94.3	1062	1060		75.5	
XI	4.7	2.5	1175	1105		2.2	
XII	30.2	19.6	689	771		10.6	
XIII	7.1	4.1	1290	1354		3.0	
XIV	11.7	7.0	1135	1138		4.7	
XV	24.0	13.9	1212	1449		10.1	
XVI	5.8	3.0	1137	1301		2.8	
Non-service industries							
II		9.9		1190	14.5441	16.3†	0.019
XVIII		11.3		2417	36.883		0.038
XVII		37.4		1076	38.101	3.8	0.021
Service sectors							
XIX		37.2				14.9*	0.026
XX		69.2				26.8*	0.035
XXI		19.0				19.7*	0.028
XXII-XXIII		100.4				7.6*	0.029
						331.6**	

† 'Blue Book' data on Companies and Public Corporation required that a composite 'Fuel and power' sector (orders II and XVIII) be used.

* Estimates produced by weighting national profits data ('Blue Book') with employment ratios shown

** Total estimated Gross Trading Profits of Companies and Public Corporations combined for West Yorkshire conurbation

For key to sectors see Table 4.2

(ii) Agriculture

The 1961 Census Workplace Tables for West Yorkshire reveal that 6,200 persons were employed (including self-employed) in sector I, (agriculture, forestry and fishing). Of this total: 1,570 were classed as farmers (employers and managers, SEG 13); 1,950 were classed as farmers (own account, SEG 14); and 2,630 were classed as agricultural workers (SEG 15). This sums to 6,150, which is within the sampling error of the order total. It is safe to assume that profits from agricultural enterprises will be covered by the item 'income from self-employment' listed as Schedule D by the Inland Revenue.

(iii) Non-manufacturing orders

There are several ways of dealing with sectors XIX-XXIV. Firstly, it is possible to use weights derived from the Ministry of Labour records (1961) and the 1961 Census Workplace Tables. Secondly, we may make estimates from the data in the 1966 Census, Economic Activity Tables, the results of which are shown in column 6 of Table 4.10. Census of Distribution data can be used as corroborative evidence to check the estimates.

4.4.5 Intermediate account totals

The intermediate account totals represent the row and column sums of the inter-industry transaction matrix, ie. excluding final demand sectors or primary input sectors. These marginal totals are of particular importance in a later stage of the model, when we come to the derivation of local input-output coefficients. If satisfactory estimates can be made of all the items described above, then marginal totals could reasonably be estimated by subtracting total primary inputs from total gross inputs (which, by definition, are the same as total gross outputs in an industry/industry model). Satisfaction with this technique will depend upon the degree to which the elements of the final demand and primary inputs sectors can be derived independently. The primary input estimates and the final demand estimates are given in Table 4.11. Clearly, the intermediate demands generated by the economy will vary according to the assumptions about technology and trading patterns which are embodied in the matrix of inter-industry coefficients. In this context three

Table 4.11 Final demand and primary input estimates, West Yorkshire conurbation, 1963 (£m)

Sector	Final demand estimates					Primary input estimates			
	Consumer Expenditure	Public Authority Expenditure	Investments		Estimated final demand	Income from employment	Gross profits	Imports (RDS)	Total primary input
			Fixed	Stocks					
I	21.4	1.1	0.1	-	22.6	1.4	5.5	1.3	8.2
II	5.7	0.6	0.4	-	6.7	9.9	-	1.1	11.0
III	45.0	1.0	-	-	42.1	12.3	19.1	16.1	47.5
IV	9.9	3.9	0.9	0.3	15.0	12.2	14.2	5.3	31.7
V	0.5	0.2	0.2	1.0	2.0	11.9	8.5	3.9	24.3
VI	3.7	17.7	54.0	1.1	76.5	62.4	47.0	15.0	124.4
VIII	8.2	5.1	6.6	-0.6	19.3	8.2	4.5	2.5	15.2
IX	3.8	0.7	2.2	0.1	6.9	11.3	10.5	5.2	27.0
X	12.0	5.5	0.1	6.3	23.9	94.3	75.5	31.4	201.2
XI	0.9	-	-	0.2	1.0	2.5	2.2	2.2	6.9
XII	6.6	1.8	-	-0.5	7.9	19.6	10.6	2.7	32.9
XIII	1.3	0.1	0.2	0.1	1.6	4.1	3.0	1.3	8.4
XIV	4.9	0.9	1.3	0.3	7.5	7.0	5.7	1.8	14.5
XV	6.8	2.4	-	0.2	9.2	13.9	10.1	2.8	26.8
XVI	3.0	0.4	0.2	0.1	3.8	3.0	2.8	1.2	7.0
XVII	11.9	8.9	69.8	-	90.7	37.4	3.8	10.1	51.3
XVIII	18.9	3.1	6.1	-	28.1	11.3	16.3	8.6	36.2
XIX	23.6	4.3	1.3	-	29.2	37.2	14.9	6.1	58.2
XX	115.6	3.6	6.7	-	125.9	69.2	26.8	9.2	105.2
XXI-XXIII	81.7	15.5	4.9	-	102.1	119.4	27.3	5.9	152.6
XXIV	-	55.6	-	-	55.6	55.6	-	-	55.6
Imports	367.2	-	-	-	367.2				
Rents (Dwellings)	50.8	-	-	-	-				

separate sets of intermediate accounts have been produced and these are presented in Tables 4.21, 4.22 and 4.23 below, while the next section explains how the relevant coefficients were derived from three different weighting procedures.

4.4.6 Estimation of model parameters

Input-output coefficients

The problem of estimating input-output coefficients for West Yorkshire basically has to be approached once again through the use of weightings derived from national data.

(a) The relative demand-supply technique (RDS)

This technique, which owes a great deal to the work of Hewings (1969), aims to provide a weighting of the national input-output coefficients matrix by using information on the relative sizes of industries in the region compared with industries in the nation. Formally, an estimate of the regional coefficient is

$$r_{ij} = a^n_{ij} \left[\frac{G^r_i}{\Sigma_j a^n_{ij} G^r_j} \Bigg/ \frac{G^n_i}{\Sigma_j a^n_{ij} G^n_j} \right] \qquad (4.25)$$

subject to

$$a^n_{ij} \geqslant r_{ij} \qquad (4.26)$$

where a^n_{ij} is the national I-O coefficient with respect to sector i and j; G^r_i is gross regional output in sector i; G^r_j is gross regional output in sector j; G^n_i is gross national output in sector i; and G^n_j is gross national output in sector j.

Where estimates of gross regional outputs are lacking, employment data can be used as follows

$$G^r_i = \frac{e^r_i}{e^n_i} G^n_i \qquad (4.27)$$

where e^r_i is employment in region r in sector i and e^n_i is employment in the nation in sector i. In the West Yorkshire model, Census of Production data have obviated the necessity to use this latter procedure for manufacturing orders, but it was used for non-manufacturing orders.

The RDS weightings, having provided estimates of the regional coefficients, r_{ij}, can then be used to derive a 'net' imports matrix. Firstly, assume

$$a^n_{ij} = a^r_{ij} = r_{ij} + m^r_{ij} \qquad (4.28)$$

so that

$$m^r_{ij} = a^n_{ij} - r_{ij} \qquad (4.29)$$

where m^r_{ij} is the imports to sector j from sector i per unit of output of sector j in region r and a^r_{ij} is the 'true' input-output coefficient representing, for the regional economy, the amount of i required per unit of output by j. Note that Equation (4.28) includes the assumption $a^n_{ij} = a^r_{ij}$ which may be reasonable since a^n_{ij} and a^r_{ij} represent elements of requirement matrices - ie. they are defined purely in terms of the industrial processes linking sectors i and j, and ignore any differences that may occur due to trading patterns between regions (this is tantamount to an assumption of uniform technology). Use of this assumption will obviously lose any indication of regional variations in the production functions of industries, but will allow some estimates of trade. The elements of the trade matrix (net imports) are given by

$$\underline{M}^r = \{m^r_{ij} G^r_j\} \qquad (4.30)$$

The above procedure has been carried out for West Yorkshire using 1963 Census of Production data on manufacturing industries and the following tables ensue:

Table 4.12: A regional inter-industry gross flows matrix; $\underline{X} = \{X_{ij}\}$.

Table 4.13: A regional input-output coefficients matrix; $\underline{r} = \{r_{ij}\}$.

Table 4.14: A regional net imports coefficients matrix; $\underline{m} = \{m_{ij}\}$.

Table 4.15: A regional imports flow matrix; $\underline{M}$

and

Table 4.16: The regional inverse matrix multiplier; $\underline{I}-\underline{r}$.

Retention of the constraint contained in Equation (4.26) above ($a^n_{ij} \geq r_{ij}$) on the regional coefficients implies that the only trade

Table 4.12 Constrained regional inter-industry gross flows matrix, West Yorkshire conurbation, 1963 (£m)

Sectors \ Sectors	I	II	III	IV	V	VI	VIII	IX	X	XI	XII	XIII	XIV	XV	XVI	XVII	XVIII	XIX	XX	XXI-XXIII
I	-	-	3.46	0.02	-	-	-	-	0.99	0.42	-	-	0.09	0.01	-	-	0.01	0.03	-	0.08
II	0.03	-	0.23	2.16	0.03	0.21	0.05	0.04	2.80	0.05	0.04	0.55	0.02	0.35	0.04	0.05	6.92	0.48	0.06	0.05
III	3.38	0.02	-	0.61	-	0.02	-	-	5.80	-	-	0.02	-	-	-	-	-	0.17	-	0.76
IV	0.85	0.25	2.03	-	2.38	2.73	0.33	0.83	17.04	0.49	0.35	0.48	0.43	0.85	1.11	1.42	1.14	1.46	0.72	1.62
V	0.06	0.64	0.46	0.59	-	19.08	3.77	11.88	0.37	0.02	0.12	0.12	0.31	0.28	0.10	3.70	0.88	0.35	0.06	0.29
VI	1.11	1.03	0.73	0.91	2.70	-	3.26	1.31	8.01	0.16	0.66	0.34	0.25	0.58	0.18	3.57	3.94	1.61	0.89	3.00
VIII	0.04	0.04	0.04	0.04	0.31	0.48	-	0.10	0.39	-	0.03	0.02	0.02	0.02	-	0.11	0.07	1.69	0.07	0.47
IX	0.30	0.11	1.67	1.06	1.03	7.51	3.11	-	1.48	0.32	1.03	0.20	0.79	0.12	0.29	1.87	0.23	0.72	1.07	1.76
X	0.11	0.22	0.15	0.13	0.02	0.80	0.31	0.20	-	0.32	19.27	0.08	0.82	0.41	0.73	0.22	0.04	-	3.05	0.32
XI	-	-	-	0.03	0.01	0.06	0.05	0.03	0.57	-	5.00	-	0.01	0.03	0.03	-	-	-	-	0.05
XII	0.01	0.08	0.32	0.01	0.01	-	0.01	-	0.17	0.02	-	-	-	0.01	0.01	0.01	0.01	0.17	0.18	0.17
XIII	0.04	0.10	0.58	0.27	0.53	1.39	0.13	0.06	0.38	-	0.02	-	0.19	0.02	0.02	7.37	0.23	0.03	-	0.08
XIV	0.06	0.23	0.24	0.13	0.09	1.47	0.44	0.13	0.39	0.02	0.08	0.10	-	0.12	0.10	5.76	0.14	0.12	0.53	0.02
XV	0.01	0.08	2.72	1.01	0.24	2.14	0.18	0.45	4.92	0.13	0.87	0.31	0.44	-	0.37	0.16	0.17	0.80	3.10	9.92
XVI	0.04	0.14	0.17	0.22	0.09	1.16	0.49	0.19	1.79	0.14	0.55	0.04	0.16	0.14	-	0.52	0.04	0.62	0.45	0.46
XVII	0.29	0.36	0.31	0.49	0.17	0.64	0.13	0.11	1.47	0.04	0.13	0.03	0.08	0.11	0.02	-	0.14	0.59	1.80	0.95
XVIII	0.20	0.59	0.69	1.52	2.11	2.56	0.38	0.99	8.11	0.13	0.36	0.49	0.23	0.50	0.19	0.31	-	0.68	2.86	2.84
XIX	0.26	0.69	2.70	3.28	3.00	2.93	0.34	1.04	1.75	0.35	1.04	0.90	0.74	1.52	0.30	1.15	2.15	-	17.11	4.60
XX	0.90	0.26	1.93	0.87	1.58	6.11	0.87	1.82	12.86	0.36	1.30	0.26	0.33	1.28	0.22	1.42	0.49	0.88	-	0.63

Table 4.13 Constrained regional input-output coefficients matrix, West Yorkshire conurbation, 1963

Sectors \ Sectors	I	II	III	IV	V	VI	VIII	IX	X	XI	XII	XIII	XIV	XV	XVI	XVII	XVIII	XIX	XX	XXI-XXIII
I	-	-	0.04	-	-	-	-	-	-	0.03	-	-	-	-	-	-	-	-	-	-
II	-	-	-	0.03	-	-	-	-	0.01	-	-	0.04	-	0.01	-	0.01	0.12	0.01	-	-
III	0.18	-	-	0.01	-	-	-	-	0.01	-	-	-	-	-	-	-	-	-	-	0.01
IV	0.05	0.01	0.02	-	0.05	0.01	0.01	0.02	0.03	0.03	0.01	0.04	0.02	0.02	0.09	0.01	0.02	0.02	-	0.01
V	-	0.03	0.01	0.01	-	0.10	0.11	0.23	-	-	-	0.01	0.01	0.01	0.01	0.04	0.02	-	-	-
VI	0.06	0.05	0.01	0.01	0.05	-	0.10	0.02	0.01	0.01	0.01	0.03	0.01	0.02	0.02	0.04	0.07	0.02	0.01	0.02
VIII	-	-	-	-	0.01	-	-	-	-	-	-	-	-	-	-	-	-	0.02	-	-
IX	0.02	0.01	0.02	0.02	0.02	0.04	0.09	-	-	0.02	0.02	0.02	0.03	-	0.02	0.02	-	0.01	0.01	0.01
X	0.01	0.01	-	-	-	-	0.01	-	-	0.02	0.28	0.01	0.03	0.01	0.06	-	-	-	0.02	-
XI	-	-	-	-	-	-	-	-	-	-	0.07	-	-	-	-	-	-	-	-	-
XIII	-	0.01	0.01	-	0.01	0.01	-	-	-	-	-	-	0.01	-	-	0.07	-	-	-	-
XIV	-	0.01	-	-	-	0.01	0.01	-	-	-	-	0.01	-	-	0.01	0.06	-	-	-	-
XVI	-	0.01	-	-	-	0.01	0.02	-	-	0.01	0.01	-	0.01	-	-	0.01	-	0.01	-	-
XVII	0.02	0.02	-	0.01	-	-	-	-	-	-	-	-	-	-	-	-	-	0.01	0.01	0.01
XVIII	0.01	0.03	0.01	0.02	0.04	0.01	0.01	0.02	0.01	0.01	0.01	0.04	0.01	0.01	0.02	-	-	0.01	0.02	0.02
XIX	0.02	0.03	0.03	0.05	0.06	0.02	0.01	0.02	-	0.02	0.02	0.07	0.03	0.04	0.03	0.01	0.04	-	0.10	0.03
XX	0.05	0.01	0.02	0.01	0.03	0.03	0.03	0.03	0.02	0.03	0.02	0.02	0.01	0.03	0.02	0.01	0.01	0.01	-	-
XXI-XXIII	0.04	0.02	0.04	0.05	0.01	0.04	0.02	0.03	0.03	0.03	0.03	0.02	0.04	0.06	0.05	0.03	0.03	0.01	0.05	-

For key to sectors see Table 4.2

Table 4.14 RDS Constrained regional net import coefficients matrix (imports per unit of output of West Yorkshire Industries) West Yorkshire conurbation, 1963

Sectors \ Sectors	I	II	III	IV	V	VI	VIII	IX	X	XI	XII	XIII	XIV	XV	XVI	XVII	XVIII	XIX	XX	XXI-XXIII
I	-	-	0.130	0.001	-	-	-	-	0.006	0.091	-	-	0.011	0.001	-	-	0.001	0.001	-	0.001
II	0.001	-	0.002	0.031	0.001	0.001	0.001	0.001	0.005	0.003	0.001	0.037	0.001	0.008	0.003	0.010	0.104	0.005	-	-
IV	0.028	0.008	0.015	-	0.028	0.008	0.006	0.010	0.018	0.021	0.003	0.021	0.011	0.013	0.056	0.009	0.012	0.010	0.002	0.006
V	0.001	0.007	0.001	0.002	-	0.021	0.025	0.050	-	-	-	0.002	0.003	0.002	0.002	0.008	0.003	0.001	-	-
VIII	0.004	0.003	0.001	0.010	0.004	-	0.003	0.001	-	0.001	0.003	0.001	0.001	-	-	0.002	0.002	0.029	0.001	0.005
XIII	0.001	0.003	0.005	0.003	0.007	0.005	0.003	0.001	-	-	-	-	0.005	-	0.001	0.049	0.003	-	-	-
XV	-	0.001	0.005	0.003	0.001	0.002	0.001	0.001	0.001	0.001	0.002	0.004	0.003	-	0.005	-	-	0.001	0.003	0.009
XVI	0.003	0.010	0.003	0.005	0.003	0.009	0.022	0.005	0.005	0.014	0.012	0.004	0.009	0.005	-	0.008	0.001	0.010	0.004	0.004
XVII	0.002	0.002	-	0.001	-	-	-	-	-	-	-	-	-	-	-	-	-	0.001	-	0.001
XVIII	0.001	0.003	0.001	0.002	0.004	0.001	0.001	0.002	0.001	0.001	0.001	0.003	0.001	0.001	0.001	0.001	-	0.001	0.002	0.002
XIX	0.003	0.007	0.007	0.011	0.012	0.003	0.002	0.004	0.001	0.005	0.003	0.014	0.006	0.008	0.005	0.002	0.007	-	0.019	0.006
XX	0.011	0.003	0.005	0.003	0.007	0.007	0.006	0.008	0.005	0.006	0.004	0.005	0.003	0.008	0.004	0.003	0.002	0.002	-	0.001
XXI-XXIII	0.016	0.007	0.016	0.020	0.005	0.015	0.009	0.013	0.012	0.011	0.012	0.006	0.017	0.024	0.021	0.010	0.008	0.005	0.019	-

For key to sectors see Table 4.2

Sectors / Sectors		To industries in West Yorkshire																	
		I	II	III	IV	V	VI	VIII	IX	X	XI	XII	XIII	XIV	XV	XVI	XVII	XVIII	XIX	XX	XXI-XXIII
From industries in the rest of the world	I	-		11.02	0.07	-	-	-	-	3.16	1.33	0.01	0.01	0.27	0.05	-	-	0.03	0.08	-	0.24
	II	0.03	-	0.21	1.96	0.03	0.19	0.04	0.04	2.54	0.05	0.04	0.50	0.02	0.32	0.04	0.95	6.26	0.44	0.05	0.05
	IV	0.52	0.15	1.24	-	1.45	1.67	0.20	0.51	10.42	0.30	0.21	0.29	0.27	0.52	0.68	0.87	0.70	0.89	0.44	1.00
	V	0.01	0.14	0.10	0.13	-	4.19	0.83	2.61	0.08	-	0.03	0.03	0.07	0.06	0.02	0.81	0.19	0.08	0.01	0.06
	VIII	0.07	0.06	0.06	0.07	0.50	0.79	-	0.16	0.64	0.01	0.05	0.04	0.03	0.04	-	0.17	0.12	2.76	0.11	0.76
	XIII	0.03	0.07	0.38	0.18	0.35	0.92	0.09	0.04	0.25	-	0.01	-	0.13	0.01	0.01	4.88	0.15	0.02	-	0.05
	XV	-	0.01	0.42	0.16	0.04	0.33	0.03	0.07	0.77	0.02	0.14	0.05	0.07	-	0.06	0.02	0.03	0.12	0.48	1.55
	XVI	0.05	0.20	0.25	0.32	0.13	1.72	0.73	0.29	2.65	0.20	0.82	0.06	0.23	0.21	-	0.77	0.06	0.91	0.66	0.68
	XVII	0.04	0.04	0.04	0.06	0.02	0.08	0.02	0.01	0.18	0.01	0.02	-	0.01	0.01	-	-	0.02	0.07	0.21	0.11
	XVIII	0.02	0.06	0.07	0.14	0.20	0.21	0.04	0.09	0.76	0.01	0.03	0.05	0.02	0.05	0.02	0.03	-	0.06	0.27	0.27
	XIX	0.05	0.14	0.55	0.67	0.61	0.60	0.07	0.21	0.36	0.07	0.21	0.18	0.15	0.31	0.06	0.24	0.44	-	3.50	0.94
	XX	0.21	0.06	0.45	0.20	0.37	1.43	0.20	0.42	3.00	0.08	0.30	0.06	0.08	0.30	0.05	0.33	0.12	0.20	-	0.15
XXI-XXIII		0.30	0.14	1.32	1.29	0.25	2.89	0.30	0.70	6.61	0.16	0.82	0.08	0.42	0.96	0.25	1.03	0.51	0.51	3.47	-

For key to sectors see Table 4.2

Table 4.16 RDS constrained inverse matrix multiplier, West Yorkshire, 1963

Sectors \ Sectors	I	II	III	IV	V	VI	VIII	IX	X	XI	XII	XIII	XIV	XV	XVI	XVII	XVIII	XIX	XX	XXI-XXIII
I	1.01	-	0.04	-	-	-	-	-	-	0.03	-	-	-	-	-	-	-	-	-	-
II	-	1.00	0.01	0.04	0.01	0.01	0.01	0.01	0.01	0.01	0.01	0.05	-	0.01	0.01	0.02	0.12	0.01	-	-
III	0.18	-	1.01	0.01	-	-	-	-	0.01	0.01	-	-	-	-	-	-	-	-	-	0.01
IV	0.06	0.02	0.03	1.01	0.05	0.02	0.02	0.03	0.03	0.04	0.02	0.04	0.02	0.03	0.10	0.02	0.03	0.02	0.01	0.01
V	0.02	0.04	0.01	0.02	1.02	0.11	0.15	0.23	0.01	0.01	0.01	0.02	0.02	0.01	0.02	0.05	0.03	0.01	0.01	0.01
VI	0.07	0.06	0.02	0.02	0.06	1.01	0.11	0.04	0.02	0.02	0.02	0.04	0.02	0.02	0.02	0.05	0.08	0.02	0.01	0.02
VIII	-	-	-	-	0.01	-	1.00	-	-	-	-	-	-	-	-	-	-	0.02	-	-
IX	0.03	0.01	0.02	0.02	0.03	0.04	0.10	1.01	0.01	0.03	0.02	0.02	0.04	0.01	0.03	0.03	0.01	0.01	0.01	0.01
X	0.01	0.01	0.01	-	-	0.01	0.01	0.01	1.00	0.03	0.29	0.01	0.03	0.01	0.06	0.01	-	-	0.02	-
XI	-	-	-	-	-	-	-	-	-	1.00	0.07	-	-	-	-	-	-	-	-	-
XII	-	-	-	-	-	-	-	-	-	-	1.00	-	-	-	-	-	-	-	-	-
XIII	0.01	0.01	0.01	0.01	0.01	0.01	0.01	0.01	-	-	-	1.00	0.01	-	-	0.08	0.01	-	-	-
XIV	0.01	0.01	-	-	-	0.01	0.02	-	-	-	-	0.01	1.00	-	0.01	0.06	0.01	-	-	-
XV	0.01	0.01	0.04	0.02	0.01	0.01	0.01	0.02	0.01	0.01	0.02	0.03	0.02	1.01	0.04	0.01	0.01	0.01	0.02	0.06
XVI	-	0.01	-	0.01	-	0.01	0.02	0.01	-	0.01	0.01	0.01	0.01	0.01	1.00	0.07	-	0.01	-	-
XVII	0.02	0.02	0.01	0.01	0.01	0.01	0.01	0.01	-	0.01	-	0.01	0.01	-	-	1.00	0.01	0.01	0.01	0.01
XVIII	0.02	0.03	0.01	0.03	0.05	0.02	0.02	0.03	0.02	0.01	0.01	0.04	0.01	0.02	0.02	0.01	1.01	0.01	0.02	0.02
XIX	0.04	0.04	0.04	0.06	0.07	0.03	0.03	0.04	0.01	0.03	0.03	0.08	0.04	0.05	0.04	0.03	0.05	1.01	0.10	0.03
XX	0.06	0.02	0.03	0.02	0.04	0.04	0.04	0.05	0.03	0.03	0.03	0.03	0.02	0.04	0.03	0.02	0.02	0.03	1.00	0.01
XXI-XXIII	0.06	0.03	0.05	0.06	0.02	0.05	0.04	0.04	0.03	0.04	0.05	0.03	0.05	0.07	0.07	0.04	0.03	0.02	0.05	1.01
[illegible]	[illegible]	[illegible]	[illegible]	[illegible]	[illegible]	[illegible]	[illegible]	1.53	[illegible]	2.31	1.60	1.40	1.31	1.28	1.47	1.42	1.39	1.17	1.28	1.22

matrix that can be derived is an imports matrix. In order to investigate the structure of an exports matrix it was decided to relax this constraint. A complementary set of five unconstrained matrices result; of these the regional imports flow matrix is presented here (Table 4.17) and can be seen to contain negative elements which represent exports.

(b) Bi-proportional models (RAS methods)

The RAS method of estimating input-output coefficients assumes that the deviation of regional coefficients from their national counterparts is explained by the simultaneous operations of a row and column vector upon an initial estimate of the regional coefficients. These regional coefficients are provided by

$$\underline{a}^r = \underline{R}\ \underline{a}^n\ \underline{S} \tag{4.31}$$

where $\underline{R}$ is now a row vector of k elements, one for each industrial sector of the economy; $\underline{S}$ is a column vector of k elements, one for each industrial sector; $\underline{a}^r$ is the regional coefficients matrix; and $\underline{a}^n$ is the national coefficients matrix; subject to:

$$(\underline{a}^r\ \underline{\hat{G}})\underline{Q} = \underline{U} \tag{4.32}$$

$$(\underline{a}^r\ \underline{\hat{G}})'\underline{Q} = \underline{V} \tag{4.33}$$

and

$$a^r_{ij} \geqslant 0 \tag{4.34}$$

where $\underline{\hat{G}}$ is a diagonal matrix from $\underline{G}$ (gross regional outputs); $\underline{Q}$ is a vector in which each element is unity; $\underline{U}$ is a vector of intermediate outputs; and $\underline{V}$ is a vector of intermediate inputs. The bi-proportional model thus solves two sets of simultaneous equations for the values of $\underline{R}$ and $\underline{S}$ using an iterative procedure.

$$\underline{U} = (\underline{a}^n\ \underline{\hat{G}}\ \underline{\hat{S}})'\underline{R} \tag{4.35}$$

$$\underline{V} = (\underline{\hat{R}}\ \underline{a}^n\ \underline{\hat{G}})\underline{S} \tag{4.36}$$

In the form given above the RAS model derives regional coefficients from minimal data sources, that is initial estimates of the regional coefficients and the marginal totals of the regional intermediate flows matrix. The model can, however, be used to update coefficient matrices in time as well as in space. Thus we postulate that

Table 4.17 RDS unconstrained import flows matrix

From industries in Rest of World: Sectors \ To industries in West Yorkshire: Sectors	I	II	II	IV	V	VI	VIII	IX	X	XI	XII	XIII	XIV	XV	YVI	XVII	XVIII	XIX	XX	XXI-XXIII	Totals
I	-	-	11.02	0.07	-	-	-	-	3.16	1.33	0.001	0.01	0.27	0.05	-	-	0.03	0.08	-	0.24	16.25
II	0.03	-	0.21	1.96	0.03	0.19	0.04	0.04	2.54	0.05	0.04	0.50	0.02	0.32	0.04	0.95	6.26	0.44	0.05	0.05	13.72
III	-2.33	-0.01	-	-0.42	-	-0.01	-	-	-4.00	-	-	-0.01	-	-	-	-	-	-0.12	-	-0.53	-7.43
IV	0.52	0.15	1.24	-	1.45	1.67	0.20	0.51	10.42	0.30	0.21	0.29	0.27	0.52	0.68	0.87	0.70	0.89	0.44	0.90	22.32
V	0.01	0.14	0.10	0.13	-	4.19	0.83	2.61	0.08	-	0.03	0.03	0.07	0.06	0.02	0.81	0.19	0.08	0.01	0.06	9.45
VI	-0.95	-0.89	-0.63	-0.78	-2.33	-	-2.81	-1.13	-6.90	-0.13	-0.57	-0.29	-0.22	-0.50	-0.15	-3.07	-3.39	-1.38	-0.77	-2.59	-29.48
VIII	0.07	0.06	0.06	0.07	0.50	0.79	-	0.16	0.64	0.01	0.05	0.04	0.03	0.04	-	0.17	0.12	2.76	0.11	0.76	6.44
IX	-0.15	-0.06	-0.82	-0.52	-0.51	-3.69	-1.52	-	-0.73	-0.16	-0.51	-0.10	-0.39	-0.06	-0.14	-0.92	-0.11	-0.35	-0.53	-0.86	-12.10
X	-0.98	-2.00	-1.30	-1.14	-0.18	-7.13	-2.74	-1.80	-	-2.87	-172.47	-0.69	-7.29	-3.65	-6.49	-1.96	-0.32	-	-27.33	-2.82	-243.17
XI	-	-	-	-0.01	-	-0.01	-0.01	-0.01	-0.11	-	-1.00	-	-	-0.01	-0.01	-	-	-	-	-0.01	-1.17
XII	-0.01	-0.06	-0.26	-0.01	-	-	-0.01	-	-0.14	-0.02	-	-	-	-0.01	-0.01	-0.01	-0.01	-0.14	-0.15	-0.14	-0.95
XIII	0.03	0.07	0.38	0.18	0.35	0.92	0.08	0.04	0.25	-	0.01	-	0.13	0.01	0.01	4.88	0.15	0.02	-	0.05	7.58
XIV	-0.03	-0.01	-0.10	-0.06	-0.04	-0.63	-0.19	-0.06	-0.17	-0.01	-0.03	-0.04	-	-0.05	-0.04	-2.48	-0.06	-0.05	-0.23	-0.01	-4.37
XV	-	0.01	0.42	0.16	0.04	0.03	0.03	0.07	0.77	0.02	0.14	0.05	0.07	-	0.06	0.02	0.03	0.12	0.48	1.55	4.37
XVI	0.05	0.20	0.25	0.32	0.13	1.71	0.73	0.29	2.65	0.20	0.82	0.06	0.23	0.21	-	0.77	0.06	0.91	0.66	0.68	10.96
XVII	0.04	0.04	0.04	0.06	0.02	0.08	0.02	0.01	0.18	0.01	0.02	-	0.01	0.01	-	-	0.02	0.07	0.21	0.11	0.94
XVIII	0.02	0.05	0.07	0.14	0.20	0.21	0.04	0.09	0.76	0.01	0.03	0.05	0.02	0.05	0.02	0.03	-	0.06	0.27	0.27	2.37
XIX	0.05	0.14	0.55	0.67	0.61	0.60	0.07	0.21	0.36	0.07	0.21	0.18	0.15	0.31	0.06	0.24	0.44	-	3.50	0.94	9.38
XX	0.21	0.06	0.45	0.20	0.37	1.43	0.20	0.42	3.00	0.08	0.30	0.06	0.08	0.30	0.05	0.33	0.11	0.20	-	0.15	8.02
XXI-XXIII	0.30	0.14	1.32	1.29	0.25	2.89	0.30	0.70	6.61	0.16	0.82	0.08	0.42	0.96	0.25	1.03	0.51	0.51	3.47	-	22.00
Totals	-3.11	-2.04	13.01	2.32	0.89	3.53	-4.74	2.17	19.35	-0.95	-171.89	0.19	-6.14	-1.44	-5.65	1.67	4.72	4.11	-19.78	-1.10	

For key to sectors see Table 4.2

$$\underline{a}_{t+T} = \underline{R}\ \underline{a}_t\ \underline{S} \tag{4.37}$$

where $\underline{a}_t$ and $\underline{a}_{t+T}$ are coefficient matrices at time t and time t+T, linked bi-proportionally by vectors of multipliers $\underline{R}$ and $\underline{S}$. It is implicit in all RAS calculations that there exist satisfactory and independent estimates of the vectors of marginal totals $\underline{U}$ and $\underline{V}$. It is advisable that these totals be independent of $\underline{G}$ (gross outputs). Some kind of interpretation of the $\underline{R}$ and $\underline{S}$ operators seems necessary. The economists' interpretation (particularly Stone's) tends to be that, over time, $\underline{R}$ represents a substitution effect and $\underline{S}$ represents a fabrication effect.

The existence now of two (1963 and 1968) national input-output tables (if the 1954 table is also used, then there are three available) imposes further constraints upon the RAS model equations which may allow a crude calibration of a modified bi-proportional model. There are two options available for calibration; firstly, we can assume that the bi-proportional hypothesis provides 'true' regional coefficients from national data in both 1963 and 1968, allowing us to fit these data to an update in time; secondly, if we take the estimates of $\underline{a}_t^r$ and $(\underline{R}\ \underline{a}_t^r\ \underline{S})$ as 'true' we may be able to fit such data to provide estimates of the parameters involved in an update over space. Conversely, this latter suggestion can be reversed to provide retro-forecasts of parameters for 1963. Tables 4.18 to 4.20 represent the set of tables giving the model parameters for the West Yorkshire conurbation using the RAS technique as a method of bi-proportional weighting to construct regional coefficients matrices from their national counterparts.

(c) Estimating trade matrices

We discuss below ways in which the trade matrices might be improved once the input-output coefficients are available. Our existing and firm knowledge about the West Yorkshire conurbation's economy may be represented by Figure 4.8. This pair of accounts in fact represent the demand pool (gross output) and the supply pool (gross purchases) concepts devised by Leontief and Strout in their multi-regional formulation of the input-output model (Leontief and Strout, 1963). Clearly, we could hypothesise that the elements of

Table 4.18 RAS weighted input-output technical coefficients matrix

Sector / Sectors	I	II	III	IV	V	VI	VIII	IX	X	XI	XII	XIII	XIV	XV	XVI	XVII	XVIII	XIX	XX	XXI-XXIII
I	-	-	0.014	-	-	-	-	-	0.008	0.001	-	-	-	-	-	-	-	0.001	-	-
II	-	-	0.001	0.006	-	-	-	-	0.014	-	-	0.002	-	-	-	0.001	0.038	0.007	-	-
III	0.019	-	-	0.002	-	-	-	-	0.044	-	-	-	-	-	-	-	-	0.004	-	-
IV	0.002	-	0.003	-	0.013	0.001	-	0.001	0.056	0.001	-	0.001	-	0.001	-	0.001	0.004	0.013	-	-
V	0.002	0.009	0.011	0.016	-	0.063	0.048	0.175	0.019	-	-	0.005	0.001	0.002	-	0.051	0.049	0.050	-	0.001
VI	0.017	0.005	0.007	0.010	0.093	-	0.017	0.008	0.164	-	-	0.006	-	0.002	-	0.020	0.090	0.094	-	0.003
VIII	-	-	-	-	0.007	-	-	-	0.005	-	-	-	-	-	-	-	0.001	0.063	-	-
IX	0.007	0.001	0.023	0.016	0.051	0.014	0.023	-	0.043	0.003	-	0.005	0.002	0.001	-	0.015	0.007	0.060	0.001	0.002
X	0.667	0.513	0.554	0.541	0.282	0.428	0.628	0.480	-	0.779	0.652	0.505	0.575	0.564	0.019	0.490	0.329	-	0.534	0.115
XI	-	-	-	0.001	-	-	-	-	0.021	-	0.001	-	-	-	-	-	-	-	-	-
XII	0.001	0.005	0.037	0.001	0.002	-	0.001	-	0.042	0.001	-	-	-	0.001	-	0.001	0.003	0.119	0.001	0.002
XIII	0.002	0.001	0.003	0.003	0.017	0.002	0.001	-	0.007	-	-	-	-	-	-	0.039	0.005	0.002	-	-
XIV	0.001	0.002	0.003	0.002	0.004	0.003	0.003	0.001	0.012	-	-	0.003	-	0.001	-	0.048	0.005	0.011	-	-
XV	-	-	0.012	0.005	0.004	0.001	-	0.001	0.044	-	-	0.002	-	- -	-	-	0.002	0.021	0.001	0.004
XVI	-	-	-	-	-	-	-	-	0.005	-	-	-	-	-	-	-	-	0.005	-	-
XVII	0.002	0.001	0.001	0.002	0.002	-	-	-	0.012	-	-	-	-	-	-	-	0.001	0.014	-	-
XVIII	0.001	0.001	0.002	0.005	0.022	0.001	0.001	0.002	0.050	-	-	0.002	-	0.001	-	0.001	-	0.012	-	0.001
XIX	0.007	0.007	0.046	0.062	0.183	0.007	0.003	0.011	0.063	0.004	-	0.026	0.002	0.009	-	0.011	0.087	-	0.013	0.007
XX	0.004	-	0.003	0.003	0.015	0.002	0.001	0.003	0.074	0.001	-	0.001	-	0.001	-	0.002	0.003	0.015	-	-
XII-XXIII	0.005	0.001	0.013	0.014	0.009	0.004	0.002	0.004	0.137	0.001	-	0.001	0.001	0.003	-	0.006	0.012	0.030	0.002	-

From industries in Rest of World / Sectors	I	II	III	IV	V	VI	VIII	IX	X	XI	XII	XIII	XIV	XV	XVI	XVII	XVIII	XIX	XX	XXI-XXIII
I	-	-	1.16	0.01	-	-	-	-	4.71	0.02	-	-	-	-	-	-	0.01	0.06	-	0.01
II	-	-	0.05	0.35	0.01	0.01	-	-	7.80	-	-	0.03	-	0.01	-	0.14	2.27	0.64	-	-
III	0.35	-	-	0.15	-	-	-	-	24.90	-	-	-	-	-	-	-	-	0.35	-	0.04
IV	0.04	0.01	0.27	-	0.68	0.12	0.01	0.04	31.96	0.01	-	0.02	-	0.02	-	0.13	0.25	1.31	0.01	0.04
V	0.04	0.19	0.93	0.99	-	12.61	1.61	9.25	10.66	-	-	0.07	0.03	0.09	-	5.08	2.96	4.73	0.01	0.11
VI	0.31	0.12	0.60	0.62	4.78	-	0.57	0.42	93.30	0.01	-	0.08	0.01	0.08	-	1.99	5.41	8.91	0.07	0.46
VIII	0.01	-	0.02	0.02	0.34	0.08	-	0.02	2.87	-	-	-	-	-	-	0.04	0.06	5.95	-	0.05
IX	0.12	0.02	1.95	1.02	2.59	2.87	0.77	-	24.47	0.04	-	0.06	0.05	0.02	-	1.49	0.45	5.64	0.12	0.38
X	12.38	10.59	47.29	34.49	14.45	85.34	21.12	25.33	-	11.29	44.54	6.86	14.56	22.55	0.23	48.79	19.83	-	97.05	19.05
XI	-	-	-	0.04	0.02	0.03	0.02	0.02	11.99	-	0.05	-	-	-	-	-	-	-	-	0.02
XII	0.02	0.11	3.16	0.05	0.11	-	0.02	-	23.60	0.02	-	-	-	0.02	-	0.06	0.20	11.16	0.17	0.30
XIII	0.01	0.01	0.45	0.18	0.89	0.36	0.02	0.02	4.15	-	-	-	-	-	-	3.91	0.30	0.15	-	0.01
XIV	0.02	0.04	0.29	0.13	0.23	0.59	0.11	0.06	6.83	-	-	0.03	-	0.02	-	4.75	0.28	1.00	0.06	-
XV	-	-	0.98	0.30	0.19	0.25	0.01	0.06	25.10	0.01	-	0.03	0.01	-	-	0.04	0.10	1.94	0.11	0.66
XVI	-	-	0.02	0.02	0.02	0.04	0.01	0.01	2.72	-	-	-	-	-	-	0.04	0.01	0.45	0.01	0.01
XVII	0.03	0.02	0.10	0.14	0.13	0.07	0.01	0.02	6.95	-	-	-	-	0.01	-	-	0.08	1.32	0.06	0.06
XVIII	0.02	0.02	0.17	0.31	1.13	0.18	0.02	0.10	28.59	-	-	0.03	-	0.02	-	0.05	-	1.14	0.07	0.13
XIX	0.13	0.15	3.92	3.95	9.40	1.39	0.11	0.58	35.99	0.05	0.01	0.35	0.06	0.37	-	1.14	5.24	-	2.42	1.24
XX	0.07	0.01	0.45	0.17	0.79	0.46	0.04	0.16	42.18	0.01	-	0.02	-	0.05	-	0.22	0.19	1.37	-	0.03
XXI-XIII	0.09	0.02	1.10	0.89	0.45	0.79	0.05	0.23	77.89	0.01	0.01	0.02	0.02	0.13	-	0.59	0.71	2.84	0.28	-

For key to sectors see Table 4.2

Table 4.20 RAS weighted inverse matrix multiplier

Sectors \ Sectors	I	II	III	IV	V	VI	VIII	IX	X	XI	XII	XIII	XIV	XV	XVI	XVII	XVIII	XIX	XX	XXI-XXIII
I	1.00	0.01	0.02	0.01	0.01	0.01	0.01	0.01	0.01	0.01	0.01	0.01	0.01	0.01	-	0.01	0.01	0.01	0.01	-
II	0.02	1.01	0.02	0.02	0.02	0.01	0.02	0.02	0.03	0.02	0.02	0.02	0.02	0.02	-	0.02	0.05	0.02	0.02	-
III	0.07	0.04	1.05	0.05	0.03	0.03	0.05	0.04	0.07	0.06	0.05	0.04	0.04	0.04	-	0.04	0.03	0.02	0.04	0.01
IV	0.07	0.05	0.07	1.06	0.06	0.05	0.07	0.06	0.09	0.07	0.06	0.05	0.06	0.05	-	0.06	0.05	0.04	0.05	0.01
V	0.06	0.05	0.07	0.07	1.07	0.11	0.11	0.23	0.08	0.07	0.05	0.05	0.05	0.05	-	0.11	0.10	0.10	0.05	0.01
VI	0.23	0.16	0.21	0.20	0.25	1.15	0.22	0.20	0.30	0.23	0.19	0.17	0.17	0.17	0.01	0.20	0.24	0.19	0.16	0.04
VIII	0.01	0.01	0.02	0.02	0.03	0.01	1.01	0.02	0.02	0.01	0.01	0.01	0.01	0.01	-	0.01	0.01	0.07	0.01	-
IX	0.07	0.05	0.08	0.08	0.11	0.06	0.09	1.07	0.09	0.08	0.06	0.06	0.06	0.05	-	0.07	0.06	0.10	0.05	0.01
X	1.12	0.85	1.03	0.95	0.73	0.76	1.08	0.91	1.60	1.25	1.04	0.84	0.92	0.91	0.03	0.94	0.73	0.45	0.86	0.20
XI	0.02	0.02	0.02	0.02	0.02	0.02	0.02	0.02	0.03	1.03	0.02	0.02	0.02	0.02	-	0.02	0.02	0.01	0.02	-
XII	0.06	0.05	0.10	0.06	0.07	0.04	0.06	0.06	0.09	0.07	1.06	0.05	0.05	0.05	-	0.06	0.06	0.15	0.06	0.01
XIII	0.01	0.01	0.02	0.01	0.03	0.01	0.01	0.01	0.02	0.01	0.01	1.01	0.01	0.01	-	0.05	0.01	0.01	0.01	-
XIV	0.02	0.02	0.02	0.02	0.02	0.02	0.02	0.02	0.02	0.02	0.02	0.02	1.04	0.02	-	0.06	0.02	0.02	0.01	-
XV	0.05	0.04	0.06	0.05	0.04	0.04	0.05	0.05	0.08	0.06	0.05	0.04	0.05	1.04	-	0.05	0.04	0.04	0.04	0.01
XVI	0.01	0.01	0.01	0.01	0.01	-	0.01	0.01	0.01	0.01	0.01	0.01	0.01	0.01	1.00	0.01	0.01	0.01	0.01	-
XVII	0.02	0.01	0.02	0.02	0.02	0.01	0.02	0.01	0.02	0.02	0.02	0.01	0.01	0.01	-	1.01	0.01	0.02	0.01	-
XVIII	0.06	0.05	0.06	0.06	0.06	0.04	0.06	0.06	0.09	0.07	0.06	0.05	0.05	0.05	-	0.05	1.04	0.04	0.05	0.01
XIX	0.11	0.08	0.14	0.15	0.26	0.09	0.11	0.13	0.14	0.12	0.09	0.10	0.08	0.09	-	0.11	0.17	1.06	0.09	0.03
XX	0.09	0.07	0.09	0.07	0.08	0.06	0.09	0.08	0.12	0.10	0.08	0.07	0.07	0.07	-	0.08	0.06	0.05	1.07	0.02
XXI-XXIII	0.17	0.12	0.16	0.15	0.12	0.11	0.16	0.14	0.23	0.18	0.15	0.12	0.13	0.14	-	0.14	0.12	0.10	0.13	1.03
Production multipliers from inverse	3.29	2.71	3.25	3.08	3.01	2.63	3.26	3.11	3.14	3.48	3.05	2.73	2.83	2.82	1.06	3.09	2.84	2.49	2.72	1.42

For key to sectors see Table 4.2

these two matrices be estimated by using the appropriate national input-output coefficients. This set of accounts tends to conceal, within one matrix of parameters, at least two sets of influences, intra-regional effects and inter-regional effects. The former are usually treated in terms of technological requirements, while the latter are normally held to be the consequences of trade between regions.

Figure 4.8 Collapsed accounts and their relationship to West Yorkshire data

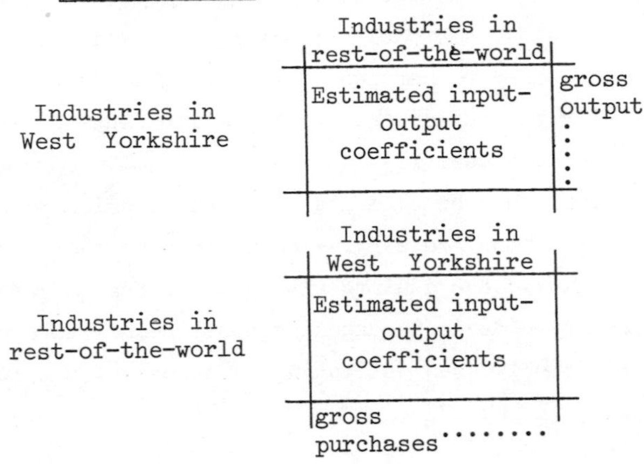

By expanding the accounts shown above we could, however, incorporate technology and trade parameters into our model. As the diagrammatic accounts set out in Figure 4.9 demonstrate, the demand and supply pools referred to earlier are, in fact, the result of adding the elements in sub-matrix A to the elements in B and C respectively. We may also represent our existing information on this diagram, since the gross outputs and gross purchases are the row and column sums of the two sub-matrices (A and B) and (A and C).

Figure 4.9 The expansion of collapsed accounts to produce a dog-leg model

	Industries in West Yorkshire	Industries in rest-of-the-world
Industries in West Yorkshire	A	B
Industries in rest-of-the-world	C	

Note This is a dog-leg model similar to the one referred to in Section 4.2.2 above.

The system of accounts presented above does allow a further series of developments, depending upon the amount of data that is available. Following the suggestions of Wilson (1970), one could estimate the elements of B and C by using singly-constrained maximum-entropy models, and then employ the usual input-output model equations as constraints upon the singly-constrained models. It should be noted, however, that the devices used to fill in the elements of B and C are not spatial interaction models, but show more affinity to the kind of projection models discussed by Bacharach (1969), Lecomber (1975) and Ferragu (1970). Broadly speaking, the estimation of the trade matrices B and C may be carried out by using a production-constrained model for the former and an attraction-constrained model for the latter. The availability of data is crucial. In our case we lack any information on the elements of B and C, which precludes any prospect of calibrating the singly-constrained models. Furthermore, in the case that we are dealing with - a two region model - the spatial interaction-type devices suggested above reduce to a cruder set of models which simply uses estimating equations of the form:

$$X_{ij}^{k} = n_{ij}^{k} G_{i}^{k} \qquad (4.38)$$

where X_{ij}^{k} is the flow of goods k from region i to j; G_{i}^{k} is total output of good k from region i; and n_{ij}^{k} is the propensity of j to import good k from region i. There are two experimental alternatives that might be tried in this situation: (i) more parameters may be introduced by raising the attraction factor (or production factor in the case of the attraction-constrained model) to a power, and then produce synthetic trade matrices by assuming a parameter value and running the model. Model outputs may then be compared with other information from diverse sources to produce what might loosely be called a calibration procedure. An additional parameter may be inserted in the term that allocates commodities to regions (analogous to the cost function in a proper spatial interaction model). Similar intuitive calibration techniques to those mentioned above might be used, although it should be borne in mind that the number of trade matrices offered as alternatives by a two parameter model increases with the square of the number of parameter-values chosen; (ii) the use of singly-constrained models is based on the assumption that no knowledge can be obtained about the input-output coefficients for the regions in question. If this assumption is dropped, then our two region example can be solved in two ways: (a) by assuming initially that both regions have identical input-output coefficient matrices. Such an assumption, in effect, provides both row and column constraints for each of the two trade matrices, which allows them to be balanced iteratively; (b) by assuming that an independent estimate of the regional input-output coefficients is available, and then solving as above. It is of interest to note that these two models are both variants of the Moses-Chenery type of trade coefficient models discussed in Section 4.2.2 above.

4.4.7 The complete accounts

We are now in a position to present three versions of an input-output table for the West Yorkshire conurbation. Tables 4.21 and 4.22 embody the inter-industry accounts based on Hewing's constrained and unconstrained RDS weightings which, it should be remembered, are the main determinants of the trade figures as shown. The construction of Table 4.21 was explained in detail in Sections 4.4.2 to 4.4.6. Table 4.22, the unconstrained version, contains estimates of exports explicitly. Table 4.23 embodies the inter-industry accounts based on the RAS weighting procedure which incorporates its own estimates of trading patterns embodied in the flows matrix. The use of alternative techniques for estimating the inter-industry coefficients, accounts for the variations displayed in the levels and patterns of inter-sectoral transactions, including external trade.

Each of the tables contains a considerable number of residual elements, a fact which reflects the fairly wide diversity of data inputs and estimation procedures used in their compilation. Ideally these residuals might be interpreted as crude estimates of trade, but at this stage of development this would seem presumptuous. The process has, however, pointed to areas where more detailed refinement and investigation might prove profitable. The control totals for the non-manufacturing sectors seem in most cases to have posed problems, particularly sector I (agriculture, forestry and fishing); clearly a more refined method than the use of employment-weighted

Table 4.21 Estimated transactions matrix, West Yorkshire conurbation, 1963, using constrained RDS weightings (£m)

Outputs / Inputs		I	II	III	IV	V	VI	VIII	IX	X	XI	XII	XIII	XIV
I		-	-	3.46	0.02	-	-	-	-	0.99	0.42	-	-	0.09
II		0.03	-	0.23	2.16	0.03	0.21	0.05	0.04	2.80	0.05	0.04	0.55	0.02
III		3.38	0.02	-	0.61	-	0.02	-	-	5.80	-	-	0.02	-
IV		0.85	0.25	2.03	-	2.37	2.73	0.33	0.83	17.04	0.49	0.35	0.47	0.43
V		0.06	0.64	0.46	0.59	-	19.08	3.77	11.88	0.37	0.02	0.12	0.12	0.31
VI		1.11	1.03	0.73	0.91	2.70	-	3.26	1.31	8.01	0.15	0.66	0.34	0.25
VIII		0.04	0.04	0.04	0.04	0.31	0.48	-	0.10	0.39	-	0.03	0.02	0.02
IX		0.30	0.11	1.67	1.06	1.03	7.51	3.11	-	1.48	0.32	1.03	0.20	0.79
X		0.11	0.22	0.15	0.13	0.02	0.80	0.31	0.20	-	0.32	19.27	0.08	0.82
XI		-	-	-	0.03	0.01	0.06	0.05	0.03	0.57	-	5.00	-	0.01
XII		0.01	0.08	0.32	0.01	0.01	-	0.01	-	0.17	0.02	-	-	-
XIII		0.04	0.10	0.58	0.28	0.53	1.39	0.13	0.06	0.38	-	0.02	-	0.19
XIV		0.06	0.23	0.24	0.13	0.09	1.47	0.44	0.13	0.40	0.02	0.08	0.10	-
XV		0.01	0.08	2.72	1.00	0.24	2.14	0.18	0.45	4.92	0.13	0.87	0.32	0.44
XVI		0.04	0.14	0.17	0.22	0.09	1.15	0.49	0.19	1.78	0.14	0.55	0.04	0.16
XVII		0.30	0.36	0.31	0.49	0.17	0.64	0.13	0.11	1.47	0.04	0.13	0.03	0.08
XVIII		0.20	0.59	0.69	1.52	2.11	2.26	0.38	0.99	8.11	0.13	0.36	0.49	0.23
XIX		0.26	0.69	2.70	3.28	3.00	2.93	0.34	1.04	1.75	0.35	1.04	0.89	0.74
XX		0.90	0.26	1.93	0.87	1.58	6.11	0.87	1.82	12.86	0.36	1.30	0.26	0.33
XXI-XIII		0.73	0.34	3.23	3.15	0.61	7.05	0.74	1.71	16.13	0.38	2.00	0.20	1.03
XXIV		-	-	-	-	-	-	-	-	-	-	-	-	-
Sub-total intermediate inputs		8.4	5.2	21.6	16.5	14.9	56.0	14.6	20.9	85.4	3.3	32.8	4.1	5.9
Income from employment		1.4*	9.9	12.3	12.2	11.9	62.4	8.2	11.3	94.3	2.5	19.6	4.1	7.0
Profits**		5.5	§	19.1	14.2	8.5	47.0	4.5	10.5	75.5	2.2	10.6	3.0	5.7
Dwellings		-	-	-	-	-	-	-	-	-	-	-	-	-
Imports	RDS	1.3	1.1	16.1	5.3	3.9	15.0	2.5	5.2	31.4	2.2	2.7	1.3	1.8
	Residuals	2.0	4.5	16.0	15.6	12.1	18.8	3.8	4.9	281.8	4.3	2.6	1.1	4.9
Sub-total primary inputs		10.2	15.5	63.5	47.3	36.4	144.5	19.0	31.9	483.0	11.2	35.5	9.5	19.4
Total inputs		18.6	20.7	85.1	63.8	51.3	199.2	33.6	52.8	568.4	14.5	68.3	13.6	25.3

* Special weights based on Woodward (1970)

** Includes taxes

§ Item included under "fuel & power", Sector XVIII

For key to sectors see Table 4.2

XVII	XVIII	XIX	XX	XXI-XXIII	XXIV	Sub-total intermediate demand	Consumer Expenditure	Public authorities expenditure	Investment		Exports		Sub-total final demand	Total output
									Fixed	Stock	RDS	Residual		
-	0.01	0.02	-	0.07	-	5.1	21.4	1.12	0.1	-		-9.2	13.5	18.6
1.05	6.92	0.48	0.06	0.05	-	15.2	5.7	0.60	0.4	-		-1.3	5.5	20.7
-	-	0.17	-	0.76	-	10.8	45.0	1.00	-	-		32.2	74.3	85.1
1.42	1.14	1.46	0.72	1.62	-	36.5	9.9	3.93	0.6	-		12.3	27.3	63.8
3.70	0.88	0.35	0.06	0.24	-	43.0	0.5	0.23	0.2	0.3		6.4	8.3	51.3
3.57	3.93	1.61	0.89	3.00	-	34.2	3.7	17.71	54.0	1.0		88.5	165.0	199.2
0.11	0.07	1.69	0.07	0.47	-	3.9	8.2	5.14	6.6	1.1		10.4	29.7	33.6
1.87	0.23	0.71	1.07	1.76	-	24.7	3.8	0.68	2.2	-0.6		21.3	28.1	52.8
0.22	0.04	-	3.05	0.32	-	27.2	12.0	5.51	0.1	0.1		517.3	541.2	568.4
-	-	-	-	0.05	-	0.9	-	-	-	6.3		7.6	8.6	14.5
0.01	0.01	0.17	0.18	0.17	-	1.2	6.6	1.80	-	0.2		59.2	67.1	68.3
7.37	0.23	0.03	-	0.08	-	11.4	1.3	-	0.2	-0.5		0.6	2.2	13.6
5.76	0.14	0.12	0.53	0.02	-	10.2	4.9	0.92	1.3	0.1		7.7	15.1	25.3
0.16	0.17	0.80	3.10	9.92	-	28.0	6.8	2.40	-	0.3		6.8	16.0	44.0
0.52	0.04	0.62	0.45	0.46	-	7.4	3.0	0.41	0.2	0.2		0.9	4.6	12.0
-	0.13	0.59	1.80	0.95	-	7.9	11.9	8.93	69.8	0.1		1.1	91.7	99.6
0.31	-	0.68	2.86	2.84	-	25.4	18.9	3.11	6.1	-		6.8	35.0	60.4
1.15	2.15	-	17.11	4.60	-	45.8	23.6	4.26	1.3	-		18.9	48.1	93.9
1.42	0.49	0.88	-	0.63	-	34.4	115.6	3.62	6.7	-		21.4	147.4	181.8
2.52	1.24	1.23	8.50	-	-	53.7	81.7	15.52	4.9	-		10.2	112.3	166.0
-	-	-	-	-	-	-	55.62	-	-	-		-	55.6	55.6
31.1	17.8	11.6	40.4	28.1	-	431.6	385.4	132.5	155.1	8.6		819.0	1,497.0	1,928.5
37.4	11.3	37.2	69.2	119.4	55.6	604.1								604.1
3.8	16.3	14.9	26.8	27.3	-	308.3								308.3
-	-	-	-	-	-	-	50.8						50.8	50.8
10.1	8.6	6.1	9.2	5.9	-	133.8	367.2						367.2	501.0
17.2	6.4	24.1	36.2	14.7	-	450.7								450.7
68.5	42.6	82.3	141.4	137.9	55.6	1,496.9	418.0						418.0	1,914.9
99.6	60.4	93.9	181.8	166.0	55.6	1,928.5	803.4	132.5	155.1	8.6		819.0	1,914.9	3,843.3

Table 4.22 Estimated transactions matrix, West Yorkshire conurbation, 1963, using unconstrained RDS weightings (£m)

Inputs \ Outputs		I	II	III	IV	V	VI	VIII	IX	X	XI	XII	XIII	XIV
I		-	-	3.46	0.02	-	-	-	-	0.99	0.42	-	-	0.08
II		0.02	-	0.23	2.16	0.03	0.21	0.04	0.04	2.80	0.05	0.04	0.55	0.02
III		5.70	0.03	-	1.03	-	0.03	-	-	9.79	-	-	0.03	-
IV		0.85	0.25	2.03	-	2.38	2.73	0.33	0.83	17.04	0.49	0.35	0.47	0.43
V		0.05	0.64	0.46	0.59	-	19.08	3.76	11.87	0.37	0.02	0.12	0.12	0.31
VI		2.06	1.91	1.36	1.69	5.03	-	6.06	2.44	14.91	0.29	1.23	0.64	0.47
VIII		0.04	0.04	0.04	0.04	0.31	0.48	-	0.09	0.39	-	0.03	0.02	0.02
IX		0.45	0.17	2.49	1.58	1.54	11.19	4.63	-	2.20	0.48	1.54	0.30	1.18
X		1.09	2.22	1.44	1.27	0.20	7.93	3.04	1.99	-	3.19	191.74	0.77	8.10
XI		-	-	-	0.04	0.01	0.07	0.05	0.03	0.68	-	6.00	-	0.01
XII		0.01	0.14	0.59	0.01	0.01	-	0.02	-	0.31	0.03	-	-	-
XIII		0.04	0.10	0.58	0.27	0.53	1.39	0.13	0.07	0.37	-	0.02	-	0.19
XIV		0.08	0.32	0.34	0.18	0.12	2.10	0.62	0.19	0.57	0.02	0.11	0.15	-
XV		0.01	0.08	2.72	1.00	0.24	2.14	0.18	0.45	4.91	0.13	0.87	0.31	0.44
XVI		0.04	0.14	0.17	0.22	0.09	1.15	0.49	0.19	1.78	0.14	0.55	0.04	0.16
XVII		0.30	0.36	0.31	0.49	0.17	0.64	0.13	0.11	1.47	0.04	0.13	0.03	0.08
XVIII		0.20	0.59	0.69	1.52	2.11	2.26	0.37	0.98	8.11	0.12	0.36	0.49	0.23
XIX		0.26	0.69	2.69	3.28	3.00	2.93	0.34	1.04	1.75	0.35	1.04	0.89	0.74
XX		0.89	0.26	1.92	0.87	1.58	6.10	0.87	1.82	12.85	0.36	1.30	0.26	0.33
XXI-XXIII		0.72	0.34	3.23	3.15	0.61	7.05	0.73	1.71	16.13	0.38	2.00	0.20	1.03
XXIV		-	-	-	-	-	-	-	-	-	-	-	-	-
Sub-total intermediate inputs		12.8	8.3	24.8	19.4	18.0	67.5	21.8	23.9	97.5	6.5	207.4	5.3	13.8
Income from employment		1.4*	9.9	12.3	12.2	11.9	62.4	8.2	11.3	94.3	2.5	19.6	4.1	7.0
Profits**		5.5		19.1	14.2	8.5	47.0	4.5	10.5	75.5	2.2	10.6	3.0	5.7
Dwellings		-	-	-	-	-	-	-	-	-	-	-	-	-
Imports	RDS	1.3	1.1	16.1	5.3	3.9	15.0	2.5	5.2	31.4	2.2	2.7	1.3	1.8
	Residuals	-2.5	1.4	12.8	12.7	9.0	7.3	-3.4	1.9	269.7	1.1	-172.0	-0.1	-0.3
Sub-total primary inputs		5.8	12.4	60.3	44.4	33.3	131.7	11.8	28.9	470.9	8.0	-139.1	8.3	11.5
Total inputs		18.6	20.7	85.1	63.8	51.3	199.2	33.6	52.8	568.4	14.5	68.3	13.6	25.3

* Special weights based on Woodward (1970)

** Includes taxes

Item included under 'fuel & power' in Sector XVIII

For key to sectors see Table 4.2

XVII	XVIII	XIX	XX	XXI-XXIII	XXIV	Sub-total intermediate demand	Consumer expenditure	Investment		Public authority expenditure	Exports		Sub-total final demand	Total output
								Fixed	Stocks		RDS	Residual		
-	-	0.02	-	0.07	-	5.1	21.4	0.1	-	1.1	-	-9.2	13.5	18.6
1.04	6.91	0.48	0.06	0.05	-	15.2	5.7	0.4	-	0.6	-	-36.6	5.5	20.7
-	-	0.28	-	1.29	-	18.2	45.0	-	-	1.0	7.4	17.4	66.9	85.1
1.41	1.13	1.46	0.72	1.61	-	36.5	9.9	0.6	0.3	3.9	-	12.3	27.3	63.8
3.70	0.87	0.35	0.06	0.28	-	43.0	0.5	0.2	1.0	0.2	-	6.4	8.3	51.3
6.64	7.32	2.98	1.66	5.59	-	63.7	3.7	54.0	1.1	17.7	29.5	29.5	135.5	199.2
0.11	0.07	1.69	0.07	0.47	-	3.9	8.2	6.6	-0.6	5.1	-	10.4	29.7	33.6
2.80	0.34	1.06	1.59	2.62	-	36.8	3.8	2.2	0.1	0.7	-	2.9	16.0	52.8
2.18	0.36	-	30.38	3.14	-	270.3	12.0	0.1	6.3	5.5	12.1	47.0	298.1	568.4
-	-	-	-	0.06	-	7.0	0.9	-	0.2	-	243.2	4.7	7.5	14.5
0.02	0.02	0.31	0.33	0.30	-	2.1	6.6	-	-0.5	1.8	1.17	57.4	66.2	68.3
7.37	0.23	0.03	-	0.08	-	11.5	1.3	0.2	0.1	-	0.95	0.5	2.1	13.6
8.23	0.20	0.17	0.75	0.02	-	14.5	4.9	1.3	0.3	0.9	-	-1.0	10.8	25.3
0.16	0.17	0.79	3.10	9.92	-	28.0	6.8	-	0.2	2.4	4.37	6.8	16.0	44.0
0.52	0.04	0.62	0.45	0.46	-	7.4	3.0	0.2	0.1	0.4	-	0.9	4.6	12.0
-	0.13	0.59	1.80	0.95	-	7.9	11.9	69.8	-	8.9	-	1.0	91.7	99.6
0.31	-	0.68	2.86	2.84	-	25.4	18.9	6.1	-	3.1	-	6.9	35.0	60.4
1.15	2.15	-	17.11	4.60	-	45.8	23.6	1.3	-	4.3	-	18.9	48.1	93.9
1.42	0.49	0.87	-	0.63	-	34.5	115.6	6.7	-	3.6	-	21.4	147.3	181.8
2.52	1.24	1.23	8.50	-	-	53.7	81.7	4.9	-	15.5	-	10.2	112.3	166.0
-	-	-	-	-	-	-	-	-	-	55.6	-	-	55.6	55.6
39.6	21.7	13.6	69.4	35.0	-	730.5	385.4	155.1	8.6	132.5	298.7	207.8	1,198.0	1,928.5
37.4	11.3	37.2	69.2	119.4	55.62	604.1	-	-	-	-	-	-	-	604.1
3.8	16.3	14.9	26.8	27.3	-	308.3	-	-	-	-	-	-	-	308.3
-	-	-	-	-	-	-	50.8	-	-	-	-	-	50.8	50.8
10.1	8.6	6.1	9.2	5.9	-	133.8	367.2	-	-	-	-	-	367.2	501.0
8.74	2.45	22.1	7.2	-21.6	-	154.5	-	-	-	-	-	-	-	154.5
60.0	38.7	80.3	112.4	131.0	55.6	1,198.0	418.0	-	-	-	-	-	418.0	1,616.0
99.6	60.4	93.9	181.8	166.0	55.6	1,928.5	803.4	155.1	8.6	132.5	298.7	207.8	1,616.0	3,544.5

Table 4.23 Extimated transactions matrix, West Yorkshire conurbation, 1963, using RAS adjustment

Inputs \ Outputs	I	II	III	IV	V	VI	VIII	IX	X	XI	XII	XIII	XIV
I	-	-	1.16	0.01	-	-	-	-	4.71	0.02	-	-	-
II	-	-	0.05	0.25	0.01	0.01	-	-	7.80	-	-	0.03	-
III	0.35	-	-	0.15	-	-	-	-	24.9	-	-	-	-
IV	0.04	0.01	0.27	-	0.68	0.12	0.01	0.04	31.96	0.01	-	0.02	-
V	0.04	0.19	0.93	0.99	-	12.61	1.61	9.25	10.66	-	-	0.07	0.03
VI	0.31	0.12	0.60	0.62	4.78	-	0.57	0.42	93.30	0.01	-	0.08	0.01
VIII	0.01	-	0.02	0.02	0.34	0.08	-	0.02	2.87	-	-	-	-
IX	0.12	0.02	1.95	1.02	2.59	2.87	0.77	-	24.47	0.04	-	0.06	0.05
X	12.38	10.59	47.29	34.49	14.45	85.34	21.12	25.33	-	11.29	44.54	6.86	14.56
XI	-	-	-	0.04	0.02	0.03	0.02	0.02	11.99	-	0.05	-	-
XII	0.02	0.11	3.16	0.05	0.11	-	0.02	-	23.60	0.02	-	-	-
XIII	0.01	0.01	0.45	0.18	0.89	0.36	0.02	0.02	4.15	-	-	-	-
XIV	0.02	0.04	0.29	0.13	0.23	0.59	0.11	0.06	6.83	-	-	-	-
XV	-	-	0.98	0.30	0.19	0.25	0.01	0.06	25.10	0.01	-	0.03	0.01
XVI	-	-	0.02	0.02	0.02	0.04	0.01	0.01	2.72	-	-	-	-
XVII	0.03	0.02	0.10	0.14	0.13	0.07	0.01	0.02	6.95	-	-	-	-
XVIII	0.02	0.02	0.17	0.31	1.13	0.18	0.02	0.10	28.59	-	-	0.03	-
XIX	0.13	0.15	3.92	3.95	9.40	1.39	0.11	0.58	25.99	0.05	0.01	0.35	0.06
XX	0.07	0.01	0.45	0.17	0.79	0.46	0.04	0.16	42.18	0.01	-	0.02	-
XXI-XXIII	0.09	0.02	1.10	0.89	0.45	0.79	0.05	0.23	77.89	0.01	0.01	0.02	0.02
XXIV	-	-	-	-	-	--	-	-	-	-	-	-	-
Sub-total intermediate inputs	13.6	11.3	62.9	43.8	36.2	105.2	24.5	36.3	466.8	11.5	44.6	7.6	14.8
Income from employment	1.4*	9.9	12.3	12.2	11.9	62.4	8.2	11.3	94.3	2.5	19.6	4.1	7.0
Profits**	5.5	§	19.1	14.2	8.5	47.0	4.5	10.5	75.5	2.2	10.6	3.0	5.7
Dwellings	-	-	-	-	-	-	-	-	-	-	-	-	-
Imports	-	-	-	-	-	-	-	-	-	-	-	-	-
Sub-total primary inputs	6.9	11.0	31.4	26.4	20.4	109.4	12.7	21.8	169.8	4.7	30.2	7.1	12.7
Residual	-2.0	-1.7	-9.2	-6.4	-5.3	-15.4	-3.6	-5.3	-68.2	-1.7	-6.5	-1.1	-2.2
Total inputs	18.6	20.7	85.1	63.8	51.3	199.2	33.6	52.8	568.4	14.5	68.3	13.6	25.3

* Special weights based on Woodward (1970)

** Includes taxes

§ Items included under 'fuel & power', Sector XVIII

For key to sectors see Table 4.2

XVII	XVIII	XIX	XX	XXI-XXIII	XXIV	Sub-total intermediate demand	Consumer expenditure	Public authority expenditure	Investment		Residuals	Sub-total final demand	Total output
									Fixed	Stocks			
-	0.01	0.06	-	0.01	-	6.0	21.4	1.1	0.1	-	-10.0	12.6	18.6
0.14	2.27	0.64	-	-	-	11.3	5.7	0.6	0.4	-	2.7	9.4	20.7
-	-	0.35	--	0.04	-	25.8	45.0	1.0	-	-	13.3	59.3	85.1
0.13	0.25	1.31	0.01	0.04	-	34.9	9.9	3.9	0.9	0.3	13.9	28.9	63.8
5.08	2.96	4.73	0.01	0.11	-	49.4	0.5	0.2	0.2	1.0	-	2.0	51.3
1.99	5.41	8.91	0.07	0.46	-	117.8	3.7	17.7	54.0	1.1	4.9	81.5	199.2
0.04	0.06	5.95	-	0.05	-	9.5	8.2	5.1	6.6	-0.6	4.8	24.1	33.6
1.49	0.45	5.64	0.12	0.38	-	42.1	3.8	0.7	2.2	0.1	3.9	10.7	52.8
48.79	19.83	-	97.05	19.05	-	535.7	12.0	5.5	0.1	6.3	8.8	32.7	568.4
-	-	-	-	0.02	-	12.8	0.9	-	-	0.2	1.2	2.3	14.5
0.06	0.02	11.16	0.17	0.30	-	39.0	6.6	1.8	-	-0.5	20.9	29.3	68.3
3.91	0.30	0.15	-	0.01	-	10.5	1.3	-	0.2	0.1	1.5	3.1	13.6
4.75	0.28	1.00	0.06	-	-	14.5	4.9	0.9	1.3	0.3	3.9	11.2	25.3
0.04	0.10	1.94	0.11	0.66	-	29.8	6.8	2.4	-	0.2	4.8	14.2	44.0
0.04	0.01	0.45	0.01	0.01	-	3.4	3.0	0.4	0.2	0.1	4.9	8.6	12.0
-	0.08	1.32	0.06	0.06	-	9.0	11.9	8.9	69.8	-	-	90.7	99.6
0.05	-	1.14	0.07	0.13	-	32.0	18.9	3.1	6.1	-	0.2	28.4	60.4
1.14	5.24	-	2.42	1.24	-	66.5	23.6	4.3	1.3	-	-1.8	27.4	93.9
0.22	0.19	1.37	-	0.03	-	46.2	115.6	3.6	6.7	-	9.6	135.5	181.8
0.59	0.71	2.84	0.20	-	-	86.1	81.7	15.5	4.9	-	-22.2	79.9	166.0
-	-	-	-	-	-	-	-	-	-	-	-	-	55.6
68.4	38.4	48.9	100.4	22.6	-	1,181.4	385.4	132.5	155.1	8.6	65.3	746.9	1,928.4
37.4	11.3	37.2	69.2	119.4	55.6	604.1	-	-	-	-	-	-	604.1
3.8	16.3	14.9	26.8	27.3	-	308.3	-	-	-	-	-	-	308.3
-	-	-	-	-	-	-	50.8	-	-	-	-	50.8	50.8
-	-	-	-	-	-	-	367.2	-	-	-	-	367.2	367.2
41.2	27.6	52.1	96.0	146.7	55.6	912.4	418.0	-	-	-	-	418.0	1,330.4
-10.0	-5.6	-7.2	-14.7	-3.3	-	-172.6	-	-	-	-	-	-172.6	-172.6
99.6	60.4	93.9	181.8	166.0	55.6	1,928.3	803.4	132.5	155.1	8.6	65.3	1,164.9	3,090.0

national data is called for. Inspection of Table 4.22 reveals that the pattern of inter-industry flows between sectors X (textiles) and XII (clothing) needs more detailed consideration, since under the assumptions of the unconstrained RDS model, the clothing sector is required to purchase more from the textiles sector than it earned.

4.5 Summary and concluding comments

There are two objectives for this concluding section: first, a summary of the progress made in the course of the chapter together with a review of future prospects based on this progress; and secondly, a preliminary evaluation of the various tables that have been generated by the different accounts and models employed.

In absolute terms, progress within the chapter has been rather limited. Without the initial formal commitment to undertake detailed survey work, any evaluation of achievement should be considered in the light of the objectives outlined in Section 4.3 above. These objectives spoke of a shift from a forecasting framework to a learning framework, and furthermore this shift implied that the final results would by no means consist of one accurate set of social accounts. Rather, it was anticipated that a range of alternative tables would be produced, each embodying a different set of assumptions which were themselves largely reactions to data deficiencies.

The bulk of the work undertaken has been concerned with the establishment of estimates of final demand and primary input data in such a form that they were consistent with known firm data; the remaining efforts were devoted to the largely mechanical process of adjusting national input-output coefficients to meet known regional constraints.

Each of the three transactions tables (4.21-4.23) contains a set of hypotheses about the structure of the West Yorkshire economy but, as hypotheses, these matrices are rather cumbersome in nature. Consequently, preliminary evaluation is attempted by looking at the different sets of production multipliers derived from the inverse of of the ($\underline{I}$-$\underline{a}$) matrices. In all, four sets of multipliers are used for comparison: the national, the unconstrained RDS, the constrained RDS, and the RAS weightings. The results are presented in Table 4.24 below.

Table 4.24 A comparison of production multipliers from West Yorkshire and national inverse coefficient matrices

Sector	Unconstrained RDS production multipliers () = ranks		Constrained RDS production multipliers () = ranks		National production multipliers () = ranks		RAS production multipliers () = ranks	
I	2.02	(3)	1.61	(1)	1.81	(1)	3.29	(2)
II	1.60	(9)	1.34	(13)	1.45	(14)	2.71	(16)
III	1.47	(15)	1.35	(11)	1.70	(5)	3.25	(4)
IV	1.44	(17)	1.34	(12)	1.49	(13)	3.08	(8)
V	1.52	(12)	1.39	(9)	1.55	(11)	3.01	(10)
VI	1.51	(14)	1.38	(10)	1.54	(12)	2.63	(17)
VIII	1.99	(4)	1.60	(2)	1.79	(2)	3.26	(3)
IX	1.67	(6)	1.53	(4)	1.74	(3)	3.11	(6)
X	1.26	(19)	1.20	(19)	1.30	(19)	3.14	(5)
XI	1.64	(7)	1.31	(14)	1.60	(9)	3.48	(1)
XII	4.89	(1)	1.60	(3)	1.73	(4)	3.05	(9)
XIII	1.56	(10)	1.40	(7)	1.59	(10)	2.73	(14)
XIV	1.74	(5)	1.31	(15)	1.45	(15)	2.83	(12)
XV	1.45	(16)	1.28	(16)	1.41	(16)	2.82	(13)
XVI	2.24	(2)	1.47	(5)	1.66	(6)	1.06	(20)
XVII	1.62	(8)	1.42	(6)	1.63	(8)	3.09	(7)
XVIII	1.54	(11)	1.39	(8)	1.64	(7)	2.84	(11)
XIX	1.24	(20)	1.17	(20)	1.30	(20)	2.49	(18)
XX	1.51	(13)	1.28	(17)	1.38	(17)	2.72	(15)
XXI-XXIV	1.32	(18)	1.22	(18)	1.30	(18)	1.42	(19)

For key to sectors see Table 4.2

One of the principal objectives of input-output analysis is the derivation of sectoral multipliers which show the direct and indirect effects of an increase of one pound's (£) worth of expenditure in the final demand sectors. These direct and indirect effects may be felt throughout the economy in at least three ways: via increased gross production by the industrial sectors, by increased levels of employment, and by increased income flows to households. Morrison's work (1973) on the Peterborough economy, drawing upon the precedents set by Hirsch (1959) for St. Louis, and Miernyk (1967) for Boulder, Colorado, demonstrates the use that can be made of these multipliers both for gaining a quantitative measure of the local multiplier effects generated by the economy, and for reviewing the prospects of the economy for expansion. Furthermore, some measure can be made of the most beneficial sectors of the economy, in terms of the increased labour demand and increased household income generated by the production sectors' expanded output. In the context of West Yorkshire, therefore, sectoral multipliers are used as aggregated indices of the complex inter-industry linkages that are assumed to exist in an urban economy as large as that of West Yorkshire.

Examination of Table 4.24 shows that the RAS-based multipliers are rather different from the remainder, both in terms of size and ranking. The size factor can be attributed to the fact that the collapsed accounts format described in Section 4.4.6(c) was used to calculate the direct coefficients table (Table 4.18). These collapsed accounts, employed in the absence of firm data on trading linkages between West Yorkshire and the rest of the world, will of course mean that the multipliers will embody direct and indirect influences that contain imports. Consequently, they should be interpreted as the level of direct and indirect effects induced within and outside West Yorkshire, for a given unit increase in the domestic final demand sectors.

Although the multipliers show considerable variations within the manufacturing sectors, an interesting contrast with Morrison's results for Peterborough emerges. Morrison found that the highest-valued multipliers were in the services and local government sectors; by contrast the three generated sets of multipliers for West Yorkshire all show that these sectors consistently have the lowest values. This would suggest that the pattern of linkages between the manufacturing and service sectors of the West Yorkshire economy are relatively under-developed, a finding that is partially substantiated elsewhere in this book (Chapter 8).

To conclude on a prospective note, it appears that without firm survey data at the local level, input-output models based on secondary data sources will prove of limited value in a strict forecasting framework. In a learning framework, however, the prospects are rather brighter. This chapter has, above all, shown the need for local-scale final demand data or, alternatively, the need for a revised set of accounts that would obviate the large exogenous data inputs required by existing models. Moreover, this chapter has aimed to show the relatively cumbersome nature of existing models <u>as sets of</u>

hypotheses. Large coefficients matrices and their inverses present the analyst with an overload of information from which it is difficult to discern the effects or the sensitivity of his original hypotheses. Further work to develop the hypothesis-testing role of input-output models requires new tools, some of which are still under investigation.

References

Almon, C. (1967) The American economy to 1975,

Artle, R. (1961) On some methods and problems in the study of metropolitan economies, Papers, Regional Science Association, 8, pp. 71-87.

Bacharach, M. (1969) Bi-proportional matrices and input-output change, University of Cambridge, Occasional Papers, Monograph Series, Cambridge University Press.

Baumol, W.J. (1958) Activity analysis in one lesson, American Economic Review, 45, pp. 837-873.

Board of Trade (1964) Report on the Census of Distribution and other Services, 1961, Part 4, Area tables, East and West Ridings Region.

Board of Trade (1970) Report on the Census of Production, 1963, Part 133, Summary Tables.

Britton, J.N.H. (1967) Regional analysis in economic geography, Bell, London.

Broadbent, T.A. (1973) Activity analysis of spatial allocation models, Environment and Planning, 6, pp. 673-691.

Brown, A.J. (1972) The framework of regional economics in the UK, Cambridge University Press.

Central Statistical Office (annually) National Income and Expenditure, HMSO, London.

Central Statistical Office (1965) Abstract of Regional Statistics, No. 1, HMSO, London.

Central Statistical Office (1970) Input-Output Tables for the UK, 1963, Studies in Official Statistics, No. 16, HMSO, London.

Central Statistical Office (1973) Input-Output Tables for the UK, 1968, Studies in Official Statistics, No. 22, HMSO, London.

Chenery, H.B., et al (1953) The structure and growth of the Italian economy, The United States Mutual Security Agency, Rome.

Chisholm, M.J. and O'Sullivan, P. (1973) Freight flows and spatial aspects of Britain's economy, Cambridge University Press.

Commissioners of Inland Revenue (1967) 109th Report, 1965/66, Cmnd 3200, HMSO, London, Appendix III, Survey of Personal Incomes, 1964/65.

Cripps, E.L., Macgill, S.M. and Wilson, A.G. (1974) Energy and material flows in the urban space economy, Transportation Research, 8, pp. 293-305.

Dean, P. (1953) Regional variation in the UK incomes from employment, Journal of Royal Statistical Society, Series A, 116, pp. 123-135.

Department of Employment and Productivity (1970) The New Earnings Survey, 1968, HMSO, London, Table 72.

Department of the Environment (1971) Survey of the Transport of Goods by Road, 1967/68, HMSO, London.

Ferragu, C. and Sakarovitch, M. (1970) A class of structural models for trip distribution, Transportation Research, 4, pp. 87-92.

General Register Office (1966) Census 1961, England and Wales, Workplace Tables, HMSO, London.

General Register Office (1968) Sample Census 1966, Economic Activity County Leaflet, Radnorshire-Yorkshire, HMSO, London.

Goldberg, M.A. (1970) An economic model of intra-metropolitan industrial location, Journal of Regional Science, 10, pp. 75-80.

Green, M.J. (1971) Investment matrices for plant and machinery, 1963 and 1968, Economic Trends, 214, HMSO, London.

Hartwick, J.M. (1971) Notes on the Isard and Chenery-Moses interregional input-output models, Journal of Regional Science, 11, pp. 73-85.

Hewings, G.J.D. (1969) Regional input-output models using national data, West Midlands, Annals of Regional Science, III, pp. 179-191.

Hewings, G.J.D. (1971) Regional input-output models in the UK. Some problems and prospects for the use of non-survey techniques, Regional Studies, 5, pp. 11-22.

Hirsch, W.Z. (1959) Inter industry relations of a metropolitan area, Review of Economics and Statistics, 41, pp. 360-369.

Isard, W. (1951) Inter-regional and regional input-output analysis: a model of a space economy, Review of Economics and Statistics, 33, pp. 318-328.

Isard, W. and Langford, T. (1971) Regional input-output study, Philadelphia input-output study: reflections and reminiscences, MIT Press, Cambridge, Massachusetts and London.

Karaska, G.J. (1968) The variation of input-output coefficients for different levels of aggregation, Journal of Regional Science, 1, pp. 215-228.

Karaska, G.J. (1969) Manufacturing linkages in the Philadelphia economy, some evidence of external agglomerating forces, Geographical Analysis, 1, pp. 354-369.

Lecomber, R. (1975) A critique of methods of adjusting, updating and projecting matrices, in Allen, R.I.G. and Gossling, V.F. (eds) Estimating and projecting input-output coefficients, pp. 1-25, The Input-Output Publishing Company, London.

Leontief, W. and Strout, A. (1963) Multi-regional input-output analysis, in Barna, T. (ed) Structural interdependence and the economy, Macmillan, London.

Linnemann, H. (1966) An econometric model of inter-national trade flows, in Contributions to Economic Analysis Series, North Holland, Amsterdam.

Lipsey, R.G. (1966) An introduction to positive economics, Weidenfield and Nicolson, London.

Meier, R.L. (1962) A communications theory of urban growth, MIT Press, Cambridge, Massachusetts.

Miernyk, W.H. (1966) The elements of input-output analysis, Random House, New York.

Miernyk, W.H. et al (1967) The impact of the space program on a local economy, West Virginia University Press.

Miernyk. W.H. et al (1970) Simulating regional economic development, Heath Lexington.

Ministry of Housing and Local Government (1966) Housing Statistics, 1, Supplementary Tables, Permanent dwellings completed, West Yorkshire Conurbation Housing Data.

Ministry of Housing and Local Government (1966) Housing Statistics, 2, Supplementary Tables, Permanent dwellings completed, West Yorkshire Conurbation Housing Data.

Ministry of Labour (1963) Family Expenditure Survey, Report for 1962, HMSO, London.

Ministry of Transport (1966) Survey of Road Goods Transport, 1962, Statistical Paper 6, Final Results, Geographical Analysis, HMSO, London.

Morrison, W.I. (1973) The development of an urban interindustry model: 2, The structure of the Peterborough economy in 1968, Environment and Planning, 5, pp. 433-460.

Moses, L.N. (1955) The stability of inter-regional trading patterns and input-output analysis, American Economic Review, 45, pp. 803-832.

Moses, L.N. and Williamson, H.F. (1967) The location of economic activity in cities, American Economic Review, 57, pp. 211-222.

Roberts, F.S. (1971) Signed digraphs and the growing demand for energy, Environment and Planning, 3, pp. 395-410.

Sadler, P. and Archer, B. (1973) Regional income multipliers: the Anglesey Study, Bangor Occasional Papers in Economics, Number 1.

Smith, T.B. (1974) A computer program for deriving final demand data for the West Yorkshire conurbation: consumers' expenditure, Technical Working Note, University of Leeds.

Starkie, D.N.M. (1967) Traffic and industry, A study of traffic generation and spatial interaction, Geographical Papers, Number 3, London School of Economics.

Stone, R. (1961) Social accounts at the regional level, a survey, in Regional Economic Planning, pp. 263-296, OEEC, Paris.

Stone, R. (1971) Mathematical models of the economy and other essays, Chapman Hall, London.

Thompson, W.R. (1968) Internal and external factors in the development of urban economies, in Perloff, H.S. and Wingo, L. (jnr) Issues in urban economics, Johns Hopkins Press, Baltimore.

University of Cambridge, Department of Applied Economics (1974) Structural change in the British economy, 1948-1968, Number 12, in A programme for growth, Chapman Hall, London.

Vernon, R. (1960) *Metropolis, 1985*, Harvard University Press, Cambridge, Massachusetts.

Wilson, A.G. (1970) *Entropy in urban and regional modelling*, Monographs in spatial and environmental systems analysis, Pion, London.

Woodward, J. (1965) *Industrial organisation theory and practice*, Oxford University Press, London.

Woodward, V.H. (1970) Regional social accounts for the United Kingdom, *NIESR Research Papers*, *I*, Cambridge University Press, Cambridge.

Chapter 5

Developments of the Lowry model

R.L. Mackett and G.D. Mountcastle

5.1 Introduction

In this chapter the development of two models of urban and regional activities and their spatial distribution are described. They are based on the Model of metropolis developed by Lowry (1964), but have been greatly modified, to make them theoretically more sound and policy oriented, and hence more effective planning tools. The modifications adopted are described in detail. The models are operational and have been tested empirically and found to give reasonable results which are described below.

One of the models has been developed for application at the city scale (and applied to Leeds). The other model has been developed for a sub-regional scale (and applied to the county of West Yorkshire). The two models are based on the same original, but were largely developed independently. Some of the characteristics of each model arise from the different scales of the study areas, others from problems encountered in applying the models. Comparison of the two models yields some interesting contrasts in possible solutions to the problems encountered in this type of model.

Lowry's model for the city of Pittsburgh may be regarded as simple in form, yet having considerable power. The original model described in the next section of this chapter incorporated population, employment, retailing (which meant the whole service sector) and land use, and yet consisted of only nine equations and three inequalities. The solution of the equation sequence requires a computer (except for trivial cases) as iterative techniques are required. A useful device to speed up solution, adopted by Lowry and here, is described in Section 5.3. Lowry's model uses gravity-type submodels to locate population and retail activity. The original versions are not very satisfactory because the models are based on a simple analogy with Newtonian physics, and they locate activities with respect to accessibility only. The entropy maximising techniques developed by Wilson (1970) are used to give an improved theoretical basis to the submodels and allow the introduction of intrinsic attraction factors. These are described in Section 5.4.

Lowry uses a constraint procedure to ensure that only as many residents as can be accommodated in a zone are located there. Unfortunately, the re-allocation of population to other zones to prevent infringement of the constraint means that the final allocation is not in accord with the original specification of the urban system. Wilson (1969) has devised a mechanism for solving this problem, which has been used in several applications in this country, for example in Bedfordshire (Cripps and Foot, 1969) and Nottinghamshire/Derbyshire (Batty, 1971-A). In this study two other similar constraints are introduced to increase the usefulness of the model. The constraint on the location of retail activity to ensure 'clustering' used by Lowry is largely made redundant by the introduction of intrinsic attraction factors and is dropped in one of these studies as in most others in this country, with the notable exception of the Nottinghamshire/Derbyshire study (Batty, 1971-A).

One of the most interesting uses of this type of model is to examine the effects of changes in the urban system on different social (or income) groups. This requires disaggregation of population and employment variables. Problems with obtaining suitable data prevent most model applications from doing this. However, because this is felt to be so important such a disaggregation is introduced into the Leeds model. The available data are far from perfect, but may be sufficient to show some important policy implications and may also help to focus attention on the need for such data. One other operational Lowry-type model that has a social group disaggregation is that in South Hampshire (Rhodes, 1969) and it has been specified theoretically in the Cheshire model (Barras, Broadbent, Cordey-Hayes, Massey and Robinson, 1971). Our methods are described in Section 5.6.

One of the main uses of this type of model is to examine the effects of planning policy controls. These can include a wide range of possibilities. The effect of holding land off the market is examined in both applications. The impact of temporary basic employment in large construction and building schemes is taken into account in the West Yorkshire model. Housing stock is incorporated into the Leeds model. This is complementary to the modelling of social groups and is particularly important at the city scale where available housing is a very real determinant of the capacity of each zone, and can give rise to substantial differences between zones in terms of quality of the environment. In the Leeds model, those in the highest social group are allowed the choice of all available housing, those in the next group choose from those houses remaining, and then the lowest group must live in the remaining houses. By introducing time as an explicit mechanism, it should be quite possible to model 'filtering' in the housing market, that is, the passing of dwellings in an area from use by the highest social group, down the social ladder as the rich move into the newest housing. Housing stock is used in the South Hampshire model, and in the model of Reading, described by Crowther and Echenique (1972) where a separate model of urban stock, based on empirical observation is used to distribute the stock which house the urban activities. The mechanism used here is described in Section 5.7.

One of the most significant developments within the Leeds model is its dynamic structure, as described in Section 5.8; that is, time is introduced into the model explicitly. Briefly, this is done by constraining the model so that a proportion of population and employment is fixed from one time period to the next. The number of jobs is computed and by subtraction, the demand for workers is found. These workers have families which must be housed; the model also allows workers to relocate residences but to keep the same job over time. The model is used to allocate the total population and employment which can be projected exogenously or computed internally using various ratios as Lowry did (although this method is not to be recommended as it places too much emphasis on rates which do not, in fact, remain constant over time). A comparable example of a dynamic Lowry model is that for Reading by Batty (1972), but it does not seem to have the stability of this model. In the West Yorkshire model dynamics are introduced via the attraction factors in the submodel.

In Section 5.9 the possibility of extending the Leeds model to include external zones is discussed. The methods for calibrating the models are described in Section 5.10. The whole Leeds model has been designed to be operational with available data. As a result of this, some of the relationships defined are cruder than might be desired. However, it is felt more important to concentrate on developing a reasonably strong model with a few weak points (which can be improved at a later date), since this will enable the user to investigate many important planning relationships, rather than attempting to refine data inputs for a poorer model.

The solution of the equation system for the Leeds model is described in Section 5.11. The data needs and availability for the models and some uses of the model are described briefly in Section 5.12. Leeds has a population that is static in overall number but not in location, consequently, the model is not designed to operate only in growth context, unlike many other models. Another particular aspect of this model is the incorporation of specific policy variables for housing, employment, population and land use. This is because the model has been designed to test planning policies and to find the effect of resulting changes in the urban system on the population disaggregated by location and social status. The introduction of an explicit dynamic structure means that these effects can be monitored over time. Alternatively, the model can be used for forecasting by giving values to all the inputs and letting the model work its way into the future, adjusting values after each time period if so desired. Other uses of the model are in impact studies to find the effect of a specific input to the urban system, and in plan design by generating several possible futures so then they may be evaluated and the optimum chosen. The chapter concludes with some results in Section 5.13.

5.2 The original model devised by Lowry

The model originally devised by Lowry for the city of Pittsburgh provides a useful starting point. The sequence of equations will follow that of Wilson (1974, Chapter 11), since this is the order for solution and aids comprehension. The notation has been changed so that it is compatible with that used later.

In essence, the model may be described as follows: basic employment is distributed exogenously and these workers are assigned to residences by a gravity model; the dependent families of these workers are generated by applying the inverse activity rate (defined as the ratio of total population to total employment); the population demands services, and these demands are met by non-basic employment, for example, in shops, and these workers are located by means of another gravity model; these workers and their dependent families are located in a similar manner, and also non-basic activities. Thus, further non-basic workers and dependent families are generated and the iteration continued until the increments are insignificant.

(a) Land use

The area of land available (a) for housing (H) in zone j (L_j^{Ha}) is given by

$$L_j^{Ha} = L_j^T - L_j^Z - L_j^B - L_j^{Ku} \quad (5.1)$$

where L_j^T is the total area of zone j; L_j^Z is the area of unusable land in zone j; L_j^B is the area of land used by basic employment in zone j; and L_j^{Ku} is the land used (u) by non-basic activity (labelled by the subscript K) in zone j.

(b) Household sector

The total population in the city (P_c) is given by:

$$P_c = g\Sigma_j E_j^T \quad (5.2)$$

where E_j^T is the total employment in zone j; and g is the inverse of the activity rate. The population in each zone (P_i) is given by:

$$P_i = G\Sigma_j E_j^T f^W(c_{ij}) \quad (5.3)$$

where c_{ij} is the distance (or cost of travel) between zone i and zone j; $f^W(c_{ij})$ is a decreasing function of c_{ij} (W is a label indicating that this function is associated with the work trip); and G is a scaling factor which ensures:

$$\Sigma_i P_i = P_c \quad (5.4)$$

A maximum density constraint is imposed:

$$P_i < D_i^H L_i^{Ha} \quad (5.5)$$

where D_i^H is the maximum residential density permitted in zone i; and L_i^{Ha} is the area of land available for housing in zone i. If this constraint is violated the values of P_i are adjusted to prevent this.

(c) Non-basic sector

Total non-basic employment in sector k (E_{ck}^K) is given by:

$$E_{ck}^K = u_k P_c \tag{5.6}$$

where u_k is the population serving ratio for sector k. A second gravity model is used to locate retail employment in each zone (E_{jk}^K):

$$E_{jk}^K = h_k\{r_k \Sigma_i P_i f_k^K(c_{ij}) + s_k E_j^T\} \tag{5.7}$$

where $f_k^K(c_{ij})$ is a decreasing function of c_{ij}; r_k and s_k determine the relative proportion of sales to shoppers from place of residence and places of work; and h_k is calculated to ensure that:

$$\Sigma_j E_{jk}^K = E_{ck}^K \tag{5.8}$$

A minimum size constraint is applied, to ensure that the retail outlets cluster in centres:

$$E_{jk}^K > E_k^{K\,\underline{min}} \tag{5.9}$$

If this constraint is violated, E_{jk}^K is set to zero. Land used by retail activity (L_j^{Ku}) is given by:

$$L_j^{Ku} = \Sigma_k d_k^K E_{jk}^K \tag{5.10}$$

where d_k^K is the mean area of land used by each worker in sector k; and L^{Ku} is adjusted to ensure that:

$$L_j^{Ku} < L_j^T - L_j^Z - L_j^B \tag{5.11}$$

If this inequality is violated, then L_j^{Ku} is set equal to the right hand side of the inequality, and over crowding is assumed to occur. Total employment in each zone (E_j^T) is given by:

$$E_j^T = E_j^B + \Sigma_k E_{jk}^K \tag{5.12}$$

The model is iterated until convergence.

5.3 Scaling up of employment

Lowry used a neat device to speed up the iterative solution of the model. He computed the total employment in the city, and used this to scale up basic employment, so that rather than generating employment, the solution is one of relocating it. It also provides a useful check on the sum of population and employment in the city. The totals are computed as follows:

from Equation (5.2):

$$P_c = gE_c^T \tag{5.13}$$

Equation (5.12) can be aggregated to

$$E_c^T = E_c^B + \Sigma_k E_{ck}^K \tag{5.14}$$

Equation (5.6) becomes:

$$E_{ck}^K = u_k P_c \tag{5.15}$$

Substituting from Equations (5.15) and (5.13) into Equation (5.14):

$$E_c^T = E_c^B + \Sigma_k u_k g E_c^T \tag{5.16}$$

so that

$$E_c^T = \frac{E_c^B}{1 - g\Sigma_k u_k} \tag{5.17}$$

Substituting from Equation (5.17) into Equation (5.13):

$$P_c = \frac{gE_c^B}{1 - g\Sigma_k u_k} \tag{5.18}$$

Substituting from Equation (5.18) into Equation (5.15):

$$E_{ck}^K = \frac{gu_k E_c^B}{1 - g\Sigma_k u_k} \tag{5.19}$$

Thus from Equations (5.17), (5.18) and (5.19), the total employment, population and retail employment in each sector can be found, and can be used to check the sums of the distribution between zones. Basic employment in each zone can be scaled up using:

$$E_j^T = E_j^B E_c^T / E_c^B \tag{5.20}$$

to give a first approximation to the total employment in each zone.

This will generate a first approximation to the total population in each zone which will demand the total retail employment. The retail employment in each zone is added onto the basic employment in each zone to give a second approximation of the total employment. This sequence is repeated until the distribution of employment or population on one iteration is not significantly different from that on the previous iteration.

The generation of total population and non-basic employment by this model is used in the West Yorkshire model. In the Leeds model, total population and non-basic employment inputs, and the inverse activity (g) and population serving (u_k) ratios are calculated in the model.

5.4 Improvements to the submodels

The gravity models used by Lowry to distribute workers to residences and retail workers to workplaces are not very satisfactory, since accessibility is the only location factor considered. By using the entropy maximising methods of Wilson (1970) more consistent equations can be obtained. These are incorporated into both the residential and non-basic submodels for the Leeds case.

Equations (5.2), (5.3) and (5.4) can be replaced by the following:

$$T_{ij} = B_j^W W_i^W E_j^T e^{-\beta^W c_{ij}} \tag{5.21}$$

where T_{ij} is the number of workers in zone j who live in zone i; E_j^T is the number of workers in zone j; W_i^W is the attraction of zone i for residential activity; c_{ij} is the distance (or cost of travel) between zone i and zone j; β^W is a parameter which determines the effect of distance on the choice of residential location; and B_j^W is a balancing factor given by:

$$B_j^W = \{\Sigma_i W_i^W e^{-\beta^W c_{ij}}\}^{-1} \tag{5.22}$$

to ensure that

$$\Sigma_i T_{ij} = E_j^T \tag{5.23}$$

that is, to ensure that the total number of work trips from zone j, is equal to the number of workers in that zone.

The number of employed residents living in zone i (R_i) is given by:

$$R_i = \Sigma_j T_{ij} \tag{5.24}$$

The population in each zone (P_i) is given by:

$$P_i = gR_i \tag{5.25}$$

where g is the inverse of the activity rate.

The retail submodel may also be replaced by a more satisfactory set of equations. One of the major difficulties in making the original version of Lowry's model operational is the values to be given to weighting factors r_k and u_k in Equation (5.7), which determine the relative proportion of sales to shoppers from places of residence and places of work. Not only would a special survey almost certainly be required, but also problems would arise with other trips, for example, trips by shoppers who have taken children to school. It is much simpler to locate retail activity with respect to residences only, but to introduce a factor representing intrinsic attractiveness of the zone for shopping. This can be interpreted as representing the various characteristics of the zone, including the number of workers there. This is also more realistic if the model is being applied to an existing area, with retail centres already there, rather than trying to generate a whole city.

So far in this chapter, the term retail, as used by Lowry and the term non-basic, have been used synonymously; in Britain the word retail is usually taken to refer to shopping activity only. From now on we will use the word 'retail' to mean this, and the word 'service' to mean other non-basic activities such as educational, medical and other services. The retail model can be developed in a similar manner to the residential location model above:

$$S_{ijr} = A^R_{ir} F_{ir} W^R_{jr} e^{-\beta^R_r c_{ij}} \tag{5.26}$$

where S_{ijr} is the sales of goods type r in zone j to residents in zone i; W^R_{jr} is the attractiveness of zone j for the purchase of goods type r; F_{ir} is the expenditure on goods type r, by residents of zone i; c_{ij} is the distance (or cost of travel) between zone i and zone j; β^R_r is a parameter which determines the effect of distance upon the choice of shopping centre; and A_{ir}^R is a balance factor given by:

$$A_{ir}^R = \{\Sigma_j W_{jr}^R e^{-\beta_r^R c_{ij}}\}^{-1} \qquad (5.27)$$

to ensure that

$$\Sigma_j S_{ijr} = F_{ir} \qquad (5.28)$$

that is, that the sale of goods to shoppers from zone i is equal to the total expenditure by residents of zone i, for goods type r. F_{ir} in Equation (5.26) is given by:

$$F_{ir} = P_i e_r \qquad (5.29)$$

where e_r is the mean expenditure per head on goods type r; and P_i is the population of zone i. It will be noticed that this version of the model permits the introduction of sales, thus increasing the number of useful outputs from the model. It may be noticed that Equation (5.26) resembles the retail model devised by Lakshmanan and Hansen (1965). Employment in zone j in retail sector r (E_{jr}^R) is given by:

$$E_{jr}^R = b_r \Sigma_i S_{ijr} \qquad (5.30)$$

where b_r is the inverse of the sales per retail worker for sector r.

The service demand model is given by:

$$J_{ijk} = A_{ik}^K {}_k P_i W_{jk}^K e^{-\beta_k^K c_{ij}} \qquad (5.31)$$

where J_{ijk} is the demand for service activity k in zone j by residents of zone i, measured in employment units; v_k is the population serving ratio for sector k; W_{jk}^K is the attractiveness of zone j for service activity k; P_i is the population of zone i; c_{ij} is the distance (or cost of travel) between zone i and zone j; β_k^K is the parameter which determines the effect of distance from population on the location of service activity k; and A_{ik}^K is a balancing factor given by:

$$A_{ik}^K = \{\Sigma_j W_{jk}^K e^{-\beta_k^K c_{ij}}\}^{-1} \qquad (5.32)$$

to ensure that

$$\Sigma_j J_{ijk} = v_k P_i \tag{5.33}$$

that is, that the total service activity k generated by residents of zone i is equal to the demand for it in zone i. Employment in service section k (E^K_{jk}) is given by:

$$E^K_{jk} = \Sigma_i J_{ijk} \tag{5.34}$$

Total employment in zone j (E^T_j) is given by:

$$E^T_j = E^B_j + \Sigma_r E^R_{jr} + \Sigma_k E^K_{jk} \tag{5.35}$$

Land use by non-basic activity (L^{Gu}_j) is given by:

$$L^{Gu}_j = \Sigma_r d^R_r E^R_{jr} + \Sigma_k d^K_k E^K_{jk} \tag{5.36}$$

where d^R_r is the land used by retail workers in sector r; d^K_k is the land used by service workers in sector k; and L^{Gu}_j is used in a constraint similar to Equation (5.11) to ensure that as much land is used by non-basic activity as is available.

In the West Yorkshire model tests began with the original model and initially simpler improvements were added serially from such a basis. In West Yorkshire, the zones vary greatly in size and the potential and submodels of the original formulation of the Lowry model were unable to allow for this. Particular attention had to be paid to this point. In this study area, Heckmondwike Urban District for example, is less than 700 acres, while Nidderdale Rural District is over 75,000 acres. As far as the residential location potential model is concerned, both these zones have the same attraction to a householder. With the smallest zones the density constraint reduces any overestimation of population but these zones will then be full to capacity. In order to allow for overestimation of smaller zone populations and underestimation of large zone populations which may have a relatively small basic employment, the area available for housing was included in the potential model as an attractiveness factor, giving

$$P_i = G_1 \Sigma_j E^T_j L^{Ha}_i c_{ij}^{-\beta^W} \tag{5.37}$$

where

$$G_1 = \frac{P_c}{\Sigma_j \Sigma_i E_j^T L_i^{Ha} c_{ij}^{-\beta^W}} \tag{5.38}$$

L_i^{Ha} is initially set to the total land area excluding unusable and basic industrial land and in later iterations is set to the land available for housing. Initially

$$L_i^{Ha} = L_i^T - L_i^Z - L_i^B \tag{5.39}$$

and succeeding iterations

$$L_i^{Ha} = L_i^T - L_i^Z - L_i^B - L_i^{Ku} \tag{5.40}$$

L_i^Z includes land too steep for building, badly drained or mineral workings unfit for building. The retail employment submodel like the residential location submodel takes no account of zone size. It was decided therefore to include an area attractiveness factor in both the home to shop and work to shop trip equations. The initial value in a model run was taken to be a third of L_j^{Ha} the land available for housing, but in later iterations was the retail land predicted from the previous iteration. Initially then

$$L_j^{Ku} = \tfrac{1}{3}L_j^{Ha} = \tfrac{1}{3}(L_j^T - L_j^Z - L_j^B) \tag{5.41}$$

In succeeding iterations

$$L_j^{Ku} = \Sigma_k d_k^K E_{jk}^K \tag{5.42}$$

The original Lowry model allowed for overcrowding of services if

$$\Sigma_k d_k^K E_{jk}^K > L_j^T - L_j^Z - L_j^B \tag{5.43}$$

and then L_j^{Ku} was set to

$$L_j^{Ku} = L_j^T - L_j^Z - L_j^B \tag{5.44}$$

Zones where such overcrowding occurred would have a zero household population. With the large zones of West Yorkshire all of which contain some population the model restricted retail land use to only one third of the land available. So if

$$\Sigma_k d_k^K E_{jk}^K > \tfrac{1}{3}(L_j^T - L_j^Z - L_j^B) \tag{5.45}$$

we set

$$L_j^{Ku} = \tfrac{1}{3}(L_j^T - L_j^Z - L_j^B) \qquad (5.46)$$

This allowed for every zone always to have some population. The new retail employment equations were then

$$E_{jk}^{HK} = h_k(\Sigma_i r_k P_i L_j^{Ku} c_{ij}^{-\beta_k^K}) \qquad (5.47)$$

$$E_{jk}^{WK} = h_k s_k E_j^T L_j^{Ku} \qquad (5.48)$$

$$h_k = \frac{E_{ck}^K}{\Sigma_j(\Sigma_i r_k P_i L_j^{Ku} c_{ij}^{-\beta_k^K} + s_k E_j^T L_j^{Ku})} \qquad (5.49)$$

$$E_{jk}^K = E_{jk}^{HK} + E_{jk}^{WK} \qquad (5.50)$$

where E_{jk}^{WK} is retail employment generated from workplace; and E_{jk}^{HK} is retail employment generated from home.

A minimum size of L_j^{Ku} of 30 acres was specified to cater for zones which may have very small predicted retail employment. If very small values for L_j^{Ku} existed this would cause the related zone's retail employment to become progressively smaller for the local services in zones where the minimum size constraint did not allow any other type of services.

Thus, if

$$\Sigma_k d_k^K E_j^K < 30 \qquad (5.51)$$

we put

$$L_j^{Ku} = 30 \qquad (5.52)$$

This last problem can be dealt with by dividing the retail land area between the various k types. A minimum size of 10 acres for each type could then be used to prevent zeros appearing in the attractiveness factors which would of course result in a predicted zero employment, so that

$$L_{jk}^{Ku} = 10 \quad \text{if} \quad d_k^K E_j^K < 10 \qquad (5.53)$$

for any k. The retail employment potential model would then become:

$$E_{jk}^{HK} = h_k(\Sigma_i r_k P_i L_{jk}^{Ku} c_{ij}^{-\beta_k^K}) \tag{5.54}$$

$$E_{jk}^{WK} = h_k(s_k E_j^T L_{jk}^{Ku}) \tag{5.55}$$

$$h_k = \frac{E_{ck}^K}{\Sigma_j(\Sigma_i r_k P_i L_{jk}^{Ku} c_{ij}^{-\beta_k^K} + s_k E_j^T L_k^{Ku})} \tag{5.56}$$

In the West Yorkshire model a further modification to the attraction factors is introduced, since trips are not directly proportional to the area available for housing which is used as an attractiveness factor. An α parameter has been introduced into the residential location model to reduce the dominance of the area attractiveness factor over the population predicted. As with the β parameter only one is defined for the whole region but there may be a case for zone specific values of α. The revised submodel then becomes

$$P_i = G_1 \Sigma_j \{E_j^T (L_j^{Ha})^{\alpha^W} c_{ij}^{-\beta^W}\} \tag{5.57}$$

where

$$G_1 = \frac{P_c}{\Sigma_i \Sigma_j \{E_j^T (L_i^{Ha})^{\alpha^W} c_{ij}^{-\beta^W}\}} \tag{5.58}$$

The same principle applies to the retail employment submodel for which the area attractiveness factors are included. A separate parameter is defined for each service type:

$$E_{jk}^{HK} = h_k \Sigma_i r_k P_i (L_{jk}^{Ku})^{\alpha_k^K} c_{ij}^{-\beta_k^K} \tag{5.59}$$

$$E_{jk}^{WK} = h_k s_k E_j^T (L_{jk}^{Ku})^{\alpha_k^K} \tag{5.60}$$

$$h_k = \frac{E_{ck}^K}{\Sigma_j \{\Sigma_i r_k P_i (L_{jk}^{Ku})^{\alpha_k^K} c_{ij}^{-\beta_k^K} + s_k E_j^T (L_{jk}^{Ku})^{\alpha_k^K}\}} \tag{5.61}$$

5.5 Constraints in the submodels

In the West Yorkshire application, the original Lowry model was applied initially with the sequence of equations outlined in Section 5.2 and the density and retail minimum size constraints applied at the end of each iteration. The procedure used for the constraints at first distributed any excess population or retail employment from one zone to its nearest neighbour. The zones and redistributions were dealt with in zone number order thus making the order of the numbering of the zones significant. It also meant that the final distribution of population was not in accordance with Equation (5.3).

To remove these two means of distortion the constraint procedure outlined by Wilson (1969, 1974, Chapter 11) was used. For the residential location potential model, this requires the definition of sets Z_1 - zones with a population infringing the density constraint:

$$P_i > L_i^{Ha} D_i^H \tag{5.62}$$

and Z_2, with zones satisfying the density constraint:

$$P_i < L_i^{Ha} D_i^H \tag{5.63}$$

The union of these sets is $Z = Z_1 U Z_2$, which is, of course, all zones. For zones in set Z_1, P_i is set equal to $L_i^{Ha} D_i^H$ and the excess population is distributed to zones in set Z_2 using the same residential location model with a new total population and smaller sets of zones. That is

$$P_i = L_i^{Ha} D_i^H \quad \text{for} \quad i \varepsilon Z_1 \tag{5.64}$$

$$P_i = G_2 \Sigma_i T_{ij} \quad \text{for} \quad i \varepsilon Z_2 \tag{5.65}$$

where

$$G_2 = \frac{P_c - \Sigma_{i \varepsilon Z_1} L_i^{Ha} D_i^H}{\Sigma_{i \varepsilon Z_2} \Sigma_j T_{ij}} \tag{5.66}$$

T_{ij} is the journey to work matrix and P_c is the total population in the region. The equations are solved iteratively until Z_1 is the null set. In the improved residential location submodel used in the Leeds model the method used was for zones in set Z_1 to have the population fixed exogenously by means of the constraint

$$\Sigma_j T_{ij} = R_i \quad \text{for} \quad i\varepsilon Z_1 \tag{5.67}$$

where T_{ij} is the number of workers in zone j who live in zone i; and R_i is the number of employed residents in zone i. A constraint of the form of Equation (5.27) applies:

$$\Sigma_i T_{ij} = E_j^T \quad \text{for all j} \tag{5.68}$$

The residential location model is given by:

$$T_{ij} = A_i^W B_j^W R_i E_j^T e^{-\beta^W c_{ij}} \quad \text{for} \quad i\varepsilon Z_1 \tag{5.69}$$

and

$$T_{ij} = B_j^W W_i^W E_j^T e^{-\beta^W c_{ij}} \quad \text{for} \quad i\varepsilon Z_2 \tag{5.70}$$

where A_i^W is a balancing factor given by:

$$A_i^W = \{\Sigma_j B_j^W E_j^T e^{-\beta^W c_{ij}}\} \quad \text{for } i\varepsilon Z_1 \tag{5.71}$$

to ensure constraint (5.67) is met, and B_j^W is a balancing factor given by

$$B_j^W = \{\Sigma_{i\varepsilon Z_1} A_i^W R_i e^{-\beta^W c_{ij}} + \Sigma_{i\varepsilon Z_2} W_i^W e^{-\beta^W c_{ij}}\}^{-1} \tag{5.72}$$

to ensure constraint (5.68) is met. The number of employed residents in zones in the unconstrained set is given by:

$$R_i = \Sigma_j T_{ij} \quad \text{for} \quad i\varepsilon Z_2 \tag{5.73}$$

Population (P_i) is then given by:

$$P_i = gR_i \tag{5.74}$$

where g is the inverse of the activity rate. The population must meet the constraints equivalent to Equation (5.5), that is

$$P_i < L_i^{Ha} D_i^H \tag{5.75}$$

where L_i^{Ha} is the area of land available for housing in zone i; and D_i^H is the density of housing in zone i. This constraint ensures that only the population that can be accommodated in a zone is allocated to it. It is possible to define two other similar constraints:

$$P_i < P_i^{\underline{max}} \tag{5.76}$$

$$P_i > P_i^{min} \quad (5.77)$$

where P_i^{max} is the maximum desired population in zone i; and P_i^{min} is the minimum desired population in zone i. These two constraints can be used to test the effect of certain policy decisions by setting a population maximum or minimum and ensuring that the model meets these constraints. Note that the right hand side of constraint (5.75) varies as the area of land varies in the model solution. When the population has been fixed by one of these constraints, the zone is transferred to set Z_1 and the values of R_i for Equation (5.69) is found from

$$R_i = P_i/g \quad (5.78)$$

The redistribution of the excess population may cause one or more of the constraints to be violated in other zones, so the process is repeated until none of the constraints is violated.

A similar mechanism is introduced into the non-basic submodel in the West Yorkshire model. For service employment, taking each service type separately, the employment of the zone with the smallest employment of the particular type (k) is redistributed to the other zones if it is less than the minimum size constraint. The next smallest employment is then redistributed and so on until the smallest employment in any one zone is equal to or greater than the minimum size constraint. For each of these redistributions or iterations sets Z_3 and Z_4 are defined: $j \varepsilon Z_3^K$ if $E_{jk}^K < E_k^{K\,min}$ is the minimum size constraint for service k and $E_{jk}^K < X_p^K$ where X_p^K is the pth from minimum of the total set E_{jk}^K. The remaining zones are in set Z_4, and for these we define

$$h_k' = \frac{E_{ck}^K}{\Sigma_{j \varepsilon Z_4^K} S_{jk}^K} \quad (5.79)$$

Then

$$E_{jk}^K = 0 \quad \text{if} \quad j \varepsilon Z_3^K \quad (5.80)$$

$$= h_k' S_{ij} \quad \text{if} \quad j \varepsilon Z_4^K \quad (5.81)$$

where

$$S_{jk}^K = c^K \Sigma_i P_i f_k^K(c_{ij}) + s_k E_j^T \quad (5.82)$$

For each service type, Equations (5.79) to (5.82) are solved iteratively until a p value is reached such that $X_p^K > E_k^{K\ min}$. If one or more E_{jk}^K's are equal this can be dealt with quite simply by dealing with the relevant zones in any order.

The density and minimum size constraints were originally checked at the end of each iteration: that is, equation order (5.12), (5.2), (5.3), (5.6), (5.7), (5.8), (5.9), (5.10), (5.1), (5.5) from Section 5.2. The density constraint was tested after the new retail employment and retail land area was produced. However, the retail employment is dependent on population in each zone. It is therefore more sensible to test the density constraints using the retail land area from the previous iteration before the retail submodel. The precise zonal populations would then be used in the retail submodel for each iteration. The equation sequence would then be (5.12), (5.2), (5.3), (5.1), (5.5), (5.6), (5.7), (5.10), (5.11), (5.9).

The value of the minimum size constraint for service employment $E_k^{K\ min}$ can have a significant effect on the results of the model. Zones in set $j \varepsilon Z_3^K$ defined in the subsection above will have a reduced population potential compared with $j \varepsilon Z_4^K$ for any service type k. In practice the minimum size constraint for local services has set Z_3^1 as a null set, but for neighbourhood services a minimum size constraint of 150 persons leaves Z_3^2 as a null set but one of 300 persons results in Z_3^2 including upwards of six zones. By referring to the Minimum List Headings for the service industries for each zone, two or three zones could be said not to contain any significant neighbourhood service employment. A minimum size constraint of 250 persons was defined by using some form of calibration to be described later.

For the third type of services - metropolitan - the set Z_4^3 is particularly significant. From the Minimum List Headings five zones would in practice appear to contain metropolitan services but using Lowry's minimum size constraint of 10,000 employees only Leeds and Bradford will fall into this category. One of 7,000 produces four zones but a fifth zone (Wakefield County Borough) is not defined as containing Metropolitan services until the constraint is reduced to 3,500 and then not on every run of the model (with different parameter values). The case of Wakefield County

Borough will be discussed in detail later. The constraints were taken as having the following sizes: 30, 250 and 3,500 for the three service types defined for West Yorkshire.

Also significant for the service employment distribution is the total size of each category E^K_{ck}. This in turn is related to the basic employment definition. The latter was defined largely by the generally accepted collection of categories and Minimum List Headings, that is categories 1-16 excluding printing and publishing and air transport, sea transport and several small Minimum List Headings included in the service categories. This definition was however refined since certain zones had excessively large numbers employed in headings normally found in the service sectors. Examples of these were railways in some mining areas, national government in Wakefield, and construction in areas with new motorways and power stations. Large amounts of employment of this kind was defined as basic. For banks, insurance and further education a minimum requirement analysis was undertaken and any excess over the minimum requirements was defined as basic.

Any alteration to the basic employment of any zone affects the total employment in the service sectors. These were distinguished largely by distributing the total employment in each Minimum List Heading between each sector according to the proportion of total employment of the heading in different zone sizes. For example motor repairers may occupy 3% of the employment in Denholme Urban District but 4% in Leeds County Borough. As Denholme from observed data (for a previous time period) would not satisfy the minimum size constraint for neighbourhood services motor repairers would be divided into 75% for the local services and 25% between the other types. In practice the calculation is more complex and may perhaps be a little arbitary for some Minimum List Headings for a 10% sample of a small population (the case in 1966). Any adjustment to the basic employment in large zones usually affects the metropolitan type services but for smaller zones no particular trend can be observed.

5.6 Social group disaggregation

The models defined so far do not differentiate between different groups in the population. If the model is being used in policy analysis the impact can only be considered in spatial terms, but by disaggregating by social groups (which may be regarded as a proxy for income), another dimension of impact can be examined. This disaggregation is illustrated by the Leeds model.

The simplest way to disaggregate is to distinguish different values of β^W; that is, to model the different effects of distance in the work trip characteristics on the social groups, since the higher the social group, the higher the income, and so the longer the trip length and the wider the choice of residential location can be. Equations (5.69), (5.70), (5.71), (5.72), (5.73) and (5.74) with the subscript q for social group can be written as

$$T_{ijq} = A^W_{iq} B^W_{jq} R_{iq} E^T_{jq} e^{-\beta^W_q c_{ij}} \quad \text{for } i\varepsilon Z_1 \tag{5.83}$$

$$T_{ijq} = B^W_{jq} W^W_{iq} E^T_{jq} e^{-\beta^W_q c_{ij}} \quad \text{for } i\varepsilon Z_2 \tag{5.84}$$

$$A^W_{iq} = \{\Sigma_j B^W_{jq} E^T_{jq} e^{-\beta^W_q c_{ij}}\}^{-1} \quad \text{for } i\varepsilon Z_1 \tag{5.85}$$

$$B^W_{jq} = \{\Sigma_{i\varepsilon Z_1} A^W_{iq} R_{iq} e^{-\beta^W_q c_{ij}} + \Sigma_{i\varepsilon Z_2} W^W_{iq} e^{-\beta^W_q c_{ij}}\}^{-1} \tag{5.86}$$

$$R_{iq} = \Sigma_j T_{ijq} \quad \text{for } i\varepsilon Z_2 \tag{5.87}$$

$$P_{iq} = g_q R_{iq} \tag{5.88}$$

where T_{ijq} is the number of workers in a social group q who work in zone j and live in zone i; R_{iq} is the number of employed residents in social group q who live in zone i; E^T_{jq} is the total employment in social group q in zone j; c_{ij} is the distance (or cost of travel) between zone i and zone j; β^W_q is a parameter which determines the effect of distance on the choice of residential location for social group q; and A^W_{iq} and B^W_{jq} are balancing factors to ensure that the constraints

$$\Sigma_j T_{ijq} = R_{iq} \tag{5.89}$$

$$\Sigma_i T_{ijq} = E^T_{jq} \tag{5.90}$$

are met respectively. Total population in each zone (P_i) is given by:

$$P_i = \Sigma_q P_{iq} \tag{5.91}$$

It would be quite possible to disaggregate the retail and service submodels in a similar manner, modelling different spatial behaviour for each social group, but the increased demands for data and computer time and storage would probably not be justified by the fairly small effect on the overall shape of the city. Thus, these two submodels are not disaggregated. The expenditure term, however, can be refined slightly: total expenditure on goods type r in zone i (F_{ir}) for Equation (5.26) is now given by

$$F_{ir} = \Sigma_q P_{iq} e_{rq} \tag{5.92}$$

where e_{rq} is the mean expenditure per head in social group q on goods type r. Total population in each zone, for Equation (5.31) is given by Equation (5.91).

5.7 Some model developments to reflect policy controls

In Section 4 above, land areas were introduced as attractiveness factors. Several of the zones in West Yorkshire are rural, with large land areas which in the submodels of the West Yorkshire model will become extremely attractive to residential and service use. In reality, the land in these areas would be suitable for residential use, but is not 'on the market' for development. We therefore introduce a further type of land use L_i^h - land zoned off the market - which can be added to the unusable and basic industrial land as not available for housing or services. Equation (5.40) then becomes

$$L_i^{Ha} = L_i^T - L_i^Z - L_i^B - L_i^h \tag{5.93}$$

for the first iteration. Subsequently, in further iterations Equation (5.41) becomes:

$$L_i^{Ha} = L_i^T - L_i^Z - L_i^B - L_i^h - L_j^{Ku} \tag{5.94}$$

Similarly, Equation (5.42) for the first iteration becomes:

$$L_i^{Ku} = \frac{1}{3}(L_i^{Ha}) = \frac{1}{3}(L_i^T - L_i^Z - L_i^B - L_i^h) \tag{5.95}$$

In the dynamic model the areas zoned off the market will be progressively released through time as could be expected to occur in the real situation.

The density constraint and area zoned off the market can be used as policy controls within the model. As will be seen in the results section, they turn out to be significant. An additional constraint was introduced into the West Yorkshire model to cater for large amounts of temporary basic employment which needs to be discounted as a generator of population. This temporary basic employment E_j^{Bt} was used for a few zones containing large construction and building schemes such as motorways and power stations. A set of zones Z_5 was defined with this type of employment. Equation (5.57) becomes, for set $j \varepsilon Z_5$, where $E_j^{Bt} > 0$

$$P_i = G_1 \Sigma_j \{(E_j^T - E_j^{Bt})(L_i^{Ha})^{\alpha^W} c_{ij}^{-\beta^W}\} \qquad (5.96)$$

$$G_1 = \frac{P_c}{\Sigma_i \Sigma_j (E_j^T - E_j^{Bt})(L_i^{Ha})^{\alpha^W} c_{ij}^{-\beta^W}} \qquad (5.97)$$

In practice, the temporary basic employment for zones in set Z_5 is subtracted at the beginning of the first iteration and it takes no part in the iteration procedure. After convergence the E_j^{Bt}'s are added to the total employment to give a correct total.

Many of the applications of the Lowry-type models in Britain have been at the sub-regional scale, using local authority areas as zones. Lowry's original application in Pittsburgh was at the urban or city scale, and it is here that most trips are made. Only a small proportion of work trips cross local authority area boundaries. Also, if policy analysis is being considered, a study area containing zones under the control of many authorities will show conflicts which partly arise because of the number of authorities concerned, and probably little change can be brought about since resources cannot be freely moved. However, in a city under a single authority, there is a much greater chance of the model being a useful planning tool since resources can be concentr-ated where they are most needed. One of the most important aspects of policy is housing. In terms of the Lowry model at the city scale, therefore, it is important to incorporate housing stock explicitly since this represents an important constraint on residential location. With the social group disaggregation introduced in the previous section, the model can then be used to examine the relationships between social status and residential choice. Thus, housing stock was introduced into the Leeds model via constraint (5.75)

$$P_{iq} < H^{a}_{iq} o_q \qquad (5.98)$$

where P_{iq} is the population in social group q in zone i; H^{a}_{iq} is the number of houses available to social group q in zone i; and o_q is the occupancy rate for social group q, that is the mean number of residents per dwelling. The attraction of a zone for residence for social group q (W^{W}_{iq}) may be taken to be the number of houses available for that social group (H^{a}_{iq}) that is[1]:

$$W^{W}_{iq} = H^{a}_{iq} \qquad (5.99)$$

It seems realistic to permit those in the highest social group to have the first choice of housing, let the next social group have the choice of the remaining housing stock, and so on, until the group at the bottom of the social scale have to live in the remaining housing stock, which has not attracted other residents. Thus, for a city with three distinguishable social groups the number of houses available for each social group is given by

$$H^{a}_{iq} = H^{V}_{i} \quad \text{for} \quad q = 1 \qquad (5.100)$$

$$H^{a}_{iq} = H^{V}_{i} - P_{i1}/o_1 \quad \text{for} \quad q = 2 \qquad (5.101)$$

$$H^{a}_{iq} = H^{V}_{i} - P_{i1}/o_1 - P_{i2}/o_2 \quad \text{for } q = 3 \qquad (5.102)$$

where H^{V}_{i} is the number of vacant houses in zone i. Houses may be vacant because they have been vacated by out-migrants (H^{M}_{i}) or because they are new (H^{N}_{i}):

$$H^{V}_{i} = H^{M}_{i} + H^{N}_{i} \qquad (5.103)$$

---

[1] A possible modification to be tested later would be to take W^{W}_{iq} as $H^{a}_{iq} W^{W'}_{iq}$, where $W^{W'}_{iq}$ represented features of attractiveness other than availability - such as quality and price.

5.8 Dynamics

For a dynamic model, a fundamental alteration was made to the submodels and the structure of the West Yorkshire model. In place of the potential models used by Lowry, spatial interaction models with attractiveness factors of the type described for the Leeds model in Section 5.4 were introduced. Then, for each time period the model is iterated until convergence is reached after which new population totals, basic employment data, land use data and parameters are new model inputs. The model which has developed so far requires most of the data to be generated afresh for every time period. It is hoped that in later versions more endogenous data can be used, generated from one time period to the next, so that attractiveness factors, for example, can relate to the results of the previous time period. The total area of each zone, permanently unusable land and distance matrix are held constant for the whole span of the model, although the last could in principle be altered.

The dynamic features introduced into this version are related mainly to the attractiveness variables W_i^W and W_{jk}^{HK}, W_{jk}^{WK}. At first, they were taken to be the area available for housing from the previous time period, but later were represented as general accessibility variables with the possibility of other factors being introduced as multiples. That is

$$W_i^W(t) = L_i^V(t)\{\Sigma_j E_j^T(t-1)f^W(c_{ij})(t-1)\}^{\alpha^W} \tag{5.104}$$

where $L_i^V(t)$ is vacant land $\{L_i^{Ha}$ from Equation (5.93)$\}$ and also

$$W_{jk}^K(t) = L_i^V(t)\{\Sigma_j E_{jk}^K(t-1)f_k^K(c_{ij})(t-1)^{\alpha_k^K} \tag{5.105}$$

Residential location was then given as an attraction constrained spatial interaction model

$$T_{ij} = B_j^W W_i^W E_j^T f^W(c_{ij}) \tag{5.106}$$

where W_i^W is the attractiveness factor for residence.

$$B_j^W = \{\Sigma_i W_i^W f^W(c_{ij})\}^{-1} \tag{5.107}$$

$$P_i = g\Sigma_j T_{ij} \tag{5.108}$$

$$g = \frac{P_c}{\Sigma_i \Sigma_j T_{ij}} \tag{5.109}$$

where g is the usual constant to make sure the population sums to the given population P. Other factors will be introduced that can be added to the model as required. There is also the usual density constraint:

$$P_i < D_i^H L_i^{Ha} \tag{5.110}$$

where

$$L_i^{Ha} = L_i^T - L_i^Z - L_i^B - L_i^h - L_i^{Ku} \tag{5.111}$$

As before, define sets Z_1 and Z_2 such that $i \epsilon Z_1$ where $P_i > L_i^{Ha} D_i^H$ and $i \epsilon Z_2$ where $P_i < L_i^{Ha} D_i^H$. For $i \epsilon Z_1$, put

$$P_i = L_i^{Ha} D_i^H \tag{5.112}$$

Since workers in either set compete for the same jobs, we have

$$T_{ij} = B_j^W W_i^W E_j^T f^W(c_{ij}) \quad \text{for } i \epsilon Z_2 \tag{5.113}$$

and

$$T_{ij} = A_i^W B_j^W R_i E_j^T f^W(c_{ij}) \text{ for } i \epsilon Z_1 \tag{5.114}$$

where

$$R_i = P_i / g \tag{5.115}$$

and the balancing factors are

$$B_j^W = \{\Sigma_{i \epsilon Z_1} A_i^W R_i f^W(c_{ij}) + \Sigma_{i \epsilon Z_2} W_i^W f^W(c_{ij})\}^{-1} \tag{5.116}$$

$$A_i^W = \{\Sigma_j B_j^W E_j^T f^W(c_{ij})\}^{-1} \tag{5.117}$$

Equations (5.116) and (5.117) are iterated until A_i^W and B_j^W converge. g and P_i are calculated from Equations (5.109) and (5.108).

The home to service model becomes

$$T_{ijk}^{HK} = r_k e_{ik}^{HK} P_i A_{ik}^{HK} W_{jk}^{HK} f_k^{HK}(c_{ij}) \tag{5.118}$$

where e_{ik}^{HK} is expenditure on services of type k per person in zone i for home to service trips; W_{jk}^{HK} is attractiveness of zone j for service type k for home to service trip; and r_k is a factor representing the relative importance of home to service trips. The balancing factors of this singly constrained model are

$$A_{ik}^{HK} = \{\Sigma_j W_{jk}^{HK} f_k^{HK}(c_{ij})\}^{-1} \tag{5.119}$$

and retail employment generated from residences can then be calculated as

$$E^{HK}_{jk} = v^H_k \Sigma_i T^{HK}_{ijk} \tag{5.120}$$

where

$$v^H_k = \frac{r_k E^K_{ck}}{\Sigma_i \Sigma_j T_{ijk}} \tag{5.121}$$

A 'work to service' term was also added to this model, as a more general version of Lowry's original:

$$T^{WK}_{ijk} = s_k e^{WK}_{ik} E^T_i A^{WK}_{ik} W^{WK}_{jk} f^{WK}_k (c_{ij}) \tag{5.122}$$

where e^{WK}_{ik} is expenditure on services type k per person in zone i for work to service trips; W^{WK}_{jk} is attractiveness of zone j for service type k for home to service trips; and s_k is relative importance of work to service trips. The balancing factors are

$$A^{WK}_{ik} = \{\Sigma_j W^{WK}_{jk} f^{WK}_k (c_{ij})\}^{-1} \tag{5.123}$$

and the contribution to service employment is

$$E^{WK}_{jk} = v^W_k \Sigma_i T^{WK}_{ijk} \tag{5.124}$$

where

$$v^W_k = \frac{s_k E^K_{ck}}{\Sigma_i \Sigma_j T^{WK}_{ijk}} \tag{5.125}$$

so that total service employment is

$$E^K_{jk} = E^{HK}_{jk} + E^{WK}_{jk} \tag{5.126}$$

This is subject to the minimum size constraint

$$E^K_{jk} > E^{K\,\underline{min}}_k \tag{5.127}$$

As described for the static version of the model starting with the smallest zonal employment of all the zones, providing it does not satisfy the constraints, the excess employment is redistributed among the other zones. This procedure continues until

$$X^K_p > E^{K\,\underline{min}}_k \tag{5.128}$$

where X^K_p is the pth from smallest of the employment totals.

Set Z_3^K then comprises zones where $E_j^K > X_{p-1}^K$ where p-1 is the number of zones not satisfying the minimum size constraint. For set Z_3^K we set,

$$E_{jk}^K = 0 \tag{5.129}$$

and for $j \varepsilon Z_4^K$:

$$T_{ijk}^{HK} = r_k e_{ik}^{HK} P_i A_{ik}^{HK} W_{jk}^{HK} f_k^{HK}(c_{ij}) \tag{5.130}$$

$$T_{ijk}^{WK} = s_k e_{ik}^{WK} E_i^T A_{ik}^{WK} W_{jk}^{WK} f_k^{WK}(c_{ij}) \tag{5.131}$$

where

$$v_k^H = \frac{r_k E_{ck}^K}{\Sigma_i \Sigma_{j\varepsilon Z_4^K} T_{ijk}^{HK}} \tag{5.132}$$

$$v_k^W = \frac{s_k E_{ck}^K}{\Sigma_i \Sigma_{j\varepsilon Z_4^K} T_{ijk}^{WK}} \tag{5.133}$$

$$A_{ik}^{HK} = \{\Sigma_{j\varepsilon Z_4^K} W_{jk}^{HK} f_k^{HK}(c_{ij})\}^{-1} \tag{5.134}$$

$$A_{ik}^{WK} = \{\Sigma_{j\varepsilon Z_4^K} W_{jk}^{WK} f_k^{WK}(c_{ij})\}^{-1} \tag{5.135}$$

Service land use is given by

$$L_i^{Ku} = \Sigma_k d_k^K E_{jk}^K \tag{5.136}$$

As with the previous versions this land use is restricted to one third of possible land available:

$$L_i^{Ku} < \tfrac{1}{3}(L_i^T - L_i^B - L_i^Z - L_i^h) \tag{5.137}$$

If this constraint is infringed, we put

$$L_i^{Ku} = \tfrac{1}{3}(L_i^T - L_i^B - L_i^Z - L_i^h) \tag{5.138}$$

Finally, total employment can be obtained as

$$E_j^T = E_j^B + \Sigma_k E_{jk}^K \tag{5.139}$$

The equations are iterated from residential location to the above equation {(5.106)-(5.139)} until convergence is reached. Initially E_j^T is set equal to E_j^B in the usual way and

$$L_j^{Ha} = L_i^T - L_i^B - L_i^Z - L_i^h \tag{5.140}$$

In the Leeds model because of the social group disaggregation, the dynamic version allows the simulation of 'filtering' in the housing stock; that is, the gradual decline in the status of the housing in an area as the rich move further and further out, so that their places are taken by the next group and so on. The oldest houses, which tend to be near the city centre often accommodate the very poor, and other deprived groups.

In a given time period, people living and working in the city can change one or both of their place of residence and work, thus four types of mover behaviour can be considered (following Wilson, 1970): (i) those with new place of residence and place of work; (ii) those with new place of residence, but the same place of work; (iii) those with the same place of residence, but a new place of work; and (iv) those with the same places of residence and work as at the beginning of the preceding time period. These four types must all be incorporated into the residential location model. Clearly, constraint (5.60) will apply automatically to those who have remained in the same residences over the time period, but new constraints must be introduced to ensure that the model locates correctly those who have moved. The residential location model for Leeds then becomes {replacing Equations (5.83) and (5.84)}:

$$T_{ijq}^{(1)(1)} = A_{iq}^{W} B_{jq}^{W} R_{iq}^{(1)} E_{jq}^{T(1)} e^{-\beta_q^W c_{ij}} \quad i\varepsilon Z_1 \tag{5.141}$$

$$T_{ijq}^{(1)(1)} = B_{jq}^{W} W_{iq}^{W} E_{jq}^{T(1)} e^{-\beta_q^W c_{ij}} \quad i\varepsilon Z_2 \tag{5.142}$$

$$T_{ijq}^{(1)(2)} = A_{iq}^{W} B_{jq}^{W} R_{iq}^{(1)} E_{jq}^{T(2)} e^{-\beta_q^W c_{ij}} \quad i\varepsilon Z_1 \tag{5.143}$$

$$T_{ijq}^{(1)(2)} = B_{jq}^{W} W_{iq}^{W} E_{jq}^{T(2)} e^{-\beta_q^W c_{ij}} \quad i\varepsilon Z_2 \tag{5.144}$$

$$T_{ijq}^{(2)(1)} = A_{iq}^{W} B_{jq}^{W} R_{iq}^{(2)} E_{jq}^{T(1)} e^{-\beta_q^W c_{ij}} \quad \text{all } i \tag{5.145}$$

$$T_{ijq}^{(2)(2)} = A_{iq}^{W} B_{jq}^{W} R_{iq}^{(2)} E_{jq}^{T(2)} e^{-\beta_q^W c_{ij}} \quad \text{all } i \tag{5.146}$$

where $T_{ijq}^{(1)(1)}$ is the number of workers in social group q who have newly located residences in zone i and workplace in zone j during the time period; $T_{ijq}^{(1)(2)}$ is the number of workers in social group q, who have newly located residences in zone i, but have remained at the same workplace location in zone j during the time period; $T^{(2)(1)}_{ijq}$ is the number of workers in social group q, who have remained in the same residential location, but have newly located workplace in zone j during the time period; $T^{(2)(2)}_{ijq}$ is the number of workers in social group q who have remained in the same residential location in zone i, and workplace in zone j, during the time period; $R^{(1)}_{iq}$ is the number of newly located residents in zone i, in social group q; $R^{(2)}_{iq}$ is the number of residents in zone i, in social group q, who have not changed residential location during the previous time period; $E^{T(1)}_{jq}$ is the number of workers in social group q, with a newly located workplace in zone j; $E^{T(2)}_{jq}$ is the number of workers in social group q who have remained in the same workplace location in zone j; and A^W_{iq}, B^W_{jq} are balancing factors. A^W_{iq} is given by

$$A^W_{iq} = \{\Sigma_j B^W_{jq} E^T_{jq} e^{-\beta^W_q c_{ij}}\}^{-1} \quad \text{for } i\varepsilon Z_1 \tag{5.147}$$

to ensure that

$$\Sigma_j T^{(1)(1)}_{ijq} + \Sigma_j T^{(1)(2)}_{ijq} = R^{(1)}_{iq} \text{ for } i\varepsilon Z_1 \tag{5.148}$$

and

$$\Sigma_j T^{(2)(1)}_{ijq} + \Sigma_j T^{(2)(2)}_{ijq} = R^{(2)}_{iq} \text{ for all } i \tag{5.149}$$

B^W_{jq} is given by

$$B^W_{jq} = \{\Sigma_{i\varepsilon Z_1} A^W_{iq} R^{(1)}_{iq} e^{-\beta^W_q c_{ij}} + \Sigma_{i\varepsilon Z_2} W^W_{iq} e^{-\beta^W_q c_{ij}} + \Sigma_i A^W_{iq} R^{(2)}_{iq} e^{-\beta^W_q c_{ij}}\}^{-1} \tag{5.150}$$

to ensure that

$$\Sigma_i T^{(1)(1)}_{ijq} + \Sigma_i T^{(2)(1)}_{ijq} = E^{T(1)}_{jq} \tag{5.151}$$

and

$$\Sigma_i T^{(1)(2)}_{ijq} + \Sigma_i T^{(2)(2)}_{ijq} = E^{T(2)}_{jq} \tag{5.152}$$

The number of employed residents in social group q, who have not changed residential location ($R^{(2)}_{iq}$) is given by:

$$R^{(2)}_{iq} = P^{(2)}_{iq}/g_q \tag{5.153}$$

The equivalent population ($P_{iq}^{(2)}$) is given by:

$$P_{iq}^{(2)}(t) = P_{iq}(t-1) - \{M_{cq}^{T}(t-1,t) - \Sigma_i H_{iq}^{D}(t-1,t)o_q\}P_{iq}(t-1)/P_{cq}(t-1) - H_i^{D}(t-1,t)o_q \quad (5.154)$$

where $P_{iq}(t-1)$ is the population in social group q in zone i at time t-1; $M_{cq}^{T}(t-1,t)$ is the total number of people in social group q who have moved residence during the time period t-1 to t; $H_{iq}^{D}(t-1,t)$ is the number of houses occupied by social group q in zone i, that have been demolished during the period t-1 to t; and o_q is the occupancy rate for social group q. Equation (5.154) gives the number of people who have remained in the same residential location, by subtracting voluntary migrants and forced migrants from the population at time t-1. Forced migrants are those who have had their houses demolished. Constraints (5.98), (5.76) and (5.77) are modified since the model must locate non-moving residents correctly:

$$R_{iq}^{(1)} < H_{iq}^{a}o_q/g_q \quad (5.155)$$

$$R_{iq}^{(1)} < P_{iq}^{max}/g_q - R_{iq}^{(2)} \quad (5.156)$$

$$R_{iq}^{(1)} > P_{iq}^{min}/g_q - R_{iq}^{(2)} \quad (5.157)$$

The number of houses available for each social group (H_{iq}^{a}) given by Equations (5.100), (5.101) and (5.102), must be modified to take into account non-movers to avoid double countings:

$$H_{iq}^{a} = H_i^{V} \quad \text{for } q=1 \quad (5.158)$$

$$H_{iq}^{a} = H_i^{V} - \{P_{i1} - R_{i1}^{(2)}g_1\}/o_1 \quad \text{for } q=2 \quad (5.159)$$

$$H_{iq}^{a} = H_i^{V} - \{P_{i1} - R_{i1}^{(2)}g_1\}/o_1 - \{P_{i2} - R_{i2}^{(2)}g_2\}/o_2 \quad \text{for } q=3 \quad (5.160)$$

As in the previous section, houses may be vacant because they are new or because they have been vacated by migrants; thus repeating

Equation (5.103):

$$H_i^V = H_i^M + H_i^V \qquad (5.161)$$

Houses vacated by migrants (H_i^M) are given by:

$$H_i^M = H_i^S(t-1) - \Sigma_q P_{iq}^{(2)}/o_q - \Sigma_q H_{iq}^D(t-1,t) \qquad (5.162)$$

where $H_i^S(t-1)$ is the stock of housing in zone i at time (t-1); and $P_{iq}^{(2)}$ is the number of members of social group q in zone i who have not moved place of residence during the preceding time period, given in Equation (5.154). The total number of new houses in the city at time t{ $H_c^N(t)$} is given by:

$$H_c^N(t) = \Sigma_q H_{cq}^O(t) - \Sigma_i H_i^S(t-1) + \Sigma_i \Sigma_q H_{iq}^D(t-1,t) \qquad (5.163)$$

where $H_{cq}^O(t)$ is the total number of houses occupied by social group q at time time; and $H_{iq}^D(t-1,t)$ is the number of houses occupied by social group q in zone i demolished during the time period t-1 to t. $H_{cq}^O(t)$ is given by

$$H_{cq}^O(t) = P_{cq}(t)o_q \qquad (5.164)$$

where $P_{cq}(t)$ is the total population in the city in social group q at time t, and is an exogenous input to this model. In the absence of other information, the number of new houses is distributed between zones in proportion to the potential number of houses that can be accommodated on the area of land available for housing

$$H_i^N = H_c^N L_i^{Ha} D_i^H / \Sigma_i L_i^{Ha} D_i^H \qquad (5.165)$$

where L_i^{Ha} is the land available for housing in zone i; and D_i^H is the density of housing in zone i. It may be that the model is being used to test the effect of locating a new housing development, so Equation (5.165) can be modified to take this into account

$$H_i^N = H_i^{NPX} + H_i^{NCX}$$
$$+ (H_c^N - \Sigma_j H_j^{NPX} - \Sigma_j H_j^{NCX}) L_j^{Ha} D_j^H / \Sigma_j L_j^{Ha} D_j^H \qquad (5.166)$$

where H_i^{NPX} is the number of private houses being located exogenously in zone i; and H_i^{NCX} is the number of council houses being located exogenously in zone i. The land available for houses is the area of vacant land less that used by non-basic activity, since this is given preference (as Lowry did), because in general, non-basic activity can out-bid residential activity for land in the city:

$$L_i^{Ha} = L_i^{Ga} - L_i^{Gu} \tag{5.167}$$

where L_i^{Ga} is the land available for non-basic activity and housing in zone i; and L_i^{Gu} is the land used by non-basic activity in zone i, on the previous iteration from Equation (5.36). The land available for non-basic activity and housing (L_i^{Ga}) is given by:

$$\begin{aligned} L_i^{Ga}(t) = L_i^V(t) - L_i^{Hu}(t-1) + \Sigma_q H_{iq}^D(t-1,t)/D_i^H(t) \\ - H_i^{NPX}(t)/D_i^{NPX}(t) \\ - H_i^{NCX}(t)/D_i^{NCX}(t) \end{aligned} \tag{5.168}$$

where $L_i^V(t)$ is the area of vacant land in zone i at time t; $L_i^{Hu}(t)$ is the area of land used by housing at the previous time point; D_i^{NPX} is the density of exogenously located private housing in zone i; and D_i^{NCX} is the density of exogenously located council housing in zone i. The area of vacant land in zone i (L_i^V) is given by:

$$L_i^V(t) = L_i^T - L_i^Z(t) - L_i^B(t) - L_i^h(t) \tag{5.169}$$

where L_i^T is the total area of land in zone i; $L_i^Z(t)$ is the area of unusable land in zone i at time t; $L_i^B(t)$ is the area of land used by basic employment in zone i at time t; and $L_i^H(t)$ is the area of land being held off the market in zone i at time t.

In the dynamic version the residential attraction factor (W_{iq}^W) can be modified to take into account not only the number of available houses, but also the fact that new residents tend to locate near members of their own social group:

$$W_{iq}^W(t) = H_{iq}^a(t)P_{iq}(t-1)/\Sigma_q P_{iq}(t-1) \tag{5.170}$$

(and may also have a $W_{iq}^{W'}$ factor of the type mentioned earlier). This will help to ensure that members of the higher social groups locate in 'high status' areas, rather than those most accessible to their workplaces. The number of employed residents in zones belonging to set Z_2 ($R^{(1)}_{i\cdot q}$) is given by:

$$R^{(1)}_{i\cdot q} = \Sigma_j T^{(1)(1)}_{ijq} + \Sigma_j T^{(1)(2)}_{ijq} \quad \text{for } i\varepsilon Z_2 \tag{5.171}$$

The equivalent population $P^{(1)}_{i\cdot q}$ is given by:

$$P^{(1)}_{i\cdot q} = g_q R^{(1)}_{i\cdot q} \quad \text{for } i\varepsilon Z_2 \tag{5.172}$$

After constraints (5.155) to (5.157) have been met for all zones the equivalent population is found:

$$P^{(1)}_{i\cdot q} = g_q R^{(1)}_{i\cdot q} \quad \text{for } i\varepsilon Z_1 \tag{5.173}$$

The total population in each social group in each zone ($P_{i\cdot q}$) is given by:

$$P_{i\cdot q} = P^{(1)}_{i\cdot q} + P^{(2)}_{i\cdot q} \tag{5.174}$$

In the original model derived by Lowry basic employment was an exogenous input. In practice basic employment tends to be very conservative, and to remain in the same location over time. Thus, we now allow the exogenous introduction and removal of basic employment, but assume that the rest grows or declines at the same rate in all zones. Thus basic employment is given by:

$$\begin{aligned} E^B_{i\cdot q}(t) &= E^{BNX}_{i\cdot q}(t) - E^{BDX}_{i\cdot q}(t) \\ &\quad + \{ E^B_{cq}(t) - \Sigma_j E^{BNX}_{j\cdot q}(t) \\ &\quad + \Sigma_j E^{BDX}_{j\cdot q}(t)\} \left\{ \frac{E^B_{i\cdot q}(t-1)}{\Sigma_j E^B_{j\cdot q}(t-1)} \right\} \end{aligned} \tag{5.175}$$

where $E^B_{i\cdot q}(t)$ is the basic employment in social group q in zone i at time t; $E^{BNX}_{i\cdot q}(t)$ is the new exogenously located employment in social group q in zone i at time t; and $E^{BDX}_{i\cdot q}(t)$ is the basic employment that has been exogenously removed in social group q in zone i at time t. Land used by basic employment ($L^B_{i\cdot}$) is located in proportion to employment:

$$L^B_{i\cdot}(t) = L^B_{i\cdot}(t-1)\, \Sigma_q E^B_{i\cdot q}(t) / \Sigma_q E^B_{i\cdot q}(t-1) \tag{5.176}$$

Both the retailing and service submodels must be modified to ensure that workers who have not moved are located correctly by the model. The retailing submodel is given by:

$$S_{ijr}^{(1)} = A_{i.r}^{R} F_{i.r} W_{.jr}^{R} e^{-\beta_r^R c_{ij}} \tag{5.177}$$

$$S_{ijr}^{(2)} = A_{i.r}^{R} B_{.jr}^{R} F_{i.r} S_{.jr}^{(2)} e^{-\beta_r^R c_{ij}} \tag{5.178}$$

where $S_{ijr}^{(1)}$ is the volume of sales of goods type r, in zone j to residents of zone i, by shop workers who have moved job location since the previous time period; $S_{ijr}^{(2)}$ is the volume of sales of goods type r, in zone j, to residents of zone i, by shop workers who have not moved job location since the previous time point; $S_{.jr}^{(2)}$ is the volume of sales of goods type r in zone j by workers who have not moved job location since the previous time point; $F_{i.r}$ is the expenditure on goods type r by residents of zone i; and $W_{.jr}^{R}$ is the attractiveness of zone j for sales of goods type r; this must take into account only sales by workers who have changed job location; it can also take into account sales to nearby workers:

$$W_{.jr}^{R}(t) = E_{.jr}^{R(1)}(t-1)\Sigma_q E_{.jq}^{T}(t)/\Sigma_q E_{.jq}^{T}(t-1) \tag{5.179}$$

Thus the attraction is the employment of newly located workers at time t-1, modified by the change in the overall employment distribution during the period t-1 to t. This means that while Equations (5.177) and (5.178) locate sales with respect to the distribution of population because of the function

$$e^{-\beta_r^R c_{ij}}$$

the distribution of employment also influences the distribution of sales since retail employment at the initial point in the time may be considered as a manifestation of the location of both population and employment at earlier points in time, and this term will take into account variation in the distribution of employment over time. The term $A_{i.r}^{R}$ in Equations (5.177) and (5.178) is a balancing factor given by:

$$A^R_{ir} = \{\Sigma_j W^R_{jr} e^{-\beta^R_r c_{ij}} + \Sigma_j B^R_{jr} S^{(2)}_{jr} e^{-\beta^R_r c_{ij}}\}^{-1} \tag{5.180}$$

to ensure that

$$\Sigma_j S^{(1)}_{ijr} + \Sigma_j S^{(2)}_{ijr} = F_{ir} \tag{5.181}$$

that is, that the total flow of sales to zone i is equal to the total expenditure by residents of that zone, for goods type r. The term B^R_{jr} in Equation (5.178) is a balancing factor given by:

$$B^R_{jr} = \{\Sigma_i A^R_{ir} F_{ir} e^{-\beta^R_r c_{ij}}\}^{-1} \tag{5.182}$$

to ensure that

$$\Sigma_i S^{(2)}_{ijr} = S^{(2)}_{jr} \tag{5.183}$$

that is, that the model allocates the correct volume of sales to non-moving retail workers. The volume of sales by non-moving retail workers in sector r in zone j is given by Equation (5.206) below. Total sales of goods type r in zone j (S_{jr}) are given by:

$$S_{jr} = \Sigma_i S^{(1)}_{ijr} + S^{(2)}_{jr} \tag{5.184}$$

Total employment of newly located retail workers in shops type r in zone j, ($E^{R(1)}_{jr}$) is given by:

$$E^{R(1)}_{jr} = b_r S^{(1)}_{ijr} \tag{5.185}$$

where b_r is the inverse of the sales per retail worker for sector r. Retail employment in each social group of newly located workers in each zone ($E^{R(1)}_{jrq}$) is given by:

$$E^{R(1)}_{jrq} = E^{R(1)}_{jr} E^R_{crq} / E^R_{cr} \tag{5.186}$$

where E^R_{crq} is the retail employment in each social group in the whole city. Total retail employment in sector in social group q in zone j is given by:

$$E^R_{jrq} = E^{R(1)}_{jrq} + E^{R(2)}_{jrq} \tag{5.187}$$

where $E^{R(2)}_{jrq}$ is given by Equation (5.202) for the appropriate point in time. The service submodel is given by:

$$J^{(1)}_{ijk} = A^K_{ik} v_k P_i W^K_{jk} e^{-\beta^K_k c_{ij}} \tag{5.188}$$

$$J^{(2)}_{ijk} = A^K_{ik} B^K_{jk} v_k P_i E^{K(2)}_{jk} e^{-\beta^K_k c_{ij}} \tag{5.189}$$

where $J^{(1)}_{ijk}$ is the demand for service activity k in zone j by residents of zone i, met by workers who have moved job location during the preceding time period; $J^{(2)}_{ijk}$ is the demand for service activity k in zone j by residents of zone i, met by workers who have not moved job location during the preceding time period; $E^{K(2)}_{jk}$ is the employment in sector k in zone i of workers who have not moved job location during the preceding period; P_i is the population of zone i; v_k is the population serving ratio for sector k; and W^K_{jk} is the attractiveness of zone j for service sector k; as in the retail model this must take into account the fact that it only applies to new workers; we only wish to take the effect of demand from nearby workers for service sector 1 (professional services), but not for sector 2 (education) or sector 3 (medical, dental and miscellaneous) which are located with respect to residential population, hence:

$$W^K_{jk}(t) = E^{K(1)}_{jk}(t-1)\Sigma_q E^T_{jq}(t)/\Sigma_q E^T_{jq}(t-1) \quad \text{for } k=1 \tag{5.190}$$

$$W^K_{jk}(t) = E^{K(1)}_{jk}(t-1) \quad \text{for } k=2,3 \tag{5.191}$$

The same argument about demand from nearby workers applies to sector 1 as that for retail activity. The term A^K_{ik} in Equations (5.188) and (5.189) is a balancing factor given by

$$A^K_{ik} = \{\Sigma_j W^K_{jk} e^{-\beta^K_k c_{ij}} + \Sigma_j B^K_{jk} E^{K(2)}_{jk} e^{-\beta^K_k c_{ij}}\}^{-1} \tag{5.192}$$

to ensure that

$$\Sigma_i J^{(1)}_{ijk} + \Sigma_j J^{(2)}_{ijk} = v_k P_i \tag{5.193}$$

That is, the total service requirements received by zone i for sector k, is equal to the demand for such service activity in that zone. The term B^K_{jk} in Equation (5.189) is a balancing factor given by

$$B^K_{jk} = \{\Sigma_i A^K_{ik} v_k P_i e^{-\beta^K_k c_{ij}}\}^{-1} \qquad (5.194)$$

to ensure that

$$\Sigma_i J^{(2)}_{ijk} = E^{K(2)}_{jk} \qquad (5.195)$$

That is, the supply of service activity sector k, in zone j, that is met by non-moving workers, is equal to employment in that sector in that zone. Total employment of new workers in service sector k in zone j is then given by:

$$E^{K(1)}_{jk} = \Sigma_i J^{(1)}_{ijk} \qquad (5.196)$$

Service employment of newly located workers in social group q is given by:

$$E^{K(1)}_{jkq} = E^{K(1)}_{jk} E^K_{ckq}/E_{ck} \qquad (5.197)$$

Total employment in service sector k in zone j is given by:

$$E^K_{jkq} = E^{K(1)}_{jkq} + E^{K(2)}_{jkq} \qquad (5.198)$$

where $E^{K(2)}_{jkq}$ is given by Equation (5.203) for the appropriate point in time. Total employment in each social group which has moved (E^T_{jq}) is given by:

$$E^{T(1)}_{jq} = E^{B(1)}_{jq} + \Sigma_r E^{R(1)}_{jrq} + \Sigma_k E^{K(1)}_{jkq} \qquad (5.199)$$

where $E^{B(1)}_{jq}$ is the basic employment of newly located workers in social group q in zone j, given by Equation (5.204) below; $E^{R(1)}_{jrq}$ is the retail employment of newly located workers in social group q in zone j, given by Equation (5.186); and $E^{K(1)}_{jkq}$ is the service employment of newly located workers in social group q in zone j given by Equation (5.197). Total employment in social group q in zone j at time t is given by:

$$E^T_{jq}(t) = E^B_{jq}(t) + \Sigma_r E^R_{jrq}(t) + \Sigma_k E^K_{jkq}(t) \qquad (5.200)$$

The land used by non-basic activity is given by Equation (5.36), repeated here for convenience

$$L^{Gu}_j = \Sigma_r d^R_r E^R_{jr} + \Sigma_k d^K_k E^K_{jk} \qquad (5.36)$$

The whole sequence of equations from the residential location model, through the retailing and service models is iterated until the population distribution does not vary significantly from one iteration to the next. Some variables must be calculated at the end of each time period for the next one.

A number of quantities can be calculated outside this iteration. The number of non-moving workers in each social group in each sector is given by:

$$E^{B(2)}_{jq}(t) = y_q E^B_{jq}(t-1) \qquad (5.201)$$

$$E^{R(2)}_{jrq}(t) = y_q E^R_{jrq}(t-1) \qquad (5.202)$$

$$E^{K(2)}_{jkq}(t) = y_q E^K_{jkq}(t-1) \qquad (5.203)$$

where y_q is the propensity not to move job for each social group over the time period under consideration. Newly located basic employment ($E^{B(1)}_{jq}$) is given by:

$$E^{B(1)}_{jq}(t) = E^B_{jq}(t) - E^{B(2)}_{jq}(t) \qquad (5.204)$$

where $E^B_{jq}(t)$ is the total basic employment in social group q in zone j, given by Equation (5.175). The term $E^{K(2)}_{jk}$ in Equation (5.189) is given by:

$$E^{K(2)}_{jk} = \Sigma_q E^{K(2)}_{jkq} \qquad (5.205)$$

The term $S^{(2)}_{jr}$ in Equation (5.178) is given by:

$$S^{(2)}_{jr}(t) = \Sigma_q E^{R(2)}_{jrq}(t)/b_r(t) \qquad (5.206)$$

where b_r is the sales employment ratio for sector r. Housing stock in each zone (H^S_i) is given by:

$$H^S_i(t) = H^S_i(t-1) + H^N_i(t) - \Sigma_q H^D_{iq}(t-1,t) \qquad (5.207)$$

where $H^N_i(t)$ is the number of new houses in zone i at time t, given by Equation (5.165); and $H^D_{iq}(t-1,t)$ is the number of houses occupied by social group q in zone i demolished during the time period t-1 to t; this is an exogenous variable. The area of land used by housing in each zone (L^H_i) is given by:

$$L_i^H(t) = \{H_i^S(t) - H_i^{NPX}(t-1,t) - H_i^{NCX}(t-1,t)\}/D_i^H(t)$$
$$+ H_i^{NPX}(t-1,t)/D_i^{NPX}(t-1,t)$$
$$+ H_i^{NCX}(t-1,t)/D_i^{NCX}(t-1,t) \qquad (5.208)$$

where $H_i^{NPX}(t-1,t)$ is the number of private houses located exogenously in zone i during the period t-1 to t; $H_i^{NCX}(t-1,t)$ is the number of council houses located exogenously in zone i during the period t-1 to t; D_i^H is the density of existing houses in zone i; $D_i^{NPX}(t-1,t)$ is the density of private houses located exogenously in zone i, during the period t-1 to t; and $D_i^{NCX}(t-1,t)$ is the density of council houses located exogenously in zone i during the period t-1 to t. The density of existing housing in zone i at time t $\{D_i^H(t)\}$ is given by:

$$D_i^H(t) = H_i^S(t-1)/L_i^H(t-1) \qquad (5.209)$$

The number of occupied houses in zone i (H_i^O) is given by:

$$H_i^O = \Sigma_q(P_{iq}/o_q) \qquad (5.210)$$

The number of vacant houses (H_i^V) in zone i is given by:

$$H_i^V = H_i^S - H_i^O \qquad (5.211)$$

The procedure for solving this complicated equation system for the Leeds model is outlined in Section 5.11 below.

5.9 External zones

The Leeds model has been extended to incorporate a set of external zones into the model. The mechanism used is described in detail elsewhere (Mackett, 1974). Basically it consists of defining the set of external zones in which some people reside. Only the work trips of these people are modelled, together with those of residents who live and work in internal zones, as before. The number of trips crossing the boundary in each direction is established, either from the Census of Population journey to work data or it is forecast, and then a constraint is introduced for each direction to ensure that the interaction across the boundary estimated by the model is equal to this total. The total resident population and employment in each external zone are not needed, although some forms of attraction factor are required. A similar method is used for the distribution of non-basic employment model except that, because the model is only singly constrained, only one extra constraint is required. It is also necessary to know the volumes of sales in shops to residents of external zones. Because of the difficulty in obtaining such a figure, the model is modified so that the required value is for the total volume of sales (or employment) in the main study area.

5.10 Calibration of the models

Calibration is the process of finding values of certain variables in the model which are characteristic of the study area. In the Leeds model, the variables to be calibrated are those which describe the effect of distance on the location of activities, namely, β_q^W in the residential location submodel, β_r^R in the retail submodel and β_k^K in the service submodel.

Recently, several papers have been published on the calibration of Lowry and similar models (see Hyman, 1969; Batty, 1970, 1971-B; Evans, 1971; Batty and Mackie, 1972; Batty el.al., 1973), and so calibration methodology will not be discussed here. The trip deterrence functions are calibrated by making the mean trip length of the model estimated trips equal to that obtained from data (from the Census of Population and a small household survey). This method is based on work by Hyman (1969).

Unlike some applications of the model (including the original) the model is calibrated internally: that is, the parameter value obtained is consistent with other variables within the model, rather than based on another study in the same area. An automatic calibration routine is incorporated into the model. An initial value of β is obtained, the appropriate submodel is run and the value of the mean trip length found. This is compared with the actual mean trip length. If the difference is insignificant, then this value of β is used and the next stage of the model is run; if a better value of β is required a new value is found by linear interpolation and the submodel run with this value in. This process is repeated until the value obtained is insignificantly different from the actual value.

This may be shown for the Leeds residential location model as follows. The mean trip length for journey to work by social group q (c_q^{Wm}) is

$$c_q^{Wm} = \frac{\Sigma_i \Sigma_j \{T_{ijq}^{(1)(1)} + T_{ijq}^{(1)(2)} + T_{ijq}^{(2)(1)} + T_{ijq}^{(2)(2)}\} c_{ij}}{\Sigma_i \Sigma_j \{T_{ijq}^{(1)(1)} + T_{ijq}^{(1)(2)} + T_{ijq}^{(2)(1)} + T_{ijq}^{(2)(2)}\}} \tag{5.212}$$

and where c_{ij} is the distance (or cost of travel) from zone i to zone j; and $T_{ijq}^{(1)(1)}$, $T_{ijq}^{(1)(2)}$, $T_{ijq}^{(2)(1)}$, $T_{ijq}^{(2)(2)}$ are the number of work trips from zone i to zone j by social group q for four types of locational behaviour given by Equations (5.141) to (5.146). The value of β is found from

$$\beta_q^W(I+1) = \frac{\{c_q^{Wr} - c_q^{Wm}(I_1-1)\beta_q^W(I_1)\}\{c_q^{Wr} - c_q^{Wm}(I_1)\beta_q^W(I_1-1)\}}{c_q^{Wm}(I_1) - c_q^{Wm}(I_1-1)}$$

$$\text{for } I_1 > 2 \tag{5.213}$$

where I_1 is the iteration on this calibration routine; $\beta_q^W(I_1)$ is the value of β in the residential location model for social group q on iteration I_1; and c_q^{Wr} is the actual mean trip length on the journey to work. Initially, we take

$$\beta_q^W(1) = 1.5/c_q^{Wr} \tag{5.214}$$

and then for the second iteration,

$$\beta_q^W(2) = \beta_q^W(1)c_q^{Wm}(1)/c_q^{Wr} \tag{5.215}$$

Equation (5.213) cannot be used for the first or second iteration. Convergence is deemed to have occurred when

$$\frac{c_q^{Wm}(I_1) - c_q^{Wr}}{c_q^{Wr}} < \Delta \tag{5.216}$$

where Δ is the maximum acceptable variation from the actual trip length for the model.

The retail and service models are calibrated in the same manner. The mean trip length for the retail models is given by:

$$c_r^{Rm} = \frac{\Sigma_i \Sigma_j (S_{ijr}^{(1)} + S_{ijr}^{(2)}) c_{ij}}{\Sigma_i \Sigma_j (S_{ijr}^{(1)} + S_{ijr}^{(2)})} \qquad (5.217)$$

where c_r^{Rm} is the mean trip length to shop for goods type r given by the model; and $S_{ijr}^{(1)}$, $S_{ijr}^{(2)}$ are the flows of money from residents in zone i to shops in zone j for goods type r given by Equations (5.177) and (5.178). The same method is used for the service submodel.

In the West Yorkshire model, the parameters to be estimated vary between the different versions of this model. Taking the final static version and the dynamic version as the two models put into practice the parameters required are as follows

Static $\beta^W, \alpha^W, \beta_k^K, \alpha_k^K, r_k, s_k, d_k^K, \underline{E_k^{K\,min}}$

Dynamic $\beta^W, \beta_k^{HK}, \beta_k^{WK}, r_k, s_k, d_k^K, \underline{E_k^{K\,min}}$

The β parameters are calibrated in a similar manner to those in the Leeds model. In the last version of the dynamic model regional β values were introduced enabling variation in the propensity to travel longer distances to work to be accounted for from different parts of West Yorkshire.

In the static version of the residential location model the parameter α has to be calibrated. The maximum likelihood equation is

$$\Sigma_i \Sigma_j T_{ij}^{pre} \log L_i^{Hu} = \Sigma_i \Sigma_j T_{ij}^{obs} \log L_i^{Hu} \qquad (5.218)$$

The best value of α occurs when left and right sides of the equation are as close as possible. For the service submodel, no trip data are available for Equations similar to (5.212) and (5.218). The main alternative which can be used with observed employment totals are various goodness-of-fit statistics. The main two used for the static model for β_k^{HK} and β_k^{WK} are the correlation coefficient and sum of squared deviations. For service employment of type k the correlation coefficient, R_k, is

$$R_k = \frac{\Sigma_i(E_{ik}^{K\ \underline{obs}} - \bar{E}_{ik}^{K\ \underline{obs}})(E_{ik}^{K\ \underline{pre}} - \bar{E}_{ik}^{K\ \underline{pre}})}{\sqrt{\Sigma_i(E_{ik}^{K\ \underline{obs}} - \bar{E}_{ik}^{K\ \underline{obs}})^2 \Sigma_i(E_{ik}^{K\ \underline{pre}} - \bar{E}_{ik}^{K\ \underline{pre}})^2}} \tag{5.219}$$

and the sum of squared deviations (N_k) is

$$N_k = \Sigma_i(E_{ik}^{K\ \underline{obs}} - E_{ik}^{K\ \underline{pre}})^2 \tag{5.220}$$

Parameters r_k and s_k in the static model require the same statistics for any calibration. The minimum size constraint can also be related to these statistics in both models. A complete trial and error process is necessary for the several parameters used in this model as a change in one parameter can affect the results obtained from another. Any formal procedure for calibration would require too much computer time to be practical for 50 zones and 15 parameters in an iterative general model. It is perhaps a weakness of the model that it has a large number of interdependent parameters for which the optimum set of values is difficult to estimate.

The calibration of the d_k^K parameter in the static model for land use is fairly straightforward. The total land used in the services should equal the total land observed in these uses. This equality is all that is required for this parameter. As over-crowding is allowed in zones with high service employment the total area divided by the number of employees would not give a correct value for α_k^K. The equality is therefore

$$\Sigma_i \Sigma_k L_{ik}^{Ku\ \underline{pre}} = \Sigma_i \Sigma_k L_{ik}^{Ku\ \underline{obs}} \tag{5.221}$$

With no available trip data for services the calibration of β_k^{HK} and β_k^{WK} for the home to service and work to service trips presents the same problems in the dynamic model as the β_k^K in the static model. The total employment in each zone for each service type observed can be used as before but an additional problem is introduced with the split into two types of service trips. This problem has yet to be solved in practice and may require certain assumptions about the behaviour of the two types of consumers, such as that workers are unlikely to travel very far for services compared with residents. The d_k^K parameter can be calibrated in the same way as the d_k^K for the static model for each time period. r_k and u_k parameters are closely related to the β_k^{WK} parameters. For this some additional informed assumptions can be made.

5.11 Solution of the equation system

In this section we will describe how the equation system of the Leeds model is solved. In fact, there are many ways, but the method suggested here has been found to work satisfactorily and probably cannot be greatly improved on. The equation system for the West Yorkshire model is simpler and its solution procedure was described in Section 5.8 above. The notation, whilst being fairly complex in places, has been simplified as far as possible providing ambiguity can be avoided. Time and iteration counts are only shown explicitly where they are essential to the explanation of the model solution.

Some of the equations themselves are solved iteratively: that is, by putting in an initial estimate of the variable, solving the equations, checking the output value, using this to find new input value, and repeating this process until a satisfactory solution is obtained (usually when the change from one iteration to the next is insignificantly small). There are several sets of nested iterations and the final solution is only achieved when all of those are completed. In the author's experience convergence of the equation system seems to occur satisfactorily for test runs on an actual city. However, it is of interest to note that test runs with a hypothetical three zone system suggests that convergence is not assured under all circumstances. Extreme values for some data inputs (relative to others) may prevent convergence; a trivial example of this would be a mean trip length to work greater than any inter-zonal distance would prevent a satisfactory solution being achieved. However, if the values are for a real study area such problems should not arise. The explanation of the solution of the equation system will be for the Leeds dynamic model described in Section 5.8 above. There are 29 steps in the solution procedure which are described in turn.

(1) Input of system descriptors

The following variables are input initially, and are taken to remain constant over the time period being considered: c_{ij} the distance (or cost of travel) between zone i and zone j; L_i^T the total area of zone i; and Δ the maximum acceptable variation from one iteration to the next for convergence.

(2) Inputs for initial time point

It is necessary to define explicitly the study area for the initial time point (called t=0 here). Changes over time are then based on the initial spatial distribution of activities. This permits the lagging of variables over time to simulate delayed response to stimuli. The required inputs are: L_i^{Hu} the land use for housing in zone i; L_i^B the land use by basic industry in zone i; H_i^S the stock of housing in zone i; P_{iq} the number of people in social group q living in zone i; E_{jq}^B the number of workers in basic industry in social group q in zone j; E_{jrq}^R the number of workers in retail industries in social group q in sector r in zone j; E_{jkq}^K the number of workers in non-retail services in social group q in sector k in zone j; y_q the propensity of workers in social group q not to change job during the time period under consideration; H_{cq}^O the number of houses occupied by members of social group q; L_{cr}^R the total area of land occupied by retail sector r in the city; and L_{ck}^K the total area of land occupied by service sector k in the city.

(3) Preliminary calculations

Some variables are calculated directly from the inputs above:

$$d_r^R = L_{cr}^R / \Sigma_j \Sigma_q E_{jrq}^R \tag{5.222}$$

$$d_k^K = L_{ck}^K / \Sigma_j \Sigma_q E_{jkq}^K \tag{5.223}$$

$$o_q = \Sigma_i P_{iq} / H_{cq}^O \tag{5.224}$$

$$D_i^H = H_i^S / L_i^{Hu} \tag{5.225}$$

where d_r^R is the area per worker for retail sector r; d_k^K is the area per worker for service sector k; o_q is the occupancy rate for social group q; and D_i^H is the density of housing in houses per unit area in zone i. The variables d_r^R, d_k^K, o_q are taken as constant over the time period. D_i^H is lagged one time period (and found at the end of the equation sequence for the next time point).

(4) Inputs for each time point

The following variables are input for each time point. It should be borne in mind that the model allocates total activity levels in the city between zones. These totals may be predicted exogenously, or may be policy inputs (that is, the model is being used to find the distributional effects of an overall increase in the activity level). This method has the advantage that the final solution is not completely dependent on the value of ratios such as the activity rate, which do not remain constant over time, but are assumed to do so in some model applications. The variables required are: P_{cq} the total population in social group q in the city; M_{cq}^T the number of members of social group q who moved from their residences during the preceding period; E_{cq}^B the total basic employment in social group q in the city; E_{crq}^R the total retail employment in sector r in social group q in the city; E_{ckq}^K the total service employment in sector k in social group q in the city; e_{rq} the expenditure per head of goods type r by social group q; c_q^{Wr} the mean trip length to work for social group q; c_r^{Rr} the actual mean distance to shop for goods type r; and c_k^{Kr} the actual mean distance to services for sector k. The last three variables above are required for calibration of the submodels.

(5) Policy variables

The following variables are regarded as describing policy inputs. Some or all of them may be given values; alternatively, the model could be used for forecasting without any of them. The variables are: L_i^Z the area of unusable land in zone i; L_i^h the area of land being held off the market in zone i; P_{iq}^{max} the maximum desired population in social group q in zone i; P_{iq}^{min} the minimum desired population in social group q in zone i; E_{iq}^{BNX} the number of workers in social group q in basic employment being located exogenously in zone i; E_{iq}^{BDX} the number of workers in social group q in basic employment being removed exogenously from zone i; H_i^{NPX} the number of new private houses being located exogenously in zone i; D_i^{NPX} the density of the exogenously located private houses in zone i; H_i^{NCX} the number of new council houses being located exogenously in zone i; and D_i^{NCX} the density of the exogenously located council houses in zone i.

(6) Total employment in each social group

Total employment in each social group in the city (E_{cq}^T) is found using variables from above:

$$E_{cq}^T = E_{cq}^B + \Sigma_r E_{crq}^R + \Sigma_k E_{ckq}^K \tag{5.226}$$

(7) Ratios for each time period

Some ratios, which change from one time period to the next one, are now calculated:

$$g_q = P_{cq}/E_{cq}^T \tag{5.227}$$

$$b_r = \Sigma_q E_{crq}^R / \Sigma_q P_{cq} e_{rq} \tag{5.228}$$

$$v_k = \Sigma_q E_{ckq}^K / \Sigma_q P_{cq} \tag{5.229}$$

where g_q is the inverse of the activity rate for social group q; b_r is the employment sales ratio for sector r; and v_k is the population serving ratio for sector k.

(8) Non-movers and houses vacated by migrants

$P_{iq}^{(2)}$ is found from Equation (5.154); $R_{iq}^{(2)}$ is found from Equation (5.153); and H_i^M is found from Equation (5.162).

(9) Checks

It is useful to perform the following checks, since if these inequalities are violated, no solution is possible:

$$\text{check} \quad P_{iq}^{(2)} < P_{iq}^{max} \tag{5.230}$$

$$\text{check} \quad \Sigma_i P_{iq}^{max} > P_{cq} \tag{5.231}$$

$$\text{check} \quad \Sigma_i P_{iq}^{min} < P_{cq} \tag{5.232}$$

(10) Basic employment submodel

E_{iq}^B is found from Equation (5.175); and L_i^B is found from Equation (5.176).

(11) Scaling up of basic employment

On the first iteration for each time period $E^B_{\cdot iq}$ is scaled up as described in Section 3 above. $E^{B(1)}_{\cdot jq}(t)$ is found from Equation (5.204) and then

$$E^T_{\cdot jq}(t)(1) = E^B_{\cdot jq}(t)E^T_{cq}(t)/E^B_{cq}(t) \tag{5.233}$$

and

$$E^{T(1)}_{\cdot jq}(t)(1) = E^T_{\cdot jq}(t)(1) - E^{T(2)}_{\cdot jq}(t) \tag{5.234}$$

where (1) indicates the iteration number, in this case 1.

(12) Land availability

$L^V_{\cdot i}$ is found from Equation (5.169); $L^{Ga}_{\cdot i}$ is found from Equation (5.168); $D^{NPX}_{\cdot i}$ and/or $D^{NCX}_{\cdot i}$ set equal to $D^H_{\cdot i}$ if no other value is available. We check that

$$H^{NPX}_{\cdot i}/D^{NPX}_{\cdot i} + H^{NCX}_{\cdot i}/D^{NCX}_{\cdot i} < L^V_{\cdot i} \tag{5.235}$$

(13) Housing stock

H^O_{cq} is found from Equation (5.164); and H^N_c is found from Equation (5.169). We check that

$$H^N_c > 0 \tag{5.236}$$

and

$$\Sigma_i H^{NPX}_{\cdot i} + \Sigma_i H^{NCX}_{\cdot i} < H^N_c \tag{5.237}$$

(14) Initial β values

The initial values of β for the calibration of the submodels are found from Equation (5.214).

(15) Non-basic attraction factors

$W^R_{\cdot jr}$ is found from Equation (5.179); $W^K_{\cdot jk}$ for k=1 is found from Equation (5.190); $W^K_{\cdot jk}$ for k=2 and 3 is found from Equation (5.191); and $S^{(2)}_{\cdot jr}$ is found from Equation (5.206). It should be noted that since the value of $W^R_{\cdot jr}$ and $W^K_{\cdot jk}$ for k=1 are dependent on the value of $E^T_{\cdot jq}(t)$ these values are found within the loop which locates non-basic employment and population.

(16) Residential location

The part of the model from finding the value of to calibration of the residential location submodels is performed for each social group q in turn: $L^{Ha}_{\cdot i}$ is found from Equation (5.167); $H^N_{\cdot i}$ is found from Equation (5.165) or (5.166); $H^V_{\cdot i}$ is found from Equation

(5.103); $H^{O}_{\cdot iq}$ is found from Equations (5.158) to (5.160); $W^{W}_{\cdot iq}$ is found from Equation (5.170); $A^{W}_{\cdot iq}$ is found from Equation (5.147); and $B^{W}_{\cdot iq}$ is found from Equation (5.150). These equations are solved iteratively. $T^{(1)(1)}_{ijq}$, $T^{(1)(2)}_{ijq}$, $T^{(2)(1)}_{ijq}$ and $T^{(2)(2)}_{ijq}$ are found from Equations (5.141) to (5.146). On the first iteration of the loop to ensure constraints (5.155) to (5.157) hold, only Equations (5.142), (5.144), (5.145) and (5.146) are required.

(17) Employed residents and population

$R^{(1)}_{\cdot iq}$ is found from Equation (5.172) for $i\varepsilon Z_2$. In practice because of the iterative procedure used it is sometimes found that the sum of all the trip ends does not exactly equal the known total. That is:

$$\Sigma_i \Sigma_j T^{(1)(1)}_{ijq} + \Sigma_i \Sigma_j T^{(1)(2)}_{ijq} + \Sigma_i \Sigma_j T^{(2)(1)}_{ijq} + \Sigma_i \Sigma_j T^{(2)(2)}_{ijq} \neq P_{cq}/g_q \tag{5.238}$$

To overcome this problem a factor is applied to the term $R^{(1)}_{\cdot iq}$ for $i\varepsilon Z_2$ in Equation (5.172), since the other values of $R^{(1)}_{\cdot iq}$ for $i\varepsilon Z_1$ and $R^{(2)}_{\cdot iq}$ are determined exogenously to this part of the model. The factor (G_q) is defined as:

$$G_q = \frac{E^{T}_{cq} - \Sigma_{i\varepsilon Z_1} R^{(1)}_{\cdot iq} - \Sigma_i R^{(2)}_{\cdot iq}}{\Sigma_{i\varepsilon Z_2} R^{(1)}_{\cdot iq}} \tag{5.239}$$

Then this factor is used to find an 'improved' value of $R^{(1)}_{\cdot iq}$:

$$R^{(1)}_{\cdot iq} = G_q R^{(1)}_{\cdot iq} \quad \text{for } i\varepsilon Z_2 \tag{5.240}$$

Equation (5.172) or (5.173) is used to give the value of $P^{(1)}_{\cdot iq}$ using the value of $R^{(1)}_{\cdot iq}$ for $i\varepsilon Z_1$, and $R^{(1)}_{\cdot iq}$ for $i\varepsilon Z_2$ thus:

$$P^{(1)}_{\cdot iq} = g_q R^{(1)}_{\cdot iq} \quad \text{for } i\varepsilon Z_1 \tag{5.241}$$

$$P^{(2)}_{\cdot iq} = g_q R^{(1)}_{\cdot iq} \quad \text{for } i\varepsilon Z_2 \tag{5.242}$$

(18) Residential constraints

Constraints (5.155) to (5.157) must be met, so the value of $R^{(1)}_{\cdot iq}$ is found if any of them is violated. This value is used in Equation (5.150) to find the value of $B^{W}_{\cdot jq}$; $A^{W}_{\cdot iq}$ is found from

Equation (5.147) to ensure that Equation (5.148) holds. Equations (5.141) to (5.146) are then used to find new values of $T_{ijq}^{(1)(1)}$, $T_{ijq}^{(1)(2)}$, $T_{ijq}^{(2)(1)}$ and $T_{ijq}^{(2)(2)}$. Since employed residents are allocated to other zones, one or more may now violate a constraint so the whole procedure is repeated until none of them is violated.

(19) Calibration of residential location submodel

c_q^{Wm} is found from Equation (5.212); and β_q^W is found from Equation (5.215) on the first calibration loop, and from Equation (5.213) subsequently. Inequality (5.216) is applied to the value of c_q^{Wm}; if it is not met the whole of the residential location submodel from the calculation of A_{iq}^W and B_{jq}^W is repeated. This process is continued until inequality (5.216) is met. It should be noted that on each of these iterations, all zones are set back into set Z_2, since the change in the spatial distribution of activities caused by the new value of β_q^W may mean the constraints are no longer violated, or may be violated in different zones.

(20) Convergence check on outer loop

Because the model sequence starts with the spatial distribution of employment it is sensible to check here for the convergence of the outer loop on which non-basic employment and population are generated. That is,

$$\text{check} \quad \frac{\Sigma_q R_{iq}^{(1)}(I_2) - \Sigma_q R_{iq}^{(1)}(I_2-1)}{\Sigma_q R_{iq}^{(1)}(I_2-1)} < \Delta \quad i\varepsilon Z_2 \tag{5.243}$$

where I_2 is the iteration number on this loop. This check is not applied on the first iteration, since no non-basic activity has been generated. If the inequality is met, the iterative sequence is complete and so total values are found for this time period, as described in step (28) below. Otherwise, the next step is followed.

(21) Retail submodel

F_{ir} is found from Equation (5.92); A_{ir}^R is found from Equation (5.180); B_{jr}^R is found from Equation (5.182). The A_{ir}^R and B_{ir}^R equations are solved iteratively. $S_{ijr}^{(1)}$ is found from Equation (5.177); and $S_{ijr}^{(2)}$ is found from Equation (5.178).

(22) Calibration of retail submodel

c_r^{Rr} is found from Equation (5.217). The calibration procedure is the same as that for the residential location submodel.

(23) Retail employment

$E_{jr}^{R(1)}$ is found from Equation (5.185); $E_{jrq}^{R(1)}$ is found from Equation (5.186); and E_{jrq}^{R} is found from Equation (5.187).

(24) Service submodel

A_{ik}^{K} is found from Equation (5.192); B_{jk}^{K} is found from Equation (5.194), and these equations are solved iteratively. $J_{ijk}^{(1)}$ is found from Equation (5.188); and $J_{ijk}^{(2)}$ is found from Equation (5.189).

(25) Calibration of service submodel

The calibration procedure is the same as that for the retail submodel.

(26) Service employment

$E_{jk}^{K(1)}$ is found from Equation (5.196); $E_{jkq}^{K(1)}$ is found from Equation (5.197); and E_{jkq}^{K} is found from Equation (5.198).

(27) Land employment and accounting

At the end of the main loop total employment and land used are found for use in the residential location submodel. $E_{jq}^{T(1)}$ is found from Equation (5.199); E_{jq}^{T} is found from Equation (5.200); L_j^{Gu} is found from Equation (5.36); E_{jq}^{T} is used in Equations (5.147), (5.179) and (5.190); $E_{jq}^{T(1)}$ is used in Equations (5.141), (5.142) and (5.145); and L_j^{Gu} is used in Equation (5.167). The sequence is then repeated until convergence is achieved.

(28) Totals for this time period

S_{jr} is found from Equation (5.184); H_i^S is found from Equation (5.207); L_i^H is found from Equation (5.208); H_i^O is found from Equation (5.210); and H_i^V is found from Equation (5.211).

(29) Values for the next time period

Except on the final time point, values to be used on the next time period are found. $E_{jq}^{B(2)}$ is found from Equation (5.201); $E_{jrq}^{R(2)}$ is found from Equation (5.202); $E_{jkq}^{K(2)}$ is found from Equation (5.203); D_i^H is found from Equation (5.209); and $S_{jr}^{(2)}$ is found from Equation (5.206). The whole system is then reiterated from step (4) for each time horizon being forecast.

5.12 Data needs and availability

The following is a list of data needs for the static West Yorkshire model (where n_i represents number of zones and n_k number of service types).

Data	Size
Cost matrix c_{ij}	$n_i \times n_i$
Total area of zones L_i^T	n_i
Total basic employment in each zone E_i^B	n_i
Area used in basic industry in each zone L_i^B	n_i
Area unusable in each zone L_i^Z	n_i
Total population for region P_c	1
Total employment in each service type for region E_{ck}^K	n_k
Area of zone held off the market for residential or services use in each zone L_i^h	n_i
Density constraint for each zone D_i^H	n_i
Observed trips between each zone for journey to work T_{ij}^{obs}	$n_i \times n_i$
Observed employment in each zone for each service type $E_{jk}^{K\ obs}$	$n_i \times n_k$
Observed population in each zone P_i^{obs}	n_i
Number of zones with temporary basic employment n_t	1
Zones in set Z_5	n_t
Amount of temporary unemployment in each zone in set Z_5	n_t

The definition of basic employment was dealt with in an earlier section (Section 5.5) and also the total service employment. The former can be calculated for each zone allowing for excesses in certain service industries which may be defined as basic. The temporary basic employment which is discounted in the calculation of population and service employment can also be defined while the basic employment is being calculated. The observed service employment in each zone requires detailed analysis of each minimum list heading to calculate the latter's division between the types. Only five zones warranted definition as metropolitan service centres. Zones such as Harrogate Metropolitan Borough have several service minimum list heading totals considerably above that of zones of similar population. The basic employment for these zones is increased accordingly and in several cases these excess amounts exceed the basic employment on the minimum requirements definition. The fundamental differences encountered between residential and industrial zones will be examined in the results section.

The population totals are readily available in Census Publications as are the total area of each zone. The population and service employment totals for the region are the sum of all the zonal totals.

For West Yorkshire land use data for 1966 (the static model first run was for this year) were published in the West Yorkshire transportation study. Land use is divided into ten types. Basic industrial land use was defined by categories for manufacturing industry and transport and unusable by open space, extractive industry and agricultural, forestry and open country, which is badly drained or very steep. The other five categories would be included for service industry - commerce, civic statutory undertakings and education - and residential use. The areas zoned off the market are therefore a proportion of the agricultural forestry and open country category not included in the unusable group.

The observed journey to work trips are published for 1966 for flows over 50 persons. The smaller flows internally within West Yorkshire or external trips can be estimated using methods described by Chilton and Poet (1973) or by intuitive guesswork. This completed matrix can then be used in the calculation of the observed mean trip length.

The density constraint D_i^H for each zone is closely related to the land zoned off the market, L_i^h. With the large zones of this application the density constraint is only brought into effect when large proportions of the land available are found in the category L_i^h. For most of the runs undertaken the D_i^H values are not varied significantly between zones. The smallest zones can allow higher densities and the largest zones lower densities.

The data need causing the greatest number of problems and playing a very significant part in the model is the cost matrix. During the testing of the static model this matrix was altered several times as errors lead to distorted results. The results will be described in the next section but the alterations made will be described here. The basic problems are caused by the zones being of different size and shape and the intra-zonal trips accounting for a large proportion of the total trips. In Pittsburg, Lowry used a grid of square zones of equal size. The potential submodels behave considerably differently if the zones are not of equal size and shape. This was partly adjusted by the introduction of area attractiveness factors. The inter-zonal distances were calculated simply by Pythagoras multiplied by 1.2 to allow for road curvature. The intra-zonal distances were originally calculated as a third of the radius of the longest dimension of the zone. This obviously meant the smallest zones had the shortest intra-zonal distance (which varied from 0.2 to 2.2 miles). However, in West Yorkshire using local authorities as zones 70% of journey to work trips are intra-zonal. A large proportion of shopping trips would also be intra-zonal although observed data are not available. The intra-zonal distances are therefore extremely important. In a submodel of the form

$$P_i = g\Sigma_j E_j^T c_{ij}^{-\beta} \tag{5.244}$$

if a small proportion of the c_{ij}'s are considerably smaller than the rest these zones can dominate the predicted trip distribution. In this region the shortest trip lengths will be for intra-zonal trips (c_{ii}) of the smallest zones. The method outlined above leads to the smallest zones dominating.

The first alternative to this method was for the c_{ii}'s to be of the same length. This, however, was too arbitrary and would not produce the correct proportion of intra-zonal trips. All workers will be inclined to live in their work zone. A method had to be devised which did not depend upon the zone size and one suggested by Wilson (1967) was used. Plotting the fraction

$$\frac{T_{ij}}{O_i D_j}$$

where T_{ij} is the observed trips between i and j, O_i is the number of residents in i and D_j the number of workers in j, against c_{ij}, for the inter-zonal trips an exponential form of curve was produced:

$$\frac{T_{ij}}{O_i D_j} \times e^{-\beta c_{ij}} = K \tag{5.245}$$

However, large differences still occurred, if an average K was obtained for all known trips and costs, in the c_{ii} values found by substitution. The zones were then divided into groups of similar population and separate K's were calculated for trips between zones of similar size for the groups as c_{ii} would obviously be between zones of the same size. Substituting O_i, D_i and T_{ii} from observed data the final c_{ii} values are calculated. These varied from 0.18 to 0.35 miles. The results from these still showed the intra-zonal trips to be too large a proportion of total trips. The final alteration, maintaining the absolute difference between the individual costs in the matrix, was to add half a mile to all trip costs as a penalty for making any trip of any type. The intra-zonal costs then varied between 0.68 and 0.85 of a mile without the shortest distances dominating the model. The shortest inter-zonal cost was 1.9 miles.

The data required to run the dynamic model in addition to the total zonal areas, total permanently unusable and control parameters (time period, no zones, etc) are necessary for each time period. They are listed above for the static model excluding those which do not vary with time: in addition the following are required: (i) attractiveness factors for residence; (ii) attractiveness factors for service trips: from work and from home; and (iii) expenditure per person on services in each zone. In a later version of the model, the first two items are calculated endogenously.

Basic employment and total employment in each service type can be calculated for 1951 and 1961 using similar methods to 1966 by analysing each zone's employment by minimum list headings and including certain excesses over minimum or normal requirements of service industries in the basic sector. For five year time periods, the figures for 1956 are usually interpolated from 1951 and 1961 Census data. Total population is the observed total for the region. Area data have to be calculated from development plan land use maps and Ordnance Survey six inch maps, as few statistics were more readily available. The area used for basic industry in each zone was then available and at first the attractiveness factors for residence and services were the residential and service land use figures of the previous time period. These of course were still exogenous inputs and were from observed data. Later runs of the dynamic model will use the endogenous input for a new time period of the land use generated from the previous time period, within the model. The attractiveness factors will obviously later be more sophisticated than just the previous land use and should include some aesthetic and density considerations.

Expenditure statistics are obtained from the Family Expenditure Survey although the figures given only differ between types of zone rather than specific zones (that is, rural, urban, metropolitan).

Observed data for calibration are also calculated in similar ways to 1966. Service employment is analysed in order to obtain the total service employment and work trip data is published in the Census of Population except for the smallest flows. These can be calculated using the methods described above.

Data for the Leeds model were obtained from many similar sources to those used in the West Yorkshire model. The inputs to this model were listed in the previous section. In many ways it is more difficult to obtain data for the intra-urban scale than the inter-urban, since the zones within the city do not represent areas for which data are normally collected in the same way that local authority areas are. There are some zone systems, such as civil wards, but unfortunately these are changed quite frequently, causing problems for dynamic models requiring data for several points in time, such as the Leeds model described in this paper. It was decided to use the 28 wards in use in Leeds over the period 1958 to 1970. Data were available from the 1961 and 1966 Census of Population for these zones. The 1961 Census County Report gives population figures for these zones for 1951, and the 1971 Census was available at an Enumeration District (ED) level. The 1971 data were aggregated to the earlier ward system by consideration of the relative location of the two sets of zones to give a good spatial correspondence. Thus some data were available for the periods 1951-1961-1966-1971 for 28 zones in Leeds.

The data required to forecast the year 1971 using 1966 as a base will be described. This is the time period for which data are most readily available. Population figures were obtained from the Census. The social group break-down was based upon the definition of socio-economic groups as follows: social group 1 was professional and managerial workers (SEG's 1, 2, 3, 4 and 13), the third group consisted of unskilled manual workers (SEG 11), while the other socio-economic groups made up the middle category. Dependents were allocated to the social group of the head of the household (since we are locating households) and members of economically inactive households were allocated in proportion to the distribution of other households in the zone. The number of out-migrants in each social group was found from the migration tables of the Census.

Employment data are much more difficult to obtain than those for population since the place of work is not normally coded at a spatial scale below that of local authorities. Fortunately, data on all work trips between all pairs of ED's in West Yorkshire in 1966 were available. These data were aggregated to give the employment in each ward in Leeds. This was for eight employment categories. Basic employment was taken to be SIC's I to XIX and XXIV. Non-basic employment was thus SIC's XX to XXIII. With such a small study area most industry will be producing goods and services for non-local purposes. The retail employment was divided between convenience and durable on the basis of information from the Census of Population and for employment from Mackett (1973-B). Unusable land was defined as land set aside for schools and public open spaces, plus other land obviously unsuitable for development such as rivers and cemeteries. Land being held off the market was taken to be Green Belt.

Housing stock information was obtained from the Census of Population. Information about demolition was based on data from Leeds County Borough Planning Department and local knowledge.

Data on expenditure per head on each type of good was based on information from the Family Expenditure Survey as described in Mackett (1973-A). The propensity of workers in each social group not to change job over the forecast period was based upon information in Table 60 of Harris (1967).

In order to allow effort to be concentrated on the more important policy considerations in the model, the inter-zonal distances were based on straight lines using a Pythagorean algorithm. Intra-zonal distances were based on consideration of the geometry of the zone. The mean trip length to work was obtained from the Census data for work trips mentioned above. The mean distances to other activities were based on a small household survey carried out in 1972 and described in Mackett (1973-A).

The above data were used to obtain the results described in the next section. Clearly, with such a complex model with large data requirements a comprehensive household survey would be needed to provide really accurate data. In the absence of such a survey the above description does illustrate how knowledge of a wide section of data sources and a certain amount of ingenuity permit at least a reasonable testing of an urban model.

5.13 Results

The first runs of the basic static models for West Yorkshire without a total population given or any of the improvements described earlier gave very small or very large populations for the region with Pudsey the largest zone! This may have been due to its position between Leeds and Bradford.

With the intra-zonal distances varying from 0.2 to 2.2 miles, the model tried to produce a metropolis in Heckmondwike, the smallest zone, although the density constraint distributed most of the population to the adjacent zones. With the variation between the intra-zonal distances reduced to 0.1 to 0.6 the zones with an intra-zonal distance of 0.1 dominated the model. As explained above this is a property of the potential submodel used by Lowry. The inverse activity ratio had to be adjusted to prevent over prediction of population in these early runs. In these early runs it also became apparent that the chronological testing of constraints with the nearest zones taking any excess caused illogical results: for example, for services Wakefield contained a few less workers in metropolitan services than the minimum size constraint and they were all redistributed to Stanley Urban District which became a metropolitan service centre!

One run with all the zones having intra-zonal distances of 0.1 miles resulted in vastly improved distribution. It was however very closely related to the basic employment distribution and too high a proportion of trips were intra-zonal. The β parameter for journey to work and g parameter were adjusted to give reasonable results but zones such as Spenborough Metropolitan Borough with high basic employment gave too high a population. The relative size of the four largest county boroughs was accurate and they also became metropolitan service centres. The density constraints for housing were adjusted considerably to see how they could affect the model. They were found to be important controls on the population of the larger employment centres.

An initial calculation of the intra-zonal distances using the method described in the previous section led to Denholme Urban District dominating the model. This was due to the function

$$\frac{T_{ij}c_{ij}}{O_i D_j} = K$$

being dealt with for all zones with one average K value. The grouping of flows into those between similar sized zones for the calculation of K gave a far more realistic result. (Denholme Urban District was the smallest zone for basic employment and population). Providing none of the zones had an intra-zonal distance considerably shorter than the rest a reasonable result was obtained for the relative populations of the zones.

The first changes in the model design were introduced with the alteration of the constraint procedure and the input of the total population and total service employment. These alterations gave an indication of the illogical order of the constraints and submodels. This order was then changed. The first runs with these alterations gave greatly improved results although again the population followed the employment distribution closely and large zones without a great deal of basic employment were under populated.

The area for housing was introduced as an attractiveness factor for the residential location submodel in the next few runs without an α parameter. This, coupled with the area used in the retail submodel, caused the populations to be taken to the opposite extreme. The largest zones in area became the largest zones in population, particularly Leeds County Borough which also had a large amount of basic employment. At one stage Leeds County Borough completely dominated the model for population and all types of service employment. A further refinement was the introduction of a minimum value for the area attractiveness variable in the retail submodel. Otherwise if no retail employment was predicted for a zone in one iteration, successive iterations would allow no retail employment as L_{ik}^{Ku} would equal zero. Separating the L_{ik}^{Ku} between types also helped as zones without metropolitan service employment would not have their local service employment reduced in relation to other zones. A minimum area of 10 acres for each service type in the retail submodel was found to give the best results.

In order to calibrate the β parameter by mean trip length a matrix of predicted trips had to be calculated. The residential location submodel does not give the actual work trips and so a doubly constrained spatial interaction model was introduced to enable the calibration to take place.

The density constraints restricted the population in the largest zones and all runs from this version of the model to the last version of the static model predicted as much population for Leeds, Bradford, Huddersfield and Halifax as the density constraint would allow.

With the general overprediction in zones which contained high basic employment and too few journey to work trips crossing zone boundaries the cost matrix was altered to cost the need to make any sort of trip at half a mile. Intra-zonal distances then varied from 0.68 to 0.85 miles. In addition the α parameters were included in the area attractiveness factors. Calibration of all the parameters was attempted as all the major alterations to the data and model design had taken place.

In succeeding runs various minor alterations were made to the basic employment and services type data with adjustment of the minimum size constraints and areas zoned off the market. The last enabled the zones with the highest population to be controlled and the other changes greatly improved the goodness-of-fit statistics which were used to calibrate the parameters. The largest zonal alterations were for Wakefield County Borough which was classified as the smallest of the metropolitan centres in observed data. The model did not predict this even though a large amount of service employment was classified as basic due to Wakefield serving as the county town of the West Riding.

Due to the large number of parameters the best overall combination was difficult to obtain and several of them may not have been calibrated precisely, particularly r_k and s_k showing the relative importance of the home to service and work to service trips. The α and β parameters were more independent and could be calibrated reasonably accurately. Once a certain degree of accuracy in the prediction had been obtained, further improvement was very difficult. A point was reached by which changes in the parameters made little difference and the results seemed to be the best the model would allow. The service employment once the population predictions were accurate could be improved upon only slightly. They depended upon zonal population and employment and area used or available for services with factors not taken into account which would affect the distribution, that is, historical, policy, transport facilities and advantages of centralisation.

The inadequacies of the final version of the static model can be related mainly to the lack of any inclusion of the factors mentioned in the last paragraph and the variation in the general functions of the zones (towns in this example): for example, Wakefield serves as a county town, Spenborough as a large employment centre and Harrogate and Ilkley as dormitory towns. The accuracy of the population predictions can be improved using density constraints and availability of land, but no amount of data manipulation will give a more accurate result for the service employment. Some results (which are displayed in Figures 5.1-5.9) have been obtained for a comparative static model run to test the submodels

Figure 5.1 Initial results of the static Lowry model without area attractiveness variables for population 1966, West Yorkshire

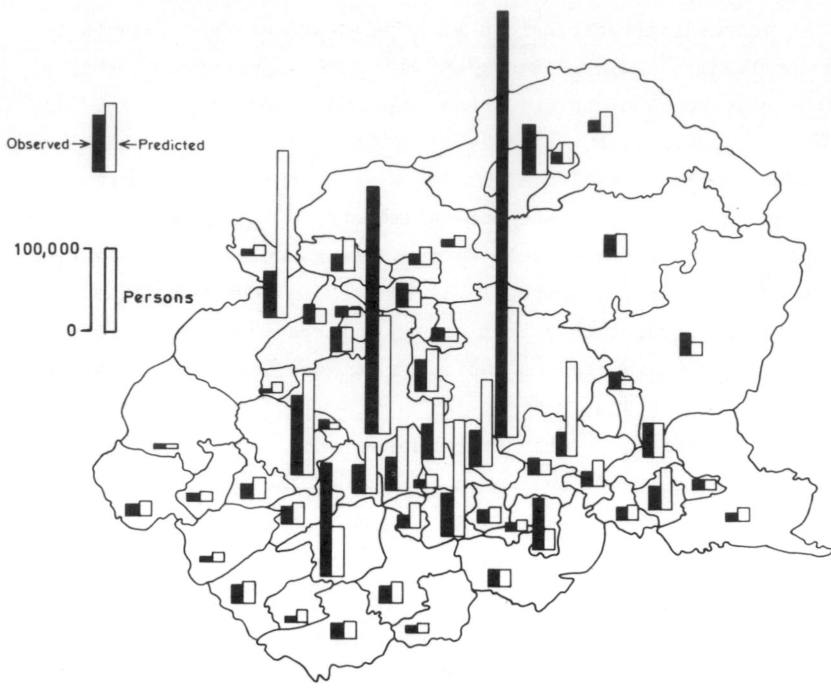

Figure 5.2 Results from the final static version with potential submodels for population 1966, West Yorkshire

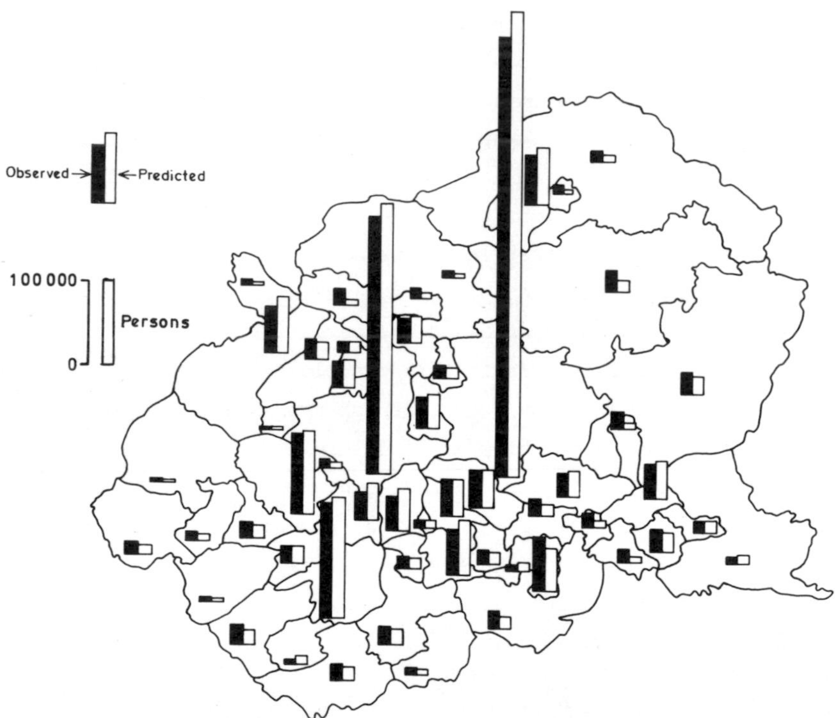

Figure 5.3 Results from the final static version with potential submodels fully calibrated for population for 1966: service type 1, West Yorkshire

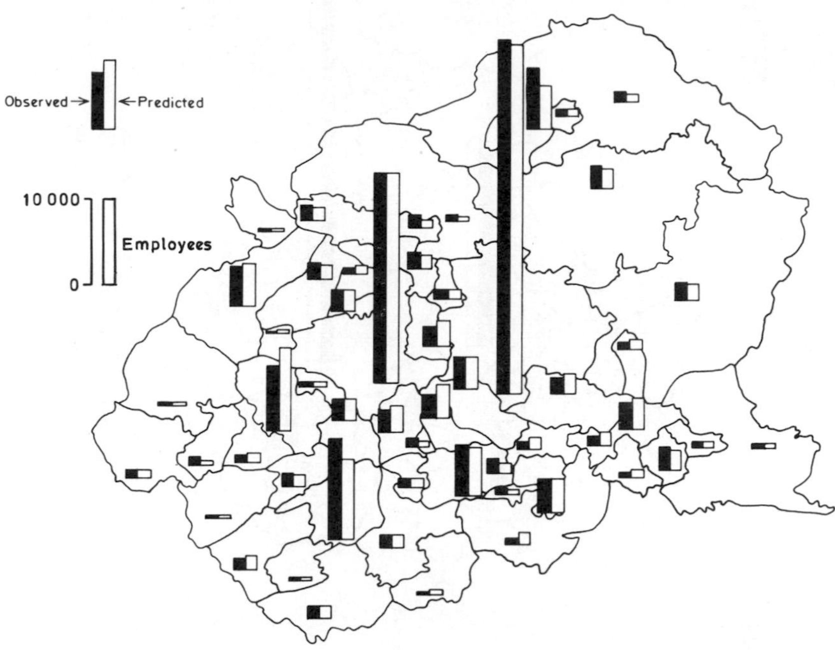

Figure 5.4 Results from the final static version with potential submodels fully calibrated for population for 1966: service type 2, West Yorkshire

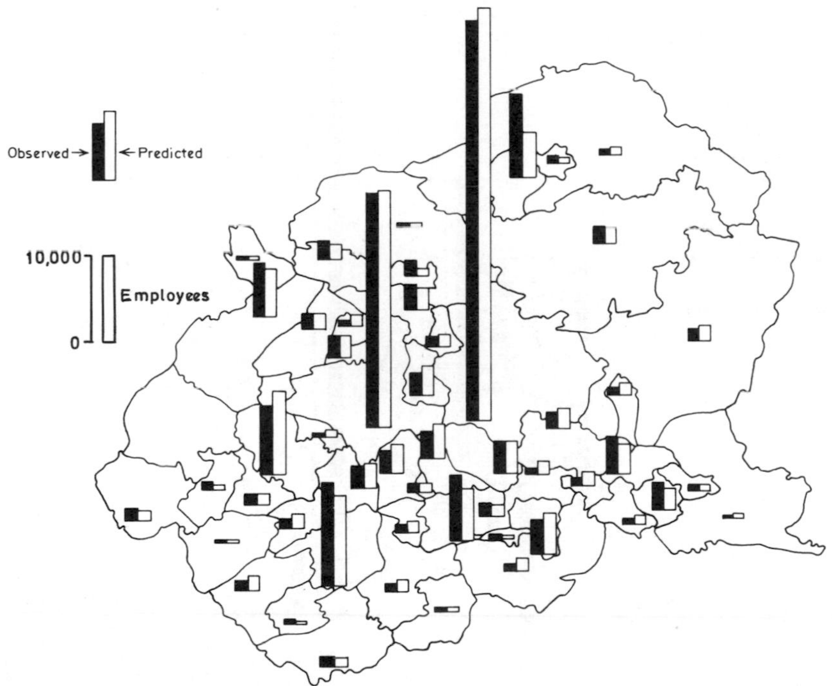

Figure 5.5 Results from the final static version with potential submodels fully calibrated for population for 1966: service type 3, West Yorkshire

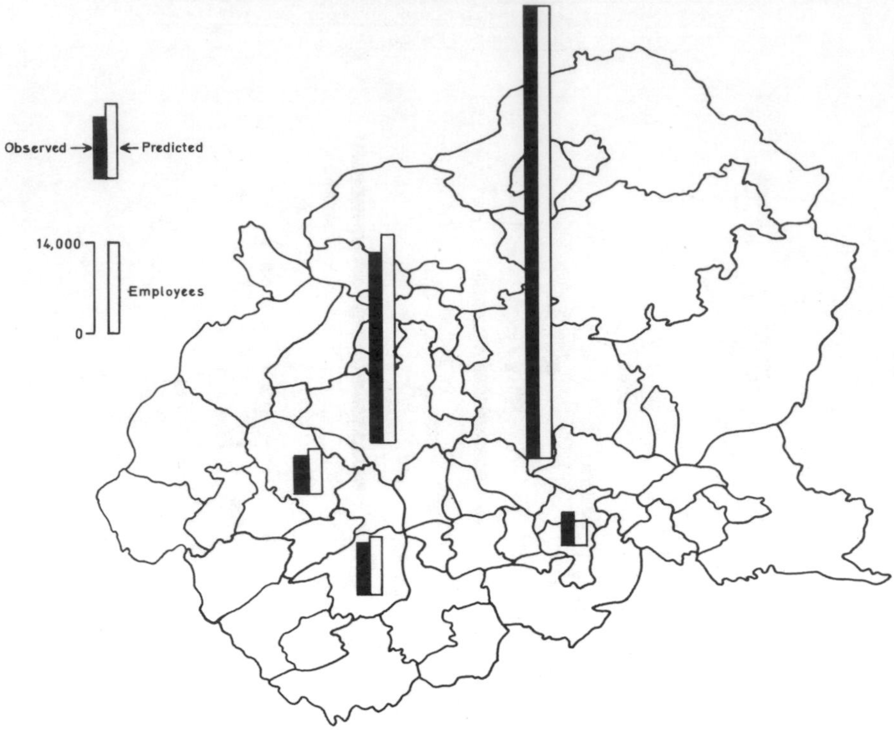

Observed → ← Predicted

14,000

Employees

0

Figure 5.6 Results of a comparative static model: population for 1951, West Yorkshire

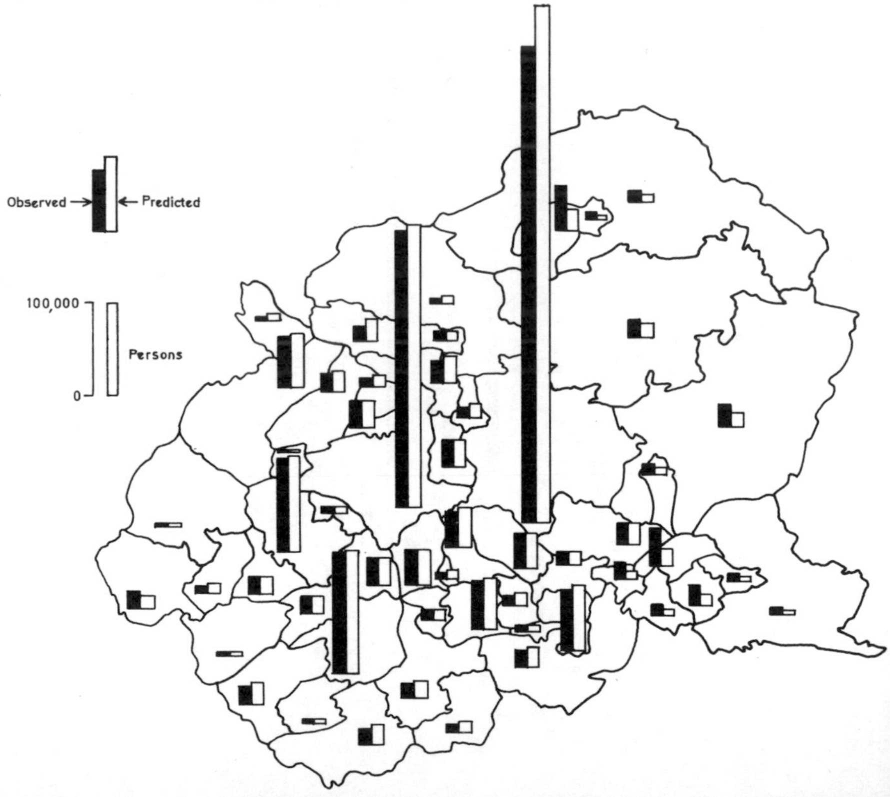

Observed → ← Predicted

100,000

Persons

0

Figure 5.7 Results of a comparative static model: population for 1956, West Yorkshire

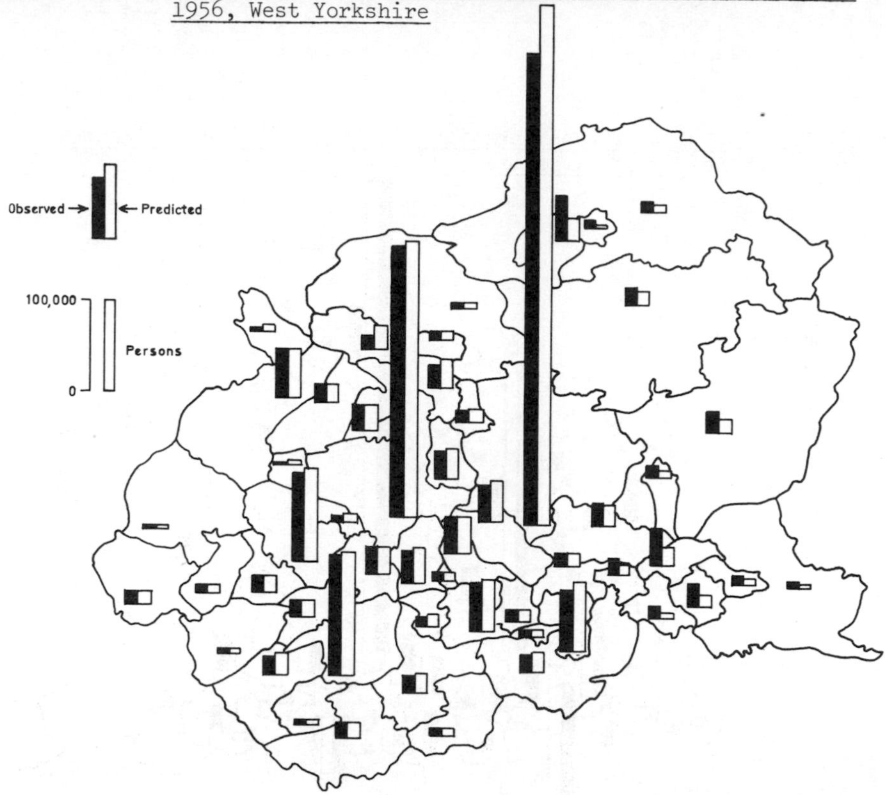

Observed → ← Predicted

100,000
0
Persons

Figure 5.8 Results of a comparative static model: population for 1961, West Yorkshire

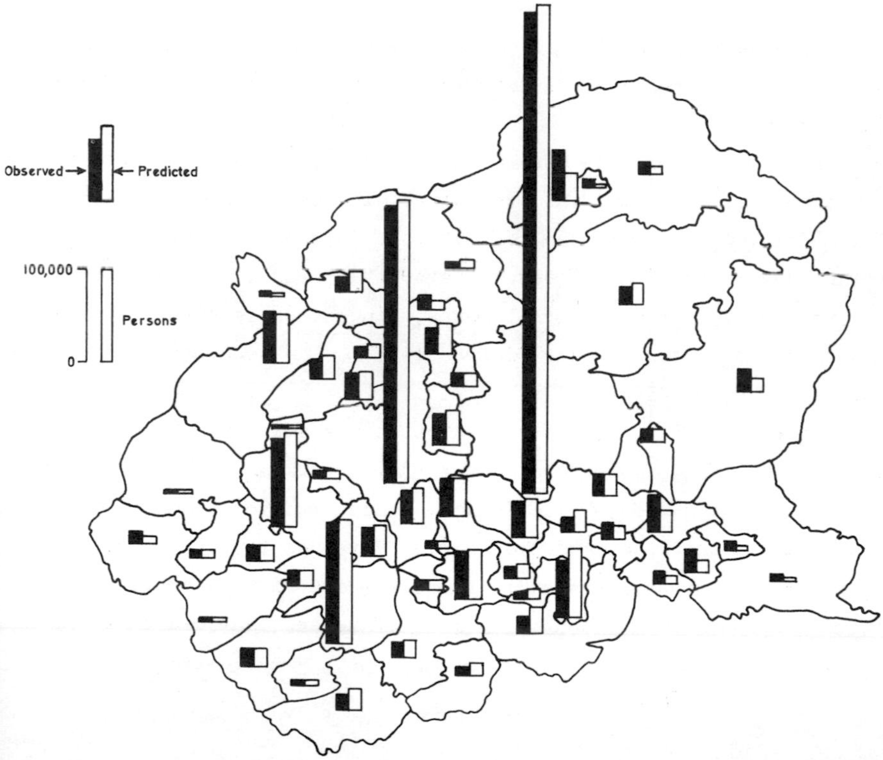

Observed → ← Predicted

100,000
0
Persons

Figure 5.9 Results of a comparative static model: population for 1966, West Yorkshire

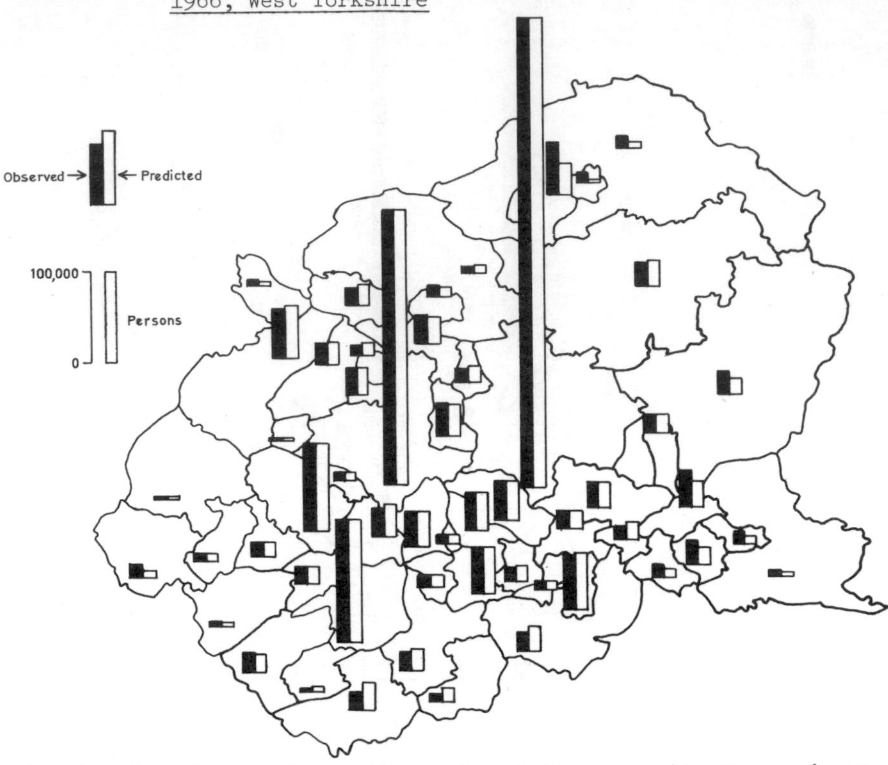

for the dynamic version. These showed the necessity for regional β values in the residential location submodel which have now been introduced.

We will now examine a test run of the Leeds model to illustrate how the model works and the sort of results that can be obtained. The model gives useful results, but these are being improved, by both model innovation and better data. The run illustrated is for the model without external zones, since this is simpler to describe and is for the period 1966-1971. The study area is shown in Figure 5.10.

In the model run the first calculations are described in Section 5.11 above, with the data read in, various ratios calculated, some useful checks on the data made, basic employment found and scaled up to the total and the initial β values found. The total number of new houses is found; these are distributed between zones in proportion to the potential number of houses that can be located in each and added on to the number of houses vacated by migrants.

Figure 5.10 Study area for the Leeds model

These houses are available for occupation by newly locating residents of social group 1; the residential attraction is based upon both the number of available houses and historic factors, since it is assumed members of a particular social group choose to locate near to other members of the same group, provided there are houses available. The residential location submodel allocates workers in this social group to available houses. None of the constraints are violated for this social group so we move directly to the calibration of the residential location model for the top social group, by comparing the model mean trip lengths with the actual value. We find a new value of β and run through the submodel again. It is not within the specified limit of 1%, so a new value of β is found. This is smaller than the first value, implying that workers in this social group have less reluctance to travel than initially implied. Again on the allocation to residences no further constraints are violated so the mean trip lengths are compared, and since it is still not near enough another, much smaller value of β is obtained by linear interpolation. Again no constraints are violated so another calibration is attempted. Again, we are not close enough for convergence so a new β value is found. This is larger than the previous value, suggesting distance may be of some importance to this social group. The mean trip length is now within the limits set of the actual value so this value of β is taken. It is now the turn of social group 2 to be allocated to residences. There are still houses available to newly located residents in all zones. The model allocates employed residents in social group 2 between the 28 zones. The housing becomes used up in zones 2, 4, 6, 7, 9, 12, 13, 14, 15, 21, 22, 25, 26 and 27. These employed residents are reallocated to zones and then constraints in the following zones become violated 3, 5, 16, 17, 20 and 28. After a further run of the submodel the housing is used up in zones 18 and 24, and then on the fourth reallocation zone 23 violates the constraint. After this capacity test there are no further violations of the constraints by the redistribution of employed residents, and so the mean trip length is found and compared with the actual value. This is not within the specified bounds and so a new value of β is found and the process repeated three times until convergence, that is the model mean trip length is sufficiently close to the actual to be acceptable. Housing has been used up in zones 2, 3, 4, 5, 6, 9, 12, 13, 14, 15, 16, 20, 22, 25, 27 and 28, so that newly located members of social group 3 cannot locate in any of these zones. The process is repeated for social group 3; this time, because the housing has been used up in certain zones, the residential attraction of these zones is set to zero. After the location of this social group the value of β is again found. The process is repeated until convergence.

This is the completion of the first iteration of the whole model. By applying the inverse activity rates to the located employed residents, the spatial distribution of population in each social group is found. The population demands services such as shops and schools, so these are located by the non-basic submodel, which is calibrated automatically for each sector in the same way as the residential location submodel. The employment in each non-basic sector is found by applying conversion factors to the demand calculated in the non-basic submodel. This is added to the basic employment to give an improved spatial distribution of jobs. Employment now takes up all available land in Harehills, so that no new houses can be built there. Because industry is given preference over housing for land (since it can usually afford higher prices for land and requires greater accessibility) we now have to run through the residential location submodel with this new distribution of jobs. We now have more employment located in the suburbs, since we are no longer merely scaling up basic industry. We start with the value of β that represented convergence for this social group on the previous iteration. After three iterations of the residential location submodel for social group 1 convergence is reached. The whole process is repeated to obtain a new population distribution. The whole model is rerun twice more until there is no significant redistribution of population from one outer loop to the next. Each time the population generates a spatial distribution of non-basic industry which is added on to the basic employment distribution to give the total employment to be located in the available housing.

The final values of β are 0.0647, 0.0690 and 0.4467 for social groups 1, 2 and 3 respectively, illustrating the relative effects of distance on the choice of residential location for the groups. Distance has least effect for social group 1, then 2 and finally social group 3, which tends to choose to locate fairly near jobs. The model calculates the number of houses actually occupied in each zone and compares this with the stock in each zone. There are no vacant houses. Thus we have found the spatial distribution of houses, population in each social group, non-basic employment and sales in shops for the year 1971. It is possible to compare the forecast and actual values for the housing and population. These are shown in Figures 5.11 to 5.15. As mentioned above these figures are largely illustrative, as further improvements are being made to both the model and the data, but it is possible to see the sort of output that the model yields.

Figure 5.11 Location of housing, Leeds

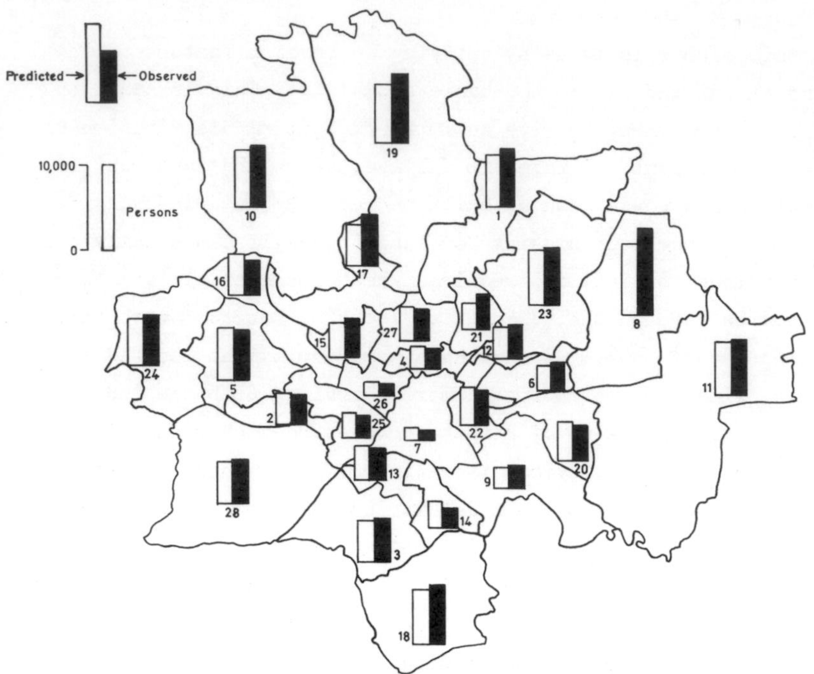

Figure 5.12 Location of population in social group 1, Leeds

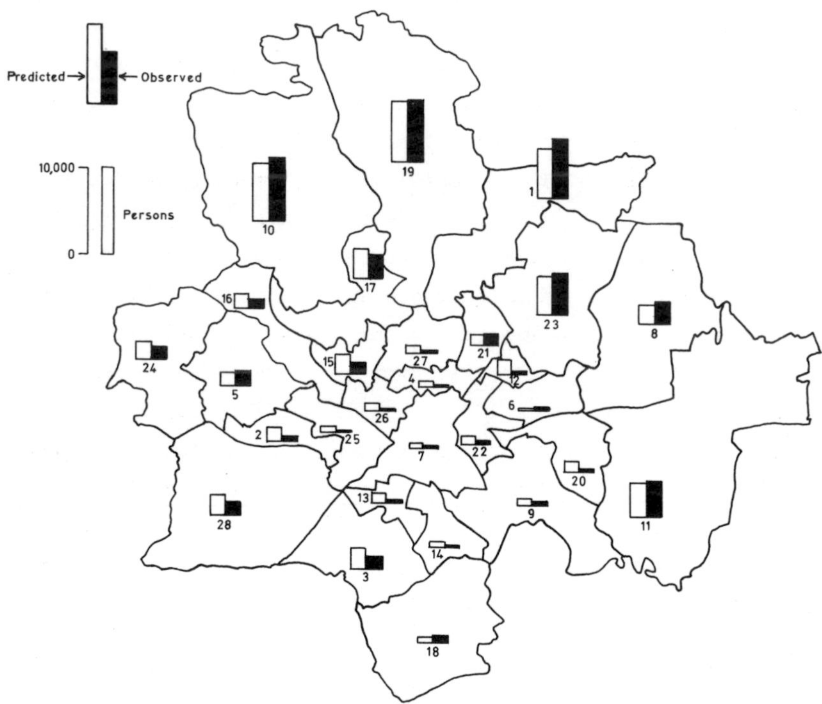

Figure 5.13 Location of population in social group 2, Leeds

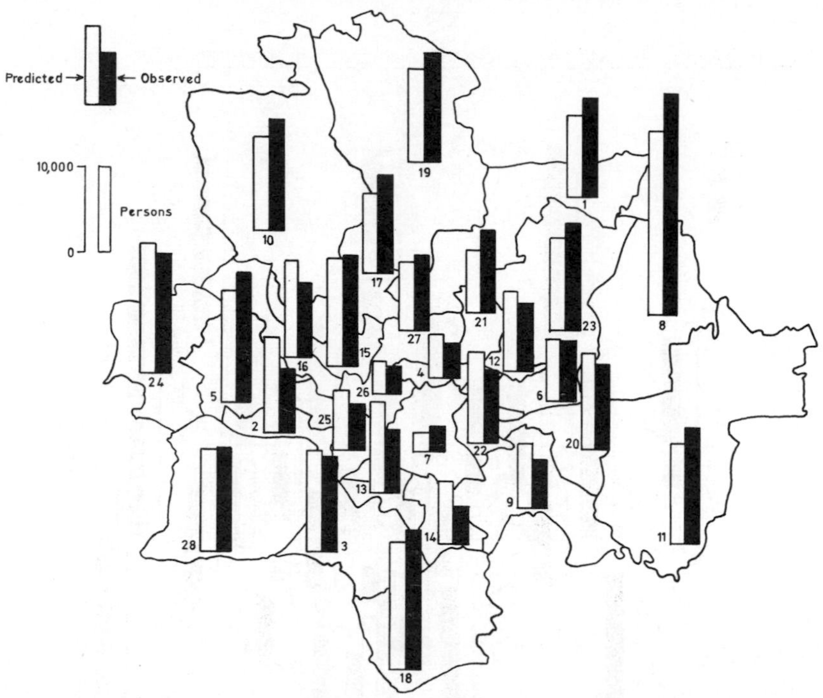

Figure 5.14 Location of population in social group 3, Leeds

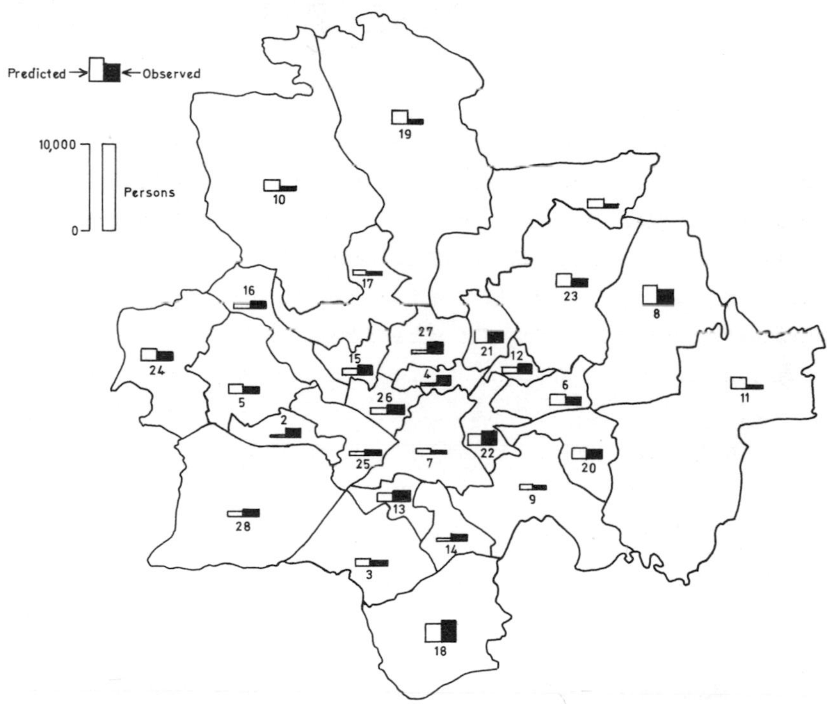

Figure 5.15 Location of total population, Leeds

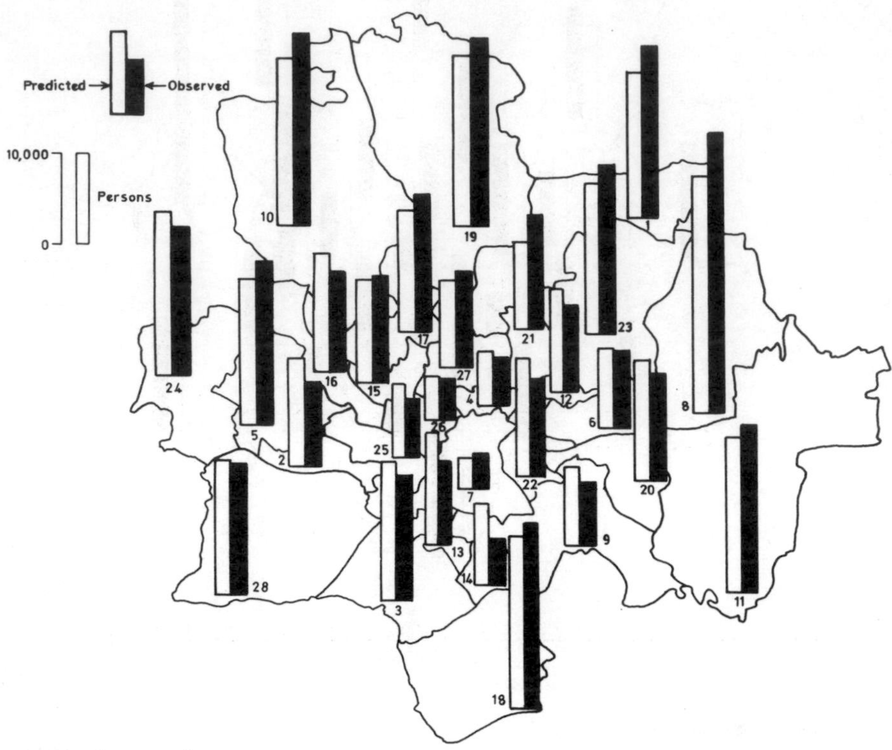

5.14 Conclusions

This chapter has described two applications developed from the original Lowry model. Both include several interesting, and probably unique, features, such as the methods of disaggregation by social group and external zones in the Leeds model. Perhaps the most interesting feature is the incorporation of explicit policy variables, and the consequent potential uses of the models in a planning context. There is still room for improvement on both models, particularly in terms of the data. However, given the potentially severe restrictions placed on model building by the lack of suitable data, these two models do demonstrate quite clearly what can be achieved with a certain amount of ingenuity in 'poor data' situations.

References

Barras, R., Broadbent, T.A., Cordey-Hayes, M., Massey, D.B. and Robinson, K. (1971) An operational urban development model of Cheshire, Environment and Planning, 3, pp. 115-234.

Batty, M. (1970) Some problems in calibrating the Lowry model, Environment and Planning, 2, pp. 95-114.

Batty, M. (1971-A) Design and construction of a subregional land use model, Socio-Economic Planning Sciences, 5, pp. 97-124.

Batty, M. (1971-B) Exploratory calibration of a retail local model using search by golden section, Environment and Planning, 3, pp. 411-432.

Batty, M. (1972) Dynamic simulation of an urban system in Wilson, A.G. (ed.) Patterns and processes in urban and regional systems, Pion, London, pp. 44-82.

Batty, M. and Mackie, S. (1972) The calibration of gravity, entropy and related models of spatial interaction, Environment and Planning, 4, pp. 131-250.

Batty, M., Foot, D., Alonso, L., Bray, G., Brehany, M., Constable, D., Dugmore, K., Ellender, R., Shepherd, J. and Williams, J. (1973) Spatial system design and fast calibration of activity interaction-allocation models, Regional Studies, 7, pp. 351-366.

Chilton, R. and Poet, R.R.W. (1973) An entropy maximising approach to the recovery of detailed migration patterns from aggregate census data, Environment and Planning, 5, pp. 135-146.

Cripps, E.L. and Foot, D.H.S. (1969) A land-use model for subregional planning, Regional Studies, 3, pp. 243-268.

Crowther, D. and Echenique, M. (1972) Development of a model of urban spatial structure, in Martin, L. and March, L. (eds.) Urban space and structure, Cambridge University Press, Cambridge, pp. 175-218.

Evans, A.W. (1971) The calibration of trip distribution models with exponential or similar functions, Transportation Research, 5, pp. 15-38.

Harris, A.I. (1967) Labour mobility in Great Britain, Government Social Survey SS330, HMSO, London.

Hyman, G.M. (1969) The calibration of trip distribution models, Environment and Planning, 1, pp. 105-112.

Lakshmanan, T.R. and Hansen, W.G. (1965) A retail market potential model, Journal of the American Institute of Planners, 31, pp. 134-143.

Lowry, I.S. (1964) A model of metropolis, RM-4035-RC, Rand Corporation, Santa Monica.

Mackett, R.L. (1973-A) Shopping in the city - the application of an intra-urban shopping model to Leeds, Working Paper 30, Department of Geography, University of Leeds.

Mackett, R.L. (1973-B) The estimation of employment in small areas within the city, Working Paper 29, Department of Geography, University of Leeds.

Mackett, R.L. (1974) A residential location model incorporating spatially varying levels of information, Regional Studies, 8, pp. 257-265.

Rhodes, T. (1969) Computer models in subregional planning, Regional Studies, 3, pp. 331-336.

Wilson, A.G. (1967) A note on intra-zonal travel times, Transportation Research, 1, p. 288.

Wilson, A.G. (1969) Developments of some elementary residential location models, Journal of Regional Science, 9, pp. 377-385.

Wilson, A.G. (1970) Entropy in urban and regional modelling, Pion, London.

Wilson, A.G. (1974) Urban and regional models in geography and planning, John Wiley, London and New York.

Chapter 6

Residential location

M.L. Senior

6.1 Developments in residential location modelling

6.1.1 Introduction

As a background to the discussion of specific residential location models some of the main features of residential modelling developments in general are reviewed briefly under the headings of urban ecological, social physics, urban economic and integrated models. (In depth reviews are given by Senior, 1973, 1974-A, 1974-B). This coverage is far from exhaustive of the variety of models proposed and used, but the above categories do represent major styles of analysis in this field.

6.1.2 Urban ecological models

Models of this 'school' first came to prominence in the 1920's with the work of a group of Chicago sociologists (Park, Burgess and McKenzie, 1925) who influenced the subsequent work of Hoyt (1939) and Harris and Ullman (1945). The outcomes of these studies were the much-debated concentric zone, sector and multiple nuclei spatial models of the city. Another group of sociologists, the Social Area Analysts, who were less spatially-minded than the earlier ecologists, hypothesised that urban society could be classified on the three dimensions of economic, family and ethnic status, and went on to demonstrate the validity of these constructs empirically (as in Bell, 1955), although their theoretical arguments have been ridiculed by Hawley and Duncan (1957). Since large scale factor analyses of residential data matrices became feasible considerable clarification and co-ordination of this previous work has been undertaken. The modern factorial ecologies have drawn together the spatial frameworks of Burgess, Hoyt, and Harris and Ullman and an expanded set of non-spatial constructs from the Social Area Analysts to give us a detailed picture of residential patterns, chiefly in westernised cities.

Essentially this approach to residential modelling is descriptive in nature and inductive in scientific style. The factorial ecology model extracts the principal dimensions of variability in residential structures, which are the outputs of processes operating in the housing system, and suggests key elements that should be incorporated in explanatory models and theories. They do however, tend to be relatively reticent about accessibility and opportunities involving spatial interaction. Factorial ecologies of a static nature have proliferated and it appears that at least for western cities future research of this kind, unless of a more specialised nature, would not repay the effort expended. However, more dynamically conceived descriptive studies may yet be worthwhile. A number of geographers have indeed turned to studying the processes causing change in residential patterns (eg. Simmons, 1968; Brown and Moore, 1970).

6.1.3 Social physics models

In contrast to urban ecological models these models are predictive, deductive in style and a spatial interaction-accessibility mechanism has often been the central feature of them. Recent developments have been playing down their spatial interaction elements.

Early models were of the static equilibrium type and aggregated over population, housing and employment types (Wilson, 1969; Cripps and Foot, 1969; Echenique, Crowther and Lindsay, 1969). Subsequent developments involved disaggregation of the variables, still within a static equilibrium framework, and attempts to specify residential attraction more fully to supplement the usual accessibility measure (Wilson, 1970-A; Senior and Wilson, 1974-A; Cripps and Cater, 1972; Anthony and Baxter, 1971). A notable attempt to operationalise a dynamic version of the aggregate models has been made by Batty (1972). The logical implications of these developments is a dynamic disaggregated model (Wilson, 1970-A), which perhaps could be made quasi-operational in the not too distant future, and some progress has now in fact been made by Ayeni (1975). The social physics models, of which the Lowry model (Lowry, 1964) is still the best known and still exerts a powerful influence on model development, have developed as operational, predictive tools and not surprisingly have lacked the depth of explanation available in more ambitious but less operational economic models (Colenutt, 1970).

6.1.4 Urban economic models

Economics, in many ways the most theoretically mature of the social sciences, has offered the most co-ordinated, comprehensive and rigorously argued theories of the housing market (Wingo, 1961; Alonso, 1960, 1964; Muth, 1969; Evans, 1973). Economists more than others have had a clearer conception of the systemic nature of the residential system which they have captured in their typical demand, supply and market-clearing framework. However, the assumptions that are associated with such theories have been fiercely criticised. Monocentric, uniform city assumptions are common for example, but others include the emphasis on a long-run static equilibrium which allows the durability and short-run inflexibility of housing supply to be ignored and attention to be focused on the spatial uniqueness of housing and the consequent price variation by location. The whole topic of residential mobility - the decision to move as opposed to the residential choice decision - is neglected. In addition externality effects in the housing market are dismissed; individual decision making is assumed independent of decisions by other consumers. Moreover, with the exception of Alonso (1964), variation in consumer preferences are suppressed in the central theoretical analyses. These assumptions among others allow economists like Muth (1969) and Beckmann (1969) to derive *analytically* the forms of the price-distance and population density functions. Alonso (1964) did not resort to the assumption of identical consumer preferences and was thus unable to derive analytically the form of such market phenomena, for which his theory has been unfairly criticised (Kirwan and Martin, 1970). However, a relaxation of the assumption of identical preferences immediately causes analytical problems as Wheaton (1972) and Wilson (1970-B, Chapter 6) have shown, and numerical methods of solution are needed.

Many aggregate models have been associated to varying extents with this theoretical work. Probably the most sophisticated is the Herbert-Stevens model (Herbert and Stevens, 1960) which employs a linear programming technique (see Section 6.2.3) to obtain an optimal solution to the market clearing problem specified by Alonso (1964, Chapter 5). Other studies include the multiple regression models of Kain (1962, 1964); the San Francisco housing model (Robinson, Wolfe and Barringer, 1965; Wolfe, 1967) and the NBER Urban Simulation model (Ingram, Kain and Ginn, 1972), which is as yet the most comprehensive model of the housing market and which, appropriately, departs substantially from the assumptions of standard micro-economic theories.

6.1.5 Integrated models

The advantage of a theoretical background to the formulation and interpretation of operational, aggregate models is evident from the above economic examples and much recent interest has been directed to incorporating economic concepts in models of the social physics style. Basically, this has involved the use of entropy maximising models, which are more flexible than the linear programming models with their optimising assumptions, but possess the accounting constraints and duality characteristics of the latter (Senior and Wilson, 1974-B). Models exemplifying these latest trends include those of Batty (1973), Eastin and Shapiro (1973), Anas (1973) and of Zoller (1972).

6.2 Choice of models for current purposes

6.2.1 Examples of model approaches

The choice of models to discuss in more detail and to test for the Leeds study area follows naturally from the above review. First, a disaggregated static equilibrium version of an elementary spatial interaction model of residential location proposed by Wilson (1970-A) illustrates developments in social physics models. Second, an example of the urban economic approach is given using a version of the Herbert-Stevens model in its linear programming form, but modified from the original to consider a fixed housing supply and the workplace connections of households. Finally, an illustration of an integrated model is conveniently derived by using the Herbert-Stevens model concepts and mechanisms in an entropy maximising (EM), rather than linear programming (LP), framework. Formal presentation of these models, which are formulated at a common level of sector-spatial resolution, is undertaken in the next three sections.

6.2.2 Model 1: A disaggregated spatial interaction model of residential location of the social physics type

Let us define an interaction variable, T_{ij}^{kwn}, to be the number of workers in location j, belonging to worker or household group w, who live in a type k house in zone i. The n superscript denotes headship of a household (n=1) or a dependent worker (n=0). The model is built by maximising an appropriate entropy function:

$$S = -\Sigma_i \Sigma_j \Sigma_k \Sigma_w \Sigma_n T_{ij}^{kwn} \ln T_{ij}^{kwn} \tag{6.1}$$

subject to constraints expressing known or hypothesised information. It is assumed that employment, E, by type of worker, w, and zone j is fixed, so:

$$\Sigma_i \Sigma_k \Sigma_n T_{ij}^{kwn} = E_j^w \tag{6.2}$$

Workers who are heads of households are assumed to be allocated to the housing stock, H_i^k, according to the availability of housing, therefore:

$$\Sigma_j \Sigma_w T_{ij}^{kw1} = H_i^k \tag{6.3}$$

and sufficient housing is thus available for dependent workers with their respective household heads:

$$\Sigma_j \Sigma_w T_{ij}^{kw0} = (r_i - 1)\, H_i^k \tag{6.4}$$

where r_i is the ratio of all workers to head workers by zone. Some commentators (eg. Cripps and Cater, 1972; Anthony and Baxter, 1971) have argued that residential trip end constraints of an equality form, like Equations (6.3) and (6.4), should not be used because they are behaviourally restrictive. In effect they force demand and supply to balance perfectly. However, such constraints have been utilised here as otherwise problems arise in the calibration process; this issue is pursued in greater length in Senior (1974-C).

Locational decisions are hypothesised to be influenced by journey-to-work expenditure, c_{ij}, expressed for each worker group w in:

$$\Sigma_i \Sigma_j \Sigma_k \Sigma_n T_{ij}^{kwn} c_{ij} = C^w \tag{6.5}$$

Heads of households are assumed to be responsible for housing expenditure and the overall attractiveness of different house types, k, in different locations, i, is taken to be reflected by their prices, p_i^k.

The attractiveness of such houses to different groups of workers depends on the divergence between housing costs and average group expenditures, where $W^w - c'_{ij}$ is income net of transport costs, and q^w is the average proportion of this income spent on housing by members of each worker group. It is hypothesised that members of each w group will have a distribution of expenditures for housing, reflecting a distribution of preferences, of which $q^w (W^w - c'_{ij})$ is only the mean value, adjusted for the differential transport costs incurred. Making the initial assumption that expenditures are normally distributed then an appropriate constraint is:

$$\Sigma_i \Sigma_j \Sigma_k T_{ij}^{kw1} \{p_i^k - q^w(W^w - c'_{ij})\}^2 = \sigma^{w^2} \quad (6.6)$$

One further constraint, relating to total heads of households by group, M^w, has been shown to be necessary for consistency and accurate calibration:

$$\Sigma_i \Sigma_j \Sigma_k T_{ij}^{kw1} = M^w \quad (6.7)$$

The resulting model is of the form:

$$T_{ij}^{kw1} = A_i^{k1} B_j^w D^w H_i^k E_j^w M^w \exp(-\beta^w c_{ij}) \exp\{-\mu^w \{p_i^k - q^w(W^w - c'_{ij})\}^2\} \quad (6.8)$$

$$T_{ij}^{kw0} = A_i^{k0} B_j^w (r_i - 1) H_i^k E_j^w \exp(-\beta^w c_{ij}) \quad (6.9)$$

where expressions for the balancing factors are:

$$A_i^{k1} = \{\Sigma_j \Sigma_w B_j^w E_j^w D^w M^w \exp(-\beta^w c_{ij}) \exp\{-\mu^w \{p_i^k - q^w(W^w - c'_{ij})\}^2\}\}^{-1} \quad (6.10)$$

$$A_i^{k0} = \{\Sigma_j \Sigma_w B_j^w E_j^w \exp(-\beta^w c_{ij})\}^{-1} \quad (6.11)$$

$$B_j^w = \{D^w M^w \Sigma_i \Sigma_k A_i^{k1} H_i^k \exp(-\beta^w c_{ij}) \times \exp\{-\mu^w \{p_i^k - q^w(W^w - c'_{ij})\}^2\} + \Sigma_i \Sigma_k A_i^{k0} (r_i - 1) H_i^k \exp(-\beta^w c_{ij})\}^{-1} \quad (6.12)$$

$$D^w = \{\Sigma_i \Sigma_j \Sigma_k A_i^{kl} H_i^k B_j^w E_j^w \exp(-\beta^w c_{ij}) \times$$

$$\exp\{-\mu^w\{p_i^k - q^w(W^w - c'_{ij})\}^2\}\}^{-1} \qquad (6.13)$$

The model's underlying hypotheses can be summarised as follows: head of household workers belonging to various groups w and with jobs in zone j choose housing according to its availability, its accessibility to workplaces, and by comparing prices with their willingness and ability to pay. Dependent workers are only affected by availability and accessibility considerations. Further interpretation of the model is pursued in Wilson (1974), Senior (1973), where the treatment of households with no workers is also dealt with, in Senior (1974-B, Sections 6.2 and 6.4), and in Senior and Wilson (1974-A). Important questions of internal consistency and calibration are discussed in the latter reference. In particular, because of the way the normal housing expenditure distribution has been formulated, it is necessary to ensure that data on consumers' housing expenditure matches data on housing costs; in other words a simple accounting identity is required. In Senior and Wilson (1974-A) it is argued that this identity can be applied only for each group w. Hence we have:

$$\Sigma_i \Sigma_j \Sigma_k T_{ij}^{kwl} q^w(W^w - c'_{ij}) = C^{Hw} = \Sigma_i \Sigma_j \Sigma_k T_{ij}^{kwl} p_i^k \qquad (6.14)$$

where the C^{Hw} are the total housing costs incurred by the w groups. If part of Equation (6.14) is adopted as an extra constraint at the model-building stage a truncated normal distribution of housing expenditures would be obtained in the model (see Senior and Wilson, 1974-A). Of course, if the normal expenditure distribution is formulated solely in terms of prices, p_i^k, then Equation (6.14) is satisfied in a more obvious manner. This can be done by sacrificing the c'_{ij} variations of mean housing expenditure, (which in any case turn out to be trivial), and by setting <u>mean</u> housing expenditure per group, $\bar{c}^{Hw}$, equal to:

$$\bar{c}^{Hw} = \Sigma_i \Sigma_j \Sigma_k T_{ij}^{kwl} p_i^k / \Sigma_i \Sigma_j \Sigma_k T_{ij}^{kwl} \qquad (6.15)$$

Hence the normal expenditure distribution would be given by:

$$\exp\{-\mu^{w}\{p_i^k - c^{-Hw}\}^2\} \tag{6.16}$$

Of course part of the calibration processes should be to determine whether the normal housing expenditure distribution is empirically valid. For example, if the distribution is positively skewed then a Γ distribution, given by:

$$(p_i^k)^{\lambda^w} \exp\{-\mu^w p_i^k\} \tag{6.17}$$

may be appropriate.

6.2.3 Model 2: A linear programming model incorporating micro-economic concepts

A number of versions of the Herbert-Stevens model (Herbert and Stevens, 1960) have been proposed (Wheaton and Harris, 1972; Senior and Wilson, 1974-B). The original was intended as an algorithmic solution to the market-clearing problem in the urban land market proposed by Alonso (1964, Chapter 5). Here we depart from some of the conditions pertaining to that model. In particular we assume a fixed housing stock, constraint (6.3), and hence consider short-run rather than long-run solutions to the market-clearing process. Also, we take demand as emanating from workers at specified workplace locations by adopting constraint (6.2); thus we relax the mono-centricity assumption of micro-economic theories by identifying multiple workplace locations explicitly unlike the original Herbert-Stevens model. Hence we have the same demand and supply constraints as the previous model; the crucial difference is that the Herbert-Stevens model uses the micro-economists' concept of bid rents/prices, b_{ij}^{kw}, to state the attractiveness of house types and locations to consumer groups[(1)]. It is conjectured that workers compete for the available residential opportunities by a bidding process. The bids offered are monetary expressions of consumers' housing and accessibility preferences subject to their budget constraints. A consumer bid price schedule defines, at a given level of utility, an indifference surface; at these offered prices the consumer is <u>indifferent</u> between all residential opportunities. In other words, the extra utility a consumer could gain by living in house A rather than house

---

[(1)] See Section 6 of Senior and Wilson (1974-B) for a suggested identification of Models 1 and 2.

B is exactly offset by the difference in his bid prices for these houses.

It is generally taken that each (j,w) consumer group is defined to have homogeneous preferences (Harris, 1966; Harris, Nathanson and Rosenburg, 1966), so every individual has an identical bid price schedule to members of his group. Alternatively it could be hypothesised that an _average_ group bid is being considered, analogous to the use of the average group housing expenditure in Model 1. However, unlike this latter model, the Herbert-Stevens model in its LP form at least would then be ignoring any intra-group preference variations. The several worker groups are regarded as competitors for scarce housing resources in a perfectly competitive housing market. Their competitive bidding pushes prices up, an effect which is captured in the primal objective function of the model, which takes total bids, Z, as being maximised subject to constraints (6.2) and (6.3)[(1)] and the non-negativity conditions:

$$T^{kw}_{ij} \geqslant 0 \tag{6.18}$$

Hence the LP objective[(2)] is to:

$$\text{Max } Z = \Sigma_i \Sigma_j \Sigma_k \Sigma_w T^{kw}_{ij} \{b^{kw}_{ij} - c'_{ij}\} \tag{6.19}$$

subject to constraints (6.2) and (6.3). Journey-to-work costs, c'_{ij}, are deducted from bids, so that the net bid is for the house only. This problem has a dual objective to minimise actual or market prices, α^k_i, paid:

$$\text{Min } Z' = \Sigma_i \Sigma_k \alpha^k_i H^k_i + \Sigma_j \Sigma_w \nu^w_j E^w_j \tag{6.20}$$

subject to:

$$\alpha^k_i + \nu^w_j \geqslant b^{kw}_{ij} - c'_{ij} \tag{6.21}$$

and

$$\alpha^k_i \geqslant 0; \quad \nu^w_j \gtreqless 0 \tag{6.22}$$

The minimisation of market prices, α^k_i, in the dual reflects the situation where suppliers are competing with each other for prospective

---

(1) The housing constraint (6.3) could be made less restrictive if a < sign replaced the equality sign.

(2) For convenience the n superscript is dropped on the T^{kwn}_{ij}'s implying only one worker per household.

tenants or purchasers. To avoid unsold or untenanted housing they will have to lower asking prices to the market price level. Hence the primal and dual problems reflect both sides of a market 'confrontation'. The other dual variables, ν_j^w, measure the differences between market prices and bids offered by consumers. They are in fact measures of consumer surpluses or losses of welfare, depending on their sign, and as such are extremely important evaluation indices. Their use in the LP model suggests that bids should be adjusted to match market prices in a linear way. However, Wheaton and Harris (1972) argue that as bids are related to levels of utility and as all realistic utility functions are nonlinear, then bids must be nonlinearly adjusted too. These arguments are reviewed in more detail in Senior (1974-B, 1974-C).

This conveniently brings us to the formulation of a demand model to estimate bid rents in the first place and subsequently to adjust them nonlinearly. Such a model was initially proposed by Harris (1965) and has been implemented by Harris, Nathanson and Rosenburg (1966) and Wheaton (1972). Briefly a sensible form for a utility function is postulated, say:

$$U^w = \ln X_i^{kw} + \Sigma_g \theta_g^{w(1)} \ln H_i^{kg} + \Sigma_j \theta_j^{w(2)} \ln d_{ij}^w \qquad (6.23)$$

where utility by worker type w is derived from expenditures on nonlocational items, X, from the 'consumption' of various attributes, g, of housing, H, by zone and type, and from accessibility, d, to sundry desinations, j. Note that the above equation is written without a constant term, as the <u>ordinal</u> form of utility is being employed (see Harris, 1965). By having unit coefficients on the expenditures, X, the whole equation can be expressed in money units; so the parameters $\theta_g^{w(1)}$ and $\theta_j^{w(2)}$ monetise respectively the housing and accessibility measures. Rearranging the variables, the utility terms U^w can be made the intercept parameters of a set of multiple regression models (one for each worker group) estimating nonlocational expenditures:

$$\ln X_i^{kw} = U^w - \Sigma_g \theta_g^{w(1)} \ln H_i^{kg} - \Sigma_j \theta_j^{w(2)} \ln d_{ij}^w \qquad (6.24)$$

This type of model can be calibrated against an observed housing market outcome assumed to be in equilibrium for some base year, where observations on X_{i}^{kw}, H_{i}^{kg} and d_{ij}^{w} are available. In a forecasting situation new housing and accessibility measures are input to the model to predict new expenditures X which, when deducted from predicted incomes for the forecast year, give new bid schedules. The Herbert-Stevens-type model can then be used to evaluate how different consumer groups fare under the new housing and accessibility policies as compared with their base year position.

6.2.4 Model 3: An integrated residential model

To obtain the best of both worlds, so to speak, this section describes the Leeds version of the Herbert-Stevens model cast within an entropy maximising framework. That is, we adopt a model building technique common to the social physics models but retain the dependence of model content on some key concepts in micro-economic theories of the housing market. This scheme has the specific advantage of avoiding the optimising and associated perfect competition assumptions that the LP procedure implies.

The model is easily derived by maximising our entropy function (6.1)[(1)] subject to the demand and supply constraints, (6.2) and (6.3), and by taking the LP objective function (6.19) as an additional behavioural constraint which is no longer necessarily optimised, but may take a suboptimal value which is known at the calibration stage (see Senior and Wilson, 1974-A, 1974-B). Forming the Lagrangian:

$$
\begin{aligned}
L = & - \sum_i \sum_j \sum_k \sum_w T_{ij}^{kw} \ln T_{ij}^{kw} - \sum_i \sum_k \lambda_i^{k(1)} \left(\sum_j \sum_w T_{ij}^{kw} - H_i^{k}\right) \\
& + \sum_j \sum_w \lambda_j^{w(2)} \left(\sum_i \sum_k T_{ij}^{kw} - E_j^{w}\right) \\
& + \mu\left\{\sum_i \sum_j \sum_k \sum_w T_{ij}^{kw}\left(b_{ij}^{kw} - c'_{ij}\right) - Z\right\}
\end{aligned}
\qquad (6.25)
$$

and differentiating, we obtain:

$$
\begin{aligned}
\frac{\partial L}{\partial T_{ij}^{kw}} = & - \ln T_{ij}^{kw} - 1 - \lambda_i^{k(1)} + \lambda_j^{w(2)} \\
& + \mu\left(b_{ij}^{kw} - c'_{ij}\right) = 0
\end{aligned}
\qquad (6.26)
$$

---

(1) See previous footnote

or in a more familiar form:

$$T_{ij}^{kw} = A_i^k H_i^k B_j^w E_j^w \exp\{\mu(b_{ij}^{kw} - c_{ij}')\} \tag{6.27}$$

The EM model will typically predict a greater diversity of residential location behaviour than an equivalent LP model, as the number of non-zero allocations in the latter model is restricted to the number of independent constraints[1]. In the EM model, (6.27), the higher the value of each bid the greater the number of allocations, T_{ij}^{kw}, provided μ is positive; also none of the T_{ij}^{kw} elements will be zero-valued although some may be trivially small.

The above equations give the primal equivalent of the LP model; we can also define an equivalent dual problem by using the arguments quoted by Balinski and Baumol (1968) and Wilson and Senior (1974). Rearranging the Lagrangian expression (6.25) we obtain:

$$L = \Sigma_i \Sigma_j \Sigma_k \Sigma_w T_{ij}^{kw}\{-\ln T_{ij}^{kw} - \lambda_i^{k(1)} + \lambda_j^{w(2)} + \mu(b_{ij}^{kw} - c_{ij}')\}$$
$$+ \Sigma_i \Sigma_k \lambda_i^{k(1)} H_i^k - \Sigma_j \Sigma_w \lambda_j^{w(2)} E_j^w - \mu Z \tag{6.28}$$

It is known from the Kuhn-Tucker conditions that for L to be a maximum in the T_{ij}^{kw}'s, the primal variables, then:

$$T_{ij}^{kw} \frac{\partial L}{\partial T_{ij}^{kw}} = 0 \tag{6.29}$$

The term in curly brackets in Equation (6.28) is equal to $(\partial L/\partial T_{ij}^{kw} + 1)$ according to Equation (6.26). So when there is a maximum in the T_{ij}^{kw}'s the first term in Equation (6.28) reduces to $\Sigma_i \Sigma_j \Sigma_k \Sigma_w T_{ij}^{kw}$, which can be expressed in terms of the Lagrangian multipliers, and the whole of Equation (6.28) then becomes the dual entropy objective function:

$$\text{Min } S' = \Sigma_i \Sigma_k \lambda_i^{k(1)} H_i^k - \Sigma_j \Sigma_w \lambda_j^{w(2)} E_j^w - \mu Z$$
$$+ \Sigma_i \Sigma_j \Sigma_k \Sigma_w e^{-\lambda_i^{k(1)} - 1 + \lambda_j^{w(2)} + \mu(b_{ij}^{kw} - c_{ij}')} \tag{6.30}$$

---

[1] The work of Suzanne Evans (1973) proves that the LP model is a limiting form of the EM model as μ tends to infinity, and some empirical 'proof' of this theorem is offered in Section 6.5.4.

provided that:

$$- \ln T_{ij}^{kw} - \lambda_i^{k(1)} + \lambda_j^{w(2)} + \mu(b_{ij}^{kw} - c_{ij}^{'}) \begin{cases} = 0 \text{ for } T_{ij}^{kw} > 0 \\ \leq 0 \text{ for } T_{ij}^{kw} = 0 \end{cases} \qquad (6.31)$$

Rewriting these constraints as:

$$\frac{\lambda_i^{k(1)}}{\mu} - \frac{\lambda_j^{w(2)}}{\mu} + \frac{\ln T_{ij}^{kw}}{\mu} = b_{ij}^{kw} - c_{ij}^{'} \qquad (6.32)$$

and comparing them with their LP equivalents (6.21) it is contended that the $\lambda_i^{k(1)}/\mu$ can be interpreted as the market prices of housing and the $\lambda_j^{w(2)}/\mu$ as the surplus or welfare terms. Observe that in (6.30) market prices are being minimised as in (6.20) and total bid rents, Z, are being maximised.

The values of the $\lambda_j^{w(2)}/\mu$ terms are affected by suboptimality in the system. In the LP solution all groups are at their optimal locations; they are all maximising consumer surpluses or minimising losses of welfare. Under imperfect market conditions, however, suboptimal allocations may entail a greater welfare loss. On the other hand the $\ln T_{ij}^{kw}/\mu$ values, which are always deducted from bids for positive μ values, represent surpluses which increase as each T_{ij}^{kw} value increases. Thus the greater the clustering of (j,w) consumers in an (i,k) house type the greater this offsetting surplus becomes. Therefore benefits may vary among members of a group according to location and house type chosen; this is in contrast to the LP model solution. These arguments are based on the assumption of identical bids by members of each consumer group. Alternatively, if the bids input to the model were taken only as summarising a distribution of bids internal to each group, then some of the variability of adjusted bids implied by the $\frac{1}{\mu} \ln T_{ij}^{kw}$ terms could be attributed to intra-group preference variations.

6.3 Methods of parameter estimation

6.3.1 Introduction

The fitting of the above models to a state of the real world involves three related tasks: (i) defining suitable and sensitive calibration statistics to optimise on parameter values; (ii) adopting and implementing efficient solution procedures for this optimisation process; and (iii) assessing the goodness-of-fit of each model's predictions obtained with the optimal parameter values; in some cases the calibration statistic might also function as a goodness-of-fit measure. These tasks are discussed in turn below.

6.3.2 Calibration statistics

For the type of EM models described in Sections 6.2.2 and 6.2.4 maximum likelihood procedures are commonly employed to obtain sensitive calibration statistics, especially where there is more than one parameter involved as in Model 1. It turns out that these maximum likelihood statistics are related to the EM constraints that give rise to the model parameters in the first place; hence for Model 1 we have separate maximum likelihood equations for β^w and μ^w, associated respectively with constraints (6.5) and (6.6):

$$\Sigma_i \Sigma_j \Sigma_k \Sigma_n T_{ij}^{kwn} c_{ij} = C^w = \Sigma_i \Sigma_j \Sigma_k \Sigma_n T_{ij}^{kwn\ \underline{obs}} c_{ij} \tag{6.33}$$

and

$$\Sigma_i \Sigma_j \Sigma_k T_{ij}^{kwl} \{p_i^k - q^w(W^w - c'_{ij})\}^2 = \sigma^{w^2}$$

$$= \Sigma_i \Sigma_j \Sigma_k T_{ij}^{kwl\ \underline{obs}} \{p_i^k - q^w(W^w - c'_{ij})\}^2 \tag{6.34}$$

For Model 3 we have a maximum likelihood equation for μ in (6.27) associated with (6.19) which, it will be recalled, was used as a constraint for Model 3. So

$$\Sigma_i \Sigma_j \Sigma_k \Sigma_w T_{ij}^{kw} (b_{ij}^{kw} - c'_{ij}) = Z$$

$$= \Sigma_i \Sigma_j \Sigma_k \Sigma_w T_{ij}^{kw\ \underline{obs}} (b_{ij}^{kw} - c'_{ij}) \tag{6.35}$$

For the solution of the LP problem, Model 2, no calibration is required. An LP algorithm such as the 'stepping-stone' method finds an optimal solution to the problem which does not infringe the constraints. There is no attempt to fit the model to the real world and clearly it may produce a poor representation of reality. However, the associated demand model (6.24), which is used to forecast bid rent, _is_ calibrated against reality. In the form specified it is a case of fitting a multiple linear regression model by the least squares method and attempting to satisfy the associated restrictions; this differs from parameter estimation in intrinsically _nonlinear_ EM models. In our empirical work we have had insufficient time and data to implement such a bid estimation model so more rough and ready approximations for bids have been made. Hence Models 2 and 3 have not been so thoroughly tested as Model 1.

A word of caution must be added about the use of the maximum likelihood statistics presented above. In all cases they are summary measures of behavioural distributions as they aggregate over indices such as i, j and k. Some exploratory calibration with two versions of Model 1 (reported in Senior, 1974-C) suggests that possibly misleading results may be obtained if the whole shapes of the observed and predicted distributions are not compared.

6.3.3 Procedures for parameter estimation

We discuss now methods for finding the parameter values in the nonlinear EM models which optimise the statistics. From the maximum likelihood criteria for optimisation given by (6.33), (6.34) and (6.35) the following conditions must be satisfied

$$\text{Min } V^w(\beta^w,\mu^w) \equiv \text{Min}|C^w - C^{w\ \underline{obs}}| = 0 \tag{6.36}$$

$$\text{Min } F^w(\beta^w,\mu^w) \equiv \text{Min}|\sigma^{w^2} - \sigma^{w^2\ \underline{obs}}| = 0 \tag{6.37}$$

$$\text{Min } G(\mu) \equiv \text{Min}|Z - Z^{\ \underline{obs}}| = 0 \tag{6.38}$$

that is, the respective parameter values are adjusted until the absolute differences between observed and predicted measures are as close to zero as we desire. Values of the functions V^w, F^w and G under different values of their associated parameters represent a set of response surfaces. The aim is to explore efficiently these unknown surfaces to find the global minima in parameter space.

One proven method for the types of residential model in Sections 6.2.2 and 6.2.4 is the Newton-Raphson procedure (Batty and Mackie, 1972). For Model 1 we wish to optimise simultaneously on the values of β^w and μ^w and therefore to satisfy both Equations (6.36) and (6.37). Starting with (hopefully) good approximations for the parameters denoted by $\beta^w(m)$ and $\mu^w(m)$, the Newton-Raphson procedure generates next best estimates as:

$$\beta^w(m+1) = \beta^w(m) + \varepsilon_1^w \tag{6.39}$$

$$\mu^w(m+1) = \mu^w(m) + \varepsilon_2^w \tag{6.40}$$

where the values of ε_1^w and ε_2^w can be found from Taylor Series expansions of (6.36) and (6.37) truncated at the first-order terms:

$$V^w\{\beta^w(m) + \varepsilon_1^w, \mu^w(m) + \varepsilon_2^w\} \simeq V^w\{\beta^w(m), \mu^w(m)\} + \varepsilon_1^w \left.\frac{\partial V^w}{\partial \beta^w}\right|_{\beta^w(m),\mu^w(m)} + \varepsilon_2^w \left.\frac{\partial V^w}{\partial \mu^w}\right|_{\beta^w(m),\mu^w(m)} \tag{6.41}$$

$$F^w\{\beta^w(m) + \varepsilon_1^w, \mu^w(m) + \varepsilon_2^w\} \simeq F^w\{\beta^w(m), \mu^w(m)\} + \varepsilon_1^w \left.\frac{\partial F^w}{\partial \beta^w}\right|_{\beta^w(m),\mu^w(m)} + \varepsilon_2^w \left.\frac{\partial F^w}{\partial \mu^w}\right|_{\beta^w(m),\mu^w(m)} \tag{6.42}$$

These two sets of simultaneous equations can be solved for ε_1^w and ε_2^w the process being iterated until these values are arbitrarily small. The derivatives can be evaluated numerically. The procedure is much simpler for the one parameter of Model 3 as only a single equation must be solved

$$G\{\mu(m) + \varepsilon_3\} \simeq G\{\mu(m)\} + \varepsilon_3 \left.\frac{\partial G}{\partial \mu}\right|_{\mu(m)} \tag{6.43}$$

6.3.4 Goodness-of-fit statistics

The calibration statistics suggested by maximum likelihood methods are not adequate measures of goodness-of-fit as they are essentially summary measures of behavioural distributions as previously mentioned. It is usual to obtain near exact fits between observed and predicted measures of those statistics, but this is not the same as measuring model performance with respect to the sector and spatial variation that these statistics sum over, namely the zonal variables i and j, and the house type variation k.

A number of goodness-of-fit measures have been used for these types of model (see Anthony and Baxter, 1971, for a review). Regressing predicted against observed values of the trip matrix, T_{ij}^{kw}, and obtaining coefficients of determination (R^2) has been undertaken. However, owing to conditions associated with the regression technique the R^2 measures have been supplemented by more straightforward measures of percentage discrepancies between observations and predictions. In addition use has been made of indices of dissimilarity and segregation to test certain features of model performance. Indices of dissimilarity can be used to reflect the extent to which the attributes, spatial and sectoral, of one w group differs from that of another group, v. Values are graduated from zero (identical) to 100 (completely dissimilar). For example we can calculate the dissimilarity (D) between the residential location patterns of two groups from:

$$D^{wv} = 50\ \Sigma_i \left| T_{i*}^{*w} / T_{**}^{*w} - T_{i*}^{*v} / T_{**}^{*v} \right| \tag{6.44}$$

where the asterisks denote summations over appropriate superscripts. Associated indices of segregation, measuring how dissimilar the spatial pattern of group w is as compared with all other groups, v, combined, can be computed from:

$$S^{wv} = 50\ \Sigma_i \left| T_{i*}^{*w} / T_{**}^{*w} - \Sigma_{v \neq w} T_{i*}^{*v} / \Sigma_{v \neq w} T_{**}^{*v} \right| \tag{6.45}$$

The remaining sections of this chapter deal with the empirical implementation and testing of the three models.

6.4 Data needs, data availability and data estimation

The chief information problems relate to data availability and compatability at required levels of sector-spatial resolution, particularly when diverse sources are utilised. The aim has been to make the best use of an ill-co-ordinated and mediocre data situation cheaply.

In the first instance, the availability of data restricted the chosen study area to the former Leeds County Borough which is somewhat smaller than the desirable city-region. The 28 wards of the city have been used as the zoning system units (labelled i and j), partly because of the size of house price samples and the information relating to local authority housing estates. Although this is not the ideal spatial framework for analysis, it does have the merit of avoiding computational problems associated with the calculation of a larger number of elements of the interaction matrix, T_{ij}^{kw}.

Data sources used included Census information for 1966, national economic series data on earnings and expenditures, and locally available information. A paper by Cripps and Cater (1972) contains a discussion of the availability and usefulness of such data for Model 1. Wilson (1970-A) intended the worker type superscript, w, to be an earnings/income categorisation, but data availability forces us to adopt the socio-economic classifications of the Census. A paper by Anthony (1970) suggests that this is in any case a more meaningful categorisation for differentiating between residential choices of worker types. The superscripted variable, W^w, thus refers to the average earnings of workers classified into the five social class groups of the Census, and E_j^w is the number of jobs falling in these five categories in each zone j. The earnings data are derived from national information provided in the Earnings Surveys for 1968 and 1970 (Department of Employment and Productivity, 1970; Department of Employment, 1971). The average proportion of income net of transport costs spent on housing, q^w, by each group was determined, with some difficulty, from the 1966 Family Expenditure Survey (Ministry of Labour, 1967). House prices have been obtained from a variety of sources: from Rent Officers' records, Housing Department rent schedules, estate agents, the local Registry of Deeds, and from newspaper advertisements. It was thought somewhat premature to attempt to represent travel costs, c_{ij}, as a generalised measure (Wilson, Hawkins, Hill and Wagon, 1969), so local public transport fares and private vehicle operating costs per mile were used. The c'_{ij} terms are weekly equivalents of these costs assuming five return journeys per week per worker.

Employment, E_j^w, housing, H_i^k, and journey-to-work, T_{ij}^{kw}, data were derived from a mixture of residential Census data for wards and Census journey-to-work information at an intra-urban scale, the latter specially prepared for the region's local authorities at the time of the West Yorkshire Transportation Study (Traffic Research Corporation, 1969). Housing types, k, were defined as joint tenure-condition categories - owner occupied and public and private rented cross-classified into two crude condition groups. Fully disaggregated housing, employment and interaction data were not available directly, so data gaps had to be filled as consistently and objectively as possible. For example the full interaction matrix T_{ij}^{kw} had to be estimated when only T_{ij}^{w}, H_i^k and r_i information was available. A best estimate was sought which was fully consistent with this known information. To avoid the assumption of complete independence, conditional probabilities of (j,w) workers living in type k housing are required. The best that could be done was to obtain the conditional joint probability of w workers in k type houses, denoted by P^{kw}, for the West Yorkshire conurbation as a whole, thus establishing the following constraints expressing known information.

$$\Sigma_k T_{ij}^{kw} = T_{ij}^{w} \tag{6.46}$$

$$\Sigma_j \Sigma_w T_{ij}^{kw} = r_i H_i^k \tag{6.47}$$

$$\Sigma_i \Sigma_j T_{ij}^{kw} = TP^{kw} \tag{6.48}$$

The following EM model then represents a best estimate of T_{ij}^{kw}:

$$T_{ij}^{kw} = A_i^k r_i H_i^k B_{ij}^w T_{ij}^w D^{kw} TP^{kw} \tag{6.49}$$

where

$$A_i^k = \{\Sigma_j \Sigma_w B_{ij}^w T_{ij}^w D^{kw} TP^{kw}\}^{-1} \tag{6.50}$$

$$B_{ij}^w = \{\Sigma_j A_i^k r_i H_i^k D^{kw} TP^{kw}\}^{-1} \tag{6.51}$$

$$D^{kw} = \{\Sigma_i \Sigma_j A_i^k r_i H_i^k B_{ij}^w T_{ij}^w\}^{-1} \tag{6.52}$$

Notice that the j variation is not strictly necessary in this estimation model and may be dropped for computational purposes if so desired and re-introduced later by a simple probability term.

It should be noted that there were no pressing *a priori* reasons for changing the hypothesised forms of the trip cost and housing expenditure distributions in Model 1. Strictly from the computational viewpoint there were strong arguments for accepting single-parameter functions.

Finally, there is the problem of estimating bid prices. Time and data quality did not permit the implementation and calibration of the Harris regression model described in Section 6.2.3, and therefore a much cruder procedure had to be used. A modified form of device suggested in Senior and Wilson (1974-B, Section 6), whereby bids are related to observed housing costs and expenditures, was used for preliminary explorations of Models 2 and 3. These models have thus not been subjected to as thorough testing as Model 1. This should be borne in mind when comparing model results in the next section. It should also be mentioned that data referred to 1966 conditions or in the case of some monetary variables was adjusted to that date.

6.5 Presentation and discussion of results

6.5.1 Model 1 results

As it happened, in the development of the empirical work, more time was devoted to the performance of Model 1. However, where relevant, tables of results present salient comparative features of some or all of the various models previously described, and reference is made to these at appropriate junctures in the text.

Table 6.1 presents best fitting parameter values and associated calibration statistics for Model 1. As anticipated parameter values are inversely related to the size of the calibration statistics.

Table 6.1 Best fitting parameter values for Model 1

Social class	Mean trip costs (new pence)	Best fitting β^W values	Housing expenditure variances (£)	Best fitting μ^W values
Professional	6.383	0.218	0-83.8	0.3595
Intermediate	6.097	0.245	0-94.5	0.3217
Skilled manual	5.399	0.29617	0-69.8	0.6317
Semi-skilled manual	5.061	0.33222	0-51.7	0.8094
Unskilled manual	4.711	0.38236	0-40.4	0.9745

Table 6.2 shows the percentage misallocations of workers of each social class group at three levels of sector-spatial disaggregation. As expected with all these aggregate models (see Table 6.7) improved performance is directly related to the degree of averaging over variability in the system modelled. As the current interest is in residential location rather than disaggregated journey-to-work predictions, then we need not concern ourselves too greatly with measures at the (i,j,k) level of resolution. Tables 6.3 to 6.5 inclusive present indices of dissimilarity between social class groups, computed separately from observed and model figures. Similarly Table 6.6 gives segregation indices for each social class group.

Table 6.2 Model 1: Percentage misallocations of all workers and heads of households of each social class group at three levels of sector-spatial resolution

Worker group (w)	Worker type	i	i-k	i-j-k
Professional	All Heads	23.291 17.482	30.69 21.259	36.309 29.841
Intermediate	All Heads	14.998 10.593	22.602 17.026	29.35 25.414
Skilled manual	All Heads	3.399 3.299	4.453 4.067	18.124 18.223
Semi-skilled manual	All Heads	7.5 6.19	10.951 8.998	21.069 20.364
Unskilled manual	All Heads	14.311 12.716	19.707 17.744	27.517 26.242

From these tables we can detect three notable weaknesses in an otherwise reasonable, and certainly not discouraging set of model results. First the predictions for dependent workers almost consistently worsen the goodness-of-fit of the model as Table 6.2 demonstrates most clearly. This effect is most marked for Professional and then Intermediate workers and least noticeable for Skilled workers. These results can be explained as follows. These high status workers cluster in the northern and eastern suburbs of Leeds which have a high proportion of the city's better owner-occupied housing. In the model for heads of households the price-expenditure mechanism is sensitive to these spatial variations. However, the dependent worker model's allocations to residential zones are based only on housing availability and the relevant trip cost impedance function. Given a strongly centralised employment pattern for Professional and Intermediate workers, dependents are allocated more symmetrically to all suburban locations. Hence total workers in these groups are typically overpredicted in southern and western zones but underrepresented in the northern and eastern zones as Figure 6.1 illustrates. Cross Gates zone is an exception because it has a lot of council housing, and as discussed below another feature of model performance is the overprediction of such workers to the public rented stock. The key problem is that dependent workers are

Figure 6.1 A comparison of observed and Model 1 figures for the distribution of professional workers by residential zone

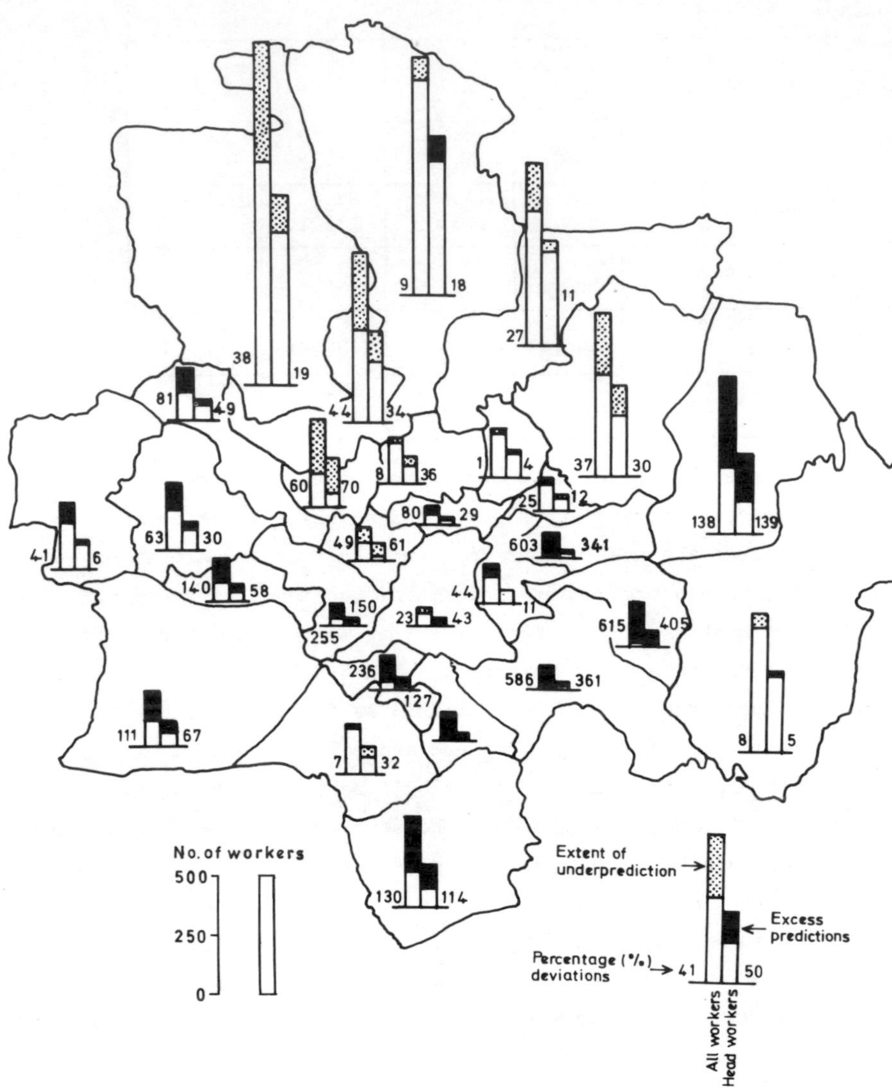

hypothesised to choose residence-workplace combinations which are not related to the residential behaviour of their respective heads of households, who are assumed solely responsible for the residential choice of the whole household. It is also important for data reasons to reformulate the model without having to disaggregate employment by head and dependent workers. A reformulated model, emphasising the workplace choice of dependent workers, is given in Senior (1977). Unfortunately, this model requires an iterative solution scheme to avoid disaggregating the employment term.

Table 6.3 Indices of dissimilarity between social class groups based on observed data for all workers

Social class	Intermediate	Skilled manual	Semi-skilled manual	Unskilled manual
Professional	16.42	42.75	50.46	55.73
Intermediate		28.94	37.07	44.78
Skilled manual			11.52	22.02
Semi-skilled manual				11.84

Table 6.4 Indices of dissimilarity between class groups based on Model 1 predictions for heads of households

Social class	Intermediate	Skilled manual	Semi-skilled manual	Unskilled manual
Professional	8.23	32.49	40.35	45.2
Intermediate		24.31	32.16	37.02
Skilled manual			7.95	13.89
Semi-skilled manual				6.2

Table 6.5 Indices of dissimilarity between social class groups based on Model 1 predictions for all workers

Social class	Intermediate	Skilled manual	Semi-skilled manual	Unskilled manual
Professional	5.48	20.52	25.75	29.55
Intermediate		15.04	20.26	24.08
Skilled manual			5.45	10.44
Semi-skilled manual				5.07

Table 6.6 Indices of segregation between social groups based on observed data and Model 1 predictions

Social class	Observed data (all workers)	Model 1 predictions	
		All workers	Heads of households
Professional	41.34	20.34	31.83
Intermediate	29.45	16.14	25.76
Skilled manual	9.95	2.82	5.01
Semi-skilled manual	14.58	7.61	11.99
Unskilled manual	23.52	11.79	16.35

Second, Tables 6.3 to 6.6 indicate that the model consistently understates the differences in locational behaviour as between social class groups. The figures, say of Table 6.6, when compared with those of Table 6.2 show the same rank ordering between the degree of 'specialisation' of residential location behaviour, measured by the index of segregation, and the poorness of model predictions in all but one instance - namely the reversal of the rank order when considering head, rather than all, workers in the Intermediate and Unskilled manual categories in the Table 6.2 results. In part, this degree of 'insensitivity' in the model is attributable to the coarseness of the classification schemes used, which, for example tend to average out house price variations. However, the fundamental issues appear to lie with the model's hypotheses and assumptions which do not capture, in sufficient detail or perhaps as accurately as desirable, the preferences and constraints which differentially condition the choice and opportunities of the worker groups. It may be that the limitations of the static equilibrium assumptions are being exposed by a dynamic disequilibrium situation in which the prior location of workers by types is an added attractiveness for subsequent locators of the same type. Consequently, the model fails to capture this 'cumulative causation' or 'social polarisation' process operating over time which would produce a higher degree of residential segregation between groups than can be reflected by a model of the type used here. Even the quasi-dynamic version of this model proposed by Wilson (1970-A) will need extending in scope to incorporate this interdependence of residential choices.

However, even within a static equilibrium framework the model's allocation mechanisms are underspecified. House prices, p_i^k, are being used as surrogate measures of attractiveness reflecting attributes of housing, of the residential environment and of general accessibility. This ensures that the model does not become directly cluttered and unmanageable with a host of individually-specified attractiveness measures, but in so doing it sacrifices a lot of detailed variation in residential attractiveness. In addition, the housing expenditure terms, $q^w(W^w - c'_{ij})$, imply that ability and willingness to pay for housing depends on income net of transport costs. They do not directly reflect consumers' varying preferences for specific house types and residential neighbourhoods, although the effects of these factors will be 'picked up' in the values of the μ^w parameters which reflect intra-group housing expenditure variations. Again though much of the explicit detail of residential attractiveness and of residential decision-making is lost in the model's variables and parameters. The whole budget term operates as a pure price-expenditure trade-off conditioned by the μ^w values, so workers are not hypothesised to discriminate between house types and neighbourhoods if house prices are identical. In fact, the allocation of workers to house types depends in an unsatisfactory way on the correlation between house prices and house types.

This brings us to a third and related weakness of the model - the misallocation of social class groups to different housing tenure types. This is partly reflected in the figures in the (i,k) column of Table 6.2, although this effect will presumably also be implicit in the figures of the (i) column as part of the aggregate mis-allocations to residential zones will be due to the tenure composition of the housing stock in each zone in addition to any 'pure' locational misplacements. In particular there are under-predictions of Professional and Intermediate workers to owner-occupied housing with corresponding overpredictions to public rented accommodation, especially the higher-priced variety; such workers are overpredicted to the latter in every zone. Model performance for Skilled workers (Table 6.2) deteriorates only slightly from the (i) to the (i,k) level, as the model gives the best results for the group most evenly represented across all house types.

As mentioned, consumer preferences for residential attributes are inadequately treated in the model, and part of the problem in this instance is that no house type and tenure preference is incorporated. However, there is a more crucial aspect of residential choice, which few predictive models have attempted to treat seriously, and that is the question of the eligibility of consumer types for housing tenure sectors. Specific constraints are imposed on residential choice by the financing of home ownership and the administrative, rather than market, allocation of public rented housing. Additionally pricing mechanisms differ as between owner-occupied, public rented and some private rented unfurnished accommodation, so the ability of price to reflect residential attractiveness is impaired in situations where private market forces are of little importance. The model assumes uniform market conditions, whereas, according to Apps' (1973/74) work, the non-uniformity arising from a multi-tenure context is responsible for considerable differences in the real price of housing between the various sectors. These arise from a tax system discriminating among households by tenure type and income, from a subsidy system related to tenure, and from mortgage allocation policies. These issues contribute to the complexity of both building realistic residential models and evaluating residential choices.

The above criticisms point to the need for a separate representation of the attractiveness of individual attributes of the residential environment to various worker groups. As explained in Senior (1974-A) this is a notable strength of the model proposed by Anthony and Baxter (1971). The problem of overcomplicating the residential location model is avoided by constructing a more manageable residential attractiveness model (Baxter and Williams, 1972) which generates weighted attractiveness indices for the location model. Something akin to this device could be used to supplement Model 1, in particular a tenure 'factor', reflecting both tenure preferences and constraints, can be incorporated in the indices. Alternatively, we could try to represent directly eligibility constraints for tenure sectors as suggested in Senior (1974-C). Hence the basic conclusions concerning Model 1 are that certain weaknesses of the model could be partially eliminated at least to improve on a reasonable forecasting model.

6.5.2 Model 2 results

We turn now to models using bid prices, b_{ij}^{kw}. One initial point to make, in light of our criticisms of Model 1, is that these bids can be made to reflect explicitly not only ability to pay, but also consumer preferences for house types and locations. However, all the models discussed here assume uniform private market conditions, and as mentioned in Section 6.2.3 Model 2 goes further by postulating perfect competition.

A feature of this LP model is, as a consequence of a well known standard theorem, the small number of non-zero allocations among the T_{ij}^{kw} which give the optimal solution - 282, in fact (140 + 143 - 1) - compared with the potential number of 20,020 (140 x 143). The observed matrix T_{ij}^{kw} had 11,376 non-zero entries, so the actual residential and journey-to-work patterns were expected to differ markedly from the optimum patterns forecast by Model 2. This is borne out by the percentage misallocations given in Table 6.7.

Table 6.7 Models 1, 2 and 3: Percentage misallocations of heads of households of each social class group at three levels of sector-spatial resolution

Worker group (w)	Model type	i	i-k	i-j-k
Professional	1	17.482	21.259	29.841
	2	50.632	59.548	76.249
	3	25.499	32.842	37.842
Intermediate	1	10.593	17.026	25.414
	2	34.327	50.322	79.349
	3	16.276	22.942	29.826
Skilled manual	1	3.299	4.067	18.223
	2	10.173	35.575	82.394
	3	4.286	7.152	18.929
Semi-skilled manual	1	6.19	8.998	20.364
	2	18.694	66.008	90.354
	3	6.602	10.974	20.93
Unskilled manual	1	12.716	17.744	26.242
	2	37.454	76.182	95.34
	3	15.791	22.685	28.302

In most cases Model 2 produces at least twice as many misplacements as its EM equivalent, Model 3. Even at the aggregate zonal level, i, the model does not give good predictions. In addition, the difference between the observed and optimal totals of bids (Z), is substantial (see Table 6.9).

In the dual, an observed common 'base-level' housing price has been used for all models to reflect the maximum price an alternative, lower bidding land user would pay. It was found that Model 2 predicted a range of prices which compared favourably with the observed ones. Aggregate values of the dual objective function terms are given in Table 6.8. Although total housing costs are predicted tolerably well, the discrepancy between total bids and the latter, measured by the welfare term, differs substantially from the observed situation.

Of course, one would expect the performance of Model 2 to be poor when applied as a static equilibrium model. Part of the discrepancy between the observed and the static equilibrium optimum total of bids may be explained by dynamic disequilibrium in the observed situation. Clearly, if Model 2 were to be used to allocate only moving households to vacant housing in a sequence of time periods, one would expect model predictions to conform more closely to reality. However, while it remains difficult to implement dynamic models, static equilibrium EM models, like Model 3, will have a distinct advantage over their LP equivalents.

6.5.3 Model 3 results

In contrast to Model 2, Model 3 is fitted to the observed situation - with a μ value of 1.5627 in Equation (6.27) - and this is reflected in improved performance measures. Calibration to a high degree of accuracy ensures that observed and predicted total bids (Z) are almost identical (Table 6.8). None of the 20,020 possible T_{ij}^{kw} elements are zero although some are trivially small as the EM model cannot be constrained to produce only integer quantities; some details are presented in the second row of Table 6.9. 8,909 allocations are of one worker or more, accounting for 107,074 workers out of a total of 110,541 for the study area. If the 3,467 workers unaccounted for are taken as single worker trips, the predicted total

Table 6.8 Aggregate values (in £) for bids, house prices and welfare terms: a comparison of observed and model values

	Observed	Model 2 (LP)	Model 3 (μ=1.5627)	Approximation to limit of Model 3 (μ=43)		
(i) Total bids (Z)	132,461.68	179,167.7	132,461.68	178,773.53	Total bids $Z = \Sigma_i \Sigma_j \Sigma_k \Sigma_w T_{ij}^{kw}(b_{ij}^{kw} - c_{ij})$	(i)
(ii) Total housing costs $\Sigma_i \Sigma_k p_i^k H_1^k$	205,713.81	215,305.68	216,978.87	211,677.89	Total housing costs $\Sigma_i \Sigma_k \alpha_i^k H_i^k$ or $\Sigma_i \Sigma_k \frac{\lambda_i^{k(1)}}{\mu} H_i^k$	(ii)
(iii) Total consumer group welfare $\Sigma_j \Sigma_w \nu_j^w E_j^w$	Not directly observable	-36,137.98	-333,511.90	-47,566.02	Total consumer group welfare $-\Sigma_j \Sigma_w \frac{\lambda_j^{w(2)}}{\mu} E_j^w$	(iii)
(iv) Total house-type dependent variable	Not directly observable	Zero (not applicable in LP model)	248,994.71	14,661.66	Total house-type dependent surplus $\Sigma_{ijkw} \frac{T_{ij}^{kw} \ln T_{ij}^{kw}}{\mu} = \frac{-S}{\mu}$	(iv)
(v) Total net welfare	-73,252.13	-36,137.98	-84,517.19	-32,904.36	Total net welfare (iii) + (iv)	(v)

Table 6.9 Total bids and the number of non-zero primal variables, T_{ij}^{kw}, for: (i) the observed situation, (ii) Model 3, (iii) $\mu \to \infty$ in Model 3, and (iv) Model 2

Value of μ	Number of allocations >0.01 of a worker	Number of allocations >0.5 of a worker	Number of allocations ≥1 worker	Total bids (Z) (in £)
Observed	11,376	11,376	11,376	132,461.68
1.5627 (Best fit in Model 3)	19,618	11,637	8,909	132,461.68
10.0 18.0 35.0 43.0 (Approximate limiting form of Model 3)	5,778 3,152 1,582 1,353	Not calculated 1,731 1,092 975	Not calculated 1,523 1,009 900	173,570.96 177,007.90 178,563.06 178,775.19
Linear programming solution (Model 2)	282	282	282	179,167.70

of non-zero allocations is 12,376, one thousand in excess of the observed number. This is a considerable improvement on Model 2. This is further substantiated by the misplacement measures in Table 6.7. The fact that these results do not quite come up to the standard of the Model 1 results is attributed partly to an as yet inadequate development of a bid estimation model and the absence of any nonlinear adjustment of bids to equilibrium, and partly to the 10 parameters, two for each social class group, in Model 1 which allow differences in residential behaviour to be 'fitted' more accurately than the single, non-disaggregated parameter of Model 3. The problems of disaggregating the μ parameter in Model 3 have been discussed in Senior and Wilson (1974-B).

It is a feature of the dual prices output by Model 3 that they display a wider range of values than those generated by Model 2. This came as a surprise as it was anticipated that, as the primal characteristics of Model 3 were more realistic than those of Model 2, this would also hold for the dual. In fact Model 3 prices are apparently more sensitive to the intensity of demand-supply pressures in the suboptimal context. It may be that a lack of perfect information and perfect competition allows some suppliers to obtain higher prices and some consumers to expend less on housing than they otherwise would under perfect conditions. This topic would certainly bear further investigation. Table 6.8 does indicate, however, that the aggregate housing costs predicted by both Models 2 and 3 do not differ substantially, and both overestimate the observed costs when the same minimum price is used. Given the discrepancy between the observed and optimum (from Model 2) totals of bids (Z) it is not surprising that Model 3 gives a more accurate prediction of net aggregate welfare in the system (Table 6.8).

Table 6.10 gives particular examples of values of dual variables for one worker group whose <u>optimal</u> residential choices are given by Model 2 as the better type of owner-occupied housing in Hyde Park and Meanwood (Zones 2 and 7). Here, such workers minimise their loss of welfare, a minimal amount (£0.11). Under imperfect conditions (Model 3) prices and welfare change. The Hyde Park accommodation represents a distinctly suboptimal choice for this group although

Table 6.10 Specific examples of dual relationships for intermediate workers employed in zone 1 (Westfield)

Model type	(Dual) price of housing $p_i^k \alpha_i^k \frac{\lambda_i^{k(1)}}{\mu}$	Bid $b_{ij}^{kw} - c_{ij}$	Dual welfare term $\nu_j^w \frac{\lambda_j^{w(2)}}{\mu}$	House-type-dependent surplus $\ln T_{ij}^{kw}/\mu$	Net welfare (c)+(d)
	(a)	(b)	(c)	(d)	(e)
Zone 2 (Hyde Park) - better owner-occupied housing					
Observed	£3.22	£3.27	na	na	-£0.05
Model 2	£3.38	£3.27	+£0.11	na	+£0.11
Model 3	£4.81	£3.27	+£2.07	-£0.53	+£1.54
Model 3 limit	£3.38	£3.27	+£0.20	-£0.09	+£0.11
Zone 7 (Meanwood) - better owner-occupied housing					
Observed	£3.23	£3.03	na	na	+£0.20
Model 2	£3.14	£3.03	+£0.11	na	+£0.11
Model 3	£2.84	£3.03	+£2.07	-£2.26	-£0.19
Model 3 limit	£3.09	£3.03	+£0.20	-£0.14	+£0.06
Zone 11 (Roundhay) - poorer private rented accommodation					
Observed	£1.39	£0.23	na	na	+£1.16
Model 2	£1.50	£0.23	+£0.11	no allocations	
Model 3	£2.28	£0.23	+£2.07	-£0.02	+£2.05
Model 3 limit	£1.50	£0.23	+£0.20	no allocations	
Zone 8 (Far Headingley) - better owner-occupied housing					
Observed	£3.64	£2.73	na	na	+£0.91
Model 2	£2.85	£2.73	+£0.11	no allocations	
Model 3	£2.38	£2.73	+£2.07	-£2.42	-£0.35
Model 3 limit	£2.83	£2.73	+£0.20	-£0.10	+£0.10

Notes (1) na = not applicable or not observable

(2) 'No allocations' indicate that market prices exceed equilibrium bids (ie original bids ± welfare term)

(3) Structure of Table based on rearranged versions of Equations (6.21) and (6.32)

one of its most suboptimal choices is the poorer private rented accommodation in Roundhay (Zone 11); very few workers from the group make these latter choices. Conversely, those still locating in the Meanwood accommodation are better off under imperfect market conditions as prices are lower and a small consumer surplus is to be had. However, it is those from the group who live in the better owner-occupied housing in Far Headingley (Zone 8) who reap the greatest surplus. It is the interpretation of the T_{ij}^{kw}/μ terms in Equation (6.32) as house-type-dependent surpluses to consumers which leads to the above explanation. Other interpretations - for example, as indicators of intra-group preference variations - are possible and should be borne in mind.

Recalling the concluding remarks on Model 2, it should be remembered that Model 3 predictions reflect implicitly true deviations from the conditions of a perfectly competitive housing market, due for example, to tenure complications and suboptimal behaviour, and disequilibrium over time caused by non-movers who have insufficiently strong incentives to continually optimise their residential choices. Now imagine that both models were to be applied quasi-dynamically to successive sets of residential movers. One would still expect Model 3 to have the superior performance because of the calibration process. However, that process would be both computationally time consuming and data demanding, especially if the most sensitive calibration statistics were used. Consequently it would be advantageous from a practical view, to employ Model 2 if its performance were not markedly inferior.

6.5.4 Limiting properties of Model 3

Mention was made in a footnote to Section 6.2.4 of Suzanne Evans' (1973) theorems, relating primal solutions from limiting forms of EM models to those from equivalent LP models. Here we report our findings when letting μ tend to a limiting value ($\mu \to \infty$) in Model 3, and compare the results with those of Model 2. Also some dual limiting properties are illustrated.

The value of μ in Model 3 was increased in arbitrary steps up to a maximum value of 43 (Table 6.9) which, when multiplied by the highest bid, gave virtually the largest value that did not exceed the capacity of the computer's exponential function. From

Table 6.9, we see that the number of non-zero allocations fall and that the value of Z approaches the Model 2 objective function value at a decreasing rate. Furthermore, a subjective comparison of the predicted trip matrices of Model 2 and of the limiting case of Model 3 indicates a high measure of agreement. A value of Z in terms of the dual variables can be derived for Model 3 by re-arranging the dual entropy expression (6.30) to:

$$Z = \Sigma_i \Sigma_j \Sigma_k \Sigma_w T_{ij}^{kw} \frac{\ln T_{ij}^{kw}}{\mu} + \Sigma_i \Sigma_k \frac{\lambda_i^{k(1)}}{\mu} H_i^k - \Sigma_j \Sigma_w \frac{\lambda_j^{w(2)}}{\mu} E_j^w \qquad (6.53)$$

It has been conjectured in Wilson and Senior (1974) that in the limit the $\ln T_{ij}^{kw}/\mu$ terms tend to zero and that the $\lambda_i^{k(1)}/\mu$ and $\lambda_j^{w(2)}/\mu$ values tend to the values of their LP equivalents, respectively α_i^k and ν_j^w in Equation (6.20). A comparison of aggregate dual values for the relevant models is available in Table 6.8. As hypothesised, it is clear that the negative entropy expression (divided by μ), the first term in Equation (6.53), does decrease markedly as μ tends to infinity in Model 3. Additionally, it is evident from rows (iii) and (v) of Table 6.8 that the aggregate welfare amounts predicted by the Model 3 limit are far closer to Model 2 values than to those of Model 3. This is confirmed more convincingly for both welfare and house price values when individual dual variable values from the results of three models are compared. This can be illustrated by referring again to Table 6.10. In all cases the properties of the limiting form of Model 3 approximate reasonably closely to the Model 2 results as expected. One of the obvious discrepancies is that Model 2 has zero allocations to Zone 8, whereas the Model 3 limit does not. Clearly a higher value of μ is needed to replicate the Model 2 results. Noticeably the Zone 8 accommodation is very nearly an optimal residential choice for the consumer group in question as the Model 2 price of £2.85 is only slightly in excess of the equilibrium bid of £2.84 (ie. original bid + welfare value). It would therefore appear that as μ is gradually increased in value in Model 3 the most suboptimal choices are eliminated first while near-optimal locations only lose their attractive power at very high μ values.

6.6 Concluding remarks

At this time, and given the present state-of-the-art, the models discussed and tested here seem to be quite promising planning tools. They are admittedly still crude representations of reality, but improve considerably on the aggregate residential component of the Lowry model. Such models should prove useful in formulating broad structure plans. However, they possess an insufficient degree of realism and explicitness to be entirely satisfactory aids to policy selection concerning key problems characteristic of urban housing markets. A medium-term aim must be to attempt more ambitious computer representations of the latter taking into account three particular requirements: (i) the need for at least a quasi-dynamic model; (ii) a more comprehensive approach, paying particular attention to tenure constraints, eligibility conditions and housing supply; and (iii) a greater attention to policy variables reflecting all the controls available to those regulating access to housing resources.

References

Alonso, W. (1960) A theory of the urban land market, Papers, Regional Science Association, 6, pp. 149-158.

Alonso, W. (1964) Location and land use, Harvard University Press, Cambridge, Massachusetts.

Anthony, J. (1970) The effect of income and socio-economic group on housing choice, Working Paper 51, Land Use and Built Form Studies, University of Cambridge.

Anthony, J. and Baxter, R. (1971) The first stage in disaggregating the residential submodel, Working Paper 58, Land Use and Built Form Studies, University of Cambridge.

Anas, A. (1973) A dynamic disequilibrium model of residential location, Environment and Planning, 5, pp. 633-647.

Apps. P.F. (1973/74) An approach to urban modelling and evaluation. A residential model: 1 Theory, 2 Implicit prices for housing services, Environment and Planning, 5, pp. 619-632 and pp. 705-717: 3 Demand equations for housing services, Environment and Planning, 6, pp. 11-31.

Ayeni, M.A.O. (1975) A predictive model of urban stock and activity: 1 theoretical considerations, Environment and Planning, 7, pp. 965-979.

Balinksi, M.L. and Baumol, W.J. (1968) The dual in nonlinear programming and its economic interpretation, Review of Economic Studies, 35, pp. 237-256.

Batty, M. (1972) Dynamic simulation of an urban system, in Wilson, A.G. (ed) London Papers in Regional Science, 3, Patterns and processes in urban and regional systems, Pion, London, pp. 44-82.

Batty, M. (1973) A probability model of the housing market based on quasi classical considerations, Socio-Economic Planning Sciences, 7, pp. 573-598.

Batty, M. and Mackie, S. (1972) The calibration of gravity, entropy and related models of spatial interaction, Environment and Planning, 4, pp. 205-233.

Baxter, R. and Williams, I. (1972) The second stage in disaggregating the residential submodel, Working Paper 65, Land Use and Built Form Studies, University of Cambridge.

Beckmann, M.J. (1969) On the distribution of urban rent and residential density, Journal of Economic Theory, 1, pp. 60-67.

Bell, W. (1955) Economic, family and ethnic status: an empirical test, American Sociological Review, 20, pp. 45-52.

Brown, L.A. and Moore, E.G. (1970) The intra-urban migration process: a perspective, Geografiska Annaler, 52B, pp. 1-13.

Colenutt, R.J. (1970) Building models of urban growth and spatial structure, in Board, C., Chorley, R.J., Haggett, P. and Stoddart, D.R. (eds) Progress in geography, 2, Edward Arnold, London, pp. 109-152.

Cripps, E.L. and Cater, E.A. (1972) The empirical development of a residential location model: some preliminary results, in Wilson, A.G. (ed) *London Papers in Regional Science*, *3*, *Patterns and processes in urban and regional systems*, Pion, London, pp. 114-145.

Cripps, E.L. and Foot, D.H.S. (1969) A land use model for subregional planning, *Regional Studies*, *3*, pp. 243-268.

Department of Employment (1971) *New Earnings Survey 1970*, HMSO, London.

Department of Employment and Productivity (1970) *New Earnings Survey 1968*, HMSO, London.

Eastin, R.V. and Shapiro, P. (1973) The design of a location experiment, *Transportation Research*, *7*, pp. 17-30.

Echenique, M., Crowther, D. and Lindsay, W. (1969) A spatial model of urban stock and activity, *Regional Studies*, *3*, pp. 281-312.

Evans, A.W. (1973) *The economics of residential location*, The MacMillan Press, London and Basingstoke.

Evans, S.P. (1973) A relationship between the gravity model for trip distribution and the transportation problem in linear programming, *Transportation Research*, *7*, pp. 39-61.

Harris, B. (1965) Notes on an approach to metropolitan housing market analysis, unpublished paper, Institute for Environmental Studies, University of Pennsylvania, Philadelphia.

Harris, B. (1966) Basic assumptions for a simulation of the urban residential housing and land market, unpublished paper, Institute for Environmental Studies, University of Pennsylvania, Philadelphia.

Harris, B., Nathanson, J. and Rosenburg, L. (1966) Research on an equilibrium model of metropolitan housing and locational choice: interim report, unpublished paper, Institute for Environmental Studies, University of Pennsylvania, Philadelphia.

Harris, C.D. and Ullman, E.L. (1945) The nature of cities, *Annals of the American Academy of Political and Social Sciences*, *242*, pp. 7-17.

Hawley, A. and Duncan, O.D. (1957) Social area analysis: a critical appraisal, *Land Economics*, *33*, pp. 337-345.

Herbert, D.J. and Stevens, B.H. (1960) A model for the distribution of residential activity in urban areas, *Journal of Regional Science*, *2*, pp. 21-36.

Hoyt, H. (1939) *The structure and growth of residential neighbourhoods in American cities*, US Government Printing Office, Washington DC.

Ingram, G.K., Kain, J.F. and Ginn, R.J. (1972) *The Detroit prototype of the NBER urban simulation model*, National Bureau of Economic Research, New York.

Kain, J.F. (1962) The journey-to-work as a determinant of residential location, *Papers, Regional Science Association*, *9*, pp. 137-160.

Kain, J.F. (1964) A contribution to the urban transportation debate: an econometric model of urban residential and travel behaviour, *Review of Economics and Statistics*, *46*, pp. 55-65.

Kirwan, R.M. and Martin, D.B. (1970) The economic basis for models of the housing market, in Housing models, Proceedings of a Planning and Transportation Research and Computation Co Seminar, London; also published by PTRC.

Lowry, I.S. (1964) A model of metropolis, RM-4215-RC, Rand Corporation, Santa Monica.

Ministry of Labour (1967) Family Expenditure Survey Report for 1966, HMSO, London.

Muth, R.F. (1969) Cities and housing, University of Chicago Press, Chicago.

Park, R.E., Burgess, E.W. and Mackenzie, R.D. (1925) The city, Chicago University Press, Chicago; reprinted 1967.

Robinson, I.M., Wolfe, H.B. and Barringer, R.L. (1965) A simulation model for renewal programming, Journal of the American Institute of Planners, 31, pp. 126-134.

Senior, M.L. (1973) Approaches to residential location modelling 1: urban ecological and spatial interaction models (a review), Environment and Planning, 5, pp. 165-197.

Senior, M.L. (1974-A) A further note on two disaggregated models of residential location, (letter to the editor), Environment and Planning, 6, pp. 355-357.

Senior, M.L. (1974-B) Approaches to residential location modelling 2: urban economic models and some recent developments (a review), Environment and Planning, 6, pp. 369-409.

Senior, M.L. (1974-C) Disaggregated residential location models, housing market models and duality, paper presented to Urban and Regional Models Seminar, PTRC, Summer Annual Meeting, in Seminar Proceedings published by PTRC, London.

Senior, M.L. (1977) Approaches to residential location modelling: empirical and theoretical developments of disaggregated models, intended Ph.D. thesis, Department of Geography, University of Leeds.

Senior, M.L. and Wilson, A.G. (1974-A) Disaggregated residential location models: some tests and further theoretical developments, in Cripps, E.L. (ed) London Papers in Regional Science, 4, Space-time concepts in regional science, Pion, London.

Senior, M.L. and Wilson, A.G. (1974-B) Explorations and syntheses of linear programming and spatial interaction models of residential location, Geographical Analysis, 6, pp. 209-238.

Simmons, J.W. (1968) Changing residence in the city, Geographical Review, 58, pp. 622-651.

Traffic Research Corporation Ltd (1969) The West Yorkshire Transportation Study, Technical Report, Leeds.

Wheaton, W. (1972) Income and urban location, Ph.D. dissertation, University of Pennsylvania, Philadelphia; also University microfilm 73-1466, Ann Arbor, Michigan.

Wheaton, W. and Harris, B. (1972) Linear programming and locational equilibrium: the Herbert-Stevens model revisited, unpublished paper, MIT, Massachusetts and University of Pennsylvania, Philadelphia.

Wilson, A.G. (1969) Developments of some elementary residential location models, Journal of Regional Science, 9, pp. 377-385.

Wilson, A.G. (1970-A) Disaggregating elementary residential location models, Papers, Regional Science Association, 24, pp. 103-125.

Wilson, A.G. (1970-B) Entropy in urban and regional modelling, Pion, London.

Wilson, A.G. (1974) Urban and regional models in geography and planning John Wiley, London.

Wilson, A.G., Hawkins, A.F., Hill, G.J. and Wagon, D.J. (1969) Calibrating and testing the SELNEC transport model, Regional Studies, 3, pp. 337-350; reprinted in Wilson, A.G. (1972) Papers in urban and regional analysis, Pion, London.

Wilson, A.G. and Senior, M.L. (1974) Some relationships between entropy maximising models, mathematical programming models and their duals, Journal of Regional Science, 14, pp. 207-215.

Wingo, L. (1961) Transportation and urban land, Johns Hopkins Press, Baltimore.

Wolfe, H.B. (1967) Model of San Francisco housing market, Socio-Economic Planning Sciences, 1, pp. 71-95.

Zoller, H.G. (1972) Localisation residentielle: decision des menages et developpment suburbian, Les Editions Vie Ouvriere, Brussels.

Chapter 7

The utilization of services

A.P. Smith, P.J. Whitehead and R.L. Mackett

7.1 Introduction: public and private goods and services

The acceptance of models as planning tools has perhaps been more complete in the field of retail shopping patterns than in any other. Recent issues of planning and related journals have contained a plethora of both theoretical and empirical papers on this topic. Moreover, many statutory planning bodies now undertake as part of their standard procedure the application of such techniques to the retail system. The reasons for this are not absolutely clear, although a major factor may be the relative ease of isolating this subsystem from the urban whole. The interest of the planner or geographer in goods and services arises from his concern about: (a) the location and size of the service points and thus their effect on urban structure; (b) the interaction that service points generate in the city; and (c) the possibility that there will arise spatial imbalances of costs and benefits incurred and received by different groups. However, in carrying out these studies, certain issues are neglected in the literature. For example, while a great deal of effort has been put into analysing retail service establishments, little time has been devoted to the problems associated with local government services. Services such as hospitals, libraries, fire protection, police and so on are important fields of study. It will be our contention that this has arisen partly because of the lack of an adequate categorisation to highlight the conceptual difficulties associated with each type of service, and partly because of the conceptual difficulties themselves. Consequently, it will be the purpose in this introduction to produce a preliminary classification appropriate to the remainder of the chapter. This draws attention to alternative frameworks and approaches.

The basis is a dichotomy between 'public' and 'private' services, together with a further distinction relating to the modes of provision: we recognise that governments as well as households and firms provide services. It was Samuelson (1954) who first drew a polar distinction between two kinds of goods: he argued that some goods and services are parcelled out among persons with one man getting more if another gets less. These goods are called private goods. On the other hand some goods and services are parcelled out such that one man's consumption does not diminish the quantity available for another. These goods are called public goods[(1)]. This distinction is fundamental to what follows. Because of its importance we shall examine critically the implications it has for the modelling alternatives to be discussed in detail later.

We first investigate the characteristics of private goods and services. Two important points must be made: first, the benefit a person derives from them depends on quantity. Assuming rationality, then a person will maximise his satisfaction by equating the marginal rates of substitution of these goods to their relative prices. In this way prices allocate private goods and services so that an individual's desired level of satisfaction is achieved by his choice in the market. Secondly, the more a person has of any good the less someone else has. This arises because the goods and services in question have a scarcity element; they are insufficient to fill completely all the wants they cater for.

For public goods and services, two corresponding points should be made: first, the benefit a person derives depends upon how much of the good exists in society. Once the good is provided for some, it is available to all and it is within reason impossible to prevent anyone from enjoying it. Like private goods, those public goods provided by governments are purchased at a price: the tax collected from individuals. However, a person cannot consume a chosen quantity of a

---

(1) The dichotomy between public and private goods can be generalised into the concept of excludability and non-excludability (Peston, 1972).

public good at a particular unit price. Second, and following on from the first, the more a good is provided for a person the more there is for everyone else. In many ways this concept of a public good is of course an abstraction from reality and we find it necessary to extend the definition and distinguish between a pure public good, the one already defined, and an impure public good. This arises because many public goods have a private aspect to them in terms of restricted availability and this is said to make them impure. Thus, although no one is excluded from benefiting from the provision of an impure public good there will be spatial variations in availability. Thus, while the power services can be considered to be spatially ubiquitous, schools or hospitals are by their nature localised. Many impure public goods cannot be provided through the normal market mechanism. As Cox (1973) points out, we will find that in many ways impure public goods are more interesting to the geographer than the pure variety.

The second major distinction is between publicly and privately provided goods and services. In many cases public goods are publicly provided while private goods are privately provided, but this correspondence is by no means exact. For instance, the building of a private supermarket can be classed as a public service while public provision of housing involves a private element in that it is not equally available. There are important differences between the two with consequences for their modelling methods and analyses. Consider fire protection and supermarkets and associated issues of location. While both could be classed as impure public goods, fire protection is provided publicly while supermarkets are provided privately. The observed pattern of fire protection points will usually have been the result of a centralised decision, while that of supermarket locations will have been formed by many individual decisions. While individual decision makers are able to locate within any jurisdiction the centralised decision taking agency will usually be limited to their corresponding local authority. In the case of the supermarket a bad location will be economically costly, and may lead to eventual bankruptcy, whereas a bad location for a fire station will not be so apparent. As Hall (1973) points out, the specific objectives to be accomplished by the choice of location will probably not be the same for the two sectors. For while private sector location decisions will include some non-economic issues they will have as their main objective the minimisation of cost or the maximisation of profit to the private owners (although this obviously involves offering something which benefits consumers!). In public sector decisions, the objective is to maximise a benefit, a social welfare function of some kind, or to minimise a cost any of which are difficult to quantify (Revelle, Marks and Liebman, 1970). This will have immediate relevance for any attempt at modelling the various services available. It may in fact restrict certain types of models to certain service sectors, though we hope to show that this need not be the case.

There are also differences in provision in relation to interaction. For example, the acquisition of privately provided goods involves, more often than not, a physical journey for the consumer between a point of consumption and one of purchase. In contrast, this is not the case for some public services, as refuse collection and electricity supply, or, if it does involve a journey, for instance a visit to the doctor, the trip characteristics may differ markedly from those of a retail nature.

More generally we can identify certain key distinctions between the economic characteristics of the two sectors which have operated historically and thus determinedthe ways in which their mathematical analyses have been pursued. The private provision of goods in our economy takes place in what approximates to a free market situation, whilst the public provision of goods and services is relatively restricted and controlled. A perfectly competitive market would be one in which a large number of sellers faced a large number of buyers and all would have perfect knowledge and mobility, so that no one buyer or seller would have any bargaining power. On both supply and demand sides the three conditions for a free market, multiplicity of factors of production or consumption, perfect knowledge, and perfect mobility, have varying degrees of applicability in the real world. However, they hold sufficiently for the free market model and its various consequences to be adhered to in some service sectors. The basis of this representation is perfect competition, on both supply and demand sides, and, as we shall see later, this is a central assumption in the use of spatial interaction models for the simulation of consumer's retailing behaviour. In the public sector, on the other hand, the system more typically approximates localised monopoly. In certain cases, such as the provision of services consumed in the home, the monopoly is virtually perfect whilst in others, such as schools and hospitals, there exist a limited number of units of production competitive only in a limited sense. What is more, there is no market for the majority of such goods and services since payment is through the rating or tax system and ideally there should be no differentiation with regard to quality of service between units. In many cases in fact the consumer is allocated a service unit on the basis of his place of residence or some similar criterion. In this situation, a programming approach may be appropriate.

This concern with the market mechanism and competition leads to a further important difference between the public and private systems of consumer provision: the nature of the associated equilibrium. The market can be considered to be in a state of equilibrium only if the price at which all consumers are prepared to purchase a certain quantity of a good or service is equal to the price at which it is available to them from the producers, including the cost of transportation involved. That is, both producers and consumers are satisfied that they are getting as good a bargain as they can expect. Their marginal rates of transformation have been equalised through competitive trading. In the private sector, the market pricing mechanism generates a tendency towards such a situation, although at any one moment in time the system is in fact in what Harvey (1973) has termed a state of differential disequilibrium. Perfect equilibrium can never be reached since the structure of the market is always changing. Notwithstanding this observation, the vast majority of model applications to the private retail system have employed this simplifying equilibrium assumption, either implicitly or explicitly. In contrast, the control of publicly provided goods and services approximates more towards a static equilibrium state. Public provision, as far as the individual is concerned, is a much more rigid affair over time with a major shift often only occurring on the change of residence of the recipient.

In the private retailing sector the equilibrium state postulated above can in fact be considered an overall 'optimum' in a perfectly competitive situation. This may of course be a suboptimal compromise for the interests of consumers and producers will rarely coincide. For the public sector, an optimum state is a much more elusive concept. The criteria involved are by no means always tangible. Typically, as we shall see, proxies such as minimisation of the mean trip distance for consumers are used, while in cases where no consumer trip is involved different criteria of social welfare must be used, such as notions of equality of provision. In the public sector a producer's solution in theory should not exist for the service exists purely for the benefit of the consumer and is in fact paid for by him, directly or indirectly. However, it is of course still the task of the operator to attempt to combine quality of service and the maximisation of public utility with efficiency of operation and financial expediency.

Thus, modellers working in these two sectors must have regard for significantly varying systems of interest with contrasting characteristics. The consequences of these and other distinctions will be discussed in the next Section, 7.2, where we discuss the range of models presently in use in this field together with a brief history of the development. In Sections 7.3 and 7.4, two examples of the application of a spatial interaction shopping model to private retailing systems for the West Yorkshire and Leeds study areas are presented Finally, in Section 7.5, we return to public goods and services and more specifically to an investigation of fire service provision in Leeds, though this is an example of one service within a broader framework.

7.2 The range of available models

7.2.1 Spatial interaction models

Spatial interaction phenomena are very common in urban and regional analysis and the service sector is no exception. Singly constrained gravity models have been widely applied in retailing studies since the pioneering work of Huff (1964) and Lakshmanan and Hansen (1965-A, 1965-B), and indeed two of the case studies to be presented in this chapter involve disaggregated versions of this kind of model. They have also been used for many other services, such as patient visits to hospitals (Morrill and Kelly, 1970). They are analogous in principle to the models already presented in Chapters 5 and 6, involving both retailing and residential location and can be built in a standard way using the entropy maximising methods of Wilson (1970). We also saw in Chapter 6 that linear programming formulations could sometimes be used as the basis of spatial interaction modelling. That chapter involved residential location, but LP methods have also been applied to the location of day centres (Holmes, Williams and Brown, 1972). It then turned out that there is a close relation to corresponding entropy maximising models: the LP models were limiting cases of EM models (Evans, 1973); and the EM models could be given new interpretations as 'imperfect market' versions of LP economic models (Wilson and Senior, 1974). Similar considerations apply in the retail and service sectors, though we shall not pursue them much further here. Another related development has been presented by Coelho and Wilson (1976): the entropy maximising model can be arranged as a non-linear programming model in such a way that 'optimum' values (say based on consumers' surplus) of shopping centre sizes can be obtained in a standard way.

7.2.2 Location-allocation models

The models mentioned in Section 7.2.1 above were mainly co cerned with the planning of privately provided facilities (with the exception of the day centres example). Different methods are needed for many public services, largely because relatively few supply points are involved. Further, there is an associated combinatorial problem of optimally selecting the service areas to consumers having selected the locations. Such problems are known as location-allocation problems and this field has developed fairly rapidly in recent years (see, for example, Cooper, 1963; Scott, 1970; Revelle, Marks and Liebman, 1970; Symons, 1971; Alperovich, 1972; Hall, 1973; Wilson, 1976). This work may go some way to meeting the call by Teitz (1968) for more work on the theory of public facility location.

7.2.3 Spatial equity and the provision of public services

Much of the third case study provided in this chapter is concerned with the spatial distribution of costs and benefits as a consequence of the ways in which public facilities are located. Attempts are made to trace the contributions to expenditures on services and the benefits received and a general framework is presented. Particular attention is paid to the Leeds Fire Service as an example. There has been a small amount of earlier work on fire service provision in the UK (Hogg, 1968) and some analogous work on libraries and similar facilities (Robertson, 1972, 1974). In Section 7.5 below we give an example of such a study for fire services in Leeds.

7.3 Application 1: shopping in West Yorkshire

7.3.1 A pilot study

The performance of various possible models and ways of using data were tested in a pilot study of the Rotherham area as a preliminary to the design of the full West Yorkshire model. This initial evaluation proved economical in time and money since it obviated the need for experimentation with the much larger system, and it was possible to produce a piece of work which was useful in its own right. The Rotherham model study and its results are discussed at length by Smith (1973) so only a brief resume is needed here. The subregion is located relative to the West Yorkshire study area in Figure 7.1. It comprises an aggregate of local authorities made up of 25 zones of origin and 22 shopping centres, seven of which are external to the study area. Following the example of the majority of similar British shopping studies, a spatial interaction model provides the basis of simulation, and in particular a disaggregated version of the model presented by Lakshmanan and Hansen (1965-A, 1965-B). Refinements were adopted in stages, thus enabling us to derive useful knowledge of its performance in response to each. Once a final form emerged, the proxies used for each of the independent variables were varied in turn to establish the sensitivity of the model to such changes. Those producing the best results then provided a starting-point for the present model application.

Figure 7.1 The West Yorkshire model system of interest

(a) Zones of origin (i)

Internal

1 Bradford County Borough
2 Dewsbury County Borough
3 Halifax County Borough
4 Huddersfield County Borough
5 Leeds County Borough
6 Wakefield County Borough
7 Aireborough
8 Baildon
9 Batley Municipal Borough
10 Bingley
11 Brighouse Municipal Borough
12 Castleford Municipal Borough
13 Colne Valley
14 Denby Dale
15 Denholme
16 Elland
17 Featherstone
18 Garforth
19 Harrogate Municipal Borough
20 Hebden Royd
21 Heckmondwike
22 Holmfirth
23 Horbury
24 Horsforth
25 Ilkley
26 Keighley
27 Kirkburton
28 Knaresborough
29 Knottingley
30 Meltham
31 Mirfield
32 Morley Municipal Borough
33 Normanton
34 Ossett Municipal Borough
36 Pontefract
37 Pudsey Municipal Borough
38 Queensbury and Shelf
39 Ripponden
40 Rothwell
41 Shipley
42 Sowerby Bridge
43 Spenborough Municipal Borough
44 Stanley
45 Todmorden Municipal Borough
46 Hepton Rural District
47 Osgoldcross Rural District
48 Tadcaster Rural District
49 Wakefield Rural District
50 Wetherby Rural District
51 Wharfedale Rural District

External

52 Skipton Urban District
Skipton Rural District
Silsden, Earby, Barnoldswick
53 Ripon Rural District
Ripon Municipal Borough
54 Nidderdale
55 York County Borough
56 Derwent Rural District
57 Selby Urban District
Selby Rural District
58 Hemsworth Urban District
Hemsworth Rural District
59 Barnsley, Darton, Royston,
Cudworth, Darfield
60 Dodworth, Penistone Urban District,
Penistone Rural District
61 Saddleworth Urban District

(b) Shopping centres (j)

Internal

1 Bradford
2 Dewsbury
3 Halifax
4 Huddersfield
5 Leeds
6 Wakefield
7 Aireborough
8 Baildon
9 Batley
10 Bingley
11 Brighouse
12 Castleford
13 Colne Valley
14 Denby Dale
15 Elland
16 Featherstone
17 Garforth
18 Harrogate
19 Hebden Royd
20 Heckmondwike
21 Holmfirth
22 Horbury
23 Horsforth
24 Ilkley
25 Keighley
26 Kirkburton
27 Knaresborough
28 Knottingley
29 Meltham
30 Mirfield
31 Morley
32 Normanton
33 Ossett
34 Otley
36 Pudsey
37 Queensbury and Shelf
38 Rothwell
39 Shipley
40 Sowerby Bridge
41 Spenborough
42 Stanley
43 Todmorden
44 Tadcaster Rural District
45 Wetherby Rural District

Inner Ring

46 Barnsley
47 York
48 Barnoldswick
49 Cudworth
50 Darton
51 Earby
52 Hemsworth Urban District
53 Penistone
54 Royston
55 Ripon
56 Saddleworth
57 Selby
58 Silsden
59 Skipton
60 Hemsworth Rural District

Outer Ring

61 Burnley
62 Colne
63 Doncaster
64 Manchester
65 Oldham
66 Rochdale
67 Rotherham

After a 1969 base year simulation of the durable retail shopping system, simple projections were obtained for each of the years 1971, 1976 and 1981 by forecasting trends in certain of the independent variables. Finally, the analysis of the results led to further modifications which were incorporated in the West Yorkshire study. Thus we were making the assumption that the Rotherham subregion retailing system, although not contained within West Yorkshire as defined here, is sufficiently representative of it for such a transfer of experience to be effected with confidence.

7.3.2 Choice of model

Based on the pilot study, the model to be used is a disaggregated version of the Lakshmanan and Hansen model. (Its derivation is described in detail in two papers by Wilson, 1967, 1969-B). The model is constrained at the production end by known data and so employs a balancing factor, A_i, in order to ensure that the predicted flows sum at the origin end to these known totals. The task of the model is to estimate S_{ij}^{kn} (the cash flows between sets of origin zones i and destination points j, by mode of transport, k, and type of good, n) from exogenous inputs. Such flows are considered as functions of similarly disaggregated measures of the relative attractiveness of the centres, the expenditure generated in each of the zones of origin, and the perceived difficulties of travel between each origin and destination pair. More formally,

$$S_{ij}^{kn} = A_i^{kn} e_i^n P_i^k W_j^{n\alpha^n} e^{-\beta^{kn} c_{ij}^{kn}} \qquad (7.1)$$

where

$$A_i^{kn} = (\Sigma_j W_j^{n\alpha^n} e^{-\beta^{kn} c_{ij}^{kn}})^{-1} \qquad (7.2)$$

and S_{ij}^{kn} is the flow of sales of type n by mode k between residential zone i and centre j; e_i^n is the average expenditure on goods of type n by households of zone i; P_i^k is the number of households of zone i shopping by mode k; W_j^n is a measure of the attractiveness of centre j for goods type n; c_{ij}^{kn} is some measure of travel deterrence between each i and j pair for persons travelling by mode k for goods of type n; α^n is a parameter governing the relative attraction of each centre j for goods of type n; and β^{kn} is a parameter governing the relationship between the 'distance' and actual deterrence of each ij trip for mode k and goods type n. The precise values of the α

and β parameters are determined by calibration. This model has been run separately for two goods' types - total and durable. The fact that one category includes the other would have presented difficulties in any attempt at simultaneous treatment, but they have been chosen because experience has shown that at this scale they are the most appropriate. Shopping patterns for convenience goods alone are dominated to a much greater extent by local trips with the result that, at a regional scale, the vast majority of sales would be intra-zonal. Modal split in spatial interaction models can be carried out at a number of alternative stages, the most popular being to combine it with trip distribution. In this case, however, we represent modal split at the trip generation stage making the simplifying assumption that car-owners use their car for shopping purposes while non car-owners use public transport. Only these two modes are recognised. This method is probably less than satisfactory largely because it omits the possibility of competition between the two modes both for the individual and for the population as a whole. The two most common impedance functions used in such models are the power and negative exponential functions. For centre attraction, the former is used while for distance deterrence the latter is chosen. If we had had sufficient data we could have derived best fitting functions empirically. The precise form of the distance deterrence function is a result of the way in which people perceive costs, or in this case time, and Wilson's (1969-B) work in the field of entropy has produced a strong theoretical preference for the negative exponential if distance perception is linear.

7.3.3 The system of interest

In choosing a base year it is necessary to balance the need to be as up-to-date as possible with the problem of data availability. In this instance, we have been able to make use of the 1971 Census, and hence to adopt 1971 as the model base year. Even so certain data inputs have had to be estimated from the most up-to-date equivalents available.

The West Yorkshire study area used here has been defined for the general purposes of the entire project, but as far as the retailing system is concerned this would appear to present no problem. The area of interest is contained wholly within the old West Riding as is illustrated in Figure 7.1, consisting of what is loosely termed the West Riding conurbation plus certain large peripheral areas displaying strong links with the conurbation. Although defined several years ago, the resulting area corresponds closely with the recently established West Yorkshire Metropolitan County. The study area comprises 51 local authorities each recognised as a separate zone, more or less System 2 of Chapter 1. These internal zones, listed in Figure 7.1, Key A, vary widely in area (from Tadcaster Rural District's 72,935 acres to Heckmondwike's 697 acres) and in population (from Leeds' 496,009 persons in 1971 to Denholme's 2,575). This variety introduces certain problems into the modelling theory as pointed out by Smith (1972) but in this case this has been considered not to justify the amount of extra work which would be generated by attempting to aggregate or disaggregate authorities.

The study area was defined in such a way as to present a system that was as closed as possible and this has been achieved quite successfully. To the west is the Pennine chain - an effective barrier, physically, psychologically and politically, to communications. To the north and east are large, sparsely-populated rural areas possessing no major centres of attraction. A more problematical boundary, however, is that to the south where the attraction of Leeds and other West Yorkshire Boroughs is in competition with that of Sheffield, Barnsley and other South Yorkshire towns. But however defined, the study area cannot be considered totally in isolation. Cross-boundary interaction is unavoidable and so, as Figure 7.2 shows, in order to close the system further, the definition of a set of external zones is necessary. These were made up of single authorities or groups, and they form a continuous ring around West Yorkshire except in the west where the Pennines intervene. The zones tend to be areally more extensive than the internal ones although to the south, because of the interaction difficulties already mentioned, they remain relatively small. Again, these external zones are listed in Figure 7.1, Key B, while Figure 7.1 presents them in their study area context.

Figure 7.2 Method of closure

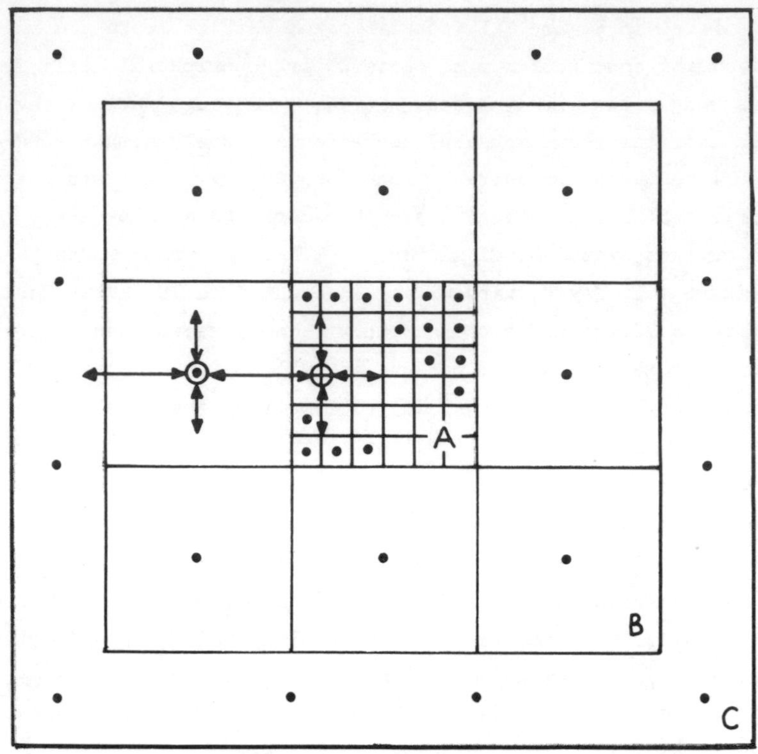

A West Yorkshire study area - residential & shopping

B External zones / External centres I - residential & shopping

C External centres II - shopping only

⟶ Shopping trips accounted for

Zones of origin

• Shopping centres

Within the study area itself the major centre of each local authority zone of origin has generally been identified with the exception of six authorities where turnover was considered for the purpose of the model to be inconsequential. This therefore leaves 45 internal retail centres and to these must be added the two rings of external centres. The inner ring, which includes all those centres considered to be significant in terms of turnover and their function as Figure 7.2 illustrates, is to account for those expenditures originating within the study area which are attracted elsewhere. But, of course, the external zones themselves require closure for this occurrence and so a second ring of external centres must be defined. In this case, however, only those (usually large) centres need be considered which compete with others of the inner study area for shopping trips originating in the intermediate zones. In choosing these second ring centres three criteria were used: (a) size in terms of observed turnover; (b) distance from the external zone system boundary; and (c) an intervening opportunities role (if in the case of any centre, another centre of at least the same size exists between it and the study area boundary then it is omitted). The definition of the system in this way, of necessity, involves several simplifications: centres under a minimum size are excluded; non-central attractions are ignored; and so on. Such steps are, however, necessary if complexity is to be reduced sufficiently for simulation purposes.

7.3.4 The independent variables

For each of the variables in turn used in the model we discuss briefly the information ideally required and compare this with what is actually available or deducible. As noted earlier, this is based on the pilot study and more details are given elsewhere by Smith (1973).

Zonal population (P_i)

It was decided to use household rather than population units in the West Yorkshire model for two reasons: first, much shopping of both durable and convenience types is carried out on a household rather than personal basis; and secondly, the household is a more convenient unit for combination with car-ownership and consumer expenditure figures. Initial model runs employed figures of total households for each of the 61 origin zones obtained from the 1971 Census of Population. For the subsequent mode-specific runs these totals were disaggregated again using Census figures into car-owning and non car-owning household groups, the latter including all households with one car or more. No disaggregation of population by socio-economic group has been employed because of the problem of compatability involved in combining various data classifications: Census definitions of socio-economic groups; expenditure by income categories; car-ownership by different income groups; and so on. Where easily compatible data is not available the returns from the use of such a population breakdown are marginal and cannot be relied upon to justify the extra effort involved.

Zonal expenditure (e_i)

Ideally we require figures of household expenditure for each constituent origin zone of the study area. Since no local expenditure survey exists for the area, however, these quantities must be estimated from nationally published figures. Using such a technique, an accurate assessment of expenditure levels for single zones is not feasible and so we must be content with an overall regional figure, together with the assumption that there is no inter-zonal variation. The 1973 Family Expenditure Survey provides average weekly household expenditure in Yorkshire and Humberside and this is the finest areal breakdown available. It is a simple matter to derive from these data a measure of annual expenditure. Such information can be obtained for a variety of expenditure classes, some of which (for instance expenditure on housing, fuel and power) are not involved in retail interaction of the type under scrutiny here. For the purpose of the model therefore convenience goods comprise food, alcoholic drink and tobacco, while durable goods are composed of clothing and footwear, durable household goods and 'other' goods. Two assumptions of note are involved in this procedure. One is that West Yorkshire expenditure is representative of the Yorkshire and Humberside region as a whole, while the other, already mentioned, relates to the neglect of internal study area variation. Obviously both of these introduce a measure of error, especially the latter since expenditure levels will in fact vary considerably between local authorities. In order to counteract this, we would need, in the absence of a survey, to employ a further disaggregation of the populations involved. However, the case against this has already been noted.

Measure of attraction (W_j)

No ideal proxy for the relative attractiveness of a shopping centre exists and selection is of necessity largely a matter of finding an empirical solution by trial and error. A variety of possible alternatives were employed in the development stage of the Rotherham model: retail square footage, numbers of establishments or employees, and so on. An evaluation of the results revealed that retail floorspace in fact provided the closest fit, other things being equal, and so this measure has been adopted for the present study. The basic information on which this input is based is the data of retail floorspace provided by the government publication Statistics for Town and Country Planning (1972). Total retail areas are here recorded for single local authorities for the year 1967. Our base year is, of course, 1971 but in the continued absence of 1971 Census of Distribution figures, no reliable means of up-dating this information exists. Further, this is also the reason behind the toleration of a further problem - that of reducing local authority figures to actual shopping centre figures. The ratio of central to total floorspace will of course vary from one authority to another but the only data with which a correction could be made is rather inadequate information regarding the centre/periphery split for a small sample of centres for the year 1966.

One further problem had to be faced. The aim was to run two models; one for total goods and one for durables only, and the latter, of course, requires adjustment of the above floorspace figures. For this task information has been obtained from three sources: (a) the Rotherham study provided for 25 centres a durable/total breakdown of sales figures for 1961 and 1969; (b) the 1961 Census of Distribution provides similar data for all the local authorities of our study area with a population in excess of 20,000; and (c) limited information is available from the Business Statistics Office on the same basis for a sample of centres in 1966. If we now make some assumptions regarding a constant durable to total sales ratio throughout the 1961/1971 period and a constant sales per square footage ratio for durable and total goods, then we can use this data to achieve the desired disaggregation. Hence for each centre zone j, we define a durable/total sales ratio, r, for 1961 such that

$$r^{j}_{1961} = t^{jd}_{1961}/t^{j*}_{1961} \qquad (7.3)$$

where t^{jd}_{1961} and t^{j*}_{1961} represent the durable and total retail turnovers respectively for centre j in 1961. Then

$$f^{jd}_{1971} = f^{j*}_{1967}r^{j}_{1961} \qquad (7.4)$$

where f^{jd}_{1971} is the required durable floorspace figure for centre j in 1971; and f^{j*}_{1967} is the corresponding recorded total floorspace for 1967. We have assumed that r^{j} is constant over the period 1961-1971, and

$$f^{j*}_{1967} = f^{j*}_{1971} \qquad (7.5)$$

and

$$t^{jd}_{1971}/f^{jd}_{1971} = t^{jd}_{1961}/f^{jd}_{1961} \qquad (7.6)$$

As hypothesised, there emerged a significant relationship between size of centre measured in floorspace and the durable/total sales ratio. From the above data, a plot of these two variables was made and a regression line fitted which enabled us to estimate the required split for those centres for which a convenient sales disaggregation did not exist. The result was therefore an estimate of durable and total retail floorspace for each centre recognised in the model.

Inter-zonal trip time matrix (c_{ij})

Dealing first with the mode aggregated model runs, the large values of journey time involved in this study relative to the Rotherham model resulted in a greater confidence in the use of rather simple trip time matrix estimation procedures. For this reason, an early decision was made to adhere to the representation of journeys in terms of time and not the more complex generalised cost units for which much necessary information was not readily available. For each of the 61 origin zones, an Ordnance Survey map can be used in order to fix the approximate population centroid in terms of a grid reference and the set can then be superimposed upon a similar set representing the positions of the 68 centres. From these grid points, a simple computer programme can determine, by use of Pythagoras' theorem, a straight line distance between each origin-destination pair. It then remains to transfer from kilometres to miles (for application of average road speeds) and to apply a road distance correction factor. For intra-zonal trips however such a procedure is inadequate; even if the population centroid and shopping centre coincide, we cannot deduce that the mean internal trip length is zero without serious consequences. Although ideally we need to take into account the population distribution, we have in this case reverted to the method employed in the Rotherham study which involves the use of the formula

$$r = \left(\frac{\text{Area of zone}}{\pi}\right)^{\frac{1}{2}} \tag{7.7}$$

where r is the radius of a circle equivalent to the area of the zone. The required mean trip distance is then taken to be $\frac{2}{3}r$, thus assuming an even spread of population. Finally, these distance figures can be converted into time units by the use of Ministry of Transport standards of average speeds for various classes of road.

As the model developed, however, a simple two-way mode split was introduced recognising public and private transport trips. Here we have been able to make use of a trip time matrix for the West Yorkshire study area already derived by colleagues working in the field of transportation (cf. Chapter 9 below). Briefly the method consisted of preparing a network of major roads for the study area and then estimating travel times along each link separately before aggregating to represent actual origin-destination trips. This was done for each mode in turn. Public transport link times are based on information from published bus timetables, while private link times are estimated from average journey speeds given the capacity of the particular link. In both cases, account has been taken of any average waiting or walking times involved. Journeys are, of course, assumed to take place along the quickest possible route, or set of links. Certain amendments have, however, been required in order to make this compatible with our requirements. The chief of these has been the need to estimate public and private trip times in cases where either the origin or destination is external to the study. This task, however, is not necessarily too demanding for these external trips require a lower level of accuracy than wholly internal ones. In fact, use has been made of the all-mode trip times estimated earlier. For journeys at the long end of the spectrum of internal trip times, these all-mode times have been compared with the public and private trip equivalents. Hence

$$c_{ij}^{car} = ac_{ij}^{*} \quad \text{where } a < 1 \quad \text{for } i \neq j \tag{7.8}$$

$$c_{ij}^{bus} = bc_{ij}^{*} \quad \text{where } b > 1 \quad \text{for } i \neq j \tag{7.9}$$

where a and b are derived empirically as just described and are used to correct the 'known' all-mode times, c_{ij}^{*}, for external journeys. In the case of intra-zonal trips, however, it has been assumed that the car looses its speed advantage over the bus over such short distances and hence

$$c_{ij}^{car} = c_{ij}^{bus} = c_{ij}^{*} \quad \text{where } i = j \tag{7.10}$$

7.3.5 Calibration

Two parameters are involved in this version of the model: the variable of retail attractiveness is raised to a power, α, while the distance deterrence function, of whichever form, requires a further parameter, β; both are required in order to define precisely the shapes of the functions involved. Various possible combinations of α and β produce a three-dimensional surface of model fit in which there is an optimum value of one for any value of the other. The problem is to find the joint optimum and this we must do for each mode considered. In fact the data is not available with which to effect a modal split of the α parameter, but the distance deterrence function can be simulated for each mode separately, thus involving two parameters, β^{car} and β^{bus}. In calibrating the SELNEC transport model it was found that only a weak interdependence existed between the two (Wilson, Hawkins, Hill and Wagon, 1969). For the purposes of this model we have therefore assumed that the effects of the parameters are independent and their values can be estimated as such.

In past studies a common assumption has been that the best statistic for measuring goodness-of-fit is some function of the sum of the deviations between observed and predicted values of the relevant flows. In the pilot study a number of alternatives was tried with varying degrees of success. Coefficients of correlation and determination and chi square values proved rather insensitive indicators of changes in parameter values and the first two never significantly varied from unity. As a result little confidence can be attached to their implications and so a further method has been sought. Following Hyman (1969), mean trip cost is increasingly regarded as the most appropriate statistic of calibration, and in particular the minimisation of the sum of squared deviations between observed and predicted values. More recently, Batty and Mackie (1972) using the principles of maximum likelihood have suggested a two-stage calibration procedure utilising measures of mean trip cost and <u>mean trip benefit</u> which enables α to be estimated as well as β and in each case aiming to minimise the sum of squared deviations. It is a version of this procedure which was finally chosen.

In theory the precise form of the equations depends on the types of functions to which the two parameters are related, and furthermore in practice it also depends on the data available for the calibration of the model. In this study, we are using a power function for centre attraction and an exponential function for distance deterrence. The mean cost statistic used for model calibration therefore takes the following form:

$$\left| \frac{\Sigma_{ij} S_{ij}^{obs} c_{ij}}{\Sigma_{ij} S_{ij}^{obs}} - \frac{\Sigma_{ij} S_{ij}^{pre} c_{ij}}{\Sigma_{ij} S_{ij}^{pre}} \right| \simeq 0 \qquad (7.11)$$

where S_{ij}^{obs}, S_{ij}^{pre} are observed and predicted sales between each ij zone pair; and c_{ij} is the travel time between each ij pair; and where the left-hand value is derived from a survey. The corresponding mean trip benefit statistic should be directly analogous but in fact it differs in two ways. Because of the use of a power rather than an exponential function of centre attraction, a natural log formulation of the statistic is required. Further, since an observed trip matrix does not exist, the S_{ij} term in the equation must be replaced by S_{*j}, inter-zonal flow summed over i. The result, shown below, is therefore perhaps not as sensitive as it might otherwise have been.

$$\left| \frac{\Sigma_j S_{*j}^{obs} \log W_j}{\Sigma_j S_{*j}^{obs}} - \frac{\Sigma_j S_{*j}^{pre} \log W_j}{\Sigma_j S_{*j}^{pre}} \right| \simeq 0 \qquad (7.12)$$

Figure 7.3 Calibration - iterative procedure

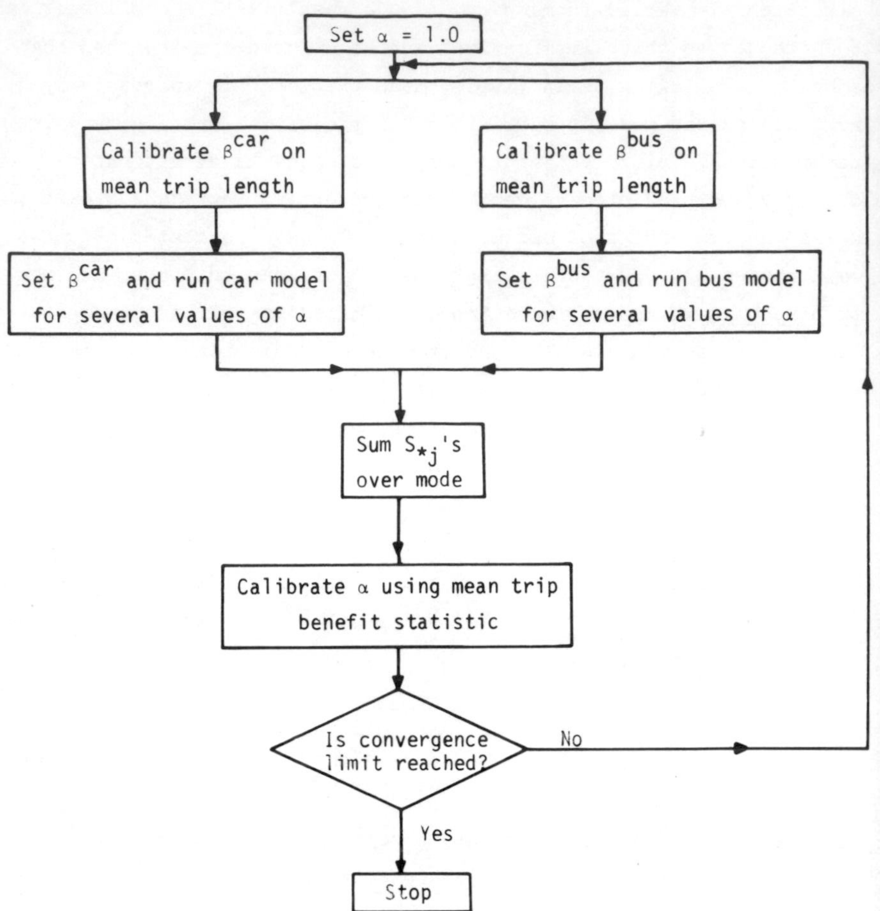

Table 7.1 Parameter values, West Yorkshire

	α	β^{car}	β^{bus}
Total sales model	0.993	0.120	0.069
Durable sales model	0.985	0.116	0.065

where S_{*j}^{obs}, S_{*j}^{pre} are observed and predicted shopping centre j turnovers; and W_j is the attraction of each centre j. Using these two statistics, calibration can be achieved iteratively, setting α initially to unity. Separate values for β^k in each iteration are produced by separate model runs for each mode, but in order to then re-estimate α the flows summed over i for each model have to be combined for comparison with a mode-aggregated, observed turnover figure for each centre. This iterative procedure is illustrated by the flow chart in Figure 7.3. There are techniques available which are theoretically more satisfying in some circumstances, but they often introduce problems of 'homing-in' on a local minimum of the particular statistic being used. Table 7.1 contains for both total and durable goods models the best fit parameter values obtained by this calibration procedure and a discussion and analysis of these will follow in Section 7.3.7.

Since information of actual sales flows, S_{ij}, is rarely available, calibration is normally carried out on the basis of flow-end data only - statistics involving S_{*j}, the observed sales of centres, or some other suitable measure. In this case, additional information was used to obtain values for the left-hand sides of the two calibration equations above. The model's β parameters are calibrated, as we have seen, by means of a mean trip length comparison. It was our initial intention to use data from a recent M62 survey (Gwilliam and Judge, 1974). However, delays in the provision of suitable information have necessitated the use of other less reliable sources involving two local surveys. A survey of mean trip times was recently carried out in Rotherham centre while a second has provided similar information for Leeds County Borough, a two mode disaggregation being employed in both. Rotherham of course is not within our study area and the fact that it is a destination end survey introduces a measure of bias. Leeds on the other hand is within the study area and yet is not really representative for it involves a more than average proportion of long trips. However, since it corresponds closely with results of other studies (Teesside, Department of the Environment, 1971; Watford, Department of the Environment, 1971) the result of these two surveys has been used to establish an average mean trip length by mode for the whole of the study area. On the whole, it must be said that this is less than satisfactory. Mean trip times are ideally required for each zone of origin separately for each will exhibit different characteristics. Moreover, because of the way in which our average figures have been arrived at, no frequency distribution of observed trip lengths can be drawn for comparison with their predicted equivalents.

We also require 1971 turnover figures for both total and durable goods for each model centre. Furthermore, we ideally require these figures to be disaggregated by mode of travel employed. This is clearly unobtainable and the method of calibration has, as we have seen, been correspondingly altered. Since the 1971 Census of Distribution is not yet available these required turnover figures must be estimated. We begin with the total turnover figures for each of the 61 authorities for 1961 provided by the Census of Distribution of that year. Using the total/durable sales ratios derived in an earlier section we can disaggregate these figures into the categories required. Thus

$$t^{jn}_{1961} = t^{j*}_{1961} r^{jn}_{1961} \tag{7.13}$$

where t^{jn} refers to the turnover of goods type n for centre j at a particular date; and r^{jn} is the total to durable sales ratio estimated earlier. However, we, of course, require data compatible with the model's 1971 base year and in effecting the required up-dating three factors require attention: (a) price level increases, 1961-1971; (b) increased expenditure levels, 1961-1971; and (c) differential rates of growth of the centres over the period. For the first of these items of information data are available in the form of an index of retail prices provided by the Annual Abstract of Statistics published by the Central Statistical Office. Taking January 1961 as 100 this index records the movement of retail prices of various categories over the period to 1971. Weights are also given for each category of goods and services based on the consumption of each. From such information, it is a simple matter to estimate weighted mean price changes for 1961-1972 for both total and durable goods; 147.0 and 133.5 respectively. Secondly, by 1971 there were substantial increases in <u>real</u> household expenditure relative to 1961.

If we assume a closed system then we are able to derive a set of factors in order to take this into account. We can sum the 1961 turnover figures to produce S_{**}^{1961}, the total expenditure of the system for that year. If we then compare this with the S_{**}^{1971} produced by the model the difference can be interpreted as a growth factor incorporating both increased real expenditure and the above price changes simultaneously. The combined effect of these two factors produces for 1961-1972 total and durable growth factors of 2.27 and 2.01. More formally

$$t_{1971}^{jn} = t_{1961}^{jn} P_{1961-1971}^{n} \qquad (7.14)$$

where $P_{1961-1971}^{n}$ represents a factor of increased expenditure levels, and is defined as

$$P_{1961-1971}^{n} = S_{1971}^{**n} / S_{1961}^{**n} \qquad (7.15)$$

S^{**} representing total sales of the system, assumed closed, for goods type n. Thirdly, only a small amount of information is available with which to make some sort of adjustment. We could make the assumption, for instance, that the larger centres have grown proportionately more than the smaller ones due to such factors as increased person mobility. However, not enough data exists in order to substantiate these claims with any confidence. Thus, differential growth is a factor which we must remember to consider when analysing the closeness-of-fit of the model results and 'observed' figures.

7.3.6 Results and analysis

The results of both the total and durable goods runs of the model are presented in tabular form in Table 7.2. For each of the 45 internal centres, the predicted 1971 turnover figures have been presented separately for each mode. Further, again for each mode, the durable sales have been subtracted from total sales in order to yield the residual convenience sales for each centre. This may not be the ideal way of achieving these figures in theory, but, bearing in mind the difficulties of applying convenience models to regional systems, it may be the best in practice. Summing the total 1971 sales for both modes, these figures are then compared in Table 7.2 with their 'observed' equivalents in order to yield the percentage error for each centre, this being contained in the extreme right-hand

Table 7.2 Comparison of observed and model simulated retai
turnover, 1971

	Local authority centre	Durable sales		Convenience sale	
		Car owners	Non car owners	Car owners	Non ca owner
1	Bradford	25403.17	33442.69	29362.14	41348.0
2	Dewsbury	4389.15	5921.49	6644.52	9399.4
3	Halifax	6941.87	10037.12	8439.70	13110.5
4	Huddersfield	11062.29	14239.21	12102.19	16658.1
5	Leeds	38965.90	59624.36	42038.08	66308.9
6	Wakefield	7121.88	10185.00	7859.47	11733.6
7	Aireborough	630.93	734.62	2292.90	2768.3
8	Baildon	43.80	45.25	491.84	532.1
9	Batley	1701.08	2212.16	4194.25	5694.0
10	Bingley	904.87	1140.12	2349.67	3177.1
11	Brighouse	133.03	1379.16	3882.23	4249.0
12	Castleford	2497.64	3051.87	3485.47	4435.9
13	Colne Valley	234.27	159.54	1621.45	1149.2
14	Denby Dale	65.09	61.17	607.81	586.3
15	Elland	343.35	337.28	1235.01	1282.6
16	Featherstone	137.56	143.38	782.65	843.6
17	Garforth	91.73	109.50	868.68	1058.8
18	Harrogate	5954.98	5265.70	6570.63	6107.6
19	Hebden Royd	164.03	235.41	825.59	1258.4
20	Heckmondwike	790.04	739.23	2577.80	2529.6
21	Holmfirth	287.73	257.12	959.65	889.6
22	Horbury	139.79	140.74	1171.08	1217.6
23	Horsforth	339.66	437.89	1476.16	1968.6
24	Ilkley	664.14	582.13	1474.17	1363.7
25	Keighley	2668.69	3771.75	4453.74	7025.
26	Kirkburton	141.84	132.74	989.90	963.8
27	Knaresborough	209.75	168.51	1107.76	925.4
28	Knottingley	84.78	90.70	714.07	792.
29	Meltham	18.89	20.43	331.90	371.
30	Mirfield	156.66	223.86	1094.72	1623.0
31	Morley	918.18	1149.70	5054.02	6547.
32	Normanton	303.90	476.14	1137.77	1828.8
33	Ossett	359.80	299.54	2014.55	1738.4
34	Otley	611.04	543.30	1665.11	1539.5
35	Pontefract	1587.65	1858.26	2560.00	3136.8
36	Pudsey	627.67	840.20	2859.80	3972.8
37	Q. & S.	62.19	54.07	696.83	636.
38	Rothwell	195.64	265.66	1507.52	2097.
39	Shipley	1487.05	1777.57	4268.69	5435.
40	Sowerby Bridge	371.46	539.24	1200.95	1845.
41	Spenborough	1176.47	995.57	3634.84	3231.0
42	Stanley	40.76	50.31	347.22	439.9
43	Todmorden	239.22	484.47	602.10	1304.
44	Tadcaster	231.66	306.63	1131.85	1507.
45	Wetherby	359.87	196.96	1303.49	741.

Notes

1. All figures in £000's
2. Only the 45 internal centres are included
   this table
3. *Convenience sales are estimated as a
   residual by subtracting durable from tota
   sales

Total sales		Total predicted sales - all modes	Total observed sales - all modes	% error
Car ners	Non car owners			
65.31	74790.69	129555.00	117216	+ 10.5
33.67	15320.92	26354.59	20559	+ 28.2
81.57	23147.67	38529.24	38899	- 1.0
64.48	30897.33	54061.81	56055	- 3.6
03.98	125933.35	206937.33	218290	- 5.2
81.35	21918.62	36899.97	32856	+ 12.3
23.83	3502.94	6426.77	6161	+ 4.3
35.64	577.42	113.06	1605	- 30.7
95.33	7906.18	13801.51	9305	+ 48.3
54.54	4317.23	7571.77	5448	+ 39.0
15.26	5628.21	10843.47	8401	+ 29.1
33.11	7487.82	13470.93	14873	- 9.4
55.72	1308.83	3164.55	4259	- 25.7
72.96	647.50	1320.46	1816	+ 27.3
78.36	1619.88	3198.24	3909	- 18.2
20.21	987.07	1907.28	2901	- 34.3
50.41	1168.38	2128.79	2794	- 23.8
25.61	11373.38	23898.99	32906	- 27.4
39.62	1493.84	2483.46	3067	- 19.0
57.84	3268.87	6636.71	4136	+ 60.4
47.38	1146.72	2394.10	4138	- 42.1
10.87	1358.37	2669.24	2002	+ 33.3
15.82	2406.49	4222.31	3580	+ 17.9
38.31	1945.84	4084.15	5920	- 31.0
22.43	10797.09	17919.52	18725	- 4.3
31.74	1096.63	2228.37	2449	- 9.0
17.51	1093.91	2411.42	3080	- 21.7
98.85	883.00	1681.85	2043	- 17.7
50.79	391.77	742.56	1083	- 31.5
51.38	1846.86	3098.24	2322	+ 33.4
72.20	7697.12	13669.32	9055	+ 51.0
1.67	2305.01	3746.68	3954	- 5.3
4.35	2037.97	4412.32	2867	+ 55.9
6.15	2082.85	4359.00	4767	- 8.6
7.67	4995.12	9142.77	11822	- 22.7
7.47	4813.03	8300.50	7475	+ 11.0
9.02	690.42	1449.44	1591	- 8.9
3.16	2362.81	4065.97	4081	- 0.4
5.74	7212.91	12968.65	9877	+ 31.3
2.41	2384.94	3957.35	4209	- 6.0
1.31	4226.59	9037.90	8444	+ 7.0
7.98	490.27	878.25	2004	- 56.2
1.32	1789.00	2630.32	4921	- 46.6
3.51	1814.40	3177.91	3382	- 6.1
3.21	938.45	2601.66	4086	- 36.3

column. We can see that a majority of centres is underestimated by varying degrees, although this is balanced by a tendency to overestimate the turnover of the small number of large centres. If these anomalies are mapped, as in Figure 7.4, they show this pattern of overestimation in the central study area with increasing underestimation towards the periphery. This spatial trend, however, is not as strong as in the case of the Rotherham subregional study, probably due to the use of external zones in the present study.

It is, of course, always possible to improve the fit achieved by refinement or sophistication of the model. For instance, we could introduce the use of zone-specific distance deterrence parameters, β^i, to produce individual functions for each origin zone. However, we must remember two points: (a) we are constrained by data availability. Possible refinements rely upon hypotheses made about behaviour and cannot be confidently put to use if this behaviour has not previously been substantiated by observation; and (b) at the limits we come up against the laws of diminishing returns whereby the effects of any model improvements become increasingly marginal. Although we have not been able to compare predicted mode-disaggregated turnover figures with their observed equivalents, our aggregate comparison gives us some justification for accepting the model findings. If we concentrate upon the generated error, however, we find that there are two types - random and systematic - superimposed upon one another with the former tending to hide the latter. The causes of these two types of error are of course different.

Random errors could arise in a number of ways. Overestimation of the sales of individual centres could be caused by a variety of factors: unexpectedly low internal incomes, poor relative accessibility, or an overestimation of the attractiveness of that particular centre. These all derive from model input data but it is also possible, in this case, that the 'observed' sales data is inaccurate. Remember the 1971 'observed' turnover figures have themselves been estimated from a 1961 base, a procedure which has involved two major omissions. First, no account has been taken of differential growth rates for the centres over the period, and secondly, the varying degree of local authority total sales attracted to the central business district has received no consideration.

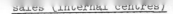

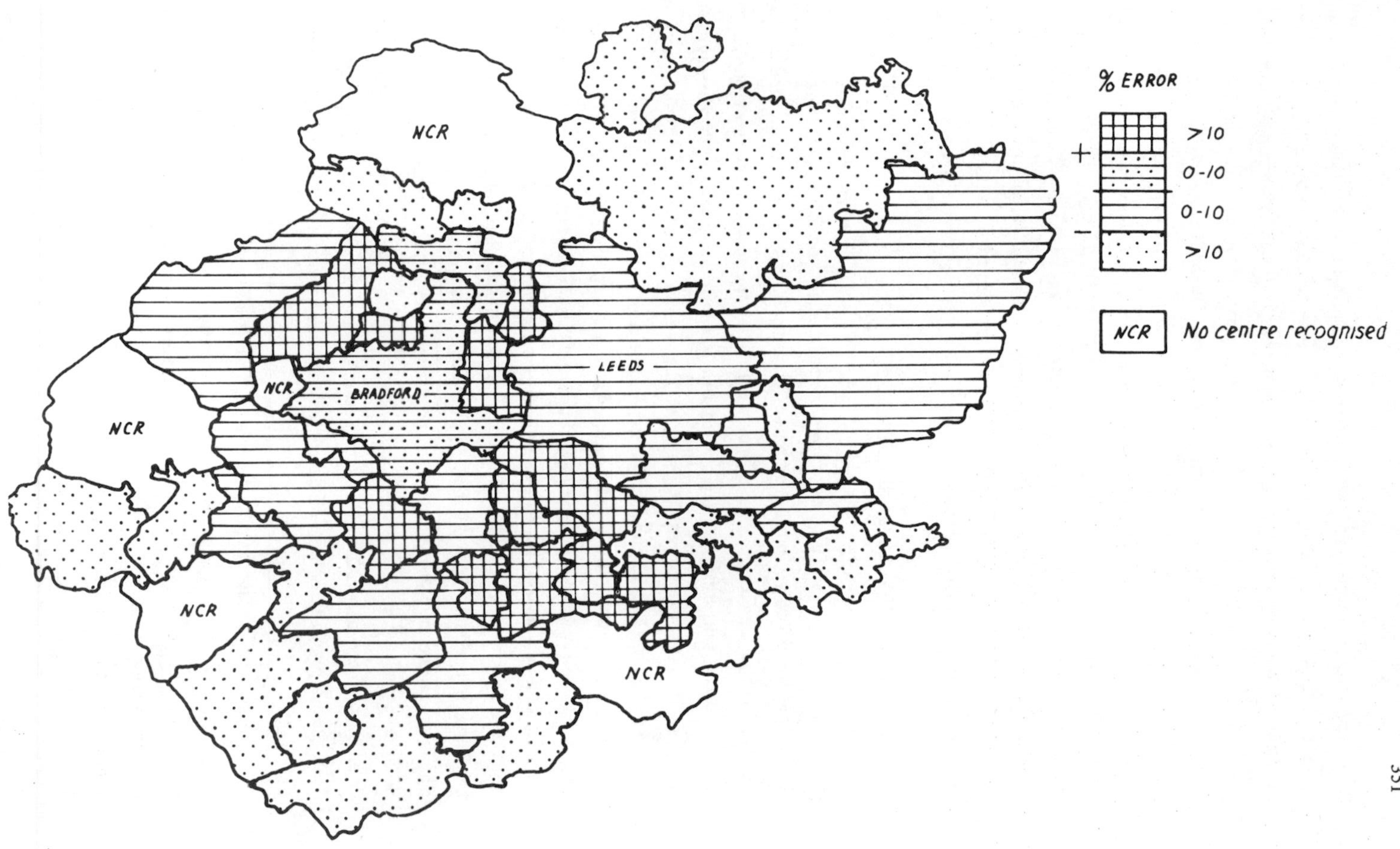

Sales (internal centres)

Systematic errors, too, can of course result from any of the factors just mentioned. However, these could also arise from model defects of a more basic nature, such as the use of wrong functions. In this West Yorkshire example, the overriding systematic error would appear to be, as already mentioned, the increasing incidence of underestimation towards the periphery of the study area. Here, possibly, the most likely explanation involves the construction of the trip time matrices, c_{ij}. In fact, this model, as with other similar ones in Chapter 5, is especially sensitive to changes in intra-zonal trip times. For instance, if all such trip times were assumed to be zero then each zone would comprise a separate self-contained retailing system.

7.3.7 Interpretation of the results

What do the model results show about retailing patterns in West Yorkshire? The matrix of flows resulting from the model can be used in a number of ways to illustrate those shopping patterns predominating in the region. We begin with some general observations. First there are certain things which we can deduce about the system as a whole. Model results as tabulated in Table 7.2 enable us to substantiate several characteristics which we might expect to be true and to reject others. To begin with we can attempt some interpretation of the parameter values obtained in calibration. Theoretically, we might have expected evidence of economies of scale in shopping centres in the form of an α value of greater than unity. The rationale behind this is the hypothesis that the 'attractiveness' of centres increases more than proportionately with their 'size'. However, as with the Rotherham pilot study, the value of α obtained does not vary significantly from unity (it is in fact slightly below 1.0) thus providing no evidence of either economies or diseconomies of scale.

A larger value for β represents a greater proportion of short trips and hence a lower mean trip length. As expected therefore the mode specific values of β are higher for total goods trips than for durable goods trips because of the inclusion of shorter convenience trips. Moreover, one would expect, for the same reason, the β value for private transport trips to be less than that for public transport trips. Non car-owners on average come from lower income groups and hence their average expenditure on trip making should be lower, and hence their β's higher. In the pilot study this was indeed the case but surprisingly the West Yorkshire model has produced the opposite relationship. In fact the private transport β values for the two models are very similar whereas there is a significant discrepancy in the public transport values. Perhaps the cause of this is to be found in the different methods employed in deriving the trip time matrices of the two models. It is interesting to note that a similar problem arose in the SELNEC transport model (Wilson, Hawkins, Hill and Wagon, 1969) where the journey-to-work was being simulated. Here it was suggested that the reason lay in the erroneous assumption that different income groups perceive time equally. They do not, of course, and because of this the average trip costs for non car-owners are often higher than those for car-owners. Hence, one would expect their value of β to be lower.

Although the method of estimating the observed mean trip length precludes any but the most coarse comparison, we can usefully illustrate and compare in diagrammatic form the trip length frequency distributions of the two modes. (Remember that the model produces cash flows not person flows and so we are assuming that the two are proportionate.) The durable trip frequency distribution of Figure 7.5 raise several observations. First, the shapes of the curves are pretty well as we would expect, with both modes peaking in a 10-15 minute median class interval. After a sharp initial rise, resulting from the spacing of durable retail facilities, the curves exhibit fairly typical exponential forms thus producing a negative skew. Secondly, it can be seen that private transport trips group more closely around the mean largely due to the relatively small number of long journey times compared with public transport. This is a function of the greater travel speeds possible by private transport. If the horizontal axis was expressed in distance units then we would find the opposite relationship with more long journeys being undertaken by car-owners than by non car-owners. Thirdly, the public transport curve further exhibits an interesting trough between journey times of 10 and 20 minutes which is absent in the private transport curve. The explanation for this phenomenon could possibly

Figure 7.5 Trip frequency distributions: both modes/durable goods

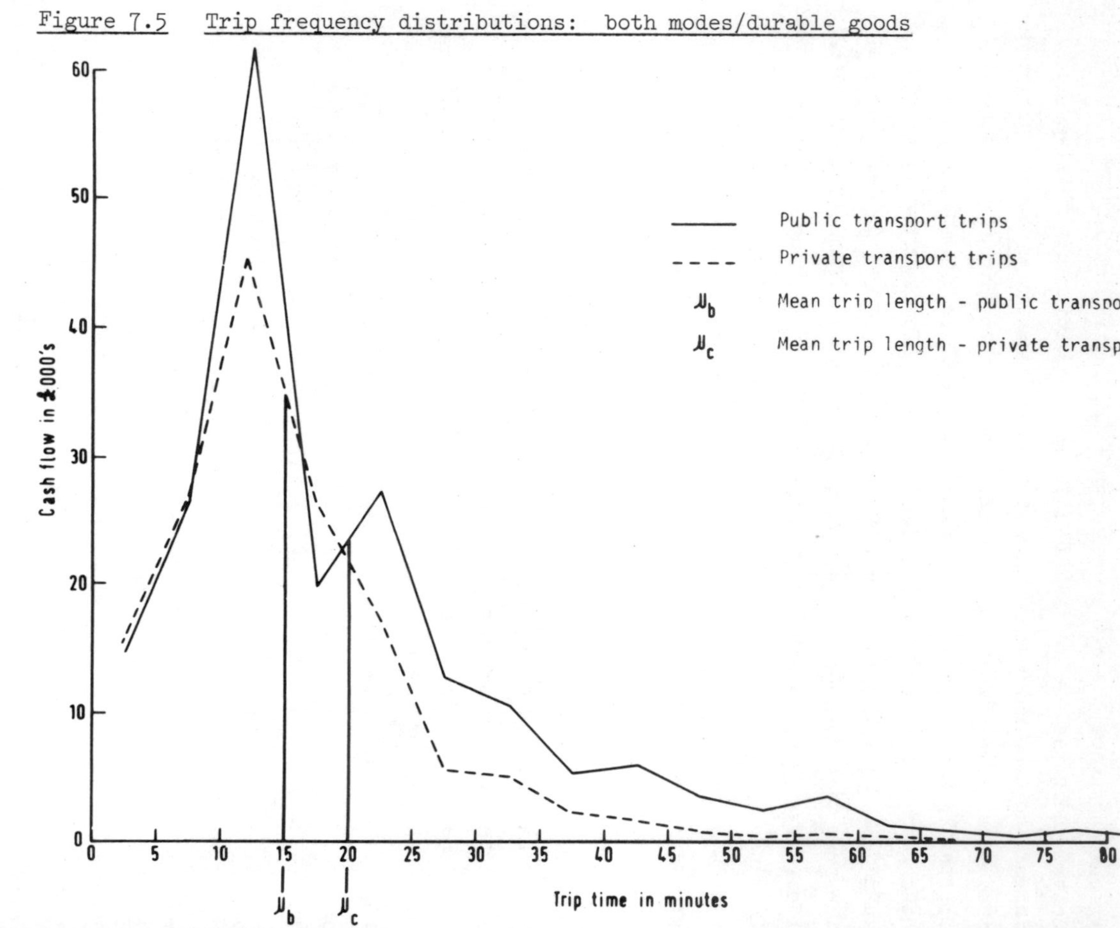

lie in the pattern of public transport provision. Journeys of up to 15 or 20 minutes are mainly intra-zonal 'local' trips carried on local service routes while journeys of over 20 minutes are probably accounted for mainly by longer inter-urban services. Between the two is an unconformity around which there is no local bus service while long distance services are not suitable. Alternatively, the trough could be a result of the greater percentage of low income groups involved in public transport journeys. These groups tend to inhabit the inner suburbs of towns and so require to undertake predominantly short journeys to their town centre or much longer inter-urban journeys to external centres. Fourthly, note that in the larger County Boroughs the sales to non car-owners tend to be significantly greater than those of car-owners, probably as a result of the more extensive public transport provision and the predominance of the lower socio-economic groups. In other areas, especially outlying rural ones, the balance is more even with, in some cases, car-owners accounting for more sales than non car-owners. Examples of towns coming in the second category are,predictably,Harrogate, Ilkley, Otley and Wetherby. Fifthly, durable sales as a percentage of the total is in most cases greater than 50, but the importance of convenience goods becomes proportionately greater in general as the size of the centre decreases. One or two exceptions, such as Harrogate and Wakefield, have a larger durable percentage than this regression would suggest. Such exceptions probably result from their peripheral location and hence their enhanced function as centres. Finally, little evidence exists for any significant difference in the car-owner:non car-owner ratio for durable and convenience goods. We might have expected a greater car-owner percentage for durable goods, but modern trends in shopping tend to work against this because of convenience shopping at supermarkets, postal shopping and so on.

Next, we look at patterns of trip distribution. We can map the flows produced by the model to show the relationships within the system of local authorities. It is more useful, however, to use this information in percentage form, expressing each inter-local authority flow as either a percentage of the total expenditure of the origin zone, or as a percentage of the total turnover of the destination zone. Using such information, we can draw up a map showing, from the retailer's viewpoint, the area of influence of any centre, or from the consumer's viewpoint the spatial distribution of expenditure. In this way the study area can be subdivided into subregions at various levels in the retail hierarchy. At each level, and for each local authority, we could construct an isoline map showing the strength of interaction with each of the surrounding zones. Or, more simply, as in Figure 7.6, we can at each level construct a map placing each zone within the hinterland of a particular centre. Using the output of the durable sales model Figure 7.6 shows the major shopping hinterlands of the West Yorkshire study area, plus the fields of attraction of the more important intermediate centres. Thus, two levels of the hierarchy are represented although, of course, this could be extended to cover lower levels also. The area of influence of each centre is defined with regard to the strength of its links with surrounding local authorities. The S_{ij} flow matrix of the model has been converted by dividing each element by the corresponding row sum - that is, expressing it as a percentage of the total expenditure of that particular zone of origin. Each zone is then assigned to that centre attracting the largest percentage of its total expenditure in durable goods. Further, these immediate hinterlands of the major centres of the study area, Leeds and Bradford, are extended to include those local authorities for whom they are also ranked second in terms of expenditure attracted. Thus it can be seen that the hinterlands of Bradford and Leeds, so defined, together cover virtually the whole of the study area plus extensive adjacent areas. As expected there is a great deal of overlap except in the east where Leeds dominates and a smaller area to the west where Bradford is more important. To the south and west we can see how their influence comes into competition with that of Sheffield and Manchester.

Within this framework the majority of County Boroughs and large Municipal Boroughs - Wakefield, Huddersfield, Harrogate and so on - also possess their own less extensive hinterlands. Some rather less expected but interesting points emerge however. Certain of these Boroughs have well defined hinterlands but do not, on the basis of our criterion, appear in it themselves. Neither Halifax nor Dewsbury are first or second ranked attractors of their own expend-

Figure 7.6 Retail hinterland - total trips, durable goods

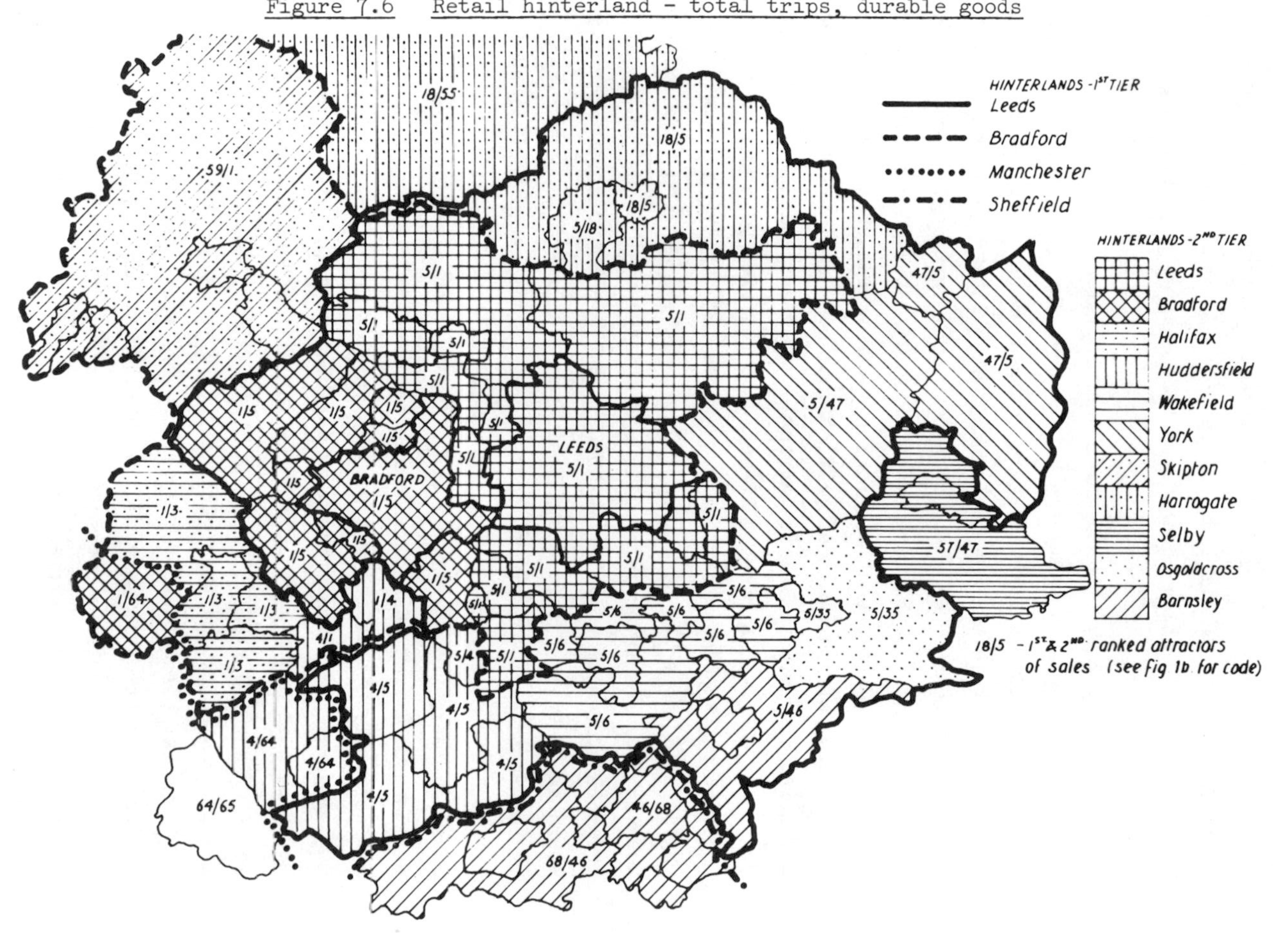

iture while Harrogate comes second to nearby Leeds. This effect is probably a result of differential ease of communication. These towns are well linked with adjacent first tier centres and therefore suffer in terms of trade retained. However, their more isolated hinterlands still primarily rely upon them for the provision of durable goods. Other centres, most notably again Dewsbury, which we would perhaps expect to maintain hinterlands are not ranked first or second in a single authority. On the other hand, less likely centres such as Pontefract appear to be able to support a hinterland. Again, this apparent paradox can be largely attributed to the communications and accessibility patterns of the region. The areas of influence so defined are, of course, a simplification. In reality, there exists a multiplicity of hinterlands arranged not hierarchically but in a continuum and overlapping. It would be relatively easy from the model output to construct isolines around each shopping centre representing contours of attraction. Whichever method is used, however, the resulting maps will be distorted by the coarseness of the zone system, especially in the extensive rural districts of the north and east. Further, the basis of each method is a ranking procedure in terms of percentages. This hides great variations in the absolute strengths of attraction exerted by the centres. For example, York, which is ranked first for its own expenditure, attracts an enormous 87% of this total while Huddersfield, also ranked first, attracts only 25% of its own population's expenditure.

Figure 7.6 is concerned with durable trips for all modes. However, this hides certain interesting differences between the patterns exhibited by each of the modes separately. Looking for example at the expenditure of Bradford we would see that although the greatest percentage of its private transport sales is attracted to its own centre, it is ranked only second behind Leeds in terms of public transport sales attracted. Finally, it should be noted that we can alternatively express each S_{ij} flow as a percentage of its corresponding <u>column</u> total; that is, as that percentage of the total turnover of a particular j centre, accounted for by each i zone of origin. Many of the patterns revealed would be similar to those already discussed but the exercise could yield further insight into the relationships between centres and their hinterlands.

We now examine individual zone mean trip lengths which are mapped in Figure 7.7. The figure confirms what one would expect to be the case: the mean trip length generally increases with distance away from the centre of the conurbation. In the case of durable shopping trips by public transport we can see that much of the central conurbation exhibits a mean trip length of under 20 minutes. This increases to over 30 minutes generally in the peripheral areas and, in one or two cases, to over 35 minutes. In general, trip lengths in the extreme east and north of the study area are greater than those in the west and south reflecting the wide spacing of settlements. In the west extreme lengths are probably avoided by the influence of adjacent Lancashire centres. A similar procedure for all mode trips would reveal closely corresponding results. However, in this case the pattern would be a function of both necessity and opportunity: necessity because of the wide spacing of shopping facilities, especially for non car-owners, and opportunity because of the increased average capability for making long trips owing to the higher incidence in the rural areas of car-ownership. We must therefore temper a little the obvious conclusions to be drawn with regard to comparative utilities of persons resident in different zones.

7.3.8 The results for two particular zones

In Section 7.3.7 we concentrated on an analysis of the West Yorkshire study area's retailing patterns as a whole, using information derived from the model output. It is possible, of course, to study these patterns in greater detail than can be successfully represented on such maps. In order to illustrate the more areally specific use to which the model output can be put, we will isolate two particularly interesting cases for further examination - Leeds and Dewsbury, beginning with Leeds.

The relevant S_{ij} flows into Leeds are expressed in such a way as to yield the percentage of the County Borough's turnover originating in each zone of origin. Total goods flows are used and for purposes of simplicity only those accounting for at least 1% of the total are included. Information presented in this way might prove useful to Leeds traders assessing the real or potential pull exerted by their centre upon the subregion. In this connection it could perhaps be

Figure 7.7 Mean shopping trip times - public transport

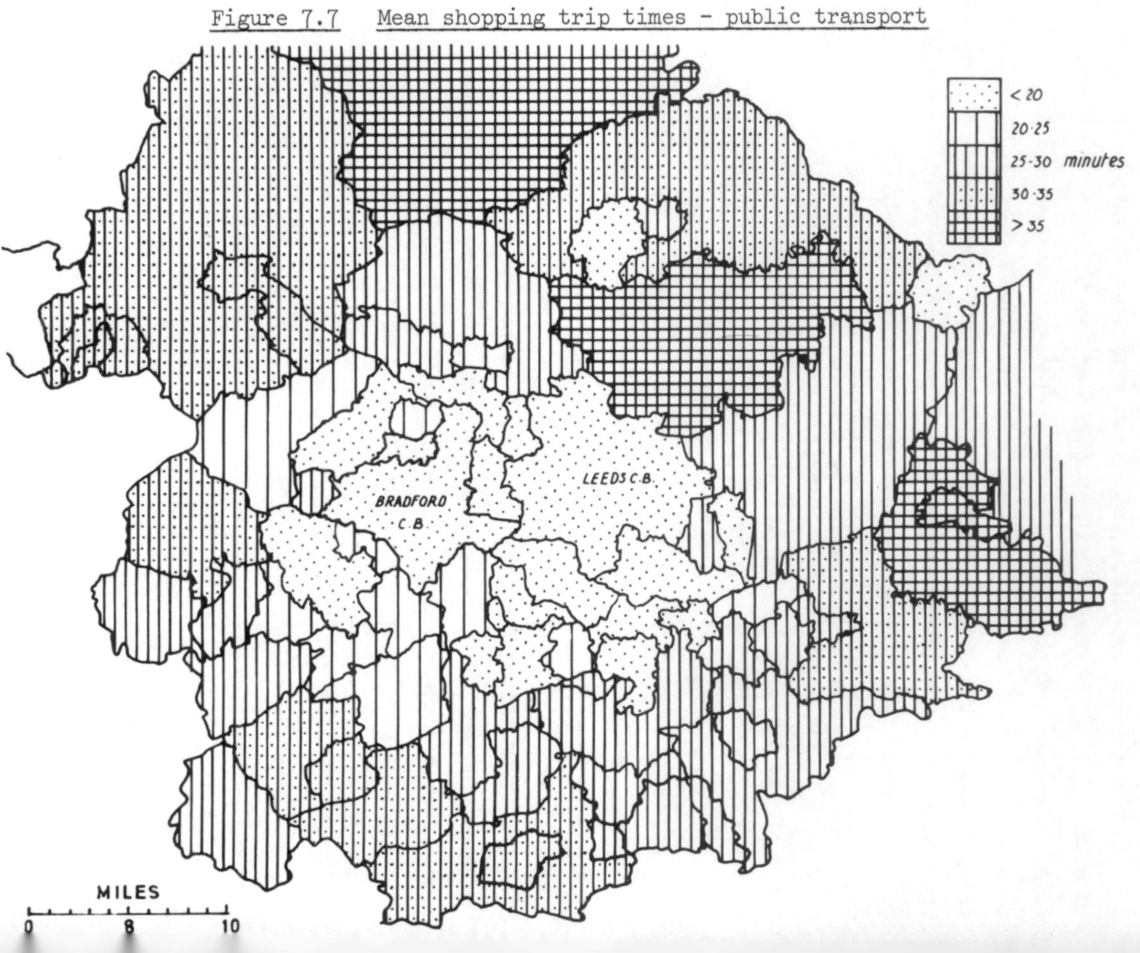

more interesting to standardise each of the flows concerned in order to take into account the populations of the zones of origin, thus giving some idea of the 'unit influence' exerted by Leeds on each of them. In Figure 7.8, however, the thickness of the arrows representing flows is proportional to the size of the flows. In addition, each arrow is accompanied by two sets of figures. At the Leeds end is presented the percentage of its total sales originating in that particular authority, while at the origin end similar figures for public (upper) and private (lower) transport trips are also presented separately. These last two cannot be compared in absolute terms, however, for they refer not to the all-mode total but to their own mode-specific totals. From the map it can be seen that almost 30% of Leeds' durable turnover originates within its own boundaries while a further 11% comes from Bradford. As one would expect, these constitute by far the two most important sources, although expenditure from other County Boroughs and large Municipal Boroughs is by no means negligible. This analysis can be taken a stage further if we consider the shopping inflows for each mode separately. Leeds' internal expenditure for the two modes is almost identical in terms of the percentage of the respective mode totals. However, although more than 13% of Leeds public transport sales originate in Bradford, only 7.4% of the corresponding private transport sales is accounted for in this way. In fact this pattern appears to be repeated for most of the large surrounding authorities, while for those less accessible there is a tendency to contribute a higher percentage of private sales. No doubt this is a function of socio-economic-group differentials and the pattern of public transport provision.

In the above Leeds example we considered the distribution of the origins of its retail turnover. On the other hand, we can take the opposite view and map the distribution of the sales originating in each zone. As an example of this latter approach we have chosen Dewsbury County Borough mainly because in the hinterland boundary exercise it was found, rather surprisingly, that the model results suggest that it does not possess a durable goods hinterland at that level. From Figure 7.9, we can see how Dewsbury's durable expenditure is in fact distributed. Approximately one-third is captured by Leeds while a further 14% is attracted by Bradford. Huddersfield and Wakefield are two other adjacent minor attractors while Dewsbury

Figure 7.8 Distributions of origins of Leeds durable goods turnover

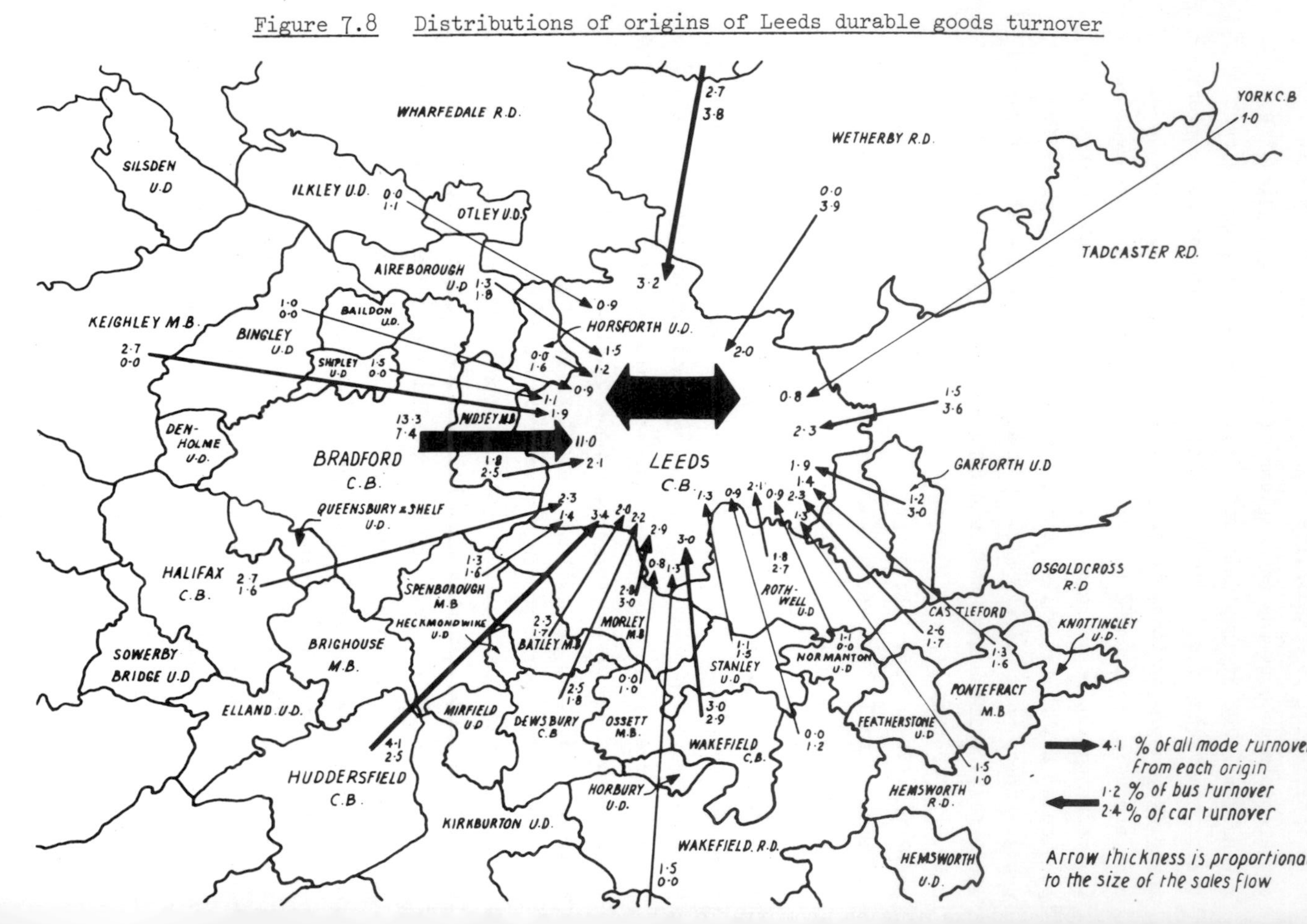

distribution of all mode durable expenditure

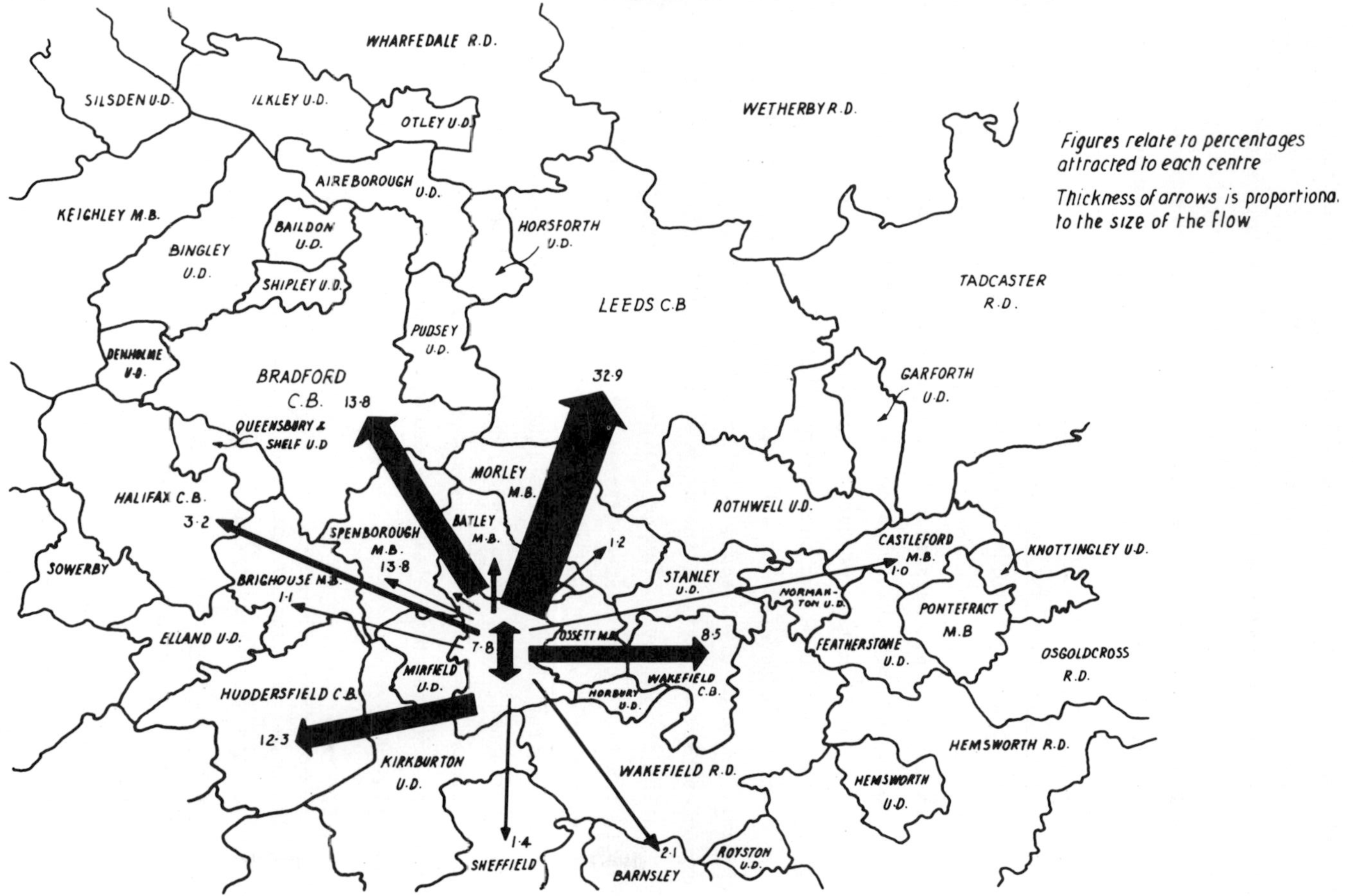

itself appears to retain less than 8% of its own expenditure on durable goods. Clearly it suffers in competition from close, more attractive centres and from its central position within a network of well-connected competitors. This hypothesis is supported by the actual flow figures which show that approximately two-thirds of the sales lost to the few above-mentioned centres are of non car-owners.

7.4 Application 2: shopping within Leeds

7.4.1 Particular problems for intra-urban models

Regional and subregional model applications of the type just described are now rather numerous. Less common, however, are studies of intra-urban retailing systems, even though such systems account for the majority of shopping trips and sales. At such a fine spatial level of resolution many of the generalisations inherent in models of spatial interaction become increasingly questionable. Statistical averaging can be carried out with less confidence, the already unstable patterns of expenditure discussed earlier become even more unpredictable, and various intangibles and qualitative factors assume increasing importance in the decision-making process of the shopper. Simple functions of distance deterrence or central attraction become less representative of reality. Nevertheless, there is still reason to believe that large urban units like Leeds, if suitable survey data can be obtained, can provide the framework for worthwhile model applications. We therefore present a discussion of such an intra-urban application, the details of which have been published separately (Mackett, 1973).

7.4.2 The form of the model

The model is formally the same as that presented in Section 7.3.2 for the West Yorkshire model. As before, the model is unconstrained at the attraction end, so that centres are competing for expenditure by users of all modes. The modal split is determined by the numbers of persons with each mode available (this again means that those without a car available use a bus or walk to the shops). The model is run separately for convenience goods and durable goods. Convenience goods' trips tend to be shorter and to a local centre, durable goods' trips are made less often, frequently to the city centre. The α_n parameter on the attraction factor has a different value for each goods type. For values greater than unity it represents theoretically a form of economy of scale in that larger centres are able to draw sales more than proportionally to their attraction factors; this is explained by the need for comparison between similar shops before purchases are made. It would be quite conceivable to have a separate α parameter for each mode (α_n^k) if the attraction factor distinguished between modes (W_{jkn}), for example, by incorporating, say, the amount of car parking space and the distance of the centre from the bus route. The explanation of 'economies of scale' for α may not hold strictly in all cases. For example, a comparison of the sales in each centre for increasing values of α_n above unity, ceteris paribus, may show that the levels of sales in centres will change at different rates, so that the smaller centres for one value of α_n may 'overtake' larger centres (in terms of sales volumes) for a larger value of α_{kn}. This may be due to the nature of the urban system being considered, and needs to be studied further.

The behaviour of the β parameter has been investigated more thoroughly as it appears in other forms of spatial interaction model. It represents decreasing interaction for increasing trip length (for β positive). The larger the value of β the greater the proportion of short trips. One would expect the value of β_{kn} to be larger for durable goods than for convenience goods since durable goods trips tend to be made to larger centres, and so are associated with a longer mean trip length.

7.4.3 Calibration

There are again two parameters to be estimated, varying with n and k, α_n and β_{kn}, giving a total of six values. As we noted earlier, most model runs in this country have used the total sales in shopping centres to calibrate the model. These are readily available (in the Census of Distribution) but such a calibration may lead to a false calibration for parameter values of $\alpha=1$, $\beta=0$, where the model will distribute sales in direct proportions to the attraction factor and distance will have no effect. This was found in the Portbury Study (Ministry of Transport, 1966) and has been described as a 'bogus calibration' by Cordey-Hayes (1968). Clearly this is unrealistic and so care must be taken to ensure that such a calibration is not used. One way to avoid it would be to use the flows of sales (S_{ij}) and fit these to actual sales. However, such data are not readily available, and would require a comprehensive household survey to find the distribution of sales from residential zones over the whole city. As we have seen, an alternative measure with a valid theoretical base is the mean trip length which can be obtained from a fairly small random survey of households. As Batty (1971) has shown, however, this alone would not suffice to produce a unique fit in the case of a two parameter model. But the same survey data can be used to compute 'mean trip benefit' and this can be used within a maximum likelihood procedure to obtain the value of α_n. Since the model is unconstrained at the retail centre end the mean trip lengths by each mode are independent and the values of β_{kn} can be fitted separately for each mode, as well as for each goods type. Although the mean trip length is related theoretically to the β parameter, it is not completely independent of the value of α_n. However, as long as the variations in the two measures for each pair of parameter values are different (that is, the surfaces generated are not parallel) the model can be calibrated by adopting the values of α_n and β_{kn} at which both measures are optimised. In this study calibration is based upon minimising the difference between the real and model values of the mean of the logarithm of trip length by each mode for each goods type, (for β_{kn}) and the mean logarithm of the attraction factors (for α_n) using the method of Batty and Mackie (1972). The observed values of the variables were found from a household survey.

Addresses of households were selected at random in Leeds from within areas defined by enumeration districts (ED's) used in the 1966 Census of Population. The ED's used were selected at random within wards or pairs of wards, using the Electoral Register. Thirty addresses were selected in each of 15 ED's, giving a total of 450. The purpose of the survey was to find the distribution of shopping sales by mode of transport and by goods type. Questions were asked about five types of convenience goods, two types of service and six types of durable goods. The groups were then aggregated into convenience and durable to provide sufficiently large samples that the mean trip length could be found for each goods type, by each mode of transport. The questionnaire results were coded at the shopping centre end using the results of a shops survey by the Leeds County Borough Planning Department which included the name, address, grid reference and type of shop for every known shop in Leeds. Since the residential address of the household was known, it was possible to define the end points of the flows of sales in the survey, and from this to find the required values of the logarithm of the trip length by each mode for each type of good and the weighted mean of the logarithm of the attraction factors. Since the household survey was areally stratified, it was necessary to weight the results of the survey to ensure spatial compatibility between these results and those from the model. Where one ED represented a pair of wards the values from the survey were divided between the zones in proportion to the total expenditure in each zone, and then weighted by these expenditures to allow for non-response.

7.4.4 Data inputs and sources

Population and the zoning system

The only comprehensive source of information about small areas within cities is the Census of Population. The last Census currently available was the sample Census of 1966, with the result that the population figures will be five years out of date, but these can be easily updated by the 1971 figures at a later stage. If the Census of Population is to be used then the zoning system at the residential end must be based upon the Census zoning system. Consequently, the 28 wards that were in use in 1966 were used as the residential zones. As we concluded earlier, the number of households is a more useful analysis unit than the number of heads, as most shopping is for the household as a unit. This information is given in the Ward and Parish Library for Leeds, which includes information for each ED.

Car availability

The number of households with a car available during the day for shopping must be found. The Census of Population gives figures for the number of households with no car, one car and two or more cars, but not the number of cars used for the journey-to-work. From the

West Yorkshire transportation survey a mean figure for the car occupancy rate for the morning work trip was found and divided into the number of people commuting by car to give the number of cars in each zone used for the work trip. The total number of cars in each zone was found and so, by subtraction the number of cars left at home during the day was calculated. This method ignores third and subsequent cars, and households with two or more cars which are all used for work but the numbers in each of these categories are small for Leeds and tend to cancel out each other.

Expenditure per head

The main source of information on expenditure is the Family Expenditure Survey (FES) which is based on a household sample and includes tables for regions, types of area and occupation group. From these tables an estimate of the average expenditure per household for each type of good for the West Yorkshire conurbation can be made:

$$e_{WYn} = \frac{e_{YHn} e_{PCn}}{e_{UKn}} \qquad (7.16)$$

where e_{WYn} is the expenditure per household on good n in the West Yorkshire conurbation; e_{YHn} is the expenditure per household on good n in the Yorkshire and Humberside region; e_{PCn} is the expenditure per household on good n in the provincial conurbation; and e_{UKn} is the expenditure per household on good n in the United Kingdom. This combines the expenditure value for the region in which Leeds is, with the type of area it is to give an estimate for the West Yorkshire conurbation, which is taken to be the same as the Leeds figure. The FES tables for occupations refer only to the nation as a whole but these can be used to find an index which represents the social structure of each zone and this can then be used to distribute zonal expenditure around the mean for the West Yorkshire conurbation.

$$\text{Zonal expenditure index} = \frac{\text{mean expenditure in zone i on good n}}{\text{mean expenditure overall on good n}}$$

$$= \frac{\Sigma_l m_{il} e_{UKnl}}{\Sigma_i m_{il}} \quad \frac{\Sigma_i \Sigma_l m_{il} e_{UKnl}}{\Sigma_i \Sigma_l m_{il}} \qquad (7.17)$$

where m_{il} is the number of people in zone i in occupation group l; and e_{UKnl} is the expenditure per household on good n by occupation group l in the United Kingdom.

$$e_{in} = e_{WYn} \frac{\Sigma_l m_{il} e_{UKnl}}{\Sigma_i m_{il}} \quad \frac{\Sigma_i \Sigma_l m_{il} e_{UKnl}}{\Sigma_i \Sigma_l m_{il}} \qquad (7.18)$$

where e_{in} is the expenditure per household on good n in zone i. The social groups are based on occupation groups in the FES and the socio-economic groups in the Census of Population, and correspond as shown in Table 7.3.

Table 7.3 Relationship of FES occupation groups to census socio-economic groups

	FES group	Census of Population group
1.	Workers in professional, administrative, managerial and leading occupations	Economically active members of socio-economic groups 1, 2, 3, 4 and 13
2.	Workers in clerical occupations	Economically active members of socio-economic groups 5 and 6
3.	Workers in manual occupations	Economically active members of socio-economic groups 7-12 and 14-17
4.	Retired and unoccupied person	Retired

The six goods groups are based on the goods used in the Family Expenditure Survey.

Every city contains a large number of corner shops and small clusters of local shops spread over the whole city. It is not practical to consider these individually, only those shops in larger centres. It seems reasonable to assume that these shops are distributed evenly over the city, and so a constant proportion of the expenditure on each goods type can be deducted from the total expenditure in each zone. The proportions were determined from the household survey. The values of the residual sales in the shopping centres being considered are 48.15% for convenience goods and 96.49% for durable goods.

The shopping centres

A total of 22 centres are used in the model and these are illustrated in relation to the population zones in Figure 7.10. They include both the main shopping centre and six centres outside the Leeds boundary. Three of these are large supermarkets owned by Associated Dairies which are indicative of the trend towards sub-urban centres and the use of the motor car for shopping trips. Away from the more traditional shopping centres, rather they stand by themselves, often in almost rural areas (with consequent lower costs in terms of rates, as well as increased accessibility for cars). These particular supermarkets are comparable in rateable value with some of the suburban centres. The Leeds city shopping centre is as defined for the Census of Distribution. Other centres were defined by the Leeds County Borough Planning Department using a 50 yard gap with no shops as the cut-off point. The actual attraction factor used is the rateable value of the shops in the centre. Although the last full rate assessment was in 1963 the value is changed whenever there is a change in land use or an extension is built or the ratepayer thinks the property value has depreciated, thus many shops will have been reassessed since 1963. There are disadvantages with all the possible available attraction factors. Floorspace tends to be slow to respond to changes in attractiveness, employment overemphasises older labour intensive shops and sales cannot be obtained from the shop owners because of confidentiality. One of the problems encountered is the use of local centres. Clearly a cut-off had to be made somewhere, and all small centres and indiv-idual shops below that cut-off regarded as local shops. There is no problem with a fairly even distribution of centres, but south Leeds, in particular lacks any large centre and so several smaller centres may perform the function of a large centre but will not be included in the model directly. This problem is unavoidable (short of including every single shop in the model) and, if one accepts the need for both large and small local centres, may not be such a disadvantage.

Figure 7.10 Leeds retail model: a map of the zones and shopping centres used

Key to zones and shopping centres on map

	Zones		Shopping Centres
1.	Allerton	A	City centre
2.	Armley	B	Crossgates
3.	Beeston	C	Headingley
4.	Blenheim	D	Seacroft
5.	Bramley	E	Armley
6.	Burmantofts	F	Harehills
7.	City	G	Morley
8.	Crossgates	H	ASDA Pudsey
9.	East Hunslet	I	Pudsey
10.	Far Headingley	J	ASDA Morley
11.	Halton	K	Bramley
12.	Harehills	L	Kirkstall Road
13.	Holbeck	M	Meanwood
14.	Hunslet Carr	N	Chapel Allerton
15.	Hyde Park	O	Horsforth-Town Street
16.	Kirkstall		
17.	Meanwood	P	Harehills Lane
18.	Middleton	Q	Oakwood
19.	Moortown	R	Moortown
20.	Osmondthorpe	S	Middleton
21.	Potternewton	T	ASDA Oldfield Lane
22.	Richmond Hill	U	Horsforth-New Road Side
23.	Roundhay	V	Halton
24.	Stanningley		
25.	Wellington		
26.	Westfield		
27.	Woodhouse		
28.	Wortley		

Travel time

As before, it was decided to use travel time as a measure of the distance between zones and centres. Clearly, if comparisons between modes are made on the basis of relative importance, then simple straight line distances and road distances between points cannot be used. Monetary cost is simple for bus travelling, but for cars the problems of fixed costs and variable costs are extremely complex - does one use overall average cost per mile (the actual cost) or perceived marginal cost (the cost one thinks about for making a single trip, if one has a car), and what values should be used? Even so, travel times do present problems, simply because an average figure must be assigned to a particular trip and this must cover trips at different times of day, congestion, waiting (for buses) and parking (for cars).

Car travel times were calculated as follows: (a) the road network was defined in terms of A roads, B roads and unclassified roads using Ordnance Survey maps; (b) the zonal centres were defined as the geometrical centre and these were joined to the nearest point or points on the network; distances were then measured from these points on the road; (c) speeds were then assigned to the roads on the basis of comparable figures published in a Road Research Laboratory Report (Marlow, 1971). Trips across the city centre were assumed to take 10 minutes, with a proportional decrease for shorter trips in the main centre; (d) distances between nodes on the network were measured on a 1 to 25,000 scale map and converted to miles; (e) distances were divided by speeds to give the travel time along the network link; (f) total travel time between zones and centres were found by addition; trips were assumed to be made by the shortest route (in terms of travel time); and (g) five minutes was added on to all travel times to allow for parking and walking to and from the car.

Bus travel times were calculated as follows: (a) the bus network was obtained from the route map published by Leeds City Transport; (b) the zonal centres were joined to the nearest bus route or routes, as above; (c) travel times were taken from the published bus timetables; (d) the times of trips between zones and shopping centres which are joined by a single bus route were measured on the assumption that people only change buses when absolutely necessary; (e) the times between zones and shopping centres which are joined by a journey involving only one change were then measured; such changes were usually made in the city centre; any dramatic reduction in travelling time caused by a change of bus, rather than a single trip was allowed as an exception to the rule that only essential changes were made; (f) the only remaining trip which required two changes was calculated; (g) walks from routes to centres and between routes up to half a mile were permitted; (h) a waiting time of five minutes for each bus was added (thus 'penalising' trips requiring a change of buses); and (i) very short trips between zones and centres were assumed to be walked where this was felt to be more realistic; walking speed is taken to be 3 mph; this means that the modal split is between car-users and non car-users.

7.4.5 Results

The model was calibrated using the results of the household survey. The flows of sales were used to find the weighted mean of the logarithm of the attraction factors for both modes of transport together, and the weighted means of the logarithm of the trip length between each residential zone and each shopping centre. A separate set of values was obtained for each mode of transport. These are shown in Table 7.4 below. The model was calibrated using a 'trial

Table 7.4 Mean attraction factors and trip lengths for calibration

	Mean of logarithm of attraction factors	Mean of logarithm of trip lengths for both modes	Mean of logarithm of trip lengths for car-users	Mean of logarithm of trip lengths for non car-users
Convenience goods	- 2.440	2.505	2.554	2.497
Durable goods	- 0.832	2.856	2.806	2.863

and error' procedure for a range of values of α_n and β_{*n}. The values of the means of the logarithms of the trip lengths for both modes combined and the attraction factors for each pair of values of the parameters were plotted; the point of intersection of the lines representing the actual values gave values of α_n and β_{*n}. In fact, several runs were required, each time containing a smaller range of possible parameter values, until the model outputs were judged to be sufficiently close to the real world values to be acceptable. Having obtained the values of α_n the model was run again for each mode separately so that the values of β_{kn} could be found. The parameter values obtained are shown in Table 7.5.

Table 7.5 Parameter values, Leeds

	α_n	β_{kn} for car-owners	β_{kn} for non car-owners
Convenience goods	1.072	2.126	2.610
Durable goods	0.913	0.667	1.847

These results offer some insights into shopping behaviour in Leeds. The values of α_n are both close to unity, implying that no great economies or diseconomies of scale occur. It might be expected that the value for convenience goods would be less than one, but it must be remembered that we are only considering sales in shopping centres, and that the model does not take into account the frequent, low value, convenience goods purchases in local shops. Consequently a substantial proportion of the convenience goods shopping that is being modelled is high value, weekly orders at supermarkets and large shops. For these types of shopping trips larger centres may be slightly more attractive than small ones, relative to their attraction factors. Economies of scale are usually regarded as more applicable to durable goods sales. In this case there appear to be slight diseconomies. As will be seen later, the city centre dominates the durable goods sales in Leeds. It may well be that the attraction factor used (rateable value) has a higher value for the city centre than sales to residents of Leeds would suggest. Quite a large proportion of the durable sales in the Leeds city centre are to non-Leeds residents giving shops there a relatively higher rateable value than the suburban centres. The value of α_n for durable goods reflects this.

The value of β represents the propensity to make trips of a certain length. The higher the value of β the greater the proportion of short trips. Thus for users of each mode there is a greater proportion of short trips for convenience goods than for durable goods, as would be expected. The corresponding values of the mean trip lengths (in minutes) are shown in Table 7.6. The figures show

Table 7.6 Mean trip lengths

	Car-users	Non car-users
Convenience goods	14.30	14.67
Durable goods	17.12	19.15

that shoppers with access to a car have an overall shorter mean trip length. The values of β_{kn} indicate that non car-owners have a greater propensity to make short trips than car-owners. Taken together these two facts suggest that in some parts of the city those without a car have to make very long trips for shopping.

The sales to Leeds' residents in the 22 shopping centres are shown in Tables 7.7 and 7.8. It should be noted that these do not represent total sales in each centre, only those to Leeds' residents. This permits comparison of the importance of different centres to users of each mode and for each goods type for households in Leeds. For both types of goods and both modes the city centre is dominant. For total sales to all customers, it is followed by Crossgates, Headingley, Seacroft and Harehills. However, there is a change in ranking when the type of goods is considered: for convenience goods, Headingley is second, followed by Crossgates and Harehills, whereas for durable goods the corresponding rankings are Crossgates, Seacroft and then Headingley. There are also differences between the users of each mode - Crossgates and Headingley are popular with car-users for both types of goods: both centres have large car parks. For non car-users Headingley and Harehills rank in popularity after the city centre for convenience goods, but for durable goods Crossgates and Seacroft are second and third. One striking difference between the two types of goods is the greater dominance of the city centre for

Table 7.7 Sales of convenience goods in shopping centres to Leeds' residents in £ per week

Shopping centres	Sales to car owners	% of convenience sales to car users	Ranking	Sales to non-car users	% of convenience sales to non-car users	Ranking	Sales to users of all modes
City Centre	26,693.93	34.75	1	147,457.40	37.96	1	174,151.32
Crossgates	8,938.18	11.63	2	26,687.72	6.87	4	35,625.91
Headingley	7,285.43	9.48	3	39,267.56	10.11	2	46,552.98
Seacroft	3,893.20	5.07	5	24,948.18	6.42	5	28,841.38
Armley	3,752.71	4.88	6	21,442.86	5.52	6	25,195.57
Harehills	4,835.95	6.29	4	28,337.43	7.29	3	33,173.38
Morley	1,484.47	1.93	12	4,660.59	1.20	16	6,145.06
ASDA - Pudsey	1,123.35	1.46	14	2,742.32	0.71	19	3,865.66
Pudsey	641.56	0.84	20	2,931.92	0.75	18	3,573.47
ASDA - Morley	468.55	0.61	22	917.03	0.24	22	1,385.58
Bramley	1,109.78	1.44	16	6,664.81	1.72	13	7,774.59
Kirkstall Road	1,381.65	1.80	13	4,892.64	1.26	15	6,274.29
Meanwood	2,238.64	2.91	9	8,329.03	2.14	12	10,567.67
Chapel Allerton	2,760.03	3.59	7	9,528.65	2.45	10	12,288.68
Horsforth - Town Street	530.38	0.69	21	1,122.95	0.29	21	1,653.33
Harehills Lane	1,606.64	2.09	11	10,101.36	2.60	9	11,708.00
Oakwood	821.27	1.07	18	4,069.29	1.05	17	4,890.56
Moortown	2,430.71	3.16	8	10,940.12	2.82	8	13,370.83
Middleton	1,853.88	2.41	10	17,201.18	4.43	7	19,055.06
ASDA - Oldfield Lane	1,118.06	1.46	15	9,129.74	2.35	11	10,247.80
Horsforth - New Road Side	1,042.12	1.36	17	1,916.56	0.49	20	2,958.68
Halton	815.81	1.06	19	5,209.25	1.34	14	6,025.06
[illegible]	[illegible]	100.00		388,498.60	100.00		465,324.90

Shopping centres	Sales to car users	% of durable sales to car users	Ranking	Sales to non-car users	% of durable sales to non-car users	Ranking	Sales to users of all modes	Total sales (convenience and durable)
City Centre	114,187.20	85.49	1	563,118.70	84.47	1	677,305.90	851,457.22
Crossgates	5,665.09	4.24	2	23,223.27	3.48	2	28,888.36	64,514.27
Headingley	2,348.67	1.75	3	14,568.90	2.19	4	16,917.57	63,470.55
Seacroft	1,684.10	1.26	4	16,625.21	2.49	3	18,309.31	47,150.69
Armley	1,435.79	1.07	5	7,457.07	1.12	6	8,892.86	34,088.43
Harehills	1,324.04	0.99	6	9,861.70	1.48	5	11,185.74	44,359.12
Morley	862.64	0.65	7	2,393.32	0.36	12	3,255.96	9,401.02
ASDA - Pudsey	483.58	0.36	13	1,112.47	0.17	19	1,596.04	5,461.70
Pudsey	588.26	0.44	8	2,142.66	0.32	15	2,730.91	6,304.38
ASDA - Morley	286.03	0.21	18	474.43	0.07	22	760.46	2,146.04
Bramley	553.76	0.41	11	3,045.10	0.46	9	3,598.86	11,373.45
Kirkstall Road	582.39	0.44	9	2,341.29	0.35	13	2,923.68	9,197.97
Meanwood	560.80	0.42	10	2,648.66	0.40	10	3,209.46	13,777.13
Chapel Allerton	512.95	0.38	12	2,457.35	0.37	11	2,970.30	15,258.98
Horsforth - Town Street	358.09	0.27	17	911.67	0.14	20	1,269.76	2,923.09
Harehills Lane	425.35	0.32	14	3,050.12	0.46	8	3,475.47	15,183.47
Oakwood	393.78	0.29	15	2,268.73	0.34	14	2,662.51	7,553.07
Moortown	362.76	0.27	16	2,077.24	0.31	16	2,440.00	15,810.83
Middleton	225.42	0.17	22	3,706.59	0.56	7	3,932.01	22,987.07
ASDA - Oldfield Lane	234.82	0.18	21	1,321.92	0.20	17	1,556.74	11,804.54
Horsforth - New Road Side	257.64	0.19	19	678.49	0.10	21	936.13	3,894.81
Halton	242.45	0.18	20	1,125.82	0.17	18	1,368.27	7,393.33
Total	133,575.60	100.00		666,610.70	100.00		800,186.30	1,265,511.20

users of both modes for durable goods with no other centre showing more than 5% of the sales. For convenience goods the distribution of sales is more even. Car-users do a greater proportion of shopping in the six centres outside Leeds than those without cars. For convenience goods, 6.89% of sales by car-users are in these centres, whereas the corresponding figure for non car-users is 3.68%. For durable goods the figures are 2.12% and 1.16% respectively. These figures emphasise the greater mobility of car-users. It would be interesting to measure these sales flows at different points in time to see if this represents a growing trend, which could lead to a substantial loss of trade in the city centre.

The mean trip lengths by each mode for each goods group and the accessibilities to shops from each zone are shown in Tables 7.9 and 7.10 respectively. These are defined as:

$$\bar{c}_{i*kn} = \frac{\Sigma_j S_{ijkn} c_{ijk}}{\Sigma_j S_{ijkn}} \qquad (7.19)$$

and

$$Q_{ikn} = \Sigma_j W_{jn}^{\alpha n} c_{ijkn}^{-\beta_{kn}} \qquad (7.20)$$

where $\bar{c}_{i*kn}$ is the mean trip length from zone i by mode k for good n; and Q_{ikn} is the accessibility to shops selling goods type n by mode k for residents of zone i. Kirby (1970) has shown that these two measures are closely related but nevertheless a study of both will add to our understanding of the retailing subsystem, since each measure consists of several components and the underlying factors may not be immediately apparent. The overall mean trip lengths by car are longer than those for non car-owners. In many of the zones the mean trip lengths by car are shorter than by bus, as would be expected, but there are some zones in which the car-trip is longer. There are five zones in which the mean trip length by car is longer for both types of goods - City, Richmond Hill, Harehills, Hunslet Carr and Crossgates. The first four are areas of old housing near to the centre of the city. Crossgates is a large council estate where many families have been rehoused as a result of redevelopment. These areas contain many households with low incomes and have low levels of car-ownership and are close to shopping centres. Since the distance between each zone and each shopping centre is as great or

Table 7.9 Mean trip lengths in minutes, by Leeds zone

Zone	Convenience goods car users	Convenience goods non-car users	Durable goods car users	Durable goods non-car users
Allerton	15.9	15.2	18.9	22.6
Armley	14.5	13.1	17.4	18.5
Beeston	18.1	18.1	17.0	16.7
Blenheim	11.7	12.7	11.5	11.4
Bramley	14.5	19.7	17.2	23.2
Burmantofts	12.6	12.9	14.3	14.2
City	8.9	8.1	7.9	7.3
Crossgates	9.6	7.3	20.3	19.5
East Hunslet	15.0	19.1	13.7	16.7
Far Headingley	17.8	18.2	20.1	25.1
Halton	13.8	14.3	17.7	21.3
Harehills	8.5	6.3	15.0	13.7
Holbeck	14.2	16.6	12.9	14.6
Hunslet Carr	16.0	15.4	14.2	13.6
Hyde Park	12.9	13.9	14.4	13.4
Kirkstall	13.2	17.5	15.3	20.7
Meanwood	12.1	12.1	14.2	18.9
Middleton	13.0	7.0	21.8	23.6
Moortown	14.6	16.7	18.5	19.9
Osmondthorpe	13.0	22.6	14.2	23.5
Potternewton	9.4	7.6	13.1	14.2
Richmond Hill	12.1	11.6	10.8	10.4
Roundhay	16.6	15.3	18.2	23.4
Stanningley	17.1	23.9	21.0	29.2
Wellington	11.9	11.7	11.8	12.3
Westfield	11.5	11.7	10.8	10.4
Woodhouse	14.5	15.6	14.7	15.4
Wortley	16.5	18.9	16.7	24.8
Mean	14.3	14.7	17.1	19.1

Table 7.10 Accessibilities to shops

Zone	Convenience goods car users	Convenience goods non-car users	Durable goods car users	Durable goods non-car users
Allerton	20.7	4.4	1498.7	32.3
Armley	23.2	5.4	1584.4	46.2
Beeston	16.4	3.3	1613.3	56.9
Blenheim	40.7	8.3	2087.6	113.2
Bramley	24.4	2.6	1597.3	30.2
Burmantofts	32.9	7.2	1811.1	76.8
City	64.1	22.2	2702.8	254.4
Crossgates	40.7	10.7	1441.5	34.6
East Hunslet	24.7	2.8	1859.1	56.1
Far Headingley	16.7	2.6	1439.3	26.6
Halton	25.7	4.6	1569.6	34.8
Harehills	54.3	20.8	1758.2	77.3
Holbeck	26.8	4.2	1935.2	72.2
Hunslet Carr	20.6	5.0	1822.9	82.4
Hyde Park	31.8	6.5	1803.1	85.1
Kirkstall	29.6	3.5	1726.6	38.2
Meanwood	35.8	6.4	1813.4	43.9
Middleton	19.7	7.1	1365.1	28.2
Moortown	24.7	3.0	1521.7	41.6
Osmondthorpe	31.9	1.9	1818.6	30.7
Potternewton	52.0	15.4	1913.7	73.4
Richmond Hill	37.8	10.2	2187.5	134.7
Roundhay	19.1	4.2	1535.5	29.7
Stanningley	17.1	1.5	1398.2	20.9
Wellington	37.6	8.4	2063.2	98.1
Westfield	41.1	9.1	2185.0	132.6
Woodhouse	25.7	4.7	1777.1	65.3
Wortley	19.6	2.5	1629.8	27.4

greater by car than by bus, this means that in these areas, those with cars are deliberately choosing to make longer trips than necessary to shop for both types of goods. The zones where bus trips are longer than car trips for both types of goods are zones on the periphery of the city with no nearby shopping centres, so that those without cars are at a greater disadvantage in terms of the length of trip to shop.

Accessibility to shops takes into account the location and size of all the centres, plus the parameter values with their associated behavioural explanations, as outlined above. The attraction factors (W_j) have been divided by the total rateable value for each goods type, so comparisons may be made between trips for each type of good. Accessibility levels are higher for durable goods than for convenience goods. This is partly because of the dominance of the City Centre for durable goods. For both types of goods car-owners have higher levels of accessibility than non car-owners. For convenience goods the zones with the highest levels of accessibility are City, Harehills and Potternewton Wards. For durable goods the corresponding areas are City, Richmond Hill and Westfield Wards, which are near the centre of the city. Despite the fact that in some zones users of public transport had shorter trip lengths than car-users, a comparison of the levels of accessibility suggest that this is a result of using a local centre or centres, rather than through choice. Thus non car-users are constrained in space to a greater extent than car-users for shopping activities.

7.5 Application 3: public services in Leeds with special reference to fire

7.5.1 Introduction: problems of the providing authority

From our introductory discussion it is recognised that many of the services we are interested in can be classed as impure public goods. We were also careful to distinguish between publicly provided and privately provided goods, and pointed out that in many cases public goods are publicly provided while private goods are privately provided but that this correspondence is by no means perfect. For the goods and services we are interested in it is difficult to determine a set of market prices and partly as a consequence such goods become part of the domain of public provision. In Britain the collective authority responsible for the provision of many of these goods is the local government, and this forms a useful basis for the development of a unified approach. We must also be aware of the problems facing the providing authority in the development of the scheme and in so doing recognise at least three relevant problems: (a) a concern that council decisions are channelling resources almost exclusively into a selected number of districts within the city; (b) a concern that rate calls will become excessive and that there is a need to examine other possible forms of finance available to local governments; and (c) a concern with rising costs that may mean a cut-back or standstill in the level of service provision to the area.

These three points are obviously interrelated. For example, if the rating system was changed and replaced by, say, a local income tax, what effect would this have on the districts that received a greater share of council resources relative to rates paid, given a changed system? Alternatively, given a cut-back in supply, then it is obviously necessary that existing facilities should be used to their utmost in terms of community benefit. What would be the optimum pattern for this usage to be achieved? It is in light of these considerations that a modelling framework has been developed and is currently in the process of being implemented for the Leeds area.

7.5.2 The modelling framework

The modelling framework developed is shown as a flow diagram form in Figure 7.11 and outlined before we go on to examine aspects of the empirical work in detail. The assumption is made that the local authority budget can be represented by a single accounting identity which takes the form:

$$GE - (SP + LI) \equiv RSGN + RSGR + LT + NRI \pm B \qquad (7.21)$$

where GE is gross expenditure; SP is specific government grants; LI is local income; RSGN is the needs element of the rate support grant; RSGR is the resource element of the rate support grant; LT is local taxation licenses; NRI is net rate income; and B is a

Figure 7.11 Modelling framework, public services

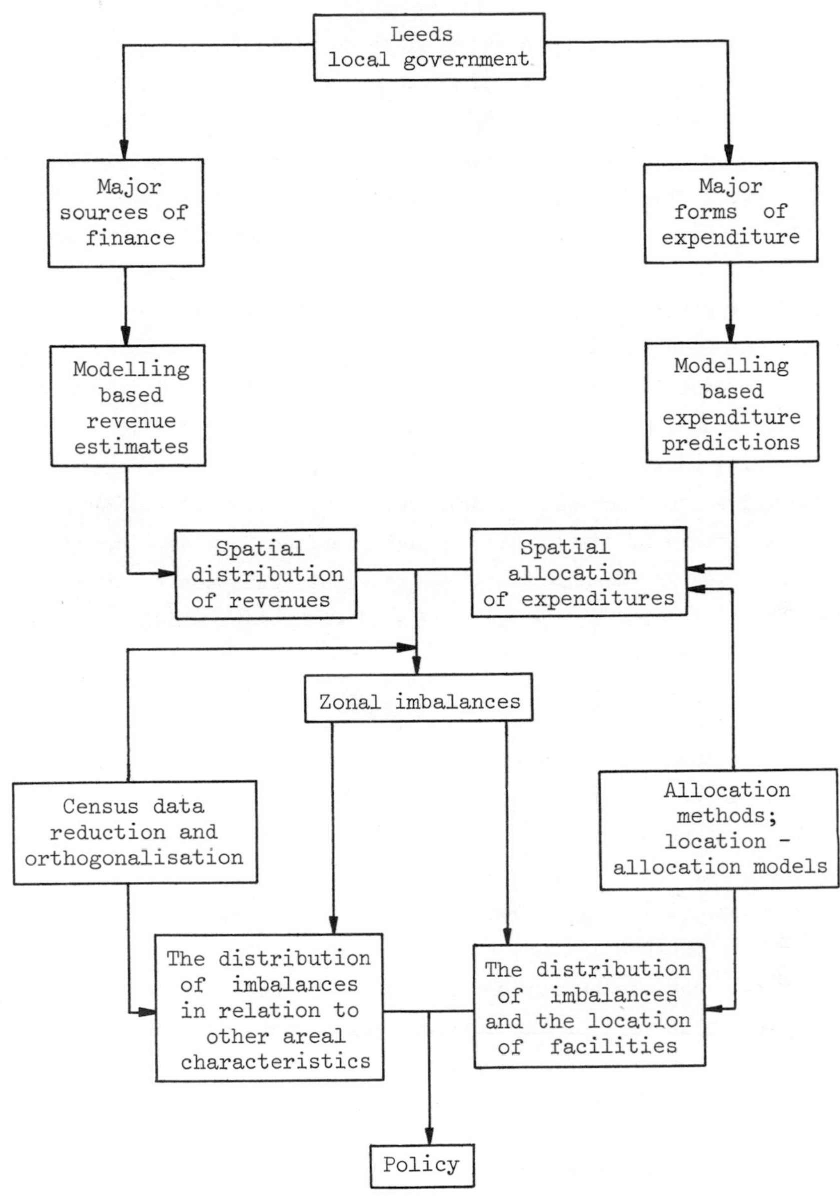

balancing figure which ensures the identity. GE - (SP + LI) is defined as net expenditure or net rate charge. Given this identity, ways of projecting the net expenditure term are examined. On the basis of these projections, the magnitude of revenue required for finance can be ascertained and a close examination of possible alternative sources can be undertaken. We then look at how the revenue is raised from various areal units of the city, concentrating particularly on 39 analysis zones defined by a principal components procedure. These analysis zones were grouped from enumeration districts using household characteristics. Similarly, we then look at how service provision is distributed throughout the city. Various methods of determining this spatial distribution were employed so that zonal imbalances could be defined and areas which exhibit an excess of expenditure received over revenue contributed (or vice versa), recognised. It is then possible to assess the location of the service points with a view to further changes being implemented to optimise some appropriate measure. Also, it will be important to look closely at the imbalance distributions on a service-by-service basis. Clearly important policy statements can then be discussed and alternative policy options assessed within the model. A more detailed discussion of the ideas presented here can be found in Whitehead (1974).

7.5.3 The analysis of imbalances

It has been pointed out that one of the problems facing the provider of public goods is the possibility that decisions taken by the authority apparently on a city-wide basis have in effect channelled resources into a selected number of districts within the city (Randall, Lomas and Newton, 1973). Coupled with this is the concern that some areas are becoming overburdened in terms of the rates paid. This particular part of the analysis, then, sets out to investigate the equality or otherwise in the spatial provision of services set within the wider context of income redistribution within the city. In so doing, an algebraic model is presented and some of the related estimation techniques discussed. The imbalance model used is, of course, developed at a finer level of spatial resolution than the macro-accounting identity presented earlier.

We define the variable $IB_i^K(t)$, as the imbalance values (in £'s) for service type K in zone i at time t. This can take either a positive or a negative value depending on whether zonal expenditure is in excess of zonal revenue or vice versa. Thus

$$IB_i^K(t) = \{\lambda_i^K(t)E^K(t) - \theta^K(t)\{\alpha(t)RV_i^D(t) + tr_i(t)Y_i(t)\}\} \quad (7.22)$$

where $\lambda_i^K(t)$ is the proportion of expenditure on service K that is allocated to zone i in time t. We note that $\Sigma_i\lambda_i^K(t) = 1$; $E^K(t)$ is the net expenditure on service type K at time t; $\theta^K(t)$ is the proportion of net rate charge which is taken by service type K at time t; $\alpha(t)$ is the rate in the pound levied at time t; $RV_i^D(t)$ is the total domestic rateable value for zone i at time t; $tr_i(t)$ is the contribution rate for zone i at time t. This can be interpreted as a local government services tax rate; and $Y_i(t)$ is the potential taxable income for zone i at time t. The set of zonal expenditure coefficients, $\lambda_i^K(t)$ reflect the proportion of expenditure on service type K that is allocated to zone i at time t. As well as being time dependent, these coefficients are both zone and service specific and their determination a matter for discussion below. The terms $\lambda_i^K(t)E^K(t)$ are thus zonal expenditure receipts for year t and from these values we must subtract the revenue estimates. Once calculated, the revenue estimates will be appropriate for all services considered, though the procedure is complex since terms appear which are not directly calculable at the zonal level. If we take local sources of revenue first, note that it is possible to estimate zonal rateable values for different time periods. These can be obtained as individual ledger totals but unfortunately not usually classified by type of hereditament. However, the information needed to obtain domestic rateable values for small areas is available, and we will assume, can be readily obtained. These values when multiplied by an exogenously determined variable defined above as $\alpha(t)$, which represents the rate per pound levied in the time period in question, give an estimate of an area's contribution to net rate income. Thus we assume

$$\Sigma_i\alpha(t)RV_i^D(t) = NRI^D(t) \quad (7.23)$$

where $NRI^D(t)$ is the contribution through domestic rates to net rate income. We recognise the possibility of refinement to take into account, for example, the domestic element of the rate support grant which acts as a subsidy to domestic rate-payers and any current rate-rebate scheme. These, however, involve severe data problems.

To estimate non-local sources of revenue, we simply multiply zonal income by an appropriate contribution rate. This rate can be interpreted as a local government services tax rate and will itself be a function of income. We assume

$$\Sigma_i tr_i(t)Y_i(t) = RSGN(t) + RSGR(t) \qquad (7.24)$$

The problems of estimating zonal income will be outlined below, together with an appropriate procedure. By summing the local and non-local sources of revenue and multiplying the results by $\theta^K(t)$, the proportion of the net rate charge taken by service type K at time t, we have the revenue estimates to be subtracted from the zonal expenditure and thus the imbalance values in Equation (7.22).

The two main estimation problems involve the zonal expenditure coefficients and zonal incomes and they are discussed in turn below. The expenditure coefficients reflect the consumption of the service in question, and therefore ideally should be related to a zone's demand for the service. However, because we are dealing with impure public goods individual demand curves are inappropriate. Consequently, we adopt the concept of participation, defined by Benson and Lund (1969) to mean all instances in which groups of households act to cause a local public service to be performed. The zonal coefficients are thus participation rates and reflect a zone's consumption of a public service. In measuring these rates we must be careful not to confuse participation with the related but conceptually different measures of standards and needs. By standards, we mean some set of criteria relevant to each service, for example, that people should be within say half a mile of a library. While standards may be relatively easy to determine for most services, they are not indicators of actual patterns of usage and thus may lead to inaccurate allocations given that any set of criteria will be somewhat artificial and not necessarily adhered to. Similarly, the concept of need is considered inappropriate since it is primarily a policy variable which reflects a value judgement rather than a set of objective criteria. It therefore provides a hypothetical allocation while participation should reflect the actual situation in that it looks at the distribution of the service as it appears in the current time period.

Consider two examples of services: fire protection and library provision. In order to estimate participation we need a measure which reflects an area's consumption of the service. In the case of the fire service, three possible measures suggest themselves: (a) the number of fires per zone; (b) the total number of personnel who are in attendance at fires per zone; and (c) the time in seconds spent bringing fires under control per zone. As fire protection does not directly involve any interaction generated on the demand side but rather a supply side response, the measures suggested for participation involve a count of instances. In fact, the type of estimation procedure which can be used is largely dependent on whether demand side interaction is generated or otherwise. In the case of the library service, participation can be defined in terms of issues, and these directly involve interaction over space. Consequently, we calculate participation for the library service using an interaction model. Participation rates are defined as:

$$\lambda_i = \Sigma_j (T_{ij} / \Sigma_k T_{kj}) \tag{7.25}$$

with

$$T_{ij} = B_j P_i D_j \exp(-\beta c_{ij}) \tag{7.26}$$

where T_{ij} is the number of issues to zone i borrowed from library j; P_i is the population in i; D_j is the number of books issued from library j; c_{ij} is a distance/cost matrix; B_j is a balancing factor to ensure $\Sigma_i T_{ij} = D_j$; and β is a parameter. It is possible to calibrate this model using a small sample of issues.

The second main estimation procedure involved in the model is that of zonal estimates of income. We recognise that while the central government's payment of the rate support grant depends on certain criteria characteristic of local authorities, it is nevertheless paid out of central funds into which contributions are received from inhabitants in the form of taxes. Taxes are paid out of income and thus zonal incomes become a prerequisite for this estimation. A suitable method can be built on the standard category analysis type of approach which is further described in Chapter 9 below. It is based on the assumption that the distribution of income can be represented by a probability function of the following form:

$$P(x) = \int_a^b \frac{\alpha N+1}{\Gamma(N+1)} x^N e^{-\alpha x} dx \qquad (7.27)$$

where P(x) is the probability of a household having income x; a, b are the upper and lower limits of x; and α is $(N+1)/\bar{X}$ where $\bar{X}$ is mean income. Mean income is generated iteratively using car-ownershi[p] data as the basic input to the model. Care is needed in the interpretation of these estimates; first to avoid confusion with other concepts of income and second to ensure they are corrected to a value appropriate for tax deductions.

7.5.4 Fire service imbalances

To illustrate the concepts outlined above, we present a worked example showing for a particular service, fire protection in the Leeds County Borough, how imbalances can be determined for small areas. The determination of an appropriate spatial zoning system presents the first problem, since wards and enumeration districts, the most often used bases, both suffer from drawbacks. A principle components analysis based on the 1966 Census enabled enumeration districts to be grouped into 39 analysis zones. The location and definition of these zones is shown as Figure 7.12. Thus, using 1966 as a base year, the macro-accounting relationships for that year are shown in Table 7.11. The General Grant and the Rate Deficiency Grant provided the local authority with the bulk of its income instead of the current Rate Support Grant. In effect, these performed similar functions to the current 'needs' and 'resources' elements respectively, the General Grant being paid on a formula basis and the Rate Deficiency Grant being designed to reduce rating inequalities. From the Net Rate Charge of £21,060,414, the fire service accounted for £389,321. Although not one of the largest services in revenue terms, it does nevertheless provide us with a useful example.

Once calculated, the revenue estimates apply generally over the range of services considered so we thus outline the methods used for these first. Initially, we are interested in domestic rateable valu[e]

Figure 7.12 Key map showing zones

Table 7.11 Leeds macro-accounts 1966

		£
Gross expenditure		35,384,008
Specific government grants and local income		14,323,594
		21,060,414
	£	
General Grant	7,491,596	
Rate Deficiency Grant	1,625,295	
Rating (Interim Relief Act, 1964)	47,605	
Local Taxation Licenses	8,589	
Net Rate Income	11,358,081	
	20,521,166	
Plus decrease in reserves	529,248	21,060,414

Ledger totals for all hereditaments were available in spatially disaggregated form for 1966. To obtain domestic rateable values a survey of the 1963 valuation list was carried out with non-domestic hereditaments being noted and then subtracted from the 1966 totals. These values were then adjusted to ensure correct addition to the control totals obtained from the macro-account. The total domestic rateable value for Leeds in 1966 was £8,900,509 and the rate in the pound levied was £0.567. By multiplying the rate in the pound by the rateable value we get an estimate of a zone's contribution to net rate income. Table 7.12 shows the values of the estimates of domestic rates paid by zone for 1966. Figure 7.13 shows the mapped

Table 7.12 Estimates of domestic rates paid by zone 1966 (£'s)

Zone	£	Zone	£	Zone	£
1	143,410	14	79,516	27	281,509
2	121,366	15	76,546	28	90,429
3	190,564	16	102,874	29	130,022
4	46,480	17	22,893	30	17,246
5	115,320	18	136,425	31	64,400
6	127,326	19	41,946	32	122,032
7	91,559	20	126,467	33	120,751
8	107,103	21	86,849	34	144,241
9	186.397	22	97,559	35	95,174
10	135,756	23	215,863	36	236,743
11	79,716	24	219,692	37	98,860
12	278,889	25	127,769	38	209,713
13	161,847	26	274,770	39	40,563

Figure 7.13 Distributions of estimated zonal contributions to total domestic rateable value - 1966

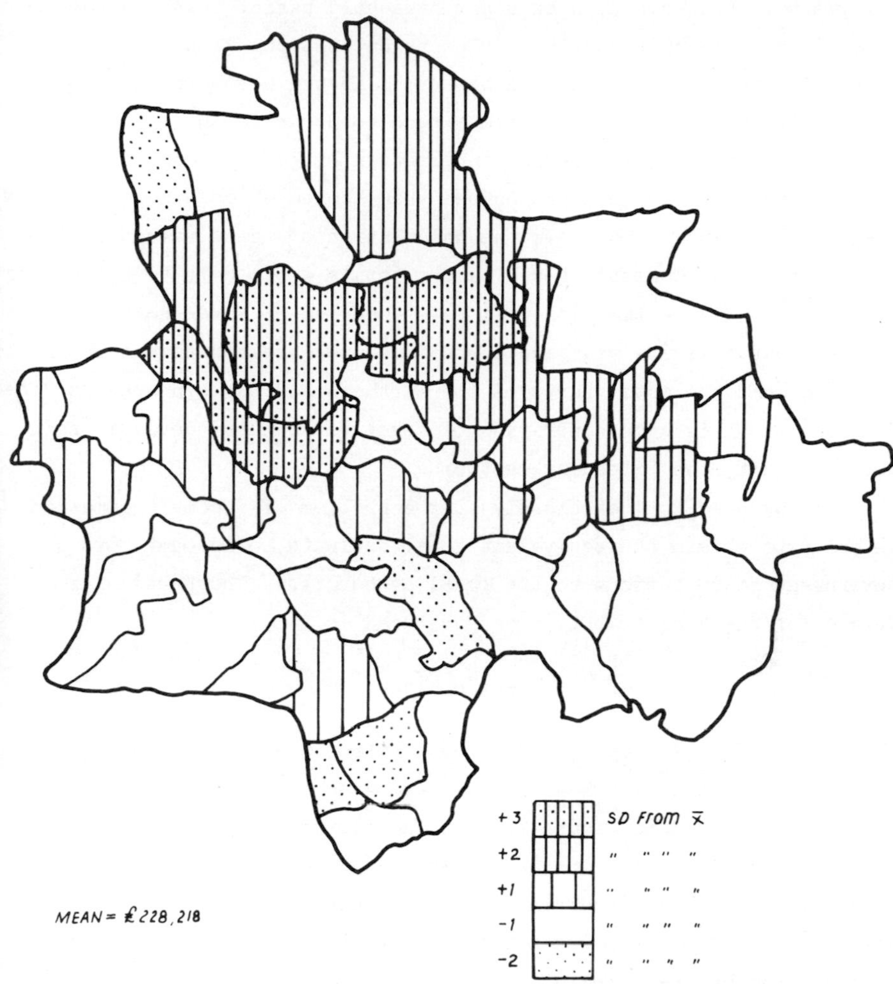

distribution of standard deviations above and below the mean zonal rate contribution of £228,218 while Figure 7.14 shows a similar distribution but this time on a per household basis. It can be seen from Figure 7.13 that the largest contributions occur in the outer zones of Allerton, Meanwood and Kirkstall in the northern part of the city, while the lower contributions tend to occur in the southern sector, for example, in Hunslet and Beeston Park. The distribution becomes considerably more pronounced when looked at on a per household basis as in Figure 7.14. In the calculation of these values it is assumed that the domestic hereditament totals apply only to households and so slight overestimation will have occurred. Nevertheless, it can be seen that positive standard deviations are confined almost wholly to a ring around the outer parts of the northern and eastern areas of the city and there is a concentration of negative standard deviations in the inner city and extending eastwards.

We now need to look closely at the problem of income estimation in order to obtain the equivalent zonal estimate to account for government contributions to the local authority. The particular version of the γ distribution we have used is

$$P(x) = \int_a^b \frac{\alpha^{2.6360}}{1.8974} x^N e^{-\alpha x} dx \qquad (7.28)$$

where the value of N as 1.6360 was taken from the West Midlands transportation study. Mean incomes are generated iteratively and all results mapped in Figure 7.15. The distribution is shown according to six income groups (remembering these apply to 1966!). The lowest estimates occur in the inner zones of Blenheim, Burmantofts and Hunslet and also in the outer areas of Middleton and Killingbeck. It is in the northern region of the city in zones like Cookridge, Adel and West Park that the highest mean incomes occur. In fact, this distribution is virtually covariant with that of household domestic rateable values, though Cookridge appears somewhat anomolous. The western parts of the city present a blanket of moderate to low income values while the east is more diversified.

These estimates are now corrected upwards so as to ensure alignment with income before tax is deducted. The potential taxable capacity of a zone is then defined by multiplying the corrected mean

Figure 7.14 Distribution of estimated domestic rateable value per household, 1966

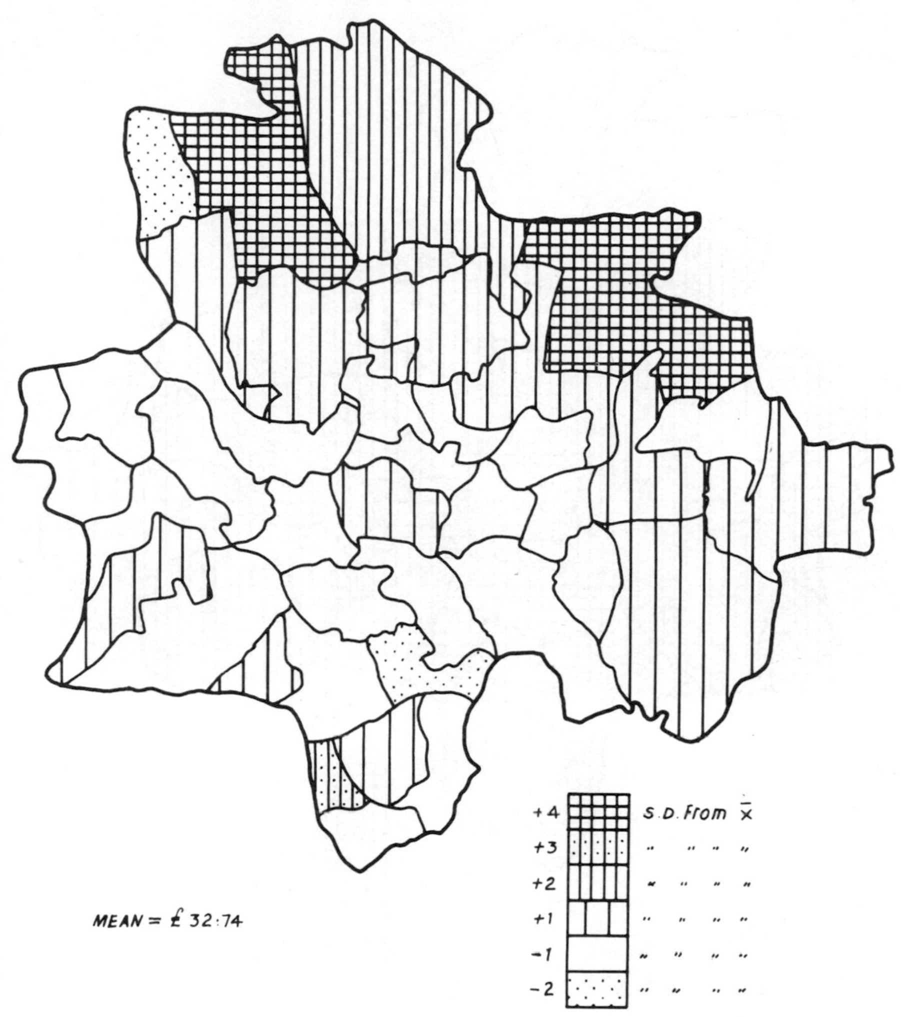

Figure 7.15 Zonal distribution of mean income estimates, 1966

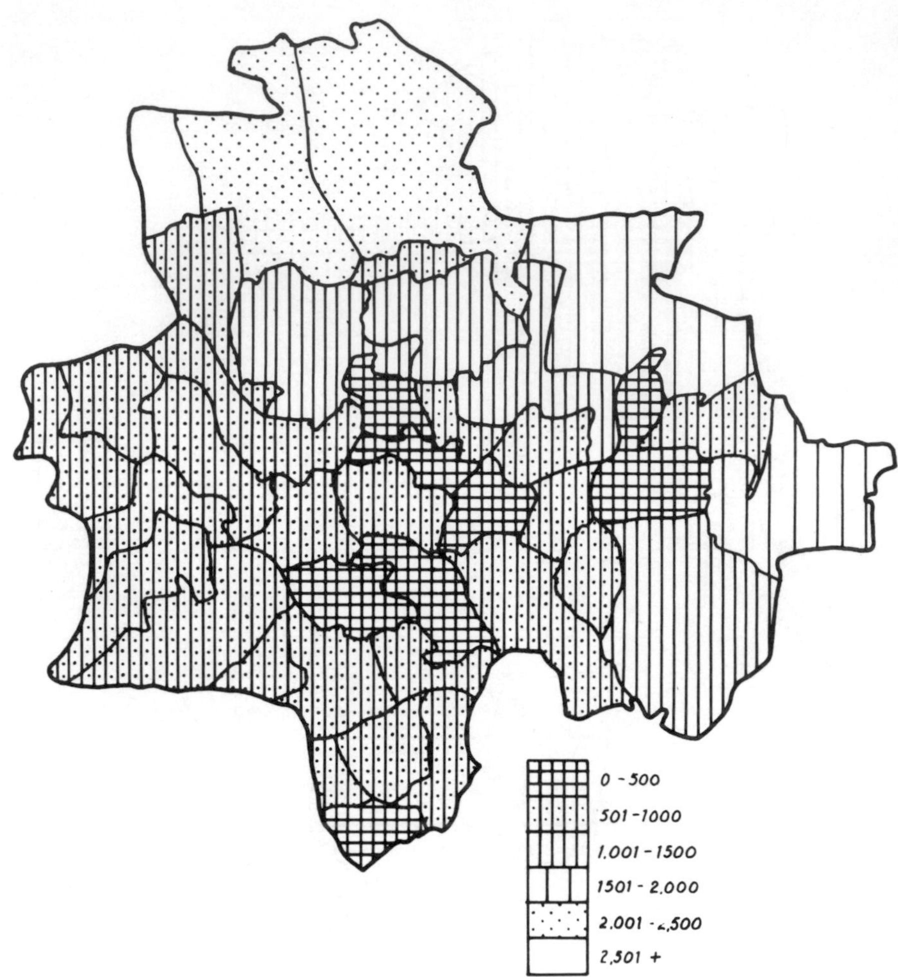

household incomes by the number of households. This involves the assumption of one taxpayer per household which can be updated at a later stage. Similarly, for this example we assume a contribution rate applied equally to all zones. Again to be refined later, this is defined as the total of government grants received divided by the total potential taxable income. By multiplying the contributory rate with the zonal potential taxable income we arrive at estimates of zonal contributions to government grants. These are shown in Table 7.13. Total zonal revenue contributions can be defined by

Table 7.13 Estimates of zonal contributions to government grants 1966 (£'s)

1	165,164	14	247,482	27	876,562
2	151,362	15	110,641	28	257,559
3	202,157	16	317,730	29	289,824
4	73,866	17	26,023	30	16,463
5	252,434	18	370,373	31	73,180
6	222,348	19	101,529	32	454,421
7	243,914	20	187,987	33	520,741
8	165,897	21	173,983	34	267,408
9	361,083	22	156,142	35	134,956
10	200,033	23	214,717	36	994,755
11	117,277	24	802,601	37	264,982
12	536,188	25	221,716	38	344,118
13	296,978	26	870,421	39	600,299

summing the values in Table 7.12 and Table 7.13. To these we apply the $\theta^K(t)$ coefficients which represent the proportion of net rate charge taken by service K, in this case, the fire service.

Turning to the zonal expenditure estimates for the fire service we begin by determining the appropriate zonal allocation coefficients. For this purpose we use the total number of personnel who were in attendance at fires per zone. The information necessary was obtained from an examination of the Fire Department's records of reports on occupied domestic property. The mean participation rate for the fire service is 0.025641 and Figure 7.16 shows the mapped distribution of standard deviations above and below the mean. It is apparent that the distribution is highly skewed and this is reflected by the concentration of fire attendances around the central and inner central areas. For example, the two inner areas of City and Hunslet receive the highest rates while peripheral zones like Adel and Middleton receive scores below the mean value. By multiplying the zones' coefficients

Figure 7.16 Fire service - zonal distribution of standard deviations from mean participation rate 1966

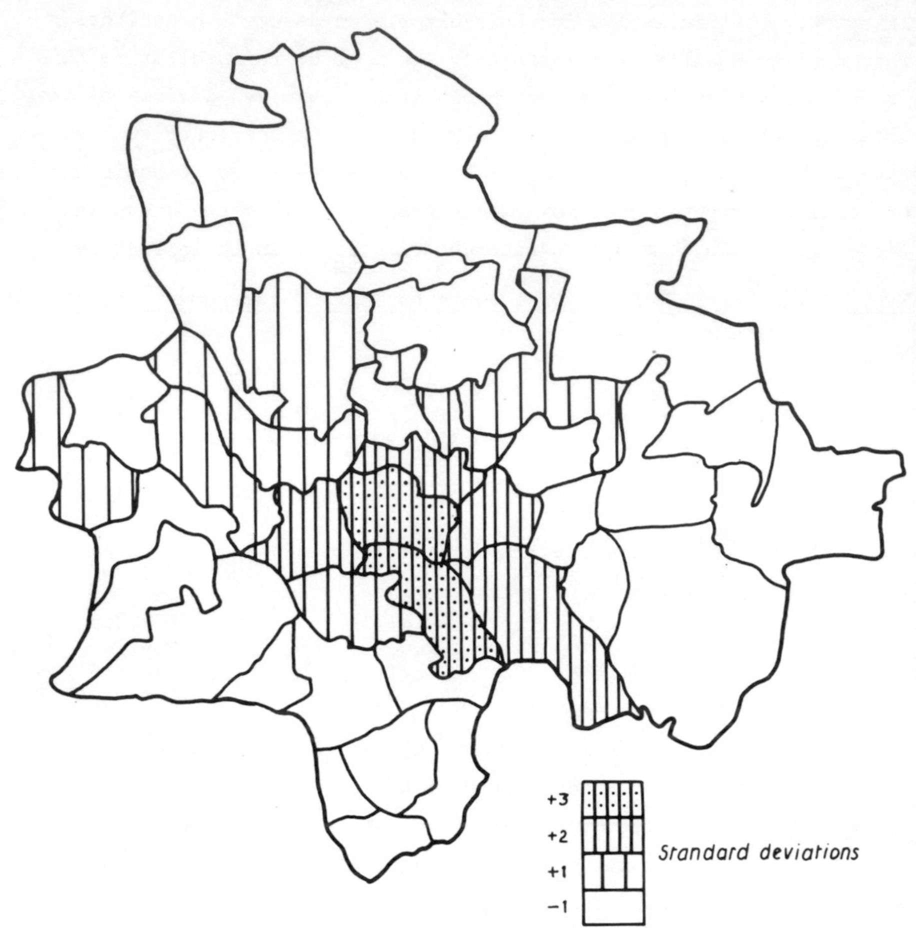

by the expenditure value, we arrive at zonal expenditure values. Imbalances are now readily determined and the calculations are shown in Table 7.14.

Table 7.14 Fire service imbalance calculation 1966

Expenditure		Revenue	Imbalance	Expenditure		Revenue	Imbalance
1	48972	7095	41877	21	21532	5997	15534
2	24801	6270	18530	22	3448	5833	-2384
3	21082	9029	12052	23	5877	9900	-4022
4	31968	2767	29201	24	9986	23505	-13519
5	24141	8455	15685	25	3658	8035	-4376
6	18323	8040	10283	26	6567	26331	-19763
7	9956	7713	2242	27	11066	26627	-15561
8	4888	6277	-1388	28	7197	8001	-804
9	7677	12588	-4910	29	10886	9653	1232
10	15984	7720	8263	30	149	775	-625
11	6927	4529	2398	31	1259	3163	-1903
12	19612	18741	871	32	5907	13254	-7346
13	12925	10549	2375	33	2369	14750	-12381
14	6207	7518	-1311	34	4588	9465	-4876
15	2369	4304	-1935	35	1169	5291	-4121
16	6777	9671	-2893	36	6267	28316	-22048
17	899	1124	-225	37	1259	8365	-7106
18	8546	11652	-3106	38	6597	12734	-6136
19	2609	3298	-689	39	1019	14735	-13715
20	3838	7230	-3391				

The distribution of fire service imbalances is mapped in Figure 7.17. The diagram is appropriate on both absolute and per household bases. It can be seen that the positive expenditure excesses over revenue are confined entirely to central and western zones. This would seem to suggest that in the example of the fire service, the inner city areas were receiving a positive subsidy from peripheral zones.

This example has served to illustrate that not only may local authority resources become channelled into certain areas of the city but that also it may be performing a substantial redistributive function through the provision of its services. The picture will become somewhat clearer when more services have been analysed and the complete framework operationalised. This will also ensure internal consistency within the model in that the imbalance values will sum to zero.

Figure 7.17 Distribution of fire service imbalances 1966

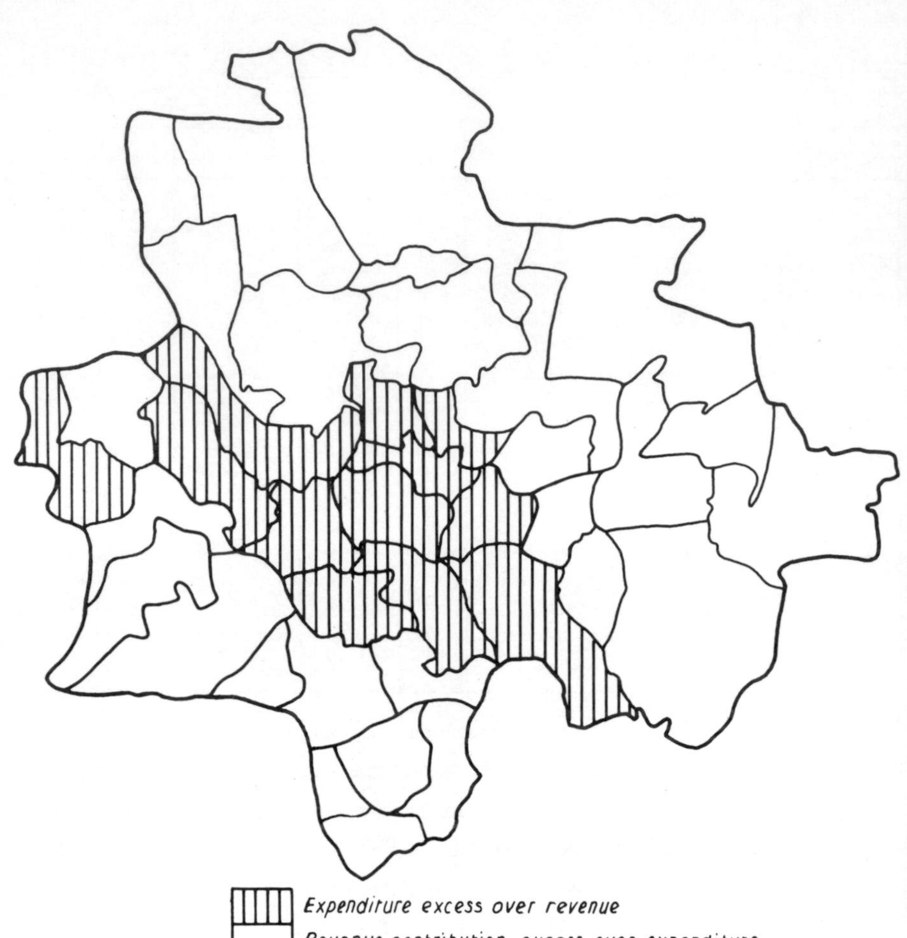

References

Alperovich, G. (1972) Welfare criteria and models for locating public facilities, Discussion Paper XIX, University of Pennsylvania.

Austin, C.M. (1974) The evaluation of urban public facility location: an alternative to benefit-cost analysis, Geographical Analysis, 6, pp. 135-145.

Batty, M. (1971) Exploratory calibration of a retail location model using search by golden section, Environment and Planning, 3, pp. 411-432.

Batty, M. and Mackie, S. (1972) The calibration of gravity, entropy and related models of spatial interaction, Environment and Planning, 4, pp. 205-233.

Benson, C. and Lund, P.B. (1969) Neighbourhood distribution of local public services, Institute of Government Studies, University of California, Berkeley.

Berry, B.J.L. (1967) Geography of market centres and retail distribution, Prentice Hall, Englewood Cliffs; New Jersey.

Central Statistical Office (1973) Annual Abstract of Statistics, HMSO, London.

Coehlo, J.D. and Wilson, A.G. (1976) The optimum location and size of shopping centres, Working Paper 136, Department of Geography, University of Leeds; to be published in Regional Studies.

Cooper, L. (1963) Location-allocation problems, Operations Research, 11, pp. 331-343.

Cordey-Hayes, M. (1968) Retail location models, Working Paper 16, Centre for Environmental Studies, London.

Cordey-Hayes, M. and Wilson, A.G. (1970) Spatial interaction, Working Paper 57, Centre for Environmental Studies, London.

Cox, K.R. (1973) Conflict power and politics in the city: a geographic view, McGraw Hill, New York.

Cullen, I.G. (1969) A mathematical study of retail impact, Discussion Paper 3, Department of Town Planning, University College London.

Davies, B. (1968) Social needs and resources in local services, Michael Joseph, London.

Davis, O.A. (1967) On the distinction between public and private goods, The American Economic Review, 57, pp. 360-373.

Daws, L.F. and Bruce, A.J. (1971) Shopping in Watford, Department of Environment, Building Research Section, Watford.

Department of Employment and Productivity (1972) Family Expenditure Survey, Report for 1968, HMSO, London.

Department of the Environment (1971) Teesside Survey and Plan, HMSO, London.

Department of the Environment/Welsh Office (1972) Statistics for Town and Country Planning, Series 11 - Floorspace, No. 2, HMSO, London.

Earickson, R. (1970) The spatial behaviour of hospital patients, Department of Geography Research Paper 124, University of Chicago, Chicago.

East Midlands Economic Planning Council (1971) Retail trade patterns in the East Midlands, 1961-1981, HMSO, London.

Evans, S.P. (1973) A relationship between the gravity model for trip distribution and the transportation problem in linear programming, Transportation Research, 7, pp. 39-61.

Gibson, M. and Pullen, M. (1972) Retail turnover in the East Midlands; a regional application of a gravity model, Regional Studies, 6, pp. 183-196.

Gwilliam, K.M. and Judge, E.J. (1974) Transport and regional development: some preliminary results of the M62 project, Working Paper 41, Institute for Transport Studies, University of Leeds.

Hall, F.L. (1973) Location criteria for high schools, Department of Geography Research Paper 150, University of Chicago, Chicago.

Harvey, D. (1973) Social justice and the city, Edward Arnold, London.

Hogg, J.M. (1968) The siting of fire stations, Operations Research Quarterly, 19, pp. 275-287.

Holmes, J., Williams, F.B. and Brown, L.A. (1972) Facility location under a maximum travel restriction: an example using day care facilities, Geographical Analysis, 4, pp. 258-266.

Huff, D.L. (1964) Defining and estimating a trading area, Journal of Marketing, 28, pp. 34-38; also reprinted in Ambrose, P. (ed)(1970) Analytical human geography, Longmans, London.

Hyman, G.M. (1969) The calibration of trip distribution models, Environment and Planning, 1, pp. 105-112.

Kirby, H.R. (1970) Normalising factors of the gravity model: an interpretation, Transportation Research, 4, pp. 37-50.

Kirwan, R. (1973) The contribution of public expenditure and finance to the problems of inner London, in Donnison, D. and Eversley, D. (eds)(1973) London: urban patterns, problems and policies, Chapter 4, pp. 119-155, Heinemann, London.

Lakshmanan, T.R. and Hansen, W.G. (1965-A) A market potential model and its application to a regional planning problem, Highway Research Record, 102, pp. 19-41.

Lakshmanan, T.R. and Hansen, W.G. (1965-B) A retail market potential model, Journal of the American Institute of Planners, 31, pp. 134-143.

Lean, W. and Goodall, B. (1966) Aspects of land economics, Estates Gazette, London.

Mackett, R.L. (1973) Shopping in the city - the application of an intra-urban shopping model to Leeds, Working Paper 30, Department of Geography, University of Leeds.

Marlow, M. (1971) Repeat traffic studies in 1967 in eight towns previously surveyed in 1963/4, Report LR 390, Road Research Laboratory, Crowthorne, Berkshire.

McIntosh, P.T. and Quarmby, D.A. (1970) Generalised cost and the estimation of movement costs and benefits in transport planning, Mathematical Advisory Unit, Note 179, Department of the Environment, London.

Ministry of Transport (1966) Portbury - reasons for the Minister's decision not to authorise the construction of a new dock at Portbury, Bristol, HMSO, London.

Morrill, R. and Kelly, M. (1970) The simulation of hospital use and the estimation of location efficiency, Geographical Analysis, 2, pp. 283-300.

Morrill, R., Earickson, R. and Rees, P.H. (1970) Factors influencing distance travelled to hospitals, Economic Geography, 46, pp. 161-171.

Murray, W. and Kennedy, M.B. (1971) Nottinghamshire/Derbyshire: a shopping model primer, Journal of the Town Planning Institute, 57, pp. 211-215.

National Economic Development Council, Distributive Trades EDC (1970) Urban models in shopping studies, National Economic Development Office, London.

Peston, M. (1972) Public goods and the public sector, Macmillan, London.

Randall, G.W., Lomas, K.W. and Newton, T. (1973) Area distribution of resources in Coventry, Local Government Finance, 77, pp. 396-400.

Reilly, W.J. (1931) The law of retail gravitation, Putnam, New York.

Revelle, C., Marks, D. and Liebman, J. (1970) An analysis of private and public sector location models, Management Science, A, 16, pp. 692-707.

Revelle, C. and Swain, R. (1970) Central facilities location, Geographical Analysis, 2, pp. 30-42.

Rhodes, T. and Whitaker, R. (1967) Forecasting shopping demand, Journal of the Town Planning Institute, 53, pp. 188-192.

Richardson, H.W. (1969) Regional economics, Weidenfeld and Nicholson, London.

Robertson, I.M.L. (1972) Population distribution and location problems: an approach by grid squares in Central Scotland, Regional Studies, 6, pp. 237-245.

Robertson, I.M.L. (1974) Road network and the location of facilities, Environment and Planning, A, 6, pp. 199-206.

Samuelson, P.A. (1954) The pure theory of public expenditure, Review of Economics and Statistics, 36, pp. 387-389.

Savas, E.S. (1969) Simulation and cost-effectiveness analysis of New York emergency ambulance service, Management Science, 15, pp. 608-627.

Scitovsky, T. (1968). Welfare and competition, Allen and Unwin, London.

Scott, A.J. (1970) Location-allocation: a review, Geographical Analysis, 2, pp. 95-120.

Scott, C.D. (1972) Forecasting local government spending, The Urban Institute, Washington.

Senior, M.L. and Wilson, A.G. (1974) Explorations and syntheses of linear programming and spatial interaction models of residential location, Geographical Analysis, 6, pp. 209-238.

Simmons, J.W. and Huebert, V.M. (1970) The location of land for public use in urban areas, The Canadian Geographer, 14, pp. 45-56.

Smith, A.P. (1972) The definition of the West Yorkshire study areas, Working Note, Department of Geography, University of Leeds.

Smith, A.P. (1973) Retail-allocation models - an investigation into problems of application to the Rotherham subregion, Working Paper 50, Department of Geography, University of Leeds.

Sunderland County Borough Council (1971) The Sunderland hypermarket survey, Sunderland.

Symons, J.G. (1971) Some comments on equity and efficiency in public facility location models, Antipode, 3, pp. 54-67.

Teitz, M.B. (1968) Toward a theory of urban public facility location, Papers, Regional Science Association, 21, pp. 35-52.

Toregas, C. and Revelle, C. (1972) Optimal location under time or distance constraints, Papers, Regional Science Association, 28, pp. 133-143.

Toregas, C., Swain, R., Revelle, C. and Bergman, L. (1971) The location of emergency facilities, Operations Research, 19, pp. 1363-1373.

University of Manchester (1966) Regional shopping centres: a planning report on north west England, Part 2, A retail shopping model, Department of Town and Country Planning, Manchester.

White, J.A. and Case, K.E. (1974) On covering problems and the central facilities location problem, Geographical Analysis, 7, pp. 281-293.

Whitehead, P.J. (1973) Public facilities: some geographical and economic considerations, Working Paper 41, Department of Geography, University of Leeds.

Whitehead, P.J. (1974) A model framework to evaluate spatial differences in local government service provision, Working Paper 96, Department of Geography, University of Leeds.

Wilson, A.G. (1969-A) Notes on some concepts in social physics, Papers, Regional Science Association, 22, pp. 159-193.

Wilson, A.G. (1969-B) The use of entropy maximising methods in the theory of trip distribution, mode split and route split, Journal of Transport Economics and Policy, 3, pp. 108-126.

Wilson, A.G. (1970) Entropy in urban and regional modelling, Pion, London.

Wilson, A.G. (1973) Further developments of entropy maximising transport models, Transportation Planning and Technology, 1, pp. 183-193.

Wilson, A.G. (1976) Retailers' profits and consumers' welfare in a spatial interaction shopping model, in Masser, I. (ed)(1976) Theory and practice in regional science, pp. 42-59, Pion, London.

Wilson, A.G., Hawkins, A.F., Hill, G.J. and Wagon, D.J. (1969) Calibrating and testing the SELNEC transport model, Regional Studies, 3, pp. 337-350.

Wilson, A.G. and Senior, M.L. (1974) Some relationships between entropy maximising models, mathematical programming models and their duals, Journal of Regional Science, 14, pp. 207-215.

Chapter 8

The spatial distribution of economic activity

C.M. Leigh and T.B. Smith

8.1 Introduction

In this chapter measures of the spatial distribution of economic activity in a regional economy are presented and illustrated with respect to West Yorkshire. A series of indices have been constructed based on the information contained in a set of disaggregated employment accounts. A number of severe constraints were imposed upon us by data deficiences in this field.

Two types of measure of economic activity can be identified: firstly 'stock data' - levels of employment, disaggregated by industrial order, by sex and by occupation; and secondly 'flow data' - levels of activity in the economy in monetary terms as reflected by data on Gross Industrial Output, by sector. These two types of measure allow analysis at different levels of spatial disaggregation. At the same time, accounting frameworks lend themselves to treatment of information at varying levels of spatial aggregation. Employment and occupation data (stocks) are readily available for fairly small zones within the West Yorkshire study area, but flow data are only available for the spatially aggregated case of the West Yorkshire conurbation. Since it is much more difficult conceptually and empirically, to disaggregate the economy spatially when using money flows, our work has been largely concerned with stock data which permit analysis of the spatial and sectoral patterns of activity in the economy, as well as allowing some simple considerations of dynamics.

8.2 Data sources

In this section we consider the sources of data that are available for analysis of the structure and distribution of economic activity in West Yorkshire, as measured by persons in employment. Two independent data sources have been used, each with its own advantages and limitations, namely the Department of Employment ER II Returns; and the Census of Population Economic Activity Tables. The relevant details concerning the breadth of coverage are given below in Figure 8.1. A further distinction has also been made between: (i) sources of data that refer to place of residence; and (ii) sources that relate to workplace. At this stage it is worth noting that the Department of Employment records are entirely workplace-based, whereas the Census of Population codes data at both workplace and place of residence. Unfortunately, the Census data tend not to be available in identical formats for successive years; for example, 1966 workplace data were available for all local authorities in West Yorkshire, and the coverage consisted of breakdowns by industrial sector (MLH's), and occupation (MLH's). In contrast, the 1961 Census did not code workplace data for local authorities with populations of less than 50,000. Not surprisingly, this did not facilitate year-to-year comparisons, and as a result the Census data were of most value when considering static, 'structural' attributes of the economy as in the principal components analysis (Section 8.5).

The two sources of information have some important differences as noted by Dodgson (1972). First, the Department of Employment data use a different system of zones, based on Employment Exchange areas. For the West Yorkshire study area the Census definition uses the 52 local authorities (Figure 8.2), whereas the ER II returns identify only 26 zones (Figure 8.3). Secondly, whereas the Census material is collected every five years, the Department of Employment data are collected annually. In our case, however, ER II returns were available only for the years 1959, 1961 and 1965-71 inclusive. The lack of year-to-year consistency in the Census data meant that for the most part the Department of Employment data form the source for most of the analysis which is carried out in this chapter.

Figure 6.1 Comparison of data sources available for the construction of employment accounts

	Census		Department of Employment
(A) SPATIALLY DISAGGREGATED WORKPLACE DATA			
Time Series	1961	1966	1959, 1961, 1965-1971
Areal Units	CB's, Harrogate, Keighley, County remainder	All local authorities in West Riding	All Labour Exchange Areas in West Riding (see map)
Sectors	Persons in Employment by Status, Industry, sector and sex (Females - married/single)	Persons in Employment by Status, Industry, sector and sex (Females - married/single). Persons in employment by occupation and sex	Total employees (in and out of employment) by industry order by sex. Unemployment by sex (June 30). For 1968 only Establishments by 5 size categories (employed persons) by MLH
(B) SPATIALLY DISAGGREGATED RESIDENCE DATA			
Time Series	Census Ward Library Data: Scales A, B, C and D		
	1961	1966	
Areal Units	Local Authorities in West Riding		
Sectors	(1) Economically active persons by sex by age group. 4 age groups used: 15-24, 25-44, 45-64, 65 & over (2) Employment by residence by sector by sex. 6 sectors used: Agriculture Mining; Manufacture & Construction; Gas, Electricity & Water; Transport; Distribution & Civilian Services; National & Local Government (3) Persons not in employment (4) Economically active and retired males, by social class. Social class groups used: I Professional, II Intermediate; III Skilled; IV Semi-skilled; V Unskilled; VI Not classified		
(C) SPATIALLY AGGREGATED ECONOMIC ACTIVITY DATA			
Time Series	Census County Economic Activity Leaflets		
	1961	1966	
Areal Units	CB's and urban areas >50,000		
Sectors	Occupation & status by sex	Economic activity by occupation by sex, by status	

Miscellaneous Sources: Census of Production: Central Statistical Office: Special Surveys, eg M62 Impact Study (Household Survey, 1969-70): West Yorkshire Transportation Survey.

Figure 8.2 The West Yorkshire study area: Census divisions

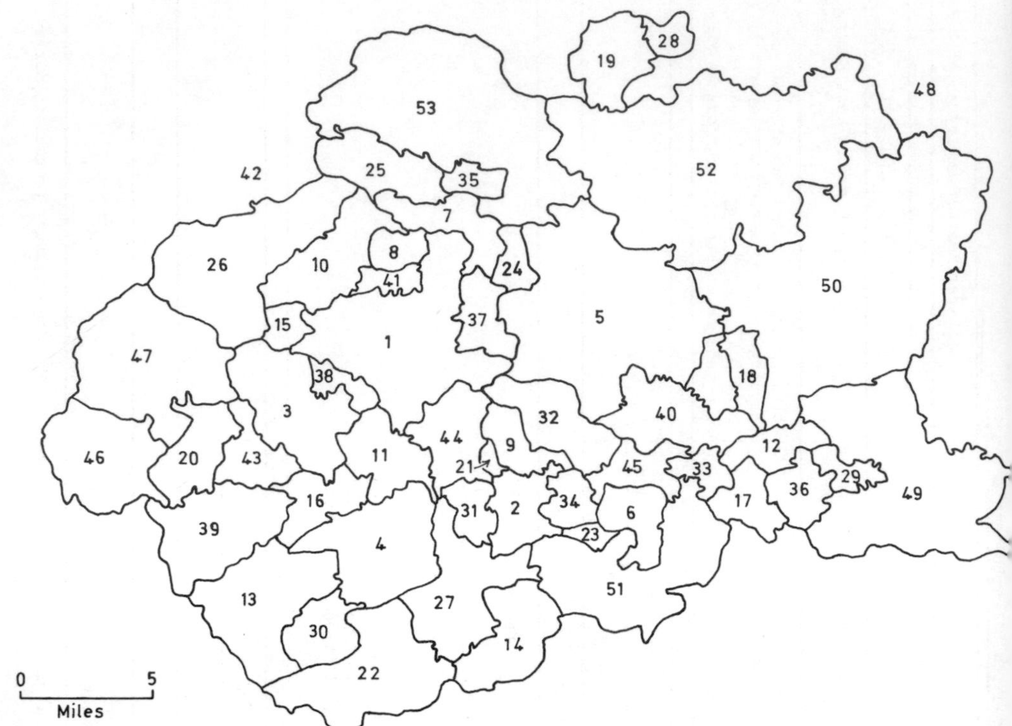

Key to Local Authorities

1 Bradford County Borough
2 Dewsbury County Borough
3 Halifax County Borough
4 Huddersfield County Borough
5 Leeds County Borough
6 Wakefield County Borough
7 Aireborough
8 Baildon
9 Batley
10 Bingley
11 Brighouse
12 Castleford
13 Colne Valley
14 Denby Dale
15 Denholme
16 Elland
17 Featherstone
18 Garforth
19 Harrogate
20 Hebden Royd
21 Heckmondwike
22 Holmfirth
23 Horbury
24 Horsforth
25 Ilkley
26 Keighley
27 Kirkburton
28 Knaresborough
29 Knottingley
30 Meltham
31 Mirfield
32 Morley
33 Normanton
34 Ossett
35 Otley
36 Pontefract
37 Pudsey
38 Queensbury and Shelf
39 Ripponden
40 Rothwell
41 Shipley
42 Silsden
43 Sowerby Bridge
44 Spenborough
45 Stanley
46 Todmorden
47 Hepton Rural District
48 Nidderdale Rural District
49 Osgoldcross Rural District
50 Tadcaster Rural District
51 Wakefield Rural District
52 Wetherby Rural District
53 Wharfedale Rural District

Figure 8.3 The West Yorkshire study area: employment exchange areas

8.3 Stock data I: workplace-based employment

8.3.1 Accounts and the derivation of indices

As shown in the previous section, the most robust source of information relating to the economy of West Yorkshire is the distribution of employees by industrial sector. Aggregate data of this kind for the whole of the West Yorkshire study area for 1959 and 1966 are given in Table 8.1. The objective here is to show how these data can be organised into an employment accounting system that will facilitate the consistent development and interpretation of indices with which to examine the spatial and economic variation of activity within the study area.

It is sensible to begin the account-building process with the smallest, ie. most disaggregated, item of information available. Let this item be represented as follows, ${}^{s}_{t}e^{km}_{i}$, where e is the number of employees; k is an industrial order or sector; m is an occupation type; s is a sex category; i is a zone; and t is a time subscript. A piece of information like this is difficult to handle in accounting terms and impossible to portray in three dimensions. For present purposes, therefore, the sex categories are dealt with separately, while the occupational dimension is left in its most aggregate form. Given these working conventions, the accounts take the form of Figure 8.4, where for convenience only male employees are depicted. The elements of such accounts may therefore be written formally as ${}^{M}_{t}e^{k*}_{i}$, where M represents males, and an asterisk replacing an index denotes summation.

Figure 8.5 shows how the occupational dimensions of the accounts can be dealt with in exactly the same way as the sectorally disaggregated data except that a typical element now has the form ${}^{M}_{t}e^{*m}_{i}$.

Unlike the distribution of employees by sector, the occupation data are available for the conurbation for 1951 and 1961. Despite the lack of time-series data, it is still possible to link the two sets of accounts shown in Figures 8.4 and 8.5, so that the information relates more realistically to jobs rather than to the occupationally heterogeneous industrial sectors. This linking of

Table 8.1 Sectoral distribution of employees, West Yorkshire study area, 1959 and 1966

	Sector	1959			1966		
		% Males	% Females	% Total	% Males	% Females	% Total
I	Agriculture	1.4	0.3	1.0	1.1	0.3	0.8
II	Mining	6.9	0.2	4.4	5.0	0.2	3.2
III	Food, Drink, Tob	2.5	3.0	2.7	2.4	3.3	2.7
IV	Chems & Allied	2.1	1.4	1.8	2.0	1.2	1.7
V	Metal Manuf	2.4	0.5	1.7	2.5	0.5	1.8
VI	Mech & Elect Eng	13.0	4.3	9.7	13.6	4.9	10.3
VII	Shipbuilding etc	0.1	0.0	0.0	0.0	0.0	0.0
VIII	Vehicles	2.0	0.5	1.4	2.5	0.7	1.8
IX	Metal Goods	2.4	1.0	1.9	2.7	1.4	2.2
X	Textiles	16.7	27.0	20.6	15.0	21.2	17.3
XI	Leather	0.5	0.5	0.5	0.4	0.5	0.4
XII	Clothing	2.6	11.2	5.9	2.4	9.8	5.2
XIII	Bricks & Pottery	1.8	0.4	1.3	1.6	0.5	1.2
XIV	Timber & Furn	1.6	0.7	1.3	1.8	0.6	1.3
XV	Paper, Print, Publ	2.2	2.6	2.4	2.5	2.9	2.6
XVI	Other Manuf	0.6	0.6	0.6	0.7	0.7	0.7
XVII	Construction	8.0	0.6	5.2	10.7	0.9	7.0
XVIII	Gas, Elect, Water	2.9	0.6	2.0	3.4	0.8	2.4
XIX	Transport & Comm	6.5	1.4	4.6	5.4	1.4	3.9
XX	Distrb Trades	9.2	14.6	11.2	8.1	14.8	10.6
XXI	Ins, Fin, Bankg	1.6	1.8	1.7	1.7	2.6	2.0
XXII	Prof & Sci Servs	4.3	13.8	7.9	5.4	17.8	10.1
XXIII	Misc Services	4.6	10.4	6.8	5.1	10.6	7.2
XXIV	Publ Admin & Def	4.3	2.7	3.7	4.2	2.5	3.5
XXV	Not Classified	0.0	0.0	0.0	0.1	0.2	0.2
Total Employed All Industries		562,561	343,742	906,303	583,663	358,622	942,285

Source: ERII Returns

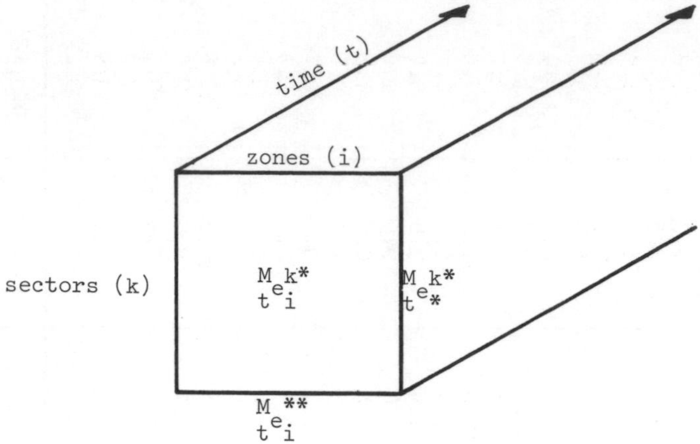

Figure 8.4 The workplace-based accounting system: structure for sectors

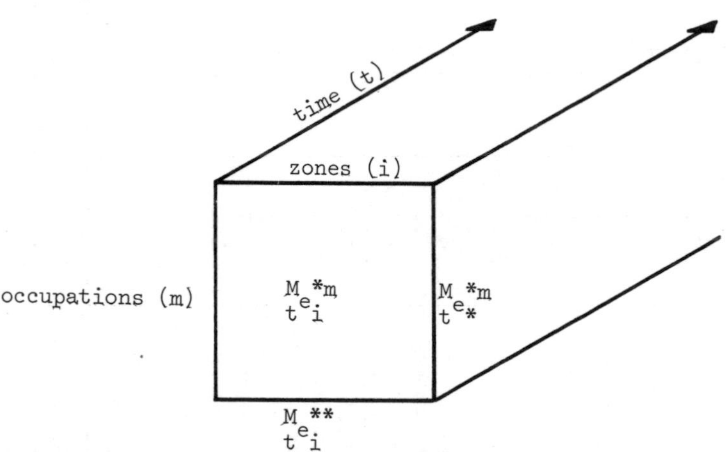

Figure 8.5 The workplace-based accounting system: structure for occupations

the two accounting systems is achieved by using a doubly-constrained conditional probability model, based on the national cross-tabulation of occupations and industrial sectors for 1966. Diagrammatically the linked accounts take the form depicted in Figure 8.6. This operation does not, of course, fully integrate sectors and occupations; in reality there is a cross-tabulation for each zone (known as a manpower-deployment matrix), which would then have the element ${}^{M}_{t}e^{km}_{i}$ referred to above. These maximally-disaggregated deployment matrices can only be estimated, and unfortunately the maximum-entropy solution is unreliable where small levels of activity are the rule. Consequently, for the purposes of index construction the deployment of manpower is dealt with at a spatially-disaggregated level only (Table 8.2).

It should be emphasised, at this point, that the model referred to above has been used in a very limited capacity. The objective is to _expand_, where necessary and appropriate, the data base; _predicting_ the content of the data base involves a more complicated application of mathematical models, more suitably dealt with by such techniques as differential shift (see Section 8.7 below).

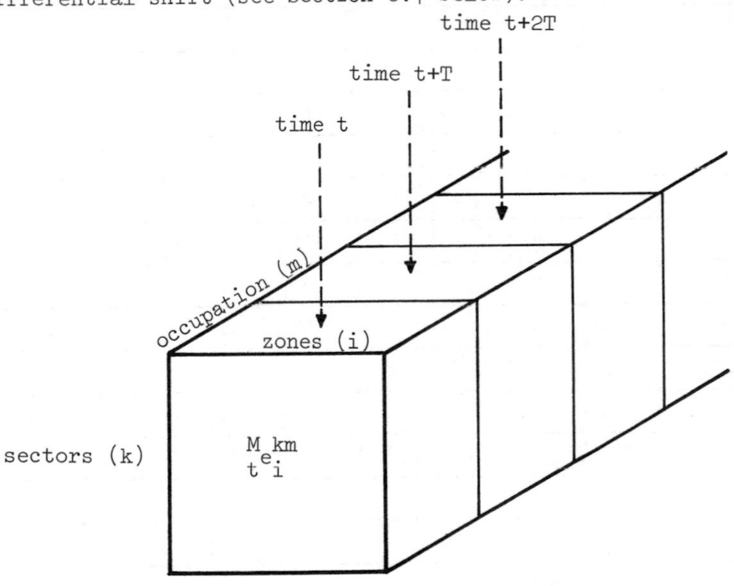

Figure 8.6 _The workplace-based accounting system: cross-tabulation of sectors by occupations_

Table 8.2 Estimated Manpower Deployment Matrix (26 occupations x 24 sectors)
Male Employees, 1966

Occupations \ Sectors	I	II	II	IV	V	VI	VII	VIII	IX	X	XI
Farmers	9,605	71	58	53	10	62	0	6	12	107	
Miners	2	20,925	0	22	2	4	0	0	1	0	
Gas, Coke, Chem	0	40	19	1,645	37	63	0	5	9	1,566	
Glass, Ceramic	1	28	3	18	8	255	0	7	4	13	
Furn, Forge, Found	6	395	8	54	4,157	2,765	5	327	37	112	
Elect, Electronic	5	1,016	161	244	277	4,359	7	253	4	603	[illegible]
Engineering Etc	84	2,646	1,066	1,949	3,705	37,601	91	1,142	6	4,043	[illegible]
Woodworkers	48	18	177	135	216	846	13	200	2	481	[illegible]
Leather Workers	0	2	0	2	0	14	0	1	2	29	[illegible]
Textile Workers	4	5	4	15	4	78	0	2	24	45,207	[illegible]
Clothing Workers	0	1	4	4	1	12	0	99	18	1,403	[illegible]
Food & Tob	21	3	3,924	48	0	2	0	1	1	9	
Paper, Printing	0	7	30	50	16	146	0	11	62	610	
Other Manuf	1	64	18	175	21	1,324	1	38	47	722	[illegible]
Construction	76	268	110	15	226	358	1	37	93	389	[illegible]
Painter, Decrtrs	8	60	135	117	69	889	6	358	260	270	
Statn Eng Drivers	23	1,349	269	338	864	1,354	4	256	236	889	[illegible]
Labourers	68	473	1,459	1,078	1,851	3,837	15	628	1,239	6,266	[illegible]
Transpt, Communc	164	1,191	1,729	690	304	1,121	3	205	347	1,346	[illegible]
Warehouse, Retail	24	361	1,390	941	501	4,143	4	673	789	6,269	[illegible]
Clerical Workers	62	803	860	877	644	4,504	6	771	591	2,655	[illegible]
Sales Workers	62	51	1,965	823	95	1,942	0	79	290	1,524	
Serv, Sport, Rec	18	322	283	270	152	759	2	150	123	882	
Admin, Management	43	508	1,079	989	418	4,456	4	323	1,061	4,449	[illegible]
Professional etc	54	638	468	1,816	624	8,325	8	1,010	635	2,180	
Armed Forces	0	0	0	0	0	0	0	0	0	0	
Totals	10,379	31,400	15,220	12,370	14,200	79,220	170	12,570	16,870	82,020	2,5[illegible]

For key to sectors see Table 8.1

II	XIII	XIV	XV	XVI	XVII	XVIII	XIX	XX	XXI	XXI	XXIII	XXIV	Totals
12	15	45	20	9	65	46	14	129	106	730	1,441	866	13,490
0	81	6	0	0	155	3	5	7	1	1	1	2	21,210
41	74	2	33	72	6	174	6	19	0	31	3	7	3,820
3	2,193	5	4	4	16	1	1	46	0	10	3	0	2,620
0	67	6	20	35	106	42	65	50	9	7	36	69	10,180
49	107	43	126	60	3,207	2,521	2,792	1,395	19	264	553	308	18,560
453	912	398	666	629	8,186	3,766	3,605	1,892	83	937	6,891	1,196	95,050
71	183	6,170	91	105	7,881	111	183	502	50	218	223	263	18,500
,620	1	4	1	7	1	0	1	42	1	5	206	1	2,610
231	31	18	11	35	3	0	5	79	0	3	33	9	45,830
,671	1	963	7	13	7	1	40	574	0	22	74	23	8,270
0	1	1	12	3	2	2	14	5,604	2	29	55	13	9,750
35	33	19	6,754	62	18	6	13	74	25	44	74	33	8,120
99	549	164	80	1,745	200	276	47	401	6	296	309	50	6,660
51	586	90	59	35	15,734	838	185	302	109	307	329	743	20,050
30	40	700	47	42	6,985	148	155	228	38	245	606	300	11,730
58	402	141	219	70	1,753	1,561	486	311	16	319	158	473	11,590
348	1,782	1,121	706	409	9,786	1,967	1,962	2,427	115	391	1,134	3,694	43,060
316	611	498	504	125	1,992	784	23,922	6,073	361	874	1,376	1,787	46,390
,252	413	374	1,163	385	525	565	878	5,242	32	344	1,262	761	28,470
498	441	345	1,006	261	1,267	1,823	3,909	3,437	4,707	2,497	2,270	5,511	39,840
539	186	271	604	220	221	555	469	32,598	4,413	98	2,889	101	50,070
774	91	49	209	65	325	280	973	682	435	4,056	14,229	6,749	31,010
,757	541	764	1,011	396	2,896	588	1,174	1,608	1,347	840	2,252	1,917	30,720
259	418	203	919	274	2,433	1,365	769	1,630	646	21,234	2,076	2,516	50,550
0	0	0	0	0	0	0	0	0	0	0	137	1,532	1,670
,030	9,760	12,390	14,270	5,050	63,770	17,420	40,670	65,350	12,520	33,800	38,620	28,920	

8.3.2 Localisation and specialisation indices

The next task is to formulate some simple hypotheses to investigate the study area. In very broad terms such working hypotheses may be classified according to Lowry's scheme (Lowry, 1967), where a distinction was made between the study of the rows of an accounting system like that shown in Figure 8.4, and the study of the columns. In Lowry's terms, an investigation of the characteristics of the rows of Figure 8.4 may be called a 'locational' approach, whereas the treatment of column attributes is known as a 'land-use' approach. While it is admitted that these two approaches are highly interdependent, with the urban or regional economy an important agent of interdependence, this distinction does allow a start to be made. The more complicated problems that arise when notions of mutual dependence are brought into the analysis are the subject matter of a later section (8.6).

In relation to the elementary accounts shown in Figure 8.4, two null hypotheses may be proposed: (i) that the spatial distribution of employment in sector k is the same as the distribution of employment in all sectors of the economy. Formally this may be written

$$ {}^{s}_{t}e^{k}_{i} \Big/ {}^{s}_{t}e^{k}_{*} = {}^{s}_{t}e^{*}_{i} \Big/ {}^{s}_{t}e^{*}_{*} \tag{8.1} $$

and (ii) that the sectoral distribution of employment in zone i is the same as the sectoral distribution of the whole economy, ie.

$$ {}^{s}_{t}e^{k}_{i} \Big/ {}^{s}_{t}e^{*}_{i} = {}^{s}_{t}e^{k}_{*} \Big/ {}^{s}_{t}e^{*}_{*} \tag{8.2} $$

Coefficient of localisation

From the first of these null hypotheses the traditional coefficient of localisation is readily derived. If the null hypothesis is true, then the LHS minus the RHS of Equation (8.1) is zero for every zone. Hence the coefficient C_k for sector k is

$$C_k = \tfrac{1}{2}\Sigma_i \left| \frac{{}_t^s e_i^k}{{}_t^s e_*^k} - \frac{{}_t^s e_i^*}{{}_t^s e_*^*} \right| \qquad (8.3)$$

The value of C_k will range between unity (maximum localisation, ie. the whole of sector k occurring in one zone) and zero (where minimum localisation occurs).

Figure 8.7 shows the range of C_k values for industrial sectors in the West Yorkshire study area, for males. Data for three dates, 1959, 1966 and 1971 were used which would allow consistent change over the study period to be identified. For male employees, most C_k values fall below 0.3, indicating a lack of localisation, especially so for sector XVII (construction) and sectors XVIII-XXIV (the services) as might be expected. The high value for mining (sector II) is readily explicable in terms of the resource distribution of the study area. Similarly shipbuilding (sector VII) which only employs 0.02% of the workforce is highly constrained spatially. The high value for clothing (sector XII) may reflect a more important spatial specialisation in the region at least for male employees. Trends through time are not strongly apparent, although a number of manufacturing sectors seem to show consistently less localisation (sectors IV, V, VI, IX, XII and XIV) whilst a number of services (sectors XVIII, XIX, XX and XXI) have increasing C_k values. A similar diagram could be drawn to show the coefficient of localisation values for female employees. These tend to be slightly higher overall than those for males, although the pattern is very similar. The sectors in which large numbers of females are employed in West Yorkshire (textiles, sector X; clothing, sector XII; and the services, sectors XX, XXII and XXIII) all have C_k values that are somewhat lower than their male counterparts and that generally show a tendency towards greater spatial dispersion through time.

Figure 8.7 The coefficient of localisation: male employees by sector, 1959, 1966, 1971

For key to sectors see Table 8.1

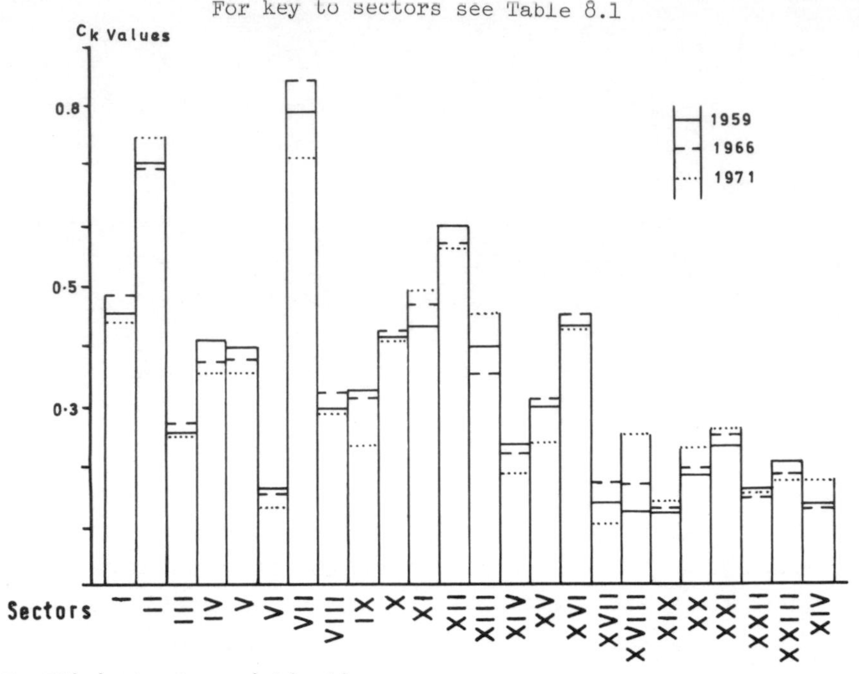

Coefficient of specialisation

The counterpart to the localisation index is derived in a similar fashion and is known as the coefficient of specialisation, a term which has an obvious land-use connotation. Formally the index may be written as

$$C_i = \tfrac{1}{2}\Sigma_k \left| \frac{{}_t^s e_i^k}{{}_t^s e_i^*} - \frac{{}_t^s e_*^k}{{}_t^s e_*^*} \right| \qquad (8.4)$$

Like C_k, this index also lies in the range unity to zero, maximally specialised to minimally specialised.

Figure 8.8 maps the distribution of C_i values for male employees in the three years, 1959, 1966 and 1971. Values range from 0.172 to 0.691 and in most areas there is a very consistent trend over time. Characteristically the six County Boroughs have low coefficients of specialisation. In five of them, these coefficients are declining but, in Halifax, which in common with the surrounding authorities in the Pennines to the west of the study area (basically the 'woollen area') shows above-average values they are also increasing, ie.

Figure 8.8 The coefficient of specialisation, 1959, 1966, 1971 males

For key to zones see Figure 8.3

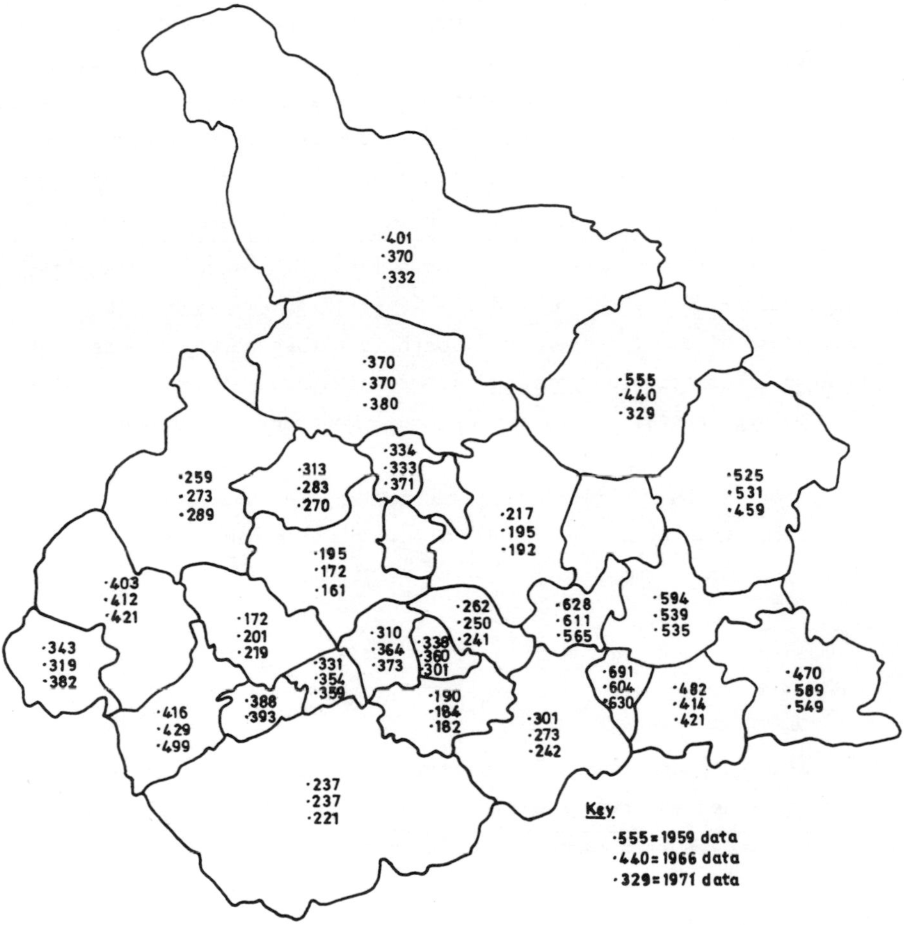

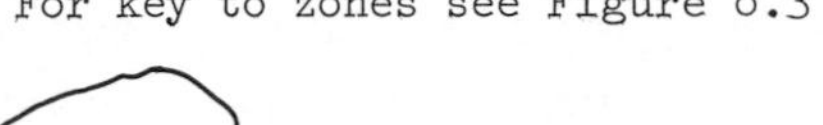

employment structures are not diversifying. High values occur in two major areas: firstly, the 'five towns' (ie. the coalfield area) and secondly the rural fringe to the north-east of the study area. In both areas the tendency is for C_i values to decline somewhat over time, ie. these areas show a tendency to diversify their employment structure.

A corresponding distribution for females would show values ranging from 0.157 to 0.680 but generally tending to be slightly lower than for their male counterparts. There is much less consistency in the trends over time and most areas show fluctuations rather than stability. The main elements of the female distribution, however, do reflect the male pattern: ie. low values in the County Boroughs, which are declining; high values in the 'five towns', though not as extreme as for their male counterparts.

8.3.3 Geographical association and structural similarity

In the form presented above, Equations (8.3) and (8.4) are very crude indices: they can provide basic statistics measuring the relative position of sectors and zones, but they reveal little about patterns of association between sectors or about patterns of similarity between zones. This can be done, however, by calculating 'cross-coefficient' indices. Firstly, one can treat the zones of the system as observations on the variables (ie. the sectors) to produce the traditional geographical association coefficient (Florence, 1948). It takes the form

$$C^{kl} = \tfrac{1}{2}\Sigma_i \left| {}_t^s e_i^k \Big/ {}_t^s e_*^k - {}_t^s e_i^l \Big/ {}_t^s e_*^l \right| \qquad (8.5)$$

where l is a second industrial sector. It may be interpreted as the degree to which industry k occurs when industry l occurs. A value of zero denotes complete association, a value of unity means no association. This index is a difficult one to portray graphically, but an attempt is made in Figure 8.9 to show, for male employees, pairs of sectors which had strong geographical association in 1966, ie. the highest C^{kl} value is plotted for each sector. It is noticeable that the manufacturing sectors have very few significant links amongst themselves whereas the services, construction and public utilities have many more strong links both between themselves and with the manufacturing sectors. The patterns of geographical association between sectors are found to be very similar for both male and female employees. Secondly, one can treat the zones as variables and arrive at an index of structural similarity between pairs of zones. Formally this is expressed as follows:

$$C_{ij} = \tfrac{1}{2}\Sigma_k \left| {}^{s}_{t}e^{k}_{i} \,/\, {}^{s}_{t}e^{*}_{i} - {}^{s}_{t}e^{k}_{j} \,/\, {}^{s}_{t}e^{*}_{j} \right| \qquad (8.6)$$

where j is another zone.

Figure 8.9 Geographical association between sectors for male employees, 1966

For key to sectors see Table 8.1

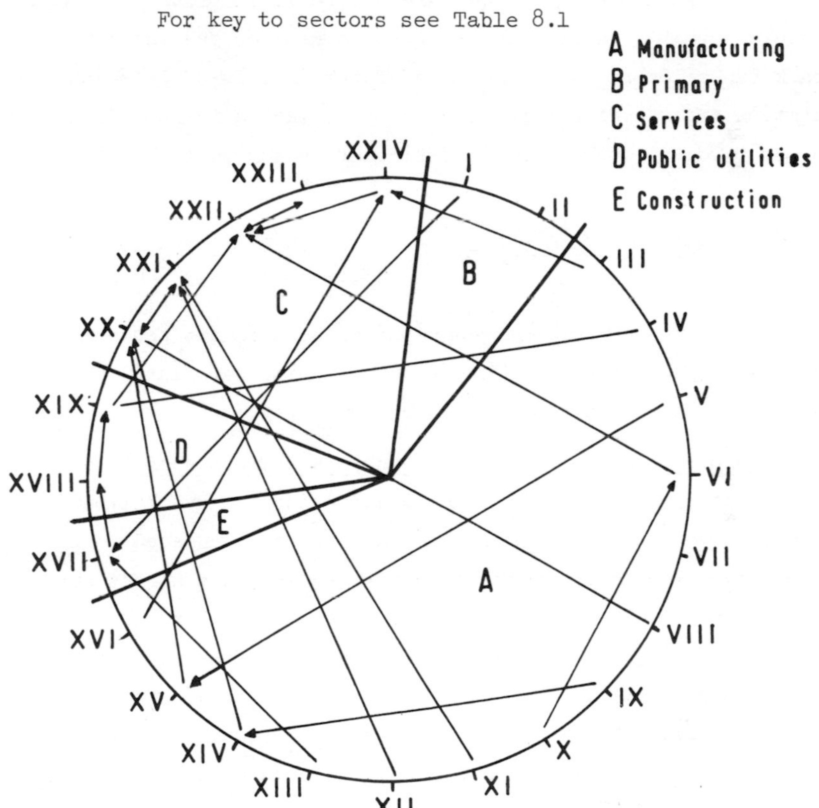

The indices have been plotted on Figure 8.10 for male employees to give some indication of the structural similarities that existed between zones in the West Yorkshire study area in 1966. This figure indicates a distinct division of the study area between Leeds and all zones to the east, which show very little similarity amongst themselves or with other zones, although the coalfield zones do show some evidence of comparable employment structure which is, however, much more marked in the western zones of the study area, in particular from Bradford westwards. This pattern is confirmed for female employees where the separation into east and west is, if anything, even more marked. The 'woollen district' again shows a high degree of structural cohesion, whilst the eastern zones, Leeds, the north-east rural fringe and the coalfield show only a limited similarity of structure.

The indices described above do suffer from the limitation that they are 'non-parametric'. They are not based on probability models that would permit significance tests to be made on the indices. This drawback can be overcome in the case of the indices of geographical association and structural similarity by replacing these indices with the product-moment correlation coefficient as suggested by Streit (1969):

$$r_{kl} = \frac{\mathrm{cov}({}_t^s e_i^k, {}_t^s e_i^l)}{\sigma e_i^k \ \sigma e_i^l} \qquad (8.7)$$

where r_{kl} is a measure of the geographical association between industry k and industry l. This index, and its corollary, are amenable to statistical testing in the usual way.

8.3.4 Alternative measures: Lorenz curve and Tress score

In addition to the indices of localisation and specialisation described above, some alternative measures were calculated to provide corroborative evidence. These alternatives were the Lorenz curve and the associated Tress score (Tress, 1938). The Lorenz curve is obtained by ranking the percentage distribution of an activity in a zone, and then plotting this ranked distribution in a cumulative fashion. If all activities in a zone made an equal percentage contribution to the total, then the Lorenz curve would be depicted

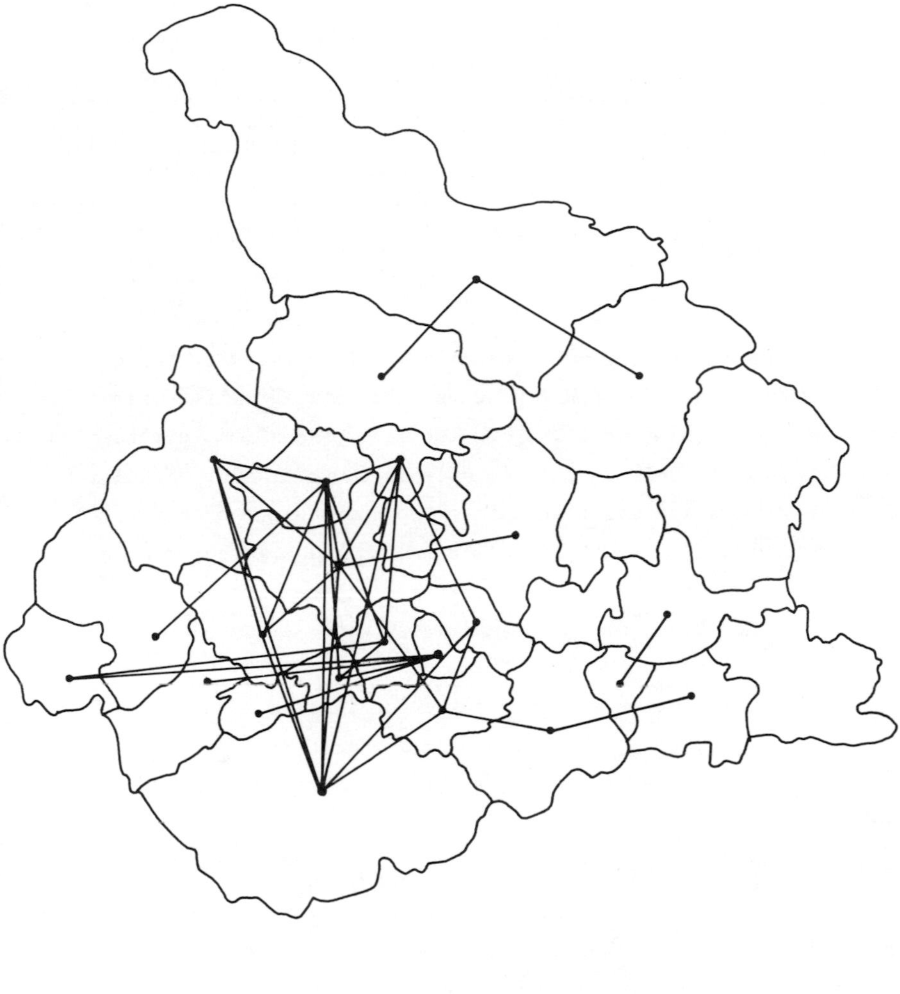

Figure 8.10 Patterns of structural similarity, male employees, 1966

For key to zones see Figure 8.3

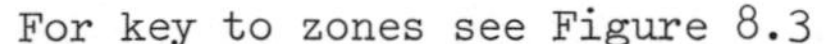

as a straight line, at 45° to either axis. The more concentrated an activity is into a few zones or sectors then the more bowed will be the corresponding Lorenz curve.

The Tress score attempts to provide a numerical measure of the 'bow' exhibited in a Lorenz curve. For example consider the following cases:

		Zones		
		1	2	3
Activities	A	25	100	50
	B	25	-	30
	C	25	-	15
	D	25	-	5
	Total	100	100	100

% employment

		Zones		
		1	2	3
Activities	A	25	100	50
	B	50	100	80
	C	75	100	95
	D	100	100	100
	Tress score	250	400	325

cumulative %

In this particular case the example of zone 1 with an equal share of all four activities would produce a 45° straight line with a Tress score of 250, whilst zone 2 shows the case of maximum localisation of activity A in zone 1 and a maximum Tress score of 400. Smaller degrees of localisation than this give intermediate scores.

Figure 8.11 gives the Lorenz curve and associated Tress scores for the 24 sectors of the West Yorkshire economy for males and females. The curve for male employees, with a Tress score of 1,799.1 (the range of possible Tress scores is from 1,259 to 2,400) is appreciably flatter than the curve for females, where the Tress score is 2,034. The change in the ranking of sectors reflects the differing importance of each sector for the two components of the labour force.

8.3.5 Employment dynamics: indices of change

All the indices discussed so far aim to give a static description of the structure and distribution of the economy at one or more points in time from which we can derive a comparative-static picture. Figure 8.12 shows how two measures of turbulence can be derived.

Figure 8.11 Lorenz curves for twenty-four sectors of the West Yorkshire economy, 1966

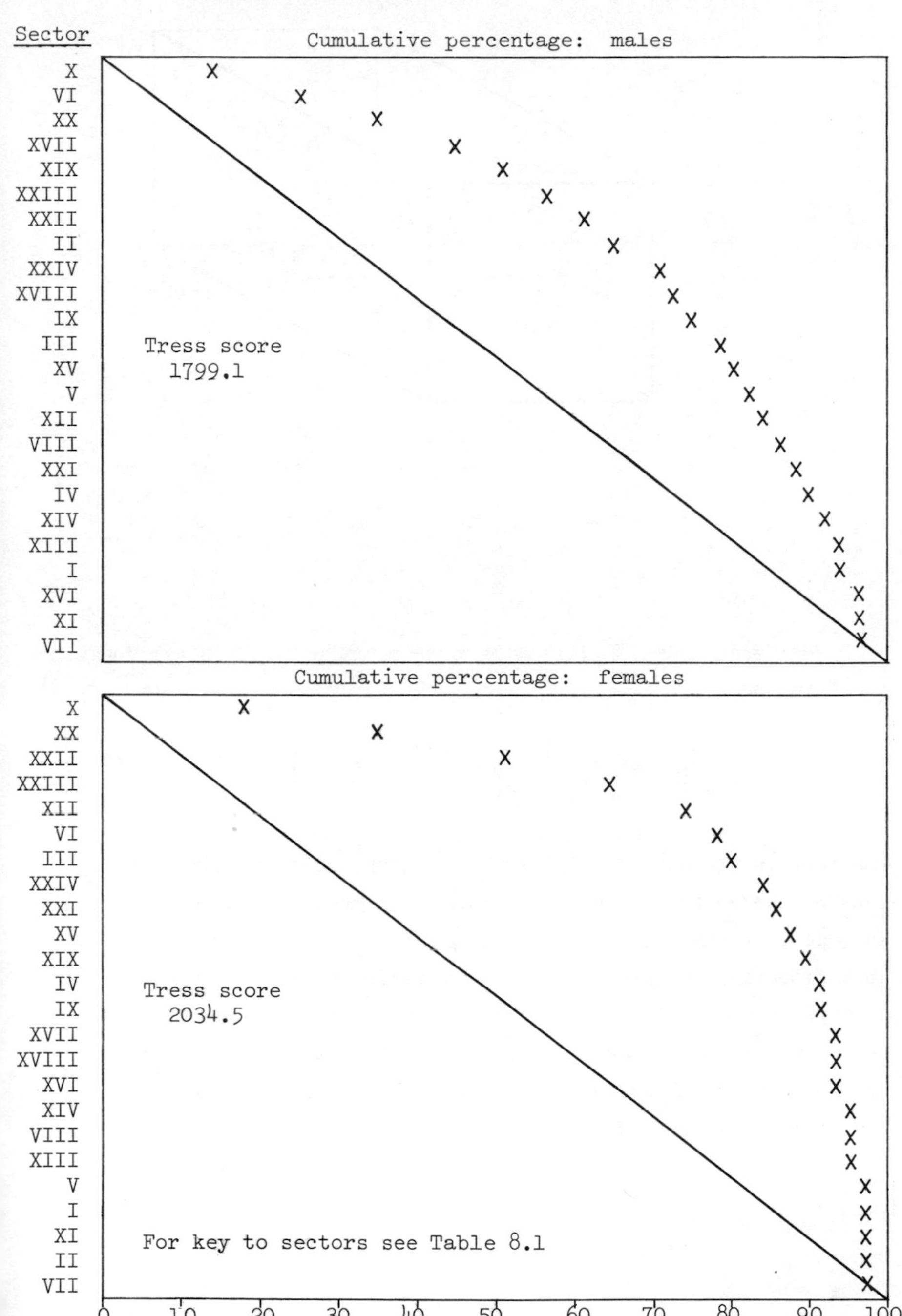

Figure 8.12 Employment dynamics: two indices of change

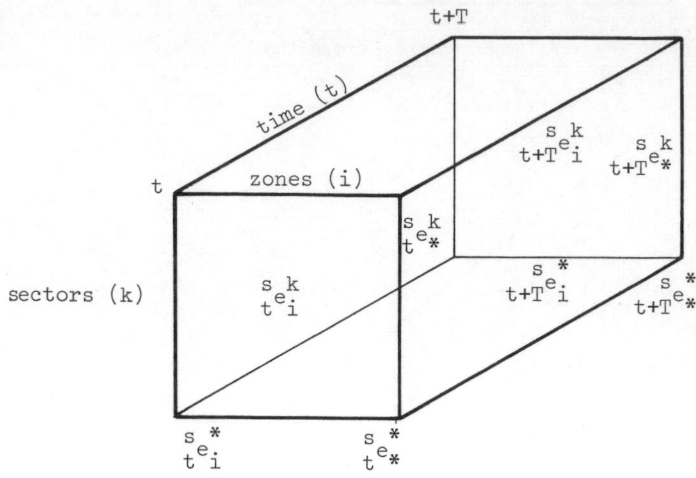

The first index, D_i, is a measure of structural change and has the form:

$$D_i = \tfrac{1}{2}\Sigma_k \left| {}^{s}_{t}e^{k}_{i} / {}^{s}_{t}e^{*}_{i} - {}^{s}_{t+T}e^{k}_{i} / {}^{s}_{t+T}e^{*}_{i} \right| \tag{8.8}$$

The term in the modulus sign represents the absolute difference between the contribution of employment in sector k to total activity in zone i at time t, and the same quantity for a later year, t+T. In a situation of no change, the two ratios would be equal for all sectors and the index would be zero. At the other extreme, if the ratio at time t were zero but unity at t+T the index would show that maximum structural change had occurred, ie. all employment in zone i had been transferred from one sector to another.

In Figure 8.13 indices of structural change for zones in the West Yorkshire study area for male employees for two time periods, 1959-66 and 1966-71 are plotted. It is significant that all D_i values are low (range 0.05 to 0.39) indicating an overall stability. There are some broad spatial distinctions to be identified. For example, there is a consistent trend towards an increase in the values of D_i in the western and north-western parts of the study area, suggesting some tendency towards change in the 'woollen area' whereas the eastern part of the study area shows a decline in D_i values through time. The County Boroughs tend, as a group, to exhibit a high degree of stability, whereas higher values occur round the fringes of the study area. This latter characteristic is also found in the pattern of D_i values for female employees over the same time periods. Although still having low values overall, (range 0.05 to 0.31), the tendency is for most areas to show an increase in the amount of structural change occurring in the period 1966-71.

The second, and concomitant, index of <u>locational change</u>, attempts to measure the degree to which the spatial distribution of an industry has changed during the time period chosen. The algebraic form is given without further elaboration, save for the comment that the index D_i is a 'column' approach, whereas D_k is its 'row' counterpart. Figure 8.12 above, lays out in diagrammatic form the relevant components of both indices

$$D_k = \tfrac{1}{2}\Sigma_i \left| {}^{s}_{t}e^{k}_{i} / {}^{s}_{t}e^{k}_{*} - {}^{s}_{t+T}e^{k}_{i} / {}^{s}_{t+T}e^{k}_{*} \right| \qquad (8.9)$$

In Figures 8.14 and 8.15 the D_k values for both males and females for 1959-66 and 1966-71 respectively are plotted. As can readily be seen, the female employees have higher indices than male employees in almost every sector, except construction (sector XVII), in both periods; agriculture (sector I), vehicles (sector VII) and other manufactures (sector XVI) in the period 1959-66; and gas, electricity and water (sector XVIII), insurance, banking and finance (sector XXI) and professional or business services (sector XXII) in the period 1966-71. It seems therefore that both structurally and

Figure 8.13 Structural change in West Yorkshire; 1959-1966 and 1966-1971: Male employees

For key to zones see Figure 8.3

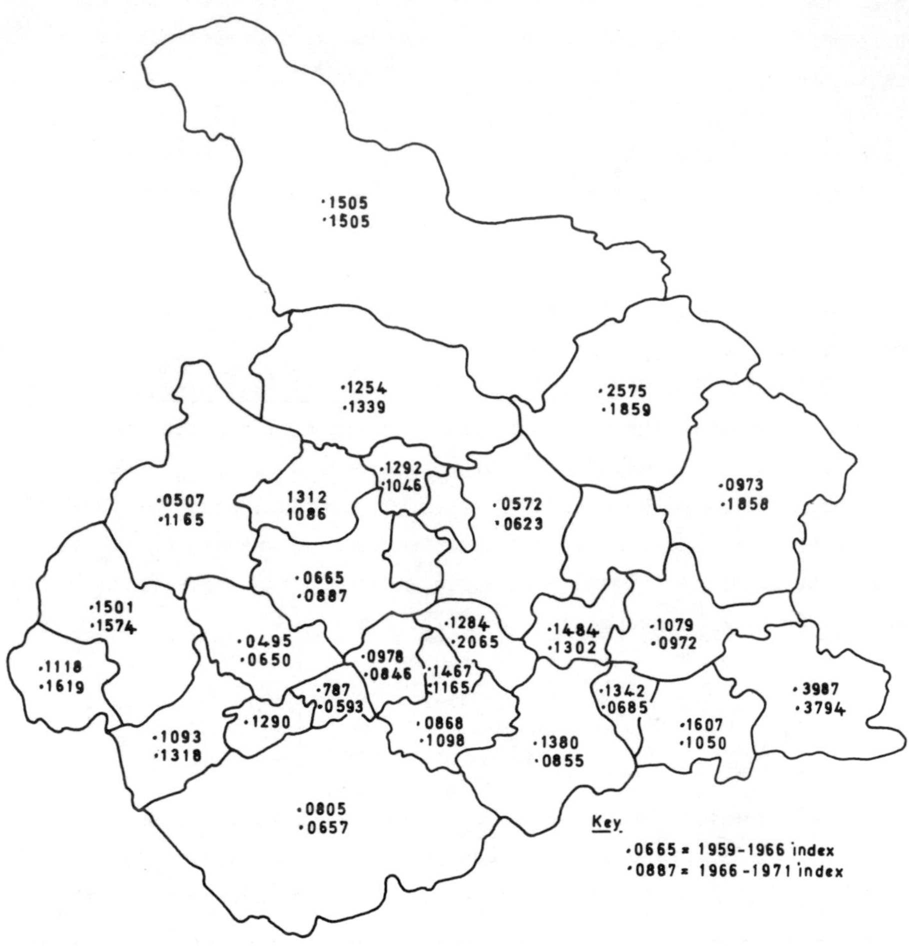

Figure 8.14 Locational change in West Yorkshire, 1959-1966

For key to sectors see Table 8.1

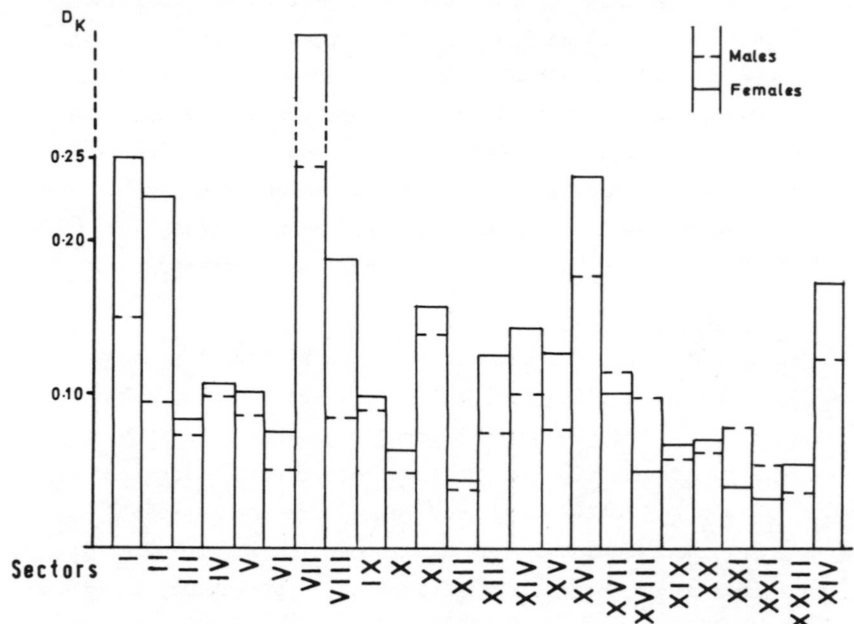

Figure 8.15 Locational change in West Yorkshire, 1966-1971

For key to sectors see Table 8.1

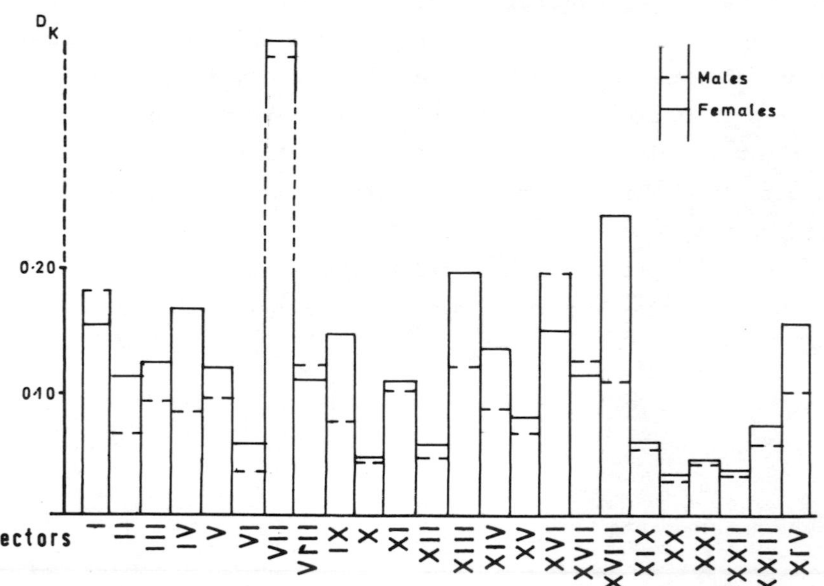

locationally female employment is more subject to change and fluctuation than male employment in West Yorkshire. Both of these indices suffer from the fact that they are 'end-point' devices. For a given time series the indices ignore changes within the time period under study. When dealing with changes between 1959 and 1966 this was relatively unavoidable since intermediate data did not exist. The period from 1966 to 1971, however, had available a full yearly series and, in this situation, a modification of the indices incorporating the notion of a 'stream-sum' constraint, devised by Robinson and Wilson (1966), would seem appropriate.

8.3.6 Shift-share technique

A similar measure of change is possible by adopting the well-documented 'shift-share' technique (Dunn, 1960; Putman, 1967; Stilwell, 1969). For the present purpose the shift-share approach can serve a purely descriptive function rather than being used as a forecasting tool. Forecasting requires a more sophisticated methodology and is discussed in some detail in Section 8.7 below. As with the other indices of change, the shift-share approach may be viewed as both a row and a column operation on the data in our workplace-based accounts. In terms of Figure 8.12, the row operation may be called a sector-shift index, whereas the column operation may be considered to be a zone-shift index.

It is helpful to set out an example of a shift-share calculation. Consider the case where we have a single activity distributed across the zones of an area. Consider also that these data exist for more than one time-point. The essence of the technique is that the base year data are inflated by the growth rate of the whole system. These expected totals are then compared with the observed data for the second time-point in order to determine which zones (in this case) grew at rates higher or lower than the system-wide growth rate.

The above sequence can be set out formally as follows:

$$\text{total shift} = {}^{s}_{t+T}e^{k}_{i} - {}^{s}_{t}e^{k}_{i} \tag{8.10}$$

$$\text{proportional share (expected value)} = {}^{s}_{t}e^{k}_{i}\left(\frac{{}^{s}_{t+T}e^{k}_{*} - {}^{s}_{t}e^{k}_{*}}{{}^{s}_{t}e^{k}_{*}}\right) - {}^{s}_{t}e^{k}_{i} \tag{8.11}$$

differential shift = total shift - proportional share, therefore

$$\begin{aligned}\text{differential shift} &= \{{}^{s}_{t+T}e^{k}_{i} - {}^{s}_{t}e^{k}_{i}\} \\ &\quad - \{{}^{s}_{t}e^{k}_{i}\left(\frac{{}^{s}_{t+T}e^{k}_{*} - {}^{s}_{t}e^{k}_{*}}{{}^{s}_{t}e^{k}_{*}}\right) - {}^{s}_{t}e^{k}_{i}\}\end{aligned} \tag{8.12}$$

$$= {}^{s}_{t+T}e^{k}_{i} - {}^{s}_{t}e^{k}_{i}\left(1 + \frac{{}^{s}_{t+T}e^{k}_{i}}{{}^{s}_{t}e^{k}_{*}}\right) \tag{8.13}$$

Note that total shift is equal, by definition, to the sum of the shift and share components and also note that the sum of the shift components for all zones is equal to zero.

The form of the shift calculation given above, however, involves the use of the system-wide growth rates as defined for <u>sectors</u> only. As with each of the other indices dealt with so far, there also exists another set of indices corresponding to the growth rates defined by the changing levels of activity in each zone. Referring back again to the accounts, the sector-shift model described above uses the sector growth rates in a row-wise inflation of the base-year data. Similar reasoning leads us to describe the alternative index as a derivation of a <u>zone-shift</u> model.

Having obtained shift data for the two types of model described above, it is notable that the shift factors show a wide variation in their sizes, the large metropolitan areas, on the whole, tend to display higher shifts than the smaller, more peripheral areas. In order to facilitate a comparative analysis, the row shift data were standardised, a process which merely involved the division of the row scores by their respective standard deviations, since by definition the mean shift score for a zone (or a sector) is zero.

The advantage of such standardised shifts is that we can now treat scores that lie in the upper and lower tails of the distribution as non-random deviations from the mean shift value (ie. zero).

For presentation, one further refinement was carried out. This involved ranking the standardisation scores and then mapping only the first and fourth quartiles. Figures 8.16 and 8.17 show some results of this process. The height of the columns represents the number of sectors that lie in the highest and lowest quartiles. In this form, the indices use only the extreme shift scores, a step that attempts to comply with the Department of Employment's warning that extreme caution be used when dealing with small year-to-year changes in employment totals.

8.4 Stock data II: the residence-based accounts activity rates

A second accounting system analogous to the workplace based accounts that we have been dealing with previously would array information showing the distribution of workers by sector of employment according to zone of residence. When using residence-based accounts we are effectively making statements about the supply side of the labour market, ie. the potential number of workers in an area as opposed to jobs. Recent work by Bowers (1970) has used this type of account to analyse the regional variation in activity rates in the UK, information which can be of particular importance when considering the areal and sectoral patterns of change in the West Yorkshire economy. Bowers has shown that variations in participation rates are largely attributable to variations in the activity rates of females; by contrast, male activity rates tend to show little areal variation. Consequently the emphasis of our supply-side analysis will be on the ways in which female rates vary with zone, and crucially with age. The attention given to this aspect of the residence accounts represent an attempt, therefore, to derive some partial indices relating to the supply side of the equation. It should be emphasised, however, that the approach is only partial, since a full treatment of labour-supply factors would require extensive integration of the demographic and economic accounting systems.

Figure 8.16 Standardised sector shifts (upper and lower quartiles) 1959-1966. Male employees. Primary and manufacturing sectors

For key to zones see Figure 8.3

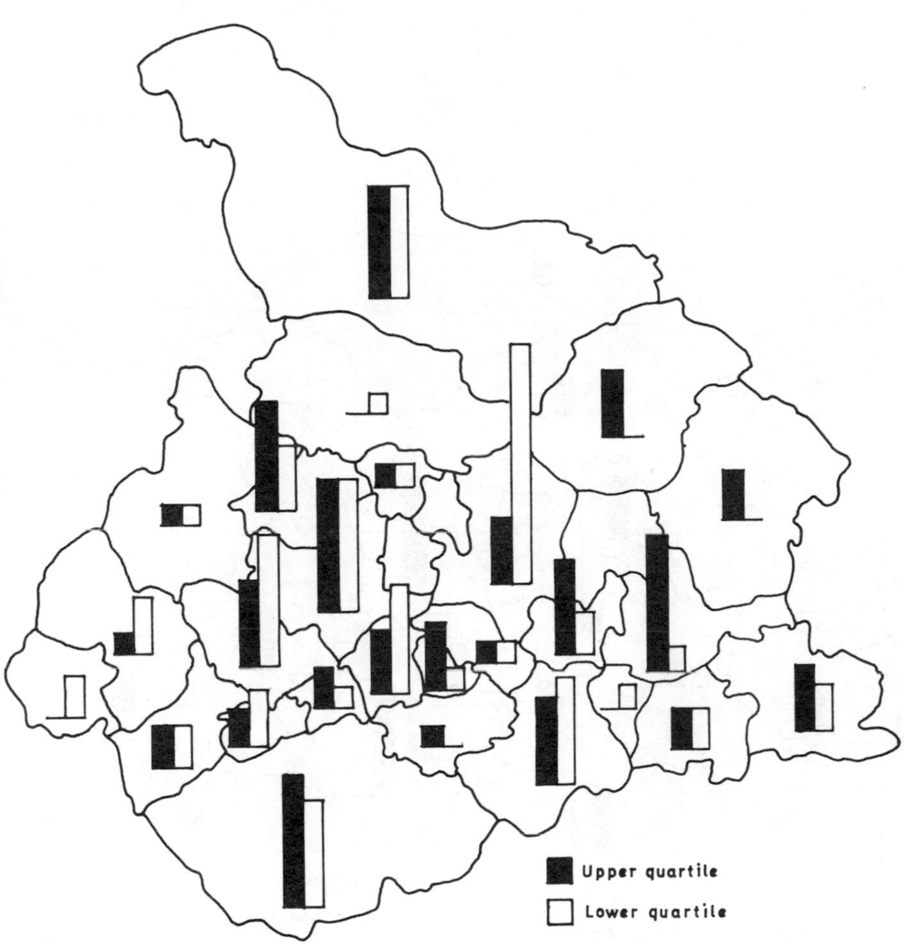

Figure 8.17 Standardised sector shifts (upper and lower quartiles) 1959-1966. Male employees. Construction, public utilities and services

For key to zones see Figure 8.3

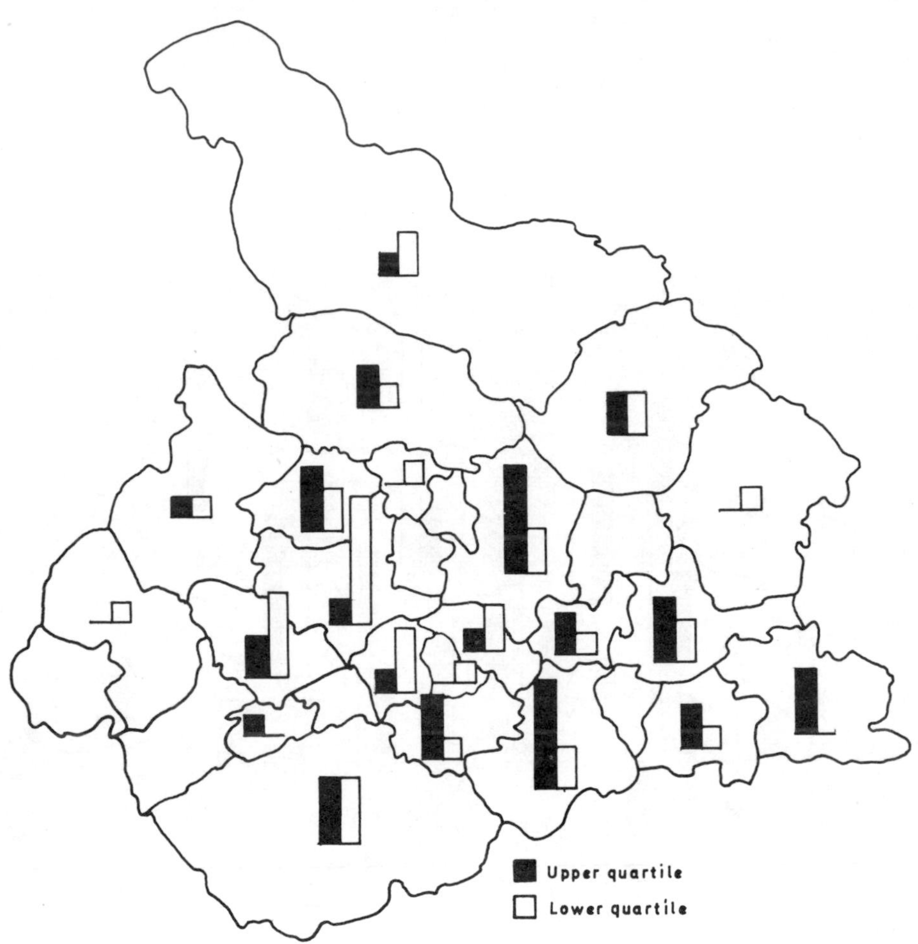

Some attempt has been made, within the constraints imposed by data availability, to disaggregate the female rates by age, so that the indices can take into account differences in the demographic structure of zones within the economy. Available data permit analysis for 1961 and 1966 and the formal structure of the index used is:

$$ {}^{F}A_{i}^{b} = {}^{F}L_{i}^{b} / {}^{F}P_{i}^{b} \qquad (8.14) $$

where ${}^{F}A_{i}^{b}$ is the age-specific female activity rate for zone i and age group b; ${}^{F}L_{i}^{b}$ is the number of economically active females in zone i and age group b; and ${}^{F}P_{i}^{b}$ is the total population in i and b. These activity rates are mapped in Figures 8.18 to 8.20 showing the spatial distribution for three age groups 15-24, 25-44 and 45-64. These three groups were determined by the Census records. They do exhibit a certain rationale: the first group includes the pre-marriage period when we might expect a high activity rate; the second group represents the child-rearing period when we would anticipate a substantial decline in women at work; and finally the 45-64, or 'post-family' period is when high rates may be expected, provided that the economic structure of the area supplies sufficient opportunities.

Activity rates for females in the first age group, 15-24 (Figure 8.18), tend to be high but declining. Median values for 1961 were around 0.72, whereas they were around 0.65 for 1966. Three-quarters of the zones show a decline in the rate between 1961 and 1966. There is no consistent spatial variation however. In contrast, the second age group, 25-44 (Figure 8.19), has an exactly opposite trend, ie. 80% of the rates are increasing, although, as expected, they start from a much lower base (median values in 1961 of 0.44 and 1966 of 0.51). This middle age group does show spatial variation within the study area, with lower rates in the eastern zones and higher rates in the west - surely a reflection of the greater job opportunities for women in the textile zone.

Figure 8.18 Female activity rates, 1961 and 1966, age group 15-24, West Yorkshire Census divisions

For key to zones see Figure 8.2

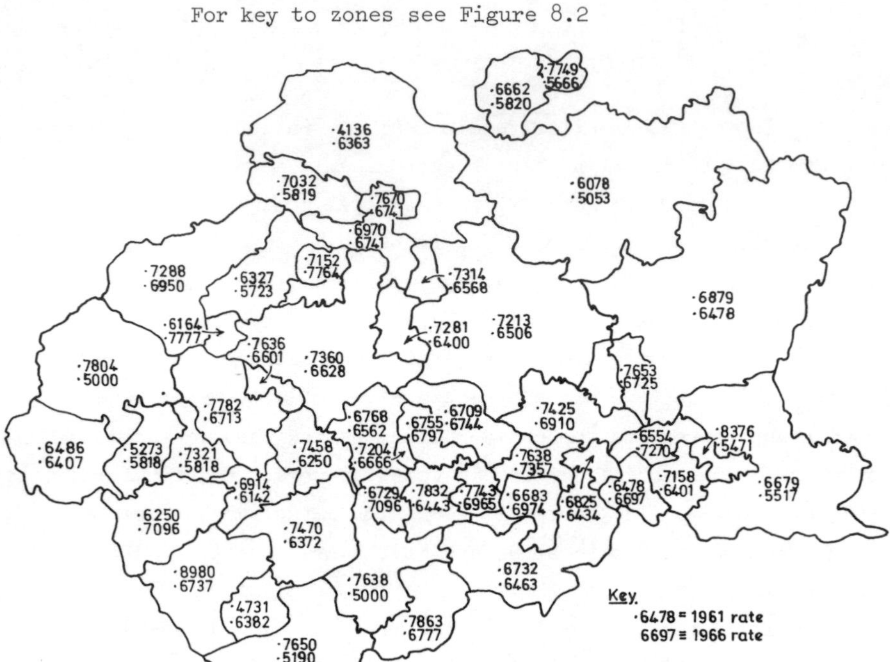

Figure 8.19 Female activity rates, 1961 and 1966, age group 25-44, West Yorkshire Census divisions

For key to zones see Figure 8.2

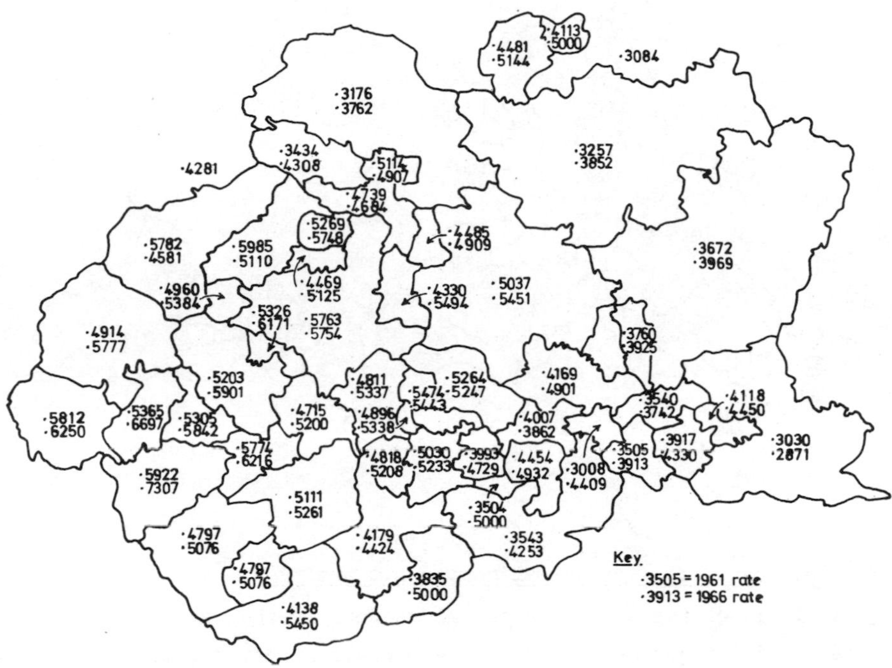

This pattern is repeated in the final age group, 45-64 (Figure 8.20), except that, overall, rates are lower still (median, 1961 of 0.40 and in 1966 of 0.48). Once again the vast majority are increasing and the highest rates are in the west.

Figure 8.20 Female activity rates, 1961 and 1966, age group 45-64, West Yorkshire Census divisions

For key to zones see Figure 8.2

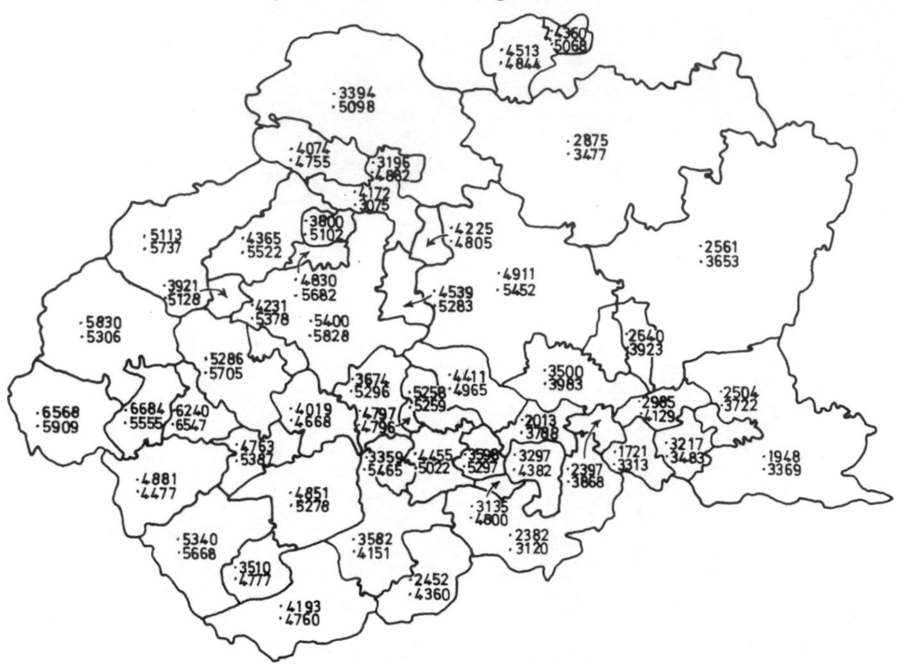

8.5 Stock data III: principal components analysis

Analysis of the way in which all sectors in the accounting system combine together to define the overall structural attributes of the West Yorkshire economy can be approached with the use of one of the members of the family of factor analysis models. The version of the workplace-based accounts which used Census data for 1966 provided the data base. Others (for example, Smith, 1968; Spence, 1968) have recently used the technique with a wider date-base to explore areas of economic health on a national or regional scale, but in our case we were more concerned with summarising and collating the static attributes towards which our earlier descriptive indices had pointed and, in particular, to construct a regionalisation of the zones in our study area.

The most appropriate of the factor analysis models for our purposes was the principal components analysis, the technical details of which need not concern us here. The analysis was carried out initially for both male employees and female employees separately, although because of the relatively small numbers of females employed in many sectors of the economy and the consequent difficulties of interpretation, it was most useful to concentrate on the analysis of male employees only.

The model used was a standard principal components analysis, using a normal varimax rotation, where components were initially identified for eigenvalues over 1 (unity) (Rummel, 1970). For male employees the analysis of the 24 variables reduced to seven components that were easily interpretable. Factor scores were computed for each of the 52 Census zones. These scores were grouped using a standard grouping algorithm which produced five distinct categories of zones. The grouping procedure did not include a contiguity constraint. Table 8.3 sets out the factor loadings matrix for male employees in West Yorkshire. Each of the factors (components) is now discussed in turn.

Factor I, explained 13.36% of the variation among the variables and was clearly a dimension which identifies the close association of the service sectors of the economy. Conversely where mining and quarrying (sector II) occur, then employment in the service sectors is weak. The distribution of high scores on this factor (Figure 8.21) points out the County Boroughs (except Halifax) as being major locations for the service sectors together with the fringe of closely linked local authorities in the north and north-east of the study area. In contrast low scores are to be found around the southern peripheries.

Factor II, which accounted for 11.10% of the variation in the variables is characterised by high scores in the construction sector (XVII) and in public utilities especially sector XVIII (gas, electricity and water). This factor also points out sector XIII (bricks, pottery and glass). High scores on this factor are limited, but areas on and around the coalfield, especially Knottingley and Osgoldcross Rural District are picked out.

Table 8.3 Factor loading matrix for principal components analysis of employment in West Yorkshire

Factors / Sectors	I	II	III	IV	V	VI	VII
I	-0.06	0.01	-0.15	0.30	0.69	0.43	0.25
II	-0.35	-0.15	-0.73	-0.01	-0.23	-0.20	-0.08
III	-0.06	-0.10	-0.04	0.83	-0.02	-0.10	-0.10
IV	0.18	0.27	-0.16	-0.18	-0.17	0.10	-0.09
V	-0.16	-0.04	0.04	0.02	0.01	-0.00	-0.01
VI	0.07	0.26	0.52	-0.05	-0.10	-0.43	-0.01
VII	-0.20	0.90	0.05	-0.05	-0.00	-0.07	-0.07
VIII	-0.19	-0.14	-0.05	-0.13	-0.06	-0.10	-0.09
IX	0.07	-0.17	0.75	0.05	-0.23	-0.10	-0.04
X	-0.22	-0.24	0.68	-0.25	-0.04	0.18	0.05
XI	-0.03	-0.14	0.24	-0.12	0.05	-0.02	-0.14
XII	0.12	-0.02	0.04	-0.08	-0.02	-0.00	0.90
XIII	-0.33	0.70	-0.03	-0.10	-0.08	-0.14	-0.11
XIV	0.04	-0.10	0.07	-0.01	-0.03	0.82	-0.02
XV	0.22	-0.08	-0.10	-0.19	0.82	-0.18	0.17
XVI	0.04	-0.06	-0.07	-0.01	-0.05	0.02	-0.01
XVII	0.18	0.60	-0.23	0.07	-0.01	0.14	-0.14
XVIII	0.05	0.81	-0.03	-0.04	0.03	-0.09	0.34
XIX	0.18	-0.12	-0.30	-0.03	-0.07	-0.33	0.05
XX	0.80	-0.14	0.15	-0.07	-0.22	0.20	-0.20
XXI	0.75	0.02	-0.04	0.10	-0.11	-0.10	0.17
XXII	0.78	-0.06	-0.01	0.01	0.14	-0.12	0.06
XXIII	0.82	-0.05	0.06	0.13	0.41	0.09	0.05
XXIV	0.40	-0.01	-0.08	0.76	0.00	0.17	0.02
% variance	13.36	11.10	8.86	6.63	6.53	6.04	4.98

For key to sectors see Table 8.1

Figure 8.21 Factor 1. The distribution of high and low scores
For key to zones see Figure 8.2

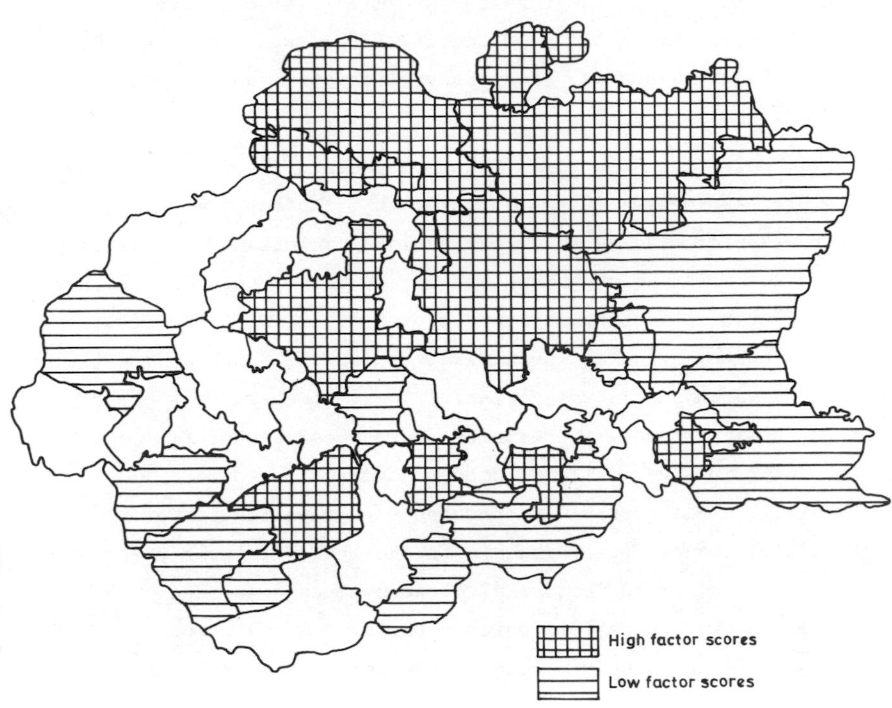

Factor III, which explains 8.86% of the variation clearly identifies the close association in the West Yorkshire economy of the engineering, metal manufacture and textile industries (sectors VI, IX and X). High employment in these sectors is not associated with mining and quarrying (sector II). The spatial distribution of high scores clearly identifies the area of the 'woollen district' in the west, ie. the major textile towns of West Yorkshire.

Factor IV, (6.63% explanation) loads highly on only two variables, sector III (food, drink and tobacco) and sector XXIV (public administration and defence). The very high scoring areas are Halifax, Wakefield, Harrogate, Pontefract, Nidderdale, Tadcaster and Wetherby; all explicable in terms of their economic specialities.

<u>Factor V</u>, (6.53% explanation) clearly identifies the rural fringe of the study area with high loadings for agriculture (sector I), paper, printing and publishing (sector XIV) and miscellaneous services (sector XXIII). Among the high scoring local authorities are Otley, Ripponden, Silsden, Hepton, Nidderdale, Tadcaster, Wetherby and Wharfedale.

<u>Factor VI</u>, reinforces the rural fringe aspects of Factor V but, as well as high employment in agriculture, it picks out timber and furniture (sector XIV) as being particularly important. Conversely these are not areas in which engineering is important. One further factor is worth mentioning, because of a specialism of the West Yorkshire economy which it identifies, <u>Factor VII</u> which only explains 5.0% of the variation in the variables does, however, very clearly identify the importance, in restricted areas, of sector XII (clothing), in particular in Leeds, Elland, Hebden Royd and Hepton.

Finally, it is possible to present a regionalisation of the local authorities of West Yorkshire on the basis of their principal component scores for 10 factors with eigenvalues over one. Figure 8.22 shows the pattern which results. Areas which fall into Group 1 are all the County Boroughs together with closely associated, often, commuter zones, eg. Ilkley, Otley, Harrogate and Horsforth. Group 2 areas all lie in the west of the study area and clearly define the Textile District. Group 3 areas are essentially the coalfield area in the south-east of the study area. Group 4 embraces the rural fringe, whilst Group 5 may be termed a 'residuals' category with only three members.

8.6 Flow data: interaction accounts and accessibilities

In this chapter, we have developed and analysed indices from the stock or structural attributes of the local economy; the attention paid to interaction has been minimal. However, this bias has often been enforced owing to the paucity of inter-zonal interaction data. It was noted in the opening paragraphs of the chapter that flow data is considerably more difficult to collect than stock data, although this obstacle should not be over-stressed as a justification for overweighting considerations of structure.

Figure 8.22 Grouping of local authorities in West Yorkshire using principal components analysis of employment data

For key to zones see Figure 8.2

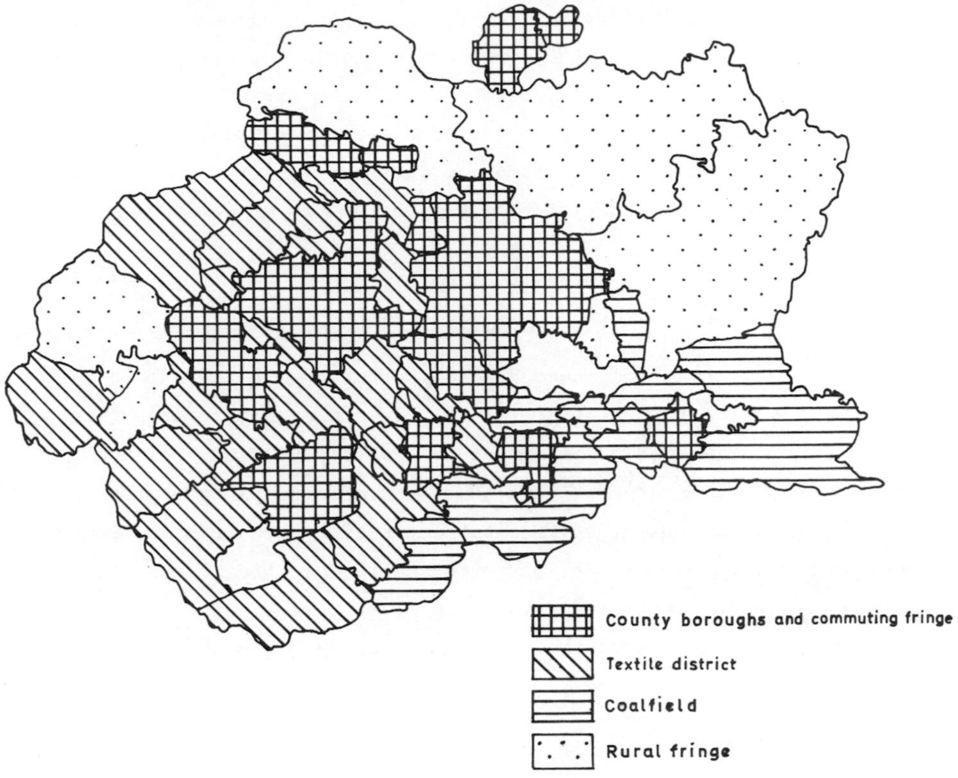

Despite these data constraints, it is nevertheless desirable to attempt a linking of the accounting frameworks used in the previous discussion with a hypothesised set of interaction accounts. An obvious contender for such an exercise is the integration of residence and workplace accounts by constructing a suitable set of journey-to-work tables. Since this is the subject of Chapter 9 the emphasis has been placed here upon inter-industry flows within the West Yorkshire economy.

Before embarking on a detailed description of the indices it should be borne in mind that the objectives of this section are rather limited: to link the structural attributes of the economy with any implicit interaction phenomena that are embodied in them, by using simple indices in an essentially descriptive fashion.

The instrument that seems most suitable for this purpose is some measure of the accessibility of activities in the West Yorkshire economy to their inputs and to their markets. Putman developed some interesting accessibility indices for his intra-regional allocation model (Putman, 1970) and they provide the basis for the West Yorkshire indices. It is interesting to note that Putman also saw these indices as links between the size and distribution of activities and the underlying sectoral flows.

The formal structure of Putman's indices is as follows:

$$A^{s}_{igt} = \Sigma_j \left\{ \frac{\Sigma_h (\alpha_{hg} \rho_h E_{jht})}{Z^{f}_{ijt}} \right\} \quad (8.15)$$

where A^{s}_{igt} is the supply accessibility of area i to the inputs required by sector g, at time t; E_{jht} is employment in area j in sector h, at time t; ρ_h is output per employed person in industry h, used to convert employment data to output measured in money terms; α_{hg} is the input-output coefficient expressing the amount of sector h output required per unit of output of sector g; and Z^{f}_{ijt} is the freight impedance between zones i and j, at time t.

The index described above measures supply accessibility; the corollary is known as the market accessibility index. It has the algebraic form:

$$A^{m}_{igt} = \Sigma_j \left\{ \frac{\Sigma_h (\alpha_{gh} \rho_h E_{jht})}{Z^{f}_{ijt}} \right\} \quad (8.16)$$

The terms have the same definitions as before, except that the subscripts of the input-output coefficient (α) are now transposed. This, in effect, states that the market index is identical to the supply index except that the matrix of input-output coefficients has been transposed. The type of index adopted in West Yorkshire differed from Putman's only in the form of the impedance term used. When describing his indices Putman noted that the cost function should properly be disaggregated for each industry type, but was unable to effect this improvement due to lack of data. Work by Chisholm and O'Sullivan (1973) on British freight-flow data has, however, made it possible to effect a disaggregation of the denominators of the indices.

The modified form of the index for the supply accessibility case is as follows:

$$A_{ig}^{s} = \Sigma_j \Sigma_i \{\alpha_{hg} \rho_h E_{jh} d_{ij}^{-\beta^{(h)}}\} \qquad (8.17)$$

where the definitions are as previously stated except that the time subscript has been dropped, d_{ij} is road distance between zones i and j; and $\beta^{(h)}$ is a parameter specifying the 'distance-decay' characteristics of the movement of goods produced by industry h. The data requirements of the new type of index necessitated the use in the first instance of national input-output coefficients. At first sight, this appears to cast doubt on the validity of the exercise; it should be noted, however, that the objectives included a *hypothesised* set of inter-industry flows. Modified coefficients could be introduced when regional data become available. Further objections are worthy of discussion here. First, the index of supply accessibility only encompasses those inputs that are required from other industries (ie. intermediate inputs) and ignores the so-called primary inputs like labour; it is also assumed that all intermediate demands can be met from within the West Yorkshire economy. While these objections must be respected, some counter-arguments can be proffered. The existing pattern of employment is incorporated implicitly in the index, since levels of employment are used as surrogates for output levels, and the numerator of the index is essentially a measure of *potential* supply. Hence although the existing mix of outputs from West Yorkshire may be inappropriate as inputs to other local industries, there may be some justification to be found from this standpoint of potential.

Clearly, a more satisfactory approach would involve a more detailed break-down of the output data, and of the input-output coefficients used. In the case of West Yorkshire, 20 industry orders, plus an aggregated 'services' sector comprising SIC orders XXI, XXII, XXIII and XXIV, were distinguished. Employment data were available at the individual MLH level for each zone of the study area for 1966, but it was considered that the dual problems of the magnitude of the sampling errors (10% sample census) and the increasing dubiety of a constant proportionate relationship between output and employment at fine levels of disaggregation, made the effort involved in such a refinement difficult to justify.

Similar arguments may be explored when discussing the market accessibility index. Again, no weight is accorded to flows (potential or real) that are destined for the final demand sectors, nor is any explicit inclusion made of goods that are delivered to external areas on intermediate account. A further partial justification is offered here. Accessibility, it may be conjectured, has many different levels of resolution; for example, accessibility to local shops would not significantly affect the locational decision of a firm intending to sell to a region-wide market. Concomitantly, an enterprise aiming at national and international markets (and possibly with a like distribution of inputs) would regard internal accessibility within West Yorkshire as a fairly minor consideration. This view of accessibility as a multi-scaled phenomenon permits the argument that the distribution of external deliveries (ie. final demands, primary inputs and trade) may not significantly effect the patterns of internal accessibility. One obvious qualification of this proposition is that where communications lines of supra-regional importance occur, it should be expected that they may be accompanied by corridors of accessibility to external influences. To embody these considerations into the descriptive indices envisaged in this section requires a multi-regional approach (and accounting system) which, although eminently desirable, is outside the present scope here.

Before describing the maps produced from the indices, some further considerations of the origins of the β-values given in the modified version is required. Note that the crudest form of the index is given when it is assumed that β is unity for all sectors; this says that road distance affects interaction uniformly and for all types of good. As mentioned earlier, Chisholm and O'Sullivan have experimented with flow data and have calibrated a gravity model of the form:

$$T_{ij} = A_i O_i D_j^{\alpha} c_{ij}^{-\beta}$$
$$A_i = \{\Sigma D_j^{\alpha} c_{ij}^{-\beta}\}^{-1} \tag{8.18}$$

where T_{ij} is the flow of goods from zone i to zone j; O_i is total goods originating in zone i; D_j is the 'attraction factor' for zone j, ie. total goods 'absorbed' by zone j; c_{ij} is the cost of transportation from zone i to j; and α and β are parameters obtained by calibration. The data resources available allowed the above authors to obtain a series of values for β, one for each traffic zone; the values varied from 0.6 to 3.1, while the relevant magnitudes for the Leeds, Barnsley, Doncaster, Sheffield and Selby zones were 1.9, 2.2, 0.6, 1.3 and 3.1 respectively. The method used to determine these numbers did not distinguish between different types of good; an alternative method did, however, allow values of β to be obtained for a limited range of commodities. Both kinds of β value have been used for calculating a range of accessibility indices; selected sectors are shown in the map series that follows, because the amount of information created by even this small number of parameter values soon outstrips the space available for presentation. Pairs of maps were constructed to allow examination and comparison of the input accessibilities that result from an assumption of values of 1.0 and the accessibilities that incorporate different β values for different sectors. The following manufacturing orders were selected for special consideration: order VI - engineering and electrical engineering; order X - textiles; and order XII - clothing and footwear.

These three orders account for over a third of all employment in the West Yorkshire study area and over 65% of the employment in manufacturing orders. At this stage it was considered that the market accessibility maps were of comparatively little value, since the major industries of West Yorkshire were known to sell to national and international markets. Input accessibilities, however, were considered to be more relevant due mainly to the emphasis given to potential accessibility to product inputs for the major industries in West Yorkshire. The effect of using varying β values was effectively to stretch the range of values in every case, otherwise the relative positions of zones remained very much the same.

Figure 8.23 shows the input accessibility surface for the textile industry using β=1.0. However a comparable map using variable β values would show essentially the same pattern, with Leeds, Bradford, Halifax and Huddersfield dominating the distribution. Other areas of high accessibility to textile inputs are

are to be found in the adjacent area to the south stretching from Spenborough to Wakefield. Castleford, Harrogate and Wakefield also have higher than usual accessibilities. When varying β values are used, areas of high accessibility are found in a slightly more fragmented pattern in the south, although the pattern is basically the same.

Figure 8.23 Input accessibilities textiles (β = 1.0)
For key to zones see Figure 8.2

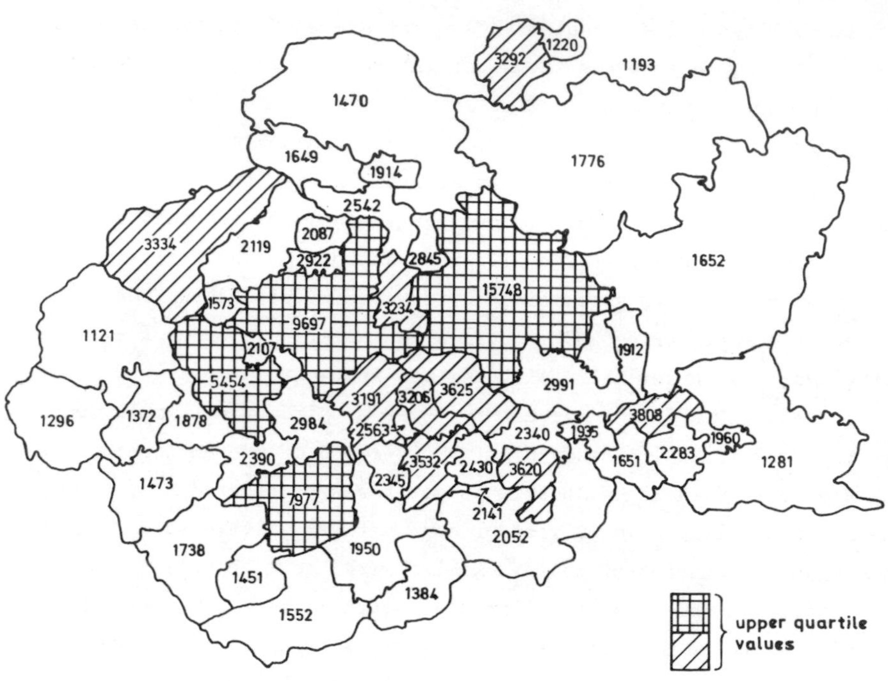

Figure 8.24 maps the fixed β distribution for sector VI (engineering and electrical engineering). Again the pattern is dominated by the County Boroughs of Leeds, Bradford, Halifax, Huddersfield and additionally, in this case, Rothwell. Other areas with high accessibility form a close-knit fringe, especially in the south, around these County Boroughs. No matter which β value is chosen, the pattern is identical, but variable β values again tend to stretch the range of values.

Figure 8.24 Input accessibilities, engineering and electrical goods (β = 1.0)

For key to zones see Figure 8.2

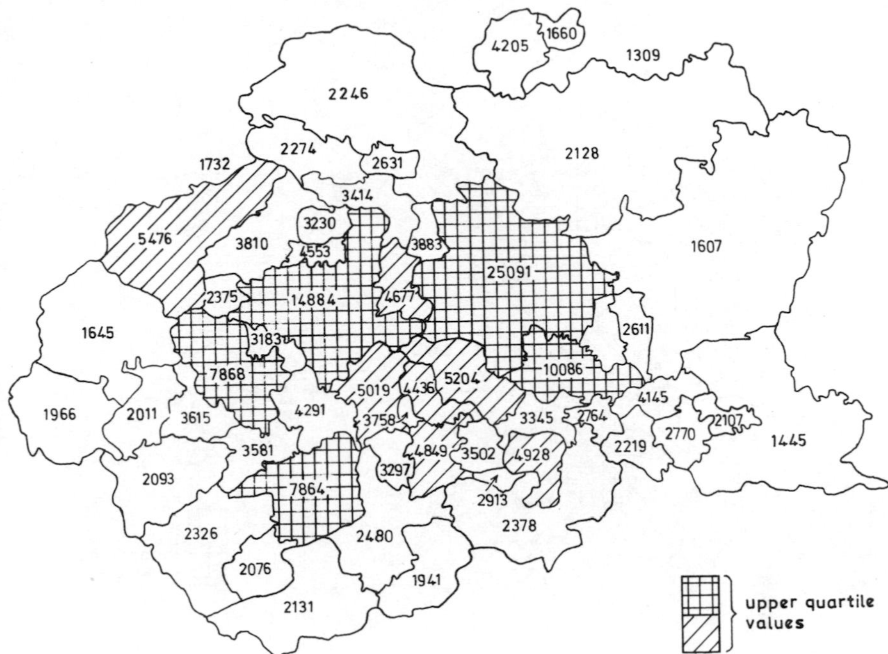

Finally, Figure 8.25 shows the input accessibilites, using variable β values, to the clothing and footwear sector. The structural pattern this time is overwhelmingly dominated by Bradford, with Halifax and Huddersfield providing secondary peaks of input accessibility. The local authorities fringing these major sources of inputs, including Leeds, are also important. As with the previous two sectors the eastern authorities in the study area, especially the rural fringe, have very low accessibility values.

Figure 8.25 Input accessibilities, clothing and footwear (variable β values)

For key to zones see Figure 8.2

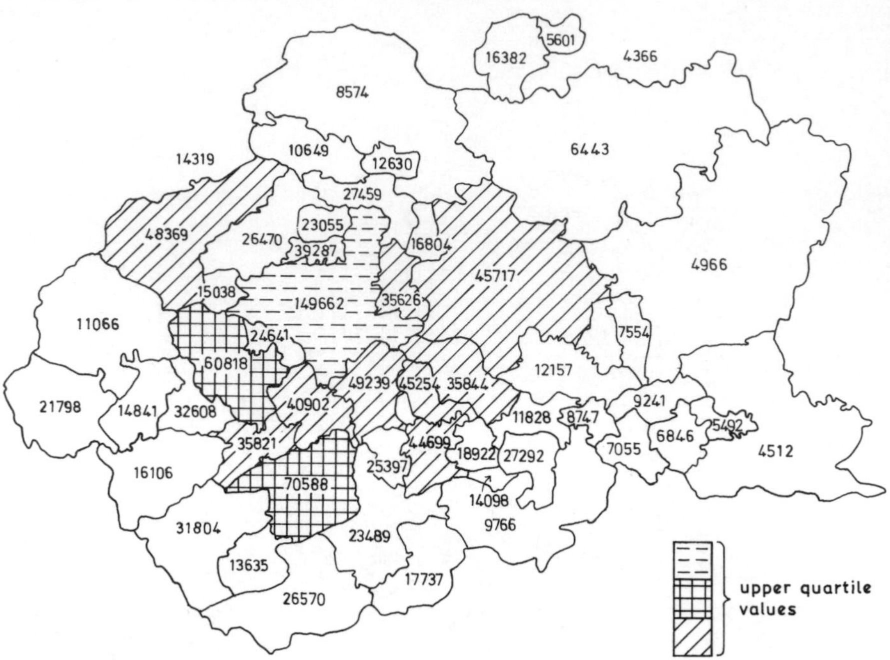

8.7 The integration of spatially-aggregated and spatially-disaggregated accounts

As a postscript to this chapter, attention is now given to the prospects for integrating the spatially-aggregated accounts and models of Chapter 4 with the spatially-disaggregated accounts which have been the theme of this chapter. The prospects are essentially concerned with the use of the shift-share methodology as a model-building strategy rather than as a descriptive device.

Lakshmanan's model of Connecticut (Lakshmanan, 1968) attempted to use the concept of differential shift as the key to the process of growth-allocation. His model, in effect, adopted a Lowry-like framework, where shifts in manufacturing employment (ie. basic employment) were assumed to determine population, service-employment and income levels in the local economy. Furthermore, Lakshmanan's model also incorporated a spatial-interaction component in the form of mutual accessibilities of constituent economic activities. This model is of interest here, not only for its obvious applicability, given the work already completed in this chapter, but also for its demonstration of the way that a spatially-aggregated economic model (ie. an economic base model), a spatially-disaggregated model (ie. the accessibility component) and a quasi-dynamic model can be incorporated into one hybrid model.

Clearly, in the case of West Yorkshire there appears to be an opportunity to experiment with the integration of an input-output model with a shift-share allocation device. Before this can be done, however, certain innovations have to be introduced into the accounting systems that underpin the two constituent models. The innovations have in effect to provide a way of converting the flow data emphasis of the input-output model to the stock data emphasis of the shift models. If this can be achieved successfully, the results would be most encouraging for builders of local input-output models. Success would essentially mean that input-output coefficients might be estimated and/or adjusted, making use of small-area employment data. Unfortunately, the innovations required are neither easy to achieve nor satisfactory in their assumptions. Nevertheless, their essential features are presented here.

Figure 8.26 summarises the argument. As noted above, previous differential shift models have tended to use shift-estimation in a Lowry-model framework, although one crucial difference is that the need for exogeneous estimates of basic employment is obviated. Nevertheless, the philosophy is essentially that of Lowry, ie. basic employment → population → service employment. Lakshmanan's model does, however, try to extend Lowry's scheme by including some equations that estimate differential shifts in incomes for household groups. The suggestion is that one replaces the Lowry accounting framework with the Keynesian income-accounting framework. In particular, it is suggested that the input-output version is adopted.

Thus, as well as containing equations for the shifts in each of the sectors already defined as constituting the economy, it is suggested that further equations are introduced to estimate differential shifts in what might be termed 'final demand' and 'primary input' sectors. These would effectively close the model. Such a

Figure 8.26 A possible framework for the integration of input-output and differential shift modelling

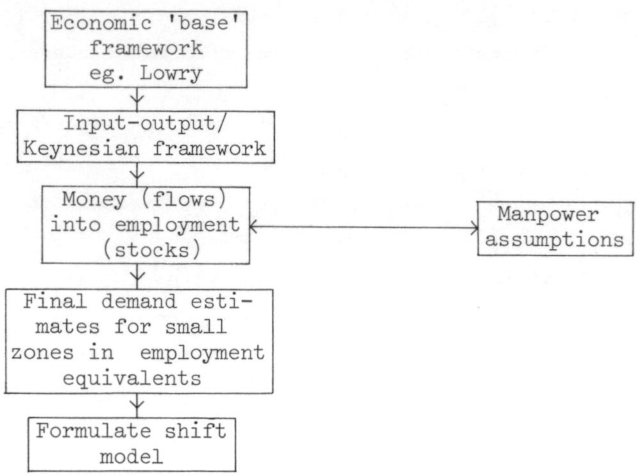

procedure requires the conversion of final demand and primary input items into their employment equivalents, in the same way that output is converted into employment units, above. Such a conversion implies a rather crudely modified set of accounts of the normal input-output type, where the usual a^{kl} coefficients are interpreted as the amount of employment in sector k that is used in the production of goods for sector l. This creates an employment indentity which very closely resembles the usual (money flows) input-output equation. This approach is obviously a very crude affair, using simple proportionality and constant coefficients. One could begin to improve this employment generation model by reconsidering the production function that is implied by the Leontief model. In particular one would have to examine the assumptions about returns to scale and elasticities of substitution, in order to ascertain whether an employment-version of the input-output model is tenable. At first sight such a model would be satisfactory in a static descriptive role, but would not perform at all well in a forecasting role. Levels of employment, for instance, reflect levels of output in a very indirect way. This is revealed to an even greater extent when one tries to deal with changes in levels of output.

The above suggestions might, therefore, lead to equations for estimating final demand sectors for example, of the following type:

DS (consumption expenditure)	= ΣDS (income)
DS (capital formation)	= ΣDS (trading income) activity level
DS (income from employment)	= ΣDS (trading income) investment
DS (gross trading income, profits, etc)	= ΣDS (consumer expenditure) exports, imports, investment
DS (government expenditure)	= exogenously estimated

DS (exports) and DS (imports) as usual present particular problems especially so since we are now concerned with small zones, and therefore their relative contribution is greater. Estimation methods require further investigation.

The data sources, of course, restrict the implementation of this model to the West Yorkshire conurbation only, with the sectors (and possibly only the manufacturing sectors) as observations. This implies that the differential shifts must be measured in terms of the aggregate growth rate of the whole economy. Having estimated the parameters of the sector-shift model we may arrange them as follows:

For each zone in a three sector model we have

$$\begin{bmatrix} DS_1 \\ DS_2 \\ DS_3 \end{bmatrix} = \begin{bmatrix} 0 & a_{12} & a_{13} \\ a_{21} & 0 & a_{23} \\ a_{31} & a_{32} & 0 \end{bmatrix} \begin{bmatrix} DS_1 \\ DS_2 \\ DS_3 \end{bmatrix} + \begin{bmatrix} b_{11} & b_{12} & b_{13} & b_{10} \\ b_{21} & b_{22} & b_{23} & b_{20} \\ b_{31} & b_{32} & b_{33} & b_{30} \end{bmatrix} \tag{8.19}$$

This can be rearranged to give an interesting form for the DS projection, ie

$$\begin{bmatrix} DS \end{bmatrix} = \begin{bmatrix} I - A \end{bmatrix}^{-1} \begin{bmatrix} b \end{bmatrix} \tag{8.20}$$

$$\begin{bmatrix} b \end{bmatrix} = \begin{bmatrix} b_{11}\ldots\ldots \\ b_{21}\ldots\ldots \\ b_{31}\ldots\ldots \end{bmatrix} i$$

and i is a unit vector. It appears that the matrix multiplier will have an inverse. Given this, we are led to quasi-input-output coefficients. What is needed now is some explanation of $|b|$ and some suitable proxy variable. This also suggests that we can use national or regional input-output coefficients as initial estimates of differential shift parameters to set up some mutual constraints procedure. This idea suggests also that at some stage of _temporal_ disaggregation (eg a year) the A matrix of the DS model and the normal input-output model are identical. A great deal more work remains to be done in this direction, however, and attention is currently being focused on this field of enquiry as part of the ongoing research generated by the work on the West Yorkshire economy as part of this project.

References

Bowers, J. (1970) The anatomy of regional activity rates in National Institute of Economic and Social Research Regional Papers I, Cambridge University Press.

Chisholm, M. and O'Sullivan, P. (1973) Freight flows and spatial aspects of the British economy, Cambridge University Press.

Department of Employment (annually) Employers Register 11.

Dodgson, J.S. (1972) Local employment statistics: West Yorkshire, M62 Impact Study, Working Paper 5, Institute for Transport Studies, University of Leeds.

Dunn, E.S. (1960) A statistical and analytical technique for regional analysis, Papers of the Regional Science Association, 6, pp. 97-112.

Florence, P.S. (1948) Investment, location and size of plant, Cambridge University Press.

General Register Office (1968) Sample Census 1966, Great Britain, Economic Activity Tables.

Lakshmanan, J.R. (1968) A model for allocating urban activities in a state, Socio-Economic Planning Sciences, 1, pp. 283-295.

Lowry, I.S. (1967) Seven models of urban development, Highways Research Board, Special Report, 97.

Putman, S.H. (1967) Intra-urban industrial location model design and implementation, Papers of the Regional Science Association, 19, pp. 199-214.

Putman, S.H. (1970) Developing and testing an intra-regional model, Regional Studies, 4,4, pp. 473-490.

Robinson, D. and Wilson, A.G. (1966) A note on calculating average compound rates of growth, Bulletin of the Oxford University Institute of Economics and Statistics, 28, pp. 241-246.

Rummel, R.J. (1970) Applied factor analysis, Northwestern University Press, Evanston, Illinois.

Smith, D.M. (1968) Identifying the grey areas: a multi-variate approach, Regional Studies, 2, pp. 183-193.

Spence, N. (1968) A multi-factor uniform regionalisation of British counties on the basis of employment data for 1961, Regional Studies, 2, pp. 87-104.

Stilwell, F.J.B. (1969) Regional growth and structural adaptation, Urban Studies, 6, pp. 162-178.

Streit, M.E. (1969) Spatial associations and economic linkages between industries, Journal of Regional Science, 9, pp. 177-188.

Tress, R.C. (1938) Unemployment and the diversification of industry, Manchester School, IX, pp. 140-152.

Chapter 9

Models for urban transport planning

P.W. Bonsall, A.F. Champernowne, E.L. Cripps, P.R. Goodman,
A. Hankin, R.L. Mackett, I. Sanderson, M.L. Senior,
F. Southworth, R. Spence, H.C.W.L. Williams and A.G. Wilson

9.1 Introduction

An example is presented in this chapter of the building of a transport model as applied to West Yorkshire. Only the barest indication is given of how such a model might be used in the development of urban transport policy. Models nonetheless are devices at the core of the urban transport planning process and as such are the tools of transportation policy-making, and this needs to be borne in mind continually. Like other urban models, they are designed to assess the impacts of policy, and though computable transportation models require a considerable effort to make them operational, their subservient role must be stressed. Since the London Travel Survey of 1962, models have been a common and controversial feature of most transportation studies in the UK (and similarly from the mid-1950's in the US). It can be argued that, in all that time, because of the difficulties of assembling the resources of money and skills, transport models, in spite of their widespread use, have not properly achieved their true place in the formulation of urban policy. Though some (who are often sceptical about all kinds of urban modelling) may think they know what to do about transportation in cities and some may know about model-building, very few teams have successfully brought the two together. Nevertheless, it can still be held that the building of an appropriate model is a prerequisite of policy testing.

The notion of a computable model of the transportation system, proposed in the previous paragraph, is best achieved through a good theory of traffic movement in urban areas. The most popular representation of such movement depicts the trip-making of members of households, for whatever purpose, and by whatever mode of transport, as a function of the costs of travel between two places, together with basic propensities to generate trips from households and other activity centres in zones of origin and destination. The trip generation of households is regarded, mainly, as a function of the levels of household income, car ownership, the size of households and the employment of household members. The attraction of home-based trips to a particular location in the city is primarily considered as proportional to the level of each activity in each location. The generation and attraction of non-home-based trips are usually assumed to be a function of the amounts of different non-home-based activities in any place and those of commercial vehicle trips are related to employment. The total number of such trips are often argued to depend on the level of economic prosperity. The sum of these trips provides a measurement of the demand for urban travel and a base from which future demand can be predicted. There are technical problems, of course, which may arise in the forecasting of certain of the variables and social, economic or technological changes may occur which make obsolete the relations which have been and are relied upon in the study of the impacts of urban transport policy. In a world of diminishing resources, can it really be expected that car-ownership will increase because families choose to spend what amounts to an ever-increasing proportion of their income on owning a motor car? In transport planning today this kind of question has to be more than rhetorical.

Despite these quite fundamental arguments, our dominant concern is with a fairly conventional theory and construction of a model of urban transportation, and with its refinement in the disaggregation of trip ends and trip lengths. The theory of travel demand has seen much sophisticated refinement in the past from several disciplines; so too, have similar computerised representations of urban transport networks. These replicate the supply of transport facilities and are matched to estimates of present travel demand, and with augmentation meet those of future travel demand. Thus, an equilibrium between demand and supply is established. Though governed by elementary concepts, the construction of the suite of transport models is a far from easy exercise. The more detailed description below will help verify this. Sections 9.2-9.5 are concerned with the conventional model, while a new model is presented in Section 9.6 which links the traditional model with some more recent innovations.

9.2 An overview of the West Yorkshire transportation model

The general characteristics and structure of urban transport models have been set out by Wilson (1974, Chapter 9). Here, the aim is to elaborate upon the features incorporated in this particular model of West Yorkshire rather than to offer some more general statement about urban transportation models.

The study area for the model, shown in Figure 9.1 and Table 9.1, was defined to cover the West Yorkshire conurbation. The population of the study area in 1966 was 2,070,170. This area was arrived at before the announcement of boundary changes under the local government reorganisation of April 1974, but corresponds closely to the West Yorkshire Metropolitan County. Twenty-eight of the zones are in the area encompassed by the old Leeds County Borough and correspond to the wards in use at the time of the 1966 Census of Population. Bradford County Borough was divided into four zones, which are aggregates of wards. The remaining 49 zones are all local authority areas as delineated prior to local government organisation. It is thus a mix of spatial Systems II and III referred to in Chapter 1. This zoning system permits the examination of intra-city policies in the Leeds area (regarding the rest of the study area as external zones) or inter-urban transport policies at the county scale. Difficulties arise, however, with the wide variation in zone size, particularly at the trip distribution stage.

The definition of the study area zoning system stems partly from the sources of data being used. Most of the data on household characteristics come from the Censuses of Population for 1966 and 1971. Trip data for calibration of the distribution and modal split submodels comes from a special coding of the workplace and transport data of the 1966 Census of Population. More detailed descriptions of data sources used are given later. On this area, the model outlined in Figure 9.2 was constructed. The submodels shown in the figure may be described briefly as follows: (i) <u>network processing</u>

Figure 9.1 The West Yorkshire study area

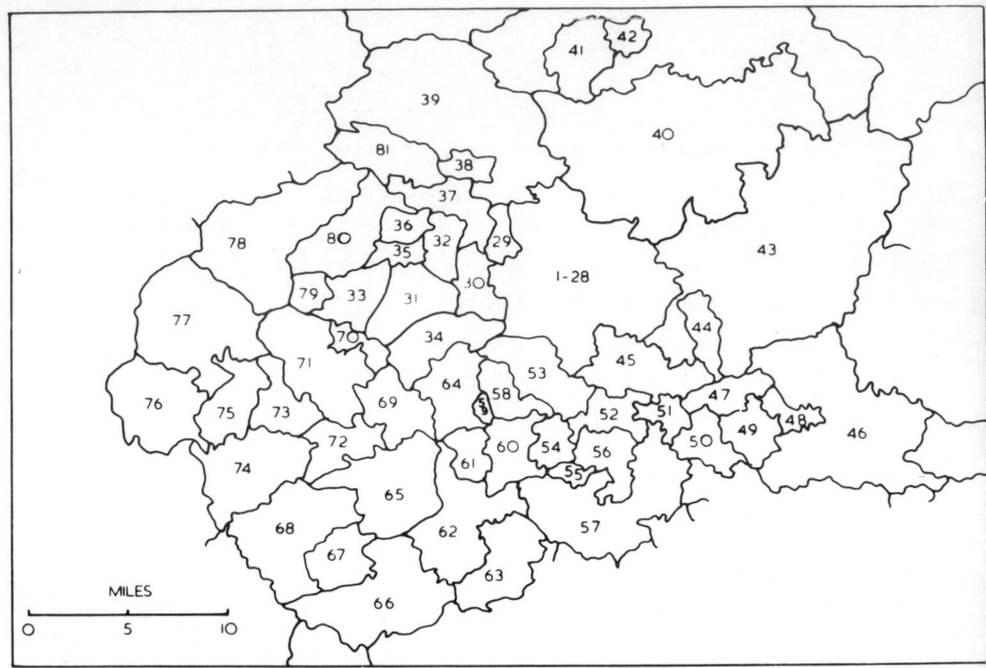

Key to Figure 9.1 Study area zones

1 to 28 Leeds Wards

1. City
2. Wellington
3. Westfield
4. Hyde Park
5. Meanwood
6. Headingley
7. Blenheim
8. Woodhouse
9. Moortown
10. Potternewton
11. Allerton
12. Roundhay
13. Richmond Hill
14. Harehills
15. Burmantofts
16. Crossgates
17. Halton
18. Osmondthorpe
19. East Hunslet
20. Hunslet Carr
21. Middleton
22. Holbeck
23. Beeston
24. Wortley
25. Armley
26. Bramley
27. Kirkstall
28. Stanningley

29 to 81 Local Authorities

29. Horsforth
30. Pudsey
31. Bradford 'A'
32. Bradford 'B'
33. Bradford 'C'
34. Bradford 'D'
35. Shipley
36. Baildon
37. Aireborough
38. Otley
39. Wharfedale
40. Wetherby
41. Harrogate
42. Knaresborough
43. Tadcaster
44. Garforth
45. Rothwell
46. Osgoldcross
47. Castleford
48. Knottingley
49. Pontefract
50. Featherstone
51. Normanton
52. Stanley
53. Morley
54. Ossett
55. Horbury
56. Wakefield CB
57. Wakefield RD
58. Batley
59. Heckmondwike
60. Dewsbury
61. Mirfield
62. Kirkburton
63. Denby Dale
64. Spenborough
65. Huddersfield
66. Holmfirth
67. Meltham
68. Colne Valley
69. Brighouse
70. Queensbury and Shelf
71. Halifax
72. Elland
73. Sowerby Bridge
74. Ripponden
75. Hebden Royd
76. Todmorden
77. Hepton
78. Keighley
79. Denholme
80. Bingley
81. Ilkley

Figure 9.2 Structure of the transport model for West Yorkshire

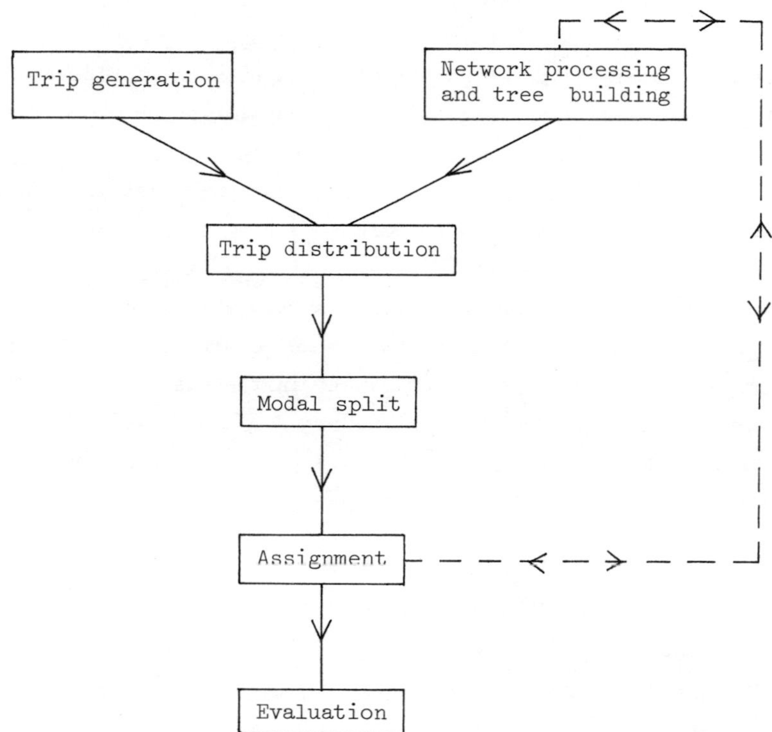

and tree building are the processes of simulating public and private transport networks in the urban system, and of finding the best paths through the networks between each pair of zones, based on the costs of travel on each link in each network. To this can be added the process of obtaining the 'skim trees' of generalised costs associated with these best paths; (ii) trip generation is the process of finding the number of trips produced in and attracted to each zone for each trip purpose in turn; (iii) trip distribution is the process of determining the number of trips between each pair of zones in the spatial system; (iv) modal split is the process of determining the mode of transport used for each trip; (v) assignment is the process of loading the trips from the trip distribution and modal split models onto each network to describe the actual pattern of movement in the urban system; and (vi) evaluation is the basis of the process of finding the optimal strategy from the set of alternative plans from the transport model outputs. This framework can be embodied - as it is to an extent in the case of the West Yorkshire model - in a modular structure for an analysis system of the type shown in Figure 9.3. Most of the parts shown in this figure were discussed above and are described in detail below. Some further elaboration of some of the levels in the diagram is useful, however.

Policy sets can be formulated to solve particular urban problems - the problems being represented by indicators. These policies will sometimes demand both refinements to the models and a particular path through such models (i.e. the way in which computer programmes which make the models work are linked together). A control programme would recognise problems and policies and sequence the programmes accordingly. A Computer MACRO for the ICL 1906A, was written in Job Command Language to achieve this for West Yorkshire. To date it only deals with network processing, trip generation, trip distribution and methods of assignment but it can be made operational for further models. Calibration means searching for the best fit in a range of values for the parameters of various models. This, of course, is part of any urban analysis system and particularly, in this case, those concerned with trip generation, trip distribution and modal split. Nowadays, such a search procedure is carried out automatic-

Figure 9.3 Possible structure for urban analysis system

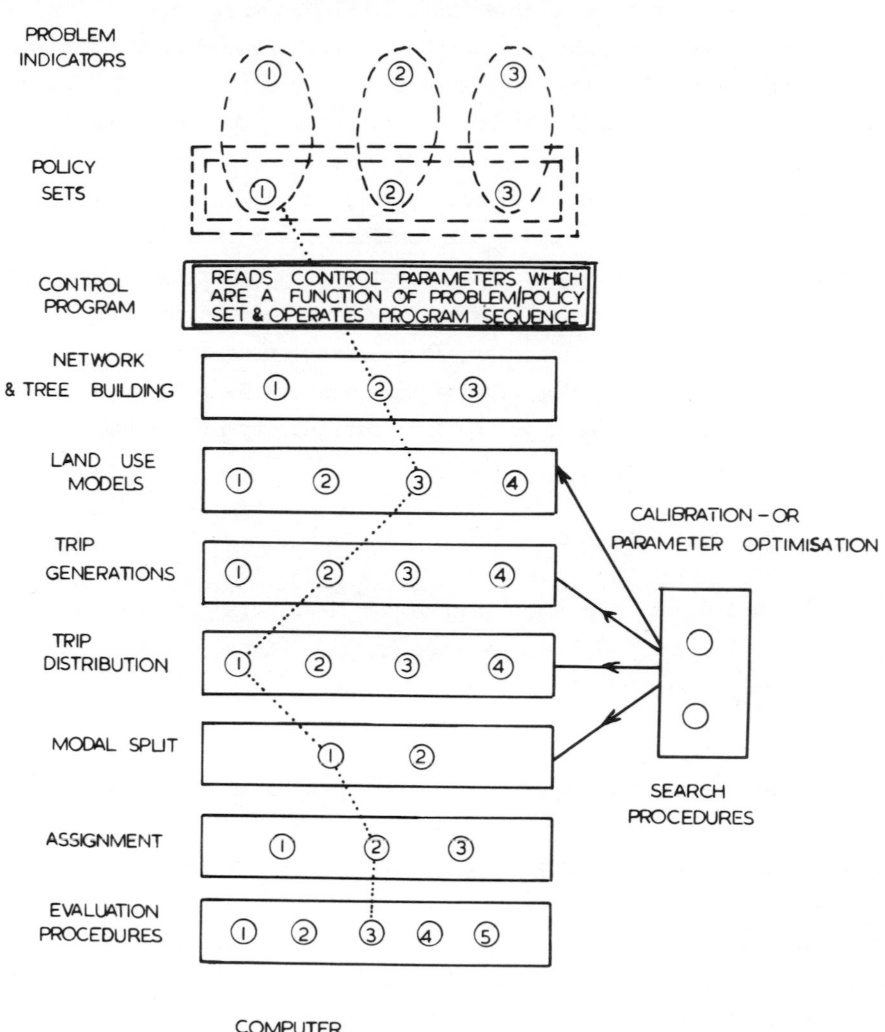

ally within a computer; hence, the need to incorporate this approach explicitly in a structure such as that of Figure 9.3.

In the example provided by the West Yorkshire model, the current version of the transportation package has not yet (August 1975) been run operationally using the MACRO as a control. The development of a variety of transport submodels has for the most part required their separate computing and calibration. Also, the demonstration of the running of a model has involved only a limited set of alternative land uses and transport options for the future. This means that, in practice, it has been almost premature to consider implementing Figure 9.3. In addition, as yet, there has been no attempt to link land use with transportation models as Putman (1973, 1974) has done. For at least these reasons, the full operationality of the MACRO is a thing of the future.

9.3 The submodels in detail

9.3.1 Introduction

We now describe the components of the West Yorkshire transportation model in turn, beginning as suggested by Figure 9.2 with network processing and tree building.

9.3.2 Network processing and tree building

In our implementation of the transport model in the West Yorkshire region we have two transport networks: a public transport network and a private transport network. These networks are represented by links and nodes. The definition file for each of the networks is made up of descriptions of the constituent links. For each link there may be stored information about: (i) the nodes it connects; (ii) its length; (iii) the time taken to traverse it; (iv) its capacity; (v) its jurisdiction code; and (vi) any excess costs associated with it, such as parking charges, transfer costs (such as waiting for a bus). The jurisdiction codes of a link describe among other things whether it is 'real' or 'notional'. For the public transport network real links represent interchanges between services and access points between the network and the zone centroids (which are the spatial centre of population distribution within a zone - where all trips are assumed to start or terminate). In the private network real links represent roads in the study area.

The network used includes all motorway and class 'A' roads together with such class 'B' roads as are necessary to ensure adequate connectivity. Notional links provide for access between the zone centroids and the network. Figure 9.4 shows the manner in which real and notional links, centroids and major intersections are incorporated in each network.

The 1966 public networks have some 550 nodes and 1,900 links. The 1966 private network has 650 nodes and 2,100 links. Figures 9.5 and 9.6 display the main elements of the train and bus networks respectively. These two networks are combined to form the public transport network. Figure 9.7 shows the main elements of the private transport network. It will be appreciated, of course, that diagrams at this scale cannot show the detail of the networks particularly within Leeds. Central Leeds, for example, has considerably greater complexity in the public transport network than indicated. The networks, described above, are used for the building of inter-zonal trees of minimum cost paths. The output of the tree building programme consists for each mode of: (i) <u>backnode tables</u>: a table is produced for each centroid and the whole collection permits the tracing of the minimum paths, through all nodes; (ii) <u>the skim trees</u>: this set of trees for each node, k, is a square matrix, c_{ij}^{k}, of all inter-zonal travel costs; and (iii) <u>the network description</u>: as well as enumerating the nodes, these tables, for each node in each of the public and private transport networks, depict whether a link is 'notional' or 'real', the length and direction of each link and any excess time incurred on a notional link. The backnode tables and skim trees are found using an algorithm first proposed by Moore (1957) and Dijkstra (1959) and reported at an expository level, for example, by Potts and Oliver (1972). For the public transport network, an innovation on the basic algorithm is introduced which allows the incorporation of a complex public transport fare function (see Bonsall, 1974, 1975-A).

As noted above, the set of skim trees provide the cost matrices c_{ij} or c_{ij}^{k} which have been much in evidence in earlier chapters, though it is usually in the context of a transport model that they are constructed properly using the methods described here. Simpler

Figure 9.4 Example of 'real' and 'notional' links

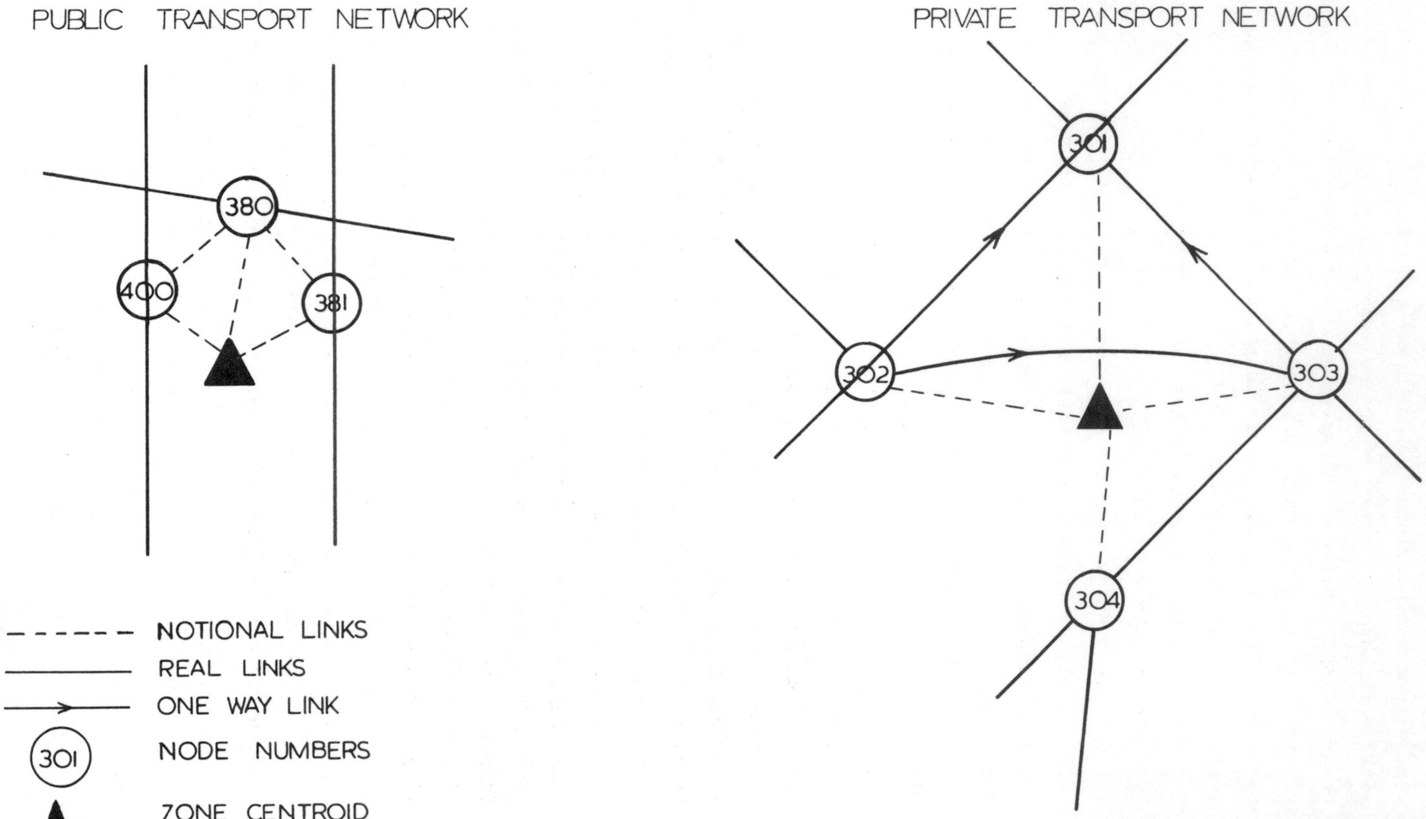

PUBLIC TRANSPORT NETWORK

380
400
381

PRIVATE TRANSPORT NETWORK

301
302
303
304

NOTIONAL LINKS
REAL LINKS
ONE WAY LINK
301 NODE NUMBERS
ZONE CENTROID

Figure 9.5 Structure of the West Yorkshire study area rail network, 1966

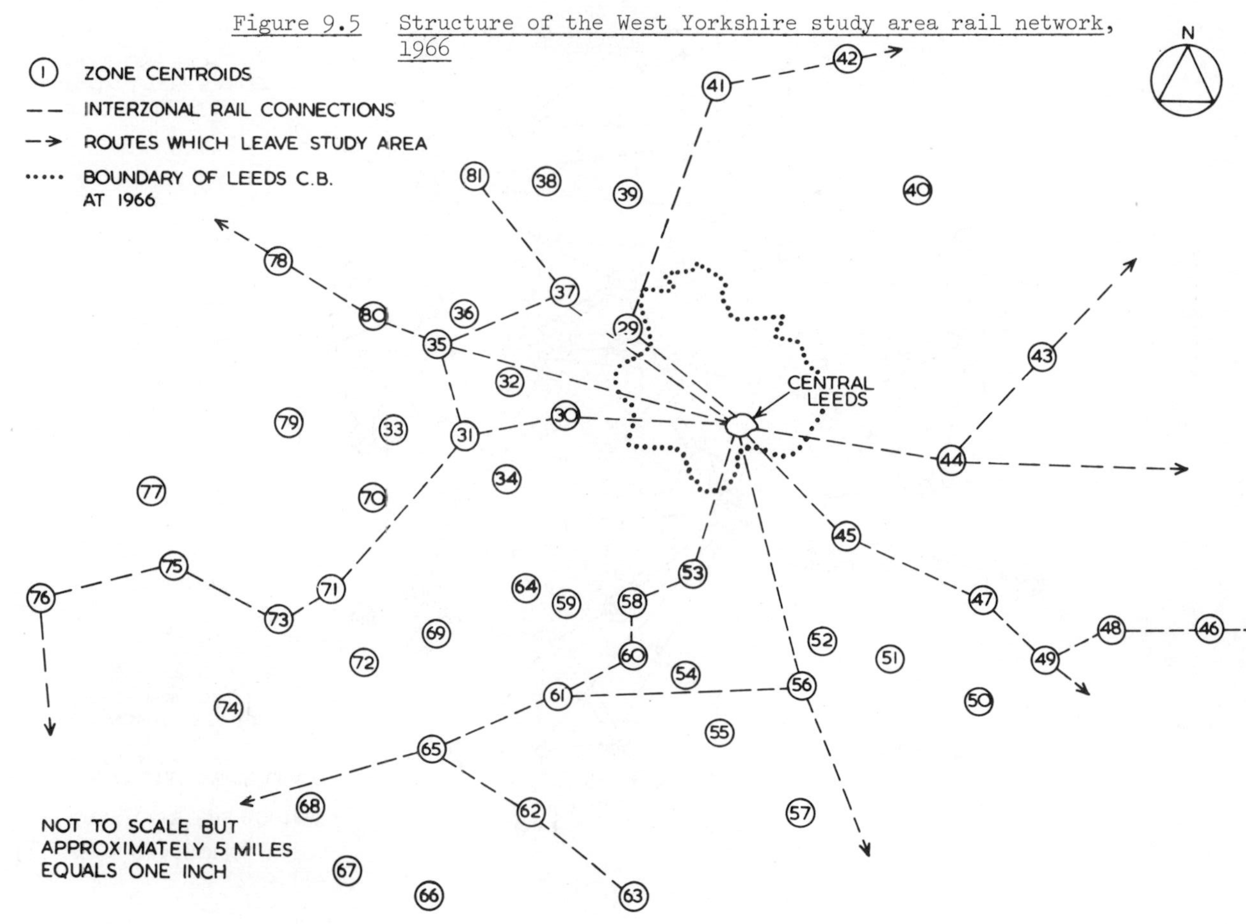

Figure 9.6 Structure of the West Yorkshire study area bus network

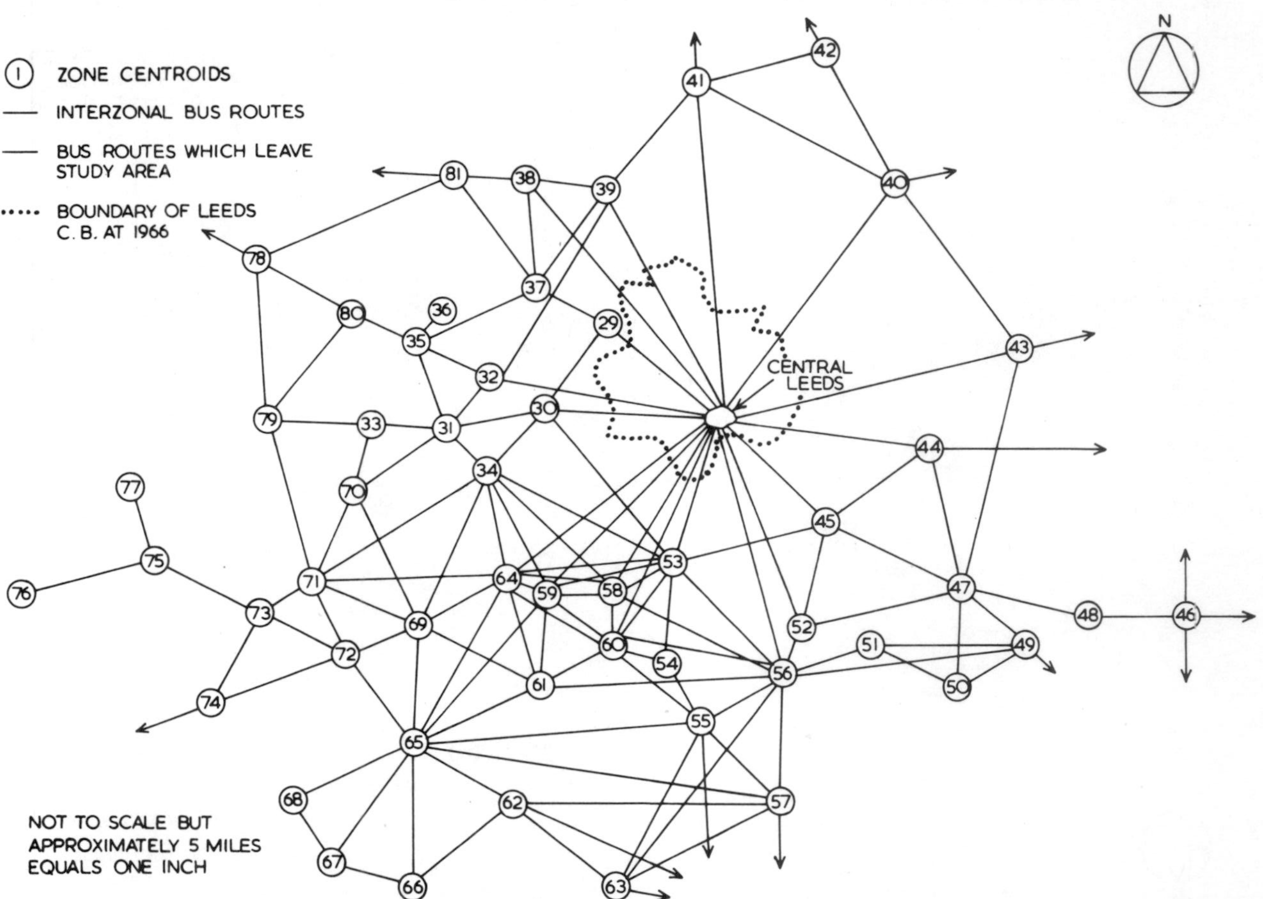

Figure 9.7 Structure of the West Yorkshire study area private transport network

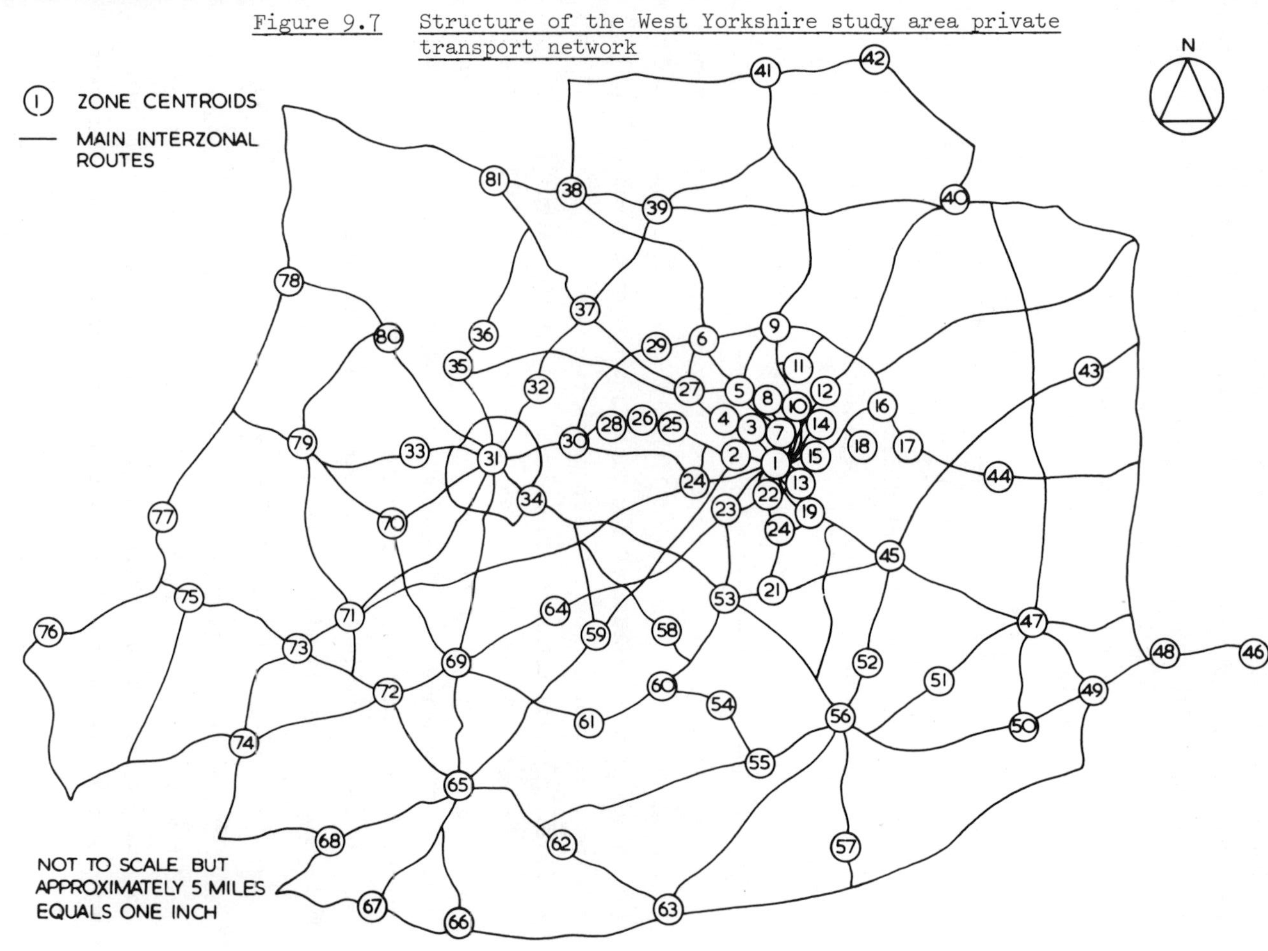

estimates are usually obtained for other models. The skim trees are built on the basis of 'generalised cost' of travel. In the case of the private network the 'generalised cost' for each link is a linear function of certain link characteristics.

The form of the generalised cost follows that suggested by McIntosh and Quarmby (1970) and may be written:

$$\begin{aligned} \text{Generalised cost} &= b_1 \text{ x in vehicle time on link} \\ &+ b_2 \text{ x distance of link} \\ &+ b_3 \text{ x excess costs of link} \end{aligned}$$

where b_1 is a perceived value of time; b_2 is a perceived operating cost per unit distance; and b_3 is a valuation of out-of-pocket costs.

In the case of the public transport network the formula is more complex because the fare paid on a public transport service per unit distance is not constant. Therefore the generalised cost cannot be expressed as a linear function of link characteristics, but only as a function of the elements of the total journey on a given public transport service. (For a fuller exposition see Bonsall, 1975-A). Analysis of public transport fare structures in West Yorkshire in 1966 revealed that the function was non-linear, but could be approximated by a piecewise linear function as shown in Figure 9.8. Each section of the curve (i.e. each piece between the points illustrated) can be described by a linear function of the form $A + Bd_{ij}^{k=2}$.

At the zone-to-zone level we can express the generalised cost of inter-zonal travel by either mode in the general formula:

$$c_{ij}^k = a_1^k t_{ij}^k + a_2^k d_{ij}^k + a_3^k e_{ij}^k + a_4 \phi_{ij}^k \qquad (9.1)$$

where c_{ij}^k, the generalised cost, is measured as a perceived generalised time in tenths of a minute and is incurred by moving from zone i to zone j by mode k, and where for k=1 such movement is by private transport and where k=2, it is by public transport. The other terms are: t_{ij}^k is the travel of time incurred between i and j by mode k in tenths of a minute; d_{ij}^k the distance between i and j by mode k, on the shortest route, in tenths of a minute; e_{ij}^k the excess time (in tenths of a minute) i.e. the waiting, walking and transfer time involved in any journey between i and j, by mode k; and ϕ_{ij}^k the

Figure 9.8 Public transport fares function

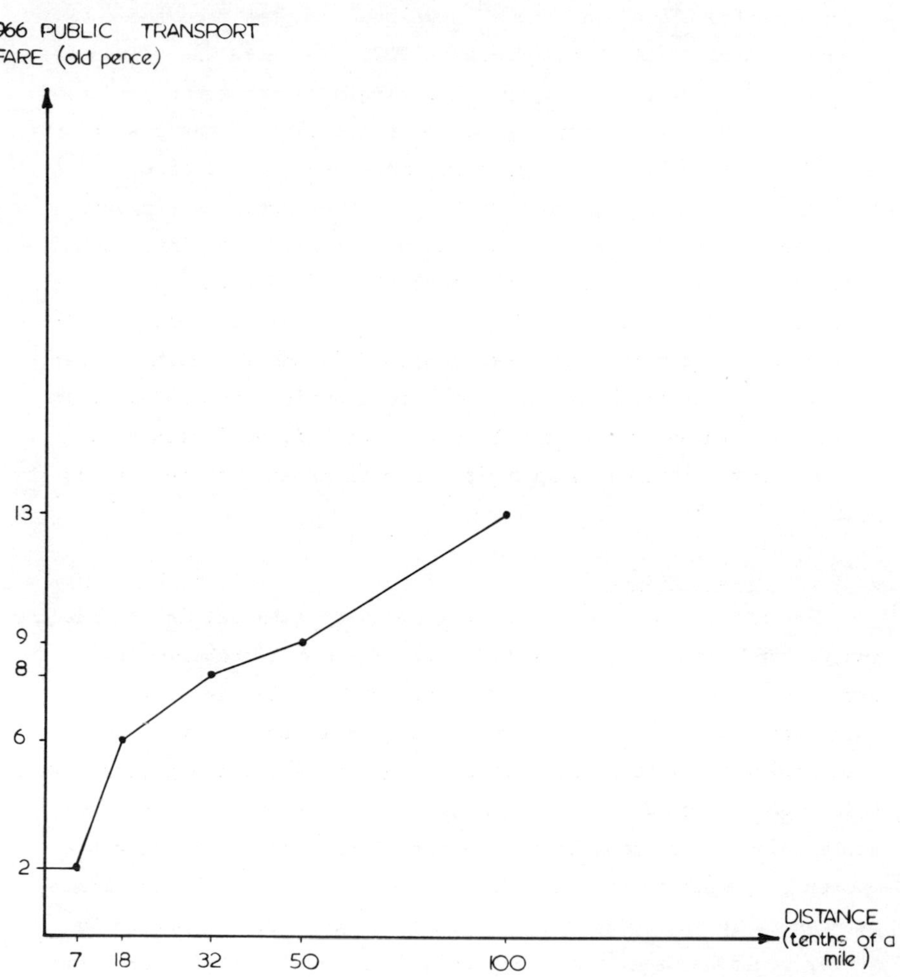

excess out-of-pocket costs (in old pence) such as parking charges incurred on a trip between i and j, by mode k. The parameters (coefficients) a_1^k, a_2^k, a_3^k and a_4^k have been adapted from those recommended by McIntosh and Quarmby (1970) and have the values set out in Section 9.5.3. The tree building programmes can produce inter-zonal costs but cannot produce an estimate of the cost of intra-zonal travel. That is to say the average cost of c_{ii} of a journey starting and terminating in the same zone. A programme has been developed (Bonsall, 1975-B) which calculates intra-zonal cost using geometric laws in the context of information available about the cost environment of the zone in question. Given that a generalised cost matrix has been computed in the foregoing manner, other tasks, particularly those of trip distribution, modal split, assignment and evaluation can be performed but, as indicated in Figure 9.2 the estimation of trip generations and attractions is the next step.

9.3.3 Trip generation

The method used for the trip generation submodel is the category analysis of Wootton and Pick (1967). The total number of trips produced in or attracted to each zone is found by dividing the population into groups using factors considered to be important in determining the total number of trips generated, and applying a mean trip rate to each group and summing over the groups for each zone. While this is conceptually simple, problems arise in finding the number of people in each group, defined in this case using income, car-ownership and household structure categories. A household survey could be used, but since this is non-existent in our example and often impractical, synthetic data for each 1966 car-ownership/ structure group were constructed. A number of probability distributions were estimated as follows.

Car ownership

The conditional probability of a household having N cars given income X, $P(N|X)$, is assumed to be a Γ distribution:

$$P(N|X) = a_N X^{b_N} e^{-dc_N X} \tag{9.2}$$

where a_N, b_N and c_N are parameters for households in groups owning

N cars. The values of a_N, b_N and c_N were taken from Wootton and Pick (1967):

		a	b	c
Number of cars owned	0	1.15	0	0.8
	1	1.64	2.29	1.31

The d parameters, which reflect different car-ownership-income relationships according to residential densities, were estimated for the West Yorkshire area as:

		d
Type of area	urban	0.6
	rural	1.1

However, in the latest work, these values are ignored and Equation (9.2) is used. The above values were used to give $P(0|X)$ and $P(1|X)$. $P(2|X)$ was found from

$$P(2|X) = 1 - P(0|X) - P(1|X) \qquad (9.3)$$

Income

The distribution of income is also portrayed by a Γ function:

$$P(X) = \int_{a_X}^{b_X} \frac{\alpha^{n+1}}{\Gamma(n+1)} X^n e^{-\alpha X} dX \qquad (9.4)$$

where $P(X)$ is the probability of a household having income X: a_X is the lower limit of the income group; b_X is the upper limit of the income group; and Γ is the standard Γ function. α and n are parameters which are functions of the mean ($\bar{X}$) and standard deviation (σ^2) of the income distribution, such that

$$\sigma^2 = \bar{X}/\alpha \qquad (9.5)$$

$$\bar{X} = (n+1)/\alpha \qquad (9.6)$$

α can be eliminated from these equations. $\bar{X}$ is found using an iterative technique and minimising the sum of the squares of the differences between the model estimate and observed values of the probabilities of households owning 0, 1 or 2+ cars. The value of n was taken from the West Midlands Transportation Study (Freeman, Fox, Wilbur Smith and Associates, 1968).

Household structure

A Poisson distribution is used for household size and a binomial distribution for employed residents. The probability of a household having n members $\phi(n)$ is given by:

$$\phi(n) = e^{-\alpha}\alpha^{n-1}/(n-1)! \tag{9.7}$$

where α is the average family size - 1. The probability that r members of an n member household are employed is given by $P(r|n)$ in Equation 9.8, where $P(n)$ is the probability that a member of an n-size household is employed:

$$P(r|n) = \frac{n!}{r!(n-r)!}\{P(n)\}^r\{1-P(n)\}^{n-r} \tag{9.8}$$

Equations (9.7) and (9.8) are multiplied together to give the probability that a household has n members of whom r are employed, $P(n,r)$:

$$P(n,r) = \frac{n!e^{-\alpha}\alpha^{n-1}}{r!(n-r)!(n-1)!}\{P(n)\}^r\{1-P(n)\}^{n-r} \tag{9.9}$$

At present, $P(n)$ is taken to be a constant z. By expanding Equation (9.9) for appropriate values of n and r the following values of the probability of being in a family structure group, $P(F)$ are obtained:

$$P(1) = e^{-\alpha}(1-z) \tag{9.10}$$

$$P(2) = (e^{-\alpha z}-e^{-\alpha})(1-z) \tag{9.11}$$

$$P(3) = e^{-\alpha}\{z+2\alpha z(1-z)\} \tag{9.12}$$

$$P(4) = e^{-\alpha z}\{z+\alpha z(1-z)\}-e^{-\alpha}\{z+2\alpha z(1-z)\} \tag{9.13}$$

$$P(5) = e^{-\alpha(1-z)}\{\alpha z(1-z)+1\}-e^{-\alpha}\{1+2\alpha z(1-z)\} \tag{9.14}$$

$$P(6) = 1-\Sigma_{f=1}^{5}P(f) \tag{9.15}$$

α is given by:

$$\alpha = \frac{\text{total household population}}{\text{total households}} \tag{9.16}$$

z is estimated from:

$$z = \frac{\text{number of employed residents}}{\text{total population}} \tag{9.17}$$

Multiplication of probabilities

The probability of a household being in category J, the combined car-ownership/income/household structure category, is found by multiplying the three probabilities together, thus:

$$P(J) = P(F)\int_{a_X}^{b_X} P(N|X)P(X)dX \qquad (9.18)$$

The number of households in category J in one zone, (N_i^J) is given by

$$N_i^J = N_i P(J) \qquad (9.19)$$

where N_i is the number of households in the zone. The number of trips generated by zone i (O_i^{pn}) is found from:

$$O_i^{pn} = \Sigma_j T^{pnJ} N_i^J \qquad (9.20)$$

where T^{pnJ} is the rate of trips made by individuals in households in category J for purpose p for person type n. Trips generated in the 1966 base year model are computed for the following purposes: work, social and recreational, shopping and 'other', which are all home-based. There is also a non-home-based category.

Trip attractions

Trip attractions are found in a similar manner to trip production:

$$D_j^p = \Sigma_L R^{Lp} E_j^L \qquad (9.21)$$

where D_j^p is the number of trips attracted in the zone for purpose p; R^{Lp} is the rate of trip attractions per unit of activity for purpose p; and E^L is the level of activity L in the zone. Since the system is assumed to be closed (and boundary crossing commuters are eliminated) the following constraint is imposed:

$$\Sigma_i O_i^p = \Sigma_j D_j^p \qquad (9.22)$$

The generation estimate is usually assumed to be more reliable than the attraction one, so $\hat{D}_j^P$ is obtained as

$$\hat{D}_j^p = D_j^p \frac{\Sigma_i O_i^p}{\Sigma_j D_j^p} \qquad (9.23)$$

Eight activities for trip attractions are defined. For education school attendance is used, for residence the number of private households is used, and for industries, utilities, transport and communications, shopping, other distribution activities and other employment, the level of employment in the appropriate sector is used.

9.3.4 Trip distribution and modal split

The distribution and modal split of trips for each purpose in turn is accomplished with a model first proposed by Wilson (1967). This is

$$T_{ij}^{kn} = A_i^n O_i^n B_j D_j \exp(-\beta^n c_{ij}^k) \tag{9.24}$$

where T_{ij}^{kn} is the number of trips which occur between origin, zone i and destination zone j by mode k and person-type n; O_i^n is the number of trips which originate in zone i by person-type n; D_j is the total number of trip destinations in zone j; c_{ij}^k is the generalised cost of travel from i to j by mode k; and β^n is the model parameter associated with trip lengths for each person-type n.

$$A_i^n = \{\Sigma_i \Sigma_{k\varepsilon M(n)} B_j D_j \exp(-\beta^n c_{ij}^k)\}^{-1} \tag{9.25}$$

$$B_j = \{\Sigma_i \Sigma_n \Sigma_{k\varepsilon M(n)} A_i^n O_i^n \exp(-\beta^n c_{ij}^k)\}^{-1} \tag{9.26}$$

$k\varepsilon M(n)$ are the modes k available to persons of type n. The A_i^n and B_j terms, which are balancing factors in the model, ensure that the following constraints are met:

$$\Sigma_j \Sigma_{k\varepsilon M(n)} T_{ij}^{kn} = O_i^n \tag{9.27}$$

and

$$\Sigma_i \Sigma_n \Sigma_{k\varepsilon M(n)} T_{ij}^{kn} = D_j \tag{9.28}$$

in addition, the model satisfies the cost constraints

$$\Sigma_i \Sigma_j \Sigma_{k\varepsilon M(n)} T_{ij}^{kn} c_{ij}^k = C^n \tag{9.29}$$

C^n is the total expenditure on travel by persons of type n, computed in terms of generalised costs. The c_{ij}^k's were calculated from the skim trees, the production of which was discussed earlier. The model outlined in Equations(9.24) to (9.29), in addition to achieving the geographical distribution of trips in the region, at the same time, estimates the modal split of these trips. The aggregate choice of mode of transport is dependent upon the type of cost function used (in the West Yorkshire case-negative exponential), difference between modal costs, and the values of the relevant β^n parameter. The modal split may be stated explicitly as:

$$M_{ij}^{kn} = \frac{T_{ij}^{kn}}{T_{ij}^{*n}} = \frac{\exp(-\beta^n c_{ij}^k)}{\Sigma_{k\varepsilon M(n)} \exp(-\beta^n c_{ij}^k)} \qquad (9.30)$$

In Equation (9.30), T_{ij}^{*n} may be regarded as T_{ij}^{kn} but now summed over all modes k, and M_{ij}^{kn} is the modal split for each person-type and each pair of zones. For two modes (as in the West Yorkshire model), Equation (9.30) can also be written for k=1 as

$$M_{ij}^{1n} = \frac{1}{1 + \exp\{-\beta^n(c_{ij}^2 - c_{ij}^1)\}} \qquad (9.31)$$

n=1 has been taken to be private transport owners, since if walking trips are omitted, (as here and as in most other large-scale computer models used in urban transport planning) these are a normally used proxy for the people with a choice of transport mode. Equations (9.24) and (9.31) form a general statement of the procedure used in the West Yorkshire study, in respect of the estimation of trip distribution and modal split.

9.3.5 Assignment

When the trips, for the West Yorkshire region have been distributed and modally split, they can be assigned to the regional public and private networks. For the purposes of the present broad discussion of the assignment procedures used, there is no need to distinguish sharply between the assignment of trips to the two kinds of networks. Generally, as Wilson (1974, Chapter 9) has pointed out, assignment may be described as a route choice problem, and, more rigorously, may be depicted, given the set of minimum paths produced earlier, $R^k(i,j)$, as:

$$x^{lk} = \Sigma_{ij \text{ such that } l\varepsilon R^k(i,j)} T_{ij}^{kn} \qquad (9.32)$$

in which x^{lk} are loadings of vehicles travelling in each mode k, on each link l. T_{ij}^{kn} now have to be vehicle trips instead of person trips. Equation (9.32) can be assumed to be a formulation of the 'all-or-nothing' procedure, like other assignment algorithms and including the capacity restrained method, follows Wardrop's (1952) principles. These are enunciated by Potts and Oliver (1972) as extremal principles of traffic flow and amount to two criteria for determining the distribution of traffic over alternative routes. These are: (i) the journey times on all routes actually used are equal, and less than those which would be experienced by a single vehicle on any unused route; and (ii) the average journey time is a minimum. Potts and Oliver call traffic patterns which are optimised according to the first principle 'user-optimised'. From the user's point of view, the first criterion achieves a 'selfish equilibrium' and as Hutchinson (1974) points out is equivalent to average cost pricing in economic theory. As is the case with most assignment algorithms Wardrop's first principle is at the root of the capacity restrained procedure adopted in the West Yorkshire model. Potts and Oliver refer to traffic patterns which can be defined as optimal according to the second principle as 'system optimised' and Hutchinson notes that in this instance, the user of the transport system is seeking to pay the marginal cost of travel. Thus, the main difference between Wardrop's first and second principles of route choice is one of the assumption made as to whether the user of the transport system thinks he is paying average or marginal costs. Since, as has already been said, most assignment methods make the first assumption the difference tends to be a theoretical one.

In addition, in all transport models, the implementation of either of these principles, as is evident from Section 9.3.2, depends on the prior determination of the minimum paths (cheapest/shortest routes) on a network. In the West Yorkshire model, where link impedances are expressed in terms of generalised costs rather than travel time, the computation of cheapest routes, through each of the public and private transport networks takes precedence over the assignment of trips. Thus, as noted above, the West Yorkshire model contains a capacity restrained procedure based on Wardrop's notion of a 'selfish equilibrium'. Being responsive to capacity restraint, the costs of travel on each link are, of necessity, flow dependent and therefore, there has to be a feedback, as indicated by Figure 9.2, so that flows of traffic initially assigned to a network affect the way in which link costs are calculated. Generalised costs thus change, via speed flow curves, in response to the volume of inter-urban flows estimated from the trip distribution and modal split models. As remarked in Section 9.3.3, specifically in Equation (9.1), generalised costs are hypothesised to be the linear sum of the travel time/distance and excess travel time on each link in a network. Travel time is clearly a function of the speed of travel and therefore of the flow of vehicles on each link. The speed of travel can clearly be related to the flow on each link and thus the effect of the changing relationship between speed and flow on generalised costs of travel can be traced. Ten relationships between speed and flow have been adopted in the capacity restrained algorithm of the West Yorkshire model. These relationships are illustrated generally by the speed/flow curve of Figure 9.9. As can be seen from Figure 9.9, the speed of travel on each link in the network (VK) is determined by its 'natural' capacity (QK), which like speed tends to decline (due to the shape of the speed/flow curve) with increasing amounts of flow (f) loaded onto a link. Since as we have already made clear the speed which a vehicle is able to travel on each link also affects travel time and therefore generalised costs, thus, an iteration between the network and tree building parts of the transport model, via the distribution/modal split submodels, becomes essential. This iteration is argued to converge when the statistic δ (Van Vliet, 1976) is less than 5%:

$$\delta = \frac{\Sigma_l r_l f_l - \Sigma_{ij} T_{ij}^{(k=1)} c_{ij}^{(k=1)}}{\Sigma_{l \varepsilon \text{ highway links in Leeds County Borough}} r_l f_l} \qquad (9.33)$$

where δ is the degree of convergence in inter-zonal and link costs. (It would be equal to 0 if there were complete convergence). It could also be taken as an indicator of the sparsity of a network. Networks in the West Yorkshire study area can be considered to be quite sparse; r_l is the cost of travel on each link in the network; f_l is the flow of vehicles on each link in the network; $T_{ij}^{(k=1)}$ is the volume of private transport trips from zones i to j; and $c_{ij}^{(k=1)}$ are the inter-zonal costs of travel. It is necessary to

Figure 9.9 A general version of the speed/flow curves used in the West Yorkshire model

V SPEED
f FLOW
QK NATURAL CAPACITY
VK SPEED AT NATURAL CAPACITY
FFL FREE FLOW LIMIT
FFV FREE FLOW SPEED

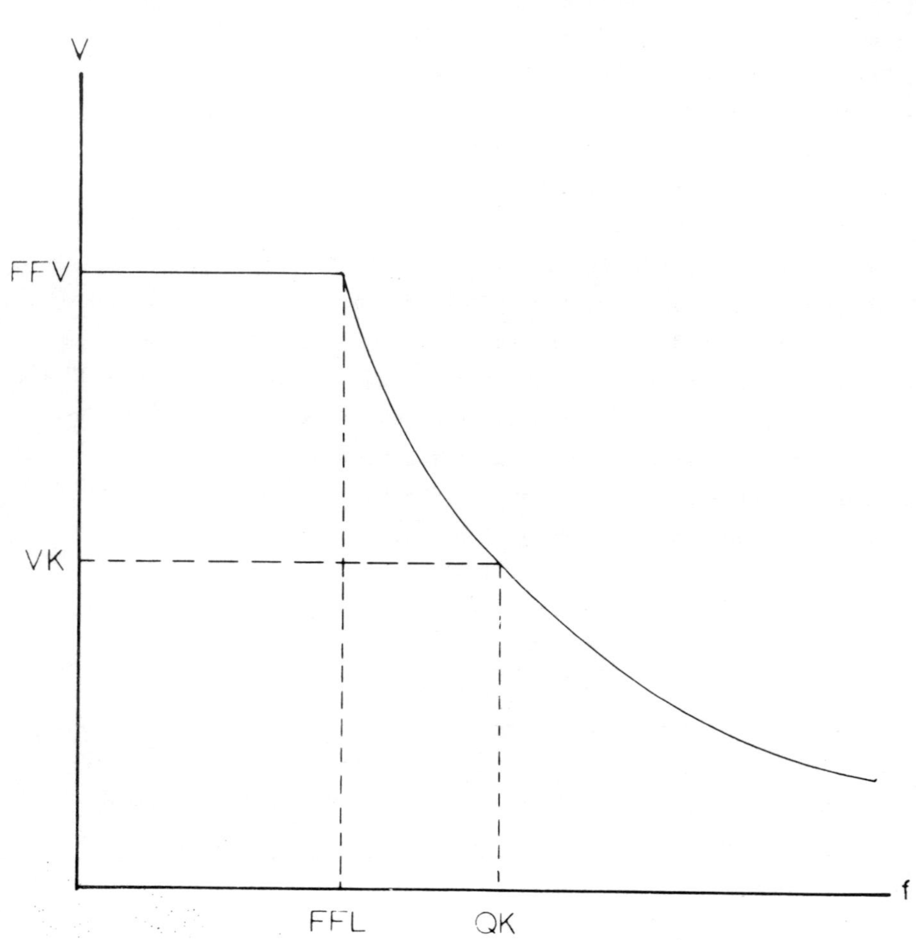

note that at the assignment stage flows are measured in passenger car units (pcu's) as opposed to the person trips of the distribution/ modal split submodel. Assigned flows may also be described as morning peak hour flows. The base year journey-to-work matrix derived from 1966 Census data was factored with West Yorkshire Transportation Study (WYTS) Traffic Research Corporation (1966) data to arrive at these morning peak hour flows. The proportions used to factor the base year Census data are discussed later.

All but one of the ten speed/flow curves, referred to, apply to different types of road in Leeds County Borough. The shape of the curve varies according to the type of road. Our road network outside Leeds is considerably sparser than it is within Leeds making individual road capacity data misleading. This fact, together with the lack of accessible data on road capacities outside Leeds, resulted in our decision not to incorporate capacity restrained procedures for links outside Leeds. For such links we have assumed that the observed speeds will hold no matter what flow passes along them.

This, in effect is 'all-or-nothing' assignment, and is applied, in this way, not only to non-Leeds County Borough private transport but to all public transport as well. In other words, at the time of writing, the West Yorkshire model assumes, rightly or wrongly, that congestion does not occur in public transport networks. Potts and Oliver have summarised the method thus: "Of the cheapest route assignment procedures, the 'all-or-nothing' assignment is the simplest and most common. Link costs are supposed constant and flow independent, and the traffic between each O-D pair is all assigned to the cheapest route between the pair and not assigned to any other route. For each centroid as home node, the cheapest route trees are loaded from all other centroids back to the home node, accumulating link flows as the calculation proceeds."

Loading trips on the network is accomplished as part of the assignment algorithm followed. In the West Yorkshire model incremental loading is used, and four increments are employed to load all trips on each link in the particular network. Incremental loading has been frowned upon in the past (Lane, Powell and Prestwood Smith, 1971) but can be argued to be a robust method of trip loading and

and proves particularly so on the, perhaps, less dense networks constructed for our West Yorkshire study area.

9.3.6 Evaluation

Figures 9.2 and 9.3 show evaluation methods to be part of the transport model and these indeed become an essential component of it when forecasts are made with the model of the impact of possible future options in transport policy. In this chapter, however, we are concerned to describe how the base year (1966) model was built, how it was calibrated, how it has performed as a base year model, (at the base year these last two matters can be deemed to be much the same thing) and how the construction of it has led on to empirical research particularly in the disaggregation of trip distribution and modal split models. Details of evaluation procedures are, therefore, not given.

9.4 A data base for the model

9.4.1 Data sources

Sections 9.2 and 9.3 of this chapter provide a brief insight into the kind of now almost traditional transport model which has been built for the Leeds and West Yorkshire area. Later, we give a brief review of a different and more detailed disaggregation of the transport model, particularly in respect of the trip distribution and modal split submodels, and describe how these were fitted to a modified data base for the region. As a preliminary, it is necessary to outline the 1966 data base for the 'traditional' model. An unusual, if not unique, feature of our data base is that it is compiled almost entirely of what has been called secondary data. It is customary to carry out household and other surveys as a precursor to the construction of an urban transport model of this type. The models, including those detailed later fitted to our amalgam of 1966 data, therefore, exhibit some of the deficiences brought about by the absence of the familiar custom-made data base. Deficiencies become glaring in the model's inability to deal realistically with other than journeys-to-work. In part reliance has to be placed on surveys made outside the region. This was especially true in estimating trip generations and attractions. As will be noticed from Section 9.4.2, probabilities

Table 9.2 Data base, 1966

Source of data	Component of computer simulation in which extensively used
1966 Sample Census of Population	
(i) Estimates from special usual workplace and residence data	Trip end data. Trip distribution and modal split
(ii) Published tables of population and employment (County Report)	Trip end data
(iii) OPCS desk analyses of household population and employment	Trip end data
(iv) Enumeration District population and employment	Trip end data
West Midlands Transportation Study	Trip rates, for trip end data
SELNEC Transportation Study	Trip rates, for trip end data
MAU note 179	Generalised costs for skim trees
M62 survey data (modified)	Private transport network
Published public transport routes; fare tables and timetables	Public transport network
1" OS maps	Public and private transport networks
Sheffield and Rotherham Land Use/Transportation Study	Speed/flow curves
WYTS	Morning peak and other purposes - assignment checking data
Leeds CB traffic cordon counts	Assignment checking data

also had to be estimated to fill out the inter-zonal trip matrix. In this sense, the empirical version of our model can only be said to be supported by at least 'semi-real' data. Nonetheless, such a model can be argued to be valid for strategic planning purposes, and is demonstrably cheaper than a survey-based model in manpower and financial resources terms. It was felt that the purposes for which the 'traditional' model was designed and built (those of strategic planning rather than the civil engineering ones of road and junction design) justify the decision to rely primarily on secondary data. If there is an inherent concern with urban strategy - the location of major land uses and their concomitant transport flows - why the capacity restrained or 'congested' form of assignment described in earlier parts of this chapter? Putman (1974) has shown that, in so far as the linking of land use and transport models is concerned, that locations are a function of congested travel in transport networks, and has drawn attention to the implications of congestion of this kind for policies which have regard to urban form. Although our particular simulation is not yet explicit about the feedback between the location of land use and transport systems, the need for congested assignment methods even in a strategic level planning model is thus clear.

9.4.2 A more detailed account of the 1966 data

Two approaches to the problem of giving a more detailed account of the data are possible. First, a somewhat prosaic list of the major variables used in our simulation and their numerical indexing could be given; second, an exposition of the major data sources used could be made. The second of these approaches is chosen, and Table 9.2 provides a resume of the data used to help verify the base year model. In Figure 9.1 and Table 9.1 the study area, its zones and zonal populations were described. In Section 9.2 the total West Yorkshire population was noted as about 2,070,000; other similar characteristics of the study area are given in Table 9.3. From Table 9.2 it is evident that the major source of data, which enables 'observed' estimates to be made of trip and planning data - information on home-based trip generations and attractions - was a variety of analyses from the 1966 Sample Census of Population.

Table 9.3 Some characteristics of the study area, 1966

Total household population	2,021,920	
Total number of households	717,940	
Total households with no car	453,427	63%
Total households with one car	234,276	33%
Total households with two or more cars	30,237	4%
Total employed residents	992,730	
Average household size	2.82	
Total number of person trips to work per day	719,170	
Income in £ estimated from the category analysis model (Mean Annual Household)	897	

Confining the testing of the category analysis to a comparison with Census data raises two problems. One has already been referred to: only the work journey purpose can be properly modelled. The second problem is one of definition: the journey-to-work data is derived from the usual work place and residence question on the Census form, and thus implies one return trip per day. The model, however, produces estimates of the actual daily trip generation. The number of trips will be greater than the number of employed residents by people who make more than one journey-to-work in a twenty-four hour period. These will be people who either work on a split shift system or return home to eat. To set against this, the trip total will be reduced by absenteeism, both due to sickness and holidays. It is assumed that these opposing effects will cancel out. In addition to problems created by the use of such a ratio, mean zonal income, necessary to a category analysis, is not available from Census material for small areas. This has had to be estimated within our model, and depends on the relationship between car-ownership and mean household income established by Lewis (1969).

In more detail, the planning data required for the trip ends estimated by the category analysis model is similar to that described in Table 9.3, but is needed for each zone. These data amount to the zone's total population, its total employed residents, its total private households, the total car-ownership in each zone and in each of the car-ownership groups defined in Table 9.3 but expressed as a number of households in each of the groups. Mean zonal income was estimated as suggested in the previous paragraph. Non-household data, in the form of aggregates of employment in some eight industrial and retail categories {the same as those used by Wootton and Pick (1967)}, are also required for the category analysis model. At the ward level, used to delineate the zone boundaries for Leeds and Bradford, the Census of Population, and in particular the Ward and Parish Library can supply these data even though SIC groupings in the Census do not match exactly those asked for by the Wootton and Pick model. At the local authority level, the employment data was extracted from published Census Economic Activity Tables. For areas with a population of less than 50,000 this kind of information is not published, but like household data for areas of this size was available as a special tabulation from the Office of Population Census and Surveys. Since the more recent type of computerisation of Census data, such information is more easily available. Most of the data required by the category analysis part of the West Yorkshire model has already been discussed. As suggested by Table 9.2 the other critical part of the data in this submodel are the trip rates. In the absence of suitable special surveys, the rates used were those reported for the SELNEC Transportation Study Area. As far as the category analysis is concerned, this is the least satisfactory aspect of the data base. Nonetheless, borrowed rates of this kind have provided adequate numbers for the model.

As can again be surmised from Table 9.2 the basis of trip distribution data was primarily the 1966 Sample Census of Population. As has already been stated, these give the numbers of 'non-peaked' interzonal work journeys, ie. at the ward and local authority levels. In our empirical implementation of the distribution and modal split model defined by Equations (9.24) to (9.31), as the reader will have discerned from previous discussion, two modes of travel are encompassed by this submodel. These we have called public and private transport. As evidenced by our network diagrams public transport covers trips made within the region by bus and train. Private transport refers to travel by private motor car and privately owned motorcycle and sidecar combinations. Private transport, however, excludes the large number of walk and cycle trips which occurred within the study area, particularly in close proximity to the central areas of the County Boroughs (e.g. roughly 17% for Central Leeds). These latter kinds of trips need to be deducted from the Census data set in order to avoid biased estimates of mean trip costs incurred by travelling by public and private vehicles. Unfortunately, the secondary sources of data available to us, and especially the Sample Census (and indeed all Censuses), only provide 'observations' of trips by mode of travel, T^{k}_{ij}, in our language, whereas the model depicted by Equations (9.25) to (9.32) requires that we 'observe' T^{kn}_{ij}, where all terms are as defined before. This fact necessitated that we synthesise data on T^{kn}_{ij} from 1966 data on T^{k}_{ij}. This was done with Equations (9.34) to (9.36) below:

$$N^{kn}_{ij} = A^{n}_{i}O^{n}_{i}B^{k}_{ij}T^{k}_{ij}p(k|n) \qquad (9.34)$$

where

$$A^{n}_{i} = \{\Sigma_{k}\Sigma_{j}B^{k}_{ij}T^{k}_{ij}p(k|n)\}^{-1} \qquad (9.35)$$

$$B^{k}_{ij} = \{\Sigma_{n}A^{n}_{i}O^{n}_{i}p(k|n)\}^{-1} \qquad (9.36)$$

and where N^{kn}_{ij} is the number of trips from origin zone i to destination zone j by mode k and by person type n; T^{k}_{ij} is the number of observed trips by mode k between i and j; O^{n}_{i} is the number of trip origins from zone i by persons of type n calculated by dividing the total observed origins in to the proportion of different household types in zone i; and p(k|n) is the probability that a person of type n will travel by mode k. Equations (9.35) and (9.36) ensure that

$$\Sigma_{jk}N^{kn}_{ij} = O^{n}_{i} \qquad (9.37)$$

and

$$\Sigma_{n}N^{kn}_{ij} = T^{k}_{ij} \qquad (9.38)$$

p(k|n), the probability of k given n was based upon information in the published report of the West Yorkshire Transportation Study (Traffic Research Corporation, 1969). If n=1, n represents car-owners and if 2, n represents non car-owners. Since there are two modes, k, described earlier, four T^{kn}_{ij} matrices are therefore possible; only three were, in fact, arrived at via the methods portrayed by our immediately preceding equations. This is because all non car-owners in the model are assumed to be captive to public transport. The 'empirical' probabilities for the modal split in 1966 arrived at by the above method were 0.31 for car-owners using public transport and 0.69 for those making use of their car for the work trip. For the calibration of the distribution/modal split submodel,

$$N^{kn}_{ij} \simeq T^{kn}_{ij} \tag{9.39}$$

but N^{kn}_{ij} is one stage removed from, in data terms, T^{k}_{ij} the only variables 'observed' in the data: hence our earlier comment about calibration to only semi-real data.

Transport network data used in this particular model, can also be argued to be semi-real in terms of transport modelling as it is usually done and written about, but only because different from usual data sources were used to build the necessary inventories. The transport networks, as in any transport model, reflect the modes of travel. For this particular simulation as noted earlier there are two networks - public and private. In order to define the public transport network (i.e. a network, which comprised a representation of the combined bus and rail networks for the region), an inventory of services on each type of route had to be compiled. This inventory was confined to services with a frequency greater than one per hour, unless the inclusion of less frequent services was deemed necessary in order to ensure connectivity between the links in the network. The 1966 inventory was collated from published information and personal communications from the following sources: (i) Leeds City Transport; (ii) West Riding Automobile Co. Ltd.; (iii) West Yorkshire Road Car Co. Ltd.; (iv) Yorkshire Woollen District Transport Co. Ltd.; (v) Yorkshire Traction Co. Ltd.; (vi) Bradford City Transport; (vii) Huddersfield Corporation Transport; (viii) Halifax and Calder Valley Passenger Transport; and (ix) British Rail Eastern Region Passenger Timetable. The inventory included: (a) service headway - the time interval between services; and (b) service time between recorded stages. Where there was more than one service between the same two stages with different service times, the time recorded for each link on such a route was calculated as the average of the times weighted by the relative frequencies of each of the services on each route. Our private transport network (our terminology for our particular representation of the region's road system) was in part extracted from a larger network for an ongoing Impact Study of the M62 trans-Pennine motorway. That particular study area was much larger than the one adopted for the West Yorkshire model (it included, for example, the Greater Manchester area), and the level of network resolution, especially in the city centres of Bradford and Leeds, was often not high enough for our purpose. This made it necessary to introduce extra links to the private transport network and these were coded using the time and distance relationships of Copley and Judge (1972). Ordnance Survey maps, especially the 1", Seventh Series, for the region were also a valuable source of supplementary data for the compilation of both public and transport networks. This has already been indicated by Table 9.2.

We have, by and large, outlined our main data sources for what we have termed a 'traditional' transport model. The remaining ones mentioned in Table 9.2 are important to the assignment phase of our transport simulation and are referred to again later when we discuss the methods used in checking the assignment algorithm of the West Yorkshire model. Suffice it to say for now that the inter-zonal person work trips produced by the distribution - modal/split submodel have to be factored to the morning peak and other purpose flows, measured as passenger car units (pcu's - 1c) prior to loading on either public or private transport networks. Data for such factoring (the proportion of work trips made between 7.00 hours and 9.00 hours and the ratios of other trips to work trips) was obtained from the West Yorkshire Transportation Study (WYTS), (Traffic Research Corporation, 1969). Data on the speed/flow curves was gleaned from the Sheffield and Rotherham Land Use Transportation Study (A.M. Voorhees and Associates, 1973). Reference was made earlier to, and a general illustration given (see Figure 9.9) of, the kind of speed/flow curves obtained from this data source. The ten types of roads, on which data are given, and which are identified in the West Yorkshire model are: Urban - (i) dual carriageway two or three lane motorways; (ii) dual carriageway two or three lane all purpose roads with limited access and an 80 km/h speed limit; (iii) dual carriageway two or three lane all purpose roads of restricted capacity with a 65 km/h speed limit; (iv) single carriageway two or three lane all purpose outer area roads with a 50 km/h speed limit; (v) single carriageway two or three lane all purpose intermediate area roads with a 50 km/h speed limit; (vi) single carriageway two or three lane all purpose central business area roads with a 50 km/h speed limit. Suburban - (vii) major radial routes or outer ringroads, with roadsides, assumed 65% development; (viii) part dual carriageway, with no major junction opposite; (ix) single (approximately 50% of each) roads with 65 km/h speed limit, with less than one major junction per km); and (x) all roads outside Leeds County Borough. An eleventh type comprising the 'notional' links (see Figure 9.4) in the road network, also referred to in Section 9.3.2, was also added. The curve used varies with the particular jurisdiction code (signifying a type of road) allocated to a transport link. Traffic flow counts provided by Leeds County Borough for various dates and cordon counts from WYTS enable a check to be made on the volume of traffic assigned to each link in the network.

9.4.3 Some general observations on the data base

It can be seen from Section 9.4.2 that data for the 1966 model's calibration was compiled from a varied collection of sources. Although such an approach in data collection offers the advantages discussed in Section 9.4.1, it can bedevil, to an extent, the calibration (described in the immediately ensuing section of this chapter) of the transport model. Many of the data sources mean that a simulation of the kind built on the West Yorkshire region, becomes much more of an approximation of the real traffic flows in the region, than a computer model usually is. A major problem with trying to amalgamate a wide variety (it is especially a wide variety in the transport model case) of data sources is that more and more error becomes built into the model and this is particularly important in an entire set of submodels in which error is readily transmitted from one to the other. Where some elements of the data needed are so inadequate, it cannot be argued that any particular theory of transport generation or flow embodied in the model is empirically substantiated. All that can be said is that the kind of use of the model proposed in Section 9.4.1 is feasible. So long as this kind of restricted use of a simulation of this type, verified only approximately by its data base, is borne in mind, and too much is not attempted with such a model, all will be well.

9.5 Calibration procedures, results and performance

9.5.1 Introduction: calibration methods

As was noted earlier in this chapter, calibration of each of the submodels is the collection of processes in which the assembled 1966 data is fitted to the theoretical models which form the basis of the West Yorkshire simulation, and which were outlined in Section 9.2. It was also pointed out in the first chapter Section 1.4, that there was a need to introduce into the transport model the kind of 'automatic' calibration methods suggested by Batty and Mackie (1972). The results of the calibration phase of the model-building exercise can also be considered as a measure of the base year performance of the model. Calibration for most of the transport submodels can be asserted to be either a non-linear maximisation or a non-linear minimisation problem (in terms of the calculus). The formal mathematical procedures are described by Box, Davies and Swann (1969), but transport calibration problems often turn out to be too untidy for analytical methods and numerical techniques have to be used. In our case, both univariate and multivariate problems emerge, and the methods used are similar to those employed on corresponding problems in earlier chapters. The procedures used in each submodel are now described, following the sequence of Figure 9.2.

9.5.2 Calibration of the category analysis model

The main calibration problem in the category analysis submodel concerned the estimation of zonal incomes. Powell's (1964) method was programmed for this purpose and worked satisfactorily. These results formed one of the main inputs.

The base year category analysis procedure, as noted in Section 9.3.3, provides estimates of generations and attractions for the usual trip purposes. However, only generations and attractions for the work trip purpose can be checked against Census data. In terms of the previous section, and of work trips only, the performance and calibration of this particular submodel has been measured and achieved by maximising the value of r^2 for zonal generations and attractions. The 'observed' set of all private transport trips on the journey-to-work, given in the 1966 Census data, are therefore used. These are not available by person type n, as we would require, and estimated trip generations for each zone, O_i^n, have to be summed over n, indicated by an * in the following equations. Thus in the case of trip generations:

$$r^2 = \left[\frac{N\Sigma_i O_i^* \hat{O}_i^* - (\Sigma_i O_i^*)(\Sigma_i \hat{O}_i^*)}{\sqrt{\{N\Sigma_i \hat{O}_i^{*2} - (\Sigma_i \hat{O}_i^*)^2\}}\sqrt{\{N\Sigma O_i^{*2} - (\Sigma_i O_i^*)^2\}}}\right]^2 \qquad (9.40)$$

and for trip attractions:

$$r^2 = \left[\frac{N\Sigma_j D_j \hat{D}_j - (\Sigma_j D_j)(\Sigma_j \hat{D}_j)}{\sqrt{\{N\Sigma_j \hat{D}_j^2 - (\Sigma \hat{D}_j)^2\}}\sqrt{\{N\Sigma_j D_j^2 - (\Sigma_j D_j)^2\}}}\right]^2 \qquad (9.41)$$

In the case of Equation (9.40), r^2 is equal to 0.9803 and for Equation (9.41), r^2 is equal to 0.9879, but it should be noted that the sum of zonal attractions was also, as is usual, scaled to correspond to total predicted trip generations within the region.

In addition to overall measures of performance given by system-wide values of r^2, the regression of the 81 zonal 'observed' and model estimated values of home-based work trip generations are illustrated in Figures 9.10 and 9.11. How well the category analysis has performed in predicting 1966 generations for each of the 81 zones in the region can also be seen from Table 9.4. As is shown these model estimates compare quite favourably with 'observed' values. This is true, even at the zonal level perhaps with the exception of zones 1 - City ward in Leeds, the central areas which has a considerable number of work trip attractions, but which are seriously underestimated by the model - and 41, 42, 65 and 66 - the latter being some of the larger towns and their environs. For the most part however, the category analysis provides a good enough estimate of work trip generations and attractions for strategic purposes.

9.5.3 The calibration and performance of the trip distribution and modal split submodel

The calibration of the combined trip distribution/modal split includes both the estimation of β^n of Equation (9.23) and of the coefficients $a_1^k - a_4^k$ of Equation (9.1). Assuming values of these

Figure 9.10 Home-work trip generations

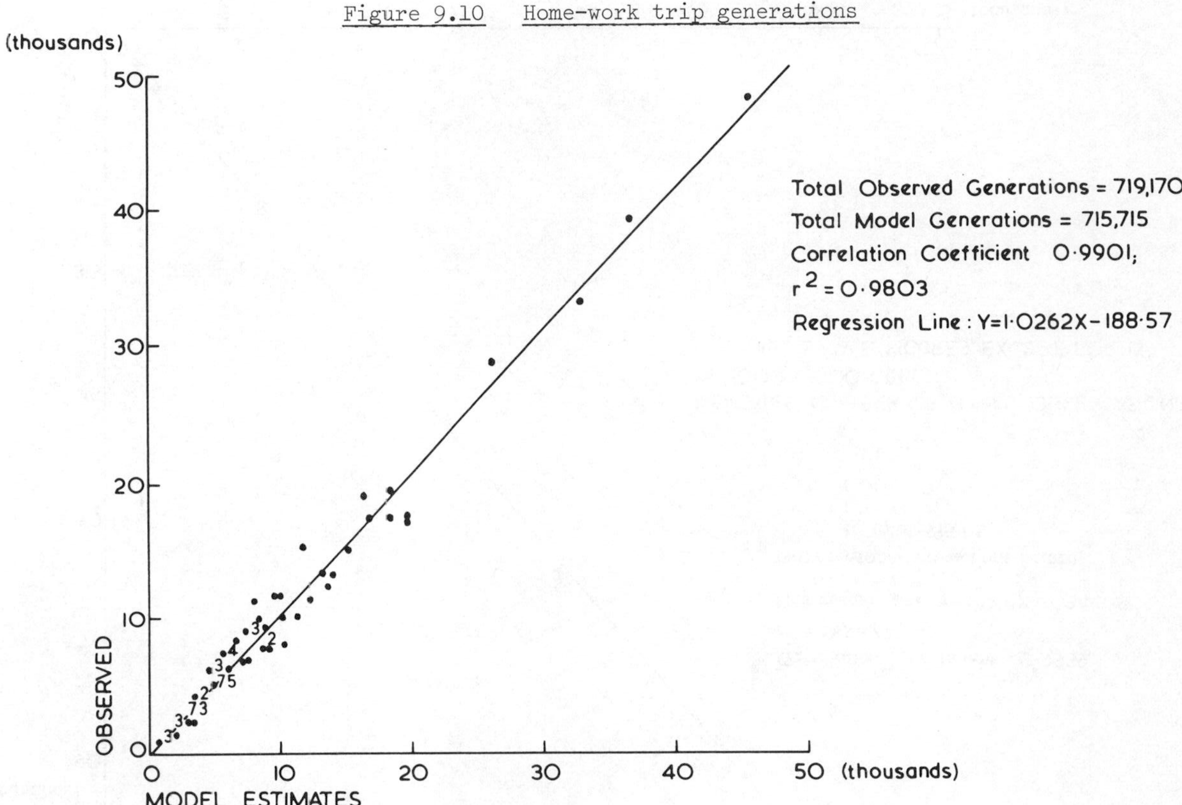

7 – INDICATES NUMBER OF ZONAL OBSERVATIONS IN 1000 X 1000 CELL (ALL SINGLE FIGURES)

Figure 9.11 Home-work trip attractions

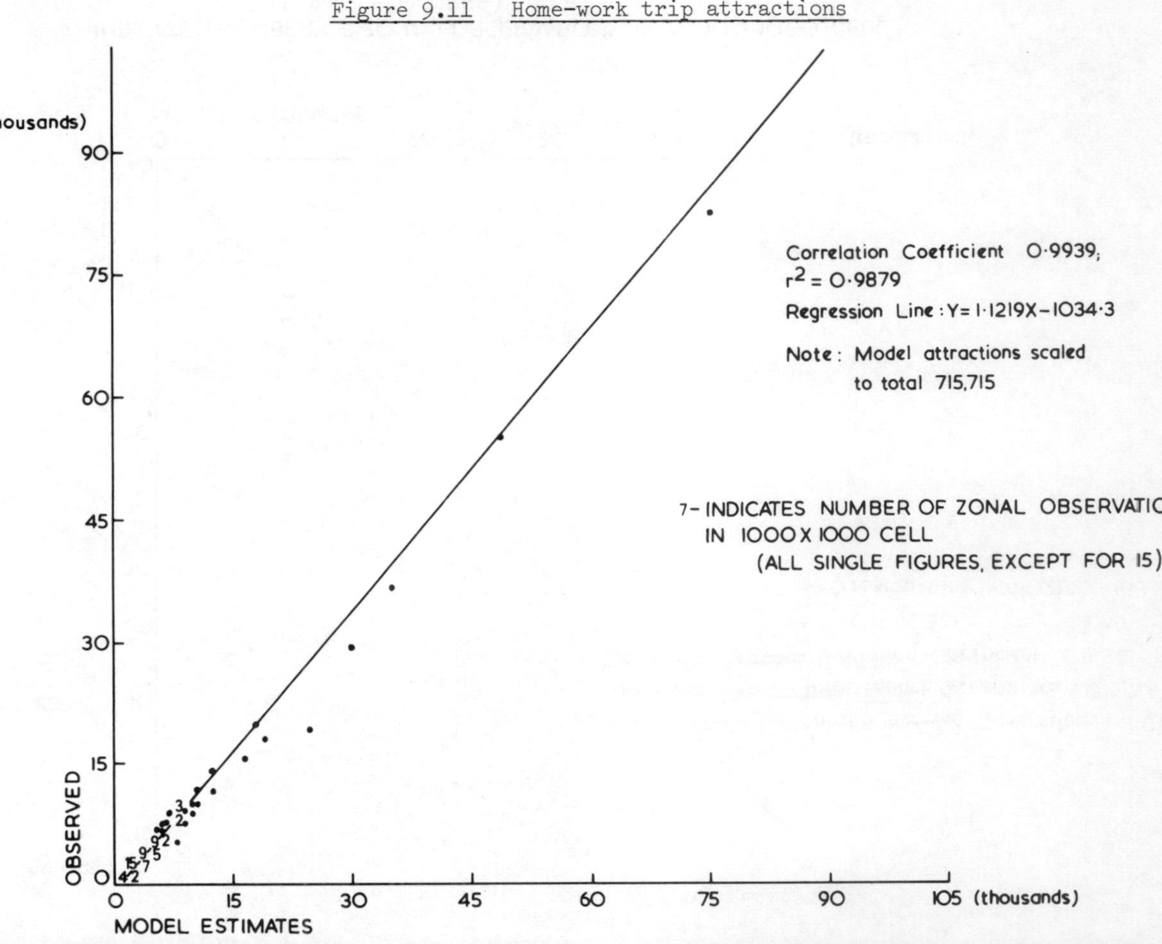

Zone	Trip generations		Trip attractions	
	'Observed'	Model estimates	'Observed'	Model estimates
1	1099	1540	104174	85898
2	3175	3148	8922	7205
3	2147	2359	10338	8590
4	5363	5109	1701	1962
5	8306	6779	2590	3021
6	11703	9969	3500	4491
7	3115	3326	7879	7159
8	6028	5541	5168	4623
9	11743	10038	1593	2273
10	6038	4758	2590	2858
11	10060	8485	1821	2448
12	9788	8318	1854	2142
13	5302	5165	9746	8645
14	4919	4866	2074	2405
15	4103	3596	7606	6055
16	15412	12125	4653	5397
17	9949	8670	2776	2998
18	7379	5863	1996	1968
19	3558	3426	6936	5857
20	3982	4067	3368	3223
21	11451	8479	1130	1377
22	5060	5208	2278	1977
23	7348	6687	4379	4078
24	7358	6714	4971	4666
25	6481	5729	2677	3016
26	9173	7538	2842	3410
27	7036	6174	5861	5497
28	9264	8449	4960	5035
29	6020	5952	2691	3168
30	13430	13632	7905	8349
31	39301	37379	82091	76754
32	28780	26675	19715	18434
33	19267	16835	5622	5257
34	19962	18866	11569	10817
35	10020	10343	9142	9258
36	4930	5031	1787	2109
37	8100	9325	7954	8875
38	3810	4499	3113	4057
39	2400	2726	1286	1782
40	7800	8758	4448	5979
41	17040	20130	19316	25248
42	3280	3520	1620	2506
43	8260	10447	5381	8036
44	7220	6848	2936	2965
45	9250	9001	9898	8571
46	2260	2803	3889	3209
47	11590	12511	11784	12726
48	3150	4371	5980	5831
49	8690	9087	7787	9109
50	4960	4831	2190	2720
51	5770	5878	1895	3158
52	6270	6150	2563	3062
53	15060	15623	10144	10870
54	5340	5969	3840	4595
55	2580	3028	3093	3256
56	17630	18782	29047	30723
57	6830	7383	6511	6209
58	13480	14207	9093	10000
59	3130	3437	4242	4206
60	17340	16972	15623	16835
61	5040	5101	2514	3143
62	5880	5698	4065	4453
63	3110	3578	2799	2859
64	12680	13941	14101	12902
65	48410	46176	54608	50070
66	5960	6934	4743	5457
67	1480	2087	2956	2610
68	6950	7860	3682	4745
69	10440	11561	9869	10187
70	3430	3632	1365	1870
71	33000	33487	36687	35945
72	5560	6979	5568	6214
73	5550	6176	4566	5110
74	1570	1805	1227	1328
75	2460	3463	3260	3834
76	5130	6057	4321	5165
77	1140	1304	344	375
78	17580	20213	18108	19105
79	930	917	461	487
80	7910	9123	5735	6895
81	5970	6602	3653	5612
Total for region	719170	715715	719170	715715

latter coefficients from other sources, the statistics to be minimised for varying β^n are:

$$\rho^n = \Sigma_{ijk} \frac{T_{ij}^{kn} c_{ij}^k}{\Sigma_{ijk} T_{ij}^{kn}} - \Sigma_{ijk} \frac{T_{ij}^{kn} c_{ij}^k}{\Sigma_{ijk} T_{ij}^{kn}} \tag{9.42}$$

$\Sigma_{ijk} \frac{T_{ij}^{kn} c_{ij}^k}{\Sigma_{ijk} T_{ij}^{kn}}$ is the average cost of travel in generalised cost units for persons of type n. β^n was found using a Newton-Raphson gradient search method outlined by Batty and Mackie (1972) and by Box, Davies and Swann (1969). In addition, r^2 statistics were used as a guide to the calibration of this particular submodel. r^2 is at a maximum when ρ^n is at a minimum. As in the case of the category analysis, model predictions for 1966 transport flows can only be compared with appropriate person movements on the respective modes of transport for the work trip purpose. r^2 for public transport travellers was 0.9311 and for private transport was 0.9497 and β^n, for n=1, car-owners, and was 0.0056 and for n=2, non car-owners was 0.0063. The a_1^k - a_4^k coefficients were adapted from those proposed by McIntosh and Quarmby (1970) and as we calculate a generalised time rather than a generalised cost the values given have been divided by the value of time. We have adopted the value of time proposed by McIntosh and Quarmby as 19% of mean household income. The values of these coefficients at calibration were: $a_1^{k=1} = 1$; $a_1^{k=2} = 1$; $a_2^{k=1} = 4.615$ (this coefficient represents perceived car operating costs in 1966 in 1/10ths of a minute); $a_2^{k=2}$ is derived from the piecewise linear of Figure 9.8, depicting public transport fare structures, as was pointed out in Section 9.3.2; $a_3^{k=1} = 2$; $a_3^{k=2} = 1.5$. This is rather than 2 as recommended by McIntosh and Quarmby, providing a better fit in the case of the West Yorkshire model; $a_4^{k=1} = 15.38$ (in tenths of a minute per old penny); and $a_4^{k=2}$ = is not applicable.

The c_{ij}^k's of Equation (9.1) are also flow dependent as described in the section on assignment and are functions of the types of road enumerated in Section 9.4.2. The performance of the distribution modal split model is partly demonstrated in Figures 9.12 to 9.15 which illustrated the flows into Zones 1 (City ward in Central Leeds)

Figure 9.12 Observed trips with destination in zone 1

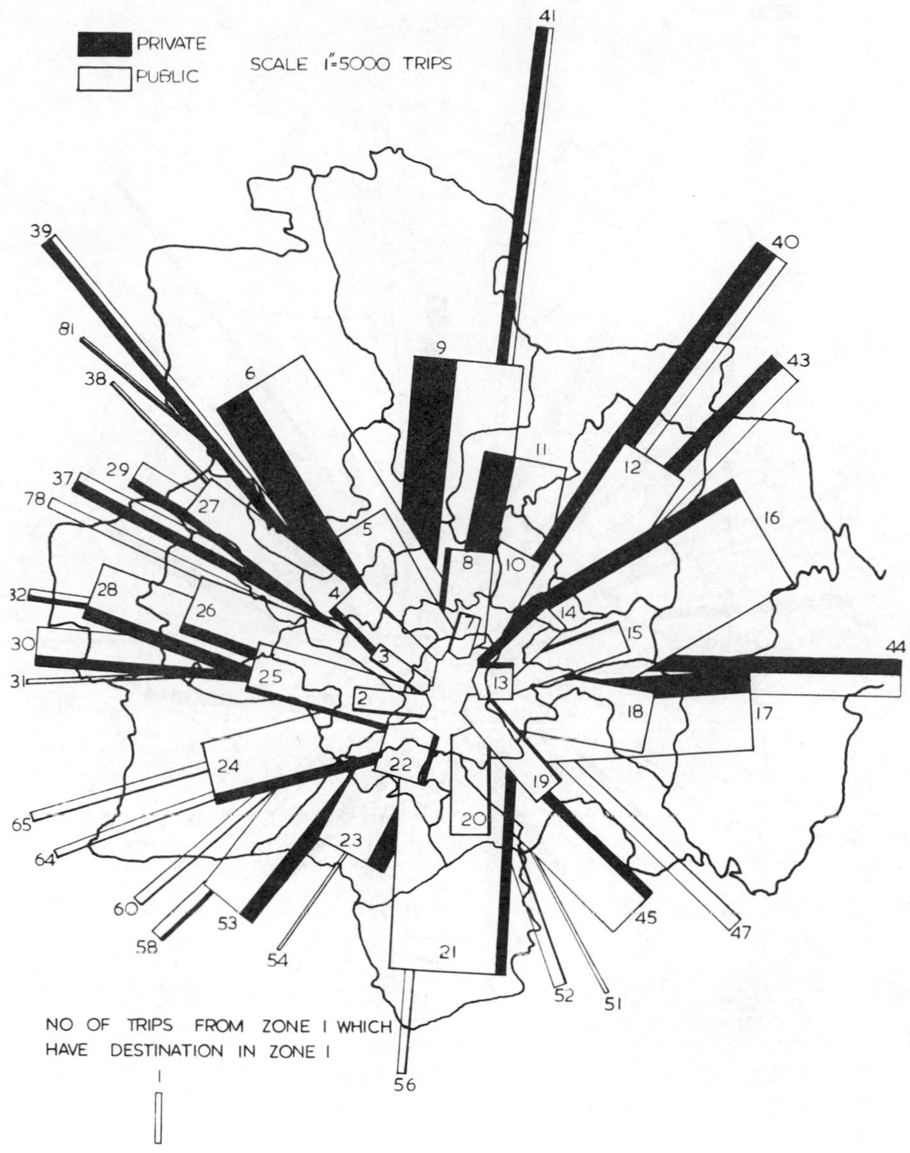

Figure 9.13 Predicted trips with destination in zone 1

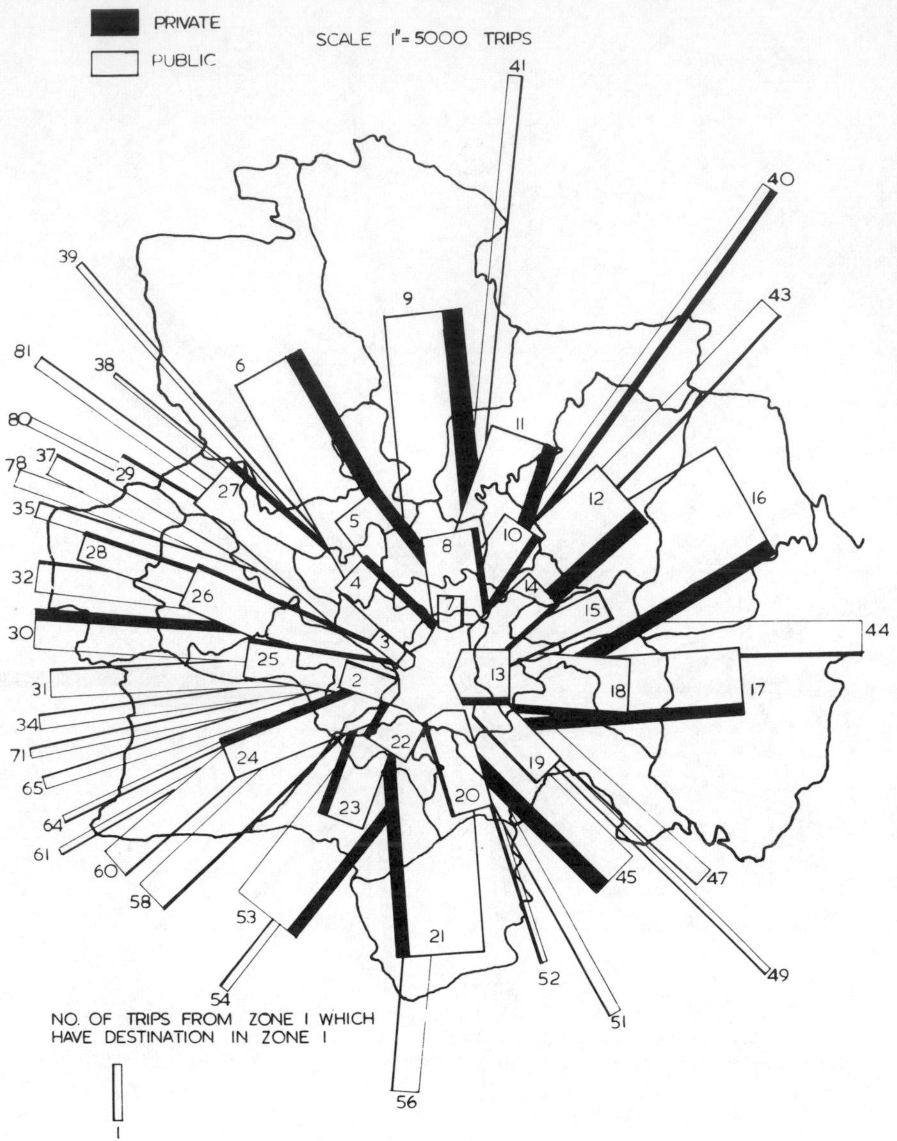

Figure 9.14 Observed trips with destination in zone 65

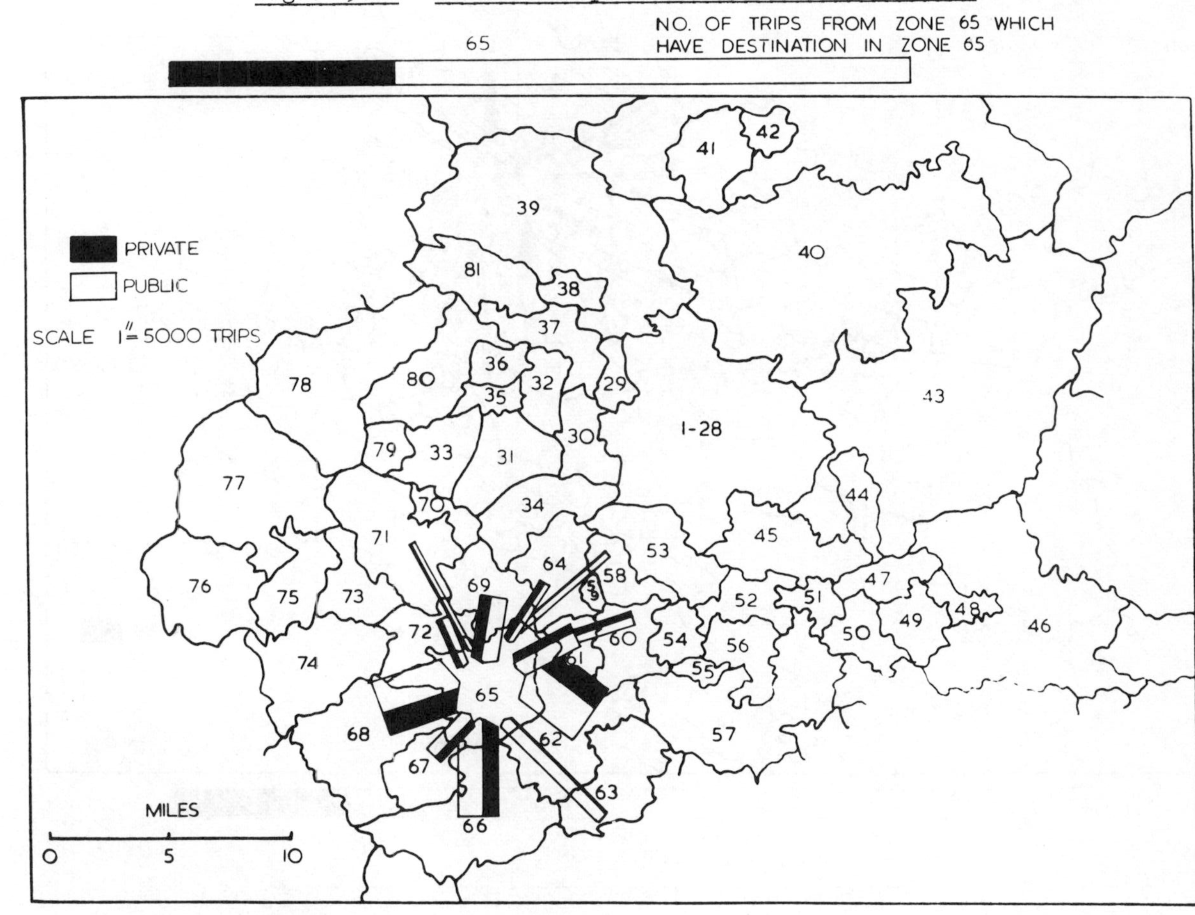

Figure 9.15 Predicted trips with destination in zone 65

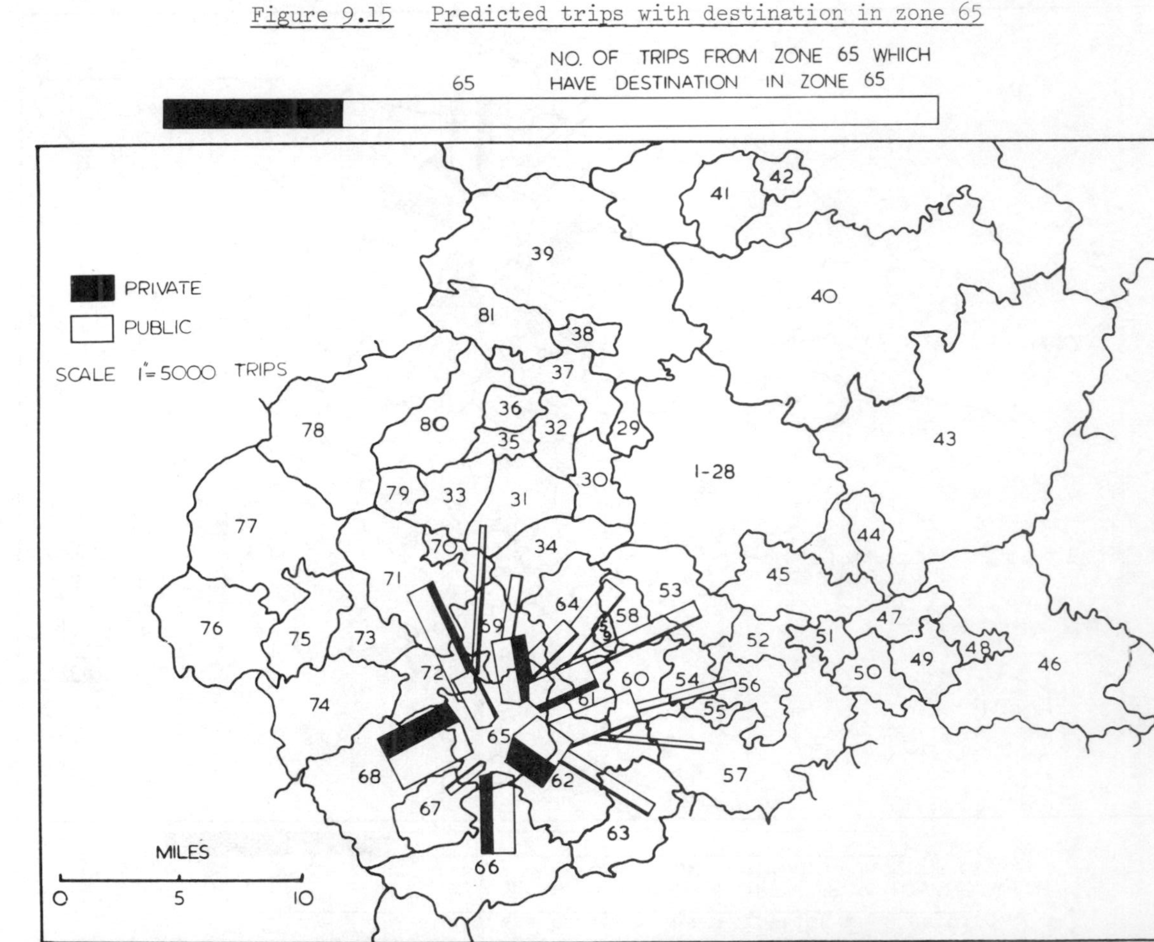

and Zone 65 (Huddersfield County Borough in 1966). Although only two zones are shown, and although there are some anomolies in the flows - for primarily data reasons - it can be seen from the diagram that the model approximates reasonably the 'observed' Census flows. In all of the figures, public and private transport flows are depicted by open and solid lines respectively. Also in both figures it should be noted, in accordance with our discussion in Section 9.4.2 in relation to the need for Equation (9.34), that all inter-zonal trips (and intra-zonals) are aggregated over person types n. Figures 9.12 to 9.14 show trips for two zones and for our two modes of transport only, therefore, and in this sense can only provide a partial indication of the performance of the combined distribution/modal split model.

The performance of the modal split aspects of the submodel are further illustrated in Table 9.5. With some exceptions, comparisons of columns (2) and (3) of this table shows a comforting correspondence between Census data and model based predictions of modal split. Over the region as a whole the proportion of car-owners travelling by car was 'observed' to be 70.9% and 'predicted' by the model to be 71.7% for the same year (1966).

9.5.4 The performance of the assignment submodel

It is almost impossible to illustrate the 'calibration' and performance of the assignment procedures used here, in the manner adopted for other submodels, particularly where much of the data, as in our case, is 'borrowed' from other sources. Our assignment of traffic flows to the public and private networks could only be crudely checked against some coarse aggregation of data from 1966 WYTS traffic counts. These do not provide a good test of the assignment procedures, nor do such comparisons adequately illustrate performance. In this case, no 'automatic' or formal calibration method was devised; however the aim of 'calibration' in the assignment procedure was to minimise the parameter δ given in Equation (9.34). For all links in the system, this had a value at 1966 of 0.0206. This figure measures the degree to which - after an iterative capacity restrained assignment of flows to the private transport network - link times (costs) predicted by the

Table 9.5 'Observed' and model estimates of modal split in trip destinations by zone

% private trip destinations of total trip destinations - car owners only			% private trip destinations of total trip destinations - car owners only		
Zone	'Observed'	Predicted (model estimates)	Zone	'Observed'	Predicted (model estimates)
1	23	14	42	67	35
2	27	29	43	54	50
3	26	25	44	48	45
4	38	41	45	39	33
5	28	33	46	67	39
6	42	43	47	29	30
7	32	31	48	51	34
8	32	38	49	31	31
9	35	39	50	28	29
10	36	33	51	31	27
11	39	33	52	49	44
12	31	32	53	38	39
13	22	29	54	41	45
14	29	34	55	40	33
15	17	32	56	36	28
16	38	28	57	47	28
17	47	38	58	32	30
18	40	36	59	30	41
19	38	25	60	31	24
20	30	32	61	36	28
21	28	23	62	40	38
22	32	30	63	46	29
23	31	26	64	35	38
24	33	31	65	30	25
25	28	35	66	43	35
26	33	35	67	43	37
27	23	37	68	28	37
28	32	34	69	39	35
29	40	44	70	38	39
30	36	33	71	30	25
31	29	23	72	39	43
32	35	37	73	35	32
33	34	36	74	37	41
34	33	34	75	38	27
35	37	32	76	29	26
36	37	35	77	38	47
37	48	47	78	35	30
38	52	44	79	34	38
39	60	47	80	36	32
40	62	51	81	54	49
41	53	35			

model, and therefore, skim trees of perceived generalised times (costs), have converged on 'observed' flows. All that can truly be said about the performance of the assignment methods, given the data base we used, is that they produced a good set of c_{ij}^k's for use in the journey-to-work distribution model.

9.5.5 Conversion of person flows to passenger car units

In order to load traffic flows onto the road network it is necessary to convert the person flows estimated by the trip distribution/modal split stage of the transport model into 'peak hour' passenger car units (pcu's) for all purposes. This was done from WYTS data, according to the following formula:

$$\zeta = \frac{2\phi\lambda}{\xi} \frac{\mu}{\tilde{\mu}} \nu \tag{9.43}$$

where ζ is morning peak hour two-way pcu's for all purposes. The factor 2 arises because the 'observed' Census O and D matrix and the equivalent model estimated O and D matrix gives only half (one-way) of all twenty-four hour journeys made to work by car and motor cycle; ϕ is 35% of twenty-four hour journeys from the model related O and D matrices made by private cars and motor cycles in the morning peak; λ is the proportion of morning peak period trips by cars and motor cycles for all purposes. This had a value of 1.28 in 1966. ξ is the car occupancy in the morning peak period. The 1966 peak was defined to be from 7.00 to 9.00 hours, and at that time ξ had a value of 1.36; μ is the total morning peak period pcu's. During the morning peak of 1966, the make up of traffic was:

60% of vehicles	= cars (pcu value = 1)	= 60.0
2% of vehicles	= motor cycles and bicycles (pcu value = 0.5)	= 1.0
15% of vehicles	= light commercial vehicles (pcu value = 1)	= 15.0
15% of vehicles	= medium commercial vehicles (pcu value = 1.5)	= 22.5
5% of vehicles	= heavy commercial vehicles (pcu value = 2)	= 10.0
3% of vehicles	= buses (pcu value = 3)	= 9.0
		117.5

$\tilde{\mu}$ is Census pcu's or Model 1 O and D pcu's (cars and motor cycles only) and which have a pcu value of some 61; and ν is the proportion of pcu's which occur in the morning peak hour. In 1966 ν was equal to $\frac{11}{19}$. Thus each person trip distributed in the private transport origin and destination matrix had a morning peak hour pcu value of 0.7349. This number also allows for the presence, for assignment requirements, of bus flows on the network. The abstraction of buses would have reduced this pcu value to 0.678.

Person trips by bus and train modes were loaded, separately, on each public transport link on an 'all-or-nothing' basis. In their case there is no need for any prior conversion to pcu's, but the pcu value of bus flows had to be accounted for in the capacity restrained assignment of vehicle trips to the private network, being part of the total vehicle flow on that network.

9.5.6 Some preliminary conclusions on the calibration of the transport model

It will be evident from what has been said in preceding sections that the fitting of the 'traditional' transport model has been partial only, in that the lack of a custom-built data base and consequent reliance primarily on Census of Population data, has meant a forced concentration on the work journey purpose. Other trip purposes, for shopping and so on, have been factored into the data, as have peak hour flows, and mainly for the assignment stage of the model. Although the same data is passed from one submodel to another, it is impossible to be precise about the accumulation of error in the various submodels although this is always suspected where models are chained together (as they are in the case of the transport model), and rules have been proposed for their discernment (for example, see Alonso, 1968). In terms of statistics used and related to fit, it proves impossible to compare like with like between submodels in the transportation simulation. In spite of these difficulties, witnessed by the various diagrams and tables of the calibration and performance section of this chapter, the general picture of transport flows, for the journey-to-work purpose, depicted by 'conventional' or 'traditional' model outputs inspires sufficient confidence for the simulation to provide an adequate tool for strategic planning, as opposed to more detailed transport facility design. The model enables an estimate to be made of the major traffic flows likely to accrue from the exogenously planned location of urban development and, via assignment, of their probable impact on public and private transport networks.

9.6 New approaches to disaggregation and the measurement of elasticities in trip distribution and modal split models

In Section 9.3.4, and particularly with Equation (9.24), we described what we called the 'conventional' approach to trip distribution and modal split. That equation suggests a particular scheme for the disaggregation of T_{ij}, the flow of people from i to j. It, especially, focuses on a model of T_{ij}^{kn}, in which k is the mode of transport used by persons of type n. In the ensuing sections of this chapter a disaggregation of the spatial interaction variables T_{ij} is explored as a possible alternative for the transportation model. Specifically, these variables are of the form T_{ij}^{ph}, where p describes the purpose of trips (which was implicit in the other definition) between i and j, and h denotes an income or other classification of people travelling between i and j. The new feature is the more detailed h-type disaggregation proposed. If an 'income' breakdown is adopted, a direct connection can be made with the income groups of the category analysis of Section 9.3.3, provided similar classifications are used. Thus, to be effective in the usual spatial structure structure of the transport model, there would have to be adequate spatial variation in average household and therefore zonal incomes, and empirical verification of the spatial homogeneity of household incomes within zones would be necessary. Alternatively, the present couplings in the transport model could be modified. The kind of summation indicated by the trip production Equation (9.20) could be largely avoided and, for each zone, most of the categories used in the trip generation model could be retained for transmission to the T_{ij}^{ph} model.

Correspondingly, the β^n's become β_i^{ph}'s, so that trip lengths become income and spatially elastic, which we inferred in the previous paragraph could amount to the same thing, as well as price elastic if T_{ij}, T_{ij}^{kn} and T_{ij}^{ph} are thought of in the appropriate models as demand functions for travel between i and j. In addition, trip generations given by the number of trip origins in i, O_i^{ph}, can be made elastic, varying notably with changes in the accessibility of a zone and/or group for each purpose p, in which case O_i^{ph} is also thought of as a demand function of several variables, comprised of a number of accessibilities. This is made more explicit in a later section.

9.6.2 An alternative trip distribution and modal split model

The considerations of Section 9.6.1 lead to a singly constrained trip distribution model of the following form (cf. Wilson, 1974, Chapter 6, for a description of such model building procedures):

$$T_{ij}^{ph} = A_i^{ph} O_i^{ph} D_j^p \exp(-\beta_i^{ph} c_{ij}^{ph}) \tag{9.44}$$

where T_{ij}^{ph} refer to the number of trips from origin zone i to destination zone j by group h and for purpose p. A_i^{ph}, like the A_i^n of Equation (9.25) is a balancing factor which ensures that:

$$\Sigma_j T_{ij}^{ph} = O_i^{ph} \tag{9.45}$$

so that

$$A_i^{ph} = \{\Sigma_j D_j^p \exp(-\beta_i^{ph} c_{ij}^{ph})\}^{-1} \tag{9.46}$$

The travel cost function is the usual negative exponential one. As foreshadowed in the previous section, there are as many trip length parameters, β_i^{ph}, estimated in the calibration of the model, as there are origin zone purposes and groups within the region. The second type of disaggregation, based on the category analysis and mentioned in Section 9.6.1 is included as the h-type disaggregation, so that although for pragmatic reasons there has had to be some aggregation of the 108 categories of the trip end model, it has been possible to select three income and two car-ownership groups based on an analysis of statistically significant differences in travel behaviour within the 108 categories. The trip costs for each purpose, c_{ij}^{ph}, for these groups, need to be estimated from the generalised modal costs

$$\gamma_{ij}^k = a_1 t_{ij}^k + a_2 e_{ij}^k + a_3 w_{ij}^k + a_4^k d_{ij}^k \tag{9.47}$$

where t_{ij}^k is travel time from i to j, by mode k, in minutes; e_{ij}^k is waiting time from i to j, by mode k, in minutes; w_{ij}^k is walking time from i to j, by mode k, in minutes; and d_{ij}^k is distance from i to j.

in miles. a_1, a_2, a_3 and a_4^k are coefficients, which convert these variables to generalised costs rather than the generalised time units we referred to earlier. Given that γ_{ij}^{k} can be calculated in this way, then c_{ij}^{ph} can be estimated using the following function (cf. Wilson, 1970, Chapter 2):

$$\exp(-\beta_i^{ph} c_{ij}^{ph}) = \Sigma_{k\varepsilon M(h)} M_{ij}^{pkh} \exp(-\beta_i^{ph} \gamma_{ij}^{k}) \qquad (9.48)$$

in which M_{ij}^{pkh} is the modal share of trips for a given purpose and household group. k, as before, denotes a mode of transport and is either public or private, and

$$M_{ij}^{pkh} = \frac{T_{ij}^{pkh}}{\Sigma_k T_{ij}^{pkh}} \qquad (9.49)$$

where T_{ij}^{pkh} is a modal disaggregation of T_{ij}^{ph}. It should be noted, however, that M_{ij}^{pkh} of Equation (9.50), used to weight the modal costs, as in Equation (9.49) is the 'observed' modal split for each household group, although other forms of weighting have been put forward (see Wilson, 1974, Chapter 9). Equations (9.48) and (9.49) suggest that an alternative modal split model may be readily incorporated into the above trip distribution framework, an alternative, that is, to the combined distribution/modal split procedure described by Equations (9.24) to (9.31). An M_{ij}^{pkh} model is probably best incorporated as a post-distribution modal split model, since a separate estimation procedure is obviously involved from that of T_{ij}^{ph}.

The particular modal split model used makes use of work by Dorrington (1971). By doing so, both awkward calibration problems are overcome, and allowance is made for data deficiencies within individual (i,j) trip elements. The modal split model is calibrated on modal cost difference intervals which may be defined for our two modes of transport as:

$$\psi_m^{2/1} = \Sigma_{d_{ij}\varepsilon m}(\gamma_{ij}^2 - \gamma_{ij}^1) \qquad (9.50)$$

and in which our new term m is a generalised cost interval.

Then, in the form of cost intervals, the logistic modal split model can be written as:

$$M_m^{pkh} = \frac{T_m^{pkh}}{\Sigma_k T_m^{pkh}} = \frac{1}{1 + \exp\{-\lambda^{ph}(\psi_m - \delta^{ph})\}} \qquad (9.51)$$

where M_m^{pkh} is now the modal split for cost difference interval m, for given p, k and ψ^m, and λ^{ph} and δ^{ph} are parameters to be estimated, and are interpreted in the usual way as relating to a traveller's sensitivity to a mode of transport and as a public transport penalty, respectively.

9.6.3 Elastic trip generation and related demand functions

In addition to the constraint given by Equation (9.45) the trip distribution model of Equation (9.44) also satisfies the constraint of

$$\Sigma_j T_{ij}^{ph} c_{ij}^{ph} = C_i^{ph} \qquad (9.52)$$

where C_i^{ph} is the expenditure on trips for purpose p by groups h living in zone i. Following an idea by Wilson (1973), the demand for trips represented by C_i^{ph} can also be expressed as a demand function in which

$$C_i^{ph} = C_i^{ph}\,(a_i^{ph1}, \ldots a_i^{ph2}, \ldots) \qquad (9.53)$$

where a_i^{ph1} and a_i^{ph2} are measures of the accessibility of given h group residents in zone i to opportunities throughout the region (for example, to shopping centres, workplaces and various entertainments) for purpose p.

Similarly, as noted in Section 9.6.1 the number of trip origins, O_i^{ph}, becomes a demand function of the form:

$$O_i^{ph} = O_i^{ph}(a_i^{ph}, \ldots C_i^{ph}, \ldots P, Q^h) \qquad (9.54)$$

where P is a price index of other goods relative to transport, Q^h is the income available to trip makers in each h group, and accessibilities, a_i^{ph} are equal to $1/A_i^{ph}$, where A_i^{ph} is defined by Equation (9.46). Accessibilities are therefore taken to be the inverse of our balancing factor in the usual way. Thus, an important link (through the a_i^{ph}'s) is established between the trip generation and distribution phases of the transport model. C_i^{ph} and O_i^{ph} can be normalised to account for differences in zonal population size, so that we can define

$$\Gamma_i^{ph} = C_i^{ph}/N_i^{ph} \qquad (9.55)$$

and

$$\Omega_{i}^{ph} = O_{i}^{ph}/N_{i}^{ph} \qquad (9.56)$$

in which N_{i}^{ph} is the population within household-group type h in origin zone i, travelling by purpose p; Γ_{i}^{ph} is an average expenditure on trips for purpose p by groups of each type h living in zone i and Ω_{i}^{ph} is an average frequency of trips generated in zone i for given p and h. Both Γ_{i}^{ph} and Ω_{i}^{ph} can be estimated by linear regression (see Southworth, 1975-A) from Equations (9.55) and (9.56) transformed as follows:

$$\ln \frac{\Gamma_{i}^{ph}}{H_{i}^{ph} - \Gamma_{i}^{ph}} = a + b \ln a_{i}^{ph} \qquad (9.57)$$

where a_{i}^{ph} is the accessibility term defined above; and H_{i}^{ph} is the higher asymptote of Γ_{i}^{ph}.

$$\Omega_{i}^{ph} = a + b\, \Gamma_{i}^{ph} \qquad (9.58)$$

Because we can measure, the accessibilities

$$a_{i}^{ph} = \Sigma_{i} D_{j}^{p} \exp\,(-\beta_{i}^{ph} c_{ij}^{ph}) \qquad (9.59)$$

either at the present or some future date it becomes possible to forecast from these Γ_{i}^{ph} and Ω_{i}^{ph}, and in iterative fashion, with values initially assumed for β_{i}^{ph} in Equation (9.59), the β_{i}^{ph}'s themselves. Values, estimated thus, for O_{i}^{ph} and β_{i}^{ph} can then be put into the model of Equation (9.44), offering a scheme which provides for consistency between the level of aggregation in the category analysis and trip distribution and modal split submodels, and through the measurement of present and future accessibilities, some prediction of elastic trip expenditure and frequencies.

9.6.4 The data-base and its additional requirements from that for the conventional model

Data requirements for the new disaggregated model outlined are similar (with some extensions and differences) to those for the earlier one. Like the previously described model, this particular scheme for trip distribution and modal split has been built and tested for the West Yorkshire study area defined in Section 9.2. The explicit addition of trip purposes and more detailed treatment of household-types in the distribution submodel demanded different combinations of some of the data sources, summarised in Table 9.2. In particular a slightly different use was made of four specific sources of information: (i) the 1966 Sample Census Usual Workplace and Residence Data; (ii) outputs of trip and estimates for different purposes from the category analysis of Section 9.3.3; (iii) M62 Trans-Pennine motorway impact study (Household survey data); and (iv) generalised cost matrices for the journey to and from work using procedures described in Section 9.3.2 (with some minor modifications) and for the two modes defined in that section. The same 'observed' trip matrices for the journey-to-work (using the same estimates of the data from Equation (9.34) were used. Other trip generations, and in particular for three shopping and social-cum-recreational trip purposes are estimated by the trip end or category analysis submodel. From this submodel too, the D_j^p's for the model of Equation (9.44) were estimated, for these three purposes. With the six h-type groups of Section 9.6.2, this meant that 18 classes of trip for each (i,j) pair were to be modelled in the system, as opposed to four classes in the usual model. The need to calibrate trip-distribution/modal split models at this highly disaggregated level led to the use of the M62 Impact Study Household Survey data to provide a sample of non-work regionwide interactions. A 1969 random sample of households in the wards of the West Yorkshire study area, made possible the abstraction of relevant 'observed' home-based trips. Travel diaries collected over one week in the summer of 1969 provide data on mode split, and inter-zonal mean trip costs by household group h in origin zone i, 'observed' values of M_i^{pkh} {see Equation (9.51)} and $\Sigma_i T_{ij}^{ph} c_{ij}^{ph} / \Sigma_j T_{ij}^{ph}$ respectively. These, adjusted to 1966, enable modal split proportions and travel cost matrices to be estimated - and in the latter case to be added to the modal cost elements for work journeys, γ_{ij}^k - from data source (iv), enumerated above.

9.6.5 Calibration of the disaggregated models

The calibration statistic used to derive the best-fit β_i^{ph} values was

$$\tau_i^{ph} = \text{Min} \quad \frac{\Sigma_j T_{ij}^{ph} c_{ij}^{ph}}{\Sigma_j T_{ij}^{ph}} - \frac{\Sigma_j T_{ij}^{ph} c_{ij}^{ph}}{\Sigma_j T_{ij}^{ph}} \tag{9.60}$$

A Newton-Raphson procedure was adopted to find τ_i^{ph}. Values for the coefficients $a_1^k - a_4^k$ in the generalised cost function were taken directly from McIntosh and Quarmby (1970) as before and consequently manipulation of the generalised cost function, given by Equation (9.47) could be avoided in the calibration of either the trip distribution or modal split models, since they could for this demonstration purpose be assumed constant.

The fitting of the disaggregated modal choice model (Southworth, 1975-B) is achieved by finding values of λ^{ph} and δ^{ph} which minimise

$$\sigma^{ph} = \left[\frac{\Sigma_{m=1} \left| V_n^{p*h} \left(\frac{V_m^{pkh}}{V_m^{p*h}} - \frac{T_m^{pkh}}{V_m^{p*h}} \right)^2 \right|}{\Sigma_{m=1} V_m^{p*h}} \right]^{\frac{1}{2}} \qquad (9.61)$$

where σ^{ph} is the standard deviation for trip group h for purpose p (Dorrington, 1971); V_m^{pkh} denotes the 'observed' number of trips for given p, k, h and m categories; n is the number of m cost intervals and * signifies summation over k modes of transport.

σ^{ph} is minimised with a routine devised by Powell (1964), described by Box, Davies and Swann (1969), and available as a Nottingham Algorithm Group subroutine on the Leeds University ICL, 1906A computer. Minimisation of Equation (9.61) also served to minimise a second 'calibration' statistic, namely:

$$\rho_*^{pkh} = \frac{T_*^{pkh}}{V_*^{pkh}} - 1 \qquad (9.62)$$

which simply compares the observed and estimated trip totals for each p, k and h. The asterisk denotes that summation occurs over all i and j on this occasion.

At this juncture in research into the efficacy of the disaggregated trip distribution and modal split models suggested in Equations (9.44) and (9.51), it has not proved possible to base regression analysis of the travel demand functions of Section 9.6.3 on the full West Yorkshire study area. Of the 81 zones delineated for that area, only data from the 28 Leeds zones were used to regress the normalised factors of trip frequency and expenditure against each other and against the natural log of the accessibility terms a_i^{ph}. Regressions on data for the full regional system have been less useful, due to such influences as the large variation in zone sizes, and the probability that the β_i^{ph} parameters are affected by factors besides trip frequencies and costs. Thus this chapter reports, in effect, a Leeds model with detailed external zone system. As before, to make use of the best available data base, results for the journey-to-work trip only are given. As was noted in Section 9.4.1, data containing a mode and appropriate group breakdown was not available, even for the journey-to-work. A 'semi'real' variable, N_{ij}^{pkh}, similar to the N_{ij}^{kn} of Equation (9.34), had to be estimated using conditional probabilities. Thus

$$T_{ij}^{ph} = \Sigma_k N_{ij}^{pkh} \tag{9.63}$$

for 'observed' values of T_{ij}^{ph} and a_i^{ph} is the inverse of A_i^{ph} in Equation (9.46), using model 'estimates' or 'calibrated' value of T_{ij}^{ph}. Since a_i^{ph} can be related in this way to N_{ij}^{pkh}, Γ_i^{ph} and Ω^{ph} can also be said to be regressed on 'semi-real' data and for this particular p, the journey-to-work. This leads to the following results:

$$\Gamma_i^{11} = \frac{2.05890}{1 + \exp\{-(13.141738-1.45674 \ln a_i^{11})\}} \tag{9.64}$$

$$\Gamma_i^{12} = \frac{2.42064}{1 + \exp\{-(11.70709-1.28365 \ln a_i^{12})\}} \tag{9.65}$$

$$\Gamma_i^{13} = \frac{2.50547}{1 + \exp\{-(10.71753-1.9945 \ln a_i^{13})\}} \tag{9.66}$$

$$\Gamma_i^{14} = \frac{2.13644}{1 + \exp\{-(14.97486-1.50255 \ln a_i^{14})\}} \tag{9.67}$$

$$\Gamma_i^{15} = \frac{2.31272}{1 + \exp\{-(12.92957-1.27700 \ln a_i^{15})\}} \tag{9.68}$$

$$\Gamma_i^{16} = \frac{2.07744}{1 + \exp\{-(10.95156-1.08728 \ln a_i^{16})\}} \tag{9.69}$$

and

$$\Omega_i^{11} = 0.2711 + 0.05559\ \Gamma_i^{11} \tag{9.70}$$

$$\Omega_i^{12} = 0.24755 + 0.05581\ \Gamma_i^{12} \tag{9.71}$$

$$\Omega_i^{13} = 0.19936 + 0.06729\ \Gamma_i^{13} \tag{9.72}$$

$$\Omega_i^{14} = 0.23312 + 0.10660\ \Gamma_i^{14} \tag{9.73}$$

$$\Omega_i^{15} = 0.026487 + 0.10948\ \Gamma_i^{15} \tag{9.74}$$

$$\Omega_i^{16} = 0.20251 + 0.12896\ \Gamma_i^{16} \tag{9.75}$$

In addition to the journey-to-work purpose, six h-groups are distinguished in the above equations. These comprise three income ranges of < £1,000, £1,000-£2,000 and >£2,000 per annum and the usual two car-owner and non car-owner groups for each (in these inflationary times) somewhat archaic income range (see Table 9.6).

Table 9.6 h-type group in disaggregated trip distribution and modal split models

Trip group	Income	Car-ownership
1	£1,000 pa	Non car-owner
2	£1,000-£2,000 pa	Non car-owner
3	£2,000 pa	Non car-owner
4	£1,000 pa	Car-owner
5	£1,000-£2,000 pa	Car-owner
6	£2,000 pa	Car-owner

The 'best fit' values for β_i^{ph} are given in Table 9.7.

For the modal split model of Equation (9.52) the calibration statistics of τ^{ph} and ρ^{pkh} are close to each other for each interval of generalised cost difference, with better values resulting in nearly all cases from the smallest cost interval. Results for the six h-groups of Table 9.6 and related to a cost difference interval of one new pence are given in Table 9.8. Note that an assumption made in this model, not made in our earlier described modal share submodel, is that non car-owners are able to use the private mode of transport. Previously only car-owners were modally split, it being assumed that non car-owners travelled by public transport and that family car-ownership approximated 'availability'. Here, we recognise that

Table 9.7 Origin Specific cost-decay parameters, β_i^{ph}, for West Yorkshire study area

Zone Numbers	Trip Group					
	1	2	3	4	5	6
1	0.31193	0.31798	0.32043	0.29114	0.30007	0.28244
2	0.19939	0.19892	0.19390	0.21495	0.21328	0.18947
3	0.14984	0.14778	-	0.14718	0.14892	0.14575
4	0.14792	0.14834	0.14624	0.17476	0.17657	0.17151
5	0.17811	0.17986	0.17856	0.21081	0.21613	0.21548
6	0.17205	0.17008	0.17176	0.22105	0.22331	0.22014
7	0.14300	0.14202	0.14051	0.14466	0.14485	0.14114
8	0.16370	0.16232	0.16016	0.19937	0.20351	0.19027
9	0.16895	0.16804	0.16650	0.23307	0.22615	0.20744
10	0.13802	0.13948	0.13841	0.17313	0.17735	0.16878
11	0.17224	0.17329	0.17050	0.21511	0.20908	0.19703
12	0.17201	0.17360	0.17106	0.21919	0.19963	0.17869
13	0.16506	0.16227	0.16340	0.16217	0.16066	0.15488
14	0.15154	0.15286	0.15163	0.16640	0.16806	0.15805
15	0.16165	0.16001	0.16134	0.16935	0.17007	0.17272
16	0.18948	0.18723	0.18887	0.20689	0.20970	0.21032
17	0.17586	0.17762	0.17617	0.19368	0.20968	0.22419
18	0.16268	0.16154	0.15949	0.19089	0.20493	0.21153
19	0.18067	0.18263	0.17738	0.16528	0.17169	0.15964
20	0.16617	0.16274	0.16103	0.14245	0.13484	-
21	0.22413	0.22040	0.22404	0.18034	0.20921	0.23645
22	0.16904	0.16575	0.16624	0.24500	0.23900	0.23645
23	0.19035	0.18673	0.18811	0.19653	0.21029	0.21013
24	0.22995	0.23080	0.22847	0.24500	0.26496	0.26858
25	0.19377	0.19116	0.19251	0.20862	0.20080	0.18874
26	0.21468	0.21342	0.21092	0.24500	0.23800	0.21715
27	0.20139	0.19937	0.19633	0.24500	0.26127	0.26206
28	0.18810	0.18594	0.18590	0.24500	0.23800	0.23645
29	0.21232	0.21413	0.21177	0.23402	0.23900	0.24858
30	0.18934	0.18841	0.18680	0.21476	0.21268	0.20857
31	0.24950	0.24459	0.24655	0.25353	0.24937	0.24377
32	0.28172	0.28170	0.27771	0.26209	0.25893	0.25275
33	0.26952	0.26661	0.26314	0.24500	0.22922	0.20314
34	0.25785	0.25833	0.25711	0.24500	0.23800	0.23645
35	0.25178	0.24647	0.24427	0.23560	0.22549	0.21541
36	0.20167	0.19936	0.19697	0.26748	0.25258	0.23645
37	0.25586	0.24949	0.24048	0.23365	0.23058	0.22764
38	0.27977	0.27850	0.27480	0.26249	0.26039	0.25856
39	0.20802	0.20711	0.20004	0.22894	0.23164	0.22626
40	0.23150	0.22080	0.20463	0.26261	0.26124	0.25931
41	0.32130	0.30686	0.29718	0.21237	0.21051	0.20872

Zone Numbers	Trip Group					
	1	2	3	4	5	6
42	0.23321	0.22730	0.22375	0.20494	0.20166	0.20009
43	0.19096	0.19175	0.19286	0.28252	0.28979	0.29405
44	0.20930	0.21078	0.20954	0.23444	0.24912	0.25572
45	0.24409	0.24225	0.24637	0.23686	0.24591	0.25299
46	0.20999	0.21690	0.22410	0.24500	0.24433	0.24305
47	0.28480	0.28730	0.28541	0.24981	0.25002	0.24938
48	0.32606	0.33109	0.33157	0.29039	0.29184	0.29199
49	0.25785	0.25328	0.25101	0.23197	0.22877	0.22482
50	0.22252	0.22073	0.21970	0.32644	0.31824	0.29929
51	0.24749	0.24596	0.24834	0.26664	0.27158	0.27681
52	0.21069	0.20699	0.20504	0.25461	0.25688	0.25458
53	0.21530	0.21573	0.21453	0.25231	0.25291	0.25276
54	0.24615	0.24444	0.24029	0.34209	0.32241	0.29237
55	0.28553	0.27640	0.26099	0.25966	0.25522	0.25162
56	0.33498	0.33256	0.32485	0.22297	0.21828	0.21480
57	0.26834	0.26310	0.25749	0.33712	0.33053	0.31460
58	0.29762	0.29220	0.28327	0.24500	0.23900	0.23645
59	0.33030	0.32893	0.32428	0.34028	0.33686	0.33249
60	0.27087	0.26783	0.26380	0.21477	0.20867	0.20279
61	0.27657	0.27407	0.26828	0.29290	0.28357	0.27238
62	0.25785	0.25853	0.25846	0.39225	0.37323	0.34720
63	0.28048	0.28170	0.27530	0.36272	0.35697	0.35063
64	0.25785	0.25242	0.25096	0.23433	0.23064	0.22666
65	0.42539	0.40840	0.40567	0.27781	0.26911	0.25947
66	0.26762	0.26688	0.26677	0.26754	0.26972	0.27160
67	0.26165	0.26070	0.28482	0.25500	0.24880	0.24854
68	0.25785	0.24170	0.22491	0.24500	0.23800	0.23645
69	0.25229	0.24985	0.24554	0.23169	0.22845	0.22501
70	0.16576	0.16488	-	0.24500	0.25837	0.25684
71	0.27966	0.28170	0.27171	0.25134	0.23800	0.22769
72	0.26900	0.26554	0.25855	0.34499	0.33937	0.33276
73	0.30052	0.29826	0.29677	0.36081	0.35319	0.34378
74	0.22099	0.21836	0.21787	0.36482	0.35812	0.34715
75	0.31831	0.31472	0.31610	0.36279	0.35892	0.35375
76	0.41617	0.41874	0.40791	0.43984	0.43443	0.42223
77	0.23645	0.23516	0.23171	0.36717	0.35551	0.33916
78	0.29764	0.29325	0.28603	0.25780	0.25144	0.24626
79	0.28024	0.28170	0.26519	0.30944	0.22226	0.15313
80	0.23174	0.22962	0.22451	0.31651	0.30247	0.24814
81	0.23504	0.22728	0.21622	0.24500	0.23800	0.23353

some non car-owners travel as car passengers. In Table 9.9 a number of comparisons are made of model estimates and 'observed' values for the same cost interval for our private mode of transport. These comparisons refer to the results achieved for private transport trip origins, private transport trip destinations and to travel by private transport on all (i,j) pairs for the whole spatial system as opposed to the zonal results given for our earlier model in Table 9.5. The results of Table 9.9 are self-evident. If r^2 is anything to go by, the empirical version of the model predicts best for the higher income car-owning groups. Southworth (1975-B) has shown that in a modal split model of this kind disaggregation to account for both tripmaker characteristics and the origin location of trips, {the incorporation of Equation (9.51) of λ_i^{ph} instead of λ^{ph}} are important influences upon the modal split at the zone level. A more detailed discussion of these results will be presented elsewhere.

Table 9.8 Parameter values and calibration statistics for disaggregated modal split submodel

	Cost difference interval, m=1 new pence					
Trip group	1	2	3	4	5	6
λ^{ph}	0.0753	0.0701	0.1159	0.0978	0.1190	0.0600
δ^{ph}	63.13	54.04	31.04	4.69	0.56	-3.64
$\frac{T_*^{pkh}}{V_*^{pkh}}$	1.017	1.025	1.016	1.006	1.003	0.997
σ^{ph}	0.522	0.989	0.919	4.370	2.320	0.540

The asterisk refers to private mode.

The development of this style of trip distribution and modal split modelling is very much part of ongoing research and more needs to be done before we can be satisfied. For example, the effect of non-transport variables located in the origin zones on trip distribution could be examined through their possible inclusion in the demand functions of Section 9.6.3 and initially the methods adopted there, of linear regression analysis could be used to examine such effects. Their effect on the modal split of trips between i and j could be looked at if λ^{ph} or λ_i^{ph} is made a function of such variables.

Table 9.9 Comparisons of observed against model estimated private transport trip matrices for disaggregated modal split model

Trip group		Cost difference interval, m=1 new pence					
		1	2	3	4	5	6
Private trip origins	Intercept	21.6482	26.7010	0.2169	108.7629	40.1127	2.1844
	Slope coefficient	0.5800	0.5880	1.0236	0.9264	0.9583	1.0063
	R^2	0.683	0.474	0.6160	0.982	0.987	0.997
Private trip destinations	Intercept	19.3370	22.5684	5.2170	117.3105	44.0963	4.8495
	Slope coefficient	0.6111	0.6328	0.8566	0.9202	0.9533	0.992
	R^2	0.897	0.8201	0.828	0.995	0.997	0.999
Zone to zone trip interchanges	Intercept	0.2635	0.3081	0.0517	1.5863	0.6077	0.0767
	Slope coefficient	0.5847	0.6070	0.8910	0.9120	0.446	0.9857
	R^2	0.770	0.635	0.658	0.985	0.990	0.997

Nevertheless, work to date has shown that consistent schemes of h-type disaggregation are possible and effective empirically, throughout the transport model, and that income elastic trip generations and trip lengths can be readily incorporated in the customary framework for the transport model. The case for h-type disaggregation is a closer connection to an adequate behavioural basis. The statistical averaging involved is less than in the usual model. A household group as well as a mode and person type breakdown is also much more informative for policy making uses than the usual mode and person type breakdown. In spite of this, it cannot be said that the T_{ij}^{ph} and M_m^{pkh} models have yet been adequately substantiated. Difficulties occur with the data base, as reported in Sections 9.4.1 and 9.4.2. Also, theoretical and empirical differences create difficulties, if not impossibilities, of comparison of the respective performances of the traditional and more disaggregated approaches. It can be shown in theory that the β's in the trip distribution model should be independent (Wilson, 1974, Chapter 9) and it has also been shown, empirically, (Southworth, 1975-A, 1975-B) that the adoption of β_i^{ph}'s and, in the disaggregated modal split model, of λ_i^{ph}'s, in preference to regional β^{ph}'s and λ^{ph}'s brings about an improvement in the fit of both models to 'observed' data. The desirability of these theoretical and empirical advances have to be set against the resources required in assembling an appropriate data base.

9.7 Some general conclusions

The differences referred to in the previous section, between the two transport modelling styles and the models developed for the West Yorkshire region, make it difficult to say that the second approach grows out of the empirical failure of the first; at this stage, this is simply a report on parallel ways of developing the transport model. The second approach, though more demanding of data, demonstrates that an income or household type disaggregation of the transport model is feasible and does permit modelling approaches to the planning of urban and regional transport facilities to address more directly some of the income-related problems faced by households in the spatial configuration of transport facilities. This chapter has not tackled directly these issues of policy, but it does demonstrate a way in which both 'conventional' and 'unconventional' models of trip generation and allocation might be built both for geographical research and for planning purposes. It further demonstrates that both kinds of model can be built on 'secondary' data bases, for some trip purposes, particularly for use in strategic planning where some error would not matter too much. Simulations of this type can be regarded as acceptable provided that broad issues of location, even concerning household groups, and their consequent transport flows are at the centre of concern, rather than either problems of detailed road design or of submodel verification. The fitting of a transport model to 'secondary' data would be too crude for such detailed work.

References

Alonso, W. (1968) Predicting best with imperfect data, Journal of American Institute of Planners, 34, pp. 248-255.

Batty, M. and Mackie, S. (1972) The calibration of gravity, entropy and related models of spatial interaction, Environment and Planning, 4, pp. 131-250.

Bonsall, P. (1974) The implementation of various cost functions in tree building algorithms, Working Paper 47, Institute for Transport Studies, University of Leeds.

Bonsall, P. (1975-A) Details of the implementation of non-linear cost functions in the tree building algorithm, Working Paper 116, Department of Geography, University of Leeds.

Bonsall, P. (1975-B) Approaches to the prediction of intra-zonal interactions, Working Paper 122, Department of Geography, University of Leeds.

Box, M.J., Davies, D. and Swann, W.H. (1969) Non-linear optimisation techniques, ICI Monograph, 5, Oliver and Boyd, Edinburgh.

Copley, D.M. and Judge, E.J. (1972) Building a network for West Riding and Lancashire, Working Paper 21, Institute for Transport Studies, University of Leeds.

Dijkstra, E.W. (1959) A note on two problems in connection with graphs, Numerishe Mathematik, 1, pp. 269-271.

Dorrington, T.E. (1971) Some new methods of applying and calibrating the SELNEC modal split model, MAU Note 233, Ministry of Transport, London.

Freeman, Fox, Wilbur Smith and Associates (1968) West Midlands Transportation Study, Birmingham.

Hutchinson, B.G. (1974) Principles of urban transport systems planning, Scripta Book Co., Washington DC.

Lane, R., Powell, T.J. and Prestwood Smith, P. (1971) Analytical transport planning, Duckworth, London.

Lewis, R.J. (1969) The use of Census data in obtaining household income distributions, Traffic Engineering and Control, 11, pp. 416-418.

McIntosh, P.T. and Quarmby, D.A. (1970) Generalised costs and the estimation of movement costs and benefits, MAU Note 179, Ministry of Transport, London.

Moore, E.F. (1957) The shortest path through a maze, International symposium on the theory of switching, Proceedings, Harvard University, 2nd-5th April.

Pick, G.W. and Gill, J. (1970) New developments in category analysis, PTRC Symposium.

Potts, R.B. and Oliver, R.M. (1972) Flows in transport networks, Academic Press, New York.

Powell, M.J.D. (1964) An efficient method of finding the minimum of a function of several variables without calculating derivatives, Computer Journal, 7, pp. 155-162.

Putman, S.H. et al (1973) The interrelationships of transportation development and land development, Department of City and Regional Planning, University of Pennsylvania, Philadelphia.

Putman, S.H. (1974) Preliminary results from an integrated transportation and land use model package, Transportation, 3, pp. 193-224.

Southworth, F. (1975-A) A disaggregated trip distribution model with elastic frequencies and expenditures, Working Paper 50, Institute for Transport Studies, University of Leeds.

Southworth, F. (1975-B) A highly disaggregated modal split model, Working Paper 58, Institute for Transport Studies, University of Leeds.

Traffic Research Corporation (1969) West Yorkshire Transportation Study, Wakefield.

Van Vliet, D. (1976) Road assignment I: principles and parameters of modal formulation, Transportation Research, 10, pp. 137-143.

Voorhees, A.M. and Associates Inc. (1973) Sheffield/Rotherham Land Use Transportation Study, Technical Memorandum 3, Speed/flow analysis and highway link classification, Sheffield.

Wardrop, J.G. (1952) Some theoretical aspects of road traffic research, Proceedings, Institution of Civil Engineers, Part II, I, pp. 325-378, London.

Wilson, A.G. (1967) A statistical theory of spatial distribution models, Transportation Research, 1, pp. 253-269.

Wilson, A.G. (1970) Entropy in urban and regional modelling, Pion, London.

Wilson, A.G. (1973) Further developments of entropy maximising transport models, Transportation Planning and Technology, 1, pp. 183-193.

Wilson, A.G. (1974) Urban and regional models in geography and planning, John Wiley, London.

Wilson, A.G., Hawkins, A.F., Hill, G.J. and Wagon, D.J. (1969) Calibrating and testing the SELNEC transport model, Regional Studies, 3, pp. 337-350; reprinted in Wilson, A.G. (1972) Papers in urban and regional analysis, Pion, London.

Wootton, H.J. and Pick, G.W. (1967) A model for trips generated by households, Journal of Transport Economics and Policy, 1, pp. 137-153.

Index